COST ACCOUNTING
A Multidimensional Emphasis

COST ACCOUNTING
A Multidimensional Emphasis

Ahmed Belkaoui, M.B.A., Ph.D.

Registered Industrial Accountant (R.I.A.)
University of Illinois at Chicago

The Dryden Press
Chicago   New York   Philadelphia   San Francisco   Montreal   Toronto
London   Sydney   Tokyo   Mexico City   Rio de Janeiro   Madrid

Acquisitions Editor: James Walsh
Developmental Editor: Susan Layton
Project Editor: Ruta Graff
Design Director: Alan Wendt
Production Manager: Mary Jarvis

Text and cover design by Alan Wendt
Copy editing by Mary Berry

Address orders to:

383 Madison Avenue
New York, New York 10017

Address editorial correspondence to:

1 Salt Creek Lane
Hinsdale, Illinois 60521

Library of Congress Catalog Card Number 82-72036
ISBN: 0-03-061121-0
Printed in the United States of America
345-144-987654321

CBS COLLEGE PUBLISHING
The Dryden Press
Holt, Rinehart and Winston
Saunders College Publishing

To Janice, Again

PREFACE

In writing *Cost Accounting: A Multidimensional Emphasis*, my goal was to create a cost accounting textbook that combines cost accounting techniques with techniques from other disciplines on the basis of their usefulness to cost accounting decisions. With this multidimensional emphasis, cost accounting emerges as a body of knowledge encompassing techniques from different disciplines and serving different users.

OBJECTIVES OF THE BOOK

This book is intended to meet the needs of at least two kinds of academic courses: first, management accounting courses in the M.B.A. program and, second, cost accounting courses in the undergraduate business program. The reader is assumed to have taken at least an introductory course in financial accounting as well as to have an elementary knowledge of mathematics and statistics.

The objectives of this book are to provide the student with a thorough exposure to both the traditional and the new dimensions of cost accounting. I believe that this book defines an expanded scope and new boundaries of cost accounting by presenting a multidimensional framework for the discipline.

First, the fields of cost accounting, economics, behavioral sciences, operations research, statistics, and mathematics provide the tools as well as the concepts necessary for the classification, accumulation, and reporting of relevant data for internal decision making as well as the tools and concepts for the interpretation and evaluation of the resulting decisions. This approach reflects the state of the art of cost accounting as a discipline involved with the choice of the best decision on the basis of the best available information.

Second, the standard cost accounting techniques are complemented by other possible approaches to problems. The organization of the material is intended to stress not only the descriptive but also the normative solutions to cost accounting problems, giving to cost accounting the status of a legitimate multidisciplinary line of inquiry.

Finally, some of the chapters include appendixes that provide a trade-off between the integration and differentiation of issues within each area of cost accounting. This will provide the reader with an opportunity to explore these new facets of cost accounting without minimizing the conventional aspects incorporated in each chapter.

Comments and suggestions from users of the book are most welcome. Please write to me care of the Dryden Press.

CONTENT AND ORGANIZATION OF THE BOOK

All major areas of cost accounting are covered in detail in fourteen chapters. Chapter 1 links cost accounting theory and techniques to other relevant disciplines by an examination of its accounting, behavioral, and decisional foundations. To understand the new role of cost accounting, an understanding of these foundations is a first and necessary step.

Chapter 2 evaluates the theoretical foundations, terminology, and treatment of the concept of *cost* in cost accounting, taking into account the behavioral patterns determined by the field of business economics. The emphasis is on cost theory, classification, and accounting and on cost concepts most relevant to business decision making.

In chapter 3, the accounting and statistical cost estimation techniques are discussed. Technical and data requirements as well as the limitations of various models are emphasized.

Chapter 4 deals with the models used to determine the breakeven point. The accounting approach to breakeven analysis is shown to be amenable to improvements and to be useful to examine and assess product mix decisions, accommodate curvilinear cost and revenue functions, and incorporate uncertainty in the analysis.

The concepts, principles, and techniques of planning are covered in chapter 5. In addition to deterministic budgeting, it discusses budgeting under uncertainty in a Bayesian framework and the behavioral considerations in budgeting.

Chapter 6 elaborates on the nature of the control process, and reviews and discusses each of the control systems (traditional, feedforward, and feedback) in terms of its technical and behavioral implications.

The learning curve is presented in chapter 7 as a legitimate and very useful cost estimation technique. The chapter provides both a review of the major computational techniques and examples of their possible applications.

Chapter 8 covers cost accumulation processes: job-order and process costing; accounting for spoilage, waste, defective units, and scrap; and accounting for payroll. The chapter's objective is to provide the essential information for certain aspects of internal decision making, namely, product costing, inventory valuation, income determination, and planning and control.

In chapter 9, the theoretical and technical implications of two inventory valuation techniques—absorption and direct costing—are discussed. The chapter covers various conceptual and operational dimensions in the areas of asset valuation, income determination, and decision making.

Chapter 10 covers issues in accounting for overhead (cost distribution, cost allocation, and cost application), as well as accounting for common product costs (both joint products and by-products). To the conventional accounting approaches are added new mathematical approaches, which highlights the conceptual complexity of allocation problems in accounting.

Capital budgeting techniques, problems of capital rationing, and capital budgeting under inflation and uncertainty are discussed in chapter 11.

Chapter 12 describes the types of leasing arrangements, the advantages of leasing, a normative model for lease evaluation, and the alternative models presented in the literature.

Chapter 13 elaborates on responsibility accounting, the types of organizational design, and the performance evaluation and transfer pricing methods needed to provide a good framework for the planning and control system of a multiproduct firm.

Finally, chapter 14 presents the formal and informal models of inventory control and valuation.

ACKNOWLEDGMENTS

No book can be written without the help of numerous individuals and organizations. I am indebted to the following professors, who influenced this book by their reviews and/or comments:

K. R. Balachandran, New York University

John Carson, University of Ottawa

James L. Chan, University of Illinois at Chicago

Sanford C. Gunn, State University of New York at Buffalo

Alfred Kahl, University of Ottawa

Philip Karpik, University of Illinois at Chicago

Bruce S. Koch, New York University

Robert W. Koehler, Pennsylvania State University

John C. Lere, University of Minnesota

Reynald Maheu, University of Ottawa

Ronald D. Picur, University of Illinois at Chicago

Jeffrey B. Sidney, University of Ottawa

William E. Simmonds, University of Illinois at Chicago

Daniel Zegal, University of Ottawa

A special note of appreciation is extended to my teaching and research assistants, Joan Baker, S. Baksi, Margaret Gonwa, Marie Holland, Vipul Kumar, and Patrick J. Slattery; to the members of the secretarial service of the Faculty of Business Administration at the University of Ottawa, and to Sarah N. Seaton, and the staff of the Word Processing Center at the College of Business Administration of the University of Illinois at Chicago for their cheerful and intelligent assistance.

Also, I thank the people at The Dryden Press: Jim Walsh, Susan Layton, Paul Psilos, Jane Perkins, Mary Jarvis, Alan Wendt, Ruta Graff, Jo-Anne Naples, Mary Berry, and Shirley Moore.

Material from the Uniform CPA Examination Questions and Unofficial Answers, copyright 1963 through 1979 by the American Institute of Certified Public Accountants, Inc., is adapted with permission.

Material from the CMA Examinations, copyright 1972 through 1979 by the National

Association of Accountants is adapted with permission. A similar permission was received from the Institute of Management Accounting of the National Association of Accountants to use problem materials from past CMA examinations.

Material from the CGA Final Examinations, copyright 1978 through 1979 by the Canadian Certified General Accountants Association (Vancouver, B.C.), is adapted with permission.

Material from the CICA Examination, copyright 1973 through 1978 by the Canadian Institute of Chartered Accountants, Toronto, Canada, is adapted with permission.

Material from the RIA Examinations, copyright 1973 through 1979 by the Society of Management Accountants of Canada, is adapted with permission.

I am grateful to the literary executor of the late Sir Ronald A. Fisher, F.R.S., to Dr. Frank Yates, F.R.S., and to Longman Group Ltd., London, for permission to reprint Table II from their book *Statistical Tables for Biological, Agricultural and Medical Research* (6th edition, 1974); to the editor of *Biometrika* for permission to reprint the "Durbin-Watson Bounds" table; to the editors of the *Accounting Review, Financial Management, Cost and Management, Journal of Finance, Journal of Accounting Research*, and *Management Accounting* for permission to adapt problems from articles or to reprint materials appearing in their journals; and to the Financial Executive Research Foundation, Haymarket Publishing Ltd., and the Conference Board for their permission to reprint material from their books.

A.B.
Chicago, Illinois

ABOUT THE AUTHOR

Ahmed Belkaoui is a professor of accounting at the University of Illinois at Chicago. He received his Ph.D. from Syracuse University and his M.B.A. from the University of Illinois at Champaign-Urbana. Professor Belkaoui is an R.I.A. from the Society of Management Accountants of Ontario. His other published books include *Accounting Theory* (Harcourt Brace Jovanovich, 1981), *Conceptual Foundations of Management Accounting* (Addison-Wesley, 1981), and *Théorie Comptable* (Presses de l'Université du Québec, 1980). Professor Belkaoui is an adjunct professor at the University of Ottawa, Ontario, Canada.

CONTENTS

COST ACCOUNTING
A Multidimensional Emphasis

1.1   THE ACCOUNTING FOUNDATIONS

1.1.1   *Classes of Accounting*

Cost accounting is traditionally and justifiably considered a unique and distinct accounting function, different from the other main accounting function, financial accounting. An understanding of the many facets of accounting will clarify the scope of cost accounting.

Accounting is a process of identifying, measuring, recording, classifying, interpreting, and communicating economic information to facilitate decision making by its users. Information is produced and disseminated for two distinct but closely related purposes: (1) reporting to those outside the organization who have a legitimate interest in its affairs (financial accounting, tax accounting, and auditing), and (2) making decisions within the organization (internal or cost accounting).

Financial accounting strives to provide necessary and specific information to external users. Its main tasks involve recording, classifying, and communicating the transactions of an entity by issuing periodic financial statements (usually annually or quarterly, but sometimes monthly). These statements include the balance sheet as an expression of the firm's financial position, the income statement as an expression of the firm's financial performance, and the statement of changes in financial position as an expression of the firm's financial conduct. Financial accounting must operate within set boundaries and must strictly adhere to *generally accepted accounting principles (GAAP)*.

Tax accounting supplies necessary information to both top management and the Internal Revenue Service. It determines the tax liability of the firm on an annual and quarterly basis. The information is conveyed in federal forms 1040 and 1120. Tax accounting rests on rules governed by the Internal Revenue Code.

Auditing provides information to top management and the public, mainly through opinions on the conformity, fairness, and consistency of the firm's financial statements. The expression of opinion, referred to as the *attest function of the auditor*, reports that the financial statements are "fairly presented, in conformity with generally accepted accounting principles, applied on a consistent basis." The auditor's opinion is prepared annually in accordance with generally accepted auditing standards.

Cost accounting strives to provide pertinent information to the firm's managers. It is charged with the following tasks:

1. Preparation and execution of plans and budgets.

2. Cost accumulation to determine inventories and cost of goods sold.

3. Income determination and reporting.

4. Preparation of performance reports to assist in the control of operations.

5. Preparation of information for short- and long-term decisions. Various questions must be considered when examining routine decision problems: What is the decision to be made? What is the best rule for making the decision? What information is required in making the decision? How accurate must that information be? How frequently should the information be supplied? What is the most logical source for generating the information? How can the information best be obtained and transmitted to the user?

Each of these cost accounting tasks is essential to managerial processes. Planning is achieved through the preparation of plans and budgets, coordinating through cost accumulation and periodic reporting, and controlling through the preparation of performance

1 *THE CONCEPTUAL FOUNDATIONS OF COST ACCOUNTING*

Accountants today occupy many of the top positions in their firms. Their role of decision maker affects every facet of the organization, whether the organization is a proprietorship, partnership, or profit or nonprofit corporation. In response to the expanding role of accountants, *cost accounting* (also called management accounting) is becoming increasingly multidimensional. It rests not only on accounting but also on organizational, behavioral, decisional, and other foundations.[1] An understanding of these foundations is necessary to an understanding of the accountants' new role.

This chapter examines the conceptual foundations of cost accounting. In doing so, it illustrates the multidimensional scope of cost accounting and establishes a frame of reference for the entire text.

Upon completion of this chapter, you should be able to do the following:

1. Differentiate between the various classes of accounting, define cost accounting, and identify the concepts and qualitative characteristics of information that form the emerging cost accounting conceptual framework.

2. Identify the elements of the organizational structure that may affect the ways cost accounting will be exercised: the organizational chart, the line and staff relationships, and the role of the controller in the organization.

3. Identify five theories of motivation and their implications for cost accounting: need theory, two-factor theory, value/expectancy theory, achievement theory, and inequity theory.

4. Identify the conceptual frameworks for viewing decisions and decision systems proposed in the cost accounting and information systems literature.

---

[1] Ahmed Belkaoui, *Conceptual Foundations of Management Accounting* (Reading, Mass.: Addison-Wesley, 1980), pp. 1–4.

reports and the comparison of budgeted and actual results. The implementation of these tasks requires the design of a cost accounting system to supply relevant and timely information for both routine and nonrecurring decisions.

In assessing the appropriateness of a cost accounting system for a routine decision area, the following deficiencies are common:

1. *Overinformation*, where too much information is supplied to the user.

2. *Underinformation*, where there is a lack of adequate information to make an appropriate decision.

3. *Untimely information* where the information comes too late for the user to benefit.

Each of these deficiencies must be corrected in the design of a cost accounting system.

1.1.2   *Toward a Cost Accounting Conceptual Framework*

In contrast to financial accounting, which rests on techniques conforming to generally accepted accounting principles, cost accounting relies on techniques from various disciplines and is not governed by generally accepted accounting principles. The Committee on Management Accounting of the American Accounting Association (AAA) developed a definition of management (cost) accounting:

The application of appropriate techniques and concepts in processing the historical and projected economic data of an entity to assist management in establishing plans for reasonable economic objectives and in the making of rational decisions with a view toward achieving these objectives. It includes the methods and concepts necessary for effective planning, for choosing among alternative business actions, and for control through the evaluation and interpretation of performance. Its study involves consideration of ways in which accounting information may be accumulated, synthesized, analyzed, and presented in relation to specific problems, decisions, and day-to-day tasks of business management.[2]

These techniques may be drawn from such fields as accounting, mathematics, sociology, psychology, and economics. A conceptual framework is necessary within which qualitative characteristics of information can guide the development of cost accounting techniques. These techniques will then be considered good not only because they are used in practice but also because they are based on accepted concepts and qualitative characteristics of information—they conform to a cost accounting conceptual framework.

Cost Accounting Concepts
An accepted, exhaustive list of cost accounting concepts does not yet exist. However, the 1972 American Accounting Association Committee on Courses in Managerial Accounting identifies measurement, communication, information, system, planning, feedback, control, and cost behavior as the cost accounting concepts that represent a necessary, if not a minimum, foundation for a cost accounting conceptual framework.[3]

---

[2] American Accounting Association, Committee on Management Accounting, "Report of the Committee on Management Accounting," *Accounting Review* (April 1959), p. 210.

[3] American Accounting Association, Committee on Courses in Managerial Accounting, "Report of the Committee on Courses in Managerial Accounting," *Accounting Review* 47 supp. (1972), pp. 7–8.

Applied to accounting, *measurement* is defined as "an assignment of numbers to an entity's past, present or future economic phenomena on the basis of past and present observation and according to rules."[4] This concept is essential to cost accounting.

Communication is also essential in cost accounting to allow movement from measurement to information. As defined by Shannon and Weaver, communication encompasses "the procedures by means of which one mechanism affects another mechanism."[5]

Data upon which action is based are *information*. The term refers to those data that reduce the user's uncertainty.

A *system* is an entity consisting of two or more interacting components, or subsystems, intended to achieve a goal. Cost accounting is generally a subsystem of the accounting information system, which is itself a subsystem of the total management information system within the organization.

Planning refers to the management function of setting objectives, establishing policies, and choosing means of accomplishment. It may occur at different levels in the organization, from strategic to operational, and may have behavioral implications.

Feedback is the output of a process that returns to become an input to initiate control. It is basically a revision of the planning process to accommodate new environmental events.

Control refers to the monitoring and evaluation of performance to determine the degree to which actions conform to plans. Ideally, planning precedes control, which is followed by a feedback corrective action or a feedforward preventive action.

A cost results from the use of an asset for production. The identification, classification, and estimation of costs—the study of *cost behavior*—are essential to any evaluation of alternative courses of action.

Qualitative Characteristics of Cost Accounting Information

To be useful, a cost accounting report must meet certain qualitative criteria. These criteria are intended to guide the cost accountant to produce the "best," or most useful, information for managers.

The Financial Accounting Standards Board (FASB), a standard-setting body for financial accounting, has proposed certain criteria for selecting and evaluating financial accounting and reporting policies.[6] These criteria, which also apply to cost accounting reports, include decision usefulness, benefits over costs, relevance, reliability, neutrality, verifiability, representational faithfulness, comparability, timeliness, understandability, completeness, and consistency. As shown in Figure 1.1, these criteria may be organized as a hierarchy of informational qualities.

Most cost accounting is concerned to some degree with decision making, so *decision usefulness* becomes the overriding criterion for choosing between cost accounting alternatives. The type of information chosen is the one which, subject to any cost considerations, appears the most useful for decision making.

Cost accounting information, like any other commodity, will be sought if the benefits to be derived from the information exceed its costs. Thus, before preparing and dis-

---

[4] American Accounting Association, Committee on Foundations of Accounting Measurement, "Report of the Committee on Foundations of Accounting Measurement," *Accounting Review* 46 supp. (1971), p. 3.

[5] Claude E. Shannon and Warren Weaver, *The Mathematical Theory of Communication* (Urbana, Ill.: University of Illinois Press, 1949), p. 95.

[6] Financial Accounting Standards Board, Exposure Draft, "Qualitative Characteristics: Criteria for Selecting and Evaluating Financial Accounting and Reporting Policies" (Stamford, Conn.: FASB, 1979).

Figure 1.1 **A Hierarchy of Qualitative Characteristics**

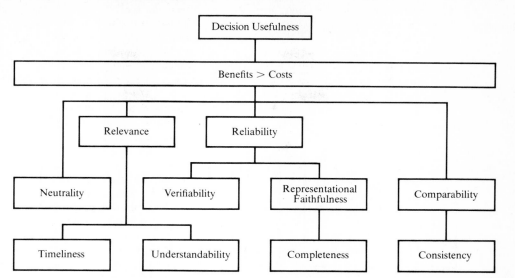

seminating the cost accounting information, the *benefits and costs* of providing the information must be compared.

Relevance has been appropriately defined as follows: "For information to meet the standard of relevance, it must bear upon or be usefully associated with the action it is designed to facilitate or the result it is desired to produce. This requires that either the information or the act of communicating it exert influence . . . on the designated actions."[7] Relevance therefore refers to the information's ability to influence the managers' decisions by changing or confirming their expectations about the results or consequences of actions or events. There can be degrees of relevance. The relevance of particular information will vary among users and will depend on their needs and the particular contexts in which the decisions are made.

Reliability refers to that "quality which permits users of data to depend upon it with confidence as representative of what it proposes to represent."[8] Thus, the reliability of information depends on its degree of faithfulness in the representation of an event. Reliability will differ between users, depending on the extent of their knowledge of the rules used to prepare the information. Similarly, different users may seek information with different degrees of reliability.

The absence of bias in the presentation of accounting reports or information is *neutrality*. Thus, neutral information is free from bias toward attaining some desired result or inducing a particular mode of behavior. This is not to imply that the preparers of information do not have a purpose in mind when preparing the reports; it only means

[7] American Accounting Association, *A Statement of Basic Accounting Theory* (Evanston, Ill.: AAA, 1966), p. 9.

[8] American Accounting Association, Committee on Concepts and Standards for External Financial Reports, *Statement of Accounting Theory and Theory Acceptance*, (Sarasota, Fla.: AAA, 1977), p. 16.

Figure 1.2 Organizational Chart of a Manufacturing Company

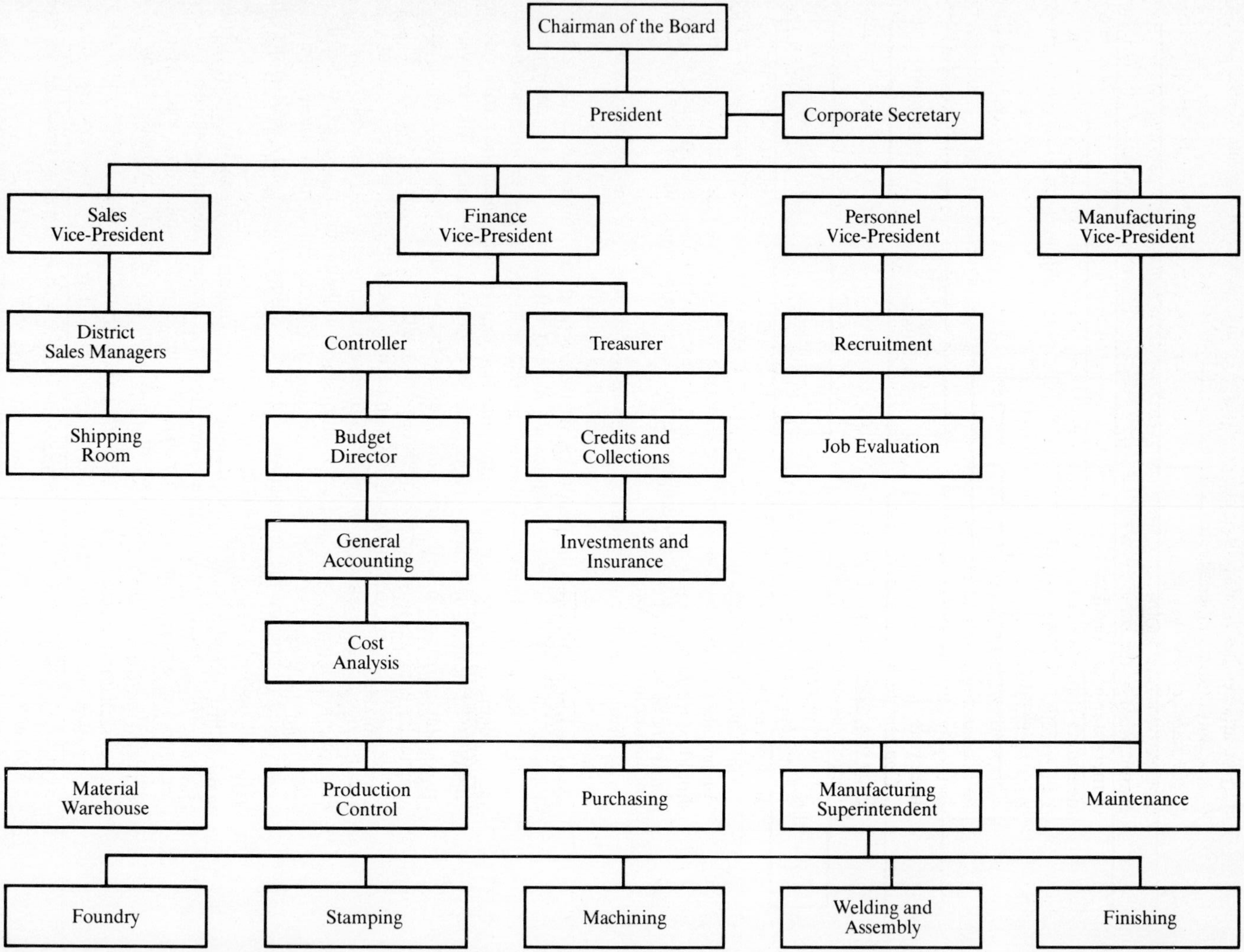

that the purpose should not influence a predetermined result. Notice that neutrality is in conflict with one of the concepts of cost accounting, namely, the feedback concept. It may be argued that cost accounting reports are intended to report on managerial performance and influence behavior and hence cannot be neutral.

Verifiability is "that attribute . . . which allows qualified individuals working independently of one another to develop essentially similar measures or conclusions from an examination of the same evidence, data, or records." [9] It implies consensus and absence of measurer bias. Verifiable information can be substantially reproduced by independent measurers using the same measurement methods. Notice that verifiability refers only to the correctness of the resulting information, not to the appropriateness of the measurement method used.

Representational faithfulness and completeness refer to the correspondence between the accounting data and the events those data are supposed to represent. If the measure portrays what it is supposed to represent, it is considered free of measurement and measurer bias.

Comparability describes the use of the same methods by different firms, and *consistency* describes the use of the same method over time by a given firm. Both qualitative characteristics are more important for financial accounting information than for cost accounting information.

Timeliness refers to the availability of data when they are needed or soon enough after the reported events. A trade-off is necessary between timeliness and precision.

The clarity of the information and ease of grasp by the users are its *understandability*. The preparer's level of understanding is generally different from the user's. Thus, efforts should be made by the preparer to increase the understandability of accounting information, in both form and content, to increase its usefulness to the user.

1.2   THE ORGANIZATIONAL FOUNDATIONS

1.2.1   Organizational Structure

Cost accounting rests not only on accounting but also on organizational foundations. It is this formal organizational structure that management often seeks to change to improve the organization's functioning. In turn, elements of the organizational structure may affect cost accounting—its techniques, approaches, and role in the firm. The strongest influences on cost accounting are the organizational chart, the line and staff relationships, and the role of the controller in the organization.

The *organizational chart* reflects the pyramidal system of relationships of an organization's staff. The chart results from deliberate, conscious planning of the areas of responsibility, specialization, and authority for each member of the organization. As shown in Figure 1.2, each vertical level in the hierarchy depicts different levels of authority. Each horizontal dimension is differentiated by specialization. This process is *departmentalization*; employees are grouped into organizational units on the basis of similar skills and specialization. A firm may departmentalize horizontally by function, by location, by process, and by product. Vertical differentiation by authority and responsibility and horizontal differentiation through departmentalization lead to the crea-

[9] American Accounting Association, *A Statement of Basic Accounting Theory*, p. 10.

tion of separate organizational units and necessitate provision for periodic planning and control. This need is met by the cost accounting system.

As shown in Figure 1.2, the lines connecting the organizational units may imply either line or staff relationships. A *line function* implies a basic hierarchical relationship as defined by the line of authority or chain of command. A *staff relationship* implies that part of the managerial task has been assigned by an executive to someone outside the chain of command. The authority relationships between the staff member and employees of the line at the same or lower levels may be one of four types: staff advice, compulsory advice, concurring authority, or limited company authority. The concepts of line and staff influence cost accounting in the following ways. First, cost accounting is supportive by nature, providing services and assistance to other units in the organization. It is basically a staff function. Second, as a staff member, the cost accountant's authority may range from purely advisory to limited authority. Third, because of its great need for the cost accountant's specialized knowledge, the organization will likely position this person rather high in the organization. In any case, cost accounting is a *decision support system*.

1.2.2   Controllership

The manager in charge of the accounting department is known as the controller. A staff member of the top management team, the controller also has a line relationship within the department. The immediate supervisor is generally the vice-president in charge of finance. As a staff person, the controller advises management in the areas of corporate reporting, planning, and control. The following are the controller's main activities:

1. Responsibility for the supervision of all facets of financial accounting leading to the publication of the annual reports.

2. Coordination of all the activities leading to the establishment of the master budget and long-term plan of the firm.

3. Maintenance of a system of control through proper circulation of performance reports.

4. Playing an essential part in the proper collection, dispersion, and channeling of pertinent and timely information as a designer and activator of the basic organizational communications system, the electronic data processing system.

As business entities increase in size and complexity, as the use of planning and control techniques grows, and as most accounting attains a multidimensional scope, the importance of the controller in the organization also increases. As an example of this new role, the organization of a modern controller's office is shown in Figure 1.3. The corporate controller has moved to center stage as the chief accounting executive.

As companies expand their operations, the duties and responsibilities of the accounting department increase, as does the size of the controller's staff. What may result is a flat organization like the one portrayed in Figure 1.3, in which all subordinates report directly to the controller. Such a structure in the controller's department may benefit downward and upward communication between the controller and subordinates. Accuracy of upward and downward communication can increase because fewer people are in the vertical chain. This reduces the likelihood of perceptual error. Communication speed can increase. Finally, the controller can initiate more direct control communication and is able to obtain firsthand information about the department performance.

The flat organizational structure may also create downward and upward communication problems. There may be increased competition for the controller's time. Too much information may obscure the pertinent information. The controller may be unable to initiate timely control communication. These negative effects, however, may be reduced by the appointment of a staff assistant for the controller. This will make it easier for the controller to adopt a democratic rather than an autocratic approach to management.

The types of functions and responsibilities assigned to the controller are generally different from those assigned to the treasurer. To avoid the confusion and distinguish between the controller and treasurer functions, the Financial Executives Institute presented the following as job responsibilities for each area:

Controllership Functions	*Treasurership Functions*
1. Planning and control	**1.** Provision of capital
2. Reporting and interpreting	**2.** Investor relations
3. Evaluating and consulting	**3.** Short-term financing
4. Tax administration	**4.** Bank and custody
5. Government reporting	**5.** Credits and collections
6. Protection of assets	**6.** Investments
7. Economic appraisal	**7.** Insurance

The primary objective of the treasurer, then, is to deal with the financing function, whereas the primary objective of the controller is to deal with the information system. Note that cost accounting is essential to the implementation of the controller's first three functions.

1.3   THE BEHAVIORAL FOUNDATIONS

Cost accounting should be built on behavioral foundations. Its explicit aim is to positively affect the behavior of individuals. To accomplish this, cost accounting must be adapted to the different characteristics shaping the "cognitive makeup" of individuals within an organization and affecting their motivation to perform. The identification of the factors and situations that may influence employees' actions allows the cost accountant to adapt the services to the realities of human behavior.

The literature on motivation identifies five theories of motivation: need theory, two-factor theory, value/expectancy theory, achievement theory, and inequity theory. Each either identifies the factors within the individual and the environment that activate high performance or attempts to explain and describe how behavior is activated, what directs it, and how it is controlled and stopped. Each of these theories of motivation has distinct implications for cost accounting.

1.3.1   Need Theory

Originally advanced by psychologist Abraham Maslow, need theory holds that people are motivated to satisfy a hierarchy of needs. These needs are as follows (in ascending order of priority):

Figure 1.3   Example of the Organization of the Controller's Department

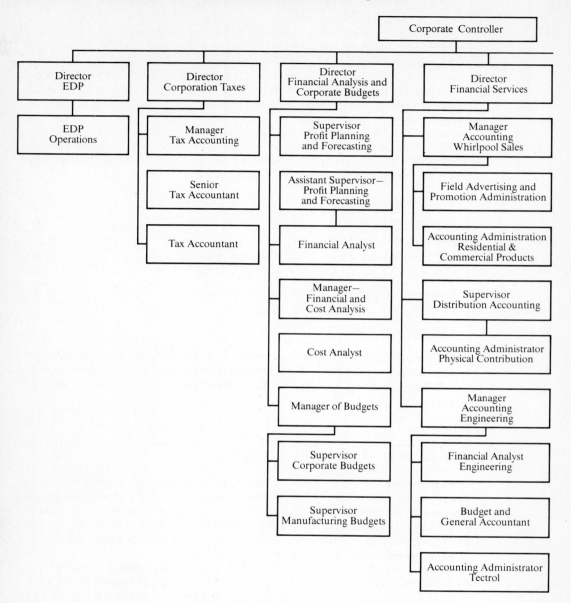

Source: National Industrial Conference Board, *Organizing the Corporate Financial Function* (New York: NICB, 1969), p. 22. Reprinted by permission.

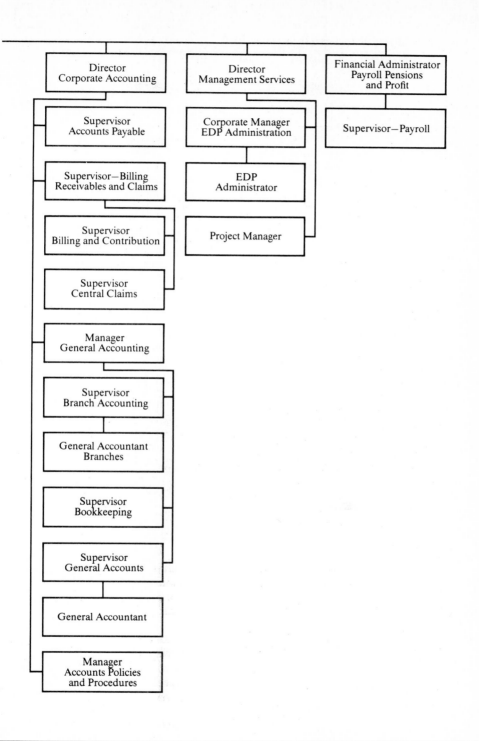

1. *The physiological needs:* food, shelter, warmth, and other bodily wants.

2. *The safety needs:* security and protection.

3. *The need for love and belongingness:* desire to both give and receive love and friendship.

4. *The need for esteem:* self-respect and the respect of others.

5. *The self-actualization need:* achieving one's full potential. [10]

People strive to satisfy these needs in a sequential fashion, starting with the physiological needs and ending with the self-actualization need. What this implies for cost accounting is that assuming individuals in the organization are well remunerated, the emphasis should be on the introduction of cost accounting techniques in general and control techniques in particular that are consistent with the satisfaction of higher-level needs. [11]

1.3.2   *Two-Factor Theory*

In a series of studies, Herzberg and his associates developed the "motivation hygiene" theory. [12] They found two factors affecting a job situation, which they labeled *satisfiers* and *dissatisfiers*. The satisfiers were related to the nature of the work itself and to rewards that flowed directly from the performance of that work. The satisfiers were (1) perceived opportunity for achievement on the job, (2) recognition, (3) a sense of performing interesting and important work, (4) responsibility, and (5) advancement. The dissatisfiers were related to the context rather than the content of the job. They were concerned with (1) company policies that foster ineffectiveness, (2) incompetent supervision, (3) interpersonal relations, (4) working conditions, (5) salaries, (6) status, and (7) job security.

The implications of Herzberg's theory for cost accounting are twofold. First, to contribute to employee motivation, cost accounting techniques should focus on better measurement and reporting of achievement, recognition, work, responsibility, and advancement. Second, given that the key to motivation is to make jobs more meaningful, cost accounting should focus on job enrichment. Managers effect job enrichment by designing tasks that create positive feelings about the job and by building in the opportunity for personal achievement, recognition, challenge, and growth.

1.3.3   *Value/Expectancy Theory*

Value/expectancy theory attempts to explain and describe how behavior is initiated, maintained, and terminated. Originally developed by Lewin, [13] and later specifically applied to work motivation by Vroom, [14] the basic tenet of the theory is that an individual chooses his or her behavior on the basis of (1) expectations that the behavior will result

---

[10] Abraham Maslow, "A Theory of Human Motivation," *Psychological Review* 50 (1943), pp. 370–396.

[11] E. H. Caplan, *Management Accounting and Behavioral Science* (Reading, Mass.: Addison-Wesley, 1971), p. 49.

[12] F. Herzberg, B. Maumer, and B. Snyderman, *The Motivation to Work*, 2d ed., (New York: Wiley, 1959).

[13] K. Lewin, *Field Theory and Social Sciences* (New York: Harper & Bros., 1951).

[14] V. H. Vroom, *Work and Motivation* (New York: Wiley, 1964).

in a specific outcome and (2) the sum of the valences (that is, personal usefulness or rewards derived from the outcome).

House's formula for the value/expectancy model can be expressed as follows: [15]

$$M = IV_b + P_1(IV_a + \sum_{i=1}^{n} P_{2i}EV_i),$$
$$i = 1, 2, \ldots, n,$$

where

M = Motivation to work

IV_a = Intrinsic valence associated with successful performance of the task

IV_b = Intrinsic valence associated with goal-directed behavior

EV_i = Extrinsic valences associated with the ith extrinsic reward contingent on accomplishment of the work goal (a given level of specified performance)

P_1 = The expectancy that goal-directed behavior will accomplish the work goal; the measure's range is $(-1, +1)$

P_{2i} = The expectancy that work goal accomplishment will lead to the ith extrinsic reward; the measure's range is $(-1, +1)$

This formula shows some of the implications of expectancy theory for cost accounting. Appropriate cost accounting techniques may be chosen to affect the independent variables of this model in the following ways:

1. By determining what extrinsic rewards (EV_i) follow work goal accomplishment.

2. By increasing through timely reports the individual's expectancy (P_{2i}) that work goal accomplishment leads to extrinsic rewards.

3. By increasing the intrinsic valence associated with work goal accomplishment (IV_a) through giving the individual a greater role in goal setting and task directing.

4. By recognizing and supporting the individual's effort, thereby influencing P_1.

5. By increasing the net intrinsic valences associated with goal-directed behavior (IV_b).

1.3.4   *Achievement Theory*

The concept of achievement motive, first introduced by McClelland and Atkinson, is based on the desire of people to be challenged, to be innovative, and to adopt an "achievement-oriented behavior" directed toward meeting a standard of excellence. The achievement-oriented individual assumes responsibility for individual achievement, seeks challenging tasks, and takes calculated risks commensurate with the probabilities of success. Therefore, such a person "will take small risks for tasks serving as stepping stones for future rewards, take intermediate risks for tasks offering opportunities for achievement, and will attempt to find situations falling somewhere between the two extremes, providing the highest probability of success, and hence maximizing his sense of

---

[15]R. J. House, "A Path-Goal Theory of Leader Effectiveness," *Administrative Science Quarterly* (September 1971), pp. 321–338.

personal achievement." [16] For cost accounting, this theory implies (1) the necessity of constructing ways to develop the achievement motive at all managerial levels, and (2) the need to introduce cost accounting techniques and to report cost accounting information that encourages and facilitates the performance of high achievers.

1.3.5   Inequity Theory

Walster and her colleagues and Adams say that individuals in a relationship have two motives: to maximize their own gains and to maintain equity in the relationship. [17] Inequity results when the rewards from a relationship are not proportional to what a person has put in. Inequity theory is based on the premise that when individuals compare their own situations with others' situations and feel they are rewarded too much or too little for their contributions, they experience increased tension and strive to reduce it.

The inequity theory suggests, then, that the employee must see rewards as fair or equitable. An appeal to equity norms can reduce conflict. Cost accounting can restore equity by insuring correct and accurate measurement and reporting of performance and the corresponding rewards. To avoid creating feelings of inequity, the methods of measuring performance and rewards should be made public to the employees.

1.4   THE DECISIONAL FOUNDATIONS

Cost accounting attempts to facilitate and support an organization's decision making. To accomplish this fundamental objective in the most appropriate areas, the cost accountant should be aware of the kinds and levels of decisions involved. Several conceptual frameworks proposed in the cost accounting and information systems literature provide a good basis for viewing the types of decisions and decision systems, the types of information needed, and the role of cost accounting.

1.4.1   Anthony's Framework

Although it is a typology of managerial activities, Anthony's framework may also be conceived as a hierarchy of decision systems—*strategic planning*, *management control*, and *operational control*. [18] Each requires different planning and control systems.

Strategic planning involves determining the objectives of the organization; the changes in these objectives; the resources used to attain the objectives; and the policies that govern the acquisition, use, and disposition of the resources. The strategic planner's main concern is the relationship between the organization and its environment, a concern expressed in the formulation of a long-range plan.

[16] D. C. McClelland, *Personality* (New York: William Sloan, 1951); McClelland, *The Achieving Society* (Princeton, N.J.: Van Nostrand, 1961); and J. W. Atkinson, "Toward Experimental Analysis of Human Motivation in Terms of Motives, Expectancies, and Incentives," in *Motives in Fantasy, Action and Society*, ed. J. W. Atkinson (Princeton, N.J.: Van Nostrand, 1958).

[17] E. Walster, E. Berscheid, and G. W. Walster, "New Directions in Equity Research," *Journal of Personality and Social Psychology* 25 (1973), pp. 151–176; and J. S. Adams, "Toward an Understanding of Inequity," *Journal of Abnormal and Social Psychology* 22 (1965), pp. 422–426.

[18] R. N. Anthony, *Planning and Control Systems: A Framework for Analysis*, Harvard University Graduate School of Business Administration Studies in Management Control (Cambridge, Mass., 1965).

Table 1.1   *Information Requirements by Decision Category*

Information Attribute	Strategic Planning	Management Control	Operational Control
Source	Externally Generated	Mostly Internally Generated	Internally Generated
Accuracy	Accurate in Magnitude Only	Accurate within Decision Bounds	Very Accurate
Scope	Summary Data	Moderately Detailed Data	Detailed Data
Frequency	Periodically Reported	Regularly Reported	Frequently Reported
Time Span	Long Range	Medium Range	Short Range
Organization	Loose	Structured	Highly Structured
Type of Information	Qualitative	Mixed	Quantitative
Age of Information	Old	Mixed	Current
Characteristic	Unique to Problem	Exception Reporting	Repetitive
Nature	Relates to Establishment of Broad Policies	Relates to the Achievement of Organizational Objectives	Relates to a Specific Task

Strategic planning formerly was the responsibility of senior managers and analysts, who approached problems on an ad hoc basis as the need for a solution arose. However, strategic planning is fast becoming an accepted, necessary, and separate management process advocated by most management consulting firms. For example, Arthur D. Little developed Strategy Center Profile techniques for integrating business planning with corporate planning as well as the "alternate futures" concepts. Boston Consulting Group advocates the experience curve, the concept of correlating relative market share with production costs, and the growth-share matrix. McKinsey and Co. developed the "shoplight" matrix with General Electric. Finally, the Strategic Planning Institute developed an expected business performance data base—Profit Impact of Marketing Strategy (PIMS)—for businesses with different characteristics.

Management control is the process by which managers insure that resources are obtained and used effectively and efficiently in the accomplishment of the organization's objectives. Managerial activities within the framework established by strategic planning sometimes require subjective interpretations and involve personal interactions. Management control involves both top management and the middle managers, who approach problems using a definite pattern and timetable to insure efficient and effective results.

Operational control insures that specific tasks or transactions are carried out effectively and efficiently. It is governed by rules and procedures derived from management control that often are expressed in terms of a mathematical model.

Anthony recognizes that the boundaries between the three decision categories often are not clear. The categories are useful, however, for the analysis of managerial activities and their information requirements. The decision categories form a continuum and require different information, summarized in Table 1.1.

Anthony's framework is simple, and it facilitates communications between individuals in the organization by categorizing different types of decisions and their information requirements. For cost accounting the framework implies a tailoring of the data to the context and category of the particular decision. It also calls for different approaches in the areas of strategic planning, management control, and operational control.

1.4.2   Simon's Framework

Like Anthony's framework, Simon's framework presents a taxonomy of decisions.[19] However, while Anthony's framework focuses on the decision making activity, Simon's framework focuses on problem solving by individuals, regardless of their position within an organization.

Simon maintains that all problem solving can be broken down into three distinct phases: intelligence, design, and choice. *Intelligence* consists of surveying the environment for situations that demand decisions. It implies an identification of one or more problems, the collection of information, and the establishment of goals and evaluative criteria. *Design* involves delineating and analyzing various courses of action to solve the problems identified in the intelligence phase. An enumeration and combination of feasible alternatives and their evaluation are based on the criteria established in the intelligence phase. Finally, *choice* involves choosing the best alternative. Although not mentioned by Simon, decision making involves a fourth phase, *implementation*, designed to insure proper execution of choice.

Simon's framework distinguishes between *programmed* and *nonprogrammed decisions*:

> *Decisions are programmed to the extent that they are repetitive and routine, to the extent that a definite procedure has been worked out for handling them so that they don't have to be treated* de novo *each time they occur. Decisions are nonprogrammed to the extent that they are novel, unstructured, and consequential. There is no cut-and-dried method of handling the problem because it hasn't arisen before, or because its precise nature and structure are elusive or complex, or because it is so important that it deserves a custom-tailored treatment. . . . By nonprogrammed I mean a response where the system has no specific procedure to deal with situations like the one at hand, but must fall back on whatever general capacity it has for intelligent, adaptive, problem-oriented action.*[20]

Because they are repetitive and routine, programmed decisions require little time in the design phase. Nonprogrammed decisions require much more time. The terms *structured* and *unstructured* are used for *programmed* and *nonprogrammed* to imply less dependence on the computer and more on the basic character of the problem solving activity in question. The two classifications advanced by Simon may be viewed as polarities in a continuum of decision making activity. For example, semistructured decisions may be those for which one or two of the intelligence, design, and choice phases are unstructured.

That decisions may fall on a continuum from structured to unstructured has implications for cost accounting. Structured decisions are solvable by analytic techniques, while unstructured decisions generally are not. The analytic techniques required for structured decisions may be based either on clerical routine and habit or formalized techniques from operations research and electronic data processing. The decision techniques required for unstructured decisions may be based either on intuition and judgment or heuristic techniques. While the role of cost accounting for structured decisions is obviously one of providing and assisting in the use of fixed routines, its role is not obvious in unstructured decisions, where the user of accounting information may rely more on decision style, intuition, or heuristic techniques.

---

[19] H. A. Simon, *The New Science of Management Decision* (New York: Harper & Row, 1960).
[20] Ibid., p. 69.

Table 1.2   ***An Expanded Example of the Gorry–Scott-Morton Framework***

	Operational Control	Management Control	Strategic Planning
Structured	Accounts Receivable	Budgeting	Tanker Fleet Mix
	Order Entry	Short-Term Forecasting	Warehouse and Plant Location
	Inventory Reordering	Engineered Costs	
		Linear Programming for Manufacturing	
Semistructured	Inventory Control	Variance Analysis	Mergers and Acquisitions
	Production Scheduling	Overall Budget	Capital Acquisition Analysis
	Bond Trading	Budget Preparation	New Product Planning
Unstructured	Cash Management	Hiring Personnel	R&D Planning
	PERT Cost Systems	Sales and Production	

1.4.3   *Gorry–Scott-Morton Framework*

Anthony's framework is based on the purpose of the decision making activity, while Simon's framework is based on the methods or techniques of problem solving. The Gorry–Scott-Morton framework combines both in a matrix that classifies decisions on both a structured-to-unstructured dimension and on an operational-to-strategic dimension.[21] Table 1.2 shows an expanded example of the matrix obtained from the synthesis provided by Gorry and Scott-Morton.

The implications for cost accounting from both the Anthony and Simon frameworks apply also to the Gorry–Scott-Morton framework. The synthesis, however, has additional implications.

First, because different information requirements and methods of data collection are required for the three decision categories borrowed from Simon, there may be three types of decisions:

1. Decisions for which adequate models are available or can be constructed and from which optimal solutions can be derived. In such cases, the decision process itself should be incorporated into the information system, thereby converting it to a control system.

2. Decisions for which adequate models can be constructed but from which optimal solutions cannot be extracted. Here heuristic procedures should be provided.

3. Decisions for which adequate models cannot be constructed. Research is required here to determine the relevant information. If decision making cannot be delayed, then judgment must be used to guess what information is relevant.[22]

---

[21]G. A. Gorry and N. S. Scott-Morton, "A Framework for Management Information Systems," *Sloan Management Review* (Fall 1971), pp. 55–70.

[22]R. L. Ackoff, "Management Misinformation Systems," *Management Science* (December 1967).

The second implication of the Gorry–Scott-Morton framework is that different organizational structures, different managerial skills and talents, and different numbers of managers may be required for each decision category. The decision process, the implementation process, and the level of analytic sophistication will differ among the three decision categories and call for different organizational structures:

On strategic problems, a task force reporting to the user and virtually independent of the computer group may make sense. The important issues are problem definition and problem structure; the implementation and computer issues are relatively simple by comparison. In management control, the single user, although still dominant in his application, has problems of interfacing with other users. An organizational design that encourages cross-functional (marketing, production, distribution, etc.) cooperation is probably desirable. In operational control, the organizational design should include the user as a major influence, but he will have to be balanced with operational systems experts, and the whole group can quite possibly stay within functional boundaries. [23]

A final implication is that model requirements may differ in the three areas, given the differences in information requirements, frequency of decisions in each area, and their relative magnitude. The operational control system calls for frequent decisions, so the models for these decisions must be efficient in running time, have ready access to current data, and be easily changed. In contrast, the models in strategic planning, and to a lesser extent management control, are infrequent, individual, and dependent on the managers involved.

Because cost accounting is a decision support system, it requires people with different skills and attitudes, different technologies, different models, and different processes to accommodate structured and unstructured decisions on one hand and strategic planning, management control, and operational control on the other.

1.5   CONCLUSION

To meet the diverse needs of today's managers, cost (or management) accounting has evolved into a multidimensional area of inquiry resting on accounting, organizational, behavioral, and decisional foundations.

The accounting foundations consist of cost accounting concepts to guide the development of cost accounting techniques. The cost accounting concepts alleged to represent a necessary, if not a minimum, foundation for cost accounting's theoretical structure include measurement, communication, information, system, planning, feedback, control, and cost behavior.

The organizational foundations include the elements of the organizational structure that shape the techniques, approaches, and role of cost accounting in the firm: the organizational chart, the line and staff relationships, and the role of the controller in the organization.

The behavioral foundations of cost accounting include the motivation theories identifying the factors and situations that may influence and coordinate employees' actions. The main theories are the need theory, the two-factor theory, the value/expectancy theory, the achievement theory, and the inequity theory.

---

[23] Gorry and Scott-Morton, "A Framework," p. 68.

The decisional foundations of cost accounting are the different conceptual frameworks for viewing types of decisions and decision systems in an organization: Anthony's framework, Simon's framework, and the Gorry–Scott-Morton framework.

To appreciate the expanding scope of the cost accountant's activities, a full grasp of these foundations is a necessary and first step in the study of cost accounting.

This expanding scope has elevated the status of cost accounting from a minor part of the accounting profession to a distinct accounting discipline. The cost accountant's right to a separate professional designation was recognized in 1972 when the National Association of Accountants (NAA is the largest association of internal accountants in the United States) established the Institute of Management Accounting to administer a program leading to the *Certificate in Management Accounting* (CMA). The objectives of this program are threefold:

1. To foster higher educational standards in the field of management accounting.

2. To establish management accounting as a recognized profession by identifying the role of the management accountant, the underlying body of knowledge, and by outlining a course of study by which such knowledge can be acquired.

3. To assist employers, educators and students by establishing an objective measure of an individual's knowledge and competence in the profession of management accounting.[24]

In recognition of the multidimensional aspect of the cost accounting discipline, the CMA qualifying examination covers (1) managerial economics and business finance; (2) organization and behavior, including ethical considerations; (3) public reporting; (4) periodic reporting for internal and external purposes; and (5) decision analysis, including modeling and information systems.[25] The CMA designation is gaining acceptance in the business world as a credential parallel to the CPA.

Two similar cost accounting programs exist in Canada that lead to the designation of Registered Industrial Accountant (RIA) or Certified General Accountant (CGA).[26] These two designations are also gaining acceptance as a credential parallel to the CA in Canada.

Several professional associations and agencies have a direct influence on cost accounting:

1. National Association of Accountants (NAA). Since 1919 the NAA has played a large role in the development of new techniques in cost accounting. The NAA publishes a monthly magazine, *Management Accounting*, and various books and monographs on cost accounting. For more information write to 919 Third Ave., New York, N.Y. 10022.

2. Cost Accounting Standards Board (CASB). This board was established by Congress in 1970 to "promulgate cost accounting standards designed to achieve uniformity and consistency in cost accounting principles followed by defense contractors under federal contracts." Consequently, its standards are only required in cost problems for govern-

---

[24] "Certificate in Management Accounting Established by NAA," *Management Accounting* (March 1977), p. 19.

[25] More information may be obtained by writing to The Institute of Management Accounting, 570 City Center Building, Ann Arbor, MI, 48108.

[26] More information on the Registered Industrial Accountant program may be obtained by writing to the Society of Management Accountants, 154 Main St. E., Box 176, Hamilton, Ontario, Canada L8N 3C3. For more information on the Certified General Accountant Program, write to the Canadian Certified General Accountants' Association, 740–1176 W. Georgia St., Vancouver, B.C., Canada V6E 4A2.

ment contracts. For more information write to 441 G St. N.W., Washington, D.C. 29548.

3. Financial Executives Institute (FEI). Since 1931 the FEI has served as a national organization for financial officers, treasurers, and controllers. It publishes a monthly magazine, *The Financial Executive*; through its research arm, the Financial Executives Research Foundation, it also publishes material relevant to cost accounting. For more information write to 633 Third Ave., New York, N.Y. 10017.

4. Society of Management Accountants of Canada. This group plays a major role in the development of new cost accounting techniques in Canada. It publishes a monthly magazine, *Cost and Management*, and various books and monographs on cost accounting. For more information write to 154 Main St. E., Box 176, Hamilton, Ontario, Canada L8N 3C3.

5. Canadian Certified General Accountants' Association. This association takes a great interest in the development of cost accounting techniques. It publishes a monthly magazine, the *Certified General Accountants' Magazine*, and various books and monographs relevant to cost accounting. For more information write to 740–1176 W. Georgia St., Vancouver, B.C., Canada V6E 4A2.

GLOSSARY

Accounting The process of identifying, measuring, recording, classifying, interpreting, and communicating economic information to facilitate decision making by users of the information.

Certificate in Management Accounting A certificate obtained upon passing the CMA examination covering (1) managerial economics and business finance; (2) organization and behavior, including ethical considerations; (3) public reporting; (4) periodic reporting for internal and external purposes; and (5) decision analysis, including modeling and information systems.

Cost Accounting (Management Accounting) The process of identifying, measuring, accumulating, analyzing, preparing, interpreting, and communicating financial information used by management to plan, evaluate, and control within an organization and to assure appropriate use of, and accountability for, its resources.

Generally Accepted Accounting Principles (GAAP) Current authoritative sources of GAAP are *Statements* issued by the Financial Accounting Standards Board, *Opinions* issued by the Accounting Principles Board, *Accounting Research Bulletins* issued by the American Institute of Certified Public Accountants Committee on Accounting Procedures, and *Accounting Series Releases* issued by the Securities and Exchange Commission.

Line Function A basic hierarchical relationship as defined by the line of authority or chain of command.

Management Control System A form of management information system that enables managers to assume that resources are obtained and used effectively and efficiently in the accomplishment of the organization's objectives.

Operational Control System A form of management information system that enables managers to insure that specific tasks are carried out effectively and efficiently.

Organizational Chart A diagram that depicts the system of relationships of an organization's staff.

Programmed Decision A decision is programmed to the extent that it is repetitive and routine and to the extent that a definite procedure has been worked out for handling it so it will not have to be treated de novo each time it occurs. A decision is nonprogrammed to the extent that it is novel, unstructured, and consequential.

Strategic Planning System A form of management information system concerned with deciding on (1) the objectives of the organization, (2) changes in these objectives, (3) the resources used to obtain these objectives, and (4) the policies that are to govern the acquisition, use, and disposition of these resources.

SELECTED READINGS

Ackoff, R. L., "Management Misinformation Systems," *Management Science* (December 1967), pp. 147–156.

American Accounting Association, Committee on Courses in Managerial Accounting, "Report of the Committee on Courses in Managerial Accounting," *Accounting Review* 47 supp. (1972), pp. 1–14.

American Accounting Association, Committee on Internal Measurement and Reporting, "Report of the Committee on Internal Measurement and Reporting, 1972," *Accounting Review* 48 supp. (1973), pp. 209–242.

Anthony, R. N., *Planning and Control Systems: A Framework for Analysis.* Harvard University Graduate School of Business Administration Studies in Management Control (Cambridge, Mass., 1965).

Belkaoui, Ahmed, *The Conceptual Foundations of Management Accounting* (Reading, Mass.: Addison-Wesley, 1980).

Benston, G. J., "The Role of the Firm's Accounting System for Motivation," *Accounting Review* (April 1963), pp. 347–354.

Caplan, E. H., *Management Accounting and Behavioral Science* (Reading, Mass.: Addison-Wesley, 1971).

Chatfield, Michael, "The Origins of Cost Accounting," *Management Accounting* (June 1971), pp. 11–20.

Collins, F., "Management Accounting and Motivation: The Relationship," *Management Accounting* (March 1979), pp. 22–26.

Donbrovski, Willis J., "Management Accounting: A Frame of Reference," *Management Accounting* (August 1965), pp. 20–25.

Donnelly, Robert N., "The Controller's Role in Corporate Planning," *Management Accounting* (September 1981), pp. 13–26.

Earnest, Kenneth R., "Applying Motivational Theory in Management Accounting," *Management Accounting* (December 1979), pp. 441–444.

Elnicki, Richard A., "The Genesis of Management Accounting," *Management Accounting* (April 1971), pp. 30–36.

Fertakis, John P., "Toward a Systems-Oriented Concept of Controllership," *Management Accounting* (December 1968), pp. 20–26.

Francia, Arthur J.; Grossman, Steven D.; and Strawser, Robert H., "The Attitudes of Management Accountants," *Management Accounting* (November 1978), pp. 35–40.

Fourke, D. V., "The Emerging Controllership," *Cost and Management* (November–December 1970), pp. 20–25.

Giacomino, Don E., "University Controllers: Are They Management Accountants?" *Management Accounting* (June 1980), pp. 32–35.

Gibson, J. L., "Accounting in the Decision Making Process: Some Empirical Evidence," *Accounting Review* (July 1963), pp. 492–500.

Giesler, Conrad, "Compensating Sales Reps," *Management Accounting* (April 1980), pp. 34–36.

Goodman, Sam R., and Reece, James S., *Controller's Handbook* (Homewood, Ill.: Dow Jones-Irwin, 1978).

Grinnell, Jacques D., and Kochanek, Richard F., "Capabilities and Role of the Contemporary Management Accountant," *Cost and Management* (July–August 1976), pp. 40–43.

Hale, Jack A., and Ryan, Larry J., "Decision Science and the Management Accountant," *Management Accounting* (January 1979), pp. 42–45.

Hayes, David, "The Contingency Theory of Managerial Accounting," *Accounting Review* (January 1977), pp. 22–39.

Hernandez, William H., "Is the Controller an Endangered Species?" *Management Accounting* (August 1978), pp. 48–52.

Horngren, C. T., "Choosing Accounting Practices for Reporting to Management," *NAA Bulletin*, (September 1962), pp. 3–15.

Imhoff, Eugene A. Jr., "Management Accounting Techniques: A Survey," *Management Accounting* (November 1978), pp. 41–45.

Janell, Paul A., and Kinnemen, Raymond M., "Portrait of the Divisional Controller," *Management Accounting* (June 1980), pp. 15–19, 24.

Johnson, Eugene A., "The Controllership Function," *Management Accounting* (March 1972), pp. 13–20.

Keller, Wayne I., "The Link between Accounting and Management," *Management Accounting* (June 1969), pp. 13–16.

Killough, Larry N., "Does Management Accounting Have a Theoretical Structure?" *Management Accounting* (April 1972), pp. 13–19.

Kotchian, A. C., "A President's View of the Chief Financial Officer," *Financial Executive* (May 1978), pp. 18–24.

Krogstad, J. L., and Harris, J. K., "The CMA Examination: A Content Analysis," *Management Accounting* (October 1974), pp. 21–23.

Lewis, Eldon C., "Successful Interface between Accounting and Management," *Management Accounting* (March 1969), pp. 12–16.

Livingstone, Leslie, ed., *Management Accounting: The Behavioral Foundations* (Columbus, Ohio: Grid, 1975).

Madden, D. L., "The CMA Examination: A Step toward Professionalism," *Management Accounting* (October 1974), pp. 17–20.

"MAP Committee Promulgates Definition of Management Accounting," *Management Accounting* (January 1981), pp. 58–60.

Meagher, Gary N., "Motivating Accountants," *Management Accounting* (March 1979), pp. 27–30.

Moller, George, "The Financial Executive: His Role in Over-all Company Planning," *Controller* (January 1968), pp. 17–18, 22.

Murray, Daniel R., "How Management Accountants Can Make a Manufacturing Control System Effective," *Management Accounting* (July 1981), pp. 25–31.

Plummer, George F., "The Financial Executive: His Role in the Corporate Organization," *Controller* (January 1962), pp. 16, 34.

Sauer, John R., "Psychology and Accounting: The Odd Couple?" *Management Accounting* (August 1980), pp. 14–17.

Seed, Allen H. III, "Strategic Planning: The Cutting Edge of Management Accounting," *Management Accounting* (May 1980), pp. 10–16.

Shenkir, William G.; Welsch, Glenn A.; and Bear, James A. Jr., "Thomas Jefferson: Management Accountant," *Journal of Accountancy* (April 1972), pp. 12–14.

Simon, H. A., *The New Science of Management Decision* (New York: Harper & Row, 1960).

Van Zante, Neal R., "Educating Management Accountants: What Do CMAs Think?" *Management Accounting* (August 1980), pp. 18–21.

Young, W. M. Jr., "The Challenge of Change: How NAA Is Meeting It," *Management Accounting* (January 1980), pp. 52–57.

QUESTIONS, EXERCISES, AND PROBLEMS

1.1   What are the main differences between (1) financial accounting, (2) tax accounting, (3) auditing, and (4) cost accounting?

1.2   Why is a cost accounting conceptual framework needed?

1.3   List and define the cost accounting concepts that represent a necessary, if not a minimum, foundation for a cost accounting conceptual framework.

1.4   List and define the qualitative characteristics of cost accounting information.

1.5   List the elements of the organizational structure that may affect the ways the cost accounting function will be exercised.

1.6   What are the differences between line and staff functions?

1.7   What is the role of the controller?

1.8   What motivates people to seek and retain membership in an organization? In answering this question, refer to the following motivation theories: need theory, two-factor theory, value/expectancy theory, achievement theory, and inequity theory.

1.9   At what level of the management structure (strategic planning, management control, or operational control) are the following cost accounting techniques needed?

1. Cost accumulation.   **9.** Performance evaluation.

2. Cost classification.   **10.** Transfer pricing.

3. Cost estimation.   **11.** Capital budgeting.

4. Cost allocation.   **12.** Inventory control.

5. Job-order costing.   **13.** Buy versus lease.

6. Process costing.   **14.** Cost-volume-profit analysis.

7. Variance analysis.   **15.** Linear programming.

8. Budgeting.

1.10   List the different information requirements of each of the processes of a planning and control system (strategic, management, and operational).

1.11   One characteristic may be applied to a member of an organization's staff. He or she may have a limited authority relationship. Elaborate on the relative usefulness of this characteristic of staff work when applied to the controller.

1.12   A production supervisor once commented, "These accountants seem to be confusing between line and staff functions. I maintain they serve purely as advisory resources when it comes to the production field. These people should stop coming down here and asking for all these useless statistics." Do you agree? Defend your decision.

1.13   Prepare an organizational chart depicting a structure with the following positions:

Purchasing   Vice-President, Manufacturing
President   Financial accountant
Receiving and stores   Cost accountant
Assembly, Superintendent   Internal auditor
Mixing, Superintendent   Vice-President, Personnel
Region—Sales manager
    Shipping manager
    Vice-President, Sales   Controller
    Advertising and sales
    promotion
                                  Production, Superintendent
                                  Finishing, Superintendent
Treasurer

1.14   Which one of the following statements is true of the relationship between financial accounting and management accounting?

1. A management accounting practice that is not consistent with financial accounting principles should not be used for internal purposes.

2. Financial accounting sacrifices usefulness to gain objectivity.

3. The purpose of financial accounting is to provide information that is useful to management.

4. Management accounting is necessary, whereas financial accounting is optional.

(SMA adapted)

1.15   You have just been appointed comptroller and chief financial officer of a large manufacturing company. The plant manager, a valued senior employee for many years, made the following comment after welcoming you to the company: "As I see it, you and the accounting department may be needed to keep the records for our shareholders and for the government, but I hope that you and your staff will try to keep your noses out of my day-to-day operations. I do my best; no pencil pusher knows enough about my responsibilities to be of any use to me."

Required:
In point form, prepare your response to the plant manager.

(SMA adapted)

1.16   It is sometimes said that the usefulness of accounting information in making intelligent decisions (by shareholders, managers, or anyone else) is severely limited both by the inherent limitations of accounting as an information resource and by the human characteristics of the decision makers themselves, who are seldom, if ever, the "rational men" of economic theory.

Required:
What are the "inherent limitations of accounting" and "human characteristics of decision makers" to which the above statement refers?

(CICA adapted)

1.17   In assessing the appropriateness of the accounting information system of a company, a number of common deficiencies exist in the information supply to the routine decision area.

1. Name and briefly explain some of these deficiencies. How would you attempt to correct them?

2. Suggest a few questions that an accountant must consider when applying the accounting viewpoint for decision making to routine decisions.

(SMA adapted)

1.18   Allen H. Seed III, a former NAA vice-president, stated: "However, in my opinion, too much strategic planning is undertaken without even the participation of management accounting, or without any linkage to the operating planning and control systems that are already in place. This is a serious deficiency when it is the case." [27]

Required:
1. Do you agree with the above statement?

2. What could be the role of management accounting in strategic planning?

1.19   ***Motivating Factors*** Tom Nelson is a young and aggressive management accountant employed by Essex Inc., a highly decentralized corporation with plants throughout the United States. Nelson was promoted to controller of the Burns Plant last year after only two years with the company. His salary provides his family comfortable living, includ-

---

[27] Allen H. Seed III, "Strategic Planning: The Cutting Edge of Management Accounting," *Management Accounting* (May 1980), p. 11.

ing an attractive home in one of the city's nice subdivisions. Essex encourages employees to continue their education, and reimburses them for tuition and fees as part of their benefit programs. Nelson has been enrolled in the night MBA program at a local university the past two years and hopes to receive his degree next year. He is the only employee on the financial staff of the Burns Plant to take advantage of this employee benefit.

Nelson regularly has sent memoranda to his superiors indicating potential improvements in the operations of the controller's department as well as in other aspects of the plant's operations. A recent memorandum sent to the plant manager and the corporate controller included recommendations to improve the reporting systems used to communicate with corporate headquarters. The ideas embodied in the recommendation resulted from knowledge acquired in the MBA program. During the recent salary review the corporate controller complimented Nelson on the fine ideas contained in his recommendations. Nelson was disappointed to learn that none had yet been implemented or even scheduled for implementation, but he guessed that the delay was due to the fact that his memorandum had not recommended either implementation steps or further study.

Earlier this year Nelson presented the plant manager (who had previously served as plant controller) with proposals to devise the plant's production scheduling and cost accounting system. The plant manager agreed that the proposals were good although they did not describe implementation procedures. The manager has not yet submitted the proposals for corporate review, even though she said she would do so. Nelson has not asked about the proposals since he introduced them.

Nelson is the newest and youngest member of the plant top management: the others have been with Burns Plant for five to twelve years. When the plant management meets, Nelson's ideas appear well conceived and presented and are seldom criticized. However, the other members of the plant management tend to view and refer to Nelson as "the new head bookkeeper" and "idea man."

Nelson has been offered a similar position by another firm. He is seriously considering the position, even though the salary and employee benefits are not as attractive as in his present employment.

Required:

1. Explain the needs that serve as motivating factors for individuals in their work.

2. Identify and explain the problems and factors that influenced Tom Nelson to consider seriously changing jobs.

(CMA adapted)

1.20   *Organizational Structure and Management Accounting*   Parisi describes the management structure of Exxon as follows:

The management committee runs the sprawling Exxon empire more or less the way Rome governed its far-flung holdings. Exxon's resources are concentrated in 13 autonomous operating companies, or affiliates. The majority, the oil-related affiliates, are organized according to geography; they include Esso Middle-East, Esso Europe and Exxon U.S.A., the largest of them all.

. . . The nonoil affiliates include Exxon Chemical, responsible for the corporation's chemical business worldwide; Exxon Enterprises, which handles the company's budding line of office equipment and other new products, and the Reliance Electric Company, the motor manufacturer purchased (in 1979). The heads of the 13 affiliates oversee their territories like provincial governors, sovereigns in their own lands but with an authority stemming from the power center in New York. The management committee exacts its

tribute (the affiliate's profits from current operations) and issues doles (the money needed to substain and expand those operations).

There is, in addition, another layer of authority consisting of 17 staff departments centered in New York. The vice presidents who run them make up what might be thought of as Exxon's cabinet. In addition to watching over such ancillary activities as corporate planning, law and public affairs, they advise the affiliates on such functions as crude-oil production, refining, or marketing. The governors in the field may command far greater resources with their 13 operating facilities, but the cabinet officers gain a special authority from their proximity to the real seat of power.[28]

1. What are the main disadvantages of Exxon's management structure?

2. What are the main advantages of Exxon's management structure?

3. What are the main functions of the staff departments from a management accounting point of view?

1.21   ***Controllership Function***   Contronics Inc. is a large electrical component manufacturer that has grown substantially in the last four years. As the company has expanded its operations, the duties and responsibilities of the accounting department have also increased. The size of the controller's staff has increased, and the department has added more responsibility centers as the department has expanded.

Each responsibility center manager reports directly to the company controller. An organization structure in which all subordinates report directly to a single supervisor is referred to as a flat organization. The organization chart presented here represents the controllership function of Contronics Inc.

Each manager of a responsibility center supervises a moderate-sized staff and is responsible for undertaking the tasks assigned to the position to accomplish the designated objectives for the individual responsibility center. The managers depend on the controller for direction in coordinating their separate activities.

Required:

1. Identify and explain briefly how a flat organization structure such as the one employed by Contronics Inc. in its accounting department might benefit downward and upward communication between the controller and his subordinates.

2. Identify and explain briefly the downward and upward communication problems which can result from the flat organization structure in Contronic's accounting department.

3. Recommend how to reduce the negative effects of a flat organization structure and discuss the impact your recommendation(s) would have on the upward communication process of Contronic's controllership function.

(CMA adapted)

1.22   ***Compensation Plan and Motivation***   Alum Company manufactures and sells costume jewelry and men's and women's toiletries. Alum's sales are seasonal, with the major sales volume to retailers in the months preceding Mother's Day, Father's Day, and Christmas. The company is planning to revise its method for compensating its sales force to encourage salespersons to increase their sales efforts.

---

[28] Anthony J. Parisi, "Inside Exxon," *New York Times*, August 3, 1980, pp. 24–25.

Figure 1   Controller's Department

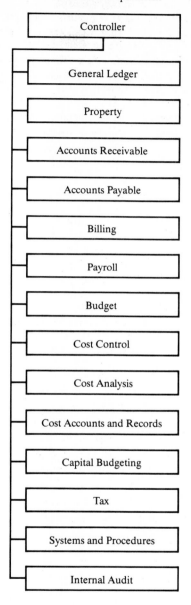

Controller's Department

- Controller
  - General Ledger
  - Property
  - Accounts Receivable
  - Accounts Payable
  - Billing
  - Payroll
  - Budget
  - Cost Control
  - Cost Analysis
  - Cost Accounts and Records
  - Capital Budgeting
  - Tax
  - Systems and Procedures
  - Internal Audit

One compensation system under consideration is a combination salary, commission, and bonus plan. Each salesperson would receive a monthly (base) salary on the first of the month. A 5 percent commission on all sales would be earned in two installments—one-half in the month of delivery and the remaining one-half on the fifteenth of the following month. In addition, salespersons could earn a bonus if the sales for the month exceeded the monthly sales quota. The bonus would be equal to 2 percent of the commission earned for sales delivered during the month and would be paid on the fifteenth of the following month (the same time as the regular commission).

The base salary and sales quotas would be established at the beginning of the year. The base salary would be reevaluated annually for each salesperson, considering such factors as cost of living, sales performance in the most recent and prior years, and length of service with Alum. An annual sales quota would be prepared for each sales territory based upon management's expectations for sales in each territory. The monthly sales quota for each territory would then be determined by dividing the annual sales quota by twelve.

Required:
Identify and discuss the strengths and weaknesses of Alum Company's compensation plan for its sales force in terms of the behavioral and motivational factors that influence employees' actions.

(CMA adapted)

1.23   ***Design of a Management Information System***   Giant Forest Products Ltd. is one of the largest North American companies in its industry, consisting of over thirty divisions of lumber, plywood, logging, and pulp and paper operations. The company has an intensive computerized management information system that provides management at all levels with detailed, timely information on all segments of company activity.

This system reflects the vice-president of finance's views: a management information system in a firm of this size should provide all managers, especially the senior ones, with up-to-date, detailed information on all aspects of the company's operations for consideration in formulating overall corporate strategies. The vice-president also believes that knowledge of what other departments are doing will induce better performance at the various operating levels.

In line with this vice-president's views, it has been the company's policy not to hire any staff assistants to work with top-level managers on the grounds that such assistants would not perform any meaningful function.

Required:
1. Discuss in detail the weaknesses inherent in the beliefs of the vice-president of finance.

2. Suggest a procedure for designing a management information system.

(SMA adapted)

1.24   ***Management Style***   Management style theoretically can range from an autocratic approach to a democratic approach. In the autocratic approach, decisions are made and announced by management, whereas decisions are reached by a majority vote in the democratic approach. While management's approach to any given decision may fall anywhere along this continuum, a predominant management style will be established through time. The behavior of individuals, with respect to such variables as goal attainment, motivation, and productivity, tends to vary depending on management style.

Required:

1. Discuss the major strengths and weaknesses of the autocratic approach to management.

2. Discuss the major strengths and weaknesses of the democratic approach to management.

3. What influences cause organizations to evolve toward a particular management style?

(CMA adapted)

COST THEORY, CLASSIFICATION, AND ACCOUNTING

The general idea of cost covers a number of different meanings. . . . A great deal of controversy [exists] as to whether certain items are properly costs at all. Most of this controversy will disappear if we carry our study far enough to recognize that there are different kinds of problems for which we need information about costs, and the particular information we need differs from one problem to another.[1]

A firm's production activities center around the relationships between two decision variables: inputs and outputs. The transformation of inputs, or scarce resources, into outputs, or goods and services, creates a cost to the firm. The concept of cost is complex, with differing scopes and classification schemes in response to the different needs of economics, accounting, finance, engineering, and law.

This chapter will evaluate the theoretical foundations, the terminology, and the treatment of cost in cost accounting, taking into account implications from these other disciplines.

Upon completion of this chapter, you should be able to do the following:

1. Differentiate between the economic and accounting theories of cost and between the notions of asset, *cost*, expense, and *loss*.

2. Identify the cost classification scheme for a particular decision and/or information need. Costs may be classified according to a natural classification, the time when computed, the degree of averaging, the behavior in relation to the volume of activity, the management function, the ease of traceability, the degree of control, the timing of charges against revenues, the relation to managerial policies, and the relation to decisions to be made.

3. Identify the cost classification on financial statements, the cost accounting cycle, and the possible format and content of the manufacturing and income statements of a manufacturing concern.

---

[1]J. Maurice Clark, *Studies in the Economics of Overhead Costs* (Chicago: University of Chicago Press, 1923), p. 35.

2.1   *COST THEORY*

2.1.1   *The Economic Theory of Cost*

The economic theory of cost deals with the relationship between input and output. Letting x be the input and y the output, the most general statement of the cost function of a firm is $(x_1 + x_2 + \ldots + x_n) - (y_1 + y_2 + \ldots + y_n) = 0$. In other words, inputs equal outputs. Although the level of the cost curve will be affected by different factors such as prices, lot size, plant utilization, etc., the theoretical approach is to assume first that these factors are constant, and second that a unique functional relationship exists between total cost and output.

The curvature of the cost curve will depend on the nature of the underlying production function. Thus, as depicted by Figure 2.1, the total cost curve is linear in the case of constant productivity and parabolic with increasing or decreasing productivity. Figure 2.1a shows that an assumption of constant productivity implies that for each additional unit of input there is a constant additional amount of output and cost. The assumption of increasing returns in Figure 2.1b implies that each additional unit of input adds more additional output and leads to less cost per unit of output. In Figure 2.1c, each additional unit of input adds less to total output, resulting in higher cost per unit. However, given the changing nature of production over time, three phases of returns—constant, increasing, and decreasing—may lead to the total cost function as depicted in Figure 2.2. Point Q_2 is the point of diminishing returns; Q_3 is the point of absolute diminishing returns.

2.1.2   *The Accounting Theory of Cost*

The term *cost* has different meanings to accountants, economists, engineers, and others facing managerial problems. Consider the following definitions from the cost accounting literature:

Figure 2.1   *Three Kinds of Short-Run Cost Functions*

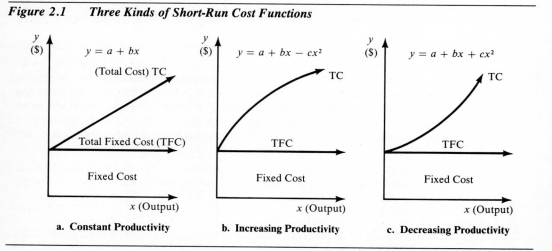

a. **Constant Productivity**   b. **Increasing Productivity**   c. **Decreasing Productivity**

Figure 2.2   **Conventional Short-Run Total Cost Function**

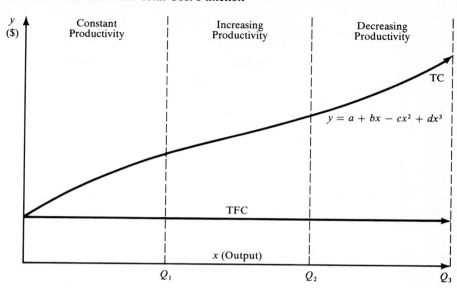

The term cost would seem to refer to some type of measured sacrifice evolving from an operational sequence of events and centering upon a particular activity or product.[2]

Cost is a foregoing, measured in monetary terms, incurred or potentially to be incurred to achieve a specific objective.[3]

The amount, measured in money, of cash expended or other property transferred, capital stock issued, services performed, or a liability incurred, in consideration of goods and services received or to be received. Costs can be classified as unexpired or expired. Unexpired costs (assets) are those which are applicable to the production of future revenues. . . . Expired costs are those which are not applicable to the production of future revenues, and for that reason are treated as deduction from current revenues, or charged against retained earnings. . . .[4]

In a cost accounting context, cost corresponds to a sacrifice resulting from the use of assets. A basic distinction should be made between unexpired cost (asset) and expired cost (cost), as well as between cost and expense. According to the third definition, cost results from the use of assets toward the creation of revenues, and as long as the assets are idle no cost is created. Cost also must be distinguished from the term *expense*. The AICPA *Accounting Research Study No. 3* defines expense as follows:

[2] Wilber E. Haseman, "An Interpretive Framework of Cost," *Accounting Review* (October 1968), pp. 738–752.

[3] American Accounting Association, Committee on Cost Concepts and Standards, "Report of the Committee on Cost Concepts and Standards," *Accounting Review* (April 1952), p. 176.

[4] Accounting Principles Board, *Statement No. 4*, "Basic Concepts and Accounting Principles Underlying Financial Statements of Business Enterprises" (New York: AICPA, 1970).

Figure 2.3   Asset-Expense-Loss Differences

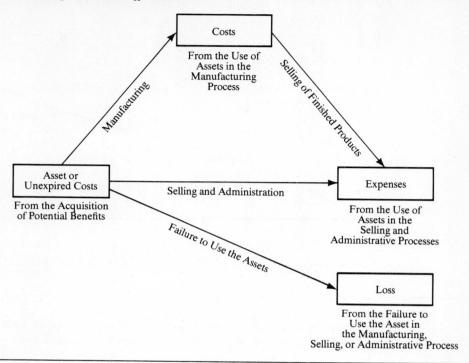

The decrease in net assets as a result of the use of economic services in the creation of revenues or of the imposition of taxes by government units.

Expense is measured by the amount of the decrease in assets or the increase in liabilities related to the production and delivery of goods and the rendering of services. . . . In its broadest sense expense *includes all expired costs which are deductible from revenues. In income statements, distinctions are made between various types of expired costs by captions or titles including such terms as cost, expense, or loss; e.g., cost of goods or services sold, operating expenses, marketing and administrative expenses, and loss on sale of property.*[5]

Here cost appears synonymous with expense. Four case analyses of costs, as depicted in Figure 2.3, may help avoid confusion between cost, expense, loss, and asset.

Case 1   The acquisition of resources with potential benefits results in the creation of *assets* or *unexpired costs.*

Case 2   The use of the assets in the manufacturing process results in the *cost* of a product. The eventual selling of the product transforms this cost into an *expense* to be matched with sales.

[5]R. T. Sprouse and M. Moonitz, *Accounting Research Study No. 3: A Tentative Set of Broad Accounting Principles for Business Enterprises* (New York: AICPA, 1962), p. 25.

Case 3   The use of the assets in the selling and administrative processes results in an *expense* to be matched with sales.

Case 4   The failure to use the assets in the manufacturing, selling, or administrative process and a misuse of the assets result in a *loss*.

These case analyses illustrate the flow of costs in a manufacturing firm. Haseman depicts this flow as follows:

> *In the process of recording events as they occur within an enterprise, costs are used as the valuation base for goods and services purchased by an enterprise. As purchased goods and services gradually are used to create other goods and services, costs originally belonging to what was purchased are transferred, following the concept of cost flow, so that they now become the valuation base for the newly created goods and services. Eventually these same costs are expensed, matched with revenue in the process of income determination. Thus, for example, costs originally identified as purchased labor, supplies, and plant and equipment may now be identified as parts of the cost of a newly created service, "maintenance," and, also (through overhead applications in one or more steps), as parts of the cost of a newly created product for sale. Eventually, when goods are sold, the same cost elements are identified as expense (cost of goods sold).*[6]

Thus, events in manufacturing occur in the following sequence: (1) acquisition creates an *asset*, (2) manufacturing creates a *cost* of a product or activity, (3) expiration or allocation creates an *expense*, and (4) misuse creates a *loss*.

2.2   COST CLASSIFICATION SCHEMES

Once identified, costs must be classified and reported. The existence of different decision making models with different information needs results in a variety of classification schemes. Each system arises to resolve a given organizational problem. Referring to the variety of cost classification schemes, Haseman states:

> *Thus, an enterprise which incurred $100,000 of costs during a period of time for purchased goods and services might recoup these costs in such a way as to identify (1) "What we purchased" (natural classes), (2) "What activities we generated with what we purchased" (functional classes), (3) "What assets, whether still on hand or not, resulted from the activities performed" (product classes), (4) "What part of the period's costs should be treated as expenses and losses and what part as assets" (expense-loss-asset classification), (5) "What costs are the result of different ventures or projects" (project classes), (6) "Which costs are responsive to changes in volume and which are not" (variability classes), and (7) "Which costs are responsive to the decisions and actions of specific managers" (responsibility classes).*[7]

A given group of costs may be classified in a variety of ways, depending on the choice of the *cost objective*, or activity for which a cost is desired.

---

[6] Haseman, "Interpretive Framework," p. 739.
[7] Ibid., pp. 739–740.

Decision usefulness generally governs the choice of a cost objective. At one time, most cost accounting systems emphasized one single cost objective, namely, product costing for inventory valuation and income determination. Because of the expanding and complex needs of modern organizations, however, many cost objectives are now considered pertinent in managerial decision making. This has generated new ways of classifying costs: a natural classification, time when computed, behavior in relation to the volume of activity, management function, ease of traceability, degree of control, timing of charges against revenues, relation to managerial policies, and relation to decisions to be made. Because decision making emphasizes the proper classification of costs, each of these classifications is examined next.

2.2.1   Natural Classification

The natural classification refers to the basic "physical" aspects of cost. Hence the accountant classifies costs as either direct labor, direct material, or manufacturing overhead.

Direct material refers to all materials that become an integral part of a finished product. In general, the ease of traceability of a material to the finished product is the determinant for its classification as a direct material. For example, wood is the direct material in a piece of wooden furniture. Materials that are not significant on a per-unit basis are *indirect materials*; glue, nails, rivets, and screws are examples.

Direct labor is the labor expended directly upon the direct material. It constitutes, then, the labor easily traceable to a finished product. For example, the wages of the production line workers constitute direct labor. *Indirect labor* cannot easily be identified with a finished product; examples include the wages of supervisors, janitors, and inspectors.

Manufacturing overhead (also called *factory overhead*) refers to all costs necessary for the manufacturing and operation of a product except direct labor and direct material. It consists of the costs of indirect material; indirect labor; and all other manufacturing costs that cannot easily be traced to a specific product, including plant depreciation, machinery and equipment depreciation, rent, insurance, taxes, maintenance, power, heat, light, supplies, small tools. Direct labor combined with direct material generally is referred to as *prime cost*. Direct labor and manufacturing overhead are what converts the direct material into a finished product. Thus, direct labor combined with manufacturing overhead is *conversion cost*.

Idle time, overtime premiums, and payroll fringe benefits in labor are not easily classified. Idle time represents wages paid for unproductive time due to machine breakdowns, material shortages, and any work stoppage. For example, if a press operator earning $5 per hour of straight time has worked thirty-five hours and was idle five hours because of material shortages, the earnings would be computed as follows:

Direct Labor ($5 × 35 Hours)	$175
Idle Time (Manufacturing Overhead) ($5 × 5 Hours)	25
Total Earnings	$200

Similarly, an overtime premium represents the cost of direct labor and indirect labor due for time beyond the straight time of the regular workday (as specified in some labor union contracts) or time over the forty-hour workweek. Overtime premium is considered indirect labor unless caused by a specific job. Thus, a job worked on during the overtime period is not attributed the overtime premium that applies to all the jobs of the period. For example, if a press operator worked forty hours at $5 per hour and ten over-time hours at an additional $3 per overtime hour, the earnings would be computed as follows:

Direct Labor ($5 × 50 Hours)	$250
Overtime Premium ($3 × 10 Hours)	30
Total Earnings	$280

Finally, payroll fringe benefits include various employment-related costs such as contributions to Social Security, employee insurance programs, life insurance, hospitalization plans, pension plans, and annuity and retirement plans. These costs are classified as direct labor, indirect labor, or partly direct labor and partly indirect labor.

2.2.2   *Time When Computed*

Costs may be classified as historical or budgeted according to the time when they are computed.

Historical costs are past costs valued at the acquisition costs of the asset. Conventional financial accounting records assets on the books at their acquisition or historical cost. Historical costs have the basic advantage of conforming to generally accepted accounting principles and so are presumed to be objective, verifiable, and free from bias.

Budgeted or standard costs express the future trend of historical costs and result from prediction models. Useful for planning and control, budgeted costs set yardsticks for future performance. They depend, however, on the accuracy of the estimation techniques used for their derivation. There are three basic approaches to their estimation: (1) qualitative judgments, (2) quantitative models, considering external variables, and (3) time series quantitative models. The cost estimation problem is fully investigated in chapter 3.

2.2.3   *Degree of Averaging*

Costs may be classified as either total, unit (average), or marginal. A *total cost* (TC) encompasses the total level of activity. A *unit cost* (UC) is related to a single unit of activity, so UC is simply TC divided by the total level of activity. Figure 2.4 illustrates the derivation of UC. The unit total cost (UTC) is equal to the slope of the line passing through the origin and tangent to the curve (Figure 2.4a), and the unit variable cost (UVC) is equal to a similar tangent line starting at the fixed cost level (Figure 2.4b). These slopes decrease up to the point of absolute diminishing returns and increase thereafter. As illustrated in Figure 2.4c, the UTC falls, reaches a minimum, and rises thereafter. Similarly, the UVC, equal to the UTC minus the unit fixed cost (UFC), has the same behavior. So, UVC is always smaller than UTC.

Similarly, the *marginal cost* (MC) is the additional outlay needed to add one unit of output. It is equal to the first derivative of TC. At the stage of increasing returns MC will be decreasing, and at the stage of diminishing returns MC will be increasing. Consequently, MC will be at a minimum at the point of diminishing returns. The concepts of MC, UTC, and UVC are illustrated in Figure 2.5. When UTC and UVC are falling, UTC and UVC are equal to MC, and when UTC and UVC are rising, UTC and UVC are equal to MC. Consequently, $MC = UVC$ at the minimum unit variable cost, and $MC = UTC$ at the minimum total cost.

Figure 2.4   Derivation of Unit Cost Curves

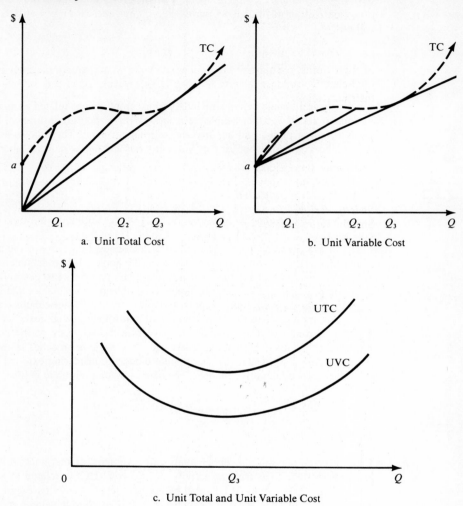

a. Unit Total Cost

b. Unit Variable Cost

c. Unit Total and Unit Variable Cost

Since these costs are depicted in terms of their relation to output, the concept of *elasticity* may be used to measure the sensitivity between cost and output. In the following equation, the *elasticity*, *e*, of total cost measures the percentage change in *TC* created by a small change in output, *X*:

$$e_{TC} = \frac{\frac{\Delta TC}{TC}}{\frac{\Delta X}{X}} = \frac{X\Delta TC}{TC\Delta X} \; .$$

Given that $MC = \Delta TC/\Delta X$ and $UC = TC/X$, this formula could be expressed as follows:

$$e_{TC} = \frac{\dfrac{\Delta TC}{\Delta X}}{\dfrac{TC}{X}} = \frac{MC}{UC} \ .$$

In other words, the elasticity of total cost is equal to the ratio of marginal cost to average total cost. These cost relationships are illustrated in Figure 2.6, and Table 2.1 shows their derivation.

2.2.4   *Behavior in Relation to the Volume of Activity*

Costs may also be classified in terms of their behavior in relation to the volume of activity. Thus, costs may be strictly variable, strictly fixed, semivariable, or semifixed.

Strictly Variable Costs
Strictly variable costs vary directly and in proportion to the volume of activity. They may be expressed as $y = bx$, where y = total variable costs, x = level of activity, and b = unit variable cost.

Figure 2.5 *Graphic Relationship between Unit Total Cost, Unit Variable Cost, and Marginal Cost*

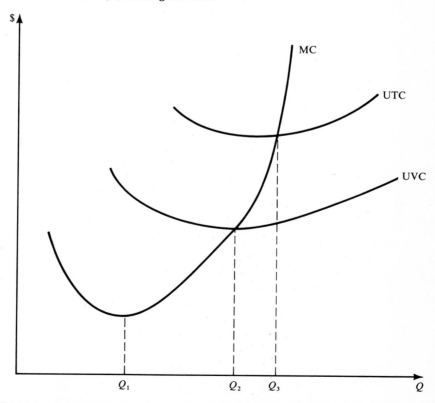

Figure 2.6   Behavior of Cost Elasticity

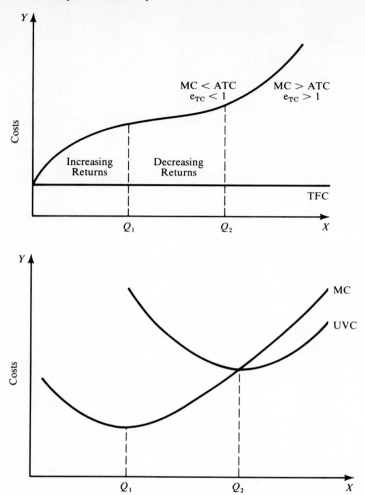

Table 2.1   Derivation of Cost Schedules

Level of Activity (1)	Total Cost (2)	Total Fixed Cost (3)	Total Variable Cost (4)	Unit Total Cost (5)	Unit Variable Cost (6)	Unit Fixed Cost (7)	Marginal Cost (8)	Cost Elasticity (9)
X	TC	TFC	TVC = (2) − (3)	(2)/(1) = UTC	(4)/(1) = UVC	(3)/(1) = UFC	$\Delta(2)/\Delta(1)$ = MC	(8)/(5) = CE
0	$ 200	$200	$ 0	—	—	—	—	—
10	300	200	100	$30.0	$10	$20.0	$10	0.33
20	380	200	180	19.0	9	10.0	8	0.44
30	440	200	240	14.6	8	6.6	6	0.41
50	500	200	300	10.0	6	4.0	3	0.30
100	700	200	500	7.0	5	2.0	4	0.57
150	1200	200	1000	8.0	7	1.0	10	1.20
200	2200	200	2000	11.0	10	1.0	20	1.80

Figure 2.7   *Total Strictly Variable Costs*

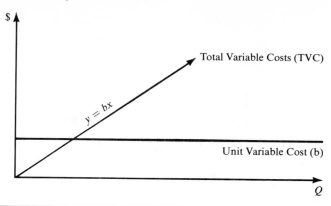

Consequently, the total variable cost, y, is equal to zero when $x = 0$. Assuming constant productivity, the total variable costs are linear, and the unit variable cost ($b = y/x$) is fixed. The slope of the cost line is b; it is equal to $(y_2 - y_1)/(x_2 - x_1)$. Figure 2.7 illustrates the strictly variable cost.

Examples of strictly variable costs are direct material and direct labor, which occur in the manufacturing of any product. The amount of direct material and/or direct labor fluctuates in direct proportion to the operating volume or level of activity. Suppose, for example, that a firm pays salespeople solely on commission. As the volume of sales increases, the commissions will increase proportionally. Thus, the commissions are a variable cost arising from sales. If the firm pays as commission 10 percent of its dollar sales, the total commission paid for three months is as follows:

Month	Sales in Dollars	Commission Paid
1	$ 1,000	$ 100
2	20,000	2,000
3	30,000	3,000

Notice that the total commission paid (total variable cost) varies proportionally to the volume of activity as expressed by the sales dollars, while the commission rate (unit variable cost) is fixed.

Strictly Fixed Costs

Strictly fixed costs, or strictly total fixed costs (TFC), do not vary with the level of activity; however, unit fixed costs (UFC) do vary with the level of activity, as shown in Figure 2.8. TFC may be expressed as $y = M$, where y = total fixed costs and M = lump sum. Similarly, $UFC = y/x = M/x$. Therefore, UFC decreases proportionally with the level of activity.

The concept of total fixed costs as independent of changes in the volume of activity includes two basic assumptions: the time period and the *relevant range* of activity. In other words, the accountant may conceive of a relevant range of activity and a time period for which the total fixed cost concept is definable. Property taxes, depreciation expense, insurance expense, and time and motion studies are examples of fixed costs. To illustrate, assume that a plant is leased for $10,000 per month. The lease cost is a *capacity cost*: it is necessary to provide or maintain the current operating capacity.

Figure 2.8   *Fixed Cost Curves*

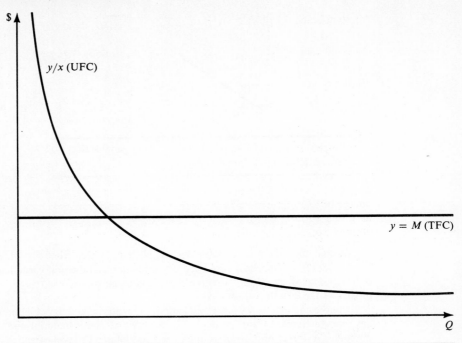

Suppose, however, that the use of the capacity varies each month. For output levels of 1,000, 5,000, and 10,000 units, the average fixed cost (UFC) will be as follows:

Month	Total Rental Cost	Level of Activity	Average Fixed Cost
1	$10,000	1,000 Units	$10
2	$10,000	5,000 Units	$ 2
3	$10,000	10,000 Units	$ 1

The capacity costs may be further classified. The *standby costs* are those capacity costs that would be incurred even if the productive facilities closed down. They are fixed whether or not any work is performed. The *enabling costs* are those capacity costs which would not be incurred in a shutdown.

Semivariable Costs
Semivariable costs include both a fixed and a variable component. They may be linear, quadratic, or cubic.

If the total cost of the fixed and variable quantities is denoted by y, then $y = a + bx$ represents a *linear cost function*. The equation's mathematical properties are as follows:

Total fixed costs (TFC) = a.

Unit cost (UTC) $= \dfrac{y}{x} = \dfrac{a}{x} + b.$

Unit variable cost (UVC) $= b =$ constant.

Marginal cost (MC) $= \dfrac{\Delta y}{\Delta x} =$ constant.

Elasticity $(e_{TC}) = \dfrac{b}{\dfrac{a}{x} + b}.$

Figure 2.9 illustrates the linear total cost function curve and its properties. The relevant range dichotomizes the semivariable costs into fixed and variable components.

The cost of equipment maintenance and repairs is semivariable. One part of the cost varies with the use of the equipment, and another part represents standby costs. For example, if the cost of repairs and maintenance amounts to $1,000 a month plus a repair charge of $20 per hour, the cost of equipment maintenance and repairs may be expressed as $y = \$1,000 + \$20x$, where $y =$ cost of maintenance and repairs, and $x =$ level of activity expressed in direct labor hours.

The quadratic cost function is represented by the equation $y = a + bx + cx^2$. Its distinct mathematical properties, shown in Figure 2.10, are as follows:

$$UTC = \dfrac{y}{x} = \dfrac{a}{x} + b + cx.$$

$$MC = \dfrac{\Delta y}{\Delta x} = b + 2cx.$$

Figure 2.9   *Linear Total Cost Function Curve*

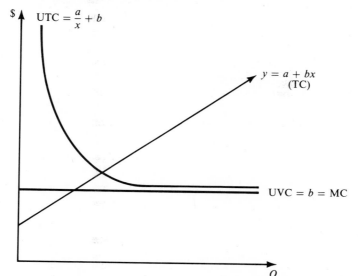

$$UTC = \dfrac{a}{x} + b$$

$$y = a + bx \quad (TC)$$

$$UVC = b = MC$$

Q
(Activity Level or Relevant Range)

Figure 2.10   Quadratic Cost Curve Properties

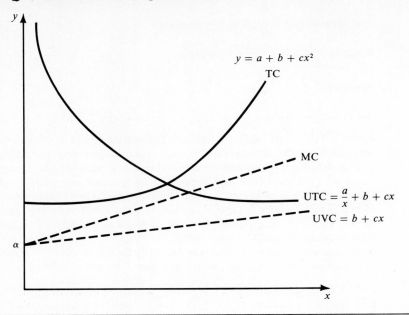

$$e_{TC} = \frac{b + 2cx}{\dfrac{a}{x} + b + cx}.$$

With increasing productivity, the following equation represents the quadratic cost curve: $y = a + bx - cx^2$. Its mathematical properties are as follows:

Table 2.2   Properties of Semivariable Cost Functions

Nature of the Equation	Form of the Equation	Total Fixed Costs	Total Variable Costs	Marginal Cost
Linear	$y = 5 + 2x$	5	$2x$	2
Quadratic I	$y = 5 + 2x + 3x^2$	5	$2x + 3x^2$	$2 + 6x$
Quadratic II	$y = 5 + 2x - 3x^2$	5	$2x - 3x^2$	$2 - 6x$
Cubic	$y = 5 + 2x - 3x^2 + 6x^3$	5	$2x - 3x^2 + 6x^3$	$2 - 6x + 18x^2$

$$UTC = \frac{y}{x} = \frac{a}{x} + b - cx.$$

$$MC = \frac{y}{x} = b - 2cx.$$

$$e_{TC} = \frac{b - 2cx}{\frac{a}{x} + b - cx}.$$

The *cubic cost function* is expressed by the now familiar equation $y = a + bx - cx^2 + dx^3$ shown in Figure 2.2. Its mathematical properties are as follows:

$$UTC = \frac{y}{x} = \frac{a}{x} + \frac{b}{x} - cx + dx^2.$$

$$MC = \frac{\Delta y}{\Delta x} = b - 2cx + 3dx^2.$$

$$e_{TC} = \frac{b - 2cx + 3dx^2}{\frac{a}{x} + \frac{b}{x} - cx + dx^2}.$$

Table 2.2 summarizes the properties of all the semivariable cost functions in a theoretical example. In practice, however, the task of classifying the semivariable costs as linear, quadratic, or cubic is very difficult. One popular simplification is to assume the cost behavior pattern to be linear rather than quadratic or cubic.

This approach is not without limitations. First, the linear approximation may oversimplify the true relationship between costs and the activity level and thus may lead to incorrect decisions or evaluations. Second, the conditions necessary for simple linearity may be difficult to achieve in cases such as the following:

1. The raw material goes through various physical processes before becoming a finished product.

Unit Total Cost	Unit Variable Cost	Unit Fixed Cost	Cost Elasticity
$\frac{5}{x} + 2$	2	$\frac{5}{x}$	$\dfrac{2}{\frac{5}{x} + 2}$
$\frac{5}{x} + 2 + 3x$	$2 + 3x$	$\frac{5}{x}$	$\dfrac{2 + 6x}{\frac{5}{x} + 2 + 3x}$
$\frac{5}{x} + 2 - 3x$	$2 - 3x$	$\frac{5}{x}$	$\dfrac{2 - 6x}{\frac{5}{x} + 2 - 3x}$
$\frac{5}{x} + 2 - 3x + 6x^2$	$2 - 3x + 6x^2$	$\frac{5}{x}$	$\dfrac{2 - 6x + 18x^2}{\frac{5}{x} + 2 - 3x + 6x^2}$

Figure 2.11   **Semifixed Cost**

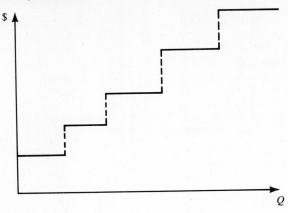

2. The cost of acquiring each input is a function of the amount purchased. It could be an exponential increasing function (in the case of scarce resources) or a decreasing function of the amount purchased (when quantity discounts apply).

3. Other intervening variables exist to affect the relationship between costs and the activity level.[8]

Semifixed Costs

Semifixed or step costs are fixed for a given level of activity and eventually increase by a constant amount at some critical points (see Figure 2.11). This level of activity must be large enough to avoid confusion with the strictly fixed cost.

The salary of the basic supervisory staff rises in steps. Assume that the supervisory staff can inspect 1,000 units a day. The addition of personnel for any activity level above 1,000 units raises the cost of supervision to a higher plateau.

In practice, the discontinuity of the stepped costs may be ignored to facilitate decision making. If the activity increments are relatively small, the semifixed cost may be approximated by a strictly variable cost. Economists favor this alternative. If the increments are relatively large, each increment may be considered a relevant range of activity and the semifixed cost approximated by a strictly fixed cost. Executives and accountants prefer this treatment.

For practical purposes the only measure of activity level used in this chapter has been the number of units produced. Other indexes of volume that may be used when classifying costs in terms of their behavioral patterns include direct labor hours, machine hours, materials quantity, and direct labor cost. Accounting criteria for choosing the activity index for allocation will be presented in a subsequent chapter. A major criteria is the possibility of measuring the organization's overall efficiency. Because such a *macro-activity index* should lead to motivational behavioral patterns, its potential for socially beneficial results must be considered.

---

[8] P. S. Singh and G. L. Chapman, "Is Linear Approximation Good Enough?" *Management Accounting* (January 1978), pp. 53–55.

2.2.5 Management Function

It is generally agreed that the management function within a firm involves manufacturing, selling, and administrative activities. The firm may classify costs as either manufacturing, selling, or administrative costs.

The *manufacturing costs* are related to the production function or input mix. They generally cover the direct material, direct labor, and manufacturing overhead discussed in a previous section.

The *nonmanufacturing costs* fall into two broad classifications: (1) selling overhead, and (2) administrative overhead. *Selling overhead* is costs incurred after the manufacturing process. It encompasses all expenses necessary for the transition of the product from the manufacturer to the immediate buyer. *Administrative overhead* includes all expenses necessary for the maintenance of an efficient management administration.

2.2.6 Ease of Traceability

Costs are classified on the basis of traceability relative to an object of costing, such as a product line. A *direct cost* is easily identified and traceable to an object of costing. The prime cost and some overhead are usually directly traceable to a product, department, or segment of the firm. A cost that cannot be identified and traced to one segment of a firm is an *indirect cost* and is usually associated with several segments of the firm. Therefore, the salary of a given worker may be a direct charge to a department but an indirect charge to a product.

The distinction between direct and indirect costs facilitates decisions in areas such as product line and pricing policy. Table 2.3 shows the distinction between direct and indirect costs and between variable and fixed costs for a given product line (product X). Notice that even a fixed cost may be either direct or indirect in terms of its association with an object of costing.

Organizations also use the direct and indirect costs concept in performance evaluation, pricing, and resource allocation. In general, the degree of traceability of cost rests on the delimitation of responsibility in *cost centers*, units that control the incurrence of cost rather than sales. The whole corporation may be perceived as a cost center, or all other segments of the firm—divisions, departments, branches, shops, and machines—may be cost centers. The total configuration of cost centers within the organization de-

Table 2.3   *Product Line Income Statement (Product X)*

Sales		$10,000
Minus Direct Costs		
Direct Variable Costs	$1,000	
Direct Fixed Costs	2,000	3,000
Equals Excess of Sales over Direct Costs		$ 7,000
Minus Indirect Costs		
Indirect Variable Costs	$2,000	
Indirect Fixed Costs	3,000	5,000
Equals Product X's Net Income		$ 2,000

Figure 2.12   Distinctions between Product and Period Costs

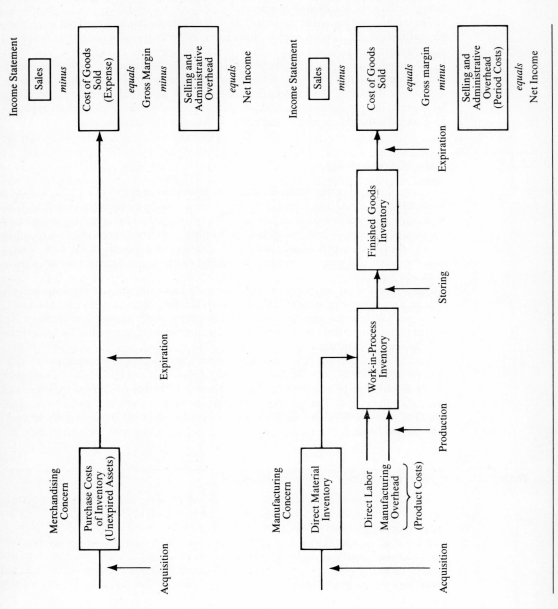

termines the traceability of costs. In general, direct costs are incurred within and for the cost center, while indirect costs are external to the center and can be identified with it only through allocation.

Direct costs may also be classified as *common* or *joint costs* if used by more than one costing unit. The common or joint costs refer to services provided to more than one costing object, and as such ought to be allocated on an objective basis. Joint or common costs arise when one input goes into a process yielding several outputs. They refer to services required for the production of different outputs. The cost allocation problem is investigated in chapter 10.

2.2.7   *Degree of Control*

Classifying costs as either *controllable* or *noncontrollable* assigns responsibility and provides a basis for cost control. A cost is called controllable by a given entity if it is under that entity's direct influence. A controllable cost's source of incurrence and responsibility are known. Consequently, the classification of a cost as controllable or noncontrollable depends on the following time period and point-of-reference assumptions: (1) for any given organization, there is always in the organizational hierarchy an individual with the power to authorize a given cost, and (2) the longer the time span, the more controllable a given cost will become. In the long run, someone in the organization can be held responsible for the ultimate decision concerning the incurrence of any cost. Note that an organization must objectively justify the assignment of controllability of a given cost to avoid a negative effect on morale. This implies that for any given responsibility center some unallocated costs should be listed separately and identified as uncontrollable.

A few fallacies concerning controllability should be recognized:

1. All variable costs are controllable, and all fixed costs are noncontrollable.

2. All direct costs are controllable, and all indirect costs are noncontrollable.

3. All long-run costs are controllable, and all short-run costs are noncontrollable.

In other words, controllability should not be confused with ease of traceability, cost behavior, and time.

2.2.8   *Timing of Charges against Revenues*

The classification of costs according to the timing of charges against revenues depends on whether the costs are considered *product* or *period costs*. Product costs—unexpired or inventoriable costs—relate to the products on hand, either unsold finished goods or semifinished goods. They are inventoried and carried forward as assets until the goods to which they relate are sold; then they are matched against sales. Period costs—expenses or losses—are costs that are associated with the revenues of the current period. They are not assigned directly to the products on hand because they do not represent value added to any specific product.

The classification as product or period costs varies between merchandising accounting and manufacturing accounting, as shown in Figure 2.12. In merchandising accounting the purchase costs of inventory are product costs, while the selling and administrative overhead are period costs. In manufacturing accounting the manufacturing costs are product costs, while the selling and administrative overhead are period costs.

2.2.9   Relation to Managerial Policies

Fixed or capacity costs are fixed for various reasons and can be divided in two categories: *committed* or *discretionary costs*.

The committed fixed costs are those fixed, unavoidable costs necessary for maintaining a basic organization and a productive capacity. Their incurrence continues even if the volume of activity is zero. Examples of committed costs are depreciation, property taxes, rent, insurance, and so on.

The discretionary, managed, engineered, or programmed fixed costs reflect a given management policy or philosophy. Because management initiates and can change discretionary costs, they are often the first costs examined in the introduction of a cost reduction program or a new managerial policy.

The distinction between discretionary and committed fixed costs may be useful for a decision concerning the elimination of a segment of the firm. For such decisions the variable costs obviously must be examined. The relevance of the fixed costs will depend on the following scheme:

	Separable	Joint
Discretionary	Relevant	Not Relevant
Committed	Not Relevant	Not Relevant

In other words, for the short-run decision affecting a segment of a firm, only the variable costs and the *separable* discretionary costs are relevant. However, in the long-term decision, all costs are discretionary and hence relevant.

The taxonomy of costs shown in Table 2.4 summarizes most of the cost classification schemes discussed so far.

2.2.10   Relation to Decisions to Be Made

Cost Concepts for Decision Making

Costs may be either relevant or irrelevant for decision making purposes. Their relevance depends on the identification of the costs as (1) sunk or *out-of-pocket costs*, (2) marginal, incremental, or differential costs, (3) historical or *opportunity costs*, and/or (4) escapable or inescapable costs.

Sunk costs are past expenditures already incurred and not relevant to a particular decision, while *out-of-pocket costs* are the possible outlays resulting from a decision. A sunk cost is irrelevant to any decision because it cannot be changed by a present or future decision. For example, outlays already spent on research and development are sunk costs for the purpose of deciding whether to produce a product.

The *incremental* or *differential costs* are the expected future costs that differ as a consequence of choosing one alternative over another. The change in costs resulting from a change in the operating level is an incremental cost. The *marginal cost* is a unit concept; it refers to the cost created by the production of one additional unit. In other words, if Y_1 and Y_2 are the costs associated with the output levels X_1 and X_2, then

$$Y_2 - Y_1 = \text{incremental cost}$$

and

$$\frac{Y_2 - Y_1}{X_2 - X_1} = \text{marginal cost.}$$

Table 2.4	Taxonomy of Costs

A. Manufacturing Costs

1. Prime Costs

1.1. Direct Material

1.2. Direct Labor

2. Variable Manufacturing Overhead

2.1. Indirect Material

2.2. Indirect Labor

2.3. Others (Overtime, Idle Time, Payroll Fringe Costs, and So Forth)

3. Fixed Manufacturing Overhead

3.1. Fixed Discretionary Manufacturing Overhead

3.2. Fixed Committed Manufacturing Overhead

B. Selling Costs

1. Variable Selling Overhead

2. Fixed Selling Overhead

2.1. Fixed Discretionary Selling Overhead

2.2. Fixed Committed Selling Overhead

C. Administrative Costs

1. Variable Administrative Overhead

2. Fixed Administrative Overhead

2.1. Fixed Discretionary Administrative Overhead

2.2. Fixed Committed Administrative Overhead

To explore the use of incremental or differential costs, assume that five years ago the ABEL Manufacturing Company purchased a cutting machine for $20,000; it has accumulated depreciation of $10,000 and has five remaining years of useful life. This machine may be sold for $5,000 now and will have no disposal value at the end of the five years. The management, realizing that the old machine no longer has its original operating advantages, decided to buy a new machine. After detailed analysis management is considering a new machine costing $12,000 with a useful life of five years; it could reduce the operating costs from $6,000 to $4,000 annually, and it would have a $5,000 disposal value at the end of the five years.

Table 2.5 presents a summary of the cost comparison for the equipment replacement. The book value of the old equipment is irrelevant to the decision and does not appear in the analysis. The disposal value of both the old and new equipment are relevant as future revenues that differ with the two alternatives. The difference column shows that the purchase of the new machine yields an $8,000 five-year cost savings, or a cost savings of $1,000 a year.[9]

Although the book value of the old equipment did not appear in the above analysis, it will appear in the computation of the formal income statement. Hence the income statement will show a $5,000 loss on disposal ($5,000 disposal value − $10,000 book value). Notice that a manager may be reluctant to replace the equipment to avoid recognizing this loss on disposal. Needless to say, such an attitude emphasizing short-run

---

[9]Ordinarily, income tax considerations and the effect of the interest value of money should be considered in analyzing whether to buy the new equipment or to keep the old equipment. In any case, the book value will still be considered as a sunk cost, and only the tax cash flow will be the basis of analysis.

Table 2.5   Cost Comparison for Replacement of Equipment

Accounts	Five Years Together			One-Year Analysis		
	Old Machine	New Machine	Difference	Old Machine	New Machine	Difference
Cash Operating Costs	$30,000	$20,000	$10,000	$6,000	$4,000	$2,000
Old Equipment (Book Value)						
Periodic Depreciation	10,000			2,000		
or						
Write-off		10,000[a]			2,000	
Disposal Value (Old Equipment)		−5,000[a]	+5,000		−1,000	+1,000
New Machine						
Periodic Depreciation		12,000	−12,000		2,400	−2,400
Disposal Value (New Equipment)		−5,000	+5,000		−1,000	+1,000
Total Costs	$40,000	$32,000	$8,000	$8,000	$6,400	$1,600

[a] The two items may be combined as Loss on Disposal of $5,000.

profit to the detriment of long-run profit is a form of suboptimization harmful to the company.

Opportunity costs refer to the benefits forgone by the choice of one alternative over the next best alternative. Because resources are always limited, any decision to produce a given commodity implies doing without some other commodity. As an example on the social level, when a tank is produced an implicit decision has been made not to produce ten tractors with the material, labor, and overhead used by the production of the tank. Thus, the opportunity cost of one tank is ten tractors. The opportunity cost doctrine prevalent in economic analysis views problems of social choice in terms of all alternatives of economic progress.

At the microeconomic level, the doctrine may be used in the context of profit maximization. Hence the opportunity cost may be the difference between the profits earned in two managerial alternatives in a profit situation, or the difference in the costs incurred in a cost situation. Suppose a firm can either use a machine to make product X or product Y. The production of Y can be sold for $20,000, with corresponding direct costs of $15,000. The opportunity cost of producing X is, therefore, $5,000 ($20,000 − $15,000). Thus, the opportunity cost of using the machine to produce X is the sacrifice of earnings from Y that might be produced using the machine.

Although used in decision making, opportunity costs are not entered in accounting records. The concept of opportunity costs requires the measurement of sacrifices associated with alternatives, which may be difficult. For example, opportunity costs of capacities are difficult to measure, so the cost accountant resorts to allocation, which is equivalent to imputing the capacities' opportunity costs to the activities undertaken (cost allocation is examined in chapter 10).

An *escapable cost* can be avoided by a structural or operational change. For instance, if the cost of labor is reduced by a curtailment of activities, such a cost may be considered an escapable or *avoidable cost*. The opposite *inescapable cost* must be incurred in spite of structural or operational changes.

In the context of an abandonment decision, Shillinglaw suggests the concept of *attributable cost*, "the cost per unit that could be avoided, on the average, if a product or function were discontinued entirely without changing the supporting organization struc-

Figure 2.13   *Graphic Presentation of Marginal Analysis*

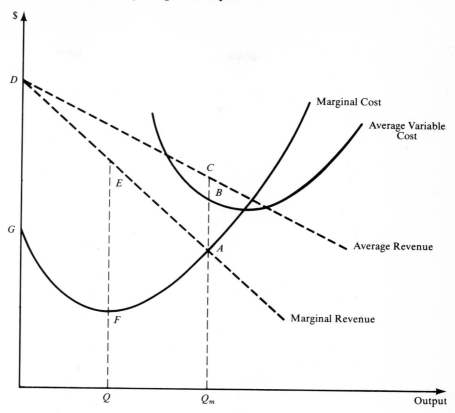

ture. The costing unit may be either a physical product or a unit of service performed." [10] Attributable cost is the long-run equivalent to avoidable cost and includes both the variable out-of-pocket costs and fixed department costs that may result from the abandonment of a product.

In general, the out-of-pocket, the incremental, the marginal, the opportunity, and the escapable costs are relevant costs for decision making.

Marginal Analysis: The Economic Approach

Economists use the marginal classification of costs in decision making. Marginal cost analysis attempts to determine pricing and output decisions. Economic analysis assumes that a firm is trying to maximize its total profits. Marginal analysis proposes that no firm can achieve maximum profit unless its marginal cost and marginal revenue are equal; in other words, unless the cost of the additional unit of output produced brings enough additional revenue to make the marginal profitability equal zero.

Marginal analysis may be explained with the aid of Figure 2.13. At any rate of output, *OQ*, total revenue is expressed by the area *OQED* under the marginal revenue

[10]Gordon Shillinglaw, "The Concept of Attributable Cost," *Journal of Accounting Research* (Spring 1963), p. 77.

curve. Total cost is expressed by the area *OQFG* under the marginal cost curve. The profit, which is equal to the difference between the areas of total revenue and total cost, is expressed by area *FEGD*. It is obvious that moving *Q* to the right will increase the profit *FEGD* to the Point Q_m where it will reach a maximum. At Point Q_m the marginal cost is equal to the marginal revenue.

The marginal analysis may also be performed algebraically. Assume a demand function $P = 200 - 0.02Q$, where *Q* is the weekly production,[11] and a total cost function $C = 60Q + 20,000$. It is easy to deduce the following:

Total revenue $= PQ = 200Q - 0.02Q^2$.

Marginal revenue $= dPQ/Q = 200 - 0.04Q$.

Marginal cost $= \dfrac{dC}{dQ} = 60$.

The marginal analysis requires as a profit maximization objective that marginal costs equal marginal revenue. Thus, $60 = 200 - 0.04Q$, or $Q = 140/0.04 = 3,500$ units per week. Consequently, the price will be $P = 200 - 0.02Q = \$130$, and total profit per week will be $\mu = PQ - C = (\$130 \times 3,500) - (20,000 + 60 \times 3,500) = \$225,000$.

Differential Analysis: The Accounting Approach
The accountant uses the incremental classification of costs in decision making. Differential or incremental cost analysis is similar to the economist's marginal analysis except that the accountant is interested in the additional cost of a change in the level of production rather than the cost of an additional unit. This approach has also been labeled the *relevant cost approach*. It is particularly applicable to short-term decisions such as dropping or adding products, setting prices, selecting equipment, selling manufactured products or processing them further, special order decisions, rationing scarce capacity, and make or buy decisions. The differential analysis approach consists of determining the relevant costs, *those expected future costs that will differ among alternatives*. For example, suppose that firm X decides to increase its level of production because the sales price offered, \$4, was more than the new per-unit cost of production. The following information was provided:

	Cost of Production	
	Old Activity Level (20,000 Units)	**New Activity Level (30,000 Units)**
Variable Costs	$20,000	$45,000
Fixed Costs	20,000	30,000
	$40,000	$75,000
Cost per Unit	$2.00	$2.50

The differential analysis will proceed as follows:

Added Revenues (10,000 × $4)	$40,000
Incremental Costs ($75,000 − $40,000)	35,000
Added Contribution	$ 5,000

---

[11]This means that price must fall by 2 percent for every one hundred additional units appearing on the market every week.

If we make the assumption that all incremental costs are out-of-pocket costs, then the decision to increase the level of production is beneficial because it increases the firm's total wealth.

In conclusion, it may be said that the differential costs are those costs that change between alternatives. Variable costs are the main differential costs. However, some fixed costs may be differential costs if they are added as a result of the new production, and some variable costs may not be differential costs in some contexts.

2.3   MANUFACTURING ACCOUNTING

2.3.1   Cost Classification on Financial Statements

The basic difference between manufacturing and merchandising accounting stems from the fact that a merchant buys and sells merchandise in a finished state, while the manufacturer transforms different inputs into a final output to be sold. Therefore, both the balance sheets and income statements of merchandisers and manufacturers will differ in format and content.

The balance sheet will differ mainly with respect to inventories. The merchandise inventory is replaced in a manufacturing firm by three inventory accounts: Direct Material Inventory account, Work-in-Process Inventory account or Goods-in-Process Inventory account, and Finished Goods Inventory account. The balance sheet content and format, consequently, will be different for the current asset section:

Current Asset Section of Balance Sheet

Manufacturer			Merchandiser	
Cash		$ 5,000	Cash	$ 5,000
Receivables		5,000	Receivables	5,000
Finished Goods	$10,000		Merchandise Inventory	29,000
Work-in-Process	5,000		Other Current Assets	6,000
Direct Material	4,000		Total Current Assets	$45,000
Total Inventory		19,000		
Other Current Assets		1,000		
Total Current Assets		$30,000		

The income statements will differ with respect to the *cost of goods sold*. For a merchandising firm, the cost of goods sold eventually comprises the purchase costs of goods, including freight in, that have been purchased and sold. For a manufacturer, the manufacturing cost of goods sold comprises a proportion of the three major elements of costs: direct labor, direct material, and manufacturing overhead. The computation of the manufacturing cost of goods sold will be examined in both the next section and chapter 8.

2.3.2   Cost Accounting Cycle

The accounting system used by a manufacturer may be either the so-called *general accounting system* or a *cost accounting system*. The general accounting system is a non-cost system. It uses *periodic* physical inventories for raw materials, goods-in-process, and finished goods that do not require a day-to-day recording of inventory changes. A periodic inventory system determines the costs of goods sold by adding the period man-

Table 2.6   *A Cost Accounting System for a Manufacturing Concern*

Raw Materials Inventory

Beginning Inventory	(2a) Direct Raw Material Used in Production
(1) Purchase of Raw Materials	(2b) Indirect Raw Material Used in Production
Ending Inventory	

Payroll

(3) Wages Incurred	(3a) Direct Labor Used
	(3b) Indirect Labor Used

Manufacturing Overhead

(2b) Indirect Material	(5) Applied Overhead
(3b) Indirect Labor	
(4) Overhead Services	

Work-in-Process Inventory

Beginning Inventory	(6) Cost of Goods Manufactured and Transferred
(2a) Direct Raw Material Used	
(3a) Direct Labor Used	
(5) Applied Overhead	
Ending Inventory	

Cost of Goods Sold		**Finished Goods Inventory**	
(7) Cost of Goods Sold		Beginning Inventory	(7) Cost of Goods Sold
		(6) Cost of Goods Manufactured and Transferred	

ufacturing costs to beginning inventory (obtained by physical count) and subtracting the ending inventory (obtained by physical count). This system is used mainly by drugstores, grocery stores, and others specializing in the sale of low-priced items.

A cost accounting system uses a perpetual inventory system of accounting for goods on hand and sold. Such a system determines the costs of goods sold during a period, as well as the ending inventory, from the accounting records without a physical inventory. This system facilitates management control and the preparation of interim financial statements. In a cost accounting system, the orderly sequence of bookkeeping is as follows: (1) assets become costs, (2) costs become goods-in-process, and (3) goods-in-process are completed and transferred to the Finished Goods Inventory account as *cost of goods manufactured*.

Table 2.6 depicts a simple cost accounting system for a manufacturing concern. The entries in the accounts are keyed to the following explanations:

1. The purchase of raw materials is debited to the Raw Materials Inventory account. A corresponding entry is made either to Cash or to Accounts Payable (if purchased on credit).

2. The direct material used in production is debited to the Work-in-Process Inventory, and the indirect material is debited to the Manufacturing Overhead account.

3. The cost of direct labor previously debited to the Payroll account is debited to Work-in-Process Inventory, while the indirect labor is debited to the Manufacturing Overhead account.

4. The charges for factory overhead services are debited to the Manufacturing Overhead account.

5. A proportion of Manufacturing Overhead is "applied" to Work-in-Process Inventory on the basis of an overhead rate.

6. The cost of goods completed is transferred as a debit to the Finished Goods Inventory.

7. The cost of goods sold is transferred to the income statement as a period expense to be matched with the period revenues.

8. Selling and administrative overhead are transferred to the income statement as a period expense.

9. Finally, the net operating income is computed.

Step 6 leads to the production of a *manufacturing statement*, as illustrated in Table 2.7, and step 9 leads to an *earnings statement*, as illustrated in Table 2.8. This earnings state-

Table 2.7   *ABEL Manufacturing Company, Ltd., Manufacturing Statement for the Year Ended December 31, 19X6*

Manufacturing Statement for the Year Ended December 31, 19X6

Raw Materials			
Raw Materials Inventory, Jan. 1, 19X6		$15,000	
Raw Materials Purchased	$30,000		
Freight on Raw Materials Purchased	2,000		
Delivered Cost of Raw Materials Purchased		32,000	
Raw Materials Available for Use		$47,000	
Raw Materials Inventory, Dec. 31, 19X6		22,000	
Raw Materials Used			$25,000
Direct Labor			$50,000
Factory Overhead Costs			
Indirect Labor		$ 1,500	
Indirect Material		1,000	
Power		1,000	
Repairs and Maintenance		1,000	
Factory Taxes		500	
Supervision		1,500	
Factory Insurance Expired		200	
Small Tools Written Off		200	
Depreciation of Equipment		800	
Depreciation of Building		1,800	
Total Factory Overhead Costs			$ 9,500
Total Manufacturing Costs			$84,500
Add: Goods-in-Process Inventory, Jan. 1, 19X6			11,500
Total Goods-in-Process during the Year			$96,000
Deduct: Goods-in-Process Inventory, Dec. 31, 19X6			36,000
Cost of Goods Manufactured and Transferred			$60,000

Table 2.8   **ABEL Manufacturing Company, Ltd., Earnings Statement for the Year Ended December 19X6**

Net Sales			$300,000
Cost of Goods Sold			
Finished Goods Inventory, Jan. 1, 19X6		$20,000	
Cost of Goods Manufactured		60,000	
Goods Available for Sale		$80,000	
Finished Goods Inventory, Dec. 31, 19X6		15,000	
Cost of Goods Sold			65,000
Gross Profit			$235,000
Operating Expenses			
Administrative and General Expenses			
Office Salaries Expense	$22,500		
Miscellaneous General Expense	6,500		
Bad Debts Expense	3,500		
Depreciation Expense, Office Equipment	5,250		
Office Supplies Expense	7,250		
Total Administrative and General Expenses		$45,000	
Selling Expenses			
Sales Salaries Expense	$11,500		
Advertising Expense	2,500		
Delivery Wages Expense	6,500		
Shipping Supplies Expense	2,500		
Delivery Equipment Insurance Expense	7,500		
Depreciation Expense, Delivery Equipment	5,500		
Total Selling Expenses		36,000	
Total Operating Expenses			$ 81,000
Operating Earnings			$154,000
Nonoperating (Irregular) Income			
Earnings from Joint Venture of Limited Duration		$100,000	
Interest Income		50,000	
Gain on Sale of Assets		60,000	
Total			$210,000
Nonoperating (Irregular) Expenses			
Research and Development		30,000	
Cost of Discontinuing Product Line		20,000	
Foreign Currency Translation Loss		54,000	
Total			$204,000
Earnings before Interest and Taxation			$160,000
Financial Expense			
Mortgage Interest Expense		4,000	
Long-Term Debt Expense		10,000	
Other		16,000	
Total			$ 30,000
Income Taxes			$ 60,000
Net Earnings			$ 70,000
Net Earnings per Share (10,000 Shares Outstanding)			$7.00

ment uses a multiple-step format that presents various levels of earnings while offering more disclosure of both irregular items and items not related to the enterprise's main activities.

2.4   CONCLUSION

Management accounting attempts to provide necessary information for all the normative decision models of its many internal users. Consequently, there are several concepts of costs, which differ depending on managerial uses and viewpoints. The particular object of costing justifies a cost's classification. Although the object of costing may differ between such groups as accountants, economists, and engineers, all view cost as a "sacrifice" and associate cost with decision alternatives, an activity, or an action. Staubus states:

> *Costing is the process of determining the cost of doing something, e.g., the cost of manufacturing an article, rendering a service, or performing a function. The article manufactured, service rendered, or function performed is known as the object of costing. . . . Objects of costing are always activities. We want to know the cost of doing something. We may, however, find ourselves speaking of the cost of a product as an abbreviation for the cost of acquiring or manufacturing the product.*[12]

GLOSSARY

Avoidable Cost A cost that can be eliminated by ceasing to perform an activity.

Committed Cost A cost necessary to maintain a basic organization.

Controllable Cost A cost that a given responsible person has the authority and ability to incur within an operating period.

Conversion Cost The sum of Direct Labor and Factory Overhead directly or indirectly necessary for the conversion of materials into finished products.

Cost The amount, measured in money, of cash expended, other property transferred, capital stock issued, services performed, or a liability incurred, in consideration of goods and services received or to be received.

Cost of Goods Manufactured The total materials, labor, and factory overhead used in the production process.

Cost of Goods Sold The cost of the units sold.

Differential Cost The difference in the net costs and benefits between two or more alternative courses of action.

Direct Labor All labor expended directly upon the direct material and easily traceable to a finished product.

Direct Material All material directly used in production and easily traceable to a finished product.

Discretionary Cost A recurring cost that can be avoided at the discretion of management.

Factory Overhead (Manufacturing Overhead) All of the manufacturing costs other than direct labor and direct material.

Fixed Cost A cost that remains constant over a relevant range of output.

Indirect Labor All labor used in the production of a product other than direct labor.

---

[12]George J. Staubus, *Activity Costing and Input-Output Accounting* (Homewood, Ill.: Irwin, 1971), p. 1.

Indirect Material All material used in the production of a product other than direct material.

Loss An asset that became valueless without rendering any benefit.

Opportunity Cost The net cash inflow that may have resulted from the use of the resource for the most desirable alternative.

Out-of-Pocket Cost A cost that generates negative cash flow.

Period Cost A cost unrelated to the production of a product.

Prime Cost The sum of direct labor and direct material.

Product Cost A cost related to the production of a product.

Relevant Range The span of an activity level for which standard revenue and cost relationships are constant.

Semivariable Cost A cost that contains a fixed component and a variable component.

Variable Cost A cost that varies proportionally with the level of activity.

SELECTED READINGS

American Accounting Association, Committee on Cost Concepts and Standards, "Report of the Committee on Cost Concepts and Standards," *Accounting Review* (January 1952), pp. 174–180.

American Accounting Association, 1955 Committee on Cost Concepts Underlying Reports for Management Purposes, "Tentative Statements of Costs Underlying Reports for Management Purposes," *Accounting Review* (April 1956), pp. 182–183.

Anthony, Robert N., "Cost Concepts for Control," *Accounting Review* (April 1957), pp. 229–234.

Bedford, Norton M., "The Nature of Business Costs: General Concepts," *Accounting Review* (January 1957), pp. 18–24. Reprinted in H. Anton and P. Firmin, *Contemporary Issues in Cost Accounting* (Boston: Houghton Mifflin, 1966), pp. 21–30.

Bisgay, Louis, "Report on Fiscal and Variable Expense Research," *Management Accounting* (June 1980), pp. 43–50.

Clark, J. M., *Studies in the Economics of Overhead Costs* (Chicago: Chicago University Press, 1923), chaps. 3 and 9.

Connolly, H. Andrew, "Planning a New Cost System: The 'Unfreezing' Stage," *Management Accounting* (November 1979), pp. 19–24.

Demski, J. S.; Feltham, G. A.; Horngren, C. T.; and Jaedicke, R. K., *A Conceptual Approach to Cost Determination* (Iowa: Iowa State Press, forthcoming).

Dickey, R. I., ed., *Accountants' Cost Handbook* (New York: Ronald Press, 1960), secs. 1 and 2.

Haseman, Wilber E., "An Interpretive Framework of Cost," *Accounting Review* (October 1968), pp. 738–752.

Hazelton, W. A., "How to Cost Labor Settlements," *Management Accounting* (May 1979), pp. 19–23.

Herman, Michael P., "Uniform Cost Accounting Standards: Are They Necessary?" *Management Accounting* (April 1972), pp. 15–19.

Horngren, Charles T., "Choosing Accounting Practices for Reporting to Management," *NAA Bulletin* (September 1962), pp. 3–15.

Leininger, Wayne, "Opportunity Costs: Some Definitions and Examples," *Accounting Review* (January 1977), pp. 248–251.

McRae, T. W., "Opportunity and Incremental Cost: An Attempt to Define in System Terms," *Accounting Review* (April 1970), pp. 315–321.

Nestor, Joseph, "How Cost Accountants Can Improve Public Housing Programs," *Management Accounting* (October 1979), pp. 40–42.

Rayburn, Gayle L., "Marketing Costs: Accountants to the Rescue," *Management Accounting* (January 1981), pp. 37–41.

Shillinglaw, Gordon, "The Concept of Attributable Cost," *Journal of Accounting Research* (Spring 1963), pp. 73–85.

Spencer, Milton H.; Seo, K. K.; and Simkin, Mark G., *Managerial Economics: Text, Problems and Short Cases*, 4th ed. (Homewood, Ill.: Irwin, 1975).

"The Uses and Classifications of Costs," *Research Series No. 7*, reprinted in *NAA Bulletin* (May 1946), pp. 10–13.

Wallace, Edward L., "Some Comments on the Statement of Planning Costs," *Accounting Review* (July 1957), pp. 448–466.

Wallace, Witt, "Work Measurement of Indirect Labor," *Management Accounting* (November 1971), pp. 31–34.

QUESTIONS, EXERCISES, AND PROBLEMS

2.1   Differentiate between the economic and accounting theory of cost.

2.2   **1.** If $TC = y = a + bx$, what are the total variable costs, total fixed costs, marginal cost, unit total cost, unit variable cost, unit fixed cost, and cost elasticity?
Repeat for

   2. $y = a + bx + cx^2$.
   3. $y = a + bx - cx^2$.
   4. $y = a + bx - cx^2 + dx^3$.

2.3   The total maintenance cost, y, for operating a manufacturing plant was found to be $y = 30 + 2x - 0.002x^2$, where x = level of production in units.
What is the equation for

   1. Total variable costs?   **5.** Unit variable cost?
   2. Total fixed costs?   **6.** Unit fixed cost?
   3. Marginal cost?   **7.** Cost elasticity?
   4. Unit total cost?

2.4   What is meant by

   1. A product cost?   **8.** An out-of-pocket cost?
   2. A period cost?   **9.** A marginal cost?
   3. A direct cost?   **10.** An incremental cost?
   4. An indirect cost?   **11.** An opportunity cost?
   5. A controllable cost?   **12.** An escapable cost?
   6. An uncontrollable cost?   **13.** A historical cost?
   7. A sunk cost?   **14.** An attributable cost?

2.5   Explain the differences between periodic and perpetual inventory systems, and indicate the relative merits and limitations of each.

2.6   The mathematical notation for the total cost function for a business is $4X^3 + 6X^2 + 2X + 10$, where X equals production volume. Which of the following is the mathematical notation for the average cost function for that business?

   1. $2(2X^2 + 3X + 2)$.   **3.** $0.4X^3 + 0.6X^2 + 0.2X + 1$.
   2. $2X^3 + 3X^2 + X + 5$.   **4.** $4X^2 + 6X + 2 + 10/X$.

(AICPA adapted)

2.7   State the distinction between the following costs:

   1. Opportunity costs and outlay costs.

   2. Past costs and future costs.

   3. Short-run costs and long-run costs.

   4. Variable costs and fixed costs.

   5. Traceable costs and common costs.

   6. Out-of-pocket costs and book costs.

   7. Incremental costs and sunk costs.

   8. Escapable costs and unavoidable costs.

   9. Controllable costs and noncontrollable costs.

   10. Replacement costs and historical costs.

2.8   *Cost Behavior*   Fill in the following cost schedule for a manufacturer of children's toys. Then, on a single chart, sketch the graphs of UTC, UVC, UFC, and MC.

Table 1   *Cost Schedule of a Toy Manufacturer*

Volume of Production	Total Variable Cost (TVC)	Total Fixed Cost (TFC)	Total Cost (TC)	Unit Fixed Cost (UFC)	Unit Average Cost (UAC)	Unit Total Cost (UTC)	Marginal Cost (MC)
1		$100	$ 110.00				
2		100	116.00				
3		100	121.00				
4		100	126.00				
5		100	130.00				
6		100	136.00				
7		100	145.50				
8		100	156.00				
9		100	172.00				
10		100	190.00				
11		100	209.00				
12		100	230.40				
13		100	260.00				
14		100	298.20				
15		100	349.50				
16		100	424.00				
17		100	518.50				
18		100	639.00				
19		100	798.00				
20		100	1000.00				

2.9   *Cost Behavior*   An ore-mining company needs both capital and labor to produce or mine ore. It uses equipment of various sizes and measures each piece by horsepower rating (Y). Each piece of equipment is operated by labor crews of various sizes (X). The per-unit costs of labor and capital are $40 and $.30, respectively.

Required:
Complete the following table:

Required:

1. Prepare a manufacturing statement for the company for 19X1.

2. Prepare a statement of cost of goods manufactured and sold for 19X1.

3. Prepare an income statement for 19X1.

4. Compute the net earnings per share for 19X1.

2.14   ***Manufacturing and Income Statements***   Vasantha Manufacturing Company's profits jumped at the end of 19X9. The company's net sales increased by 25 percent of its previous year's sales of $482 million. Thanks to the new production management strategies, the cost of goods sold had decreased to 80 percent of sales in 19X9. The ending inventory of finished goods was only 60 percent of the beginning inventory of finished goods. The costs and expenses of the company for the year were as follows:

Materials Used	$132,000,000
Direct Labor	$ 70,000,000
Fixed Factory Overhead	$ 20,000,000
Variable Factory Overhead	$2.50 per Direct-Labor Dollar
Sales Salaries	$ 30,000,000
Office Salaries	$ 48,000,000
Mortgage Interest	$ 7,000,000
Depreciation on Delivery Trucks	$ 3,000,000
Advertising	$ 2,000,000
Depreciation on Office Equipment	$ 1,500,000

The beginning work-in-process was $154,000,000, and the ending work-in-process was reduced to 50 percent of the beginning amount.

Examination of transactions shows that Vasantha sold an industrial lot for a gain of $3,000,000 and lost $1,000,000 in discontinuing its old product line.

Required:

1. Prepare a manufacturing schedule.

2. Prepare an income statement separating operating, nonoperating, and financial activities.

2.15   ***Cost Classification***   Select the graph that matches the numbered factory cost or expense data, and identify by letter which of the graphs best fits each of the situations or items described.

1. Depreciation of equipment, where the amount of depreciation charged is computed by the machine hours method.

2. Electricity bill—a flat fixed charge, plus a variable cost after a certain number of kilowatt hours are used.

3. City water bill, which is computed using the following method:

First 1,000,000 gallons or less, $1,000 flat fee.
Next 10,000 gallons, $.003 per gallon used.
Next 10,000 gallons, $.006 per gallon used.
Next 10,000 gallons, $.009 per gallon used.

4. Cost of lubricant for machines, where cost per unit decreases with each pound of lubricant used (for example, if 1 pound is used, the cost is $10.00; if 2 pounds are used,

Figure 1

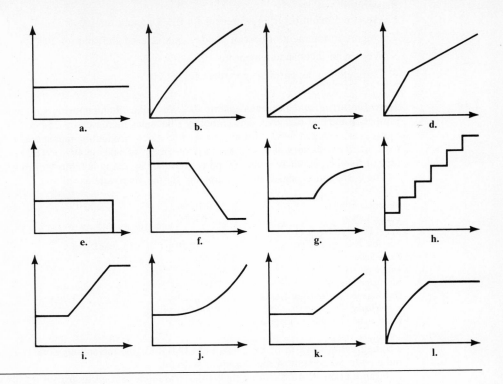

the cost is $19.98; if 3 pounds are used, the cost is $29.94; and the minimum cost per pound is $9.25).

5. Depreciation of the equipment, where the amount is computed by the straight-line method. When the depreciation rate was established it was anticipated the obsolescence factor would be greater than the wear and tear factor.

6. Rent on a factory building donated by the city, where the agreement calls for a fixed fee payment unless 200,000 labor hours are worked, in which case no rent need be paid.

7. Salaries of repair workers, where one person is needed for every 1,000 machine hours or less (that is, 0 to 1,000 hours requires one worker, 1,001 to 2,000 hours requires two workers, and so forth).

8. Federal unemployment compensation taxes for the year, where the labor force is constant in number throughout year (average annual salary is $6,000 per worker).

9. Cost of raw materials used.

10. Rent on a factory building donated by the county, where an agreement calls for rent of $100,000 less $1 for each direct labor hour worked in excess of 200,000 hours, but a minimum rental payment of $20,000 must be paid.

(AICPA adapted)

2.16   *Imputed Opportunity Cost*   The Stambaugh Manufacturing Company is considering a proposal to start a new product. Cost analysis determines the following for the proposed project:

Marginal Cost of Sales	$13,000
Normal Sales Markup of Existing Products	35%
Sales Dollars Would Then Be	$20,000
Gross Margin Is Therefore	$ 7,000
Fixed Cost on Building and Equipment	$ 2,000
Gross Profit	$ 5,000
Expected Production Volume (in Units)	2,000
Selling Price per Unit	$10
Square Feet of Existing Building	1,600
Gross Margin per Square Foot	$ 4.38

Keeping in mind that 1,600 square feet of existing business is being sacrificed to the new project, should the Stambaugh Manufacturing Company accept the project?

(Adapted with permission from D. M. Stambaugh, "Imputed Opportunity Costs," *Management Accounting* (December 1974), pp. 39–40.

2.17 **Sunk Costs and Opportunity Costs** The Paretta Manufacturing Company has 20,000 defective units of a product that cost $2 per unit to manufacture. Two options are open to management.

1. The units can be sold as they are at $1 each.

2. The units may be rebuilt at an additional cost of $1.20 and sold at their full price of $3 per unit.

Required:

1. Which option should the company choose?

2. Suppose that to rebuild the defective units, the company has to forgo the manufacturing of 20,000 new units. On the basis of this new information, which option should the company choose?

2.18 **Different Cost Terms** Match each of the nine numbered items that follow with the one term (A through R) listed here that most specifically identifies the cost concept indicated parenthetically. (*Caution:* An item of cost may be classified in several ways, depending on the purpose of the classification. For example, the commissions on sales of a proposed new product line might be classified as direct, variable, and marginal, among others. However, if such costs are being considered specifically as to the amount of cash outlay required in making a decision concerning adoption of the new line, the commissions are out-of-pocket costs. That would be the most appropriate answer in the context.) The same term may be used more than once.

Indicate your choice of answer for each item by choosing the letter that precedes the correct term.

Terms

a. By-product cost.	**g.** Historical cost.	**m.** Out-of-pocket cost.
b. Common or joint cost.	**h.** Imputed cost.	**n.** Prime cost.
c. Controllable cost.	**i.** Differential cost.	**o.** Replacement cost.
d. Direct cost.	**j.** Indirect cost.	**p.** Standard cost.
e. Estimated cost.	**k.** Opportunity cost.	**q.** Sunk cost.
f. Fixed cost.	**l.** Original cost.	**r.** Variable cost.

Items

1. The management of a corporation is considering replacing a machine that is operating satisfactorily with a more efficient new model. Depreciation on the cost of the existing machine is omitted from the data used in judging the proposal, because it has little or no significance to such a decision. (The omitted cost.)

2. One of the problems encountered by a bank in attempting to establish the cost of a commercial deposit account is the fact that many facilities and services are shared by many revenue-producing activities. (Costs of the shared facilities and services.)

3. A company declined an offer received to rent one of its warehouses and elected to use the warehouse for storage of extra raw materials to insure uninterrupted production. Storage cost has been charged with the monthly amount of the rental offered. (This cost.)

4. A manufacturing company excludes all fixed costs from its valuation of inventories, assigning to inventory only applicable portions of costs that vary with changes in volume of product. (The term employed for the variable costs in this context by advocates of this costing procedure.)

5. The sales department urges an increase in production of a product and, as part of the data presented in support of its proposal, indicates the total additional cost involved for the volume level it proposes. (The increase in total cost.)

6. A CPA takes exception to his client's inclusion, in the cost of a fixed asset, of an "interest" charge based on the client's own funds invested in the asset. The client states that the charge was intended to obtain a cost comparable to what would have been the case if funds had been borrowed to finance the acquisition. (The term that describes such interest charges.)

7. The direct production cost of a unit includes those portions of factory overhead, labor, and materials that are obviously traceable directly to the unit. (The term used to specify the last two of the named components.)

8. Calling upon the special facilities of the production, planning, personnel, and other departments, a firm estimated its future unit cost of production and used this cost (analyzed by cost elements) in its accounts. (The term used to specify this scientifically predetermined estimate.)

9. A chemical manufacturing company produces three products from the same initial material mix. Each product gains a separate identity part way through processing and requires additional processing after the "split." Each contributes a significant share of revenue. The company plans to spread the costs up to the split among the three products by the use of relative market values. (The term used to specify the costs accumulated up to the point of the split.)

(AICPA adapted)

2.19   *Acceptance of Offer*   T Manufacturing Ltd. produces several products and sells them directly to consumers under its own T brand name. It sells one product, Troys, at $16 per unit. While the company has operated at a profitable level for the past several years, a decline in sales activity in 19X1 has resulted in the company's first operating loss. During 19X1, sales of Troys averaged 4,000 units per month, which represents one-third of the firm's normal productive capacity for this product.

Mr. K, the president, received an offer from a chain store for 5,000 Troys per month beginning in January and ending in December 19X2. The units would carry the chain label and would be packed and shipped at the chain's expense. The chain offered $6.80 per unit on the basis of a one-year contract.

The management of T Manufacturing anticipated an upturn in their consumer sales beginning in 19X3 but forecast 19X2 sales at 4,000 units per month. They do not believe the chain store offer would replace the existing volume of sales, nor would the offer increase selling or administrative expenses. If the offer is accepted, T Manufacturing Ltd. would enter into such an arrangement only for the one-year period.

Mr. K called together his managers to discuss the offer. The comptroller presented 19X1 budgeted figures on manufacturing, selling, and administrative expenses for Troys at two production levels, 4,000 and 8,000 units per month. The comptroller stated that the budgeted figures were based on the existing cost structure, and, apart from the need for a second supervisor at the 6,000-unit level, there would be no incremental fixed costs in moving from a capacity of 4,000 units to 12,000 units per month. The marginal manufacturing cost per unit would be the same above the 8,000-unit production level as in the 4,000- to 8,000-unit production range.

The production manager noted that minor design modifications for this order would involve $20,000 for special tooling. A review of 19X1 cost data indicated that irrespective of the proposed contract's acceptance, there would be no cost change for 19X2, with the exception of a direct labor increase of 10 percent, an increase in property taxes of 15 percent, and a decrease in direct material cost of 4 percent over or under 19X1 budgeted levels.

Mr. K has another problem he would like resolved. In developing the budget for 19X2, he would like an estimate of the costs involved to ship another of the company's products, Retros. Mr. K has not had any training in statistics but understands that there are quantitative techniques that can be used to help management predict and control costs.

Required:
What effect would acceptance of the offer from the chain store have on T Manufacturing Ltd.'s income before income taxes for the year 19X2? Submit the necessary calculations and schedules to support your conclusion.

(CICA adapted)

2.20   ***Differential Analysis***   Mary Jarvis operates a small machine shop that manufactures one standard product available from many other similar businesses as well as products to customer order. Her accountant prepared the annual income statement shown here:

	Custom Sales	Standard Sales	Total
Sales	$50,000	$25,000	$75,000
Material	$10,000	$ 8,000	$18,000
Labor	20,000	9,000	29,000
Depreciation	6,300	3,600	9,900
Power	700	400	1,100
Rent	6,000	1,000	7,000
Heat and Light	600	100	700
Other	400	900	1,300
Total Expenses	$44,000	$23,000	$67,000
Net Income	$ 6,000	$ 2,000	$ 8,000

The depreciation charges are for machines used in the respective product lines. The power charge is apportioned on the estimate of power consumed. The rent is for the building space, which has been leased for ten years at $7,000 per year. The rent as well as heat and light are apportioned to the product lines based on the amount of floor space occupied. All other costs are current expenses identified with the product line causing them.

A valued custom parts customer has asked Jarvis if her shop would manufacture 5,000 special units. Jarvis is working at capacity and would have to give up some other business in order to take this business. She cannot renege on custom orders already agreed to, but she could reduce the output of her standard product by about one-half for one year while producing the specially requested custom part. The customer is willing to pay $7 for each part. The material cost will be about $2 per unit, and the labor will be $3.60 per unit. Jarvis will have to spend $2,000 for a special device, which will be discarded when the job is done.

Required:
1. Calculate and present the following costs:

  a. The incremental cost of the order.

  b. The full cost of the order.

  c. The opportunity cost of taking the order.

  d. The sunk costs related to the order.

2. Should Jarvis take the order? Explain your answer.

(CMA adapted)

2.21   ***Determining the Cost of Goods Manufactured***   The Helper Corporation manufactures one product and accounts for costs by a job-order-cost system. You have obtained the following information for the year ended December 31, 19X3, from the corporation's books and records:

1. The total manufacturing cost added during 19X3 (sometimes called *cost to manufacture*) was $1,000,000, based on actual direct material, actual direct labor, and applied factory overhead on actual direct-labor dollars.

2. The cost of goods manufactured was $970,000, also based on actual direct material, actual direct labor, and applied factory overhead.

3. The factory overhead was applied to work-in-process at 75 percent of direct-labor dollars. Applied factory overhead for the year was 27 percent of the total manufacturing cost.

4. The beginning work-in-process inventory, January 1, was 80 percent of the ending work-in-process inventory, December 31.

Required:
Prepare a formal statement of the cost of goods manufactured for the year ended December 31, 19X3, for Helper Corporation. Use actual direct material used, actual direct labor, and applied factory overhead.

(AICPA adapted)

2.22   ***Marginal Analysis under Pure Competition***   The wholesale meat industry in the western region of the United States is characterized by a very large number of firms with no one firm dominating the market. The Perry Wholesale Meat Company is interested in expanding its production of ground beef because of available capacity and the rapid growth of franchise hamburger outlets in its market area.

Perry management have found that they can sell all of the ground beef they can produce at $.99 per pound. The controller's office estimated the total costs, including a normal return on investment, for various levels of production:

Company's Ground Beef Production (in Pounds)	Company's Total Estimated Production Costs, Including a Normal Return on Investment (in Dollars)
120,000	120,000
150,000	149,000
180,000	178,200
210,000	207,900
240,000	238,000

Each production level requires a slightly larger investment than the next smaller production level.

Required:

1. What selling price should the Perry Wholesale Meat Company charge for the ground beef? Explain your answer.

2. What level of production will maximize total return on investment for the Perry Wholesale Meat Company? Explain your answer.

3. What pricing and output strategy should the Perry Wholesale Meat Company use if it were the exclusive distributor of ground beef in the western region of the United States? Explain your answer.

(CMA adapted)

2.23   ***Determining the Work-in-Process***   On June 30, 19X8, a flash flood damaged the warehouse and factory of Padway Corporation, completely destroying the work-in-process inventory. There was no damage to either the raw materials or finished goods inventories. A physical inventory taken after the flood revealed the following valuations:

Raw Materials	$ 62,000
Work-in-Process	0
Finished Goods	119,000

The inventory on January 1, 19X8, consisted of the following:

Raw Materials	$ 30,000
Work-in-Process	100,000
Finished Goods	140,000
	$270,000

A review of the books and records disclosed that the gross profit margin historically approximated 25 percent of sales. The sales for the first six months of 19X8 were $340,000. Raw material purchases were $115,000. Direct labor costs for this period were $80,000, and manufacturing overhead has historically been applied at 50 percent of direct labor.

Required:
Compute the value of the work-in-process inventory lost at June 30, 19X8.

(AICPA adapted)

Man who relies only on the seat-of-his-pants to predict the future may soon lose his shirt.[1]

Most cost accounting decisions depend on the reliability of the information produced by the accounting system. This information consists of *anticipated* data on different alternatives. In response to these information needs, business forecasting has developed as an integral part of the cost accounting discipline. Because business forecasting emphasizes cost reduction and control, *cost estimation* is at its center. A knowledge of future costs and the behavior of costs over time may be useful for a *structural analysis* of costs, which determines the structural relationships between costs and the factors most likely to affect them; *budget forecasting* of costs, which builds on the structural relationships to extrapolate the behavior of costs in the future; and *cost control*, which compares the actual behavior of costs with the predetermined costs.

The forecasting activities, therefore, consist of three temporally interrelated phases: (1) a structural phase to determine the independent variables affecting the behavior of costs (or cost estimation), (2) a prediction phase to forecast the future behavior of costs based on the results of the structural analysis (or cost prediction), and (3) a control phase to evaluate the reliability of the prediction phase. The success of these phases depends on the definition of an adequate theoretical or other relationship between costs and other variables, and on the choice of an estimation technique. This chapter will evaluate each of these problems.

3.1   STRUCTURE OF THE COST ESTIMATION MODEL

A cost estimation model relates to a set of structures that are defined by relationships between economic variables. Each structure is defined by a set of equations according to which of the following type of relationship exists:

---

[1] Attributed to Confucius. K. H. Chan, F. L. Sbrocchi, and N. R. VanZante, "Forecasting Methods and the Management Accountant," *Cost and Management* (January–February 1980), p. 44.

1. Definitions or identities which need no further proof for their existence, e.g.,
Sales Revenue = Price × Quantity Sold

2. Technological relationships determined by the "state of the arts" as may be given, e.g.,
Output = F (Labor, Capital)

3. Institutional or historical relations, which are incorporated by virtue of belonging to the given society, e.g.,
Sales Tax Revenue = Tax Rate × Volume of Sales,
where the tax rate is determined by the appropriate governmental institution.

4. Behavioral relationships, which describe how particular variables in the economic behavior of an individual or a group respond to changes in other variables, e.g.,
Aggregate Consumption = F (Aggregate Income).[2]

A structure based on any of these relationships will be specified by the dependent variable, or costs, and the independent variables. The structure or set of relationships determines the functional relationship of the model. These relationships may take the following forms, resulting in different equations:

1. A positive linear relationship between costs and one independent variable may be expressed as $y = a + bx$, where, for example, a is the total fixed cost, b the unit variable cost, and x the total level of activity.

2. A strictly linear relationship between costs and one independent variable may be expressed as $y = bx$, with $a = 0$ and $b = dy/dx > 0$.

3. The polynomial model $y = a + bx + cx^2$ depicts a relationship between costs and output with *decreasing* productivity.

4. The polynomial model $y = a + bx - cx^2$ depicts a relationship between costs and output with *increasing* productivity.

5. The total long-run cost of a firm may be depicted as $y = a + bx + cx^2 + dx^3$.

6. Other forms of curves may be transformed into straight lines by the use of transformations:

Log $y = a + bx$ becomes $Z = a + bx$ if Log $y = Z$.

$y = a + b$ Log x becomes $y = a + bw$ if Log $X = w$.

$y = ax^b$ becomes Log $y = $ Log $a + b$ Log X.

$y = \dfrac{1}{a + bx}$ becomes $Z = a + bx$ if $Z = 1/y$.

$= a + b\dfrac{1}{x}$ becomes $y = a + bw$ if $w = 1/x$.

The transformations do not change the fundamental properties of the relationships of the variables.

---

[2]M. Dutta, *Econometric Methods* (Cincinnati, Ohio: South-Western Publishing, 1975), p. 10.

These equations imply a perfect relationship between the variations of the dependent and independent variables. Most of the time, however, some variations remain unexplained. Consequently, the structural relationship will be as follows:

$$y = f(x, \mu),$$

where μ is a symbolic variable representing the random variations. It is called the *disturbance term*, the shock term, the error term, or the stochastic term.

3.2   COST ESTIMATION TECHNIQUES

The accountant faced with the choice of cost estimation techniques needs selection criteria. One obvious criterion is the *predictive ability* of the model. Another may be that the improvement in the quality of the decision must exceed the cost of obtaining the information. In other words, the choice of a cost estimation technique must involve a *cost-benefit analysis*.

There are two main estimation techniques: intuitive or judgmental forecasting and quantitative forecasting. The judgmental method is based on the collection of experiences, opinions, and feelings about the subject which may be translated into a considered judgment or a prediction. Examples of this approach are opinion polls, panels of experts, and the more refined delphi method. Statisticians and psychologists have criticized the judgmental method, and it may be impractical, unappealing, and cumbersome when applied to cost estimation.

The quantitative method is based on a model representing the real-life situation involving the cost object. This model may be either statistical (least squares method) or nonstatistical, and the following discussion reflects this dichotomy in cost estimation techniques.

The nonstatistical techniques identified in the literature and in practice as particularly useful to the cost estimation problem are the *engineering method*, the *accounts method*, the *high-low method*, and the *visual curve fitting method*.

3.2.1   Engineering Method

The engineering approach to estimation bases its results on the input-output relationships implied by the production function. For every output mix, the engineering specifications, or input mix, indicate the particular mix of material, labor, and capital equipment. Consequently, given a study of the input mix—the physical relationships between quantities of inputs and each unit of output (what the economist calls the "production function")—the total cost of material and labor may be estimated.

For example, suppose a given product, alpha, uses material, labor, and capital equipment. The production function or input mix specifies that 2 pounds of material are needed for each unit of output. A time and motion study (or any other engineering study) shows that 3 hours of direct labor are needed for the completion of a unit of output. The estimated price of material is $5 per pound, and the wage rate is $4 per hour. On the basis of this information derived from the engineering study, the total prime cost (TPC) per unit of output will be $TPC = (2 \text{ pounds} \times \$5) + (3 \text{ hours} \times \$4) = \$22$. The input mix and output mix derived from engineering studies are used to estimate the total prime cost used in future periods for prediction.

Engineering methods can also be used to predict overhead costs. For example, plant design work requires estimates of overhead costs using engineering principles.

The engineering method, although fairly accurate, presents some serious problems:

1. The final cost of any product should include a fair share of the overhead costs. These are, by definition, indirect costs to the final product, so they cannot be linked directly to an individual product and estimated by an engineering study. The engineering method is generally useful for the estimation of the prime costs of the product and may ignore secondary relationships between the inputs and outputs. The method is most applicable when the direct costs make up a large proportion of total costs and when the input mix is fairly stable over time.

2. The material and labor estimates made by the engineering method are ideal estimates: They do not take into account possible material waste and labor inefficiency. The total prime cost estimated by the engineering method, to be more accurate, should include additional allowances for material waste and labor inefficiency.

3. The engineering method implicitly assumes that the actual input and/or output mixes are optimal mixes. The method ignores other possible input or output mixes which may be more beneficial to the firm in terms of cost reduction, better product quality, imposed productivity, and even improved morale.

4. The engineering method may be costly to use.

The engineering method, therefore, is most useful with the concurrent use of other estimation techniques. An NAA report describes its use as follows:

The industrial engineering approach to determination of how costs should vary with volume proceeds by a systematic study of materials, labor, services, and facilities needed at varying volumes. The aim is to find the best way to obtain the desired production. These studies generally make use of past experience, but it is used as a guide or as a check upon the results obtained by direct study of the production methods and facilities. Where no past experience is available, as with a new product, plant, or method, this approach can be applied to estimate the changes in cost that will accompany changes in volume.[3]

3.2.2   *Accounts Method*

The accounts method relies on the existence of past accounting records and the expert judgment of the cost accountant. The steps in applying the method are as follows:

1. The cost accountant classifies the total cost at a given level of activity (for example, x_o) into either a fixed or a variable category on the basis of past experience and knowledge.

2. The variable category total is an estimation of the total variable costs (for example, $\Sigma_i VC_i$), and the fixed category total is an estimation of the total fixed costs (for example, $\Sigma_i FC_i$).

---

[3]National Association of Accountants, Research Report No. 16, "The Analysis of Cost-Volume-Profit Relationships," (New York: NAA, 1965), p. 17.

Table 3.1   **NANEX, Inc.: Total Costs for Department X**

Account	Total	Variable	Fixed
Direct Labor	$ 5,000	$ 5,000	
Direct Material	10,000	10,000	
Indirect Labor	5,000	5,000	
Indirect Material	12,000	12,000	
Depreciation	2,000		$ 2,000
Power	3,000	3,000	
Maintenance	5,000		5,000
Selling Overhead	10,000		10,000
Miscellaneous Items	3,000		3,000
		$35,000	$20,000
Volume of Activity	5,000 units		

3. The unit variable cost (b) is computed as follows:

$$b = (\sum_i VC_i)/x_o.$$

4. The total fixed cost (a) is equal to $\Sigma_i FC_i$.

5. The total cost equation (TC) is expressed as follows:

$$TC = a + bx$$

or

$$TC = \sum_i FC_i + \left[(\sum_i VC_i)/x_o\right]x.$$

To illustrate, suppose that the cost accountant of NANEX, Inc., classified total costs at an output of 5,000 units, as shown in Table 3.1. Based on the accounts method, the cost equation would be

$$TC = \$20,000 + \frac{\$35,000}{5,000}x$$
$$= \$20,000 + \$7x.$$

The accounts method although expedient and rather inexpensive, suffers from serious drawbacks:

1. It relies heavily on the intuitive judgment of the cost analyst. The reliability of the estimates is difficult to evaluate, and another cost accountant is very likely to come up with different classifications.

2. The classification of costs as either fixed or variable is at best restrictive, if not unrealistic. Assuming linearity, costs may be either fixed, variable, or semivariable; the semivariable category, ignored in the accounts method, is most suitable to most overhead items. If semivariable costs are classified as either fixed or variable, the unit variable cost and total fixed costs could be overestimated or underestimated.

3. The accounts method depends heavily on the financial accounting and recording system. For example, the recording of a transaction into given accounts may influence the classification of the accounts as variable or fixed, which will affect the resulting unit variable cost and total fixed costs.

In conclusion although the accounts method is inexpensive and expedient, it should be used with caution and when only crude approximations of cost behavior are needed.

To illustrate the application of the following methods for the estimation of the structural relationships of a mixed cost, one theoretical problem will be used. Assume that JABEX, Inc., which manufactures and sells widgets, wants to estimate its production costs. The labor hours and production costs for the 12 months of 19X9 are shown in Table 3.2 and plotted in Figure 3.1. The problem is to estimate the semi-variable equation $y = a + bx$, where y = total cost of production, a = total fixed costs, b = unit variable cost, and x = level of activity.

3.2.3   *High-Low Method*

The high-low method is an estimation technique which relies on the relationship between the highest and lowest observed values of costs. The steps in this method are as follows:

1. The highest and lowest levels of costs are determined. In our example, the lowest level of activity is 1 unit with $5 in production cost, and the highest level of activity is 6 units with $15 in production cost.

2. If the two extreme observations identified in step 1 are assumed to be representative of the cost relationships, then the parameters of the equation line which connects them

Table 3.2   **JABEX, Inc.: Total Labor Hours and Production Costs for 19X9**

Month (t)	Labor Hours (x)	Total Production Costs (y)
January	2	7
February	1	5
March	3	10
April	4	12
May	2	8
June	3	11
July	5	13
August	6	15
September	2	9
October	4	10
November	5	11
December	3	9
$n = 12$	$40 = \Sigma x$	$120 = \Sigma y$

Figure 3.1   JABEX, Inc.: Plotting of Direct-Labor Hours and Production Costs

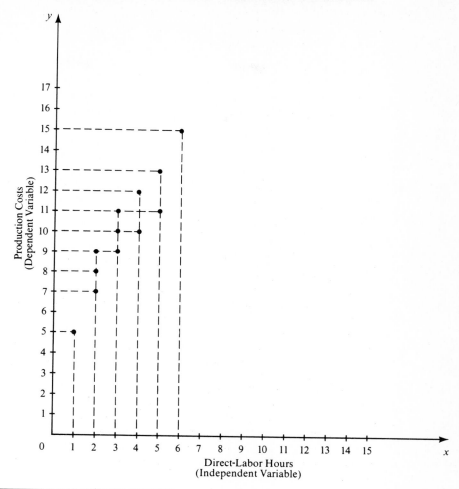

may be determined as follows. The unit variable cost will be the slope of the equation line and, consequently, will be equal to the difference between the highest and lowest values of cost divided by the differences in the corresponding values of the dependent variable: b = unit variable cost = $(\$15 - 5)/(6 - 1) = \$2$. The total fixed cost will be the intersection of the equation line with the y-axis. Consequently, it may be computed on the basis of either an equation based on the lowest observation, $\$5 = a + \$2 \times 1$, or an equation based on the highest observation, $\$15 = a + \$2 \times 6$. In either case the total fixed cost (a) is equal to $\$3$.

3. It may be concluded that the basis of the high-low method, the equation line estimating the production costs of JABEX, Inc., is $y = \$3 + \$2x$.

The cost line resulting from the high-low technique is depicted in Figure 3.2.

   Like the accounts method, the high-low method may be inexpensive and expedient. However, it relies heavily on the observation of the two extremes and, consequently,

Figure 3.2   *JABEX, Inc.: Cost Line Resulting from the High-Low Method*

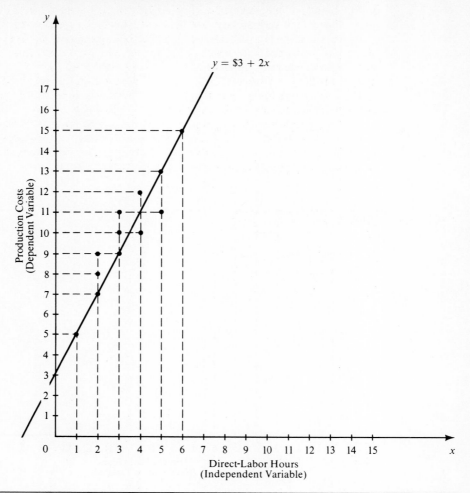

may ignore the information included in the remaining observations. Furthermore, the high and the low cost values are, by definition, extreme situations which might reflect more an abnormal than a normal cost situation. The reliability of the method depends on how representative the high and low cost values are. Therefore, the high-low method should only be used when crude, general approximations rather than precise estimates are needed.

3.2.4   *Visual Curve Fitting Method*

The visual curve fitting method is an estimating technique which relies on the general trend of the plotted points on a *scattergraph*, or scatter diagram. When the total costs observed at various levels of activity are plotted on a graph, a *regression line*, passing by the maximum number of plotted points and in line with the general trend of the plotted points, is fitted by simple visual inspection. The slope of such a line is considered to be the unit variable cost, and the intercept with the y-axis is the total fixed cost.

Figure 3.3 presents a scattergraph for the JABEX, Inc., problem. The regression line strikes the y-axis at $5.30, which represents the total fixed cost. This *arbitrary* trend line is also drawn through points $x = 2$, $y = \$8$, and $x = 5$, $y = \$13$. The unit variable cost is $(\$13 - \$8)/(5 - 2) = 1.66$, and the equation line is $y = \$5.30 + 1.66x$.

The visual curve fitting method has serious limitations. To be useful, the scattergraph and regression line must be drawn by a very experienced cost analyst. A knowledge of extraordinary events leading to adjustment of the cost behavior (strikes, natural disasters, wars, and so forth) is necessary to insure the accuracy of the regression line. The regression line obtained through the visual curve fitting method is subjective: Using the same data, another cost accountant is likely to draw a different line.

Figure 3.3   JABEX, Inc.: Scatter Diagram

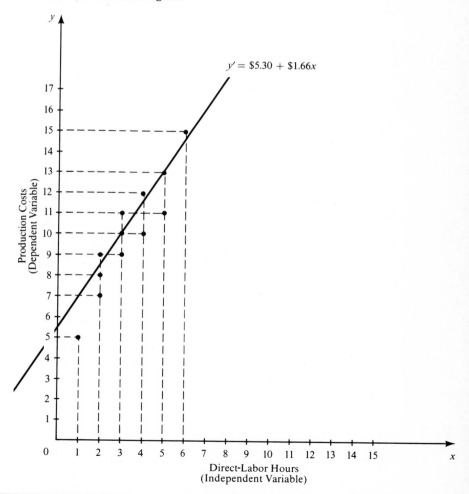

3.2.5   *Simple Regression Method*

The regression method is a statistical estimating technique which determines relationships between variables. In its simplest form, the *simple regression method*, it relates one dependent variable to one independent variable:

$$y = a + bx + \mu.$$

The total variation in y (described as the dependent, endogenous, regressed, or explained variable) is equal to a systematic variation associated with variation in the independent variable (x) and a random variation (μ) attributed to unknown factors.

In the technique's more complex form, the *multiple regression method*, it relates one dependent variable to more than one independent variable. Both simple and multiple regression analyses determine the equation relating the independent variable to the dependent variable(s) by estimating the unknown parameters a and b. The mathematical technique used is the *least squares method*, or more precisely, the ordinary least squares (OLS) regression method.

Least Squares Method

The least squares regression method is a mathematical technique that estimates the regression parameters a and b and provides an exact fit between the independent and dependent variables. This method determines a straight line that minimizes the sum of the squared deviations ($\Sigma \mu_i^2$).

The mathematics of the least squares method are as follows:

1. The least squares linear model is written as

$$y_i = a + bx_i + \mu_i,$$

where y_i denotes the dependent variable and x_i, the independent variable.

2. The deviations μ_i, which are the vertical distances between the observations y_i and the regression line, are written as

$$\mu_i = y_i - (a + bx_i)$$
$$= y_i - a - bx_i.$$

3. The regression parameters a and b are obtained by minimizing the sum of squared deviations as follows:

$$\Sigma \mu_i^2 = (y_i - a - bx_i)^2 \rightarrow \text{a minimum.}$$

4. By taking the partial derivatives with respect to a and b and setting them equal to zero for minimizing the sum of squares, "normal equations" will be obtained:

$$\frac{\partial \sum_{i=1}^{n} \mu_i^2}{\partial a} = -2 \sum_{i=1}^{n} (y_i - a - bx_i) = 0$$

and

$$\frac{\partial \sum_{i=1}^{n} \mu_i^2}{\partial b} = -2 \sum_{i=1}^{n} x_i (y_i - a - bx_i) = 0.$$

The two normal equations also can be stated as follows:

$$\Sigma y = na + b\Sigma x.$$
$$\Sigma xy = a\Sigma x + b\Sigma x^2.$$

These normal equations can be solved either by successive substitution or using matrix algebra.

5. Successive substitution (or Cramer's rule) produces the following:

$$a = \frac{(\Sigma y)(\Sigma x^2) - (\Sigma x)(\Sigma xy)}{n(\Sigma x^2) - (\Sigma x)^2}$$

and

$$b = \frac{n(\Sigma xy) - (\Sigma x)(\Sigma y)}{n(\Sigma x^2) - (\Sigma x)^2}.$$

By inserting the values from the JABEX problem, the values of a and b will equal

$$a = \frac{(120)(158) - (40)(441)}{12(158) - (40)^2} = \$4.45.$$

$$b = \frac{(12)(441) - (40)(120)}{12(158) - (40)^2} = \$1.66.$$

Table 3.3 shows the detailed computations. Placing the values of a and b in the equation of the least squares line produces $y' = \$4.45 + \$1.66x$, where y' is the predicted production cost for a given month and x the direct-labor hours (y' is shown in Figure 3.4). The least squares equation may be used for prediction. Thus, for estimated direct-labor hours of 10, the predicted production costs will equal $\$4.45 + \$1.66 \times 10 = \$21.05$.

6. In matrix form, the system of equations becomes

$$\begin{bmatrix} n & \Sigma x \\ \Sigma x & \Sigma x^2 \end{bmatrix} \begin{bmatrix} a \\ b \end{bmatrix} = \begin{bmatrix} \Sigma Y \\ \Sigma xY \end{bmatrix}$$

or

$$(X'X)B = [X'Y]$$
$$(X'X)^{-1}(X'X)B = (X'X)^{-1}(X'Y)$$
$$B = (X'X)^{-1}(X'Y).$$

Table 3.3   *JABEX, Inc.: Computations for Least Squares*

(1)	(2)	(3)	(4)	(5)
Month (*t*)	**Labor Hours** (*x*)	**Production Costs** (*y*)	*xy*	x^2
1	2	7	14	4
2	1	5	5	1
3	3	10	30	9
4	4	12	48	16
5	2	8	16	4
6	3	11	33	9
7	5	13	65	25
8	6	15	90	36
9	2	9	18	4
10	4	10	40	16
11	5	11	55	25
12	3	9	27	9
$n = 12$	$x = 40$	$y = 120$	$xy = 441$	$x^2 = 158$

By inserting the values from the JABEX example, we obtain:

$$
\overset{X^1}{\begin{bmatrix} 1 & 1 & \ldots & 1 & 1 \\ 2 & 1 & \ldots & 5 & 3 \end{bmatrix}}
\overset{X}{\begin{bmatrix} 1 & 2 \\ 1 & 1 \\ . & . \\ . & . \\ . & . \\ 1 & 5 \\ 1 & 3 \end{bmatrix}}
= \overset{X^1 X}{\begin{bmatrix} 12 & & 40 \\ & & \\ 40 & & 158 \end{bmatrix}}.
$$

$$
\overset{X'}{\begin{bmatrix} 1 & 1 & \ldots & 1 & 1 \\ 2 & 1 & \ldots & 5 & 3 \end{bmatrix}}
\overset{Y}{\begin{bmatrix} 7 \\ 5 \\ . \\ . \\ . \\ 11 \\ 9 \end{bmatrix}}
= \overset{X\,Y}{\begin{bmatrix} 120 \\ \\ 441 \end{bmatrix}}.
$$

$$
B = (X^1 X)^{-1} (X'Y)
$$

$$
= \begin{bmatrix} 12 & 40 \\ 40 & 158 \end{bmatrix}^{-1} \begin{bmatrix} 120 \\ 441 \end{bmatrix} = \begin{bmatrix} 0.53378 & -0.13513 \\ -0.13513 & 0.04054 \end{bmatrix} \begin{bmatrix} 120 \\ 441 \end{bmatrix}
$$

$$
= \begin{bmatrix} 4.45 \\ 1.66 \end{bmatrix}.
$$

Assumptions in Regression Analysis

Although apparently mechanical and objective, the regression method is only reliable when the assumptions of regression are met. The assumptions on the disturbance term or deviation in a regression model are as follows:

1. $E(\mu_i) = 0$, $i = 1, 2, \ldots, N$

specifies that the expected value of μ_i is zero for any value of the dependent variable x_i.

2. $E(\mu_i\mu_j) = 0$, $i \neq j$

means that no two μs are correlated. The distribution is referred to as *free from serial correlation*.

3. $E(\mu_i\mu_j) = 6_\mu^2$, $i = j$

means that the standard deviation and variance of the μs are constant. This constancy of variance is known as the *homoscedasticity* assumption.

Figure 3.4   JABEX, Inc.: The Least Squares Regression Line

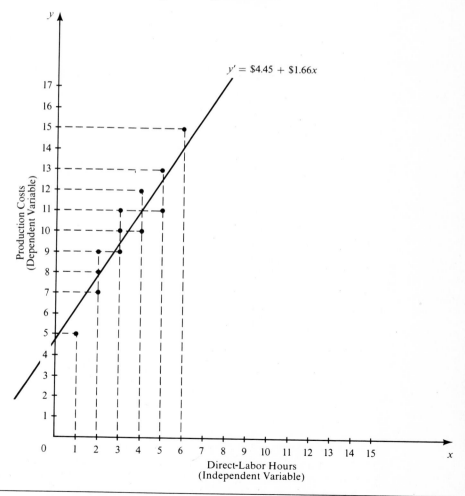

4. $E(x_i\mu_j) = 0$

specifies that x_i is independent of μ_i. It specifically implies that the direction of dependence is from x to y, and no feedback effect from y to x exists.

5. $\mu_i \approx N(0, 6^2)$

specifies that μ_i is normally distributed and hence permits statistical testing and inferences.

Specification analysis, the process of insuring that these assumptions are met, is essential before valid inferences can be made from sample data about population relationships. If any of these conditions are not met, the results of the regression analysis are inappropriate for cost estimation and prediction. When these assumptions are satisfied, the regression coefficients obtained through the examined sample of observations are the best available estimate of the population parameters.

Descriptive Statistics in Regression Analysis
The preceding sections demonstrated how the least squares regression method can be used to compute the relationship between a dependent and an independent variable. For the JABEX, Inc., example presented in Figure 3.1, the regression summarized the relationship as $y = \$4.45 + 1.66 + \mu$. When the assumptions of regression analysis are met, the next steps determine (1) the degree of association between the variables and (2) the reliability of the estimates provided by the least squares equation.

Coefficient of Determination (R^2)   The values on the equation line (y') differ from the actual values (y). These variations depend partially on chance and partially on the relationship between x and y. The *coefficient of determination* (R^2) measures the degree of association between the variables. Operationally, it measures closeness as the percentage of total variation in the dependent variable explained by the regression line. Figure 3.5 illustrates the explained and unexplained variations for a given observation. The explained variation is the difference between the mean ($\bar{y}$) and the value on the line (y'). The unexplained variation is the difference between the actual value (y) and the value on the line (y'). In other words, ($y' - \bar{y}$) is explained by x, while ($y - y'$) is unexplained by x.

The formal definition of R^2 is the following:[4]

$$R^2 = 1 - \frac{\text{Unexplained variation}}{\text{Total variation}}$$

$$= 1 - \frac{\Sigma (y - y')^2}{\Sigma (y - \bar{y})^2}.$$

The range of R^2 is $0 \leq R^2 \leq 1$.

---

[4] R^2 can be derived as follows:

1. The total variation relationship can be expressed as $y - \bar{y} = (y - y') + (y' - \bar{y})$. Total variation = unexplained variation + explained variation.
2. The goodness of fit relationship for all observations can be expressed as follows:

Figure 3.5   Variations around the Mean ȳ

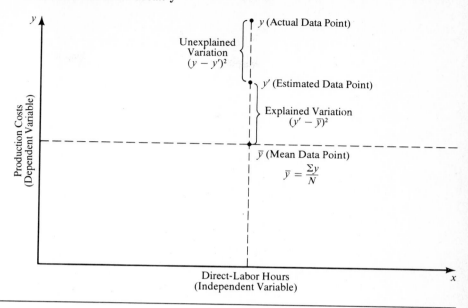

Table 3.4 presents a worksheet for the computation of the coefficient of determination for the JABEX, Inc., problem. Direct-labor hours explained about 85.18 percent of the change in total production costs, leaving 14.82 percent unexplained.

Standard Error of Estimate   How accurate is the least squares line for prediction? This question arises because the least squares line is based on a sample of observations rather than the total population of observations. In other words, using the JABEX, Inc., problem, \$4.45, \$1.66, and $y = \$4.45 + \$1.66x$ are only estimates of the true values of the total fixed cost, unit variable cost, and total cost, respectively. The accuracy of each of these estimates must be determined.

The standard error of estimate (S_e) measures the accuracy of the regression line. It indicates the size of the forecasting errors which may result from the use of a given

---

$$\Sigma(y - \bar{y})^2 = \Sigma(y - y')^2 + \Sigma(y' - \bar{y})^2.$$

Total sum of squares (TSS) = sum of squares regression (SSR) + sum of squares error (SSE), or

$$1 = \frac{\Sigma(y - y')^2}{\Sigma(y - \bar{y})} + \frac{\Sigma(y' - \bar{y})^2}{\Sigma(y - \bar{y})^2}.$$

1 = unexplained sum of squares + explained sum of squares.

3. R^2 can be derived as equal to the explained sum of squares, as follows:

$$R^2 = 1 - \frac{\Sigma(y - y')^2}{\Sigma(y - \bar{y})^2} = \frac{\Sigma(y' - \bar{y})^2}{\Sigma(y - \bar{y})^2}.$$

4. $r = \sqrt{R^2}$ is often given as the sample correlation coefficient.

Table 3.4   JABEX, Inc.: Correlation Analysis

(1)	(2)	(3)	(4)	(5)	(6)
Month (t)	Labor Hours (x)	Production Costs (y)	y'	$(y - y')^2$	$(y - \bar{y})^2$
1	2	7	7.77	0.5929	9
2	1	5	6.11	1.2321	25
3	3	10	9.43	0.3249	0
4	4	12	11.09	0.8281	4
5	2	8	7.77	0.0529	4
6	3	11	9.43	2.4649	1
7	5	13	12.75	0.0625	9
8	6	15	14.41	0.3481	25
9	2	9	7.77	1.5129	1
10	4	10	11.09	1.1881	0
11	5	11	12.75	3.0625	1
12	3	9	9.43	0.1849	1
$n = 12$	$\Sigma x = 40$	$\Sigma y = 120$		$\Sigma(y - y')^2 = 11.854$	$\Sigma(y - \bar{y})^2 = 80$

$$R^2 = 1 - \frac{11.854}{80} = 0.8518$$

regression equation and measures the scatter of the actual observations (y values) about the values on the y' line. The S_e is computed as follows:

$$S_e = \sqrt{\frac{\text{Unexplained variation}}{n - 2}}$$
$$= \sqrt{\frac{\Sigma(y - y')^2}{n - 2}},$$

where n is the size of the sample. The $n - 2$ represents the degrees of freedom around the regression line, because, based on the sample of observations, the values of *two* regression coefficients, a and b, were estimated.

If all the assumptions of regression analysis are met, the following confidence in the predictions can be stated:

$y_i' \pm 1S_e$ has a 68 percent chance of including the actual value.

$y_i' \pm 2S_e$ has a 95 percent chance of including the actual value.

$y_i' \pm 3S_e$ has a 99.7 percent chance of including the actual value.

Thus, for the JABEX, Inc., problem, the standard error of estimate is computed as

$$S_e = \sqrt{\frac{\Sigma(y - y')^2}{n - 2}} = \sqrt{\frac{11.852}{12 - 2}} = 1.08.$$

Similarly, for 7 direct-labor hours, the total cost and confidence intervals will be as follows:

$$y' = \$4.45 + \$1.66(7) = 16.07,$$

and

1. $16.07 \pm 1 \times 1.08$ ($\$17.15 \geq y' \geq \$14.99$) has a 68 percent chance of including the actual value.
2. $16.07 \pm 2 \times 1.08$ ($\$18.23 \geq y' \geq \$13.91$) has a 95 percent chance of including the actual value.
3. $16.07 \pm 3 \times 1.08$ ($\$19.31 \geq y' \geq \$12.83$) has a 99.7 percent chance of including the actual value.

Sampling Errors and Regression Coefficients   As stated earlier, the regression line y is based on a sample of observations rather than the total population. How well does each of the coefficients a and b explain the relationships between x and y? If there were no relationship, b would equal zero. The problem, then, becomes to test the null hypothesis that $b = 0$ and the alternate hypothesis that $b \neq 0$.[5]

To test these hypotheses, compute the standard error of the b regression coefficient as follows:

$$S_b = \frac{S_e}{\sqrt{\Sigma x^2 - \bar{x}\Sigma x}}$$

or

$$S_b = \frac{S_e}{\sqrt{\Sigma (x - \bar{x})^2}} \ .$$

S_b is a measure of the sampling error of the regression coefficient. In our example, the standard error of b is

$$S_b = \frac{1.08}{\sqrt{24.67}} = 0.217.$$

Accordingly, to test the hypothesis that $b = 0$, a t value is computed as follows:

$$t_b = \frac{b - 0}{S_b} = \frac{\$1.66 - 0}{0.217} = 7.649.$$

The table value of t for df $(12 - 2)$ at the 95 percent confidence level is 2.228 (see Appendix 3.A). The statistical evidence indicates that it is safe to reject the null hypoth-

---

[5]Appendix 3.A presents an explanation of hypothesis testing.

esis at the 95 percent confidence level for b. For the 10 degrees of freedom, the confidence interval equals $b \pm t_{0.025} S_b = 1.66 \pm 2.228(0.217) = 1.66 \pm 0.483$.

Similarly, the t value for a may be computed as follows:

$$S_a = S_e \sqrt{\frac{1}{n} + \frac{\bar{x}^2}{\Sigma(x - \bar{x})^2}}.$$

$$S_a = 1.08 \sqrt{\frac{1}{12} + \frac{10.98}{24.48}} = 0.77.$$

$$t_a = \frac{4.45 - 0}{0.77} = 5.7.$$

The statistical evidence again indicates that it is safe to reject the null hypothesis $a = 0$ at the 95 percent confidence level. For 10 degrees of freedom, the confidence interval is computed as follows: $a \pm t_{0.025} S_a = 4.45 \pm 2.228 (0.77) = 4.45 \pm 1.715$.

3.2.6   Multiple Regression Cost Estimation Model

Cost estimation is a determinant step in the budgeting process. The cost object as a dependent variable is subject to the influence of independent variables, and multiple regression techniques enable the cost accountant to estimate these relationships. Although very helpful to estimation and prediction of cost, the techniques can lead to useless results if the assumptions are not satisfied and the limitations not recognized.

Description of a General Regression Cost Estimation Model

Multiple regression analysis as a technique enables the cost accountant to estimate the amount by which various cost-causing factors affect costs. For example, the cost C_j for Branch j during a given accounting period may be described as

$$C_j = b_1 + b_2 x_{2j} + b_3 x_{3j} + \ldots + b_m x_{mj} + \mu_j \text{ for } j = 1, 2, \ldots, n.$$

The operating cost C_j is assumed to be a linear function of $m - 1$ variables (causal variables) x_{ij} plus a disturbance term μ_j arising from unexplainable variations in the model. Such a disturbance term may be explained by the regression model failing to include all the explanatory variables affecting the costs. It also could be the result of measurement errors in the causal variables of the model.

The terms $b_1, b_2, \ldots, b_m$ represent the *net regression coefficients*. Each measures the changes in C_j per unit change in each explanatory variable while holding all the others constant. As an example, suppose that a given firm manufactures a widget and several other products, using the services of different departments.[6] In one department two products are produced: Gammas and Alphas. Gammas are produced in batches, while Alphas are assembled singly. Weekly observations of cost and output are punched on cards. A graph is prepared that indicates the presence of a linear relationship. Furthermore, the cost of producing Gammas is not believed to be a function of Alpha production or other causal variables. Therefore, the following regression is computed:

---

[6] Adapted with permission from George J. Benston, "Multiple Regression Analysis of Cost Behavior," *Accounting Review* (October 1966), pp. 670–671.

$$\hat{C} = 110.3 + 8.21N - 7.83B + 12.32D + 235S + 523W - 136A,$$
$$(40.8) \quad (0.53) \quad (1.69) \quad (2.10) \quad (100) \quad (204) \quad (154)$$

where

$\hat{C}$ = Expected cost.
N = Number of Gammas.
B = Average number of Gammas in a batch.
D = Number of Alphas.
S = Summer dummy variable, where $S = 1$ for summer, 0 for other seasons.
W = Winter dummy variable, where $W = 1$ for winter, 0 for other seasons.
A = Autumn dummy variable, where $A = 1$ for autumn, 0 for other seasons.
$R^2 = 0.892$ (the coefficient of multiple determination).
Number of observations = 156.
Standard error of estimate = 420.83, which is 5 percent of the dependent variable cost.

The numbers in parentheses beneath the coefficients are the standard errors of the coefficients. For example, 0.53 is the sampling error associated with the estimate 8.21, or the standard error of the coefficient 8.21. This standard error of the coefficient, 0.53, allows assessment of a probability of 0.67 that the "true" marginal cost is between 7.68 and 8.74 (8.21 ± 0.53) and a probability of 0.95 that it is between 7.15 and 9.27 (8.21 ± 1.06).[7]

The predictive ability of the explanatory variable can be ascertained by computing t. In this case, the t value of N is $8.21 \div 0.53 = 15.49$. Such a high value of t demonstrates the importance of the variable N.

The regression can be used in forecasting. For example, suppose the following were production levels for a given week: $N = 532$, $B = 20$, $D = 321$, and $S =$ summer $= 1$. If this week were representative of past experience, total costs would be $110.3 + 8.21(532) - 7.83(20) + 12.32(321) + 235(1) = 8511.14$.

The forecast amount does not necessarily equal the actual amount. However, we can compute the probability that actual cost is within some range around the expected cost. Given an adjusted standard error of estimate equal to 592.61, we can assess a probability of 0.67 that the actual costs incurred will be between 7918.53 and 9103.75 (8511.14 ± 592.61); a probability of 0.95 that they will be between 9696.36 and 7325.92 (8511.14 ± 2 × 592.61); and a probability of 0.99 that they will be between 10,288.97 and 6733.31 (8511.14 ± 3 × 592.61).

Determination of the Model Parameters

The regression equation for the cost of Branch j with m independent variables can be expressed as follows: $y_j = a + b_1x_{1j} + b_2x_{2j} + \ldots + b_{mj}x_{mj} + e_j$, where y is the variable to be predicted; $x_{1j}, x_{2j}, \ldots, x_{mj}$ are the independent variables on which the prediction is to be based; $a, b_1, b_2, \ldots, b_m$ are unknown regression coefficients of the explanatory variables; and e_j is the disturbance term including the effects of all other variables.

Using matrix notation, the cost estimation model may be stated as follows: $y = X B + C$, where for n branches and m variables we have:

---

[7]The statements about probability are based on a Bayesian approach, with normality and diffuse prior distribution assumed.

$$
\begin{bmatrix} Y_1 \\ Y_2 \\ Y_3 \\ \cdot \\ \cdot \\ \cdot \\ Y_n \end{bmatrix} = \begin{bmatrix} 1 & X_{11} & X_{12} & \cdots & X_{1m} \\ 1 & X_{21} & X_{22} & \cdots & X_{2m} \\ 1 & X_{31} & X_{32} & \cdots & X_{3m} \\ \cdot & \cdot & \cdot & & \cdot \\ \cdot & \cdot & \cdot & & \cdot \\ \cdot & \cdot & \cdot & & \cdot \\ 1 & X_{n1} & X_{n2} & & X_{nm} \end{bmatrix} \begin{bmatrix} a \\ b_1 \\ b_2 \\ b_3 \\ \cdot \\ \cdot \\ \cdot \\ b_m \end{bmatrix} + \begin{bmatrix} e_1 \\ e_2 \\ e_3 \\ \cdot \\ \cdot \\ \cdot \\ e_m \end{bmatrix}
$$

$y = a \ (n \times 1)$, vector of observations on the dependent variables.

$X = a \ (n \times m + 1)$, matrix of observations on the independent variables.

$B = a \ (k + 1 \times 1)$, vector of the regression coefficients.

$e = a \ (n \times 1)$, vector of the error terms.

The regression coefficients in B are not known and must be estimated using reported branch data for the accounting period to arrive at least squares estimates b_i for $i = 1$, $2, \ldots, n$. The least squares estimates are given by the following:

$$
B = \begin{bmatrix} a \\ b_1 \\ b_2 \\ \cdot \\ \cdot \\ \cdot \\ b_n \end{bmatrix} = (X'X)^{-1} X'Y.
$$

Computer programs could provide these estimates with high speed and accuracy.

Once the regression line is found, determine how well it estimates y given some values of x. The relevant statistics presented for the simple regression analysis are computed in the multiple regression analysis as follows:

1. The standard error of the estimate can still be found as

$$
S_e = \sqrt{\frac{\Sigma(y - y')^2}{n - m - 1}} \ .
$$

2. The standard error of the b_j regression coefficients may be expressed as

$$
S_{bj} = S_e \sqrt{S_{jj}},
$$

where S_{jj} is the jth diagonal element of the $(X'X)^{-1}$ matrix. Accordingly, the t test used to determine if the b_j value is significantly different from zero is $t = b_j / S_{bj}$, which has a t distribution with $n - m - 1$ degrees of freedom. The confidence interval equals

$$
b_j \pm t_{(1 - \alpha)/2} \ S_{bj}.
$$

3. Just as the t ratio is used to test the null hypothesis $b_j = 0$, the F ratio allows the cost analyst to test for the simultaneous effects of all the independent variables by computing the ratio of the mean squares of the sum of squares regression (SSR) and the sum of squares error (SSE):

$$F = \frac{\dfrac{SSR}{m}}{\dfrac{SSE}{n-m-1}} = \frac{\dfrac{\Sigma(Y'-\bar{Y})^2}{m}}{\dfrac{\Sigma(Y-Y')^2}{n-m-1}},$$

which has an F distribution with m and $n-m-1$ degrees of freedom. If the F ratio is greater than the F statistic (obtainable from an F table), the null hypothesis that the regression coefficients of the cost model taken into combination are equal to zero can be rejected.[8]

Data Problems in Regression Analysis

Certain data requirements must be met to insure the usefulness of the regression analysis. If the data originate in the cost accounting recording system, the user should be aware of all possible data problems.

Data Characteristics To be useful, the data on both the dependent and the independent variables should represent the same periods, which in turn should meet the following general criteria:

1. The periods should be long enough to allow a proper matching of the output produced in a period with its related production costs. Any lag in reporting either costs or production must be corrected. The periods also should be small enough to catch wide variation in the production during the period, which may obscure the true relationship between the cost and the independent variables.

2. There should be a sufficient number of time periods. In general, the number of observations should exceed the number of coefficients in the regression by one. In other words, the number of degrees of freedom equals the number of observations minus the number of coefficients in the regression being estimated. Naturally, many more observations are needed to assess the significance of the "true" relationship between the cost and cost-related factors.

3. The periods should represent the widest possible range of variability. A greater variation from period to period in the dependent and independent variables will insure a better estimation of the "true" relationship.

4. All cost-related factors should be specified and included in the analysis. For example, changes in the price of the input factors require adjustment of the data to account for the specific price changes. Similarly, changes in technology and capacity, seasonal differences, and other change factors must be accounted for by the inclusion or exclusion of variables in the regression model.

All these requirements emphasize the necessity of properly defining the time periods in terms of their length and number and the range of observations. As a rule of thumb, time periods of no longer than one month and no shorter than one week allow effective analysis of the relationship between cost and the independent variables.

---

[8]The degrees of freedom are expressed by two numbers, the first equal to the number of regression coefficients in the cost model and the second equal to the number of observations on the cost data (n) minus the number of regression coefficients found in the cost model.

Data Forms   The data used in every previous example are known as *time series data*, since they have been generated for a single costing unit at different points in time. When analysts seek knowledge of the cost behavior patterns of other costing units, they use *cross-sectional data* generated from several similar but different costing units at one or different points in time. Regression analysis techniques and interpretations are similar for both time series data and cross-sectional data. However, certain requirements must be kept in mind:

1. The costing units should be homogeneous enough to allow pooling of the data, which implies that technological and even behavioral factors be sufficiently similar.

2. When the costing units are observed at a single point in time (which may often be the case), behavior is more random than when the costing units are observed over time. As a result, independent and dependent variables have more systematic movements in time series data, leading to a higher coefficient of determination (R^2).

3. The assumption of the homogeneity of variances is violated more often in cross-sectional data than in time series data.

Measurement Errors   The dependent and independent variables are subject to measurement errors, and they must be measured accurately. The impact of these errors on the usefulness of regression analysis varies. If an inaccurate measurement of the dependent variable, cost, includes an error (∂), then the cost equation will be as follows:

$$C + \partial = b_0 + b_1 x_1 + \mu$$

or

$$C = b_0 + b_1 x_1 + \mu - \partial.$$

As we see from the equation, only the disturbance term and the predictive ability of the cost equation are affected—the estimate of the regression coefficient is not.

   If, instead, any independent variable (x) is inaccurately measured and includes an error (ϕ), then the cost equation will be as follows:

$$C = b_0 + b_1(x_1 + \phi) + \mu$$

or

$$C = b_0 + b_1 x_1 + b_1 \phi + \mu.$$

Inaccurate measurement of x affects the regression coefficient, leading to correlation between the independent variable and the residual μ, as well as an underestimation of the regression coefficient. The measurement errors may be caused by either of the following:

1. The failure to record the production costs in the same period the output was produced. Benston gives as an example overtime pay for production workers in the week following their work.

2. Recording errors, such as recording costs in the wrong account or wrong period, failing to expense previously capitalized costs, or allocating specific cost accounts to time periods bearing no relation to production.

Dummy Variables   Although most independent variables included in cost models are quantitative, some qualitative variables are often used. Seasonal adjustment is a good example in the cost estimation model: Production costs hypothetically differ between the seasons. To measure the impact of qualitative variables, *dummy variables* included in the regression equations take the value of 1 for the presence of the qualitative attribute and 0 for the absence of the given attribute. For example, if a company wanted to measure the impact of the regional location of its divisions on the behavioral pattern of their production costs, the following model may be assumed:

$$C_i = b_0 + b_1 R_i(1) + b_2 R_i(2) + b_3 R_i(3) + \mu_i,$$

where

C_i = Production costs of division i.

$$R_i = \text{Region of the division } i \left[\begin{array}{l} \underline{\hspace{1cm}} 1 = \text{Northeast.} \\ \underline{\hspace{1cm}} 2 = \text{Midwest.} \\ \underline{\hspace{1cm}} 3 = \text{West.} \\ \underline{\hspace{1cm}} 4 = \text{South.} \end{array} \right.$$

$R_i(1)$ = 1 if the division is in region 1.
       = 0 otherwise.
$R_i(2)$ = 1 if the division is in region 2.
       = 0 otherwise.
$R_i(3)$ = 1 if the division is in region 3.
       = 0 otherwise.

From equation C_i we may derive the following statements:

$E(C_i) = b_0$ when $R_i(1) = R_i(2) = R_i(3) = 0$, that is, the ith division belongs to region 4.

$E(C_i) = b_0 + b_1$ when the ith division belongs to region 1.

$E(C_i) = b_0 + b_2$ when the ith division belongs to region 2.

$E(C_i) = b_0 + b_3$ when the ith division belongs to region 3.

This example serves as a warning about what is known as the *dummy variable trap*. In general, whenever dummy variables are included using the zero-one technique (binary dummy variables) and there is an intercept term in the equation, such as b_0 in this example, the number of such dummy variables should be one less than the number of different ways the dummy variable under consideration is expected to affect the dependent variable.

Lagged Factor Reaction   In cost estimation we can sometimes assume that cost today depends on what happened yesterday. As an example, the production costs in a given period may be partly determined by the patterns of production in previous periods.[9] Such a model, in which the dependent variables are lagged values, is known as an *autoregressive model*. The simplest case of such a model can be expressed as follows:

---

[9] In the economics "habit formation" hypothesis, the consumption of nondurable goods and services is affected by patterns of consumption in previous periods.

$$C_t = b_0 + b_1 x_{t-1} + \mu_y, \; t = 1, 2, \ldots, T.$$

Such a model often violates the assumptions of regression analysis. It is likely that the residuals and the dependent variables are not independent, so special estimating techniques are required. Given the complexity of the problem, the reader should consult references on autoregressive and lag models.

Requirements for the Implementation of the Regression Model   Because of the data problems discussed in previous sections, adjustments and preparatory steps are necessary before the accounting data can be used in a regression analysis cost estimation model. The data should be examined to detect any bias introduced by the accounting policies. To do so, some guidelines must be followed: (1) the cost data and activity data should be of the same period, (2) the data should be properly classified by costing unit, (3) the extent to which costs of the costing unit are the result of accounting allocations should be determined, and (4) the time period under consideration should be long enough to permit collection of meaningful data but short enough to reflect different rates of activity. The data should be examined to determine if they come from a stationary or homogeneous process. They should be homogeneous. The independent variables should be selected on the logical basis of physical or reasonable evidence. Finally, the data are plotted to determine the nature of the relationship between the cost factor and the output or decision variables presumed to be causal variables.

Statistical Problems in Regression Analysis

Heteroscedasticity   If the homoscedasticity assumption of constant variance of the disturbance term is violated, the test of significance for the efficiency of the estimating coefficients is not appropriate. In this condition, referred to as *heteroscedasticity*, the disturbance variance increases with the square of one of the explanatory variables; that is, $E(\mu_j) = 6^2 f_{ij}$.

The practical significance of heteroscedasticity derives from its tendency to inflate the sampling errors of the least squares estimators of $b_{1j}, b_{2j}, \ldots, b_{mj}, \mu_j$. Traditional tests of hypotheses concerning these estimators can no longer be made, since their sampling variances are biased.

Testing for heteroscedasticity is essential to the successful application of the regression analysis cost estimation mode. Different tests have been advocated in the literature.[10]

Multicollinearity   Multicollinearity exists when the independent variables in a regression coefficient are highly correlated with one another. The computed coefficients of the independent variables are entangled and have very large standard errors. In cost estimation models, multicollinearity exists in varying degrees. As a rule of thumb, Lawrence R. Klein suggests that multicollinearity is severe if $r_{ij} > R_y$, where r_{ij} = zero-order correlation between the two independent variables x_i and x_j ($i \neq j$), and R_y = multiple correlation coefficient between the dependent variable (y) and all the independent variables (x).[11]

---

[10]For an expanded discussion of this problem, see Dutta, *Econometric Methods*, chap. 5; and S. M. Goldfield and R. E. Quandt, "Some Tests for Homoscedasticity," *Journal of the American Statistical Association* (July 1966), pp. 539–547.

[11]Lawrence R. Klein, *An Introduction to Econometrics* (Englewood Cliffs, N.J.: Prentice-Hall, 1962), pp. 64, 101.

Table 3.5 **Direct-Labor Hours Worked on Refrigerators, Freezers, and Washing Machines during a Five-Week Period**

Week	Refrigerator	Freezer	Washing Machine
1	6	2	4
2	12	4	8
3	15	5	10
4	9	3	6
5	6	2	4

To understand the multicollinearity problem, consider the hypothetical observations in Table 3.5 on the number of direct-labor hours worked on refrigerators, freezers, and washing machines. The production times, in terms of direct-labor hours for each week, reflect a construct ratio of 3:1:2. In this extreme case, an increase in the size of the standard errors of the estimated coefficients makes it more likely that the correlated independent variables will be found to be not significantly different from zero.

One test for multicollinearity is based on the correlation coefficients between the dependent variables. For example, consider the following fictional results:

	Production Costs	Direct-Labor Hours	Number of Units Produced
Production Costs	1,000	0.8636	0.8540
Direct-Labor Hours	0.8636	1,000	0.9050
Number of Units Produced	0.8540	0.9050	1,000

Assuming the correlation coefficients have a bivariate normal distribution with $n - m - 1$ degrees of freedom, the t statistic is as follows:

$$t = \frac{R}{\sqrt{\dfrac{1 - R^2}{n - 2 - 1}}}.$$

The multicollinearity between the direct-labor hours and machine hours may be tested on the basis of the following computed t value (assuming $n = 10$):

$$t = \frac{0.9050}{\sqrt{\dfrac{1 - 0.9050^2}{10 - 2 - 1}}} = 5.63.$$

The confidence interval at the 95 percent level of significance for a two-tail test and 10 degrees of freedom (derived from Table 3.8 in Appendix 3.A) is

$$P\,(5.63 - 2.228 < t < 5.63 + 2.228) = 0.95.$$
$$P\,(3.40 < t < 7.86) = 0.95.$$

Therefore, the t coefficient of 5.63 is significant; it indicates the existence of multicollinearity between direct-labor hours and the number of units produced.

Different methods have been proposed to eliminate multicollinearity:

1. When multicollinearity is suspected, omit one of the highly correlated variables from the regression.

2. George J. Benston suggests that you construct an index of output in which the different types of output are weighted by a factor (such as labor hours) that serves to describe their relationship to cost.[12] For example, our firm produced 300 refrigerators, 100 freezers, and 200 washers. The 600 units produced are equivalent to 100 units of the product mix $3:1:2$, that is, a "bundle" of output in a mix of $3:1:2$.

3. Benston also suggests that you first allocate cost to cost centers where a single output is produced, and second compute a regression for each cost center.[13]

4. Collect new information: The variables may be multicollinear in one sample but not in another.

5. Transform the observed time series data to first differences.

Serial Correlation   Serial correlation, or autocorrelation, refers to the correlation of successive residual terms. The correlation is positive or negative, depending on whether the residual terms are positively or negatively correlated. Autocorrelation causes an underestimation of the standard error of the regression coefficient, which influences the accuracy of the outcome of the hypothesis-testing procedure.

In general, autocorrelation is tested by the *Durbin-Watson statistic* (d), which has the following formulation:

$$d = \sum_{i=1}^{n}(\mu_t - \mu_{t-1})^2 / \sum_{i=1}^{n}\mu_t^2,$$

where

μ_t = residual term = $y_t' - y_t$, for $t = 1, 2, 3, \ldots, n$.

A Durbin-Watson table appears in Table 3.6. If correlation is a problem, then $M_t = \rho M_{t-1}$ + error when $|\rho| < 1$. The null hypothesis is H_0: $\rho = 0$ against the alternate hypothesis H_1: $\rho > 0$. The Durbin-Watson table is used as follows: If $d < d_L$, reject H_0; if $4 - d < d_L$, reject H_0; and if $d_U < d < 4 - d_U$, accept H_0.

As an example, assume that $n = 15$, $k = 2$ (number of independent variables), and that the Durbin-Watson statistic is 1.85. From Table 3.6, the d_L and d_U values are, respectively, $1.85 < 0.83$, $4 - 1.85 < 0.83$, and $1.40 < 1.85 < 4 - 1.40$. Consequently, the d statistic is not significant, and there is no serial correlation.

Different solutions have been proposed for the problem of serial correlation. It may be resolved by the addition of a dummy variable. Another possible solution is the "first difference method," in which the changes in the dependent variables are regressed against the changes in the independent variables. Other methods—the Cochrane-Orcutt method, the generalized least squares method, and the Durbin method—may be found in any standard econometric textbook.[14]

---

[12] Benston, "Multiple Regression of Cost Behavior," pp. 666–667.

[13] Ibid.

[14] Dutta, *Econometric Methods*, pp. 117–126.

Table 3.6   Durbin-Watson Bounds

K = Number of Independent Variables

Values of d_L and d_U from Durbin and Watson

Sample Size (T)	Probability in Upper Tail	K = 1		K = 2		K = 3		K = 4		K = 5	
		d_L	d_U	d_L	d_U	d_L	d_U	d_L	d_U	d_L	d_U
15	0.01	0.81	1.07	0.70	1.25	0.59	1.46	0.49	1.70	0.39	1.96
	0.025	0.95	1.23	0.83	1.40	0.71	1.61	0.59	1.84	0.48	2.09
	0.05	1.08	1.36	0.95	1.54	0.82	1.75	0.69	1.97	0.56	2.21
20	0.01	0.95	1.15	0.86	1.27	0.77	1.41	0.68	1.57	0.60	1.74
	0.025	1.08	1.28	0.99	1.41	0.89	1.55	0.79	1.70	0.70	1.87
	0.05	1.20	1.41	1.10	1.54	1.00	1.68	0.90	1.83	0.79	1.99
25	0.01	1.05	1.21	0.98	1.30	0.90	1.41	0.83	1.52	0.75	1.65
	0.025	1.18	1.34	1.10	1.43	1.02	1.54	0.94	1.65	0.86	1.77
	0.05	1.29	1.45	1.21	1.55	1.12	1.66	1.04	1.77	0.95	1.89
30	0.01	1.13	1.26	1.07	1.34	1.01	1.42	0.94	1.51	0.88	1.61
	0.025	1.25	1.38	1.18	1.46	1.12	1.54	1.05	1.63	0.98	1.73
	0.05	1.35	1.49	1.28	1.57	1.21	1.65	1.14	1.74	1.07	1.83
40	0.01	1.25	1.34	1.20	1.40	1.15	1.46	1.10	1.52	1.05	1.58
	0.025	1.35	1.45	1.30	1.51	1.25	1.57	1.20	1.63	1.15	1.69
	0.05	1.44	1.54	1.39	1.60	1.34	1.66	1.29	1.72	1.23	1.79
50	0.01	1.32	1.40	1.28	1.45	1.24	1.49	1.20	1.54	1.16	1.59
	0.025	1.42	1.50	1.38	1.54	1.34	1.59	1.30	1.64	1.26	1.69
	0.05	1.50	1.59	1.46	1.63	1.42	1.67	1.38	1.72	1.34	1.77
60	0.01	1.38	1.45	1.35	1.48	1.32	1.52	1.28	1.56	1.25	1.60
	0.025	1.47	1.54	1.44	1.57	1.40	1.61	1.37	1.65	1.33	1.69
	0.05	1.55	1.62	1.51	1.65	1.48	1.69	1.44	1.73	1.41	1.77
80	0.01	1.47	1.52	1.44	1.54	1.42	1.57	1.39	1.60	1.36	1.62
	0.025	1.54	1.59	1.52	1.62	1.49	1.65	1.47	1.67	1.44	1.70
	0.05	1.61	1.66	1.59	1.69	1.56	1.72	1.53	1.74	1.51	1.77
100	0.01	1.52	1.56	1.50	1.58	1.48	1.60	1.46	1.63	1.44	1.65
	0.025	1.59	1.63	1.57	1.65	1.55	1.67	1.53	1.70	1.51	1.72
	0.05	1.65	1.69	1.63	1.72	1.61	1.74	1.59	1.76	1.57	1.78

Source: J. Durbin and S. Watson, "Testing for Serial Correlation in Least-Squares Regression," part 2, *Biometrika* (1951), pp. 173–175. Reprinted by permission.

3.3   CONCLUSION

The most popular methods to develop a cost estimation model include the engineering method, accounts method, high-low method, visual curve fitting method, simple regression method, multiple regression method, and exponential smoothing method (see Appendix 3.B). Be attentive to the potential technical and data requirements and limitations of each method: Check the data and statistical properties before you draw inferences from the cost estimation model. You should fully understand two requirements: (1) properly defined structural relationships between costs and the chosen independent variables, and (2) properly defined data to precede the use of the many available library computer programs on estimation.

3.A   APPENDIX: HYPOTHESIS TESTING

Because most tests are designed to reject a hypothesis, a null hypothesis is created. In the cost estimation model, for example, the main hypothesis is that production costs change as direct-labor hours change. This is equivalent to the null hypothesis that the population value of b is not equal to zero. In the example of the production costs in section 3.2.5 with a \$4.45 regression coefficient, the null hypothesis is that the true mean regression coefficient of the population is zero. This is a one-tailed test in the sense that we are determining if the sample mean (\$4.45) is so far above the hypothesized mean (\$0) that we can reject the hypothesis. In case we were testing above or below, the test would be a two-tail test.

In either case, the interval constructed around the estimate is a confidence interval, or, in probability terms, the level of confidence. The criteria for testing the null hypothesis are (1) reject the null hypothesis if it does not lie in the confidence interval, and (2) accept the null hypothesis if it lies in the confidence interval.

Accordingly, the procedures for hypothesis testing are as follows. First, compute the sample mean. In our cost estimation case, it was equal to a regression coefficient of \$4.45.

Next, determine the standard deviation of the sampling distribution. In our example, it was the standard error of the regression coefficient, equal to 0.217.

The inference procedures now depend on whether or not the sample size is greater than 30. If it does exceed 30, the third step is to transform the difference between the sample mean and the hypothesized mean into normalized standard deviations. Called a Z transformation, it is Z = (sample mean − hypothesized mean) / standard deviation of the sampling distribution. Table 3.7 shows the areas under the standard normal curve tail. The fourth step is to determine if the sample result on Z lies in the confidence interval.

When the sample size is smaller than 30, the third step is to use a t distribution (Student's t) in a manner similar to using the Z statistic. The t statistic in our example is equal to t = (\$1.66 − 0) / 0.217 = 7.649. The fourth step in this case is to check if the sample result, 7.649, lies in the confidence interval defined by a 95 percent level of confidence. With a one-tailed test, Table 3.8 shows a t value for 10 degrees of freedom in the $t_{0.025}$ column equal to 2.228. The null hypothesis b = 0 is rejected.

3.B   APPENDIX: EXPONENTIAL SMOOTHING

Another cost estimation technique, exponential smoothing, has as its basic formula

$$X_i' = \alpha X_i + (1 - \alpha)X_{i-1}',$$

where

X_i' = Exponentially smoothed weighted average in period i.

Table 3.7   *Areas in One Tail of the Normal Curve*

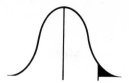

z	0.00	0.01	0.02	0.03	0.04	0.05	0.06	0.07	0.08	0.09
0.0	0.5000	0.4960	0.4920	0.4880	0.4840	0.4801	0.4761	0.4721	0.4681	0.4641
0.1	0.4602	0.4562	0.4522	0.4483	0.4443	0.4404	0.4364	0.4325	0.4286	0.4247
0.2	0.4207	0.4168	0.4129	0.4090	0.4052	0.4013	0.3974	0.3936	0.3897	0.3859
0.3	0.3821	0.3783	0.3745	0.3707	0.3669	0.3632	0.3594	0.3557	0.3520	0.3483
0.4	0.3446	0.3409	0.3372	0.3336	0.3300	0.3264	0.3228	0.3192	0.3156	0.3121
0.5	0.3085	0.3050	0.3015	0.2981	0.2946	0.2912	0.2877	0.2843	0.2810	0.2776
0.6	0.2743	0.2709	0.2676	0.2643	0.2611	0.2578	0.2546	0.2514	0.2483	0.2451
0.7	0.2420	0.2389	0.2358	0.2327	0.2296	0.2266	0.2236	0.2206	0.2177	0.2148
0.8	0.2119	0.2090	0.2061	0.2033	0.2005	0.1977	0.1949	0.1921	0.1894	0.1867
0.9	0.1841	0.1814	0.1788	0.1762	0.1736	0.1711	0.1685	0.1660	0.1635	0.1611
1.0	0.1587	0.1562	0.1539	0.1515	0.1492	0.1469	0.1446	0.1423	0.1401	0.1379
1.1	0.1357	0.1335	0.1314	0.1292	0.1271	0.1251	0.1230	0.1210	0.1190	0.1170
1.2	0.1151	0.1131	0.1112	0.1093	0.1075	0.1056	0.1038	0.1020	0.1003	0.0985
1.3	0.0968	0.0951	0.0934	0.0918	0.0901	0.0885	0.0869	0.0853	0.0838	0.0823
1.4	0.0808	0.0793	0.0778	0.0764	0.0749	0.0735	0.0721	0.0708	0.0694	0.0681
1.5	0.0668	0.0655	0.0643	0.0630	0.0618	0.0606	0.0594	0.0582	0.0570	0.0559
1.6	0.0548	0.0537	0.0526	0.0515	0.0505	0.0495	0.0485	0.0475	0.0465	0.0455
1.7	0.0446	0.0436	0.0427	0.0418	0.0409	0.0401	0.0392	0.0384	0.0375	0.0367
1.8	0.0359	0.0351	0.0344	0.0336	0.0329	0.0322	0.0314	0.0307	0.0300	0.0294
1.9	0.0287	0.0281	0.0274	0.0268	0.0262	0.0256	0.0250	0.0244	0.0238	0.0233
2.0	0.0227	0.0222	0.0217	0.0212	0.0207	0.0202	0.0197	0.0192	0.0188	0.0183
2.1	0.0179	0.0174	0.0170	0.0166	0.0162	0.0158	0.0154	0.0150	0.0146	0.0143
2.2	0.0139	0.0135	0.0132	0.0129	0.0125	0.0122	0.0119	0.0116	0.0113	0.0110
2.3	0.0107	0.0104	0.0102	0.0099	0.0096	0.0094	0.0091	0.0089	0.0087	0.0084
2.4	0.0082	0.0080	0.0078	0.0075	0.0073	0.0071	0.0069	0.0068	0.0066	0.0064
2.5	0.0062	0.0060	0.0059	0.0057	0.0055	0.0054	0.0052	0.0051	0.0049	0.0048
2.6	0.0047	0.0045	0.0044	0.0043	0.0041	0.0040	0.0039	0.0038	0.0037	0.0036
2.7	0.0035	0.0034	0.0033	0.0032	0.0031	0.0030	0.0029	0.0028	0.0027	0.0026
2.8	0.0025	0.0025	0.0024	0.0023	0.0022	0.0022	0.0021	0.0020	0.0020	0.0019
2.9	0.0019	0.0018	0.0017	0.0017	0.0016	0.0016	0.0015	0.0015	0.0015	0.0014
3.0	0.0013	0.0013	0.0013	0.0012	0.0012	0.0011	0.0011	0.0011	0.0010	0.0010
3.1	0.0010	0.0009	0.0009	0.0009	0.0008	0.0008	0.0008	0.0008	0.0007	0.0007
3.2	0.0007	0.0007	0.0006	0.0006	0.0006	0.0006	0.0006	0.0005	0.0005	0.0005
3.3	0.0005	0.0005	0.0004	0.0004	0.0004	0.0004	0.0004	0.0004	0.0004	0.0003
3.4	0.0003	0.0003	0.0003	0.0003	0.0003	0.0003	0.0003	0.0003	0.0002	0.0002
3.5	0.0002	0.0002	0.0002	0.0002	0.0002	0.0002	0.0002	0.0002	0.0002	0.0002
3.6	0.0002	0.0001	0.0001	0.0001	0.0001	0.0001	0.0001	0.0001	0.0001	0.0001
3.7	0.0001	0.0001	0.0001	0.0001	0.0001	0.0001	0.0001	0.0001	0.0001	0.0001
3.8	0.0001	0.0001	0.0001	0.0001	0.0001	0.0001	0.0001	0.0000	0.0000	0.0000
3.9	0.0000	0.0000	0.0000	0.0000	0.0000	0.0000	0.0000	0.0000	0.0000	0.0000
4.0	0.0000	0.0000	0.0000	0.0000	0.0000	0.0000	0.0000	0.0000	0.0000	0.0000

Table 3.8   *Values of* t

df	$t_{0.100}$	$t_{0.050}$	$t_{0.025}$	$t_{0.010}$	$t_{0.005}$
1	3.078	6.314	12.706	31.821	63.657
2	1.886	2.920	4.303	6.965	9.925
3	1.638	2.353	3.182	4.541	5.841
4	1.533	2.132	2.776	3.747	4.604
5	1.476	2.015	2.571	3.365	4.032
6	1.440	1.943	2.447	3.143	3.707
7	1.415	1.895	2.365	2.998	3.499
8	1.397	1.860	2.306	2.896	3.355
9	1.383	1.833	2.262	2.821	3.250
10	1.372	1.812	2.228	2.764	3.169
11	1.363	1.796	2.201	2.718	3.106
12	1.356	1.782	2.179	2.681	3.055
13	1.350	1.771	2.160	2.650	3.012
14	1.345	1.761	2.145	2.624	2.977
15	1.341	1.753	2.131	2.602	2.947
16	1.337	1.746	2.120	2.583	2.921
17	1.333	1.740	2.110	2.567	2.898
18	1.330	1.734	2.101	2.552	2.878
19	1.328	1.729	2.093	2.539	2.861
20	1.325	1.725	2.086	2.528	2.845
21	1.323	1.721	2.080	2.518	2.831
22	1.321	1.717	2.074	2.508	2.819
23	1.319	1.714	2.069	2.500	2.807
24	1.318	1.711	2.064	2.492	2.797
25	1.316	1.708	2.060	2.485	2.787
26	1.315	1.706	2.056	2.479	2.779
27	1.314	1.703	2.052	2.473	2.771
28	1.313	1.701	2.048	2.467	2.763
29	1.311	1.699	2.045	2.462	2.756
inf.	1.282	1.645	1.960	2.326	2.576

Source: The data of this table was taken from Table III of Fisher and Yates, *Statistical Tables for Biological, Agricultural and Medical Research*, (6th edition, Longman 1974) page 46, published by Longman Group Ltd. London. (previously published by Oliver & Boyd Ltd. Edinburgh) and by permission of the authors and publishers.

$0 \leq \alpha \leq 1$ = Smoothing constant.

X_i = Most recent observation.

The exponentially smoothed average for a given period is equal to α times the actual observation for the period plus $1 - \alpha$ times the previous period's exponentially smoothed weighted average. Therefore, the method rests on two values, the most recent observation and the previous period's weighted average.

For example, the production cost in period i is designated by X_i. We can estimate the production cost for the ensuing period, assuming $\alpha = 0.3$, by the following formula:

$$X_i' = 0.3X_i + 0.7X_{i-1}'.$$

Then we find

i	X_i	$0.3X_i + 0.7X'_{i-1}$	X'_i
1	50		50
2	60	$0.3(60) + 0.7(50)$	53
3	70	$0.3(70) + 0.7(53)$	58.1
4	80	$0.3(80) + 0.7(58.1)$	64.67
5	80	$0.3(80) + 0.7(64.67)$	69.26
6	80	$0.3(80) + 0.7(69.26)$	72.48

To evaluate the efficiency of the system, we compute the forecasting error as follows:

i	X_i	X'_i	Δ_i	Δ_i/X_i (% error)
1	50	50	0	—
2	60	53	-7	-0.11
3	70	58.1	-11.9	-0.17
4	80	64.67	-15.33	-0.19
5	80	69.26	-10.74	-0.13
6	80	72.48	-7.52	-0.09

If the forecasting error is not satisfactory, we can choose a higher smoothing constant that will weigh the most recent observations more heavily. In general, α is usually taken to be close to zero rather than close to one. If α is small, the estimate will be stable and the effect of short-term fluctuation depressed.

3.C   APPENDIX: AN INTRODUCTION TO MATRIX ALGEBRA

3.C.1   Definition

A matrix is an array of numbers arranged in rows and columns. The size, or order, of the matrix is defined by the number of rows and columns it includes. The following matrix, X, has the order (2×4):

$$X = \begin{bmatrix} 3 & 5 & 2 & 3 \\ 4 & 6 & 1 & 1 \end{bmatrix}.$$

Subscripts are usually used to describe and locate each element of a matrix. Hence a complete description of matrix X is

$a_{1,1} = 3, \ a_{1,2} = 5, \ a_{1,3} = 2, \ a_{1,4} = 3$

$a_{2,1} = 4, \ a_{2,2} = 6, \ a_{2,3} = 1, \ a_{2,4} = 1.$

In other words,

$$X = \begin{bmatrix} a_{1,1}, & a_{1,2}, & a_{1,3}, & a_{1,4} \\ a_{2,1}, & a_{2,2}, & a_{2,3}, & a_{2,4} \end{bmatrix} = \begin{bmatrix} 3 & 5 & 2 & 3 \\ 4 & 6 & 1 & 1 \end{bmatrix}.$$

Special matrices include the null or zero matrix and the identity matrix:

1. If the elements of a matrix are 0, the matrix is a null or zero matrix. An example is

$$Y = \begin{bmatrix} 0 & 0 & 0 \\ 0 & 0 & 0 \\ 0 & 0 & 0 \end{bmatrix}.$$

2. If all the elements on the right diagonals are 1 and all other elements are 0, the matrix is an identity matrix. An example is

$$Z = \begin{bmatrix} 1 & 0 & 0 \\ 0 & 1 & 0 \\ 0 & 0 & 1 \end{bmatrix}.$$

3.C.2   *Basic Operations*

Addition
Only matrices of the same size can be added by summing their respective elements. For example, if

$$X = \begin{bmatrix} 3 & 6 \\ 2 & 2 \end{bmatrix},$$

and

$$Y = \begin{bmatrix} 2 & 5 \\ 4 & 2 \end{bmatrix},$$

then the matrix $X + Y$ is formed as follows:

$$X + Y = \begin{bmatrix} 3 + 2 & 6 + 5 \\ 2 + 4 & 2 + 2 \end{bmatrix} = \begin{bmatrix} 5 & 11 \\ 6 & 4 \end{bmatrix}.$$

Subtraction
Only matrices of the same size can be subtracted by subtracting their respective elements. Using the matrices X and Y from the preceding example, we obtain

$$\begin{bmatrix} X - Y \end{bmatrix} = \begin{bmatrix} 3 - 2 & 6 - 5 \\ 2 - 4 & 2 - 2 \end{bmatrix} = \begin{bmatrix} 1 & 1 \\ -2 & 0 \end{bmatrix}.$$

Multiplication
Only "conformable" matrices can be multiplied: The number of columns of the first matrix must equal the number of rows of the second matrix. Multiplication of two conformable matrices results in a matrix having the same number of rows as the first matrix and the same number of columns as the second matrix. Thus, if matrix X is $k \times p$, and matrix Y is $p \times t$, then the product is a matrix of size $k \times t$.

Multiply each element of a row of the first matrix by the corresponding element in the column of the second matrix, and sum the result to obtain an element of the product matrix. Consider the following matrix multiplication:

$$\begin{bmatrix} 2 & 4 \\ 3 & 5 \end{bmatrix} \begin{bmatrix} 3 & 5 & 2 \\ 2 & 2 & 4 \end{bmatrix} = \begin{bmatrix} [(2 \times 3) + (4 \times 2)] & [(2 \times 5) + (4 \times 2)] & [(2 \times 2) + (4 \times 4)] \\ [(3 \times 3) + (5 \times 2)] & [(3 \times 5) + (5 \times 2)] & [(3 \times 2) + (5 \times 4)] \end{bmatrix}$$

$$= \begin{bmatrix} 14 & 18 & 20 \\ 15 & 25 & 26 \end{bmatrix}.$$

Inversion

The inverse of a matrix X is the reciprocal $1/X$, or X^{-1}. The inverse can be computed for any square nonsingular matrix X such that $X \times X^{-1} = I$ (identity matrix). The procedure for the computation of the inverse of any square nonsingular matrix will be illustrated with the matrix

$$X = \begin{bmatrix} 4 & 3 \\ 6 & 5 \end{bmatrix} = \begin{bmatrix} a_{11} & a_{12} \\ a_{21} & a_{22} \end{bmatrix}.$$

Step 1 Determine the augmented matrix $[X/I]$:

$$\begin{bmatrix} 4 & 3 & | & 1 & 0 \\ 6 & 5 & | & 0 & 1 \end{bmatrix}.$$

Step 2 Multiply the second row by $1/5$ to bring 1 into the a_{22} position:

$$\begin{bmatrix} 4 & 3 & | & 1 & 0 \\ \dfrac{6}{5} & 1 & | & 0 & \dfrac{1}{5} \end{bmatrix}.$$

Step 3 Multiply the second row by -3 and add it to the first row to bring a 0 into the a_{12} position:

$$\begin{bmatrix} \dfrac{2}{5} & 0 & | & 1 & -\dfrac{3}{5} \\ \dfrac{6}{5} & 1 & | & 0 & \dfrac{1}{5} \end{bmatrix}.$$

Step 4 Multiply the first row by -3 and add it to the second row to bring a 0 into the a_{21} position:

$$\begin{bmatrix} \dfrac{2}{5} & 0 & | & 1 & -\dfrac{3}{5} \\ 0 & 1 & | & -3 & \dfrac{10}{5} \end{bmatrix}.$$

Step 5 Multiply the first row by $5/2$ to bring a 1 into the a_{11} position:

$$\begin{bmatrix} 1 & 0 & \dfrac{5}{2} & -\dfrac{3}{2} \\ 0 & 1 & -3 & \dfrac{10}{5} \end{bmatrix}.$$

The process is completed, because the left half of the augmented matrix is now an identity matrix. The right half of the augmented matrix is the inverse. To check, verify that $X \times X = I$:

$$
\begin{bmatrix} 4 & 3 \\ 6 & 5 \end{bmatrix}
\begin{bmatrix} \dfrac{5}{2} & -\dfrac{3}{2} \\ -3 & \dfrac{10}{5} \end{bmatrix}
=
\begin{bmatrix} [(4 \times \frac{5}{2}) + (3 \times -3)] & [(4 \times -\frac{3}{2}) + (3 \times \frac{10}{5})] \\ [(6 \times \frac{5}{2}) + (5 \times -3)] & [(6 \times -\frac{3}{2}) + (5 \times \frac{10}{5})] \end{bmatrix}
$$

$$
= \begin{bmatrix} 1 & 0 \\ 0 & 1 \end{bmatrix}.
$$

3.C.3   Applications

This chapter and others on cost allocation explore one of the applications of matrix algebra to accounting. For examples of applications in financial accounting, the student should consult the following books: W. E. Leininger, *Quantitative Methods in Accounting* (New York: Van Nostrand, 1980); and J. Shank, *Matrix Methods in Accounting* (Reading, Mass.: Addison-Wesley, 1972).

GLOSSARY

Accounts Method The cost estimation technique which first classifies costs into variable and fixed costs, second divides total variable costs by the level of activity to determine the unit variable cost, and third sums the fixed costs to determine the total fixed costs.

Cost Estimation The process of measuring future costs and specifying a relationship between y and x.

Cross-sectional Data Data generated from different costing units at one point in time or at different points in time.

Engineering Method The cost estimation technique which bases its results on the input-output relationships implied by the production function.

High-Low Method The cost estimation technique which relies on the line linking the highest and lowest observed values of cost to estimated cost in a scatter diagram.

Homoscedasticity The property of the constancy of variance.

Multicollinearity Exists when the independent variables in a regression coefficient are highly correlated with one another.

Multiple Regression Method The cost estimation technique which relates one dependent variable to more than one independent variable and relies on the least squares method.

Serial Correlation (Autocorrelation) Refers to the correlation of successive residual terms.

Simple Regression Method The cost estimation technique which relates one dependent variable to one independent variable and determines the parameters of the relationship on the basis of the least squares method.

Time Series Data Data generated for a single costing unit at different points in time.

Visual Curve Fitting Method The cost estimation technique which relies on the general trend of the plotted points on a scattergraph.

SELECTED READINGS

Association of American Railroads, *A Guide to Railroad Cost Analysis* (Washington, D.C.: Bureau of Railway Economics, AAR, 1964).

Benston, George J., "Economics of Scale and Marginal Costs in Banking Operations," *National Banking Review* (July 1965), pp. 507–549.

Benston, George J., "Multiple Regression Analysis of Cost Behavior," *Accounting Review* (October 1966), pp. 657–672.

Cerullo, Michael J., "Use a Flow Chart to Interpret Regression Analysis Computer Output," *Cost and Management* (May–June 1979), pp. 37–41.

Chan, K. H.; Sbrocchi, F. L.; and VanZante, N. R., "Forecasting Methods and the Management Accountant," *Cost and Management* (January–February 1980), pp. 40–45.

Dutta, M., *Econometric Methods* (Cincinnati, Ohio: South-Western Publishing, 1975).

Gynther, R. S., "Improving Separation of Fixed and Variable Expenses," *NAA Bulletin* (June 1963), pp. 25–38.

Hicks, J., "The Application of Exponential Smoothing to Standard Cost Systems," *Management Accounting* (September 1978), pp. 28–32, 53.

Jensen, Robert, "A Multiple Regression Model for Cost Control: Assumptions and Limitations," *Accounting Review* (April 1967), pp. 265–273.

Johnson, J., *Statistical Cost Analysis* (New York: McGraw-Hill, 1960).

Knapp, Robert A., "Forecasting and Measuring with Correlation Analysis," *Financial Executive* (May 1963), pp. 13–19.

Leininger, W. E., *Quantitative Methods in Accounting* (New York: Van Nostrand, 1980), chap. 6.

McClenon, Paul R., "Cost Finding through Multiple Correlation Analysis," *Accounting Review* (July 1963), pp. 540–547.

Naphtali, Michael W., "Improving Cost Forecasting," *Cost and Management* (June 1974), pp. 13–20.

National Association of Accountants, *Accounting Practice Report No. 10*, "Separating and Using Costs as Fixed and Variable" (New York: NAA, 1960), in *NAA Bulletin* (June 1960), sec. 3.

Oliver, F. R., "A Cross-section Study of Marginal Cost," *Applied Statistics* (June 1962), pp. 65–78.

Pierce, Richard F., "The Importance of the Distinction between Fixed and Variable Costs," *NAA Bulletin* (May 1964), pp. 19–26.

Tingey, Sherman, "Difficulties in Identifying Fixed and Variable Costs," *Budgeting* (March–April 1968), pp. 25–28.

QUESTIONS, EXERCISES, AND PROBLEMS

3.1   Cost estimation may be achieved through (1) the engineering method, (2) the accounts method, (3) the high-low method, (4) the visual curve method, and (5) the simple regression method. Explain the main characteristics of each method.

3.2   What requirements are necessary for the implementation of a regression model?

3.3   What are the three phases of cost estimation?

3.4   Discuss the operational usefulness of the following description statistics:

1. The coefficient of determination.
2. The standard error of estimate.
3. The t value.
4. The F value.

3.5   Discuss the main data problems occurring in regression analysis, using the following headings:

1. Data characteristics.   **4.** Dummy variables.

2. Data forms.   **5.** Lagged factor reaction.

3. Measurement errors.

3.6   *Accounting Applications of Matrix Algebra*

Required:
Select the best answer for the following situation. Dancy, Inc., is going to produce a new chemical cleaner by combining alcohol, peroxide, and enzyme. Each quart of the new cleaner will require one-half quart of alcohol, one quart of peroxide, and one-third quart of enzyme. The costs per quart are $.40 for alcohol, $.60 for peroxide, and $.20 for enzyme. The matrix operation to determine the cost of producing one quart of cleaner is

1. $[\frac{1}{2}, 1, \frac{1}{3}] \begin{bmatrix} 0.40 \\ 0.60 \\ 0.20 \end{bmatrix}$.

2. $\begin{bmatrix} \frac{1}{2} \\ 1 \\ \frac{1}{3} \end{bmatrix} \begin{bmatrix} 0.40 \\ 0.60 \\ 0.20 \end{bmatrix}$.

3. $[\frac{1}{2}, 1, \frac{1}{3}]$ $[0.40, 0.60, 0.20]$.

4. $\begin{bmatrix} 0.40 \\ 0.60 \\ 0.20 \end{bmatrix}$ $[\frac{1}{2}, 1, \frac{1}{3}]$.

5. None of the above.

(AICPA adapted)

3.7   Regression analysis is considered one of the most powerful tools available to the cost accountant for both cost estimation and cost prediction.

Required:
1. Distinguish between cost estimation and cost prediction. Provide a simple example showing how regression analysis can be used for both.

2. Briefly describe the crucial assumptions underlying regression analysis that are necessary to make valid inferences from sample data about population relationships.

3. One of the problems associated with multiple regression is multicollinearity. What are the principal consequences of the presence of multicollinearity in an estimated equation?

(SMA adapted)

3.8   *Exponential Smoothing* Exponential smoothing is commonly used for short-term forecasting. One example would be forecasting weekly sales to improve control of the inventory level.

Required:

Explain why the value of α in the exponential smoothing formula is usually taken to be close to zero (say 0.1) rather than close to one.

(CGA adapted)

3.9   Fairchild Appliances Ltd. sells a full line of complementary products; that is, an increase in demand of one product will increase the demand of other products in the line. The appliance industry is capital intensive, and competition is extremely keen. Therefore, costs such as depreciation and advertising may decline when volume declines.

Required:

1. Regression analysis has two troublesome aspects. Name and discuss the two problems of specification analysis in Fairchild's case when multiple regression analysis is used to determine cost.

2. If Fairchild resorts to simple regression using one independent variable, what criteria should be met if regression is to be helpful?

(SMA adapted)

3.10   Enumerate the procedures available for testing heteroscedasticity in the cost estimation model.

3.11   Explain the "dummy variable trap."

3.12   ***Exponential Smoothing***   You have been provided with weekly sales statistics for the past year. The actual sales for the week just completed are 107 units, and the sales estimate for that week was 102 units. The sales manager has assured you that seasonal effects can safely be ignored. You must take into account the long-term trend in sales of +1.1 units per week.

Required:

Using a value of $\alpha = 0.12$, calculate the sales estimate for the following week (to two decimal places).

(CGA adapted)

3.13   ***Choice of a Prediction Equation***   The Bright Company produces widgets and gadgets. Each widget requires 4 direct-labor hours and 0.4 machine hours. Each gadget requires 5 direct-labor hours and 0.2 machine hours. The company wishes to predict total overhead for the year, and a computer printout concerning overhead cost incurrence reads as follows:

Independent Variable	Coefficient	S_e	t Value	R^2
Intercept	15,000.000	500.000	30.000	
Direct-Labor Hours	7.000	1.000	6.000	
				0.832
Intercept	8,400.000	8.400	10.000	
Machine Hours	17.000	4.250	4.000	
				0.929

The computer analysis was based on information from the March monthly financial statements. Annual production is 6,000 widgets and 8,000 gadgets.

Required:

1. With this data available, which prediction equation should be selected? Indicate the factors which should be considered in such a selection.

2. Assuming that March is a representative month, predict the total annual overhead. Show all computations.

(SMA adapted)

3.14   ***Cost Estimation***   The following relationship was found to exist between total factory overhead and changes in direct-labor hours: $Y = \$1000 + \$2X$.

1. This equation was probably found through the use of which of the following mathematical techniques?
   a. Linear programming.   **d.** Dynamic programming.
   b. Multiple regression analysis.   **e.** None of the above.
   c. Simple regression analysis.

2. The relationship shown in the equation is
   a. Parabolic.   **d.** Probabilistic.
   b. Curvilinear.   **e.** None of the above.
   c. Linear.

3. In the equation, Y is an estimate of
   a. Total variable costs.   **d.** Total direct-labor hours.
   b. Total factory overhead.   **e.** None of the above.
   c. Total fixed costs.

4. The $2 in the equation is an estimate of
   a. Total fixed costs.   **d.** Fixed costs per direct-labor hour.
   b. Variable costs per direct-labor hour.   **e.** None of the above.
   c. Total variable costs.

5. The use of such a relationship of total factory overhead to changes in direct-labor hours is said to be valid only within the relevant range. The phrase *relevant range* means
   a. Within a reasonable dollar amount for labor costs.
   b. Within the range of observations of the analysis.
   c. Within the range of reasonableness as judged by the department supervisor.
   d. Within the budget allowance for overhead.
   e. None of the above.

3.15   ***Rudiments of Simple Linear Regression***   Answer the questions that follow this information concerning overhead costs and direct-labor hours:

Overhead Cost	Direct-Labor Hours
$16	4
20	8
22	10
25	12
30	16
35	20

1. Determine an equation to estimate overhead costs consistent with least squares regression analysis.

2. Compute the coefficient of determination (R^2).

3. Compute the standard error of estimate (S_e). Assume that there are 25 estimated direct-labor hours for the next period. Compute a point estimate and a prediction interval of overhead costs for the next period using a 95 percent confidence coefficient.

4. Test to see if a significant relationship exists between the direct-labor hours on one hand and overhead costs on the other. Determine a 95 percent confidence interval for the *b* coefficient of the regression coefficient.

3.16   ***Rudiments of Multiple Regression***   You have been asked to assist in the estimation of the overhead costs for the Garcia Manufacturing Company. The following data were provided:

Period	Overhead Cost	Direct-Labor Hours	Machine Hours
1	250	3	9
2	300	7	13
3	370	11	15
4	350	9	25
5	520	14	30
6	280	6	11
7	190	5	12
8	390	9	20
9	480	10	25
10	510	12	23
11	460	11	22
12	320	7	11
13	350	10	18
14	410	11	18
15	280	4	10

Required:

1. Determine the best equation for estimating overhead cost.

2. Compute the standard error of the estimate.

3. Test to see if a significant relationship exists between the direct-labor hours and machine hours on one hand and overhead cost on the other. Determine a 95 percent confidence interval for the *b* coefficients of the regression equation.

4. Test the significance of the regression equation using the *F* test.

5. Compute the coefficient of determination, R^2.

6. Test for multicollinearity.

7. Test for serial correlation using the Durbin-Watson statistic.

3.17   ***Regression Analysis***   A company has analyzed the relationship between labor hours and production output for two departments that produce the same products but are located in two different plants. Department A recently has been modernized with new equipment and has three times the capacity of department B. The data in both cases refer to a range of output from 2,500 to 7,500 units per day. The least squares method was used to calculate linear regression equations of the form $Y = a + bX$, where X is production output in thousands of units, and Y is labor hours.

Department A	Department B
$Y = 33 + 3.4X$	$Y = -18 + 13.6X$
$S_{yx} = 7.5$	$S_{yx} = 12.5$
$\bar{Y} = 50$	$\bar{Y} = 50$
$r = 0.8$	$r = 0.4$

Required:
1. What information does the standard error of estimate provide? What does it indicate in this example?

2. What information does the coefficient of correlation provide? What does it indicate in this example?

3. How would you interpret the regression coefficients a and b (in the equation $Y = a + bX$) in this example?

4. In both departments the mean of labor hours equals 50. What output in each department is associated with that level of labor input? If both departments had been operating at that level and both decided to reduce production by 1,000 units, which department would require the greater decrease of labor input?

(CGA adapted)

3.18   ***Cost Behavior Patterns***   MacKenzie Park Company manufactures and sells trivets. Labor hours and production costs for the last four months of 19X9, which you believe are representative for the year, were as follows:

Month	Labor Hours	Total Production Costs
September	2,500	$ 20,000
October	3,500	25,000
November	4,500	30,000
December	3,500	25,000
	14,000	$100,000

Required:
Based on this information, and using the least squares method of computation with the following letters, select the best answer for each of questions 1 through 5.

Let

a = Fixed production costs per month.
b = Variable production costs per labor hour.
n = Number of months.
x = Labor hours per month.
y = Total monthly production costs.
Σ = Summation.

1. The equation(s) required for applying the least squares method of computation of fixed and variable production costs could be expressed as
    a. $\Sigma xy = a\Sigma x + b\Sigma x^2$.   **d.** $\Sigma xy = a\Sigma x + b\Sigma x^2$
    b. $\Sigma y = na + b\Sigma x$. $\Sigma y = na + b\Sigma x$.
    c. $y = a + bx^2$
        $\Sigma y = na + b\Sigma x^2$.

2. The cost function derived by the least squares method
    a. Would be linear.
    b. Must be tested for minima and maxima.
    c. Would be parabolic.
    d. Would indicate maximum costs at the function's point of inflection.

3. Monthly production costs could be expressed as
    a. $y = ax + b$.   **c.** $y = b + ax$.
    b. $y = a + bx$.   **d.** $y = \Sigma a + bx$.

4. Using the least squares method of computation, the fixed monthly production cost of trivets is approximately
    a. $10,000.   **c.** $7,500.
    b. $ 9,500.   **d.** $5,000.

5. Using the least squares method of computation, the variable production cost per labor hour is
    a. $6.   **c.** $3.
    b. $5.   **d.** $2.

(AICPA adapted)

3.19

Regression Analysis   Mr. Gene Leeb, a manufacturer of widgets, has kept a careful weekly record of production volume (in units), electric power used, and labor hours. The range of output for which data were compiled was 1,000 to 4,000 units per week. The following statistics were computed for electric power: $Y = 1,500 + 1.7X$, $S_{yx} = 240$, and $S_y = 410$, where Y is electric power and X is units of production. The following statistics were computed for labor: $Y = 100 + 0.7X$, $S_{yx} = 150$, and $S_y = 170$, where Y is labor hours and X is units of production.

Required:
1. Calculate R (coefficient of correlation) for both electric power and labor.

2. If output were increased by 1,000 units, what would be the best estimate of the increase in electric power and in labor?

3. Indicate which of the following statements are true, and amend any that are incorrect.
    a. A smaller proportion of the total variation can be explained by the calculated regression equation for labor than for electric power, as indicated by the smaller value of S_{yx}.
    b. It is valid to use the regression equation to estimate labor requirements outside the range 1,000 to 4,000 units only if S_{yx} is small, as in this case, and if a is positive.
    c. If the standard deviation and the standard error of estimate were equal, it would indicate perfect correlation.
    d. When the coefficient of correlation is close to 1, you can be confident that the relationship is not spurious.
    e. Even if a is negative, as in electric power—indicating that over a wide range of output, a curve or step function may be required within the limited range of output used—a straight line may be a reasonable approximation of the relationship between output and electric power.

(CGA adapted)

3.20

Multiple Regression and Cost Estimation   Centrex Co. Ltd. manufactures three industrial products called A, B, and C. The manufacturing facilities of the company are arranged in divisions by product line. The management of Centrex wants to use multiple regression to predict manufacturing overhead (total and divisional) for the coming month. The following equation was estimated using historical monthly data; standard errors appear in parentheses.

$$M(t) = 2450.0 + 10.0Q_A(t) + 6.0Q_B(t) + 12.0Q_C(t) \quad R^2 = 0.84$$
$$\quad\quad\quad (125.0) \quad\quad (4.0) \quad\quad\quad (3.6) \quad\quad\quad (6.25)$$

where

$M(t)$ = Total manufacturing overhead (in dollars) in month t.
$Q_A(t)$ = Number of units of A produced in month t.
$Q_B(t)$ = Number of units of B produced in month t.
$Q_C(t)$ = Number of units of C produced in month t.

The manufacturing budget calls for a production of 2,000, 3,000, and 1,000 units of A, B, and C, respectively, in the coming month.

Required:
Refer to the estimated regression equation to answer the following:

1. From an economic point of view, what *exactly* do the numbers 10.0, 6.0, and 12.0 represent?

2. Compute the t values of the net regression coefficients (independent variables only), and briefly state any inferences that can be made.

3. What percentage of the variability in overhead is explained by the regression?

4. Under what conditions can one say that fixed overhead is $2,450?

5. Predict next month's total manufacturing overhead.

(SMA adapted)

3.21   ***Regression Analysis***   You have been provided with the following weekly statistics on the use of labor and the corresponding output in units of production.

Week	Output in Units (X)	Labor (Y)	Week	Output in Units (X)	Labor (Y)
1	15	40	11	45	50
2	22	42	12	20	30
3	29	50	13	50	90
4	35	80	14	60	100
5	48	115	15	55	110
6	55	110	16	70	185
7	50	160	17	75	200
8	70	190	18	85	190
9	75	220	19	90	230
10	80	210	20	95	220

A least squares linear regression equation fitted to this data is Y (labor) $= -23.60 + 2.75X$ (output). $R^2 = 0.88$, and $S_y = 68.30$.

Required:
1. Calculate the standard error of estimate.

2. Comment on the significance of the standard error of estimate.

3. Comment on the significance of the coefficient of correlation.

4. Comment on the significance of the value of a in the equation $Y = a + bX$.

(CGA adapted)

3.22   ***Choice of a Cost Estimation Technique***   The Ramon Co. manufactures a wide range of products at several different plant locations. Its Franklin Plant, which manufactures electrical components, has been experiencing some difficulties with fluctuating monthly overhead costs. The fluctuations have made it difficult to estimate the level of overhead that will be incurred for any one month.

Management wants to be able to estimate overhead costs accurately to better plan its operation and financial needs. A trade association publication to which Ramon Co. subscribes indicates that, for companies manufacturing electrical components, overhead tends to vary with direct-labor hours.

One member of the accounting staff proposed that the cost behavior pattern of the overhead costs be determined. Then overhead costs could be predicted from the budgeted direct-labor hours. Another member of the accounting staff suggested that a good starting place for determining the cost behavior pattern of overhead costs would be an analysis of the historical cost behavior pattern as a basis for estimating future overhead costs. Ramon Co. decided to employ the high-low method, the scattergraph method, and simple linear regression to determine the cost behavior pattern. Data on direct-labor hours and the respective overhead costs incurred were collected for the past two years. The raw data prepared from the data are as follows:

	Direct-Labor Hours		Overhead Costs	
	19X3	19X4	19X3	19X4
January	20,000	21,000	$84,000	$86,000
February	25,000	24,000	99,000	93,000
March	22,000	23,000	89,500	93,000
April	23,000	22,000	90,000	87,000
May	20,000	20,000	81,500	80,000
June	19,000	18,000	75,500	76,500
July	14,000	12,000	70,500	67,500
August	10,000	13,000	64,500	71,000
September	12,000	15,000	69,000	73,500
October	17,000	17,000	75,000	72,500
November	16,000	15,000	71,500	71,000
December	19,000	18,000	78,000	75,000

The following data were obtained using linear regression:

Coefficient of Determination	0.9109
Coefficient of Correlation	0.9544
Coefficients of the Regression Equation	
Constant	39,859
Independent Variable	2.1549
Standard Error of the Estimate	2,840
Standard Error of the Regression Coefficient for the Independent Variable	0.1437
True *t* statistic for a 95 percent Confidence Interval (22 Degrees of Freedom)	2.074

Required:

1. Using the high-low method, determine the cost behavior pattern of the overhead costs for the Franklin Plant.

2. Using the results of the regression analysis, calculate the estimated overhead costs for 22,500 direct-labor hours.

3. Of the three proposed methods (high-low, scattergraph, and linear regression), which one should Ramon Co. use to determine the historical cost behavior pattern of Franklin Plant's overhead costs? Explain your answer completely, indicating the reasons why the other methods should not be used.

(CMA adapted)

3.23   ***Cost Estimation and Prediction***   The Johnstar Co. makes a very expensive chemical product, with costs averaging about $1,000 per pound and the material selling for $2,500 per pound. The material is very dangerous; therefore, it is made daily to fill the customer orders for the day. Failure to deliver the quantity required results in a shutdown for the customers and a high-cost penalty for Johnstar (plus customer ill will).

Predicting the final weight of a batch of the chemical being processed has been a serious problem. This is critical because of the large cost of failure to meet customer needs. A consultant recommended that the batches be weighed halfway through the six-hour processing period. He proposed the use of linear regression to predict the final weight from the midpoint weight. If the prediction indicated that too little of the chemical would be available, a new batch could be started and still delivered in time to satisfy customers' needs for the day. Included in the report of a study made by the consultant during a one-week period were the following items:

Observation Number	Weight (3 Hrs.)	Final Weight	Observation Number	Weight (3 Hrs.)	Final Weight
1	55	90	11	60	80
2	45	75	12	35	60
3	40	80	13	35	80
4	60	80	14	55	60
5	40	45	15	35	75
6	60	80	16	50	90
7	50	80	17	30	60
8	55	95	18	60	105
9	50	100	19	50	60
10	35	75	20	20	30

Data from the regression analysis follow:

Coefficient of Determination	0.4126
Coefficient of Correlation	0.6424
Coefficients of the Regression Equation	
Constant	+28.6
Independent Variable	+1.008
Standard Error of the Estimate	14.2
Standard Error of the Regression Coefficient for the Independent Variable	0.2796
The t Statistic for a 95 Percent Confidence Interval (18 Degrees of Freedom)	2.101

Required:

1. Using the results of the consultant's regression analysis, estimate today's first batch, which weighs 42 pounds at the end of three hours' processing time.

2. Customer orders for today total 68 pounds. The nature of the process is such that the smallest batch that can be started will weigh at least 20 pounds at the end of six hours. Using only the data from the regression analysis, would you start another batch? (Remember that today's first batch weighed 42 pounds at the end of three hours).

3. Is the relationship between the variables such that this regression analysis provides an adequate prediction model for the Johnstar Co.? Explain your answer.

(CMA adapted)

3.24   ***Sales Forecasting***   Brown Company employs twenty salespeople to market its products in well-defined sales territories. The company, analyzing the weekly sales order-getting costs for the past year using regression analysis, derived the following: $C = \$6,000$

+ $\$.50M$ + $\$6.00S$, where C = weekly sales order-getting costs, M = number of miles driven per week by the sales force, and S = number of sales calls completed per week. The standard error of the estimate for C, given the values for M and S, equals 400.

Required:

1. The sales department has estimated that the sales force will drive 10,000 miles and make five hundred calls during the first week in July. Calculate the estimated sales order-getting costs for the week. What criteria should be met before Brown's sales department relies on this estimate?

2. What does the value for the standard error of the estimate for C (400) mean, and how might it be used in cost estimation?

(CMA adapted)

Cost-volume-profit analysis involves an examination of cost and revenue behavioral patterns and their relationships with profit. The analysis separates costs into fixed and variable components and determines the level of activity where costs and revenues are in equilibrium. The cost-volume-profit analysis is a normative model for understanding the relationships between the cost, revenue, and profit structures of a firm. It is a key factor in all decisions based on selling prices, variable costs, and fixed costs. Acquisitions, resource utilization and disposition, product mix determination, product pricing, and even fixed assets acquisitions are decisions in which an understanding of cost-volume-profit relationships may avoid undesirable results.

This chapter first covers the accounting approach to breakeven analysis. It extends the analysis to the multiproduct firm both without constraint and with many resource constraints, where it describes the linear programming approach. Next, it contrasts the economic approach, in the form of the curvilinear breakeven analysis, with the conventional approach. Finally, it introduces uncertainty in the breakeven analysis, assuming first a discrete-variable approach, and then a continuous-variable approach. The cost-volume-profit analysis, or breakeven analysis, is a useful managerial decision making tool that can be adapted to specific situations by relaxing any of the limiting and typical assumptions of the conventional breakeven analysis.

4.1 ACCOUNTING APPROACH TO BREAKEVEN ANALYSIS

The cost accountant uses the cost-volume-profit analysis, commonly known as *breakeven analysis*, to compute the volume or level of activity for which the profit generated is zero and beyond which any increase in production will lead to a positive result, or profit. The *breakeven point* corresponds to the volume of activity at which total revenues equal total costs.

4.1.1   *Breakeven Formulae*

In algebraic terms, profit or loss may be given by

$$\mu = Pq - (F + Vq),$$

where

μ = Profit before income taxes.
P = Unit selling price.
q = Sales volume in units.
F = Total fixed costs.
V = Unit variable cost.

The breakeven point at which sales equal total costs and profit equals zero may be found as follows: $Pq^* - (F + Vq^*) = 0$, where q^* = breakeven volume. Consequently, we may write

$$\boxed{q^* = \frac{F}{P - V},}$$

where $P - V$ = *contribution margin* per unit. Therefore, the breakeven point equals the ratio of total fixed costs (F) divided by the contribution margin per unit ($P - V$).

To convert q^* to dollar terms, multiply both sides of the q^* formula by P as follows:

$$Y = Pq^* = \frac{PF}{P - V},$$

or

$$\boxed{Y = \frac{F}{1 - \dfrac{V}{P}},}$$

where

Y = Breakeven sales.
$1 - \dfrac{V}{P}$ = Contribution margin ratio.

The last formula expresses the breakeven sales or breakeven point in dollars. It equals the ratio of the fixed costs (F) divided by the contribution margin ratio, also referred to as the variable profit ratio

$$\left(1 - \frac{V}{P}\right).$$

To illustrate, consider the following example. Clara Smith plans to open a frozen yogurt business. She determined the following revenue and expense relationships:

	Dollars	Percent
Sales Price per Cup of Yogurt	.50	100
Variable Expense per Cup	.30	60
Monthly Fixed Expenses		
Rent	1,000	
Wages for Two Employees	1,500	
Payroll Fringe Costs	500	
Liability Insurance	50	
Other Fixed Costs	6,450	
Electricity	500	
	10,000	

The breakeven analysis proceeds as follows:

1. The unit contribution margin, or excess of unit sales price over unit variable cost:

$$P - V = \$.50 - \$.30 = \$.20.$$

2. The breakeven point in terms of units sold:

$$q^* = \frac{\$10,000}{\$.20} = 50,000 \text{ cups per month.}$$

3. The contribution margin ratio, or variable profit ratio:

$$1 - \frac{V}{P} = 1 - \frac{\$.30}{\$.50} = 40\%.$$

4. The breakeven sales:

$$y = \frac{\$10,000}{0.40} = \$25,000,$$

or $y = Pq^* = \$.50 \times 50,000$ cups $= \$25,000$.

4.1.2   *Breakeven Charts*

The profit structure of a company may be portrayed in a simple *breakeven chart* depicting the interactions between the cost and revenue structures. Figure 4.1 is a breakeven chart showing the relationship between sales volume as an independent variable and total costs as a dependent variable. The main breakeven point is the intersection between the total revenues line and the total cost line. The area between the total revenues line and the total cost line at a volume below the breakeven point represents the loss area. The corresponding area above the breakeven point represents the profit area. Whereas Figure 4.1 presents the breakeven chart in total dollars, Figure 4.2 presents it in average dollars.

Another approach to graphic cost-volume-profit analysis is shown in Figure 4.3. Known as the *profit graph approach*, it portrays the relationships between profit as a dependent variable and sales volume, or dollar sales, as an independent variable. Where the profit line crosses the sales volume axis is the breakeven point.

4.1.3   Limiting Assumptions of Breakeven Analysis

The user of breakeven analysis must be aware of the limiting assumptions or simplifications of the model:

1. Expenses may be dichotomized into variable and fixed categories.

2. The behavior of revenues and expenses is accurately portrayed and is linear. This is possible when (a) unit selling price will not change with volume (for example, the firm does not adopt any discriminatory pricing); (b) unit variable cost will not change with volume; and (c) some costs are fixed for a given period and over a particular level of activity (the relevant range).

3. The difference between beginning and ending inventory is insignificant.

4. A single product is produced.

5. The situation is deterministic, and the values are known with certainty.

6. The analysis is intended to satisfice rather than optimize a profit motive.

7. The cost of capital is absent in the analysis.

8. The implications of the elasticity of the product and demand are not included in the analysis.

These assumptions or simplifications implied in the accountant's model are justified if they are assumed to lead to the same or better decisions than might be provided by more

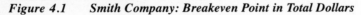

Figure 4.1   Smith Company: Breakeven Point in Total Dollars

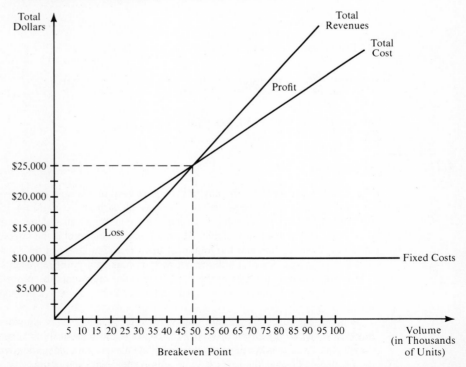

Figure 4.2   Smith Company: Breakeven Point in Average Dollars

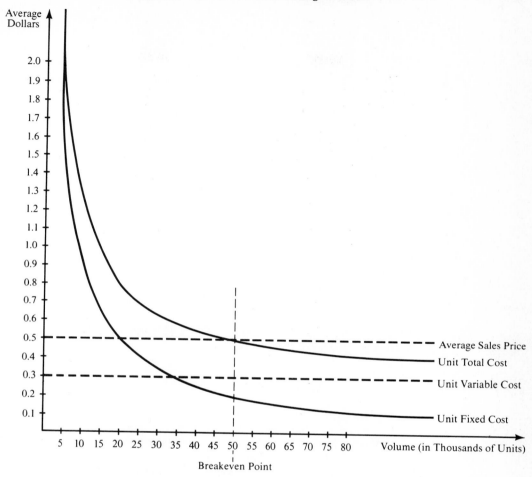

realistic, complex, and costly models. The sections that follow present extensions to the accountant's breakeven analysis on the basis of the relaxing of some of these assumptions. The added benefits and better decision making are assumed to outweigh the additional costs of these more complex models.

4.2   USEFULNESS OF THE ACCOUNTING APPROACH

A knowledge of the breakeven structure, the proposed changes in revenue, and the operating characteristics of a firm permits the identification of areas of cost, revenue, and profit fluctuations, as well as evaluation of the breakeven area. In other words, an analysis of the changes in each of the parameters and variables of the breakeven formulae allows assessment of the significance of possible estimation errors in the breakeven

Figure 4.3   Smith Company: Profit Graph

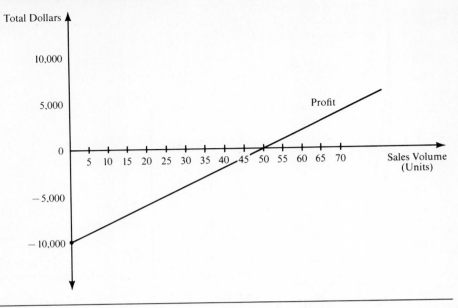

point. Each possible change may also be identified with a managerial problem. The sections that follow discuss these problems.

4.2.1   Change in the Unit Selling Price

An increase in the selling price will raise the contribution margin and, consequently, decrease the breakeven volume. To illustrate, suppose that Smith decides to decrease the selling price from $.50 to $.40, and all other variables remain unchanged. What is the monthly breakeven point in number of cups? In dollar sales?

These questions can be answered by turning to breakeven formulae for q^* and y:

$$q^* = \frac{\$10,000}{\$.40 - \$.30} = 100,000 \text{ cups per month,}$$

and $y = 100,000 \text{ cups} \times \$.40 = \$40,000$, or

$$y = \frac{\$10,000}{1 - \dfrac{\$.30}{\$.40}} = \$40,000.$$

4.2.2   Change in the Unit Variable Cost

An increase in the unit variable cost leads to a decline in the unit contribution margin and an increase in the breakeven volume. Similarly, a decrease in the unit variable cost will decrease the breakeven volume.

To illustrate, suppose that Smith decides to pay the manager $.10 per cup as a commission, and the other variables remain unchanged. What is the monthly breakeven point in number of cups? In dollar sales? The question can be answered by turning again to breakeven formulae for q^* and y:

$$q^* = \frac{\$10,000}{\$.50 - \$.40} = 100,000 \text{ cups per month,}$$

and $y = 100,000$ cups $\times$ $.50 = $50,000, or

$$y = \frac{\$10,000}{1 - \dfrac{\$.40}{\$.50}} = \$50,000.$$

4.2.3   *Change in the Total Fixed Costs*

An increase in the total fixed costs will result in an increase in the breakeven volume. Similarly, a decrease in the total fixed costs will result in a decrease in the breakeven volume.

To illustrate, suppose Smith's rent was tripled and she wanted to determine the breakeven point in terms of cups and dollar sales. The breakeven formulae are again used to solve the problem:

$$q^* = \frac{\$10,000 + \$2,000}{\$.50 - \$.30} = 60,000 \text{ cups per month,}$$

and $y = 60,000$ cups $\times$ $.50 = $30,000, or

$$y = \frac{\$12,000}{1 - \dfrac{\$.30}{\$.50}} = \$30,000.$$

4.2.4   *Target Sales for a Given Target Profit*

The breakeven formulae can be adapted to determine the sales volume necessary to achieve a desired net income. The conventional formula for computing a profit before taxes (μ) is as follows:

$$\mu = Pq - (Vq + F).$$

To soive for the volume q necessary to achieve μ, the formula may be rearranged as follows:

$$q = \frac{F + \mu}{P - V}.$$

In other words, the sales volume necessary for a desired net income before taxes equals the ratio of fixed assets plus the desired net income before taxes divided by the contribution margin per unit.

To find the sales dollars needed to achieve the desired net income before taxes, adjust the formula for the sales volume as follows:[1]

$$y = \frac{F + \mu}{1 - \dfrac{V}{P}}.$$

The sales dollars necessary for a desired net income before taxes equals the ratio of the fixed costs plus the desired net income before taxes divided by the contribution margin ratio.

Given a tax rate equal to t, formulae for both q and y can be adjusted to determine the sales volume or sales dollars necessary to achieve an after-tax profit Z. The formulae are rearranged as follows:

$$q = \frac{F + \dfrac{Z}{1 - t}}{P - V},$$

and

$$y = \frac{F + \dfrac{Z}{1 - t}}{1 - \dfrac{V}{P}}.$$

To illustrate, what sales must Smith try to achieve to obtain a net income after taxes of $20,000 if the tax rate is 50 percent? The formula for the sales volume necessary to achieve a given profit yields

$$y = \frac{\$10,000 + \dfrac{\$20,000}{1 - \$.50}}{1 - \dfrac{\$.30}{\$.50}} = \$125,000.$$

---

[1] The profit formula (μ) may be rearranged to solve for other variables. To solve for P:

$$P = V + \frac{F + \mu}{q}.$$

To solve for V:

$$V = P - \frac{F + \mu}{q}.$$

To solve for F:

$$F = q(P - V) - \mu.$$

4.2.5 *Operating Profit at a Given Sales Volume*

Given that the operating profit before taxes at the breakeven volume equals zero, the operating profit for any given sales volume greater than the breakeven volume equals the profit realized by the additional volume beyond the breakeven volume.

Consequently, the operating profit for any given sales volume q', given a breakeven volume of q^*, equals $(q' - q^*)(P - V)$. In other words, it equals the difference between the volume of sales desired and the breakeven volume, multiplied by the contribution margin per unit.

You will recall that Smith Company's breakeven volume was found to equal 50,000 cups. Smith now wants to find the profit before taxes associated with sales volumes of 60,000 cups, 70,000 cups, and 80,000 cups. Operating profit for 60,000 cups sold $= (60,000 - 50,000)(\$.50 - \$.30) = \$2,000$. Operating profit for 70,000 cups sold $= (70,000 - 50,000)(\$.50 - \$.30) = \$4,000$. Operating profit for 80,000 cups sold $= (80,000 - 50,000)(\$.50 - \$.30) = \$6,000$.

4.2.6 *Effects of Multiple Changes*

If the interaction of volume, selling price, variable costs, and fixed costs are taken into account, the breakeven formulae can be adapted to reflect the simultaneous changes in all relevant variables. For example, assume that Smith is considering the impact of different changes on her original estimates. She believes that a decrease of 20 percent per unit in the selling price may lead to a 30 percent increase in the sales volume. She also believes than an improvement in production techniques would lead to a decrease of 90 percent per unit in the unit variable cost and an increase of $46,500 per year in the fixed costs. What level of sales dollars must Smith achieve to attain an after-tax net income of $18,000 if the current tax rate is still 50 percent?

All these changes may be shown in one formula, as follows:

$$q = \frac{F + \Delta F \pm \dfrac{Z}{(1 - t)}}{1 - \dfrac{V \pm \Delta V}{P \pm \Delta P}},$$

where Δ stands for changes. This is calculated as follows:

$$q = \frac{\$10,000 + \$46,500 + \dfrac{\$18,000}{(1 - \$.50)}}{1 - \dfrac{\$.30(1 - \$.90)}{\$.50(1 - \$.20)}} = \$100,000.$$

4.2.7 *Other Cost-Volume-Profit Relationships*

In addition to predicting the impact of changes in relevant variables, as discussed in the preceding section, breakeven analysis can provide additional insight into a firm's planning and control processes by furnishing information such as the margin of safety and the margin of safety ratio. The *margin of safety* is given sales less breakeven sales. The *margin of safety ratio* is the margin of safety expressed as a percentage of sales:

Margin of safety = Given sales figure − Breakeven sales.

$$\text{Margin of safety ratio} = \frac{\text{Given sales figure} - \text{Breakeven sales}}{\text{Given sales figure}}.$$

For the data in section 4.1.1, and with sales equaling $50,000, the margin of safety and the margin of safety ratio are as follows:

Margin of safety = $50,000 − $25,000 = $25,000.

$$\text{Margin of safety ratio} = \frac{\$50,000 - \$25,000}{\$50,000} = 50\%.$$

In other words, sales have to decrease by 50 percent before the company suffers a loss. In summary, the main cost-volume-profit relationships include the following:

1. Contribution margin (CM) = Unit selling price − Unit variable cost.

2. Contribution margin ratio (CMR) = $\dfrac{\text{CM}}{\text{Unit selling price}}$.

3. Breakeven volume (BEV) = $\dfrac{\text{Fixed costs}}{\text{CM}}$.

4. Breakeven sales (BES) = $\dfrac{\text{Fixed costs}}{\text{CMR}}$.

5. Margin of safety (MS) = Sales − BES.

6. Margin of safety ratio (MSR) = $\dfrac{\text{MS}}{\text{Sales}}$.

7. Variable cost ratio (VCR) = $\dfrac{\text{Unit variable cost}}{\text{Unit selling price}}$.

8. Net income ratio (NIR) = $\dfrac{\text{Net income}}{\text{Sales}}$.

9. Net income ratio (NIR) = CMR × MSR.

4.3   BREAKEVEN ANALYSIS FOR THE MULTIPRODUCT FIRM

4.3.1   In the Absence of Constraints

The previous analysis assumed a single-product firm. However, most manufacturers make more than one product. Each of the products has its own contribution margin, and any changes in one product's contribution margin will affect the total contribution margin. To assess the impact of the product mix on the overall profit rates, a knowledge of the breakeven point for the product mix is useful.

For a single-product firm, the contribution margin ratio may be expressed as

$$\frac{P - V}{P}.$$

Given the existence of a sales mix, the contribution margin ratio for a multiproduct firm will be equal to a weighted summation of the individual contribution margin ratios. If n is the number of products included in the product mix, the overall contribution margin ratio is given by

$$\sum_{i=1}^{n} [q_i(P_i - V_i)] / \sum_{i=n}^{n} P_i q_i,$$

where

n = Number of different products ($i = 1, \ldots, n$).
q_i = Estimated sales volume for the ith product.
P_i = Unit selling price for the ith product.
V_i = Unit variable cost for the ith product.

Thus, the breakeven sales for a multiproduct firm are given by

$$\text{Breakeven sales} = \frac{\text{Fixed cost}}{\text{Overall contribution margin}}$$

$$= \frac{F}{\sum_{i=1}^{n} [q_i(P_i - V_i)] / \sum_{i=1}^{n} P_i q_i}.$$

To illustrate the above formulae, consider the following information on a three-product firm:

Product	Alpha	Beta	Gamma
Sales (Units)	6,000	5,000	4,000
Unit Selling Price	$5	$6	$15
Unit Variable Cost	$3	$2	$ 8

Fixed Expenses: $30,000

The overall contribution margin ratio is equal to

$$\frac{6,000(\$5 - \$3) + 5,000(\$6 - \$2) + 4,000(\$15 - \$8)}{(6,000 \times \$5) + (5,000 \times \$6) + (4,000 \times \$15)} = \frac{60,000}{120,000} = 50\%.$$

$$\frac{\$30,000}{50\%} = \$60,000.$$

This analysis does not allow the inclusion of resource constraints. Since a firm's product mix decision generally is constrained by the limited supply of diverse resources, an adequate framework for product mix decisions must consider the impact of these limiting factors.

4.3.2   *Product Mix Decisions with One Resource Constraint*

Every company has at least one limiting factor, and its optimal use is an important consideration in product mix decisions. The firm's objective is to secure maximum profit, which depends on achieving the highest contribution margin per unit of the limiting factor. When a firm has one resource constraint, the optimal product mix may be derived as follows:

1. Determine the contribution margin per unit of output.

2. Calculate the contribution per unit of the constraining factor by dividing the contribution margin per unit of output by the number of units of the constraining factor required for each unit of output.

3. Rank the products on the basis of the size of their contribution margin per unit of the constraining factor.

This procedure establishes the preferred order in which products should be manufactured. For example, assume that plant hours is the factor constraining the volume of production at the XYZ Company. The contribution margin per hour is computed as shown in Table 4.1. To maximize the contribution to profit per unit of the constraining factor, the XYZ Company should produce its products in the following order of priority: C, D, B, and finally A.

Assume that the labor hour capacity is limited to 47,000 hours per month, and the following monthly sales estimates are provided:

Table 4.1   *Contribution Margin per Hour*

Product	Contribution Margin per Unit	Labor Hours per Unit	Contribution Margin per Labor Hour	Ranking
A	$15	5	$3	4
B	$12	3	$4	3
C	$14	2	$7	1
D	$15	3	$5	2

Table 4.2   *Allocations of Capacity on the Basis of the Contribution Margin per Unit*

Product	Contribution Margin per Unit	Labor Hours per Unit	Monthly Sales	Total Hours	Contribution Margin
C	$14	2	4,000	8,000	$ 56,000
D	$15	3	6,000	18,000	90,000
B	$12	3	2,000	6,000	24,000
A	$15	5	3,000	15,000	45,000
			Total Supply of Labor Needed	47,000	
			Total Contribution Margin		$215,000
			− Total Fixed Costs (Given)		$115,000
			Total Profit per Month		$100,000

Product	Monthly Sales Estimates	Hours Required
A	5,000	25,000
B	2,000	6,000
C	4,000	8,000
D	6,000	18,000
	17,000	57,000

The optimal plant capacity can be computed as shown in Table 4.2, which takes into account both the preference order established by the ranking of the contribution margin per hour and the limited supply of hours. This analysis assumes that the firm elects to produce only 3,000 units of A at a time, when sales of A could be 5,000 units.

4.3.3   Product Mix Decisions with Many Resource Constraints

The XYZ Company, with one resource constraint, decided to maximize the contribution margin per unit of the scarce factor. A firm with many resource constraints maximizes the total contribution margin subject to the limitations imposed by the scarce factors. *Linear programming* is a useful method for solving such product mix problems.

Linear Programming Model

Linear programming is an operational research technique which allows the determination of an optimal solution to a maximization or a minimization objective, taking into consideration a set of limited resources. Linear programming may be applied to the product mix problems a decision maker faces when attempting to allocate limited resources to definite segments while at the same time meeting a given objective. *Limited resources* pertains mainly to the availability of capital, material, labor, space, and so forth. The *definite segments* are represented by the output mix to which the limited resources are to be allocated. The objective or criteria on which the allocation of resources is made is expressed as either a profit maximization or a cost minimization. Thus, a linear programming problem exists each time the cost accountant faces the decisions involved in allocating limited resources to the production of an output mix while at the same time satisfying the appropriate performance indicator of the firm.

The methodology the accountant follows in setting up the linear programming model includes determining the required data, formulating the objective and constraint functions, and resolving the model to obtain an optimal solution. In the case of a product mix problem, the objective function expresses either profit or cost. The profit expression is generally more popular in theory and in practice. It is expressed as a maximization (max.) of the total contribution margin of the firm. Given a knowledge of the contribution margins of a set of products, CM_i, the objective function may be expressed as

$$\text{Max. } Z = CM_1X_1 + CM_2X_2, \ldots, CM_iX_i,$$

where $X_1, X_2, \ldots, X_i$ represent the quantities of each of the products.

The constraint functions express the limited capacity and availability of resources. In general, these constraints pertain to the various factors of production, such as material, labor, capital, and so forth. Each unit of output requires a given number of units of the scarce resources. Consequently, the data required are (1) the production coefficients of each output, which specify the technological requirements of each unit of output in terms of the scarce factors; and (2) the capacity or supply of resources for the period under analysis. The derivation of these data leads to the expression of the linear programming model. For example, assume firm A produces three products: $\bar{X}_1$, $\bar{X}_2$, and $\bar{X}_3$, with their respective contribution margins CM_1, CM_2, and CM_3. The objective function is to maximize the total contribution margin of the firm. Thus, the first equation will be

$$\text{Max. } Z = CM_1X_1 + CM_2X_2 + CM_3X_3 \,, \tag{1}$$

where X_1, X_2, and X_3 represent the volume of production for the three products, $\bar{X}_1$, $\bar{X}_2$, and $\bar{X}_3$. The constraints are in terms of labor and material. Assuming that (1) the production coefficients for the three products are M_1, M_2, and M_3 for material and L_1, L_2, and L_3 for labor and (2) the material and labor capacities equal M and L, the constraint functions can be expressed as follows:

$$\text{Material constraint: } M_1X_1 + M_2X_2 + M_3X_3 \leq M, \tag{2}$$

and

$$\text{Labor constraint: } L_1X_1 + L_2X_2 + L_3X_3 \leq L. \tag{3}$$

The system of equations 1, 2, and 3 expresses the product mix problem in a linear programming context.

The model represents the so-called primal solution in the sense that

$$\text{Max. } Z = CM_1X_1 + CM_2X_2 + CM_3X_3,$$

subject to

$$M_1X_1 + M_2X_2 + M_3X_3 \leq M,$$
$$L_1X_1 + L_2X_2 + L_3X_3 \leq L,$$

allows the determination of two important results: (1) the optimal product mix (X_1, X_2, X_3) and (2) the optimal contribution margin. Both results may be easily obtained by applying the simplex method (see Appendix 4.A).

To illustrate a linear programming analysis, assume the following information. Company A produces two products, Alpha and Beta. The contribution margin per unit is $6 for Alpha and $7 for Beta. The production of both products requires labor and material: 4 hours and 4 units of material are needed to produce 1 unit of Alpha, and 2 hours and 6 units of material are needed to produce 1 unit of Beta. For the period under analysis, 16 hours of time and 24 units of material are available for production. The management wants to determine the optimal production mix for the period. The linear model is set up as follows:

$$\text{Objective function: Max. } Z = 6X_1 + 7X_2,$$

subject to

$$\text{Material constraint: } 4X_1 + 6X_2 \leq 24 \text{ units,}$$

$$\text{Labor constraint: } 4X_1 + 2X_2 \leq 16 \text{ hours,}$$

Nonnegativity constraint: X_1, $X_2 \geqslant 0$,

where X_1 and X_2 are the quantities of products Alpha and Beta, respectively. The solution to this problem may be obtained graphically.

Graphic Solution

The company wants to determine the production levels of X_1 and X_2 that will maximize the contribution margin of $6X_1 + 7X_2$ subject to the following constraints:

$4X_1 + 6X_2 \leqslant 24$ units of material.

$4X_1 + 2X_2 \leqslant 16$ hours of labor.

$X_1, X_2 \geqslant 0$, because negative production is impossible.

A graph is drawn showing the constraints, as illustrated in Figure 4.4. The constraints define the solution space on the graph. When $X_1 = 0$, then $X_2 \leqslant 4$ (material constraint),

Figure 4.4   *A Linear Programming Graphic Solution*

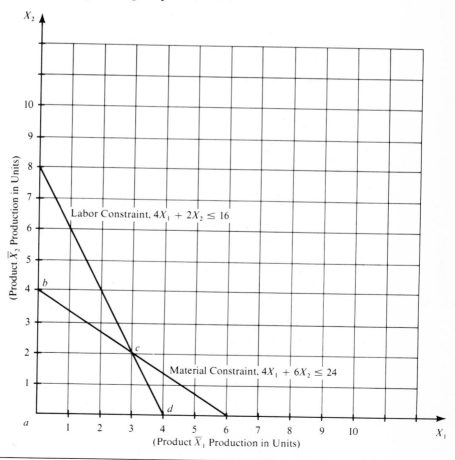

and $X_2 \leqslant 8$ (labor constraint). When $X_2 = 0$, then $X_1 \leqslant 6$ (material constraint), and $X_1 \leqslant 4$ (labor constraint). The section on the graph, bounded by the corner points a, b, c, and d represents the area of feasible product combinations, or the *feasible region*.

The optimal product mix can be determined as follows: The best feasible solutions must lie on one of the corner points. Consequently, by trial and error the corner yielding the highest contribution margin can be found, which corresponds to the optimal product mix. The computations for each corner are as follows:

		Combination	
Corner	X_1	X_2	Total Contribution Margin
(0, 4)	0	4	$6.00(0) + $7.00(4) = $28
(4, 0)	4	0	$6.00(4) + $7.00(0) = $24
(3, 2)	3	2	$6.00(3) + $7.00(2) = $32

Therefore, Company A should produce 3 units of X_1 and 2 units of X_2, which gives a total contribution margin of $32.

Shadow Prices

Company A is also interested in expanding its capacity to meet an increased demand for one of its products. The value of an additional unit of the constraining factor now becomes important. In our fictional example, we must determine the value of an additional unit of material and time, which will increase the total contribution margin. Therefore, the value of a marginal unit of the constraining factor equals the additional contribution margin obtained by relaxing the constraint and increasing it by 1 unit. This value is referred to as the *shadow price* of a constraint. It measures the benefit forgone by failing to use one more unit of the constraining factor.

To illustrate the computation of shadow prices, let us return to the data used in the previous example. The original constraints were expressed as follows: $4X_1 + 6X_2 \leqslant 24$ (material constraint), and $4X_1 + 2X_2 \leqslant 16$ (labor constraint).

The shadow price of the material constraint equals the difference in the total contribution margin that results from relaxing the material constraint by 1 unit of material. Therefore, the constraints are now expressed as follows: $4X_1 + 6X_2 \leqslant 25$ (increased from 24 units), $4X_1 + 2X_2 \leqslant 16$ (unchanged), and $X_1, X_2 \geqslant 0$. Solving these constraint equations for new values for X_1 and X_2 gives $X_2 = 2.25$ units and $X_1 = 2.875$ units. In other words, the increased material capacity from 24 to 25 units allows the production of 2.875 units of X_1 and 2.25 units of X_2. This new production mix will have an impact on the total contribution margin as follows:

$$Z = 6X_1 + 7X_2$$

$$= 6(2.875) + 7(2.25)$$

$$= 33.$$

Therefore, with an increase from 24 to 25 units of material, Company A can increase the total contribution margin from $32 to $33. The material shadow price is computed as follows:

Material shadow price = New total contribution margain − Old total contribution margin

$$= \$33 - \$32$$

$$= \$1.$$

This result implies that if the cost of an additional unit of material is less than $1, the firm should proceed with its expansion policies.

The shadow price of the labor constraint equals the difference in the total contribution margin that results from relaxing the labor constraint by 1 unit of labor. The constraints are now expressed as follows: $4X_1 + 6X_2 \leq 24$, and $4X_1 + 2X_2 \leq 17$. Solving these new constraint equations for new values of X_1 and X_2 gives $X_1 = 3.375$ units and $X_2 = 1.75$ units. In other words, increasing the labor capacity from 16 to 17 units allows the production of 3.375 units of X_1 and 1.75 units of X_2. This new production mix will affect the total contribution margin as follows:

$$Z = 6X_1 + 7X_2$$
$$= 6(3.375) + 7(1.75)$$
$$= 32.50.$$

Therefore, with an increase from 16 to 17 units of labor, Company A can increase its total contribution margin from $32 to $32.50. The shadow price associated with labor is $.50. This implies that if the cost of an additional unit of labor is less than $.50, the firm should proceed with its expansion policies.

Having determined the shadow prices of material and labor, is it important to determine the range of values for the constraints over which these shadow prices apply? In other words, does the total contribution margin continue to increase by $1 (or $.50) as more material (or labor) is added? The material constraint limits are illustrated in Figure 4.5. The total contribution margin will improve with one additional unit of material, and this improvement will continue until the material constraint prevents production of

Figure 4.5   *Material Constraint Limits*

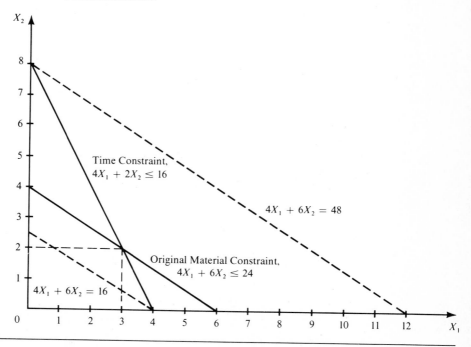

Figure 4.6   **Time Constraint Limits**

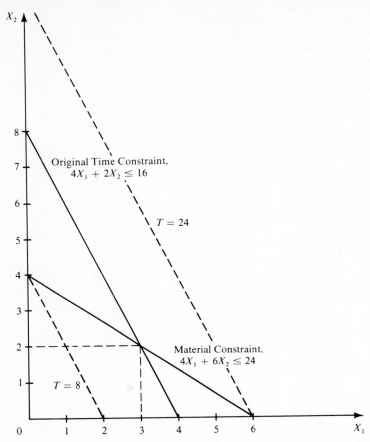

X_2

Original Time Constraint,
$4X_1 + 2X_2 \leq 16$

$T = 24$

$T = 8$

Material Constraint,
$4X_1 + 6X_2 \leq 24$

X_1

either X_1 or X_2. As shown in Figure 4.5, the material constraint limits reach a maximum of 48 and a minimum of 16.

The time constraint limits are illustrated in Figure 4.6. With one additional unit of labor, the total contribution margin will improve, and this improvement will continue until the labor constraint prevents production of either X_1 or X_2. Figure 4.6 shows that the labor constraint limits reach a maximum of 24 and a minimum of 8.

In summary, shadow prices constitute appropriate expressions of the opportunity costs, provided that the basic solution is not altered.

4.4   ECONOMIC APPROACH TO BREAKEVEN ANALYSIS

4.4.1   *Economic Framework to Breakeven Analysis*

Businesspeople and economists examine similar problems differently, and breakeven analysis exemplifies their varying approaches. As suggested by Douglas Vickers, the

Figure 4.7   *Economic Breakeven Analysis*

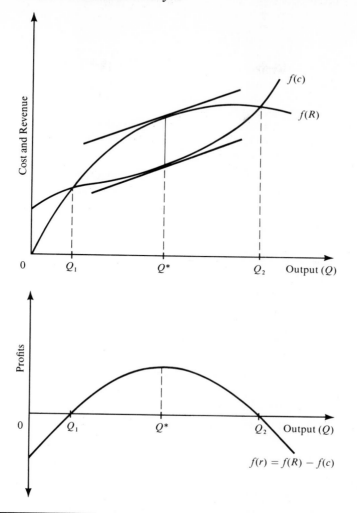

difference "relates to the use by business of the method of cost-volume-profit analysis, and of pricing and volume adjustments, which is referred to as breakeven analysis and which, *prima facie*, ignores the economists' generalized theorems of cost and revenue behavior."[2]

The accountant assumes that the firm charges a constant selling price per unit of the output and incurs a constant variable cost per unit. The economist, whose analysis of cost and revenue behavior extends beyond the accountant's relevant range, accounts for the variability of both the unit selling price and the unit variable cost.

In the *economic model*, the revenue curve will have a curvilinear (inverted U–shaped) form that depicts the fact that the firm can sell more output only by lowering the price.

---

[2]Douglas Vickers, "On the Economics of Break-Even," *Accounting Review* (July 1960), p. 405.

The cost curve has a cubic shape, because it is based on the classic production function of increasing-decreasing returns (law of variable proportions). The cost curve's shape indicates that with increasing returns, total costs rise at a decreasing rate up to a point where, with decreasing returns, total costs rise at an increasing rate. The economist assumes that the marginal productivity of labor initially is rising as labor is utilized and the fixed capital is underutilized. The short-run variable costs rise less rapidly as the output expands, so initially the total cost curve will be concave downward. Beyond some output level the fixed capital tends to become overutilized, the marginal productivity of labor begins to decline, and the total costs rise rapidly as the output expands. The total cost curve becomes concave upward. Both curves are illustrated in Figure 4.7, where $f(R)$ represents the revenue curve, $f(c)$ the cost curve, and $f(r)$ the profit curve. Several characteristics should be noted:

1. Where the marginal revenue equals the marginal cost, the profit reaches a maximum (Q^*). This occurs when the slope of the cost function (marginal cost) equals the slope of the revenue function (marginal revenue).

2. The breakeven points occur at two different output levels, Q_1 and Q_2.

3. Between Q_1 and Q_2 profit will be realized, since the total revenue exceeds the total cost. Below Q_1 and above Q_2 losses will be incurred, since the total revenue is less than the total cost.

4.4.2   *Example of Curvilinear Breakeven Analysis*

This section will illustrate the application of the curvilinear breakeven analysis that arises from the nonlinear character of the economist's cost and revenue data. Assume the following revenue and cost estimates for company X:

Production Volume	Total Revenues	Total Costs
5	8.5	6.7
6	9.6	8.0
4	7.2	5.6
11	12.1	17.5
20	4.0	47.2
15	10.5	28.7
10	12.0	15.2

To compute the breakeven point, you must determine both the revenue and costs functions. Given an a priori ignorance of the form of these functions, you will find it useful to plot the data on a graph, as in Figure 4.8. You will then notice that the form of the functions is parabolic, which corresponds to the economist's assumptions of variability of both the unit selling price and the unit variable cost.

Next, determine the regression coefficient of both the revenue and cost functions by the least squares method, which requires the computation of the "normal equations." In this case, the normal parabolic equations will be as follows:

$$Na + b\Sigma x + c\Sigma x^2 = \Sigma y,$$

$$a\Sigma x + b\Sigma x^2 + c\Sigma x^3 = \Sigma xy,$$

$$a\Sigma x^2 + b\Sigma x^3 + c\Sigma x^4 = \Sigma x^2 y,$$

Figure 4.8 **Curvilinear Breakeven Analysis**

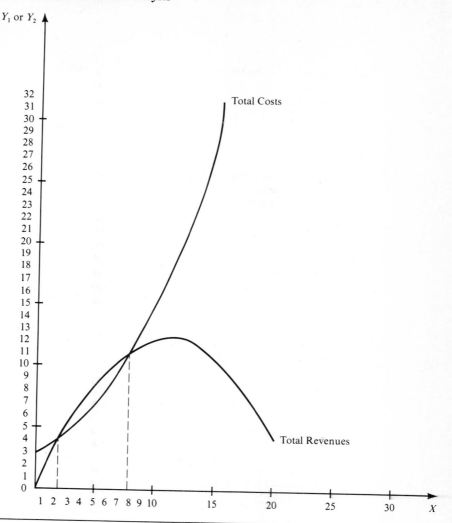

where x = production volume, y = cost or revenue in dollars, and n = number of observations.

Using the data of company X and the normal equations' relationships, both the total revenue (TR) and the total cost (TC) functions will be as follows: $Y_1 = TR = 2.2x - 0.1x^2$, and $Y_2 = TC = 3.2 + 0.2x + 0.1x^2$. Given these two functions, it is possible to compute the breakeven point(s) by setting TR equal to TC. Therefore, $3.2 + 0.2x + 0.1x^2 = 2.2x - 0.1x^2$, or $3.2 - 2x + 0.2x^2 = 0$. Solving for x yields two breakeven points, $x_1 = 2$ units and $x_2 = 8$ units. In other words, the economic approach to breakeven analysis enables the computation of two breakeven points.

Figure 4.8 shows the existence of a profit zone between the two breakeven points and two loss zones. What would be the optimal production volume? According to microeconomic theory it could be stated that the optimal profit corresponds to the volume of output where the marginal revenue equals the marginal cost ($MR = MC$). Therefore,

$$\frac{dTR}{dx} = \frac{dTC}{dx} \; ,$$

or $0.2 + 0.2x = 2.2 - 0.2x$. Solving for x (subject to $x \geqslant 0$ and taking into account the fact that the second-order condition is met) yields $x^* = 5$. Consequently, the economic approach to the breakeven analysis allows both the computation of two breakeven points and a simple profit maximization search.

4.5   COST-VOLUME-PROFIT ANALYSIS UNDER UNCERTAINTY

The cost-volume-profit analysis under uncertainty considers one of two cases:

Case 1   A discrete range of probabilities is assumed associated with each of the breakeven variables.

Case 2   A continuous range of probabilities is assumed associated with each of the breakeven variables.

4.5.1   Discrete Variable Approach

One approach to cost-volume-profit relationships under uncertainty is the discrete variable approach based on a *probability tree analysis*, in which probability estimates are made for every level of the variables in the model. In a breakeven context, probabilities are assigned to different levels of the unit selling price, unit variable cost, and total fixed cost. The analysis then proceeds as follows:

1. Divide each fixed cost estimate by the different contribution margin estimates to obtain combinations of breakeven volumes.

2. For each of these breakeven combinations, assign a joint probability by multiplying the probabilities of the fixed cost, unit selling price, and unit variable cost used in the combination.

3. Multiply each of the breakeven combinations by its joint probability and sum the results, which yields the mean or expected value of the breakeven point.

Figure 4.9 illustrates such an analysis. The decision tree shows the values and probabilities associated with two alternative unit selling prices, three alternative unit variable costs, and two alternative fixed costs. Column IV indicates that there are twelve possible combinations of breakeven volumes. Columns V and VI show, respectively, the breakeven combinations and the corresponding joint probabilities. Column VII gives each breakeven combination multiplied by its corresponding joint probability, which corresponds to the amount that each case contributes to the expected value of the breakeven volume. Finally, column VII shows that the expected breakeven volume in this example is 7,968 units.

Figure 4.9   Decision Tree, Cost-Volume-Profit Relationships

I Price	II Variable Costs	III Fixed Costs	IV Case Number	V Break-even Point	VI Joint Probability	VII Expected Value Break-even Point
		$20,000 $p = 0.8$	1	10,000	0.28	2,800
	$6 $p = 0.5$	$10,000 $p = 0.2$	2	5,000	0.07	350
$8 $p = 0.7$	$4 $p = 0.3$	$20,000 $p = 0.8$	3	5,000	0.168	840
		$10,000 $p = 0.2$	4	2,500	0.042	105
	$2 $p = 0.2$	$20,000 $p = 0.8$	5	3,333	0.012	373
		$10,000 $p = 0.2$	6	1,666	0.028	46
		$20,000 $p = 0.8$	7	20,000	0.12	2,400
	$6 $p = 0.5$	$10,000 $p = 0.2$	8	10,000	0.03	300
$7 $p = 0.3$	$4 $p = 0.3$	$20,000 $p = 0.8$	9	6,666	0.072	479
		$10,000 $p = 0.2$	10	3,333	0.018	59
	$2 $p = 0.2$	$20,000 $p = 0.8$	11	4,000	0.048	192
		$20,000 $p = 0.2$	12	2,000	0.012	24

Expected Value Break-even Volume

7,968 Units

4.5.2   Continuous Variable Approach

Probabilistic Framework

Robert K. Jaedicke and Alexander A. Robichek were among the first to suggest the use of probability concepts in cost-volume-profit analysis.[3] They agreed that traditional cost-volume-profit analysis does not include adjustments for risk and uncertainty, which may severely limit its usefulness. Thus, most of the variables included in the breakeven formulae are subject to a wide range of possible outcomes due to chance variations. These variables are (1) the selling price per unit, (2) the variable cost per unit, (3) the total fixed cost, and (4) the expected sales volume for each product. In a probabilistic breakeven analysis, one or several of these variables may be treated as a random variable. For

[3]Robert K. Jaedicke and Alexander A. Robichek, "Cost-Volume-Profit Analysis under Conditions of Uncertainty," *Accounting Review* (October 1964), pp. 917–926.

each random variable it is possible to estimate the probability distribution indicating the likelihood that it will take on various possible values.

This concept of uncertainty can be illustrated by considering two sales proposals from the records of the Smith Company, which the cost accountant believes will take the following probability distribution:

Sales Proposal A		Sales Proposal B	
Probability	Demand (Units)	Probability	Demand (Units)
0.05	2,000	0.05	2,000
0.25	3,000	0.25	3,000
0.30	4,000	0.30	4,500
0.25	5,000	0.25	5,000
0.15	6,000	0.15	10,000

The cost accountant should choose the proposal with the highest mean or expected value. The formula for the mean is as follows:

$$\bar{y} = \sum_{i=1}^{n} Y_i P_i,$$

where Y_i is the outcome for the ith event, P_i is the probability of the ith event, and $\bar{y}$ is the expected value. Based on the expected value approach, the cost accountant should choose sales proposal B rather than A. The expected values of each sales proposal are as follows:

$$E(A) = (2,000 \times 0.05) + (3,000 \times 0.25) + (4,000 \times 0.30) + (5,000 \times 0.25) + (6,000 \times 0.15) = \$4,200.$$

$$E(B) = (2,000 \times 0.05) + (3,000 \times 0.25) + (4,500 \times 0.30) + (5,000 \times 0.25) + (10,000 \times 0.15) = \$4,950.$$

Two summary measures of the distribution generally are provided to help the decision maker: the standard deviation and the coefficient of variation. The *standard deviation* measures the dispersion of the individual observations about the mean of all the observations. The larger the standard deviation, the more widely spread is the distribution and the riskier the outcome. The formula for the standard deviation is as follows:

$$\sigma = \sqrt{\sum_{i=1}^{n} (Y_i - \bar{y})^2 P_i}.$$

The standard deviation for each sales proposal follows:

For A: $\sigma_A = \sqrt{(2,000 - 4,200)^2 \times 0.05 + (3,000 - 4,200)^2 \times 0.25 + (4,000 - 4,200)^2 \times 0.30 + (5,000 - 4,200)^2 \times 0.25 + (6,000 - 4,200)^2 \times 0.15}$
$\sigma_A = \$1,122.50.$

For B: $\sigma_B = \sqrt{(2,000 - 4,950)^2 \times 0.05 + (3,000 - 4,950)^2 \times 0.25 + (4,500 - 4,950)^2 \times 0.30 + (5,000 - 4,950)^2 \times 0.25 + (10,000 - 4,950)^2 \times 0.15}$
$\sigma_B = \$2,296.19.$

Probabilistic Breakeven Analysis

The unit selling price, unit variable cost, and total fixed costs are given, known values with certainty (deterministic), and the sales volume is a random variable (stochastic). Therefore, the profit equations may be written $E(Y) = E(Q)(P - V) - F$, where

Y = total profits, Q = sales volume, P = unit selling price, V = unit variable cost, F = total fixed costs, $E(Y)$ = expected value of profits, and $E(Q)$ = expected value of sales.

To illustrate the probabilistic breakeven analysis, assume that Smith Company could sell the expected demand of product A and product B at $10 per unit, with a variable cost of $5 per unit and a fixed cost of $10,000. The expected demand for products A and B is 2,400 units and 2,100 units, respectively, with a standard deviation of 200 units and 125 units. The expected profit for products A and B is calculated as follows:

$$E(A) = 2,400(\$10 - \$5) - \$10,000 = \$2,000.$$

$$E(B) = 2,100(\$10 - \$5) - \$10,000 = \$500.$$

The standard deviation of the profit for products A and B is

$$\sigma_A = 200 \times \$5 = \$1,000.$$

$$\sigma_B = 125 \times \$5 = \$625.$$

Based on the expected value criterion, product A should be preferred, although it is riskier in terms of standard deviation. In other words, the final choice may depend on the risk attitudes of management. The expected profit equation may be also written as

Expected profit $= \sigma CD$,

where

σ = Standard deviation of sales probability distribution.
C = Contribution margin per unit.
D = Breakeven's distance from mean sales (in standard deviations).[4]

Thus, for Smith Company, computations using the expected profit equation are as follows:

X_A = Breakeven $10,000 \div (\$10 - \$5) = \$2,000.$
σ_A = 200 units.
$C = \$10 - \$5 = \$5.$
$D_A = \dfrac{\bar{x}_A - \bar{x}_B}{\sigma} = \dfrac{2,100 - 2,000}{125} = 0.8.$
$E(B) = \sigma_B CD_B = 125 \times \$5 \times 0.8 = \$500.$

---

[4] For a derivation of this formula see Harold Bierman, Jr., *Topics in Cost Accounting and Decisions* (New York: McGraw-Hill, 1963), pp. 44–46. A simple derivation of this formula follows:

Expected profit = (Mean sales − Breakeven sales) × Contribution margin per unit.

= Standard deviation of sales (Mean sales − Breakeven sales) × Contribution margin per unit.

$= \sigma \times D \times C.$

Figure 4.10   Cost-Volume-Profit Chart

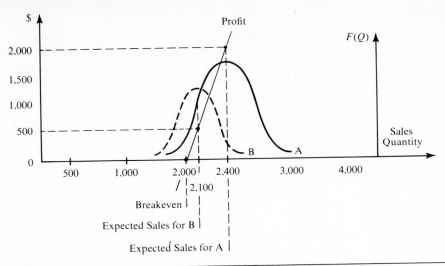

Probabilistic breakeven analysis is illustrated in Figure 4.10, which superimposes the distribution of sales on the profit portion of the traditional cost-volume-profit chart. The distributions show the likelihood of selling different amounts of products A and B. Figure 4.10 has two scales on the y-axis: The left vertical axis measures dollars of income, while the right vertical axis measures the probability of sales, or $F(Q)$. The area under the curve is equal to one and also permits the determination of the probability of sales being less than or greater than any given amount. Unlike the example in section 4.5.1, here the distribution is assumed to be continuous and unimodal. In the next section the distribution is assumed to be normal.

Assumptions of Normality

If sales are normally distributed and, consequently, profits are also normally distributed, different probability statements may be made about the expected level of profit. One important feature of any normal distribution is that approximately 0.50 percent of the area lies within ±0.67 standard deviations of the mean, and 0.68 percent of the area lies within ±1.96 standard deviations of the mean. For example, if the sales manager feels that there is roughly a two-thirds (that is, 0.667) chance that the actual costs will be within $500 of the mean, the standard deviation can be set equal to $500, given that two-thirds of the area under a normal curve lies within 1 standard deviation.

Another important feature of a normal distribution is that it may be standardized, leading to a practical use of the table of normal probabilities. The following formula may be used to standardize a normal distribution:

$$Z = \frac{\text{Actual profits} - \text{Mean profits}}{\text{Standard deviation of profits}}$$

$$= \frac{Y - E(y)}{\sigma y} ,$$

where Z is the number of standard deviations from the mean. Once Z is determined, a table of normal probabilities such as Table 4.3 may be used to determine the probability

Table 4.3   Areas in One Tail of the Normal Curve

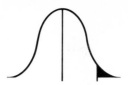

z	0.00	0.01	0.02	0.03	0.04	0.05	0.06	0.07	0.08	0.09
0.0	0.5000	0.4960	0.4920	0.4880	0.4840	0.4801	0.4761	0.4721	0.4681	0.4641
0.1	0.4602	0.4562	0.4522	0.4483	0.4443	0.4404	0.4364	0.4325	0.4286	0.4247
0.2	0.4207	0.4168	0.4129	0.4090	0.4052	0.4013	0.3974	0.3936	0.3897	0.3859
0.3	0.3821	0.3783	0.3745	0.3707	0.3669	0.3632	0.3594	0.3557	0.3520	0.3483
0.4	0.3446	0.3409	0.3372	0.3336	0.3300	0.3264	0.3228	0.3192	0.3156	0.3121
0.5	0.3085	0.3050	0.3015	0.2981	0.2946	0.2912	0.2877	0.2843	0.2810	0.2776
0.6	0.2743	0.2709	0.2676	0.2643	0.2611	0.2578	0.2546	0.2514	0.2483	0.2451
0.7	0.2420	0.2389	0.2358	0.2327	0.2296	0.2266	0.2236	0.2206	0.2177	0.2148
0.8	0.2119	0.2090	0.2061	0.2033	0.2005	0.1977	0.1949	0.1921	0.1894	0.1867
0.9	0.1841	0.1814	0.1788	0.1762	0.1736	0.1711	0.1685	0.1660	0.1635	0.1611
1.0	0.1587	0.1562	0.1539	0.1515	0.1492	0.1469	0.1446	0.1423	0.1401	0.1379
1.1	0.1357	0.1335	0.1314	0.1292	0.1271	0.1251	0.1230	0.1210	0.1190	0.1170
1.2	0.1151	0.1131	0.1112	0.1093	0.1075	0.1056	0.1038	0.1020	0.1003	0.0985
1.3	0.0968	0.0951	0.0934	0.0918	0.0901	0.0885	0.0869	0.0853	0.0838	0.0823
1.4	0.0808	0.0793	0.0778	0.0764	0.0749	0.0735	0.0721	0.0708	0.0694	0.0681
1.5	0.0668	0.0655	0.0643	0.0630	0.0618	0.0606	0.0594	0.0582	0.0570	0.0559
1.6	0.0548	0.0537	0.0526	0.0515	0.0505	0.0495	0.0485	0.0475	0.0465	0.0455
1.7	0.0446	0.0436	0.0427	0.0418	0.0409	0.0401	0.0392	0.0384	0.0375	0.0367
1.8	0.0359	0.0351	0.0344	0.0336	0.0329	0.0322	0.0314	0.0307	0.0300	0.0294
1.9	0.0287	0.0281	0.0274	0.0268	0.0262	0.0256	0.0250	0.0244	0.0238	0.0233
2.0	0.0227	0.0222	0.0217	0.0212	0.0207	0.0202	0.0197	0.0192	0.0188	0.0183
2.1	0.0179	0.0174	0.0170	0.0166	0.0162	0.0158	0.0154	0.0150	0.0146	0.0143
2.2	0.0139	0.0135	0.0132	0.0129	0.0125	0.0122	0.0119	0.0116	0.0113	0.0110
2.3	0.0107	0.0104	0.0102	0.0099	0.0096	0.0094	0.0091	0.0089	0.0087	0.0084
2.4	0.0082	0.0080	0.0078	0.0075	0.0073	0.0071	0.0069	0.0068	0.0066	0.0064
2.5	0.0062	0.0060	0.0059	0.0057	0.0055	0.0054	0.0052	0.0051	0.0049	0.0048
2.6	0.0047	0.0045	0.0044	0.0043	0.0041	0.0040	0.0039	0.0038	0.0037	0.0036
2.7	0.0035	0.0034	0.0033	0.0032	0.0031	0.0030	0.0029	0.0028	0.0027	0.0026
2.8	0.0025	0.0025	0.0024	0.0023	0.0022	0.0022	0.0021	0.0020	0.0020	0.0019
2.9	0.0019	0.0018	0.0017	0.0017	0.0016	0.0016	0.0015	0.0015	0.0015	0.0014
3.0	0.0013	0.0013	0.0013	0.0012	0.0012	0.0011	0.0011	0.0011	0.0010	0.0010
3.1	0.0010	0.0009	0.0009	0.0009	0.0008	0.0008	0.0008	0.0008	0.0007	0.0007
3.2	0.0007	0.0007	0.0006	0.0006	0.0006	0.0006	0.0006	0.0005	0.0005	0.0005
3.3	0.0005	0.0005	0.0004	0.0004	0.0004	0.0004	0.0004	0.0004	0.0004	0.0003
3.4	0.0003	0.0003	0.0003	0.0003	0.0003	0.0003	0.0003	0.0003	0.0002	0.0002
3.5	0.0002	0.0002	0.0002	0.0002	0.0002	0.0002	0.0002	0.0002	0.0002	0.0002
3.6	0.0002	0.0001	0.0001	0.0001	0.0001	0.0001	0.0001	0.0001	0.0001	0.0001
3.7	0.0001	0.0001	0.0001	0.0001	0.0001	0.0001	0.0001	0.0001	0.0001	0.0001
3.8	0.0001	0.0001	0.0001	0.0001	0.0001	0.0001	0.0001	0.0000	0.0000	0.0000
3.9	0.0000	0.0000	0.0000	0.0000	0.0000	0.0000	0.0000	0.0000	0.0000	0.0000
4.0	0.0000	0.0000	0.0000	0.0000	0.0000	0.0000	0.0000	0.0000	0.0000	0.0000

of a profit greater than Z standard deviations from the mean. Thus, Table 4.3 shows the right tail of the distributions, that is, the probability of the variable being greater than X standard deviations from the mean.

The following paragraphs describe situations in which the table of normal probabilities can be used.

Suppose the cost accountant at the Smith Company wants to know the probability that profits from products A and B will be greater than zero. The Z values are computed as follows:

$$Z_A = \frac{\$0 - \$2,000}{\$1,000} = -2.$$

$$Z_B = \frac{\$0 - \$500}{\$625} = -0.8.$$

Zero profits for A and B fall 2 and 0.8, respectively, to the left of the mean. Table 4.3 may be used to read both the left- and right-tail probabilities. Hence the probabilities of profits being less than zero for A and B are

P (Profits of A $> -2\sigma$ from the mean) $=$

$1 - P$ (Profits of A $> 2\sigma$ from the mean).

Therefore, P (Profits of A > 0) $= 1 - 0.0228 = 0.9712$. Similarly,

P (Profits of B $> -0.8\sigma$ from the mean) $=$

$1 - P$ (Profits of B $> 0.8\sigma$ from the mean).

Therefore, P (Profits of B > 0) $= 1 - 0.2119 = 0.7881$.

Suppose the cost accountant at the Smith Company wants to know the probability that the profits of A and B would each be greater than \$2,375. He can compute the Z values again as follows:

$$Z_A = \frac{\$2,375 - \$2,000}{\$1,000} = 0.375.$$

$$Z_B = \frac{\$2,375 - \$500}{\$625} = 3.$$

Therefore, using Table 4.3 he can state that P (Profits of A $> \$2,375$) $= 0.3557$, and P (Profits of B $> \$2,375$) $= 0.0013$.

Suppose instead that the cost accountant of Smith Company wants to know the probability that the profits of A and B would equal \$2,375. Table 4.4 gives the relative heights of the normal curve at distances from the mean measured by Z values. Thus,

$Z_A = 0.375$, and $P(Z_A) = 0.3726$.

$Z_B = 3$, and $P(Z_B) = 0.0044$.

Table 4.4   Ordinates of the Normal Curve

z	0.00	0.01	0.02	0.03	0.04	0.05	0.06	0.07	0.08	0.09
0.0	0.3989	0.3989	0.3989	0.3988	0.3986	0.3984	0.3982	0.3980	0.3977	0.3973
0.1	0.3970	0.3965	0.3961	0.3956	0.3951	0.3945	0.3939	0.3932	0.3925	0.3918
0.2	0.3910	0.3902	0.3894	0.3885	0.3876	0.3867	0.3857	0.3847	0.3836	0.3825
0.3	0.3814	0.3802	0.3790	0.3778	0.3765	0.3752	0.3739	0.3726	0.3712	0.3697
0.4	0.3683	0.3668	0.3653	0.3637	0.3621	0.3605	0.3589	0.3572	0.3555	0.3538
0.5	0.3521	0.3503	0.3485	0.3467	0.3448	0.3430	0.3411	0.3391	0.3372	0.3352
0.6	0.3332	0.3312	0.3292	0.3271	0.3251	0.3230	0.3209	0.3187	0.3166	0.3144
0.7	0.3123	0.3101	0.3079	0.3056	0.3034	0.3011	0.2989	0.2966	0.2943	0.2920
0.8	0.2897	0.2874	0.2850	0.2827	0.2803	0.2780	0.2756	0.2732	0.2709	0.2685
0.9	0.2661	0.2637	0.2613	0.2589	0.2565	0.2541	0.2516	0.2492	0.2468	0.2444
1.0	0.2420	0.2396	0.2371	0.2347	0.2323	0.2299	0.2275	0.2251	0.2227	0.2203
1.1	0.2179	0.2155	0.2131	0.2107	0.2083	0.2059	0.2036	0.2012	0.1989	0.1965
1.2	0.1942	0.1919	0.1895	0.1872	0.1849	0.1827	0.1804	0.1781	0.1759	0.1736
1.3	0.1714	0.1691	0.1669	0.1647	0.1626	0.1604	0.1582	0.1561	0.1540	0.1518
1.4	0.1497	0.1476	0.1456	0.1435	0.1415	0.1394	0.1374	0.1354	0.1334	0.1315
1.5	0.1295	0.1276	0.1257	0.1238	0.1219	0.1200	0.1182	0.1163	0.1145	0.1127
1.6	0.1109	0.1092	0.1074	0.1057	0.1040	0.1023	0.1006	0.0989	0.0973	0.0957
1.7	0.0941	0.0925	0.0909	0.0893	0.0878	0.0863	0.0848	0.0833	0.0818	0.0804
1.8	0.0790	0.0775	0.0761	0.0748	0.0734	0.0721	0.0707	0.0694	0.0681	0.0669
1.9	0.0656	0.0644	0.0632	0.0620	0.0608	0.0596	0.0584	0.0573	0.0562	0.0551
2.0	0.0540	0.0529	0.0519	0.0508	0.0498	0.0488	0.0478	0.0468	0.0459	0.0449
2.1	0.0440	0.0431	0.0422	0.0413	0.0404	0.0396	0.0387	0.0379	0.0371	0.0363
2.2	0.0355	0.0347	0.0339	0.0332	0.0325	0.0317	0.0310	0.0303	0.0297	0.0290
2.3	0.0283	0.0277	0.0270	0.0264	0.0258	0.0252	0.0246	0.0241	0.0235	0.0229
2.4	0.0224	0.0219	0.0213	0.0208	0.0203	0.0198	0.0194	0.0189	0.0184	0.0180
2.5	0.0175	0.0171	0.0167	0.0163	0.0158	0.0154	0.0151	0.0147	0.0143	0.0139
2.6	0.0136	0.0132	0.0129	0.0126	0.0122	0.0119	0.0116	0.0113	0.0110	0.0107
2.7	0.0104	0.0101	0.0099	0.0096	0.0093	0.0091	0.0088	0.0086	0.0084	0.0081
2.8	0.0079	0.0077	0.0075	0.0073	0.0071	0.0069	0.0067	0.0065	0.0063	0.0061
2.9	0.0060	0.0058	0.0056	0.0055	0.0053	0.0051	0.0050	0.0048	0.0047	0.0046
3.0	0.0044	0.0043	0.0042	0.0040	0.0039	0.0038	0.0037	0.0036	0.0035	0.0034
3.1	0.0033	0.0032	0.0031	0.0030	0.0029	0.0028	0.0027	0.0026	0.0025	0.0025
3.2	0.0024	0.0023	0.0022	0.0022	0.0021	0.0020	0.0020	0.0019	0.0018	0.0018
3.3	0.0017	0.0017	0.0016	0.0016	0.0015	0.0015	0.0014	0.0014	0.0013	0.0013
3.4	0.0012	0.0012	0.0012	0.0011	0.0011	0.0010	0.0010	0.0010	0.0010	0.0009
3.5	0.0009	0.0008	0.0008	0.0008	0.0008	0.0007	0.0007	0.0007	0.0007	0.0006
3.6	0.0006	0.0006	0.0006	0.0005	0.0005	0.0005	0.0005	0.0005	0.0005	0.0004
3.7	0.0004	0.0004	0.0004	0.0004	0.0004	0.0004	0.0003	0.0003	0.0003	0.0003
3.8	0.0003	0.0003	0.0003	0.0003	0.0003	0.0002	0.0002	0.0002	0.0002	0.0002
3.9	0.0002	0.0002	0.0002	0.0002	0.0002	0.0002	0.0002	0.0002	0.0001	0.0001
4.0	0.0001	0.0001	0.0001	0.0001	0.0001	0.0001	0.0001	0.0001	0.0001	0.0001

Assumptions of Nonnormality

Probabilistic breakeven analysis can be extended to include all inputs as random variables. The inputs can be assumed to be normally distributed and mutually independent. As a result of the independence assumption, the expected profit and standard deviation can be expressed as follows:

$$E(Y) = E(Q)[E(P) - E(V)] - E(F),$$

and

$$\sigma = \sqrt{\sigma_Q^2 (\sigma_P^2 + \sigma_V^2) + E^2(Q)(\sigma_P^2 + \sigma_V^2) + [E(P) - E(V)]^2\sigma_Q^2 + \sigma_F^2}.$$

The expected profit is assumed to be normally distributed. However, as pointed out in the theorem of C. C. Craig and L. A. Aroian, the product of two normally distributed and statistically independent random variables approximates the normal distribution only when their coefficients of variation approach zero.[5] W. L. Ferrara, Jack C. Hayya, and D. A. Nachman show that the normality assumption for the profit cannot be rejected at the 0.05 level if the sum of the coefficients of variation for Y and $P - V$ is less than or equal to 12 percent.[6] Thus, probabilistic breakeven analysis is sound only for small coefficients of variation or when P and V are deterministic.

Because of these limitations, various methods other than normal distribution have been proposed for use in probabilistic breakeven analysis. They include statistical distributions, such as the log normal[7] and beta distributions;[8] several distribution-free methods, such as the Tchebycheff inequality;[9] and model sampling and curve fitting techniques.[10] The study of these techniques to analyze the random behavior of profits is beyond the scope of this book.

4.6   CONCLUSION

Breakeven analysis is a useful cost accounting technique for situations that involve the relationships between costs, revenues, and profits. The accounting approach to breakeven analysis can be supplemented to (1) examine and assess product mix decisions, (2) accommodate curvilinear cost and revenue functions, and (3) incorporate uncertainty in the analysis.

4.A   APPENDIX: THE SIMPLEX METHOD ILLUSTRATED

The simplex method is one of the techniques used to solve linear programming problems. It is an iterative procedure that improves a feasible solution until the optimal solution is obtained.

The example described in section 4.3.3 will be used to illustrate the simplex method.

[5] L. A. Aroian, "The Probability Function of the Product of Two Normally Distributed Variables," *Annals of Mathematical Statistics* (October 1947), pp. 265–271; and C. C. Craig, "On the Frequency Function of XY," *Annals of Mathematical Statistics* (October 1936), pp. 1–15.

[6] W. L. Ferrara, Jack C. Hayya, and D. A. Nachman, "Normalcy of Profit in the Jaedicke-Robichek Model," *Accounting Review* (April 1972), pp. 299–307.

[7] J. E. Hilliard and R. A. Leitch, "Cost-Volume-Profit Analysis under Uncertainty: A Log Normal Approach," *Accounting Review* (January 1975), pp. 69–80.

[8] R. Tersine and C. Altimus, "Probabilistic Profit Planning: A Feasible Approach," *Management Advisor* (May–June 1974), pp. 46–50.

[9] S. L. Buzby, "Extending the Applicability of Probabilistic Management Planning and Control Models," *Accounting Review* (January 1974), pp. 42–49.

[10] M. Liao, "Model Sampling: A Stochastic Cost-Volume-Profit Analysis," *Accounting Review* (October 1975), pp. 780–790.

This example requires the maximization of the contribution margin of two products with different resource requirements: Product A, 4 hours of time and 4 units of material; and Product B, 2 hours of time and 6 units of material. For the period under analysis, 16 hours of time and 24 units of material are available for production.

The simplex method applied to this problem consists of the following steps.

Step 1   Set the objective function and the constraint inequalities:

Objective function: Max. $Z = 6X_1 + 7X_2$,

subject to

Material constraint: $4X_1 + 6X_2 \leq 24$ units.

Labor constraint: $4X_1 + 2X_2 \leq 16$ hours.

Nonnegativity constraint: $X_1, X_2 \geq 0$.

Step 2   Because the simplex method requires equations rather than inequalities, transform the inequalities into equations by adding the arbitrary variables, called *slack variables*, X_1 and X_2. The constraint equations, then, are as follows:

$4X_1 + 6X_2 + X_3 + 0X_4 = 24$ units.

$4X_1 + 2X_2 + 0X_3 + X_4 = 16$ hours.

The objective function becomes

Max. $Z = 6X_1 + 7X_2 + 0X_3 + 0X_4$.

Step 3   Arrange the data in an initial simplex tableau as follows:

C_j	Variables Allocated	Quantity	$6 X_1	$7 X_2	$0 X_3	$0 X_4	
							◀——— Objective Row
							◀——— Variable Row
\$0	X_3	24	4	⑥	1	0	◀ Problem Rows
\$0	X_4	16	4	2	0	1	◀
	Z_j	\$0	\$0	\$0	\$0	\$0	◀ Index Rows
	$C_j - Z_j$		+\$6	+\$7	\$0	\$0	◀

Optimal or Key Column
Quantity Column
Variable Column
Objective Column

The $C_j - Z_j$ row gives the net profit from adding 1 unit of a profit, so the presence of at least one positive number in the $C_j - Z_j$ row indicates that profit can be improved. Absence of a positive number in that row indicates that profit cannot be improved—that is, the optimal solution has been obtained. In this example the numbers in the $C_j - Z_j$ row are positive, which indicates that the solution could be improved.

Step 4 Determine the entering and departing variables.

1. To find the entering variable, the *key column* is selected, which has the highest positive value in the $C_j - Z_j$ row. In this example, the X_2 variable is the entering variable ($C_j - Z_j = +\$7$).

2. To find the departing variable, the *key row* is selected, which contains the smallest positive ratio obtained by dividing the quantities of X_3 and X_4 (in the quantity column) by their corresponding entries in the key column. X_3 row = $^{24}\!/_6$ = 4. X_4 row = $^{16}\!/_2$ = 8. The smaller of the two ratios is 4, which corresponds to X_3. Therefore, the key row is X_3, which is the departing variable.

Step 5 Compute a revised tableau as follows. Determine the X_2 row of the revised tableau by dividing each amount in the X_3 row (the departing row) by the element in the optimal column of the replaced row, which is 6 in this example. Thus, the X_2 row will be $^{24}\!/_6$, $^4\!/_6$, $^6\!/_6$, $^1\!/_6$, $^0\!/_6$, or 4, $^2\!/_3$, 1, $^1\!/_6$, 0.

Compute all the remaining rows of the variables in the tableau using the formula

$$\text{Element in old row} - \left(\begin{array}{c} \text{Element of old row} \\ \text{in optimal column} \end{array} \times \begin{array}{c} \text{Corresponding} \\ \text{element in replacing row} \end{array} \right).$$

For this example, compute the new values for the X_4 row as follows:

Element in Old Row	Minus	Element of Old Row in Optimal Column	Times	Corresponding Element in Replacing Row	Equals	New Values of X_4
16	−	(2	×	4)	=	8
4	−	(2	×	⅔)	=	8/3
2	−	(2	×	1)	=	0
0	−	(2	×	⅙)	=	−⅓
1	−	(2	×	0)	=	1

Compute the new profit:

Z_j = Total profit = ($\$0 \times 8$) + ($\$4 \times 7$) = $28.

Z_j for X_1 = ($\$0 \times 8/3$) + ($\$7 \times ⅔$) = $14⅓.

Z_j for X_2 = ($\$0 \times 0$) + ($\$7 \times 1$) = $7.

Z_j for X_3 = ($\$0 \times -⅓$) + ($\$7 \times ⅙$) = $7/6.

Z_j for X_4 = ($\$0 \times 1$) + ($\$7 \times 0$) = $0.

The revised tableau is as follows:

C_j	Variables	Quantity	6 X_1	7 X_2	0 X_3	0 X_4
$7	X_2	4	2/3	1	1/6	0
◄ $0	X_4	8	(8/3)	0	−1/3	1
	Z_j	$28	$14/13	$7	$7/6	$0
	$C_j - Z_j$		$4/3	$0	−$7/6	$0

Step 6 Determine the entering and departing variables. The entering variable is X_1, because the maximum positive value in the $C_j - Z_j$ row is $\frac{4}{3}$. The departing variable is X_4, because $X_2 = 4/(\frac{8}{3}) = 6$, and $X_4 = 8/(\frac{8}{3}) = 3$. The smaller of the two ratios is 3, which corresponds to X_4.

Step 7 Compute a revised tableau as follows. Determine the X_1 row by dividing each amount in the X_4 row (the departing row) by the element in the optimal column of the replaced row, which is $\frac{8}{3}$ in this example. Thus, the new X_1 row will be

$$\frac{8}{\frac{8}{3}}, \frac{\frac{8}{3}}{\frac{8}{3}}, \frac{0}{\frac{8}{3}}, \frac{-\frac{1}{3}}{\frac{8}{3}}, \frac{1}{\frac{8}{3}}, \text{ or } 3, 1, 0, -\frac{1}{8}, \frac{3}{8}.$$

Compute the remaining row (X_2) as follows:

Element in Old Row	Minus	Element of Old Row in Optimal Column	Times	Corresponding Element in Replacing Row	Equals	New Values of X_2
4	−	($\frac{2}{3}$	×	3)	=	2
$\frac{2}{3}$	−	($\frac{2}{3}$	×	1)	=	0
1	−	($\frac{2}{3}$	×	0)	=	1
$\frac{1}{6}$	−	($\frac{2}{3}$	×	$-\frac{1}{8}$)	=	$\frac{1}{4}$
0	−	($\frac{2}{3}$	×	$\frac{3}{8}$)	=	$-\frac{1}{4}$

Compute the new profit as follows:

$Z_j = $ Total profit $= (\$6 \times 3)\quad + (\$7 \times 2)\quad = \$32.$

Z_j for $X_1 \qquad = (\$6 \times 1)\quad + (\$7 \times 0)\quad = \$6.$

Z_j for $X_2 \qquad = (\$6 \times 0)\quad + (\$7 \times 1)\quad = \$7.$

Z_j for $X_3 \qquad = (\$6 \times -\frac{1}{8}) + (\$7 \times \frac{1}{4})\quad = \$1.$

Z_j for $X_4 \qquad = (\$6 \times \frac{3}{8})\quad + (\$7 \times -\frac{1}{4}) = \$\frac{1}{2}.$

The revised tableau is as follows:

C_j	Variables	Quantity	$6 X_1	$7 X_2	$0 X_3	$0 X_4
$7	X_2	2	0	1	$\frac{1}{4}$	$-\frac{1}{4}$
$6	X_1	3	1	0	$-\frac{1}{8}$	$\frac{3}{8}$
	Z_j	$32	$6	$7	$1	$\frac{1}{2}$
	$C_j - Z_j$		$0	$0	$-$1	$-$\frac{1}{2}$

In this tableau all the elements of the $C_j - Z_j$ row are less than or equal to zero. Therefore, this constitutes the final tableau for the maximization problem. It shows that the optimal solution is to produce 2 units of X_2 and 3 units of X_1, which yields a maximum contribution of $32.

An important property of the net evaluation row is that the negative of the $C_j - Z_j$ row values for a slack variable associated with a constraint tells us how much the objective function will increase if one additional unit above the initial amount of the resource corresponding to the constraint is made available. These are the shadow prices of the resources, so the shadow price of material is $1 and the shadow price of labor is $.50.

They may be interpreted as the maximum value or price the company would be willing to pay to obtain one additional unit of the resource.

Step 8 Find the range over which the shadow prices of $1 and $.50 for material and labor are valid as follows. For the lower limit of the range, divide each unit in the solution mix by the coefficients in the slack variable columns. The smallest positive number that results is the maximum decrease in the constraint.

(1) Product	(2) Units	(3) Material	(4) Labor	(5) = (2) ÷ (3) Material	(6) = (2) ÷ (4) Labor
X_2	2	¼	−¼	8	−8
X_1	3	−⅛	⅜	−24	8

For the material constraint, the decrease is 8 units. Since the original number available is 24 units, the lower limit is 16 (24 − 8). For the labor constraint, the decrease is 8 hours. Since the original number available is 16 hours, the lower limit is 8 (16 − 8).

For the upper limit of the range, multiply each coefficient by −1, and repeat the process you used to find the lower limit of the range. The smallest positive number in the results is the maximum increase in the constraint:

(1) Product	(2) Units	(3) Material	(4) Labor	(5) Material	(6) Labor
X_2	2	−¼	¼	−8	8
X_1	3	⅛	−⅜	24	−8

For the material constraint, the increase is 24 units. Thus, the upper limit is 48 (24 + 24). For the labor constraint, the increase is 8 hours. Thus, the upper limit is 24 (16 + 8).

In summary, the lower and upper constraint limits are

	Current Value	Upper Limit	Lower Limit
Material	24	48 Units	16 Units
Labor	16	24 Hours	8 Hours

4.B   *APPENDIX: THE DUAL PROBLEM*

For every linear programming problem there is a second linear programming problem referred to as the *dual*. When the first, or *primal*, problem involves the *maximization* of an objective function, the dual problem involves the *minimization* of the same objective function, and vice versa. The dual problem provides a solution which minimizes the opportunity cost (or lost profit) due to the choice of the primal solution rather than the best of the other available alternative solutions. The dual variable of each factor of production is interpreted as its marginal profit contribution. For example, the dual variable of the labor constraint indicates the contribution to the profit of the use of one additional unit of labor.

The dual problem is completely symmetrical to the primal problem, and the solution of one problem provides full information for the solution of the other problem. The correspondence between both problems is as follows:

Primal Problem

Constants in Constraints
Coefficients in the Objective Function
Inequality Signs of Constraints
ith Row of Coefficients in Constraints

Dual Problem

Coefficients in the Objective Function
Constants in Constraints
Inequality Signs of Constraints Reversed
ith Column of Coefficients in Constraints

The primal and dual problems can be stated as follows:

Primal Method

$AX \leq b$

Max. $z = cX$

Dual Method

$A'W \geq C'$

Min. $Z = b'W$

The parameters of the dual problem can be computed easily from the following tableau:

Columns			1	2	3
	Primal		**Maximum**		**Constraints**
Rows	**Dual**		X_1	X_2	
1	Minimum	W_1	$M_1 = 4$	$M_2 = 6$	≤ 24
2		W_2	$L_1 = 4$	$L_2 = 2$	≤ 16
3	Decision Rule		V	V	Optimal Solution
	Contribution Margin		$CM_1 = 6$	$CM_2 = 7$	32

This tableau provides a practical way to convert a primal to a dual problem. It can be constructed as follows:

1. Row 1 specifies the material constraints.

2. Row 2 specifies the labor constraints.

3. Row 3 specifies the contribution margin of each product.

4. The primal problem, then, is as follows:

Row 3, objective function: Max. $6X_1 + 7X_2$,

subject to

Row 1, material constraint: $4X_1 + 6X_2 \leq 24$.

Row 2, labor constraint: $4X_1 + 2X_2 \leq 16$.

5. The dual problem may be derived from the columns as follows:

Column 3, objective function: Min. $24W_1 + 16W_2$,

subject to

Column 1: $4W_1 + 4W_2 \geq 6$.

Column 2: $6W_1 + 2W_2 \geq 7$.

This can be restated:

1. When the primal problem has n decision variables, the dual problem will have n constraints. The first constraint in the dual is associated with variable X_1 in the primal, the second with variable X_2, and so on.

2. The values on the right side of the primal problem constitute the objective function coefficients of the dual problem.

3. The objective function coefficients of the primal problem constitute the values on the right side of the dual problem.

4. The constraint coefficients of the ith primal variable constitute the coefficients in the ith constraint of the dual primal variable.

5. The solution to either the primal or the dual problem also provides the solution to the other, as follows:

    a. The values of the dual variables and the shadow prices are the same. The dual variables in the preceding example are $W_1 = \$1$ and $W_2 = \$.50$, which correspond to the shadow prices of the resources.

    b. The values of the optimal solutions to the dual and the primal problems are the same. The optimal solution to the dual problem in the preceding example is $24(\$1) + 16(\$.50) = \$32$, which corresponds to the optimal solution of the primal problem.

6. Whenever computational time and cost are important considerations in solving linear programs, decision makers have the option of solving either the primal or the dual problem, depending upon which is easier.

GLOSSARY

Breakeven Chart A graphic representation of the behavior of and relationships between cost, revenue, and profit, and pinpointing the breakeven point.

Breakeven Point The volume of activity at which total revenues equal total costs.

Contribution Margin The excess of sales over variable expenses.

Economic Model The economist's analysis of cost and revenue behavior that accounts for variability of both the unit selling price and the unit variable cost.

Linear Programming The operational research technique of allocating scarce resources among various alternative options to achieve a stated objective within the constraints reflecting the use of resources.

Margin of Safety A given sales figure less breakeven sales.

Shadow Price The value of a marginal unit of the constraining factor, which equals the additional contribution margin obtained by releasing the constraint and increasing it by one unit.

SELECTED READINGS

Adar, Z.; Barnea, A.; and Lev, B., "A Comprehensive Cost-Volume-Profit Analysis under Uncertainty," *Accounting Review* (January 1977), pp. 137–149.

Anderson, Lane K., "Expanded Breakeven Analysis for a Multi-product Company," *Management Accounting* (July 1975), pp. 16–20.

Buzby, S. L., "Extending the Applicability of Probabilistic Management Planning and Control Models," *Accounting Review* (January 1974), pp. 42–49.

Chan, K. H., and Laughland, Alan, "Towards Probabilistic Break-Even Analysis," *Cost and Management* (July–August 1976), pp. 44–47.

Charnes, A.; Cooper, W. W.; and Ijiri, Y., "Breakeven Budgeting and Programming to Goals," *Journal of Accounting Research* (Spring 1963), pp. 16–43.

Chasteen, L. G., "A Graphical Approach to Linear Programming Shadow Prices," *Accounting Review* (October 1972), pp. 819–823.

4.6   ***Probability Tree Analysis***   The Rushing Enterprises Company manufactures the industrial chemical product Conscousate and has excess production capacity for the coming
year. The company received an order that could generate sales of either $50,000,
$60,000, or $70,000. The management of Rushing Enterprises Company wants to know
if the order should be accepted. The following data on Conscousate are provided:

Sales (Anticipated)	$50,000	$60,000	$70,000
Probability of Sales	0.2	0.4	0.4

Total Costs (Anticipated): $50,000 or $60,000

Probability of Costs	0.5	0.5

Required:
Compute the expected profit by accepting the special order (submit all computations).

(Adapted with permission from Ahmed Belkaoui, "Planification Budgétaire dans l'Incertitude," *Cost and
Management*, March–April 1974, pp. 25–79.)

4.7   ***Probability Tree Analysis***   Management of the Soussi Company, which sells bicycles,
is considering opening a new store in a suburb. The following data are offered for
analysis:

1. The company estimates the selling price per unit to be either $100 with a probability
of 0.7, or $90 with a probability of 0.3.

2. The company estimates the invoice cost per unit to be either $70 with a probability of
0.6, $80 with a probability of 0.3, or $70 with a probability of 0.1.

3. The company estimates the fixed costs to be either $2,000 with a probability of 0.5,
$3,000 with a probability of 0.2, or $4,000 with a probability of 0.3.

Required:
Estimate the expected breakeven point in units of the new store.

4.8   ***Evaluation of Degree of Risk: Standard Deviation and Coefficient of Variation***   Assume that as a manager of T Company you must choose between the production of two
products, Alpha and Gamma. You are provided the following discrete probability distributions of the demands in the next five years:

Product Alpha		Product Beta	
Probability	**Demand (in Units)**	**Probability**	**Demand (in Units)**
0.12	2,000	0.12	500
0.23	3,000	0.23	1,500
0.32	4,000	0.32	2,000
0.23	6,000	0.23	3,000
0.10	7,000	0.10	4,000

Required:
1. For each product, compute (a) the expected demand, (b) the standard deviation, and
(c) the coefficient of variation.

2. Which product should T Company produce? Why?

4.9   ***Formulate Objective Function***   Z Ltd. produces two products, A and B. Product A sells for $50 per unit and requires 3 hours of direct-labor time to produce. Product B sells for $30 per unit and requires 2 hours of direct-labor time. For simplicity, assume that direct labor is the only variable production cost. The cost of direct labor is $7 per hour. Fixed costs of Z Ltd. are $500 per period.

Because of the specialized nature of Z Ltd.'s direct-labor requirements, the amount of direct labor available for production cannot be varied in the short run. For the next period the maximum number of direct-labor hours available is 120 hours. Z Ltd.'s marketing expert advises that the maximum number of units that could be sold next period is 30 units of product A and 45 units of product B.

Required:

1. Z Ltd. must decide how many units of products A and B to produce next period to maximize its profit. To assist in this decision problem, you are asked to formulate it as a linear programming problem—that is, set up the objective function and the constraints. You are not required to solve the problem.

2. A linear programming problem is a deterministic model; that is, the various numbers and relationships within the model are assumed to be known with certainty. However, given that most firms operate in an uncertain environment, do you think it wise to ignore uncertainty in decisions such as this? Why?

(SMA adapted)

4.10   ***Effect on Profits of Change in Price***   The Canadian Zinc Die-Casting Company is one of several suppliers of part X to an automobile manufacturing firm. Orders are distributed to the various die-casting companies on a fairly even basis; however, the sales manager of Canadian Zinc believes that with a reduction in price, he could secure another 30 percent increase in units sold. The general manager has asked you to analyze the sales manager's proposal and submit your recommendation. The following data are available:

	Present	**Proposed**
Unit Price	$2.50	$2.00
Unit Sales Volume	200,000 units	Plus 30%
Variable Cost (Total)	$350,000	Same Unit Variable Cost
Fixed Cost	$120,000	$120,000
Profit	$ 30,000	?

Required:

1. Determine the net profit or loss based on the sales manager's proposal.

2. Determine the unit sales required under the proposed price to make the original $30,000 profit.

(SMA adapted)

4.11   ***Cost-Volume Relationships, Income Taxes***   R. A. Ro and Company, maker of quality handmade pipes, has experienced a steady growth in sales for the past five years. However, increased competition has led Mr. Ro, the president, to believe that an aggressive advertising campaign will be necessary next year to maintain the company's present growth. To prepare for next year's advertising campaign, the company's accountant has gathered and presented Ro with the following data for the current year, 19X2:

Variable Costs (per Pipe)	
Direct Labor	$ 8.00
Direct Materials	3.25
Variable Overhead	2.50
Total Variable Costs	$ 13.75
Fixed Costs	
Manufacturing	$ 25,000
Selling	40,000
Administrative	70,000
Total Fixed Costs	$135,000
Selling Price (per Pipe)	$ 25
Expected Sales, 19X2 (20,000 Units)	$500,000
Tax Rate	40%

Ro has set the 19X3 sales target at a level of $550,000 (or 22,000 pipes).

Required:

1. What is the projected after-tax net income for 19X2?

2. What is the breakeven point in units for 19X2?

3. Ro believes an additional selling expense of $11,250 for advertising in 19X3, with all other costs remaining constant, will be necessary to attain the sales target. What will be the after-tax net income for 19X3 if the additional $11,250 is spent?

4. What will be the breakeven point in dollar sales for 19X3 if the additional $11,250 is spent for advertising?

5. If the additional $11,250 is spent for advertising in 19X3, what sales level in dollar sales will be required to equal 19X2's after-tax net income?

6. At a sales level of 22,000 units, what maximum amount can be spent on advertising if an after-tax net income of $60,000 is desired?

(CMA adapted)

4.12
Fixed Costs, Variable Costs, Relevant Range, Breakeven Point, Margin of Safety, and Sales Mix Cost-volume-earnings analysis (breakeven analysis) is used to determine and express the interrelationships of different volumes of activity (sales), costs, sales prices, and sales mix to earnings. More specifically, the analysis determines the effect on earnings of changes in sales volume, sales prices, sales mix, and costs.

Required:

1. Certain terms are fundamental to cost-volume-earnings analysis. Explain the meaning of each of the following terms:

a. Fixed costs.
b. Variable costs.
c. Relevant range.

d. Breakeven point.
e. Margin of safety.
f. Sales mix.

2. Which assumptions are implicit in cost-volume-earnings analysis?

3. In a recent period, Zero Company had the following activity:

	Fixed	Variable	
Sales (10,000 Units @ $200)			$2,000,000
Costs			
Direct Material	$ —	$ 200,000	
Direct Labor	—	400,000	
Factory Overhead	160,000	600,000	
Administrative Expenses	180,000	80,000	
Other Expenses	200,000	120,000	
Total Costs	$540,000	$1,400,000	1,940,000
Net Income			$ 60,000

Answer each of the following questions independently:

a. Calculate the breakeven point for Zero Company in terms of units and sales dollars. Show your calculations.

b. What sales volume would be required to generate a net income of $96,000? Show your calculations.

c. What is the breakeven point if management makes a decision which increases fixed costs by $18,000? Show your calculations.

(AICPA adapted)

4.13   ***Breakeven Analysis***   Anderson Co. Ltd. produces a product with the following variable costs per unit: direct materials, $10; direct labor, $20; and variable overhead, $6. Fixed overhead costs are expected to be $72,000 for a range of output from 10,000 to 20,000 units. Variable selling expenses are $4 per unit. Fixed administrative expenses will total $18,000. Anderson's income tax rate is 40 percent.

Required:

1. At a sales price of $46 per unit, compute the breakeven point in units.

2. At a sales price of $50 per unit, how many units would Anderson Co. have to sell to produce a net income after tax of $30,000?

3. Another company has offered to supply this product to Anderson at a unit price of $39. If annual sales will be 18,000 units, should Anderson accept this offer?

4. Annual sales to regular customers are expected to be 15,000 units at $50 per unit. Should Anderson accept a special order for 3,000 units at $40 per unit? Variable selling expenses on this special order would be $2 per unit.

(CGA adapted)

4.14   ***Breakeven Analysis***   Theta Co. Ltd. has analyzed the costs of producing and selling 5,000 units of its sole product as follows:

Direct Materials	$60,000
Direct Labor	40,000
Variable Overhead	20,000
Fixed Overhead	30,000
Variable Selling and Administrative Expenses	10,000
Fixed Selling and Administrative Expenses	15,000

Required:

1. At a sales price of $38.50 per unit, how many units would Theta have to sell to break even?

2. At a sales price of $40 per unit, how many units would Theta have to sell to produce a profit of $18,000?

3. Theta's plant has the capacity to produce 7,000 units. Sales to regular customers will not exceed 5,000 units. Should Theta accept a special order for 1,500 units at $30 per unit?

4. If 5,000 units were produced and sold, what price would Theta have to charge to produce a profit equal to 20 percent of sales?

(CGA adapted)

4.15   *Comprehensive Cost-Profit-Volume Analysis*   Mr. Calderone started a pizza restaurant in 1970. He rented a building for $400 per month. He hired two people to work full-time at the restaurant and six people to work thirty hours per week delivering pizza. Calderone also hired an outside accountant at $300 per month for tax and bookkeeping purposes. He purchased the necessary restaurant equipment and delivery cars with cash. Expenses for utilities and supplies have been rather constant.

     Calderone increased his business between 19X0 and 19X3. Profits have more than doubled since 19X0, and he does not understand why profits have increased faster than volume. A projected income statement for 19X4 has been prepared by the accountant:

Calderone Company
Projected Income Statement
for the Year Ended December 31, 19X4

Sales		$95,000
Cost of Food Sold	$28,500	
Wages and Fringe Benefits of Restaurant Staff	8,150	
Wages and Fringe Benefits of Delivery Staff	17,300	
Rent	4,800	
Accounting Services	3,600	
Depreciation of Delivery Equipment	5,000	
Depreciation of Restaurant Equipment	3,000	
Utilities	2,325	
Supplies (Soap, Floor Wax, etc.)	1,200	73,875
Net Income before Taxes		$21,125
Income Taxes		6,338
Net Income		$14,787

Note: The average pizza sells for $2.50. Assume that Calderone pays out 30 percent of his income in income taxes.

Required:

1. What is the breakeven point in the number of pizzas that must be sold?

2. What is the cash flow breakeven point in the number of pizzas that must be sold?

3. If Calderone withdraws $4,800 for personal use, how much cash will be left from the 19X4 income-producing activities?

4. Calderone would like an after-tax net income of $20,000. What volume must be reached in the number of pizzas sold to obtain the desired income?

5. Briefly explain to Calderone why his profits have increased at a faster rate than his sales.

6. Briefly explain to Calderone why his cash flow for 19X4 will exceed his profits.

(CMA adapted)

4.16   ***Breakeven Analysis for Two Products***   The Dooley Company manufactures two products, baubles and trinkets. The following are projections for the coming year:

	Baubles		Trinkets		
	Units	Amount	Units	Amount	Total
Sales	10,000	$10,000	7,500	$10,000	$20,000
Costs					
Fixed		2,000		5,600	7,600
Variable		6,000		3,000	9,000
		8,000		8,600	16,600
Income before Taxes		$ 2,000		$ 1,400	$ 3,400

Required:
Select the best answer for each of the following items:

1. Assuming that the production facilities are not jointly used, the breakeven output (in units) for baubles would be
   a. 8,000.   **c.** 6,000.
   b. 7,000.   **d.** 5,000.

2. The breakeven volume (in dollars) for trinkets would be
   a. $8,000.   **c.** $6,000.
   b. $7,000.   **d.** $5,000.

3. Assuming that consumers purchase composite units of four baubles and three trinkets, the composite unit contribution margin would be
   a. $4.40.   **c.** $1.33.
   b. $4.00.   **d.** $1.10.

4. If consumers purchased composite units of four baubles and three trinkets, the breakeven output for the two products would be
   a. 6,909 baubles and 6,909 trinkets.   **c.** 5,000 baubles and 8,000 trinkets.
   b. 6,909 baubles and 5,182 trinkets.   **d.** 5,000 baubles and 6,000 trinkets.

5. If baubles and trinkets become one-to-one complements and there is no change in Dooley Company's cost function, the breakeven volume would be
   a. $22,500.   **c.** $13,300.
   b. $15,750.   **d.** $10,858.

6. If a composite unit is defined as one bauble and one trinket, the composite contribution margin ratio would be
   a. $7/10$.   **c.** $2/5$.
   b. $4/7$.   **d.** $10/50$.

(AICPA adapted)

4.17   ***Probabilistic Decision Making***   You have been provided with the following information about the life of three brands of tires: A, B, and C. The data are the results of extensive tests of the three brands by an independent testing bureau under normal conditions of use. The three brands sell for the same price. Assume that the manufacturers do not accept returns and do not offer any warranty. Unless another policy is specifically stated, assume that the tires are used until they are worn out. Data are given in miles.

	Brand A	Brand B	Brand C
Mean	27,000	31,000	32,000
Median	a	a	28,000
Standard Deviation	2,000	3,000	a

a Information not provided by the testing bureau. Brands A and B are normally distributed.

Required:

1. If you were to purchase one tire, what is the probability that you would obtain 28,000 miles or more of use

    a. If it were brand A?

    b. If it were brand B?

    c. If it were brand C?

2. If you purchased three tires (one of brand A, one of brand B, and one of brand C), what is the probability that *none* would exceed 28,000 miles?

(CGA adapted)

4.18   ***Optimal Production with Single Constraint*** Standard costs and other data for two component parts used by Griffon Electronics are as follows:

	Part A4	Part B5
Direct Material	$0.40	$8.00
Direct Labor	1.00	4.70
Factory Overhead	4.00	2.00
Unit Standard Cost	$5.40	$14.70
Units Needed per Year	6,000	8,000
Machine Hours per Unit	4	2
Unit Cost If Purchased	$5.00	$15.00

In past years, Griffon has manufactured all its required components; however, in 19Y4 only 30,000 hours of otherwise idle machine time can be devoted to the production of components. Accordingly, some of the parts must be purchased from outside suppliers. When Griffon produces parts, factory overhead is applied at $1 per standard machine hour. Fixed capacity costs, which will not be affected by any make-buy decision, represent 60 percent of the applied overhead.

Required:

Assuming that the allocation of machine time is based on potential cost savings per machine hour, determine the number of units of A4 and B5 Griffon should produce.

(AICPA adapted)

4.19   ***Probabilistic Decision Making*** Three brands of paint—A, B, and C—were tested under normal use conditions to determine the area one gallon would cover. The three brands sell for the same price. The following statistics were derived (in square feet):

	Brand A	Brand B	Brand C
Mean	875	850	900
Median	875	850	825
Standard Deviation	100	65	a

a Information not provided by the testing bureau. Brands A and B are normally distributed.

Required:

1. If you were planning to purchase 1 gallon to paint a room of 825 square feet, which brand would you choose? Explain with supporting calculations.

2. If you purchased 1 gallon of each brand, and each gallon were to be used to paint a room of 825 square feet (each room to be painted a different color), what is the probability that you would *not* run short of paint?

(CGA adapted)

4.20   ***Probability Tree Analysis***   The Zribi Corporation produces a single product. In preparing a profit budget for the coming year, the cost accountant developed the following estimates:

1. The sales volume may be 80,000 units with a probability of 0.3, 100,000 units with a probability of 0.5, or 110,000 units with a probability of 0.2.

2. The variable manufacturing costs per unit may be $5.10 with a probability of 0.2, $5.00 with a probability of 0.6, or $4.80 with a probability of 0.2.

3. The managed costs and the committed costs are $45,000 and $280,000, respectively, if the sales volume is 80,000 units, $70,000 and $280,000 if the sales volume is 100,000 units, or $80,000 and $280,000 if the sales volume is 110,000 units.

Required:

Assuming the unit selling price is $10 and the tax rate 50 percent, compute the expected value of net income after tax using a probability tree analysis.

(Adapted with permission from W. L. Ferrara and Jack C. Hayya, "Probabilistic Profit Budgets," Management Accounting, October 1970, p. 27.)

4.21   ***Probability Tree Analysis***   Langdon Enterprises Ltd., manufacturer of the industrial chemical product Zincate, has excess production capacity for the coming year. The firm recently received a special order for Chloromine at $3 per gallon. Subsequent discussions with the prospective buyer indicated that while the purchase order would be effective for the coming year only, the total quantity to be supplied could be expected to range between 40,000 and 80,000 gallons. Management must decide whether the special order should be accepted, and it has provided the following data on Chloromine:

1.

	Anticipated Sales Volume (Gallons)		
	40,000	**60,000**	**80,000**
Probability	0.40	0.50	0.10

2.

	Anticipated Variable Costs per Gallon	
	$2.20	**$2.60**
Probability	0.6	0.4

3. Fixed production costs are expected to amount to $33,000, representing anticipated out-of-pocket outlays for equipment, supplies, and so forth, in connection with the special order. The equipment will be scrapped once the order is filled. No other costs are expected to be incurred.

Noting that there are six possible states (outcomes) for sales volume and variable costs, the president requests your advice regarding the special order as described in Figure 1.

Figure 1   Decision Tree

	Sales Volume	Variable Costs	State
	40,000	2.20	1
		2.60	2
Accept Order	60,000	2.20	3
		2.60	4
	80,000	2.20	5
		2.60	6

Required:

1. Prepare a comparative statement that shows the following for each of the six states that may occur (if the order is accepted):

    a. Incremental income (profit). Submit all computations.

    b. Probability of occurrence. Submit all computations.

2. What is the probability that incremental income from the special order will be negative?

3. Compute the *expected* incremental income (profit) obtained by accepting the special order. Submit all computations.

4. Should Langdon accept the special order? Discuss your reasons briefly.

Note: You will save considerable time if you work with contribution margin per gallon rather than total sales and total variable costs.

(SMA adapted)

4.22   *Linear Programming Formulation*   The Frey Company manufactures and sells two products, a toddler bike and a toy high chair. The company uses linear programming to determine the best production and sales mix of bikes and chairs. This approach allows Frey to speculate on economic changes. For example, management often wants to know how variations in selling price, resource cost, resource availability, and marketing strategy would affect the company's performance.

The demand for bikes and chairs is relatively constant throughout the year. The following economic data pertain to the two products:

	Bicycle (B)	Chair (C)
Selling Price per Unit	$12	$10
Variable Cost per Unit	8	7
Contribution Margin per Unit	$ 4	$ 3
Raw Materials Required		
Wood	1 board foot	2 board feet
Plastic	2 pounds	1 pound
Direct Labor Required	2 hours	2 hours

Estimates of the resource quantities available in a nonvacation month during the year are wood, 10,000 board feet; plastic, 10,000 pounds; and direct labor, 12,000 hours.

The graphic formulation of the constraints of the linear programming model Frey

Figure 2   *Decision Analysis*

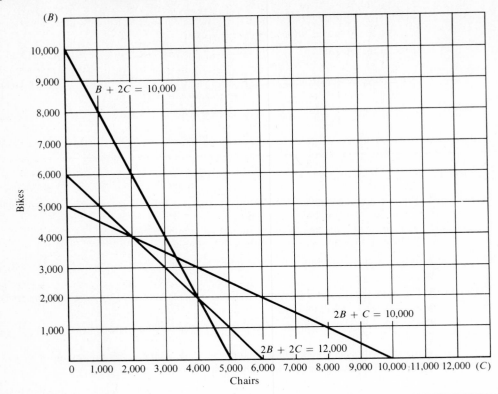

Company has developed for nonvacation months is presented in Figure 2. The algebraic formulation of the model for the nonvacation months is as follows:

Objective function: Max. $Z = 4B + 3C$.

Constraints:

$B + 2C \leq 10,000$ board feet.

$2B + C \leq 10,000$ pounds.

$2B + 2C \leq 12,000$ direct-labor hours.

$B, C \geq 0$.

The results from the linear programming model indicate that Frey Company can maximize its contribution margin (and, thus, its profits) for a nonvacation month by producing and selling 4,000 toddler bikes and 2,000 toy high chairs. This sales mix will yield a total contribution margin of $22,000 in a month.

Required:
1. Due to vacations during June, July, and August, the total direct-labor hours available are reduced from 12,000 to 10,000.

a. What would be the best product mix and maximum total contribution margin during a month when only 10,000 direct-labor hours are available?

b. Based upon your solution for part a, what is the shadow price of direct-labor hours in the original model for a nonvacation month?

2. Competition in the toy market is very strong, so the prices of the two products tend to fluctuate. Can analysis of data from the linear programming model provide information to management that will indicate when price changes made to meet market conditions will alter the optimum product mix? Explain your answer.

(CMA adapted)

4.23

Marginal Income Calculations with Probabilities   Commercial Products Corporation, an audit client, requested your assistance in determining the potential loss on a binding purchase contract that will be in effect at the end of the corporation's fiscal year. The corporation produces a chemical compound that deteriorates and must be discarded if not sold by the end of the month it is produced.

The total variable cost of the manufactured compound is $25 per unit, and it is sold for $40 per unit. The compound can be purchased from a vertically integrated competitor at $40 per unit, plus $5 freight per unit. It is estimated that failure to fill orders would result in the complete loss of eight out of ten customers placing orders for the compound.

Commercial Products has sold the compound for the past thirty months. Demand has been irregular, and there is no sales trend. During this period, sales per month have been the following:

Units Sold per Month	Number of Months [a]
4,000	6
5,000	15
6,000	9

[a] Occurred in random sequence.

1. Prepare a schedule (with supporting computations in good form) for each of the following:

a. Probability of sales of 4,000, 5,000, or 6,000 units in any month.

b. Marginal income if sales of 4,000, 5,000, or 6,000 units are made in one month and 4,000, 5,000, or 6,000 units are manufactured for sale in the same month. Assume all sales orders are filled. (Such a schedule is sometimes called a *payoff table*.)

c. Average monthly marginal income the corporation should expect over the long run if 5,000 units are manufactured every month and all sales orders are filled.

The primary ingredient used to manufacture the compound costs $12 per unit of compound. There is a 60 percent chance that the plant supplying this ingredient will be shut down indefinitely by a strike. A substitute ingredient is available at $18 per unit of compound, but Commercial Products must contract immediately to purchase the substitute, or it will be unavailable when needed. A firm purchase contract for either the primary or substitute ingredient must now be made with one of the suppliers for production next month. If an order were placed for the primary ingredient and a strike should occur, Commercial Products would be released from the contract, and management would purchase the compound from the competitor. Assume that 5,000 units are to be manufactured, and all sales orders are to be filled.

2. Compute the monthly marginal income from sales of 4,000, 5,000, and 6,000 units if the substitute ingredient were ordered.

3. Prepare a schedule computing the average monthly marginal income the corporation could expect if the primary ingredient were ordered with the existing probability of a strike at the supplier's plant. Assume that the expected average monthly marginal income from manufacturing will be $65,000 using the primary ingredient or $35,000 using the substitute, and the expected average monthly loss from purchasing from the competitor will be $25,000.

4. Should management order the primary or substitute ingredient during the anticipated strike period (under the assumptions stated in part 3)? Why?

5. Should management purchase the compound from the competitor to fill sales orders when the orders cannot otherwise be filled? Why?

(AICPA adapted)

4.24 ***Linear Programming Formulation*** The Witchell Corporation manufactures and sells three grades of a single wood product: A, B and C. Each grade must be processed through three phases—cutting, fitting, and finishing—before it is sold. The following unit information is provided:

	A	**B**	**C**
Selling Price	$10.00	$15.00	$20.00
Direct Labor	5.00	6.00	9.00
Direct Materials	0.70	0.70	1.00
Variable Overhead	1.00	1.20	1.80
Fixed Overhead	0.60	0.72	1.08
Materials Requirements (in Board Feet)	7	7	10
Labor Requirements (in Hours)			
Cutting	3/6	3/6	4/6
Fitting	1/6	1/6	2/6
Finishing	1/6	2/6	3/6

Only 5,000 board feet can be obtained per week. The cutting department has 180 hours of labor available each week, whereas the fitting and finishing departments each have 120 hours. No overtime is allowed. Contract commitments require the company to make 50 units of grade A per week. In addition, company policy is to produce at least 50 additional units of grade A, 50 units of B, and 50 units of C each week to actively remain in each of the three markets. Because of competition, only 130 units of grade C can be sold each week.

Required:

1. Formulate and label the linear objective function and the constraint functions necessary to maximize the contribution margin.

2. The graph in Figure 3 presents the constraint functions for a chair manufacturing company whose production problem can be solved by linear programming. The company earns $8 for each kitchen chair sold and $5 for each office chair.

What is the profit-maximizing production schedule? How did you select this production schedule?

(CMA adapted)

4.25 ***Weather Predictions and Profitability*** Food Products, Inc., has the following problem and requests guidelines that can be applied in the future to obtain the largest net income.

Figure 3   Linear Programming Graph

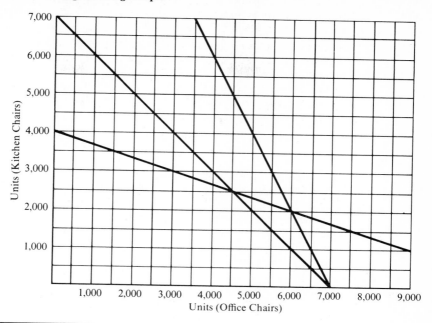

A Food Products plant on the coast produces a food product and ships its production of 10,000 units per day in an airplane owned by Food Products. The area is sometimes fogbound, and shipment then can be made only by rail. The plant does not operate unless shipments are made. Extra preparation costs for rail shipment reduce the marginal contribution of this product from $.40 per unit to $.18 per unit, and there is an additional fixed cost of $3,100 for modification of packaging facilities to convert to rail shipment (incurred only once per conversion). The fog may last for several days; Food Products normally starts shipping by rail only after rail shipments become necessary to meet commitments to customers.

A meteorological report reveals that during the past ten years, the area has been fogbound 250 times for one day, and fog continued 100 times for a second consecutive day, 40 times for a third consecutive day, 20 times for a fourth consecutive day, and 10 times for a fifth consecutive day. Occurrences and lengths of fog were both random. Fog never continued more than five days, and there were never two separate occurrences of fog in any six-day period.

Required:
1. Prepare a schedule presenting the computation of the daily marginal contribution (ignoring fixed conversion cost)
  a. When there is no fog and shipment is made by air.
  b. When there is fog and shipment is made by rail.

2. Prepare a schedule presenting the computation of the probabilities of the possible combinations of foggy and clear weather on the days following a fogbound day. Your schedule should show the probability that, if fog first occurs on a particular day,
  a. The next four days will be foggy.
  b. The next three days will be foggy, and the fifth day will be clear.

c. The next two days will be foggy, and the fourth and fifth days will be clear.

d. The next day will be foggy, and the third, fourth, and fifth days will be clear.

e. The next four days will be clear.

3. Assume you determine it is probable that it would be unprofitable to start shipping by rail on either the fourth or fifth consecutive foggy day. Prepare a schedule presenting the computation of the probable marginal income or loss that should be expected from rail shipments if they were started on the third consecutive foggy day and the probability that the next two days will be foggy is 0.25; if the probability that the next day will be foggy and the fifth day clear is 0.25; and if the probability that the next two days will be clear is 0.50.

(AICPA adapted)

4.26   *Hospital Breakeven*   The Columbus Hospital operates a general hospital but rents space and beds to separate entities for specialized areas such as pediatrics, maternity, psychiatric, and so on. Columbus charges each separate entity for common services to its patients such as meals and laundry and for administrative services such as billings, collections, and so on. All uncollectible accounts are charged directly to the entity. Space and bed rentals are fixed for the year.

For the entire year ended June 30, 19X3, the pediatrics department at Columbus Hospital charged each patient an average of $65 per day, had a capacity of 60 beds, operated 24 hours per day for 365 days, and had revenue of $1,138,800.

Expenses charged by the hospital to the pediatrics department for the year ended June 30, 19X3, were as follows:

	Basis of Allocation	
	Patient Days	Bed Capacity
Dietary	$ 42,952	
Janitorial		$ 12,800
Laundry	28,000	
Laboratory, Other Than Direct Charges to Patients	47,800	
Pharmacy	33,800	
Repairs and Maintenance	5,200	7,140
General Administrative Services		131,760
Rent		275,320
Billings and Collections	40,000	
Bad Debt Expense	47,000	
Other	18,048	25,980
	$262,800	$453,000

The only personnel directly employed by the pediatrics department are supervising nurses, nurses, and aides. The hospital has minimum personnel requirements based on total annual patient days. Hospital requirements beginning at the minimum expected level of operation follow:

Annual Patient Days	Aides	Nurses	Supervising Nurses
10,000–14,000	21	11	4
14,001–17,000	22	12	4
17,001–23,725	22	13	4
23,726–25,550	25	14	5
25,551–27,375	26	14	5
27,376–29,200	29	16	6

These staffing levels represent full-time equivalents, and it should be assumed that the pediatrics department always employs only the minimum number of required full-time equivalent personnel.

Annual salaries for each class of employee are supervising nurses, $18,000; nurses, $13,000; and aides, $5,000. Salary expense for the year ended June 30, 19X3, for supervising nurses, nurses, and aides was $72,000, $169,000, and $110,000, respectively.

The pediatrics department operated at 100 percent capacity during 111 days for the past year. It is estimated that during 90 of these capacity days, the demand averaged 17 patients more than capacity and even went as high as 20 patients more on some days. The hospital has an additional 20 beds available for rent for the year ending June 30, 19X4.

Required:

1. Calculate the minimum number of patient days required for the pediatrics department to break even for the year ending June 30, 19X4, if the additional 20 beds are not rented. Patient demand is unknown, but assume that revenue per patient day, cost per bed, and employee salary rates will remain the same as for the year ended June 30, 19X3. Present calculations in good form.

2. Assume for purposes of this problem that patient demand, revenue per patient day, cost per patient day, cost per bed, and employee salary rates for the year ending June 30, 19X4, remain the same as for the year ended June 30, 19X3. Should the pediatrics department rent the additional 20 beds? Show the annual gain or loss from the additional beds. Present calculations in good form.

(AICPA adapted)

4.27   ***Linear Programming: Graphic Solution and Simplex Method***   The Berry Company produces electric toothbrushes and electric toys, each of which is processed through two operating departments. The maximum machine time in department 1 is 120 hours and in department 2, 180 hours. Machine time for processing a unit in each department follows:

Department	Hours Required by 1 Unit of	
	Electric Brush	Electric Toy
1	6	4
2	3	10

The unit contribution margin is $55 for an electric toy and $45 for an electric toothbrush.

Required:

1. Formulate an objective function to maximize the contribution margin and all the constraints applicable to this function.

2. Determine graphically the number of electric toothbrushes and electric toys that should be manufactured to maximize the total contribution margin.

3. Solve the linear programming problem using the simplex method.

4.28   ***Economic Breakeven Model***   The Hassan Manufacturing Company has the following cost and revenue structure:

Volume of Production	Total Cost	Total Revenue
5	8	7
20	21	14
15	17	10
10	12	7
20	23	16
10	14	9
15	19	12
5	6	5

Required:

1. Using the least squares method, estimate the total cost and the total revenue functions.

2. Determine the breakeven volume and optimal volume of production.

4.29   ***Shadow Prices***   The KingKong Company produces two toys, King and Kong, which contribute $10 and $5 per unit, respectively, to profits. The maximum machine time available is 100 hours. The maximum amount of material Z is 30 units. Each unit of King requires 10 machine hours, and each unit of Kong requires 4 machine hours. Only Kong requires material; each unit of Kong requires 2 units of material Z.

Required:

1. Formulate the objective function to maximize the profits and the constraints applicable to that function.

2. Solve the problem using the simplex method.

3. Determine the range over which the shadow prices are valid.

Of all possible organizational styles of management, the ones most likely to create problems are the "fire fighting" and "tunnel vision" approaches. Fire fighting consists of reacting to events and crises when they appear; tunnel vision is a selective perception of what constitutes the organization's concern.

Planning is an effective mechanism to counter both the fire fighting and tunnel vision management styles. It allows the organization to define its relationship with the environment and is "a method of guiding managers so that their decisions and actions are set to the future of the organization in a consistent and rational manner, and in a way desired by top management."[1] Planning has also been defined as "a process which begins with objectives; defines strategies, policies and detailed plans to achieve them; which establishes an organization to implement decisions; and feedback to introduce a new planning cycle."[2]

These definitions describe planning as the process of collecting information on objectives and making decisions on the best way to achieve them. Planning is vital to an organization's future success. Stanley Thune and Robert House analyzed the planning function in thirty-six similar firms in six industries. They concluded that (1) those firms which rely on a formal planning department were more successful than those which rely on informal planning, and (2) those firms which rely on a formal planning department perform more successfully after the system is instituted than previously.[3] Planning prepares firms to operate in a dynamic world and to adapt to the ensuing changes in technology, financing, resource availability, economic conditions, and so forth. Because of the benefits of planning, it is not surprising that most firms of all sizes and industries rely on some type of formal planning system.[4]

---

[1] David W. Ewing, *The Practice of Planning* (New York: Harper & Row, 1968).

[2] G. A. Steiner, *Top Management Planning* (New York: Macmillan, 1969).

[3] Stanley Thune and Robert House, "Where Long-range Planning Pays Off," *Business Horizons* (October 1970), pp. 81–87.

[4] J. Bacon, *Planning and Forecasting in the Smaller Company* (New York: Conference Board, 1971). In a study of ninety-three companies, each with two thousand or fewer employees, Bacon found that only four do not plan at all.

This chapter elaborates on planning principles and examines budgeting as a formalization of planning in the organization. It illustrates the technical preparation of the master budget and describes budgeting under uncertainty in a Bayesian framework. The chapter concludes with an examination of the behavioral considerations in budgeting.

5.1   GOAL CONGRUENCE:
THE MAIN OBJECTIVE OF PLANNING AND CONTROL

Cost accounting systems, also known as management control systems or control systems, consist of rules and procedures aimed at the accumulation and communication of relevant cost information for internal decision making. These control systems formalize the objectives of the organization and express them operationally as performance criteria to be met by the individuals in the organization. Central to the efficient working of the control systems is goal congruence, that is, the harmonization of the individual and group objectives within the organization and the objectives of the organization as a whole. Robert N. Anthony was perhaps the first to stress the importance of goal congruence. In 1964 he wrote

Essentially, therefore, the control system should be designed so that actions that it leads people to take, in accordance with their perceived self-interest, are actions that are also in the best interests of the company. In the language of social psychology, the system should encourage goal congruence. . . . Perfect congruence between individual goals and organizational goals does not exist, but as a minimum the system should not encourage the individual to act against the best interests of the company.[5]

Goal congruence is achieved when individuals in the organization strive or are induced to strive toward the company goals. This assumes, of course, that the individuals are aware of the company goals and the derivative performance criteria.

The essence of a company's goals is conveyed by the planning process, which expresses these goals in terms of *budgets*, standards, and other formal measures of performance. Management must tailor the planning activities to encourage goal congruence at various levels of management. To achieve goal congruence the following ideas are important.[6]

First, the firm should be viewed as a pluralist entity where coalitions of individuals seek to express their own aspirations within the structure of the firm. Personnel cannot be viewed only as people sharing the same goal, but also as people striving for such rewards as power, security, survival, and autonomy.[7] K. J. Arrow observes:

An organization is a group of individuals seeking to achieve some common goals, or, in different language, to maximize an objective function. Each member has objectives of his own, in general not coincident with those of the organization. Each member also has some range of decisions to make within limits set partly by the environment external to the organization and partly by the decisions of other members. Finally, some but not all

---

[5] Robert N. Anthony, *Management Accounting*, 3d ed. (Homewood, Ill.: Irwin, 1964), p. 362.

[6] Lee D. Parker, "Goal Congruence: A Misguided Concept," *Abacus* (June 1976), pp. 3–13.

[7] C. Perrow, *Complex Organizations: A Critical Essay* (Glenview, Ill.: Scott, Foresman, 1972), pp. 160–163.

observations about the workings of the organization and about the external world are communicated from one member to another.[8]

Second, while profit maximization has long been considered the single goal of the firm, in reality, corporations pursue a range of goals. For example, the General Electric Company emphasizes multiple goals by stressing that organizational performance be measured in the following eight areas: (1) profitability, (2) market position, (3) productivity, (4) product leadership, (5) personnel development, (6) employee attitudes, (7) public responsibility, and (8) a balance between short-range and long-range goals.

Third, the goals of the firm may also conflict with one another and with the individual and group objectives. A bargaining process may be necessary to reduce these conflicts in the goal-setting process.[9] In fact, the budget may be considered the key mechanism for the stabilization of that process, that is, "a bargaining medium through which individuals and groups try to further their own goals."[10]

5.2 FROM PLANNING TO BUDGETING

Anthony's decision systems framework, presented in chapter 1, distinguishes between planning and budgeting. Planning—or, precisely, strategic planning—takes place at the strategic planning level and principally involves elaboration of organizational goals and the strategies necessary to accomplish them. Planning reflects the organization's desire to face the future in a rational manner by providing a general guide to managerial decision making. In general, strategic planning is subdivided into two activities: business planning and diversification planning, which are defined as follows:

Business planning *is the process of determining the scope of organizational activities that will be undertaken toward the satisfaction of a broad consumer need, of deciding on the objectives of the organization in its defined area of operations, and of evaluating the effectiveness with which varying magnitudes of resources may be committed toward achieving those objectives.*

Diversification planning *is the process of deciding on the objectives of a corporation, including the determination of which and how many lines of business to engage in, of acquiring the resources needed to attain those objectives, and of allocating resources among the different businesses in a manner intended to achieve those objectives.*[11]

The strategic planning process is followed by a management control process the purpose of which is to insure that the long-term plans emerging from business and diversification planning are implemented over the years. The management control process, therefore, is a communication and interaction process for the implementation of strategic plans, and *its success rests on budgeting.* Budgeting, then, is the most conspicuous evidence of the planning process. The budget, the formal means by which the planning process takes

[8]K. J. Arrow, "Control in Large Organizations," *Management Science* (April 1964), pp. 397–408.
[9]R. M. Cyert and J. G. March, *A Behavioral Theory of the Firm* (Englewood Cliffs, N.J.: Prentice-Hall, 1963), pp. 4–43, 83–177.
[10]C. Perrow, *Complex Organizations*, p. 162.
[11]Robert N. Anthony, J. Dearden, and R. F. Vancil, *Management Control Systems: Text Cases and Readings* (Homewood, Ill.: Irwin, 1972), p. 466.

shape, ties together the diverse activities of the firm that are related to specific goals and specifies the means for their realization. W. J. Vatter defines budgets as follows:

Budgets state formally—in terms of expected transactions—the decisions of all levels of management about the resources to be acquired, how they are to be used, and what ought to result. Budgets put the details of management plans for operations in money units, so that the results may be projected into expected financial statements.[12]

In short, planning precedes budgeting, and budgets are quantitative, and mostly monetary, short-term expressions of plans.

5.3   BUDGETING PRINCIPLES

5.3.1   Nature of Budgeting

Most companies, large or small, prepare budgets. The budget is a quantitative monetary expression of future activities covering a specific period of time, usually one year. The budget, also called a *master budget*, is used as a tool for planning in both centralized and decentralized firms. The following are among the purposes of budgets and budgeting:

1. The budget is used to plan and coordinate the overall activities of the firm, and it forces management to quantify their expectations.

2. The budget is used to communicate to all employees the goals and objectives of the firm and the means to be used to attain them.

3. The budget is used to assign to each employee the responsibility for the performance of a given activity, task, or program, and it serves as a final guide in evaluating the adequacy of the employee's performance.

4. The budget is used to give management a chance to examine environmental conditions and changes, thereby increasing their potential to reduce uncertainty and shape the firm's future progress.

5. The budget is used to create a harmony between all functional areas of the firm (sales, marketing, production, purchasing, finance, personnel, and so forth) by specifying what each functional area manager must do to optimize the performance in other areas and in the firm as a whole.

5.3.2   Types of Budgets

Budgeting is sometimes referred to as *periodic budgeting*, because budgets are usually prepared for specific time periods, such as one year or five years. The annual profit plan is the master budget, which may be broken down by months or quarters. The master budget is a *continuous budget* if a budget for one month (or one quarter) is added as one

---

[12]W. J. Vatter, *Operating Budgets* (Belmont, Calif.: Wadsworth Publishing, 1969), pp. 15–16.

month (or one quarter) goes by. The firm then has an annual profit plan at all times. Budgets are not always connected to a time period. For example, a *project budget* or *product budget* serves as a general guideline to probable results of a project or product. It emphasizes the various stages of the project or product rather than the periods. There is a connection to periods, however, because the cash requirements for the project or product budgets are considered in the cash budget as a component of the master budget.

The *capital budget* specifies the future expenditures for fixed assets over a given number of years. It is a major component of the strategic plan outlining the long-term future of the firm. The capital budget also affects periodic budgeting, because the cash requirements for the fixed asset purchases are periodically specified in the cash budget as a component of the master budget.

5.3.3   Advantages of Budgeting

The use of budgeting has many advantages. It may lead to better performance of individuals in the organization because of better performance by the managers. Budgets may motivate managers to accomplish the organizational objectives if they are used to communicate company objectives; establish subobjectives in accord with managerial objectives; and provide a thoroughly understood, common basis for performance measurement and feedback. Thus, budgets motivate people by providing information for the comparison of expected and actual performance. When such evaluation of performance is known to result in rewards and penalties, people are more often motivated to do their best.

Because budgets are quantitative plans for action, they may force management to examine carefully the available resources and determine how these can be used efficiently.

Budgets make expectations concrete by letting people know what is expected of them. They require specific quantification of ideas.

Budgets are essential tools of coordination. They provide an integration of all the production factors and all the departments and functions of an organization; thus, the organization's joint objectives are obtained, and a congruence is insured between the goals of the individual managers and the goals of the organization as a whole. By using budgets to coordinate activities, a firm is more likely to operate at an optimal level, given the constraints on its resources. Hence the budgeting of departmental activities insures their coordination, so bottlenecks do not occur and interdepartmental conflicts are reduced.

Budgets are essential tools to communicate expectations. When a budget is distributed to those responsible for various parts of it, the individual managers become more aware of where they fit in the organization.

5.3.4   Budgeting Procedures

The budgeting procedures and the construction of a master budget usually are supervised by a budget committee, which may include members representing the firm's divisions or functions (sales, marketing, production, purchasing, finance, personnel, and so forth). A budget director, generally the controller or the chief financial officer, serves as head of the budget committee.

Although they differ from one organization to another, the budgeting procedures are likely to resemble the following:

1. Top management develops the overall goals of the organization and includes them in the firm's strategic plan.

2. Keeping in mind the overall organizational goals, the budget committee determines the basic economic forecasts outlining the future progress of the company and communicates these long-term forecasts to the divisions or departments.

3. Each division or department determines its operating budgets in line with the overall goals and basic economic forecasts outlined for the company. These operating budgets then are communicated to the budget committee.

4. The budget committee reviews and coordinates the budgets and either asks for revision or approves the submitted budgets. When all the submitted budgets are approved, the budget committee puts the master budget in final form, which is then communicated to the various departments or divisions to serve as a guide for action and control.

5.4   THE MASTER BUDGET ILLUSTRATED

As an annual profit plan, the master budget expresses the company's *financial* position and *operational* performance for the next year. The budgets comprising the master budget, accompanied by their subsidiary schedules, include the following:

I. Operating budget.
　A. Sales budget.
　B. Production budget (for manufacturing concerns).
　　1. Production budget or changes in inventory levels budget.
　　2. Material usage and purchases budget.
　　3. Direct-labor budget.
　　4. Overhead budget.
　C. Cost of goods sold budget.
　D. Budgeted income statement.
II. Financial budget.
　A. Cash budget.
　B. Budgeted balance sheet.
　C. Budgeted statement of changes in the financial position.

Section 5.4 describes the master budget of the Monti Company. The basic data are followed by a step-by-step procedure for the preparation of the master budget. Although only one draft of the budget is presented, in reality further drafts may be required before a final budget is decided on.

5.4.1   Basic Information

The Monti Company is preparing its master budget immediately after the close of the year 19XA. Ali Azhar, the budget director, together with a budget committee, has gathered the following data and requirements:

1. The balance sheet for the year just ended, 19XA, is given here:

Monti Company
Balance Sheet
December 13, 19XA

Assets			Equities		
Current Assets			**Current Liabilities**		
Cash	$ 10,000		Accounts Payable	$ 1,000	
Accounts Receivable	10,000		Wages Payable	1,000	
Material Inventory (10,000 Units)	10,000		Total Current Liabilities		$ 2,000
Finished Goods Inventory (2,500 Units)	10,000		**Stockholders' Equity**		
Total Current Assets		$ 40,000	Common Stock, No Par, 2,000 Shares Outstanding	$200,000	
			Retained Earnings	48,000	
Fixed Assets			Total Stockholders' Equity		248,000
Land	$150,000				
Buildings and Equipment	100,000		Total Equities		$250,000
Accumulated Depreciation	(40,000)	210,000			
Total Assets		$250,000			

2. The expected monthly gross sales for 19XB are as follows:

Month	Volume (in Units)	Unit Selling Price (in Dollars)
January	5,000	5
February	5,000	5
March	5,000	5
April	5,000	10
May	10,000	10
June	15,000	10
July	15,000	10
August	10,000	10
September	10,000	10
October	5,000	5
November	5,000	5
December	5,000	5
	95,000	
January 19XC	5,000	$5

3. The sales discounts, returns, and allowances are estimated to be 10 percent of gross sales. Net sales consist of 40 percent cash and 60 percent credit. All credit sales are collected in the month following the sales.

4. At the end of each month, the Monti Company desires an ending finished goods inventory equal to 50 percent of the sales of the following month.

5. There are no work-in-process inventories.

6. Each finished goods unit requires 2 units of a direct material (X), the price of which is estimated to be $1 per unit.

7. At the end of each month, the Monti Company desires an ending material inventory equal to 100 percent of the materials requirements for the following month. However, for April and May, the company wants to maintain an ending material inventory equal to 50 percent of the material requirements of the following month.

8. The purchase discounts, returns, and allowances are estimated to be equal to 10 percent of the gross purchases.

9. Each unit of finished goods requires 0.5 hour of direct labor at $2 per hour.

10. The Monti Company pays 40 percent of its direct-labor costs the same month they are incurred. It pays the 60 percent balance the following month.

11. Net purchases consist of 40 percent cash and 60 percent credit.

12. At the anticipated volume for 19XB, the company will incur the following costs:

Factory Overhead

Supplies	$10,000, to Be Paid 60% in June and 40% in December
Indirect Labor	20,000, to Be Paid 50% in June and 50% in December
Maintenance-Variable Portion	1,000, to Be Paid in June
Power-Variable Portion	1,500, to Be Paid in December
Property Taxes	500, to Be Paid in June
Depreciation	500
Payroll Fringe Costs	10,000, to Be Paid 50% in June and 50% in December
Maintenance-Fixed Portion	2,000, to Be Paid in June
Power-Fixed Portion	1,000, to Be Paid 50% in June and 50% in December
Miscellaneous-Fixed Portion	1,000, to Be Paid 50% in June and 50% in December
	$47,500

Selling and Administrative Overhead

Travel	$10,000, to Be Paid in December
Sales Commissions	4,000, to Be Paid in December
Salaries	12,000, to Be Paid $1,000 per Month
Depreciation	23,500
	$49,500

13. The Monti Company expects to issue common stock for $100,000 in August and bonds for $40,000 in December.

14. The Monti Company expects to purchase a new machine for $150,000 in April to be paid three months later.

15. Two parcels of land will be purchased in February to be paid as follows: $50,000 in April, $35,000 in May, $50,000 in June, $50,000 in July, $70,000 in August, $50,000 in September, $25,000 in October, and $25,000 in November.

16. The company borrows or repays money in multiples of $100 at an interest rate of 10 percent per year. Borrowing is generally done at the beginning of the month and repayment at the end of the month. Any excess of total cash available over total cash needed is used to repay the maximum principal and the corresponding interest. Any deficiency is corrected by borrowing the necessary cash.

17. The Monti Company expects to maintain a minimum monthly cash balance of $30,000.

18. The sales for January 19XB will be 5,000 units at $5 per unit.

5.4.2   *Sales Budget*

The first step in budgeting is the determination of the sales budget. This sets the level of anticipated activity upon which inventory levels, production, and expenses are planned. Table 5.1 shows the sales budget for the Monti Company for 19XB. The sales budget includes units expected to be sold; the selling price; the total expected gross sales; the sales discounts, returns, and allowances; the net sales; the cash and credit sales; the total cash collections; and the accounts receivable by month. The preparation of the sales budget, therefore, depends on the estimation of the following information:

1. The sales forecast in units.

2. The selling price or pricing policy of the firm.

3. The proportion of cash sales or the sales credit policy of the firm.

4. The cash collection policy, bad debt history, and average time lag between sales and collections.

5. The proportion of sales discounts, returns, and allowances.

5.4.3   *Production Budget (Changes in Inventory Levels Budget)*

Once the sales budget has been determined, the production budget can be prepared. Assuming the firm has a finished goods inventory policy, the desired monthly ending inventory can be compared with the monthly sales estimates to determine the monthly production. In equation form, the relationship is

$$\text{Units to be produced} = \text{Desired ending inventory} + \text{Estimated sales} \\ - \text{Desired beginning inventory.}$$

Table 5.2 illustrates the Monti Company's production budget for 19XB. It includes the estimated sales, ending inventory, total units needed, beginning inventory, and units to be produced by month. The preparation of the production budget, therefore, rests on an estimation of:

1. The sales forecast in units (provided now by the sales budget).

2. The inventory objectives or inventory policy of the firm.

5.4.4   *Material Usage and Purchases Budget*

Once the production budget is determined, the material usage and purchases budget can be prepared. On the basis of the estimated production and the number of units of material required to produce one unit of finished goods, the number of units of material needed for production is determined. Assuming the firm has a material inventory policy, the desired monthly ending material inventory can be compared with the monthly production estimates to determine the monthly material purchases. In equation form, the relationship is

$$\text{Units to be purchased} = \text{Desired ending material inventory} + \text{Units of material} \\ \text{needed for production} - \text{Beginning material inventory.}$$

Table 5.1 *Monti Company Sales Budget for the Year Ending December 31, 19XB*

	January	February	March	April	May
Volume	5,000	5,000	5,000	5,000	10,000
Selling Price	$ 5	$ 5	$ 5	$ 10	$ 10
Gross Sales	$25,000	$25,000	$25,000	$50,000	$100,000
Sales Discounts, Returns, and Allowances	$ 2,500	$ 2,500	$ 2,500	$ 5,000	$ 10,000
Net Sales	$22,500	$22,500	$22,500	$45,000	$ 90,000
Cash Sales, 40%	$ 9,000	$ 9,000	$ 9,000	$18,000	$ 36,000
Credit Sales, 60%	$13,500	$13,500	$13,500	$27,000	$ 54,000
Cash Collections					
1. Cash Sales This Month	$ 9,000	$ 9,000	$ 9,000	$18,000	$ 36,000
2. Credit Sales of Last Month Collected	$10,000	$13,500	$13,500	$13,500	$ 27,000
3. Total Collections	$19,000	$22,500	$22,500	$31,500	$ 63,000
Accounts Receivable	$13,500	$13,500	$13,500	$27,000	$ 54,000

Table 5.2 *Monti Company Production Budget in Units for the Year Ending December 31, 19XB*

	January	February	March	April	May
Estimated Sales	5,000	5,000	5,000	5,000	10,000
+ Ending Inventory	2,500[a]	2,500	2,500	5,000	7,500
= Total Needed	7,500	7,500	7,500	10,000	17,500
− Beginning Inventory	2,500	2,500	2,500	2,500	5,000
= Units to Be Produced	5,000	5,000	5,000	7,500	12,500

[a] 0.5 × February sales of 5,000 units.

Table 5.3 *Monti Company Material Usage and Purchases Budget for the Year Ending December 31, 19XB*

	January	February	March	April	May
Finished Goods: Units to be Produced[a]	5,000	5,000	5,000	7,500	12,500
Units of Material Needed for Production	10,000	10,000	10,000	15,000	25,000
Ending Material Inventory	10,000	10,000	15,000	12,500	15,000
Total Needed	20,000	20,000	25,000	27,500	40,000
Beginning Material Inventory	10,000	10,000	10,000	15,000	12,500
Units to Be Purchased	10,000	10,000	15,000	12,500	27,500
Gross Purchases	$10,000	$10,000	$15,000	$12,500	$27,500
Purchase Discounts, Returns, and Allowances	$ 1,000	$ 1,000	$ 1,500	$ 1,250	$ 2,750
Net Purchases	$ 9,000	$ 9,000	$13,500	$11,250	$24,750
Cash Purchases, 40%	$ 3,600	$ 3,600	$ 5,400	$ 4,500	$ 9,900
Credit Purchases, 60%	$ 5,400	$ 5,400	$ 8,100	$ 6,750	$14,850
Disbursements for Purchases					
1. Cash Purchases	$ 3,600	$ 3,600	$ 5,400	$ 4,500	$ 9,900
2. Credit Purchases of Last Month	$ 1,000	$ 5,400	$ 5,400	$ 8,100	$ 6,750
3. Total Disbursements	$ 4,600	$ 9,000	$10,800	$12,600	$16,650
Accounts Payable	$ 5,400	$ 5,400	$ 8,100	$ 6,750	$14,850

[a] From the production budget (Table 5.2).

Table 5.1   continued

June	July	August	September	October	November	December	Total
15,000	15,000	10,000	10,000	5,000	5,000	5,000	95,000
$ 10	$ 10	$ 10	$ 10	$ 5	$ 5	$ 5	
$150,000	$150,000	$100,000	$100,000	$25,000	$25,000	$25,000	$800,000
$ 15,000	$ 15,000	$ 10,000	$ 10,000	$ 2,500	$ 2,500	$ 2,500	$ 80,000
$135,000	$135,000	$ 90,000	$ 90,000	$22,500	$22,500	$22,500	$720,000
$ 54,000	$ 54,000	$ 36,000	$ 36,000	$ 9,000	$ 9,000	$ 9,000	$288,000
$ 81,000	$ 81,000	$ 54,000	$ 54,000	$13,500	$13,500	$13,500	$432,000
$ 54,000	$ 54,000	$ 36,000	$ 36,000	$ 9,000	$ 9,000	$ 9,000	$288,000
$ 54,000	$ 81,000	$ 81,000	$ 54,000	$54,000	$13,500	$13,500	$428,500
$108,000	$135,000	$117,000	$ 90,000	$63,000	$22,500	$22,500	$716,500
$ 81,000	$ 81,000	$ 54,000	$ 54,000	$13,500	$13,500	$13,500	

Table 5.2   continued

June	July	August	September	October	November	December	Total
15,000	15,000	10,000	10,000	5,000	5,000	5,000	95,000
7,500	5,000	5,000	2,500	2,500	2,500	2,500	47,500
22,500	20,000	15,000	12,500	7,500	7,500	7,500	142,500
7,500	7,500	5,000	5,000	2,500	2,500	2,500	47,500
15,000	12,500	10,000	7,500	5,000	5,000	5,000	95,000

Table 5.3   continued

June	July	August	September	October	November	December	Total
15,000	12,500	10,000	7,500	5,000	5,000	5,000	95,000
30,000	25,000	20,000	15,000	10,000	10,000	10,000	190,000
25,000	20,000	15,000	10,000	10,000	10,000	10,000	162,500
55,000	45,000	35,000	25,000	20,000	20,000	20,000	352,500
15,000	25,000	20,000	15,000	10,000	10,000	10,000	162,500
40,000	20,000	15,000	10,000	10,000	10,000	10,000	190,000
$40,000	$20,000	$15,000	$10,000	$10,000	$10,000	$10,000	$190,000
$ 4,000	$ 2,000	$ 1,500	$ 1,000	$ 1,000	$ 1,000	$ 1,000	$ 19,000
$36,000	$18,000	$13,500	$ 9,000	$ 9,000	$ 9,000	$ 9,000	$171,000
$14,400	$ 7,200	$ 5,400	$ 3,600	$ 3,600	$ 3,600	$ 3,600	$ 68,400
$21,600	$10,800	$ 8,100	$ 5,400	$ 5,400	$ 5,400	$ 5,400	$102,600
$14,400	$ 7,200	$ 5,400	$ 3,600	$ 3,600	$ 3,600	$ 3,600	$ 68,400
$14,850	$21,600	$10,800	$ 8,100	$ 5,400	$ 5,400	$ 5,400	$ 98,200
$29,250	$28,800	$16,200	$11,700	$ 9,000	$ 9,000	$ 9,000	$166,600
$21,600	$10,800	$ 8,100	$ 5,400	$ 5,400	$ 5,400	$ 5,400	$102,600

Table 5.4   *Monti Company Direct-Labor Budget for the Year Ending December 31, 19XB*

	January	February	March	April	May
Finished Goods: Units to Be Produced[a]	5,000	5,000	5,000	7,500	12,500
Total Hours Needed for Production	2,500	2,500	2,500	3,750	6,250
Total Labor Costs Expected	$5,000	$5,000	$5,000	$7,500	$12,500
Disbursements for Wages					
1. 40% of This Month's Expenses	$2,000	$2,000	$2,000	$3,000	$ 5,000
2. 60% of Last Month's Expenses	$1,000	$3,000	$3,000	$3,000	$ 4,500
3. Total Disbursements	$3,000	$5,000	$5,000	$6,000	$ 9,500

[a]From the production budget (Table 5.2).

Table 5.3 illustrates the Monti Company's material usage and purchases budget for 19XB. It includes material usage; inventory levels; units to be purchased; gross purchases; purchase discounts, returns, and allowances; net purchases; cash and credit purchases; disbursements for purchases; and accounts payable. The preparation of the material usage and purchases budget rests on the estimation of the following information:

1. Production (now provided in the production budget).
2. The material requirement for each unit of finished goods, that is, the input mix.
3. The proportion of cash purchases or the purchase credit policy.
4. The purchase price of materials.
5. The disbursement policy, the credit terms extended by suppliers, and the bill-paying habits of the firm.
6. The proportion of purchase discounts, returns, and allowances.
7. The inventory objectives or inventory policy.

5.4.5   Direct-Labor Budget

Once the production budget has been determined, the direct-labor budget can also be prepared. The total hours needed for production is determined on the basis of the estimated production and the number of direct-labor hours required to produce one unit of finished goods. The total direct-labor costs expected are based on a knowledge of the labor rates. Table 5.4 shows the direct-labor budget for the Monti Company for 19XB. It includes the labor usage, labor costs, and disbursements for wages. The direct-labor budget is based on an estimation of

1. Production (now provided in the production budget).
2. The labor rates.
3. The payroll methods or wage disbursements policy.
4. The payroll dates.

5.4.6   Overhead Budget

The overhead budget includes both a factory overhead schedule and a selling and administrative overhead schedule. Once the production level is known, the overhead budget can be prepared, as it depends on the anticipated activity level and upon the behavior of

Table 5.4   *continued*

June	July	August	September	October	November	December	Total
15,000	12,500	10,000	7,500	5,000	5,000	5,000	95,000
7,500	6,250	5,000	3,750	2,500	2,500	2,500	47,500
$15,000	$12,500	$10,000	$7,500	$5,000	$5,000	$5,000	$95,000
$ 6,000	$ 5,000	$ 4,000	$3,000	$2,000	$2,000	$2,000	$38,000
$ 7,500	$ 9,000	$ 7,500	$6,000	$4,500	$3,000	$3,000	$55,000
$13,500	$14,000	$11,500	$9,000	$6,500	$5,000	$5,000	$93,000

Table 5.5   *Monti Company Overhead Budget for the Year Ending December 31, 19XB*

Factory Overhead at an Expected Activity Level of 47,000 Direct-Labor Hours

Supplies	$10,000	
Indirect Labor	20,000	
Maintenance-Variable Portion	1,000	
Power-Variable Portion	1,500	
Payroll Fringe Costs	10,000	
Total Variable Overhead		$42,500
Property Taxes	$ 500	
Depreciation	500	
Maintenance-Fixed Portion	2,000	
Power-Fixed Portion	1,000	
Miscellaneous-Fixed Portion	1,000	
Total Fixed Overhead		$ 5,000
Total Factory Overhead		$47,500
Expected Activity Level		47,500 Direct-Labor Hours
Predetermined Overhead Application Rate		$1.00 per Direct-Labor Hour

Selling and Administrative Overhead

Travel	$10,000
Sales Commissions	4,000
Salaries	12,000
Depreciation	23,500
	$49,500

the individual expense items in relation to the level of activity. The overhead budget can be set at an expected activity level and includes both variable and fixed expenses. Table 5.5 illustrates the Monti Company's overhead budget for 19XB. It includes a detailed list of the factory overhead items, the predetermined overhead application rate, and a detailed list of the selling and administrative overhead items. Its preparation depends on an estimation of:

1. The activity level (now provided in the production budget).

2. The behavior of the individual expense items in relation to the level of activity.

3. The disbursement policy and credit terms extended by suppliers.

5.4.7 *Cost of Goods Sold Budget*

The cost of goods sold budget depends on all the information gathered in the production, material usage and purchases, direct-labor, and overhead budgets. The basic relationship is

Cost of goods sold = Total manufacturing costs
    + Beginning finished goods inventory − Ending finished goods inventory.

The Monti Company's cost of goods sold budget for 19XB is shown in Table 5.6.

5.4.8 *Cash Budget*

The cash budget, or budgeted statement of cash receipts and disbursements, may be prepared once management has prepared the sales, production, material usage and purchases, direct-labor, and overhead budgets, as well as a list of anticipated acquisitions and dispositions of fixed assets, dividend and interest payments to investors, proceeds from new financing, and outflows from long-term debt retirement and stock repurchasing. The cash budget may be considered the most important part of the master budgeting process. It allows the firm to control for its continuous solvency; that is, to have the ability to pay bills when due and to avoid unnecessary idle cash or cash deficiencies by a timely borrowing, repayment, and short-term investment policy. The cash budget, or budgeted statement of cash receipts and disbursements, for the Monti Company is illustrated in Table 5.7. Note the following sections of the cash budget.

Total Cash Available before Current Financing   In general, this is equal to the beginning cash balance, collections from customers (from the sales budget), proceeds from new financing, proceeds—including interest—from marketable securities, and proceeds from dispositions of long-term assets.

Total Disbursements   In general, this is equal to the cash outflow for operations (for purchases and other operations), routine outflows to investors (as dividend and/or interest payments), outflows for long-term debt retirement and treasury stocks, and outflows for acquisition of long-term assets.

Total Cash Needed   In general, this is equal to the total disbursements and a minimum cash balance the firm wants to keep as a security.

Table 5.6 *Monti Company Cost of Goods Sold Budget for the Year Ending December 31, 19XB*

Direct Material Used (from the Material Usage and Purchases Budget) $190,000
Direct Labor Used (from the Direct-Labor Budget) 95,000
Manufacturing Overhead (from the Factory Overhead Budget) 47,500

$332,500

Less: Purchase Discounts, Returns, and Allowances (from the Material Usage and
Purchases Budget) . . . . (19,000)

Total Manufacturing Costs $313,500
Add: Finished Goods Inventory, December 31, 19XA (from the Production Budget) . . . . . 10,000[a]

Total Needed $323,500
Less: Finished Goods Inventory, December 31, 19XB (from the Production Budget) . . . . . 10,000[a]

Cost of Goods Sold $313,500

[a] 2,500 units × $4 = $10,000.

Excess or Deficit of Cash In general, this is equal to the total cash available before current financing *minus* the total cash needed.

Total Effect of Financing In general, this is equal to the amount borrowed in case of a cash deficit, the interest and principal repaid in case of an excess of cash, and the investment in short-term marketable securities in case of an excess of cash.

Ending Cash Balance This is equal to the excess or deficit of cash *minus* the total effect of financing *plus* the minimum cash balance.

Loan Payable This is equal to the outstanding loan *minus* the short-term loan repayments and interest.

The preparation of the cash budget rests on a knowledge of the following information:

1. Cash inflows and outflows from operations.
2. Cash inflows and outflows from capital, financial, and tax activities.
3. The minimum cash balance.
4. The short-term borrowing, repayment, and investment policy. In the Monti Company example, a self-liquidating loan is assumed in the sense that cash borrowed is used for operations, and the cash inflows from operations are used to repay the loan. Known as the *working capital cycle*, this style of management consists of transforming cash into finished goods and into accounts receivable and/or cash.

5.4.9 Budgeted Income Statement

The budgeted income statement may be prepared once the sales, production, material usage and purchases, direct-labor, overhead, cost of goods sold, and cash budgets are

Table 5.7   *Monti Company Cash Budget for the Year Ending December 31, 19XB*

	January	February	March	April	May
Beginning Cash Balance	$10,000	$30,000	$30,079	$33,422	$30,022
Receipts[a]					
1. Collections from Customers	19,000	22,500	22,500	31,500	63,000
2. Issuance of Common Stock	—	—	—	—	—
3. Issuance of Bonds	—	—	—	—	—
Total Available before Current Financing	29,000	52,500	52,579	64,922	93,022
Less Disbursements					
1. For Labor[b]	3,000	5,000	5,000	6,000	9,500
2. For Materials[c]	4,600	9,000	10,800	12,600	16,650
3. For Other Manufacturing Expenses	—	—	—	—	—
4. For Other Nonmanufacturing Expenses	1,000	1,000	1,000	1,000	1,000
5. For Machinery Purchase	—	—	—	—	—
6. For Land Purchase	—	—	—	50,000	35,000
7. Total Disbursements	8,600	15,000	16,800	69,600	62,150
Minimum Cash Balance	30,000	30,000	30,000	30,000	30,000
Total Cash Needed	38,600	45,000	46,800	99,600	92,150
Excess (Deficit)	(9,600)	7,500	5,779	(34,678)	872
Financing					
1. Borrowing	9,600	—	—	34,700	—
2. Repayment	—	(7,300)	(2,300)	—	(800)
3. Interest[d]	—	(121)	(57)	—	(13)
4. Total	9,600	(7,421)	(2,357)	34,700	(813)
Ending Cash Balance	30,000	30,079	33,422	30,022	30,059
Loan Payable	9,600	2,300	0	34,700	33,900

[a] From the Sales Budget (Table 5.1)
[b] From the Direct-Labor Budget (Table 5.4)
[c] From the Material Usage and Purchases Budget (Table 5.3)
[d] Interest calculations are as follows:

```
February:  $  7,300 × 0.10 × 2/12 months = $  121
March:     $  2,300 × 0.10 × 3/12 months = $   57
May:       $    800 × 0.10 × 2/12 months = $   13
August:    $ 33,900 × 0.10 × 5/12 months = $1,412
             11,200 × 0.10 × 3/12 months = $  280
             70,300 × 0.10 × 2/12 months = $1,172
             ───────                        ──────
             $115,400                       $2,864
September: $ 17,800 × 0.10 × 3/12 months = $  445
October:   $ 20,700 × 0.10 × 4/12 months = $  690
December:  $ 11,800 × 0.10 × 2/12 months = $  197
Accrued interest payable, December 31, 19XB:
           $  5,500 × 0.10 × 2/12 months = $   92
```

available. Table 5.8 shows the budgeted income statement for the Monti Company for 19XB. It includes the following sections:

1. Gross sales (from the sales budget).

2. Sales discounts, returns, and allowances (from the sales budget).

3. Cost of goods sold (from the cost of goods sold budget).

4. Selling and administrative expenses (from the overhead budget).

5. Interest expense.

Table 5.7   continued

June	July	August	September	October	November	December
$ 30,059	$ 30,009	$ 30,009	$ 30,045	$30,100	$30,210	$30,010
108,000	135,000	117,000	90,000	63,000	22,500	22,500
—	—	100,000	—	—	—	—
—	—	—	—	—	—	40,000
138,059	165,009	247,009	120,045	93,100	52,710	92,510
13,500	14,000	11,500	9,000	6,500	5,000	5,000
29,250	28,800	16,200	11,700	9,000	9,000	9,000
25,500	—	—	—	—	—	21,500
1,000	1,000	1,000	1,000	1,000	1,000	15,000
—	150,000	—	—	—	—	—
50,000	50,000	70,000	50,000	25,000	25,000	—
119,250	243,800	98,700	71,700	41,500	40,000	50,000
30,000	30,000	30,000	30,000	30,000	30,000	30,000
149,250	273,800	128,700	101,700	71,500	70,000	80,500
(11,191)	(108,791)	118,309	18,345	21,600	(17,290)	12,010
11,200	108,800	—	—	—	17,300	—
		(115,400)	(17,800)	(20,700)	—	(11,800)
		(2,864)	(445)	(690)	—	(197)
11,200	108,800	(118,264)	(18,245)	(21,390)	17,300	(11,997)
30,009	30,009	30,045	30,100	30,210	30,010	30,013
45,100	153,900	38,500	20,700	0	17,300	5,500

5.4.10   *Budgeted Balance Sheet*

The last step in developing the master budget is the preparation of the budgeted balance sheet. Table 5.9 shows the Monti Company's budgeted balance sheet for 19XB. Each of the balance sheet items is derived from the previously computed budgets, namely, the sales, production, material and usage purchases, direct-labor, overhead, cost of goods sold, and cash budgets and the budgeted income statement. For example, the accrued interest payable would be computed by subtracting the interest expenditures (from the cash budget) from the interest expense (from the budgeted income statement).

Table 5.8   ***Monti Company Budgeted Income Statement for the Year Ending December 31, 19XB***

Gross Sales (from the Sales Budget)	$800,000
minus Sales Discounts, Returns, and Allowances (from the Sales Budget)	(80,000)
equals Net Sales	$720,000
minus Cost of Goods Sold (from the Cost of Goods Sold Budget)	313,500
equals Gross Margin	$406,500
Selling and Administrative Expenses (from the Overhead Budget) $49,500	
Interest Expense .... 4,479[a]	
Operating Expenses	$ 53,979
Net Profit before Taxes	$352,521

[a] This was derived from the summation of interest accrued on the loan payable (121 + 57 + 13 + 2864 + 445 + 690 + 197 + 92).

5.5   *COPING WITH UNCERTAINTY*

The master budget prepared in section 5.4 was based on incomplete information, since budgeting is a set of decisions under uncertainty. However, applications of Bayesian statistics have shown that there is a common structure of elements in most decisions under uncertainty, and budgeting is no exception.

The Bayesian analysis approach to a decisional problem consists of two steps. The first is an *a priori analysis*, which consists of choosing the action with the highest expected profit value based on the unconditional probabilities of the states of nature (the a priori probabilities). The second step is an *a posteriori analysis*, which consists of choosing the action with the highest expected profit value based on revised a priori probabilities. Bayes's theorem is the basic technique in reevaluating the a priori probabilities to obtain a posteriori probabilities by the incorporation of new information.

The Bayesian approach to budgeting requires the determination of several factors:

1. The desired objective, such as the maximization of the expected value of the profit or the minimization of the expected value of cost.

2. The possible actions that can be taken.

3. The actuality of possible states of nature.

4. The numerical payoff associated with each possible state of nature and decision.

To illustrate the Bayesian approach to budgeting, let us assume that firm Z is choosing a production volume. Three actions are considered possible, and the firm's objective is to choose the action that maximizes the expected profit value. The three actions are

a_1 = Pessimistic policy leading to a production volume of 800,000 units.

Table 5.9   ***Monti Company Budgeted Balance Sheet, December 31, 19XB***

Assets

Current Assets

Cash .... $ 30,013
Accounts Receivable   13,500
Material Inventory   10,000
Finished Goods Inventory   10,000

Total Current Assets .... $ 63,513

Fixed Assets

Land .... $ 505,000
Buildings and Equipment   250,000
Depreciation ....   (64,000)

Total Fixed Assets   691,000

Total Assets $754,513

Equities

Current Liabilities

Interest Payable[a] .... $ 192
Accounts Payable[b]   5,400
Loans Payable[c]   5,500
Wages Payable[d]   3,000

Total Current Liabilities .... $ 13,992

Bonds Payable   40,000

Stockholders' Equity

Common Stock .... $ 300,000
Retained Income ($48,000 + $352,521)   400,521
Total Stockholders' Equity   700,521

Total Equities $754,513

[a] The interest payable on December 31 is the accrued amount payable on the outstanding loan of $5,000 (5,500 × 10% × 3 months = $92).
[b] From Material Usage and Purchases Budget (Table 5.3).
[c] From the Cash Budget (Table 5.7).
[d] From Direct-Labor Budget (Table 5.4), 60% December labor costs outstanding (60% × $5,000 = $3,000).

a_2 = Rational policy leading to a production volume of 900,000 units.

a_3 = Optimistic policy leading to a production volume of 1,000,000 units.

The states of nature are

S_1 = Low estimate of sales that amounts to 800,000 units.

S_2 = Moderate estimate of sales that amounts to 900,000 units.

S_3 = High estimate of sales that amounts to 1,000,000 units.

The problem is to choose the most profitable of production volume, taking into account the uncertainty resulting from ignorance of the market reaction.

5.5.1   A Priori Analysis

To proceed with the a priori analysis, a payoff table like Table 5.10 is required. Such a table shows the possible states of nature, the possible actions, the possible gain from the choice of a particular decision given a state of nature, and the a priori probabilities of the states of nature.

Planning under Uncertainty
The expected profit from each action is equal to the sum of the products of each conditional profit multiplied by the corresponding a priori probability of the state of nature. Table 5.11 shows the results of these computations. The assumption that the measure of performance is to achieve the highest possible expected payoff dictates that firm Z choose a_2 and produce 900,000 units.

Planning under Certainty
Assume the information was perfect in the sense that before making a decision, firm Z knew the prevailing state of the world and thus could pass from the known state of the world plus a decision to a known outcome. If firm Z knew that the market response

Table 5.10   Payoff Table for the Choice of a Volume of Production (in Millions of Dollars)

Decisions	States of Nature		
	S_1 = 800,000 Units	S_2 = 900,000 Units	S_3 = 1,000,000 Units
a_1 = 800,000 Units	$15	$15	$15
a_2 = 900,000 Units	$15	$18	$18
a_3 = 1,000,000 Units	$10	$15	$20
A Priori Probability	0.50	0.25	0.25

Table 5.11   Planning under Uncertainty (in Millions of Dollars)

States of Nature	Probability	Volume of Production					
		800,000 Units		900,000 Units		1,000,000 Units	
		Conditional Profit	Expected Profit	Conditional Profit	Expected Profit	Conditional Profit	Expected Profit
S_1 = 800,000 Units	0.50	$15	$ 7.50	$15	$ 7.5	$10	$ 5.00
S_2 = 900,000 Units	0.25	$15	$ 3.75	$18	$ 4.5	$15	$ 3.75
S_3 = 1,000,000 Units	0.25	$15	$ 3.75	$18	$ 4.5	$20	$ 5.00
Total	1.00		$15.00		$16.5		$13.75

Table 5.12   *Opportunity Cost Table (in Millions of Dollars)*

States of Nature	Probability	Volume of Production 800,000 Units Opportunity Cost	Expected Cost	900,000 Units Opportunity Cost	Expected Cost	1,000,000 Units Opportunity Cost	Expected Cost
S_1 = 800,000 Units	0.50	$0	$0.00	$0	$0.00	$5	$2.50
S_2 = 900,000 Units	0.25	$3	$0.75	$0	$0.00	$3	$0.75
S_3 = 1,000,000 Units	0.25	$5	$1.25	$2	$0.50	$0	$0.00
Total	1.00		$2.00		$0.50		$3.25
					$0.50		

would be 900,000 units, it would produce 900,000. The same behavior would apply if the firm knew the market response would be 800,000 or 1,000,000 units. Therefore, under perfect information and certainty, the expected value of profit would be (0.50 × $15,000,000) + (0.25 × $18,000,000) + (0.25 × $20,000,000) = $17,000,000. This sum is called the *expected value with perfect information.*

Expected Value of Perfect Information
The role of information is central to a planning decision. Firm Z may wonder whether or not to "buy" more information. More explicitly, firm Z may want to know the *expected value of perfect information*, which is the upper limit it is willing to pay for the information. The expected value of perfect information is the difference between the maximum expected payoff when perfect information is available and the maximum expected payoff when only a priori information is available. Hence the maximum expected payoff under uncertainty is $16,500,000, and the maximum expected payoff under certainty is $17,000,000. The latter increases the expected gain by $500,000, which is the most firm Z is willing to pay for the privilege of perfect information, or the expected value of perfect information. If the value of perfect information is greater than its cost to firm Z, the firm should exercise the option of obtaining the information at that price.

Opportunity Costs under Uncertainty
Hidden in the entries of firm Z's payoff table are the opportunity costs. Assuming the state of nature is S_2 = 900,000 units, then the maximum profit of $18,000,000 is generated by a_2 = 900,000 units. Accordingly, the opportunity cost generated by the choice of a_3 is $3,000,000 ($18,000,000 − $15,000,000), the one generated by a_2 is $0 ($18,000,000 − $18,000,000), and the one generated by a_1 is $3,000,000 ($18,000,000 − $15,000,000). Opportunity costs are found using the payoff table by subtracting the maximum profit in each vertical row corresponding to a state of nature from each of the other values in that row. In the opportunity cost table for firm Z, shown in Table 5.12, the diagonal cells are all zero, indicating that firm Z could do no better given the prevailing state of nature. The opportunity costs below the diagonal result from not producing enough units. The costs above the diagonal result from having produced too many units. Table 5.12 yields important results:

1. The expected profit under certainty is equal to the sum of the expected profit under uncertainty and the expected opportunity loss. Hence

Expected profit under uncertainty + Expected opportunity loss = Expected profit
under certainty.

Action a_1: \$15,000,000 + \$2,000,000 = \$17,000,000.

Action a_2: \$16,500,000 +   \$500,000 = \$17,000,000.

Action a_3: \$13,750,000 + \$3,250,000 = \$17,000,000.

2. The volume of production yielding the highest expected profit also generates the lowest expected opportunity loss (so a_2 is still the optimal a priori act).

3. The expected opportunity loss of the optimal a priori act (\$500,000) corresponds to the expected value of perfect information (\$500,000).

5.5.2   A Posteriori Analysis

The expected value of perfect information was determined to be \$500,000 in the a priori analysis. This is the maximum amount firm Z should be willing to pay. Assuming the cost of new information is less than the expected value of perfect information, the a posteriori analysis proceeds as follows.

Step 1   Assume a market survey indicated that sales would be limited to $Z = 700,000$ units, and the conditional probabilities are the following:

$P(Z/S_1) = 0.6.$

$P(Z/S_2) = 0.3.$

$P(Z/S_3) = 0.1.$

Step 2   Based on the new information provided by the conditional probabilities, compute the a posteriori probabilities of the states of nature on the basis of Bayes's theorem:

$$P(S_1/Z) = \frac{P(S_1) \times P(Z/S_1)}{\sum\limits_{i=1}^{n} P(S_j) \times P(Z/S_j)},$$

where $P(S_1/Z)$ = probability of state of nature S_1 given the new evidence Z, and S_j = state of nature j. The computation of the a posteriori probability distribution is shown in Table 5.13.

Step 3   Based on the a posteriori probabilities, compute the expected profit value for each volume of production. The results are shown in Table 5.14. Again, the volume of

Table 5.13   A Posteriori Probabilities

States of Nature Si	A Priori Probabilities $P(Si)$	Conditional Probabilities $P(Z/Si)$	Marginal Probabilities $P(Si)P(Z/Si)$	A Posteriori Probabilities $P(Si/Z)$
S_1 = 800,000 Units	0.50	0.6	0.5 × 0.6 = 0.300	0.3/0.4 = 0.75
S_2 = 900,000 Units	0.25	0.3	0.25 × 0.3 = 0.075	0.075/0.4 = 0.1875
S_3 = 1,000,000 Units	0.25	0.1	0.25 × 0.1 = 0.025	0.025/0.4 = 0.0625
Total	1.00	1.0	0.400	1.00

Table 5.14   A Posteriori Analysis (in Millions of Dollars)

States of Nature	A Posteriori Probabilities	800,000 Units Conditional Profit	800,000 Units Expected Profit	900,000 Units Conditional Profit	900,000 Units Expected Profit	1,000,000 Units Conditional Profit	1,000,000 Units Expected Profit
S_1 = 800,000 Units	0.75	$15	$11.25	$15	$11.25	$10	$ 7.5
S_2 = 900,000 Units	0.1875	$15	$ 2.8125	$18	$ 3.375	$15	$ 2.8125
S_3 = 1,000,000 Units	0.0625	$15	$ 0.9375	$18	$ 1.125	$20	$ 1.25
Total	1.00		$15		$15.750		$11.5625

production that should be chosen is the one with the highest expected profit value. As Table 5.14 shows, this production volume is still a_2 = 900,000 units, with an expected profit value equal to $15,700,000.

Step 4   The value of the information provided by the market evidence is the difference between the expected value of perfect information before the market sample and the expected value of perfect information after the sample. The expected value of perfect information before the market sample was found to be $500,000. Compute the expected value of perfect information after the market sample as follows: [(0.75 × $15,000,000) + (0.1875 × $18,000,000) + (0.0625 × $20,000,000)] − $15,750,000 = $125,000. Thus, the value of information provided by the market evidence is $500,000 − $125,000 = $375,000.

5.6   BUDGETING FOR NONPROFIT ENTITIES

5.6.1   Differences to Be Considered

Many of the planning and budgeting concepts presented in this chapter are applicable to governmental units and nonprofit organizations in the private sector. Adaptations are necessary, however, according to the characteristics of these entities.

Planning and budgeting is regarded as a management function and a prerogative in business firms. In the public sector, however, budgeting often involves taxpayers, voters, service recipients, and others who take part in elections and public hearings on the budgets of some local governments. Thus, the process is much more open and political, as the budget determines who gets what services and who pays how much for the services.

Governmental and nonprofit organizations tend to produce services rather than material goods—for example, police protection, health care, and education. The identification and measurement of these services are often complicated and require specialized knowledge. This makes it difficult, but not impossible, to prepare a "production budget," as the outputs must be identified and measured. Budgeting the inputs (material, labor, and overhead) is also hampered by imprecise knowledge of the input-output relationships.

The budget in government is a legal document, the basis of public officials' authority to spend funds; it is also a public document. In contrast, the financial plans and budgets of a business firm usually are not disclosed to external parties.

The budget is not only a resource allocation device; it also serves as a basis of performance evaluation. The budgeted costs, in effect, are standard costs. Indeed, accounting standards for governmental units require that whenever there exists a formally adopted budget, financial reports should disclose actual performance in comparison with the budget. Deficits or surplus, therefore, would attract management and public attention, and possible corrective actions could be taken. This rather elementary form of cost-variance analysis is refined to a much greater extent in business firms, as described in the next chapter.

5.6.2   *The Budgeting Process and Concepts in Nonprofit Entities*

The budgeting process in nonprofit entities focuses on an estimation of the costs of the programs and activities to be performed by the various units of the entity. The budgets can be prepared and conveyed in various ways, as follows:

1. In a *line-item budget*, various expenditures necessary to perform the required activities and programs are listed in detail without any overall information on the overall cost of each activity and program. The focus is then on expenditure classifications, such as salaries, materials, and other costs; the budget actions either increase, decrease, or eliminate "lines."

2. A *program* is a group of activities undertaken to achieve an objective. Unlike the line-item budget, the *program* or *performance budget* lists the costs of the activities, functions, and programs of the entity. Program budgeting begins by requiring each department to identify the programs and activities it intends to perform. Next, budget guidelines are developed to establish next year's areas of priority and to determine the programs that meet the guidelines. Finally, the resources necessary to meet the accepted programs are determined, resulting in a program budget.

3. A *zero-based budget* is initiated to avoid the dysfunctional consequences of incremental budgeting, where next year's budget will always be larger than this year's "base," neglecting to uncover budgeting stocks built up over time. Zero-based budgeting does not assume commitments to existing programs, and it requires each *decision unit* to justify all its resource requests. It forces managers to set priorities as expressed in *decision packages*. In brief, zero-based budgeting provides the costs of the programs or decision packages. The approach is threefold. (1) Packages for old and new activities are determined for various levels of activity. A decision package lists the following information: a description of the function, the objectives of the function, specific measures of performance, the benefits expected, the projected costs, and the various options of executing the function. (2) The packages are ranked by order of importance. (3) Then the packages above an acceptable cutoff point are chosen as the final packages.

5.7   *BEHAVIORAL BUDGETING CONSIDERATIONS*

A budget cannot exist without people. An organization's budget "is prepared by people, revised by people, and its requirements must be met by people."[13] The diverse human reactions a budget elicits must receive full attention to insure success and adequate per-

[13] Ronald Beddingfield, "Human Behavior: The Key to Success in Budgeting," *Management Accounting* (September 1969), p. 54.

formance. The behavioral literature on budgeting focuses on two general areas: *slack budgeting* and the effects of budgeting on managerial attitudes and behavior.

5.7.1 *Slack Budgeting*

The budget in its dual role of planning tool and control device may give rise to slack. R. M. Cyert and J. G. March defined organizational slack as the difference between the "total resources available to the firm and the total necessary to maintain the organizational coalition."[14] Slack may be due to an imperfect allocation of resources within the organization. It may be distributed in the form of additional dividends and excessive wages beyond the minimum required to obtain a healthy coalition of all the participants in the organization, or it may be undistributed as idle cash and securities.

Schiff and Lewin described the behavioral implications of the occurrence of slack as an unintended consequence of the budget and control system.[15] Since the budget is an expression of the performance criteria, and because managers bargain and participate in its formation, the budget process may become a vehicle for slack. Thus, organizational slack is an organizational phenomenon conducive to slack budgeting behavior. In an accounting framework, slack budgeting is defined operationally as the process of understating revenues and overstating costs.

Budgetary slack can arise from conflicts between the individual and organizational goals. The individual desires integration into an organization to the point where an agreement is reached between both sets of goals.[16] Managers generally join or remain in a company where they simultaneously can fulfill their own needs—at least partially—as well as contribute to the goals of the organization itself.

However, the formation of an individual's judgment reflects the numerous relationships among the personality and environmental variables within an organization. Since these relationships are in constant flux, potential conflict exists between the individual and organizational goals. The budgeting process is partially responsible for the harmony or discord of these relationships. To maximize individual goals while meeting organizational goals, a slack environment is necessary. As O. E. Williamson suggests, managers intentionally create slack.[17]

Organizational structure also may explain the creation of slack. The traditional Tayloristic organizational structure is assumed to be more conducive to slack behavior than others. However, it is naive to assume that slack budgeting is not possible in a participative organizational structure. In fact, Edwin Caplan suggests that participative budgeting may increase the likelihood of slack.[18]

The organizational structure may be centralized or decentralized. Schiff and Lewin examined the role of the controller in creating slack.[19] They discovered that slack is incorporated in the budget whether the organizational structure was centralized or decentralized. However, each type of structure creates or handles the slack differently:

---

[14] Cyert and March, *A Behavioral Theory of the Firm*, pp. 36–38.

[15] M. Schiff and A. Y. Lewin, "The Impact of the People on Budgets," *Accounting Review* (April 1970), pp. 259–268.

[16] J. G. March and H. A. Simon, *Organizations* (New York: Wiley, 1958), pp. 84–110.

[17] O. E. Williamson, *The Economy of Discretionary Behavior: Managerial Objectives in a Theory of the Firm* (Englewood Cliffs, N.J.: Prentice-Hall, 1964).

[18] Edwin H. Caplan, *Management Accounting and Behavioral Sciences* (Reading, Mass.: Addison-Wesley, 1971), p. 85.

[19] Schiff and Lewin, "The Impact of People on Budgets," p. 264.

Specifically, it appears that in a decentralized company, slack is concentrated at the divisional management level. Moreover, the divisional controller is intimately involved in the creation and "husbanding" of slack. Conversely, in a centralized company with a weaker control system, slack is discussed through all management levels of the division.[20]

Mohamed Onsi stated that budgetary slack is created as a result of pressure and the use of budgeted profit as a main criterion in evaluating managerial performance.[21]

5.7.2   *Effects of Budgeting on Managerial Attitudes and Behavior*

Budgets have a dual role: They constitute the final outcome of the planning process and the basis of the control system. This dual role creates dysfunctional managerial attitudes and behavior, which has been the subject of most behavioral research on budgets.

The coercive nature of budgets was first discussed by Argyris. He reported on the great distrust of the entire budgeting process at the supervisory level and concluded that budgeting can be related to at least four human relations problems:

First, budget pressure tends to unite the employees against management, and tends to place the factory supervisor under tension. This tension may lead to inefficiency, aggravation, and perhaps a complete breakdown on the part of the supervisor.

Second, the finance staff can obtain feelings of success only by finding fault with factory people. These feelings of failure among factory supervisors lead to many human relations problems.

Third, the use of budgets as "needlers" by top management tends to make the factory supervisors see only the problems of their own department. The supervisors are not concerned with other people's problems. They are not "plant centered" in outlook. Finally, supervisors use budgets as a way of expressing their own patterns of leadership. When these patterns result in people getting hurt, the budget, in itself a neutral thing, often gets blamed.[22]

M. E. Wallace described the unwanted pressure created by budgets:

Budgets are not the only source of pressure but, being a concrete measure of cost and performance, they are a convenient peg on which to hang the blame for management pressure. Constant pressure leads to a gradual erosion of rationality which is replaced by mistrust, intolerance and apathy and, as such, detracts from the long-term growth prospects of the company and places the realization of company long-term goals in jeopardy.[23]

Following Argyris's pioneering study, numerous studies explored the effects of budgeting on managerial attitudes and behavior. They examined the links between a defined, independent budgetary variable (such as the budget level, budget pressure, or method of

---

[20] Ibid., p. 267.

[21] Mohamed, Onsi, "Factor Analysis of Behavioral Variables Affecting Budgetary Slack," *Accounting Review* (July 1973), pp. 535–548.

[22] C. Argyris, *The Impact of Budgets on People* (New York: Controllership Foundation, 1975). p. 25.

[23] M. E. Wallace, "Behavioral Considerations in Budgeting," *Management Accounting* (August 1966), p. 5.

budget formation) and a psychological variable (such as aspiration level) or interpersonal variable (such as leadership style) that increases job performance and/or satisfaction. G. H. Hofstede found that the way in which superiors in the hierarchy manage budget problems and the extent to which they discuss budget results with subordinates have a strong impact on the subordinates' attitudes about the budget system and their perceptions of the relevancy of the budget standards to their job.[24] In the same vein, Don T. DeCoster and John P. Fertakis examined the relationship between budget-induced pressure and a supervisor's leadership behavior. They found that supervisors, when subjected to budget-induced pressure by their superiors, tend to increase their own behavior by both initiating structure and consideration.[25] In other words, they are more likely to show greater initiative in assigning work, but also a greater amount of employee-oriented or considerate leadership behavior.

Andrew C. Stedry examined motivation through budgeting and the interactions of budgets, aspiration levels, and performance. His results point to (1) the importance of the acceptance of standards by subordinates and (2) the links between the level of difficulty of the standards and the resulting performance. Stedry found that individuals' aspiration levels affect their performance. Workers given a budget with goals lower than their aspiration level tend to lower their "aspiration level to conform to that goal." [26] One of the main conclusions drawn from Stedry's findings is that performance can be improved by setting standard levels attuned to the motivational effects on individuals. Individuals can be motivated to perform better if the budget is adjusted in light of their past performance.

5.7.3   *Participation and Budgeting*

Participation means that budget preparation starts at the lower level of the hierarchy and moves upward, allowing numerous people to make suggestions for changes to reach a coordinated plan conforming with organizational goals. Participation by subordinates in standard setting is usually considered effective in getting the subordinates to accept the standards and in achieving goal congruence.[27]

Many behavioral studies support the use of participation in task-goal setting and decision making. Selwyn Becker and David Green used the results of studies of aspiration levels to argue that a "successful program of participation can result in greater expenditure of effort on the part of employees to reach goals specified in the budget." [28] They also analyzed the use of participation in standard setting. They believe that if greater interaction of individuals leads to greater group cohesiveness, and if this cohesiveness and some incentive to produce at either a higher or lower level are positively correlated, then participation can induce higher or lower levels of performance. Similarly, if participation at an upper level creates positive attitudes on the part of supervisors, they will induce higher individual and group aspiration in their subordinates, which, it is hoped, will create higher rather than lower levels of performance.[29]

---

[24]G. H. Hofstede, *The Game of Budget Control* (New York: Van Nostrand, 1967).

[25]Don T. DeCoster and John P. Fertakis, "Budget-Induced Pressure and Its Relationship to Supervisory Behavior," *Journal of Accounting Research* (Autumn 1968), pp. 237–246.

[26]Andrew C. Stedry, *Budget Control and Cost Behavior* (Englewood Cliffs, N.J.: Prentice-Hall, 1960).

[27]G. A. Welsh, *Budgeting: Profit Planning and Control*, 3d ed. (Englewood Cliffs, N.J.: Prentice-Hall, 1960).

[28]Selwyn Becker and David Green, Jr., "Budgeting and Employee Behavior," *Journal of Business* (October 1962), p. 399.

Most empirical budgetary studies support the positive effects of participation on subordinates' attitudes. Ken Milani, for example, found positive and significant correlations between participation in budget setting and attitudes toward the job and company.[30] Hofstede's study revealed that budget participation was the variable with the strongest effect on all measures of motivation.[31] Similarly, R. J. Sweringa and R. H. Moncur found higher need satisfaction among managers who were consulted on their budget than among those who were not consulted.[32]

Although most research studies demonstrate the likelihood that participation can produce positive benefits to the organization, these are not generalizable to all firms. The success of a participative scheme in a given organization depends on factors specific to that organization. Lee D. Parker states

The effectiveness of participation in an enterprise can be affected by other factors such as management attitudes, participants' motives and personality traits and the nature of the enterprise itself. A participative scheme which has been successful in one enterprise will not automatically achieve success in other enterprises. This should not be forgotten when examining reported results of empirical studies of attempts at participation, even if the researchers responsible do try to generalize.[33]

5.8   CONCLUSION

Planning essentially involves the collection of environmental and internal information to derive an organization's objectives and make decisions on the best way to achieve them. Central to an efficient planning system is goal congruence, the harmonization of the individual and group objectives within the organization and the objectives of the organization as a whole. The budget as a formalization of planning is a key mechanism for the creation of goal congruence; it serves as a bargaining medium through which individuals and groups try to further their own goals. The budget is also used as a tool of planning, control, coordination, and communication. Used wisely, it can motivate managers to accomplish the organizational objectives.

GLOSSARY

A Posteriori Analysis Obtaining new information and reevaluating the a priori probabilities to obtain a posteriori probabilities by incorporating the new information through the use of Bayes's theorem.

A Priori Analysis Choosing the action with the highest expected profit value based on the unconditional probabilities of the states of nature.

Budget A plan of action expressed in figures.

Expected Value of Perfect Information The difference between the maximum expected payoff when

---

[29] Ibid.

[30] Ken Milani, "The Relationship of Participation in Budget-Setting to Industrial Supervisor Performance and Attitudes: A Field Study," *Accounting Review* (April 1975), pp. 274–284.

[31] Hofstede, *The Game of Budget Control.*

[32] R. J. Sweringa and R. H. Moncur, *Some Effects of Participative Budgeting on Managerial Behavior* (New York: National Association of Accountants, 1975).

[33] Lee D. Parker, "Participation in Budget Planning: The Prospects Surveyed," *Accounting and Business Research* (Spring 1979), pp. 123–139.

perfect information is available and the maximum expected payoff when only a priori information is available.

Master Budget A budget that consolidates the firm's overall plans.

Slack Budgeting Operationally defined as the process of understating revenues and overstating costs.

SELECTED READINGS

Auger, B. Y., "Presenting the Budget," *Management Accounting* (May 1981), pp. 22–27.

Becker, Selwyn, and Green, David Jr., "Budgeting and Employee Behavior," *Journal of Business* (October 1962), pp. 392–402.

Beddingfield, Ronald, "Human Behavior: The Key to Success in Budgeting," *Management Accounting* (September 1969), pp. 54–56.

Benke, Ralph L. Jr., and O'Keefe, W. Timothy, "Organizational Behavior and Operating Budgets," *Cost and Management* (July–August 1980), pp. 21–27.

Bennett, Robert B., "Motivational Aspects of Participation in the Planning and Control System," *Cost and Management* (September–October 1974), pp. 37–40.

Bradley, Hugh E., "Setting and Controlling Budgets with Regression Analysis," *Management Accounting* (November 1969), pp. 31–34, 40.

Bullock, James H., and Bakay, Virginia H., "How Las Vegas Casinos Budget," *Management Accounting* (July 1980), pp. 35–39.

Cheng, Philip C., "Humanizing the Budget Process in a Total Management System," *Cost and Management* (July–August 1976), pp. 24–28.

Cismoski, David R., and Toepfer, Frederick, "How to Allocate the College Budget Objectively," *Management Accounting* (December 1979), pp. 45–50.

Feldbush, Marvin A., "Participative Budgeting in a Hospital Setting," *Management Accounting* (September 1981), pp. 43–48.

Gunders, Henry, "Better Profit Planning," *Management Accounting* (August 1965), pp. 3–24.

Hanson, E. I., "The Budgetary Control Function," *Accounting Review* (April 1966), pp. 239–243.

Irvine, V. Bruce, "Budgeting: Functional Analysis and Behavioral Implications," *Cost and Management* (March–April 1970), pp. 6–16.

Leitch, Robert A.; Barrack, John B.; and McKinley, Sue H., "Controlling Your Cash Resources," *Management Accounting* (October 1980), pp. 58–60.

Levine, Marc, "The Behavioral Implications of Participative Budgeting," *Cost and Management* (March–April 1981), pp. 28–32.

Lowe, Larry S.; Roberts, C. Richard; and Cagley, James W., "Your Sales Forecast-Marketing Budget Relationship: Is It Consistent?" *Management Accounting* (January 1980), pp. 29–33.

Newman, M. S., "The Essence of Budgetary Control," *Management Services* (January–February 1965), pp. 19–26.

Parker, Lee D., "Participation in Budget Planning: The Prospects Surveyed," *Accounting and Business Research* (Spring 1979), pp. 123–137.

Ridgeway, V. F., "Dysfunctional Consequences of Performance Measurement," *Administrative Science Quarterly* 1 (September 1956), pp. 240–247.

Schiff, M., and Lewin, A. Y., "The Impact of People on Budgets," *Accounting Review* (April 1970), pp. 259–268.

Suver, James D., and Helmer, F. Theodore, "Developing Budgetary Models for Greater Hospital Efficiency," *Management Accounting* (July 1979), pp. 34–36, 39.

QUESTIONS, EXERCISES, AND PROBLEMS

5.1   Explain the concept of goal congruence and its importance to planning and control.

5.2   Outline the steps required in the Bayesian approach to budgeting.

5.3   Define the expected value of perfect information. Elaborate on its importance in the Bayesian approach to budgeting.

5.4   Explain the relevance of the opportunity cost concept in the Bayesian approach to budgeting.

5.5   What are the main determinants of slack budgeting?

5.6   The budget can be a powerful tool for motivating people to achieve the organization's objectives, or it can be a positive hindrance.

Required:
Analyze extensively the effects of budgeting on people, and show how budgeting can lead to either bad or good consequences according to the way it is applied in various types of organizations.

(SMA adapted)

5.7   Outline the component budgets leading up to the preparation of a budgeted income statement for a manufacturing company.

(CGA adapted)

5.8   Briefly discuss the advantages and disadvantages of single versus multiple goals.

(SMA adapted)

5.9   The operating budget is an instrument used by many businesses. While it usually is thought to be an important and necessary tool for management, it has been subject to some criticism from managers and researchers studying organizations and human behavior.

Required:
1. Describe and discuss the benefits of budgeting from the behavioral point of view.

2. Describe and discuss the criticism of the budgeting process from the behavioral point of view.

3. What solutions are recommended to overcome the criticism described in part 2?

(CMA adapted)

5.10   A budget is a device to provide greater effectiveness in achieving organizational efficiency. For the budget to be effective, however, its functional aspects must outweigh its dysfunctional aspects.

Required:
1. Briefly discuss how a budget system enables management to more effectively plan, coordinate, control, and evaluate the activities of the business.

2. Explain, using four examples, how budgets can lead to dysfunctional results.

(CMA adapted)

5.11   ***Planning under Uncertainty: Fundamentals***   Mr. Brown, the president of Saba Enterprises, is deciding whether to invest $3,000,000 in a research project designed to discover a method of converting industrial waste from the Clean Company into usable fuel. If the research project is successful, the revenues net of operating costs (excluding the $3,000,000 outlay for the research and an initial investment in equipment) are estimated as follows:

Anticipated Net Revenues	Probability
$10,000,000	0.10
20,000,000	0.25
25,000,000	0.35
30,000,000	0.20
35,000,000	0.10

Brown knows there is a 60 percent chance that the project will be unsuccessful.

Required:
Assuming Brown wishes to maximize the expected value of net cash flows, should he invest in the research project? Show all calculations.

(SMA adapted)

5.12

A Priori Analysis   The Xyrox Company manufactures low-quality garments on a mass production basis. The production vice-president knows the plant has some idle capacity. A European importer has approached Xyrox and requested it to supply a few thousand dozen stylish men's shirts at a contract price of $250 per dozen. Xyrox management is uncertain whether the order should be accepted, because the demand would be for 3,000, 4,500, or 6,000 dozen, depending on how well the European importer did the advertising. The shirts also would vary, depending on which of two different types of materials the ultimate buyers requested. The variable cost per dozen would vary between $200 per dozen and $165 per dozen, but the selling price for Xyrox would remain firm at $250 per dozen. They estimate that, if the order were accepted, incremental fixed costs would amount to $295,000.

The market research department of the European importer predicts that 75 percent of the consumers would prefer the more expensive material, while the remaining 25 percent would choose the less expensive, as it requires no ironing. They also report that there is a 90 percent chance that less than 6,000 dozen would be sold and a 30 percent chance that less than 4,500 dozen would be sold. Assume that consumer preference probabilities are independent of sales value probabilities.

Required:
1. Compute the incremental profit or loss and the probability of occurrence for the six possible states of nature.

2. What is the probability that the project would be profitable?

3. Compute the expected value if the order were accepted. Would you accept the order?

4. Assume the answer to part 2 remains as computed, and the answer to part 3 is $25,000. Discuss briefly whether you would accept the order.

(SMA adapted)

5.13

A Posteriori Analysis   Management has made the following estimates of operating costs (in millions of dollars) at various volumes (in millions of gallons):

Volume	Cost	Volume	Cost
5	$11.7	9	$15.5
6	12.5	10	17.5
7	13.3	11	20.5
8	14.2	12	24.5

The marketing vice-president believes that by spending an additional $200,000, the cumulative probability can be increased by 0.1 at each volume level from 6,000,000 to 11,000,000 gallons.

Required:
Should the $200,000 be spent? Submit detailed calculations. *Hint:* In setting volume levels, use midrange volumes: 11,500,000, 10,500,000, 9,500,000 gallons, and so forth. Assume costs behave linearly within each interval, and the upper limit is 11,500,000 gallons.

(SMA adapted)

5.14   ***Slack Budgeting***   For many years the Noton Company's comprehensive budgeting system has been a major component of the company's program to control operations and costs at its widely scattered plants. Periodically the plants' general managers gather with the top management to discuss the overall company control system.

At this year's meeting one of the most senior plant managers severely criticized the budgetary system, saying the system discriminated against the older, well-run, established plants in favor of the newer plants. This resulted in lower year-end bonuses, poor performance ratings, and lower employee morale. In this plant manager's judgment, revisions in the system were needed to make it more effective. Noton's budget system includes (1) the announcement of an annual improvement percentage target established by top management, (2) the plants' submission of budgets implementing the annual improvement target, (3) management review and revision of the proposed budget, and (4) the establishment and distribution of the final budget.

To support her arguments, the plant manager compared the budget revisions and performance results. The older plants are expected to achieve the improvement target but often are unable to meet it. On the other hand, the newer plants often are excused from meeting a portion of this target in their budgets. However, their performance is usually better than the final budget. The plant manager further argued that the company does not recognize the operating differences that make attainment of the annual improvement factor difficult in some cases, if not impossible. Her plant has been producing essentially the same product for its twenty years of existence. The machinery and equipment, which underwent many modifications in the first five years, have had no major changes in recent years. Because the machines and equipment are old, repair and maintenance costs have increased each year, and the machines are less reliable. The plant management team has been together for the last ten years and works well together. The labor force is mature, and many of the employees have the highest seniority in the company. In the plant manager's judgment, the significant improvements have been "wrung out" of the plant over the years, and now merely keeping even is difficult.

For comparison, she noted that one plant opened within the past four years would have an easier time meeting the company's expectations. The plant is new and contains modern equipment that, in some cases, is still experimental. Major modifications in its equipment and operating systems have been made each year as the plant management obtains a better understanding of the operations. The plant's management, although experienced, has been together only since its opening. The plant is located in a previously nonindustrial area and, therefore, has a relatively inexperienced work force.

Required:
1. Evaluate the plant manager's views.

2. Equitable application of a budget system requires the ability of corporate management to remove budgetary slack in plant budgets. Discuss how each plant could conceal slack in its budget.

(CMA adapted)

5.15   *Behavioral Budgeting*   Drake, Inc., is a multiproduct firm with several manufacturing plants. Management generally has been pleased with the operation of all plants but the Swan plant. Swan plant's poor operating performance has been traced to poor control over plant costs and expenses. Four plant managers have resigned or been terminated during the last three years.

     David Green was appointed the new manager of the Swan plant on February 1, 19X6. Green is a young and aggressive individual who progressed rapidly in Drake's management development program, and he performed well in lower-level management positions. Green had been recommended for the position by Steve Bradley, Green's immediate supervisor. Bradley was impressed by Green's technical ability and enthusiasm. Bradley explained to Green that his assignment as Swan plant manager was approved despite the objections of some of the other members of the top management team. Bradley told Green that he had complete confidence in him and his ability and was sure Green wanted to prove that he had made a good decision. Therefore, Bradley expected Green to have the Swan plant on budget by June 30.

     As a result of Swan plant's past difficulties, Bradley was responsible for formulating the last four annual budgets for the plant. The 19X6 budget was prepared during the last six months of 19X5—before Green had been appointed plant manager. The budget report covering the three-month period ending March 31 showed that Swan's costs and expenses were slightly over budget. At a meeting with Bradley, Green described the changes he had instituted during the previous month. Green was confident that the costs and expenses would be held in check by these changes and that the situation would get no worse for the rest of the year.

     Bradley repeated that he not only wanted the costs and expenses controlled, but he expected Swan plant to be on budget by June 30. Green pointed out that Swan plant had been in poor condition for three years and that, while he appreciated the confidence Bradley had in him, he had only been in charge two months.

     Bradley then replied, "I am expected to meet my figures. The only way that can occur is if my subordinates exercise control over their costs and expenses and achieve their budgets. Therefore, to assure that I achieve my goals, get the Swan plant on budget by June 30, and keep it on budget for the rest of the year."

Required:

1. Present a critical evaluation of the budget practices described in the problem.

2. What are the likely immediate and long-term effects on David Green and Drake, Inc., if the present method of budget administration is continued? Justify your answer.

(CMA adapted)

5.16   *Budgeting*   Tomlinson Retail seeks your assistance to develop cash and other budget information for May, June, and July 19X3. At April 30, 19X3, the company had cash of $5,500, accounts receivable of $437,000, inventories of $309,400, and accounts payable of $133,055.

     The following information is also available. Each month's sales are billed on the last day of the month. Customers are allowed a 3 percent discount if payment is made within ten days after the billing date. Receivables are booked gross. Sixty percent of the billings are collected within the discount period, 25 percent are collected by the end of the month, 9 percent are collected by the end of the second month, and 6 percent prove uncollectible.

Fifty-four percent of all purchases of material and selling, general, and administrative expenses are paid in the month of purchase, and the remainder are paid in the following month. Each month's number of units of ending inventory equals 130 percent of the next month's units of sales. The cost of each unit of inventory is $20. Selling, general, and administrative expenses—of which $2,000 is depreciation—are equal to 15 percent of the current month's sales.

Actual and projected sales are as follows:

19X3	Dollars	Units
March	$354,000	11,800
April	363,000	12,100
May	357,000	11,900
June	342,000	11,400
July	360,000	12,000
August	366,000	12,200

Required:
Select the best answer for each of the following items:

1. Budgeted cash disbursements during the month of June 19X3 are
   a. $292,900.
   b. $287,379.
   c. $294,900.
   d. $285,379.

2. Budgeted cash collections during the month of May 19X3 are
   a. $333,876.
   b. $355,116.
   c. $340,410.
   d. $355,656.

3. The budgeted number of units of inventory to be purchased during July 19X3 is
   a. 15,860.
   b. 12,260.
   c. 12,000.
   d. 15,600.

(AICPA adapted)

5.17   *Cash Budgeting*   The Dilly Company marks up all merchandise at 25 percent of the gross purchase price. All purchases are made on account with terms of 1/10, net/60. Purchase discounts, which are recorded as miscellaneous income, are always taken. Normally, 60 percent of each month's purchases are paid for in the month of purchase, while the other 40 percent are paid for during the first ten days of the first month after purchase. Inventories of merchandise at the end of each month are kept at 30 percent of the next month's projected cost of goods sold.

Terms for sales on account are 2/10, net/30. Cash sales are not subject to discount. Fifty percent of each month's sales on account are collected during the month of sale, 45 percent are collected in the succeeding month, and the remainder are usually uncollectible. Seventy percent of the collections in the month of sale are subject to discount, while 10 percent of the collections in the succeeding month are subject to discount.

Projected sales data for selected months follow:

	Sales on Account (Gross)	Cash Sales
December	$1,900,000	$400,000
January	1,500,000	250,000
February	1,700,000	350,000
March	1,600,000	300,000

Required:
Select the best answer for each of the following items:

1. Projected gross purchases for January are
   a. $1,400,000.   **d.** $1,248,000.
   b. $1,470,000.   **e.** None of the above.
   c. $1,472,000.

2. Projected inventory at the end of December is
   a. $420,000.   **d.** $393,750.
   b. $441,600.   **e.** None of the above.
   c. $552,000.

3. Projected payments to suppliers during February are
   a. $1,551,200.   **d.** $1,509,552.
   b. $1,535,688.   **e.** None of the above.
   c. $1,528,560.

4. Projected sales discounts to be taken by customers making remittances during February are
   a. $5,250.   **d.** $11,900.
   b. $15,925.   **e.** None of the above.
   c. $30,500.

5. Projected total collections from customers during February are
   a. $1,875,000.   **d.** $1,188,100.
   b. $1,861,750.   **e.** None of the above.
   c. $1,511,750.

(AICPA adapted)

5.18

Profit Planning   The Zel Company, a wholesaler, budgeted the following sales for the months indicated:

	June 19X1	July 19X1	August 19X1
Sales on Account	$1,500,000	$1,600,000	$1,700,000
Cash Sales	200,000	210,000	220,000
Total Sales	$1,700,000	$1,810,000	$1,920,000

All merchandise is marked up to sell at its invoice cost plus 25 percent. Merchandise inventories at the beginning of each month are at 30 percent of that month's projected cost of goods sold.

Required:
Select the best answer for each of the following items:

1. The cost of goods sold for June 19X1 is anticipated to be
   a. $1,530,000.   **d.** $1,190,000.
   b. $1,402,500.   **e.** None of the above.
   c. $1,275,000.

2. Merchandise purchases for July 19X1 are anticipated to be
   a. $1,605,500.   **d.** $1,382,250.
   b. $1,474,400.   **e.** None of the above.
   c. $1,448,000.

The following annual flexible budget has been prepared for use in making decisions relating to product X:

	100,000 Units	150,000 Units	200,000 Units
Sales Volume	$800,000	$1,200,000	$1,600,000
Manufacturing Costs			
Variable	300,000	450,000	600,000
Fixed	200,000	200,000	200,000
	$500,000	$ 650,000	$ 800,000
Selling and Other Expenses			
Variable	$200,000	$ 300,000	$ 400,000
Fixed	160,000	160,000	160,000
	360,000	460,000	560,000
Income (or Loss)	$ (60,000)	$ 90,000	$ 240,000

The 200,000-unit budget has been adopted and will be used for allocating fixed manufacturing costs to units of product X. At the end of the first six months, production has been completed on 120,000 units, and sales total 60,000 units. All fixed costs are budgeted and incurred uniformly throughout the year, and all costs incurred coincide with the budget. Overapplied and underapplied fixed manufacturing costs are deferred until year-end.

Required:
Select the best answer for each of the following items:

3. The amount of fixed factory costs applied to product X during the first six months under absorption costing would be

  a. Overapplied by $20,000.   **d.** Underapplied by $80,000.
  b. Equal to the fixed costs incurred.   **e.** None of the above.
  c. Underapplied by $40,000.

4. Reported net income (or loss) for the first six months under absorption costing would be

  a. $160,000.   **d.** $(40,000).
  b. $80,000.   **e.** None of the above.
  c. $40,000.

5. Reported net income (or loss) for the first six months under direct costing would be

  a. $144,000.   **d.** $(36,000).
  b. $72,000.   **e.** None of the above.
  c. $0.

6. Assuming that 90,000 units of product X were sold during the first six months and that this is to be used as a basis, the revised budget estimate for the total number of units to be sold during this year would be

  a. 360,000.   **d.** 120,000.
  b. 240,000.   **e.** None of the above.
  c. 200,000.

The following inventory data relate to the Shirley Company:

	Inventories	
	Ending	**Beginning**
Finished Goods	$95,000	$110,000
Work-in-Process	80,000	70,000
Direct Materials	95,000	90,000

Costs Incurred during the Period

Cost of Goods Available for Sale	$684,000
Total Manufacturing Costs	654,000
Factory Overhead	167,000
Direct Materials Used	193,000

Required:

Select the best answer for each of the following items:

7. Direct materials purchased during the period were
   a. $213,000.
   b. $198,000.
   c. $193,000.
   d. $188,000.
   e. None of the above, or not determinable from the above facts.

8. Direct-labor costs incurred during the period were
   a. $250,000.
   b. $234,000.
   c. $230,000.
   d. $224,000.
   e. None of the above, or not determinable from the above facts.

9. The cost of goods sold during the period was
   a. $614,000.
   b. $604,000.
   c. $594,000.
   d. $589,000.
   e. None of the above, or not determinable from the above facts.

(AICPA adapted)

5.19   *Budgeting Material Quantities*   A sales budget for the first five months of 19X3 is given for a product line manufactured by Pat Slattery Co. Ltd.:

Sales Budget
(in Units)

January	10,800
February	15,600
March	12,200
April	10,400
May	9,800

The inventory of finished products at the end of each month is to equal 25 percent of the sales estimate for the next month. On January 1, there were 2,700 units of the product on hand. No work is in process at the end of any month.

Each unit of product requires two types of materials: 4 units of material A, and 5 units of material B. Materials equal to one-half of the next month's requirements are to be on hand at the end of each month. This requirement was met on January 1, 19X3.

Required:

Prepare a budget showing the quantities of each type of material to be purchased each month for the first quarter of 19X3.

(SMA adapted)

5.20   *Comprehensive Master Budget*   Garcia Mills is a large textile manufacturing firm. Sales in 19X7 were 1,000,000 yards of tetron at $15 per yard and 1,500,000 yards of xylon at $12 per yard. Production in 19X7 was 1,000,000 yards of tetron and 1,500,000 yards of xylon.

Management feels that with a vigorous advertising campaign, sales of tetron in 19X8 could be boosted by 50 percent over their 19X7 levels without affecting the sales of xylon, which, management feels, would remain constant at their 19X7 levels.

The balance sheet for the year ending December 31, 19X7, is given in Table 1. Prices of direct materials and direct-labor wages will remain at their 19X7 levels, which are given in Table 2. Both products go through two departments during manufacturing, processing, and weaving. The material, labor, and machine time requirements are given in Table 3. Overhead costing is done on a departmental basis and is calculated for planning and application purposes according to the following relationship:

Processing department overhead cost = $100,000 + $1 × Machine hour usage.

Weaving department overhead cost = $100,000 + $2 × Direct labor hours.

Selling and administrative expenses at the expected sales volume (because of the strong marketing effort) in 19X8 are given in Table 4. Depreciation on Factory Buildings and Equipment is on a declining balance basis at the rate of 10 percent of the balance outstanding. Income taxes are calculated at the flat rate of 40 percent of income before taxes.

Table 1   ***Garcia Mills Balance Sheet, December 31, 19X7***

Assets

Current Assets			
Cash		$ 10,000	
Accounts Receivable		100,000	
Inventory			
Materials			
Cloth Fiber	$100,000		
Chemical X	10,000		
Tetron (50,000 Yards at Absorbed Costs)	379,000	489,000	$ 599,000
Fixed Assets			
Land		100,000	
Buildings and Equipment (Factory)		2,000,000	
Accumulated Depreciation (Factory)		(200,000)	$1,900,000
Total Assets			$2,499,000

Equities

Current Liabilities			
Accounts Payable			$ 10,000
Stockholders' Equity			
Capital Stock		$1,000,000	
Retained Earnings		1,489,000	2,489,000
Total Equities			$2,499,000

Table 2   **Basic Cost Data**

Materials
    Cloth Fiber $5 per Pound
    Chemical X $10 per Pound
   Labor (Direct) $5 per Hour

Table 3   **Material, Labor and Machine Time Requirements**

	Tetron per Yard	Xylon per Yard
Cloth Fiber	1.0 Pound	1.0 Pound
Chemical X	0.1 Pound	—
Direct Labor	0.2 Hour	0.1 Hour
Machine Time	0.1 Hour	0.2 Hour

Table 4   **Selling and Administrative Expenses**

Sales Commissions	5% of Gross Sales
Advertising	$1,000,000
Sales Salaries	$2,000,000
Travel	$1,000,000
Clerical and Executive Salaries	$2,000,000
Miscellaneous	1% of Gross Sales

Management feels that because of the strong marketing effort, there will be a demand for the products in 19X9 that must be met without inconvenience to customers. Therefore, the company desires an ending inventory of finished goods of 150,000 yards each of tetron and xylon. Moreover, there is a backlog of orders from 19X7 for xylon amounting to 10,000 yards, which must be accommodated in 19X8. This backlog is not included in 19X7 sales. Management expects a raw materials shortage—especially for chemical X—and, therefore, requires an ending inventory of 5,000 pounds of chemical X and 20,000 pounds of cloth fiber.

Assume there are no work-in-process inventories at the end of 19X7 or 19X8.

Required:
Giving proper explanation and using notes whenever necessary, prepare the following for 19X8:

1. **a.** Sales budget.   **d.** Factory overhead budget.
   b. Production budget.   **e.** Cost of goods sold budget.
   c. Material usage and purchases budget.
2. Budgeted income statement.

(SMA adapted)

5.21 ***Cash Budgeting***   The Jim Chan Co. manufactures a product for which the following sales forecast has been prepared:

Number of Units

January	12,000
February	10,000
March	13,000
April	11,000

Jim Chan has a policy of producing enough units so there will be a beginning inventory each month equal to 20 percent of the month's predicted sales. The standard cost per unit is as follows:

Materials: 3 Pounds @ $5	$15
Direct Labor: 1 Hour @ $6	6
Variable Overhead	2
Fixed Overhead	7
	$30

Material inventories at the beginning of each month are to equal 40 percent of that month's production requirements. All materials are purchased on account with terms of 2/10, net/30. Purchases are made evenly throughout the month. For convenience, assume that all months have thirty days.

Required:
Compute the amount of cash required in February for payment of Accounts Payable related to the purchase of materials.

(CGA adapted)

5.22 ***Cash Budgeting: Mathematical Model***   Zeghal Co. is experiencing cash management problems. It has been unable to determine its temporary cash needs on a timely basis. This has increased the cost of borrowing, because the company often has been unable to obtain desirable terms. Borrowing in advance would make better terms available at a lower cost. A review of cash flow indicates that all factors can be adequately predicted except the expenditures for hourly payroll and certain other expenditures. The cash receipts can be determined accurately, because Zeghal's customers are all reliable and pay on an identifiable schedule within the two calendar months following the sale. The payments for raw materials are similarly predictable, because they are all paid in the calendar month subsequent to the purchase. Disbursements for monthly fixed obligations, such as lease payments, salaried personnel, and so forth, are known well in advance of the payment dates.

In an attempt to better forecast cash changes for the next month, the company conducted a statistical analysis of many possible variables that might be suitable as a basis for forecasting the expenditure for payroll and other items. This analysis revealed a high correlation between the advance sales orders received in a month and those expenditures in the next month. The following relationships useful for cash forecasting have been identified, where N = the forecast month:

1. Collections on account:

$C_N = 0.9S_{N-1} + 0.1S_{N-2}$,
where S = sales.

2. Disbursements for raw material purchases:

$D_N = R_{N-1}$,
where R = raw material purchases.

3. Monthly fixed obligations:

$F_N = \$400,000$.

4. Payroll and other expenditures:

$P_N = 0.25A_{N-1} + 70,000$,
where
A = advance sales orders.

Coefficient of correlation	= 0.96.
Standard error of the estimate	= 10,000.
Standard error of the regression coefficient of the independent variable	= 0.0013.
t statistic for the 95 percent confidence interval	= 2.07.

Required:
1. Estimate the change in the cash balance for July 19X5 using the specified relationships and the following data:

	Sales (S)	Raw Material Purchases (R)	Advance Sales Orders (A)
April	$1,300,000	$300,000	$1,225,000
May	1,200,000	400,000	1,050,000
June	1,000,000	350,000	1,400,000

2. Revise your estimate of the change in the cash balance to recognize the uncertainty associated with the payroll and other expenditures.

3. How could management use this information to study alternative plans to reduce the short-term borrowing costs?

(CMA adapted)

5.23   ***Expected Value of Perfect Information*** The Nedzella Broadcasting Company has asked you to evaluate the commercial possibilities of a new record expected to appeal to the teenage segment of the population in the northern region. Based on past experience and available data, you have determined the following. Fixed outlays for setting up machinery for the record would equal $500,000. The variable cost per unit of producing, promoting, and distributing the record would be $2, and the unit selling price would be $5. You have also determined that there are three possible states of nature:

S_1 = Sales will be 100,000 records, with a probability of 0.6.

S_2 = Sales will be 150,000 records, with a probability of 0.3.

S_3 = Sales will be 10,000 records, with a probability of 0.1.

Required:

1. Should the Nedzella Broadcasting Company commercialize the record?

2. What is the expected value of perfect information?

3. Assuming the cost of obtaining additional information is estimated to be $30,000, should the Nedzella Broadcasting Company exercise the option of obtaining the information at that price?

5.24   ***Probabilistic Budgeting***   Lefoll, Inc., has been operating the concession stands at the university football stadium. The university has had successful football teams for many years; as a result, the stadium is always full. The university is located in an area with no rainfall during the football season. At times, Lefoll runs short of hot dogs, and at other times it has many left over. A review of the sales records of the past five seasons revealed the following frequency of hot dogs sold:

	Total Games
10,000 Hot Dogs	5
20,000 Hot Dogs	10
30,000 Hot Dogs	20
40,000 Hot Dogs	15
	50

Hot dogs sell for $.50 each and cost Lefoll $.30 each. Unsold hot dogs are given to a local orphanage without charge.

Required:

1. Assuming that the four quantities listed were the only ones ever sold and that the occurrences were random events, prepare a payoff table (ignoring income taxes) to represent the four possible strategies of ordering 10,000, 20,000, 30,000, or 40,000 hot dogs.

2. Using the expected value decision rule, determine the best strategy.

3. What is the dollar value of perfect information in this problem?

(CMA adapted)

5.25   ***Bayes's Theorem: Probabilistic Budgeting***   A local restaurant wants to open a stand at the local fair. Leo Gaspari, the owner, asked you to assist him in evaluating the profitability of the project. He advised you that he has three options available to him:

a_1 = He could sell only sandwiches.

a_2 = He could sell sandwiches and beer.

a_3 = He could sell only beer.

Based on past experience and available city records, you have determined the following:

	Dollars
Fixed Outlays for Setting Up the Stand	3,000
Cost of a Sandwich	1
Cost of a Beer	.20
Selling Price of a Sandwich	1.50
Selling Price of a Beer	.50

You have also determined that the project will be affected by the weather. If it rains, Gaspari's three options will be affected as follows:

a_1 = He will sell 8,000 sandwiches.

a_2 = He will sell 8,000 sandwiches and 1,000 beers.

a_3 = He will sell 8,000 beers.

If it shines, his three options will be affected as follows:

a_1 = He will sell 8,000 sandwiches.

a_2 = He will sell 8,000 sandwiches and 2,000 beers.

a_3 = He will sell 10,000 beers.

From past experience, Gaspari advised you that there is a 40 percent chance of rain on the local fair at this time of the year. After reading a barometer, you determined the following conditional probabilities:

	States of Nature	
Barometer Reading	**R = Rain**	**S = Shine**
X_1 = Rain	0.9	0.2
X_2 = Shine	0.1	0.8

What would you recommend to Gaspari if

1. Your barometer is broken?

2. It indicates rain?

3. It indicates shine?

5.26   ***Budgeted Cash Receipts***   You have been asked to assist in the preparation of a cash budget for the Maheu Co. Ltd. Maheu sells one item only at a price of $100. Budgeted unit sales are as follows: January, 5,000 units; February, 4,000 units; and March, 3,000 units. All of Maheu's customers buy on account. Of these, 75 percent take advantage of a cash discount of 3 percent. Maheu's terms are 3/10, net/30. Maheu's bad debts average 2 percent of sales on account.

Required:
Determine the budgeted cash receipts for March.

(CGA adapted)

5.27   ***Cash Budget: Mathematical Model***   Over the past several years, the Programme Corporation has encountered difficulties estimating its cash flows, which has resulted in a rather strained relationship with its banker. Programme's controller would like to develop a means of forecasting the firm's monthly operating cash flows. The following data were gathered:

1. Sales have been and are expected to increase at 0.5 percent each month.

2. Of each month's sales, 30 percent are for cash; the other 70 percent are on open account.

3. Of the credit sales, 80 percent are collected in the first month following the sale, and the remaining 20 percent are collected in the second month. There are no bad debts.

4. The gross margin on sales averages 25 percent.

5. Programme purchases enough inventory each month to cover the following month's sales.

6. All inventory purchases are paid for in the month of purchase at a 2 percent cash discount.

7. Monthly expenses are payroll, $1,500; rent, $400; depreciation, $120; and other cash expenses, 1 percent of that month's sales. There are no accruals.

8. Ignore the effects of corporate income taxes, dividends, and equipment acquisitions.

Required:
Using the data available, develop a mathematical model the controller can use for calculations. Your model should be capable of calculating the monthly operating cash inflows and outflows for any specified month.

(CMA adapted)

5.28   ***Cash Budget: Mathematical Model***   You have been requested to build a simulation model for one product line of Jensen Ltd., a small retailer, and you are provided the following data. Demand for the product is believed to be affected by its price and the advertising expenditures. Every $100 of current advertising expenditures increases demand in that month by 20 units. Also, due to a lag in the effect of advertising, every $100 of advertising expenditures in the previous month increases demand in the current month by 10 units. The effect of price on monthly demand may be expressed as 10,000/price. The actual quantity sold during the month equals quantity demanded or goods available for sale, whichever is lower. The actual quantity purchased during the current month is 120 percent of the previous month's unit sales less inventory on hand at the beginning of the current month.

Let

$I(t)$ = Inventory on hand at the end of month t.

$D(t)$ = Quantity demanded during month t.

$Q(t)$ = Quantity sold during month t.

$S(t)$ = Sales (in dollars) during month t.

$P(t)$ = Prices per unit in month t.

$A(t)$ = Total advertising expenditures in month t.

$V(t)$ = Variable cost per unit during month t.

$F(t)$ = Fixed costs during month t.

$B(t)$ = Breakeven sales volume in month t.

$E(t)$ = Net profit for month t.

Required:
Employing this notation *only*, provide an expression for each of the following in terms of other relevant variables and parameters. For example, dollar sales during month t can

be expressed as $S(t) = Q(t) \times P(t)$, and dollar sales during the previous month $(t - 1)$ as $S(t - 1) = Q(t - 1) \times P(t - 1)$. (Note: Z = Min. (x, y) indicates that Z is the lesser of x or y.)

1. Quantity demanded during month t.
2. Quantity sold during month t.
3. Inventory on hand at the end of month t.
4. Breakeven sales volume in month t.
5. Net profit for month t.

(SMA adapted)

5.29   *Quarterly Cash Budget*   As part of the company's overall planning program, the controller of the So Good Blueberry Packing Co. Ltd. prepares a cash budget by quarters each year. The company's sole operation is processing and canning the yearly crop of blueberries. As this is a seasonal commodity, all manufacturing operations take place in the quarter of October through December. Sales are made throughout the year, and the company's fiscal year ends on June 30.

The sales forecast for the coming year indicates the following (all figures in thousands): first quarter (July through September 19X1), $780; second quarter (October through December 19X1), $1,500; third quarter (January through March 19X2), $780; and fourth quarter (April through June 19X2), $780. All sales are on account. The beginning balance of receivables is expected to be collected during the first quarter. It is anticipated that subsequent collections will follow the pattern of two-thirds collected in the quarter of sales and the remaining one-third in the quarter following.

Purchases of blueberries are scheduled to be $240,000 in the first quarter and $720,000 in the second quarter. Payment is made in the quarter of purchase. Direct labor of $700,000 is incurred and paid in the second quarter. Factory overhead cost (paid in cash during the quarter it is incurred) is $860,000 in the second quarter. The standby (fixed) amount in each of the other three quarters is $200,000. Selling and administrative expenses, incurred and paid, amount to $100,000 per quarter during the year.

To finance its seasonal working capital needs, the company has obtained a line of short-term credit with the Royal Toronto Bank. The company maintains a minimum cash balance of $8,000 and borrows and repays only in multiples of $5,000. It repays as soon as it is able without impairing the minimum cash balance. Interest is at 8 percent and is paid at the time of loan repayment. It is assumed that all borrowing is made at the beginning of a quarter, and the repayments are made at the end of a quarter. (Round the interest calculations to the nearest $1,000.)

The company plans to spend the following on fixed assets: $150,000 in the third quarter and $50,000 in the fourth quarter. Account balances as of July 1, 19X1, were Cash, $8,000; and Accounts Receivable, $25,000.

Required:

1. Prepare a schedule to show the cash budget and financing requirements for each quarter and for the year ended June 30, 19X2.

2. Comment briefly on the nature and purpose of cash budgets for managerial planning.

(SMA adapted)

5.30   *Production and Cash Budget*   The Fleury Company, a manufacturer of plastic containers, is attempting to forecast inventory requirements and cash flow for March 19X6. The following information is available.

Sales were budgeted at $150,000 for March (15,000 units). The accounts receivable at the end of February are $135,000 (February sales totaled $120,000). The collection pattern is as follows. 20 percent of sales were collected during the month of sale, 50 percent during the month after the month of sale, and 30 percent during the second month after the month of sale.

Inventory plans call for a basic stock of 5,000 finished units plus 50 percent of the next month's sales requirements to be on hand at month-end. Expected sales for April, May, and June are 18,000 units per month, and units on hand at February 28 totaled 13,000 (500 units more than planned).

Production costs per unit are

Material (½ Pound @ $3)	$1.50
Labor (½ Hour @ $4)	2.00
Overhead (½ Hour @ $5)	2.50
Total Cost Per Unit	$6.00

The raw material inventory is to be maintained at the expected production requirements for the next two months to avoid any shortage. The inventory of raw materials at February 28 was 16,000 pounds, and a total of 6,500 pounds was purchased during February. The terms of purchase are net 30 days.

The overhead rate of $5 per hour is based on the following annual budget:

Variable Overhead

Indirect Materials	$ 49,000
Indirect Labor	143,000
Total	$192,000

Fixed Overhead

Salaries	$204,000
Services (Heat, Light, etc.)	36,000
Taxes (Accrued, Payable in May and November)	18,000
Insurance (Prepaid in January)	9,000
Depreciation Expenses	21,000
Total	$288,000
All totaled	$480,000

Expected Hours (192,000 Units): 96,000 Hours
Overhead Rate per Hour: $5

Variable manufacturing overhead costs are paid in the month of incurrence. Marketing and administrative expenses are estimated as 30 percent of sales, two-thirds of which is payable during the month of sale, and one-third is payable in the month following the sale.

Required:

1. Determine the number of pounds of raw materials to be purchased during March.

2. Prepare a cash forecast statement for March 19X6. The statement should show the amount of cash generated from operations during the month and the amount available for other expenditures at month-end, assuming a cash balance of $4,500 at February 28, 19X6.

(SMA adapted)

5.31   ***Master Budget***   In estimating the Brown Store's seasonal cash requirements, you made the following assumptions for the period August 1 to October 31.

Sales are 40 percent for cash and 60 percent on open book accounts. Of the credit sales, 75 percent are collected in the first month following the sale and 25 percent in the second month following the sale. The gross profit margin on sales averages 20 percent.

All inventory purchases are paid during the month in which they are made. A basic inventory of $10,000 (cost) is constantly maintained, and the store follows a policy of purchasing enough additional inventory each month to cover the following month's sales.

A minimum cash balance of $2,000 is maintained by the store. Accrued Wages and Salaries and Other Current Liabilities remain unchanged. Any additional financing necessary will be obtained in multiples of $1,000. The Brown Store is a sole proprietorship. The Brown Store's balance sheet at August 1 follows:

Cash	$ 5,100	Accrued Wages and Salaries .. $	600
Accounts Receivable	14,700	Other Current Liabilities	2,000
Inventory (Cost)	26,000	Capital	59,200
Furniture and Fixtures $20,000			
Allowance for Depreciation .. 4,000	16,000		
	$61,800		$61,800

Past sales were $18,000 in June and $20,000 in July. The Brown Store's sales budget is August, $20,000; September, $26,000; October, $24,000; and November, $40,000.

Monthly expenses for wages and salaries are August, $1,400; September, $1,600; and October, $1,600. Rent is $400 per month; depreciation is $150 per month, and other expenses make up 1 percent of sales.

Required:

1. Prepare a cash budget for the quarter ending October 31. Show beginning cash balances, cash receipts, cash disbursements, and cash balances before and after financing for each month. Indicate clearly the maximum amount of necessary borrowing during this period.

2. Prepare a pro forma balance sheet at October 31 and a pro forma income statement for the quarter ending October 31.

(SMA adapted)

5.32   ***Budgeting for the Board of Education***   The board of education of the Victoria School District is developing a budget for the school year ending June 30, 19X7. The budgeted expenditures follow:

The following data are available:

The estimated average daily school enrollment of the school district is 5,000 pupils, including 4,800 regular pupils and 200 pupils enrolled in a vocational training program.

Estimated revenues include equalizing grants-in-aid from the state of $150 per pupil. The grants were established by state law under a plan intended to encourage raising the level of education.

The federal government matches 60 percent of state grants-in-aid for pupils enrolled in a vocational training program. In addition, the federal government contributes toward the costs of bus transportation and school lunches a maximum of $12 per pupil based on

Victoria School District
Budgeted Expenditures
for the Year Ending June 30, 19X7

Current Operating Expenditures

  Instruction

    General $1,401,600

    Vocational Training 112,600 $1,513,600

  Pupil Service

    Bus Transportation ...... $ 36,300

    School Lunches ....   51,700 $ 88,000

  Attendance and Health Service   14,000

  Administration   46,000

  Operation and Maintenance of Plant   208,000

  Pensions, Insurance, etc.   154,000

  Total Current Operating Expenditures $2,023,600

Other Expenditures

  Capital Outlays from Revenues .... $ 75,000

  Debt Service (Annual Installment and Interest on

    Long-term Debt)   150,000

  Total Other Expenditures   225,000

  Total Budgeted Expenditures $2,248,600

total enrollment within the school district but not to exceed 6⅔ percent of the state per-pupil equalization grants-in-aid.

Interest on temporary investment of school tax receipts and rents of school facilities are expected to be $75,000 and are earmarked for special equipment acquisitions listed as Capital Outlays from Revenues in the budgeted expenditures. Cost of the special equipment acquisitions will be limited to the amount derived from these miscellaneous receipts.

The remaining funds needed to finance the budgeted expenditures of the school district are to be raised from local taxation. An allowance of 9 percent of the local tax levy is necessary for possible tax abatements and losses. The assessed valuation of the property located within the school district is $80,000,000.

Required:

1. Prepare a schedule computing the estimated total funds required from local taxation for the ensuing school year ending June 30, 19X7, for the Victoria School District.

2. Prepare a schedule computing the estimated current operating cost per regular pupil and per vocational pupil to be met by local tax funds. Assume that costs other than instructional costs are assignable on a per-capita basis to regular and vocational students.

3. Without prejudice to your solution to part 1, assume that the estimated total tax levy for the ensuing school year ending June 30, 19X7, is $1,092,000. Prepare a schedule computing the estimated tax rate per $100 of assessed valuation of the property within the Victoria School District.

(AICPA adapted)

The process of *control* is the attempt by a manager or accountant to reach a state of control, where actual results conform to planned results. The process of control traditionally has been visualized as a series of examinations of the deviations between actual and planned performances. However, a manager may decide to bring about control by altering the planned results to conform to the actual results—a *feedback control system*. Similarly, a manager may elect to adjust the anticipated results through a compensatory action—a *feedforward control system*. Each of these control systems has distinct conceptual and operational advantages over the traditional control system. This chapter will elaborate on the nature of the control process, reviewing and discussing each of the control systems in terms of its implications for the design and effectiveness of a standard cost accounting system and in terms of its behavioral implications.

6.1   *NATURE OF THE CONTROL PROCESS*

6.1.1   *Types of Control*

Control is a central factor in the management of any organization. Leonard Sayles illustrates its importance:

After all controls are the techniques by which the manager decides how to expand his most valuable assets, his time. Be they formal or informal, it is through controls that he knows where things are going badly that require his intervention—and where and when he can relax because things are going well. All managers from presidents to foremen make use of controls, some more effectively than others.[1]

---

[1]Leonard Sayles, "The Many Dimensions of Control," *Organizational Dynamics* (Summer 1972), p. 21.

Sayles lists four distinct types of control that serve very different functions for the manager:

1. *Reassurances to sponsors*, whereby stakeholders are informed of the efficient conduct of operations.

2. *Closing the loop*, whereby the managers are informed that both technical and legal requirements have been met.

3. *Guidance to subordinates from managers*, whereby the subordinates are informed of "what is important and what they should concentrate on."

4. *Guidance to lower-level management by higher-level management*, whereby managers are informed of "where accomplishment is lagging and management action is needed." [2]

A more operational classification is provided by W. H. Newman, who recognizes three different types of control:

1. *Steering controls*, whereby management is provided signals indicating what will happen if it continues its present operations. Steering controls enable management to take either a *corrective* or an *adaptive response* before the total operation is completed. A corrective response implies the source of the error is inside the organization and can be corrected. An adaptive response implies that the source of the error is outside the organization and cannot be corrected. In the latter case, the solution is to redesign the operations to adapt to the new environmental situations.

2. *Yes/no controls*, whereby management is provided rules indicating the conditions that must be met before work may proceed to the next step. Yes/no controls provide management with checkpoints at different levels of the total operation. The technique is a defensive strategy aimed at controlling the size of the errors to be made by lower-level management and subordinates in general. In other words, yes/no controls are comparable to safety devices.

3. *Postaction controls*, whereby management is provided with performance reports or scorecards upon completion of the operations, indicating the differences or variances between the actual and planned performance. In general, postaction controls and steering controls make use of the feedback mechanism for the correction of any deviations, except that the response in the steering controls comes before the completion of the total operation. The steering controls may be labeled as a feedback control system, while the postaction controls are a traditional control system. [3]

6.1.2   *Stages of Control*

Control is an extension of the planning process. Planning sets the standards, and control puts the actual performance in the framework of the plan. There are three stages in the control process: (1) monitoring, (2) reviewing, and (3) correcting.

Monitoring consists of the measurement of actual performance. Its expression conforms to the terms used in standard setting in particular and in the statement of objec-

---

[2] Ibid.

[3] W. H. Newman, *Constructive Control: Design and Use of Control Systems* (Englewood Cliffs, N.J.: Prentice-Hall, 1975), p. 6.

tives in general. Monitoring can be expressed in monetary forms such as profits, costs, revenues, or other accounting indicators, and in nonmonetary forms such as the quality of the product, the nature of the market response, or any other social indicator. *Reviewing* consists of comparing the actual with the planned performance. The result of the comparison or variance may be favorable or unfavorable, controllable or noncontrollable. If the variance is unfavorable and controllable, the stage involving *correcting* the deviations between the actual and planned performance may be initiated. As noted earlier, the response in the third stage may be corrective or adaptive, depending on the source of the error.

6.1.3   *Sources of Control*

One or more of five possible causes can lead to a difference between the actual and standard performance: implementation failure, prediction error, measurement error, model error, and random deviation.

1. An *implementation failure* is a human or mechanical failure to obtain or maintain a specific obtainable action or standard. For example, the ordering or use of the wrong quantity of a given input, material, labor, or overhead will result in an implementation failure. Given that the standard is assumed to be obtainable, the deviation caused by the implementation failure may be immediately corrected once its existence is known. The decision to correct such *variance* depends on a comparison between the cost of correction and the resulting savings.

2. A *prediction error* is a failure to correctly predict one of the decision model's parameter values. Again, the decision to correct the variance depends on a comparison between the cost of resolving the model and the resulting cost savings.

3. A *measurement error* in determining the actual cost of operation occurs because of improper classification, recording, or counting. The correction of the variance involves improving the work habits of employees and motivating them to maintain proper records.

4. A *model error* results from an incorrect functional representation in the decision model. The decision to correct the variance depends on a comparison between the cost of reformulating the model and the resulting cost savings.

5. A *random deviation* results from minor variations in the input or output process. It arises from the stochastic operation of some correctly specified parameters. Random deviations are inevitable and need no corrective action.[4]

These sources of variation are important to decision makers because they involve assumptions, prediction methods, managerial habits, and decision models.

6.2   TRADITIONAL CONTROL MODEL

A firm using a traditional control model first establishes performance standards for each operational activity in a budget-setting phase. At the end of the period, it compares these

---

[4]Joel S. Demski, *Information Analysis* (Reading, Mass.: Addison-Wesley, 1972), chap. 6.

standards with the actual results, using the variance analysis techniques to assess (1) the nature of the obtained deviations and (2) the possibility of any corrective action. Therefore, a proper selection of the types of standards and the variance analysis technique is essential to the success of a traditional control system.

6.2.1   Standard Setting

A standard is a norm set for a given activity in the plan. It represents the best and most operational working method for the activity, given the state of the art. Consequently, the standard represents a normative expression of the performance related to a given activity, while the actual result represents a descriptive expression. The difference between standard performance and actual performance lies in the distinction defined by management between what should be and what is acceptable behavior.

To avoid semantic problems, the standard is generally considered a *unit concept*, while the budget is a *total concept*. For example, the *standard cost* of direct labor is $3 per direct-labor hour (DLH), whereas the budgeted cost of direct labor is $24,000 if 8,000 direct-labor hours are needed at a standard cost of $3 per direct-labor hour. In general, the standard cost is used for the control of direct material and direct labor, while the budgeted cost is used for the control of overhead. This is because prime costs are identifiable with individual units of output, whereas overhead is only identifiable with total production.

Different types of standards have been presented in the literature and in practice. Standards are either basic or current. *Basic standards* are historical performance standards that are not changed unless there are important modifications in the nature or sequence of the manufacturing operations. *Current standards* might be changed to reflect environmental changes. Basic standards are useful for long-term analysis of variances, while current standards are more suited to short-run analysis.

There are three different levels of current and basic standards: expected actual standard, normal standard, and theoretical standard. The expected actual standard is set for an expected capacity for the coming year and reflects predictions about the expected actual results. The normal standard, or currently attainable standard, is set for a *normal capacity*. This is the level of operations attainable by normal operating procedures, allowing for extraordinary events such as normal spoilage, ordinary machine breakdowns, and lost time. The theoretical, or ideal, standard is the standard set for a *theoretical capacity*, the level of operations possible under the best operating conditions without any unusual events. It is a perfect, maximum efficiency standard.

There are four broad classes of current and basic standards: imposed standards, standards set through participation, standards set with consultation, and standards reinforced by financial rewards. Imposed standards are derived without any input from subordinates. They reassert the superior's power in the budgeting process and emphasize the goals of the organization. Standards set through participation are derived with direct input from subordinates. They can increase motivation, and they emphasize both the organizational and individual goals. Standards set with consultation are derived with indirect input from subordinates. They represent a trade-off between the imposed and the participative approaches to standard setting. Standards reinforced by financial rewards are derived with a commitment from subordinates secured by linking rewards to organizational performance. An often-cited example is the Scanlon plan.[5]

---

[5]F. C. Lesieur, ed., *The Scanlon Plan* (Cambridge, Mass.: MIT Press, 1958).

Basic and current standards are estimated in several ways, mainly through engineering methods, managerial estimates, collective bargaining, and the learning curve. The engineering methods consist of an examination of the engineering specifications of manufactured outputs. The production function, or the input/output, mix of a productive process indicates the amount of physical output expected from a particular mix of material, labor, and capital equipment. The engineering methods are useful to determine standard quantities of material and labor. Hence standard quantities of material are specified by the engineering department on the basis of technical requirements defined by the product design and production function. Similarly, time and motion studies establish standard quantities of labor based on observation of the actual performance of a given operating task by an actual worker of average aptitude. Managerial estimates may be necessary to estimate a standard quantity of overhead, which might be difficult to obtain through the engineering estimates. Experience, participation, involvement, and commitment are advantages to the use of managerial views for the estimation of standards. Collective bargaining agreements establish the standard labor rates, such as hourly wages, piece rates, and bonus differentials. The learning curve can be used to assess and determine the standard quantity of labor required.

6.2.2   *Direct-Cost Variances*

Models of Variance Analysis

Actual performance and standard performance can be compared within three models in *variance analysis*: the one-way model, the two-way model, and the three-way model.

The *one-way model* appraises the total performance for a given activity by combining the effects of both price and quantity decisions. It is expressed by a unique variance figure as follows:

$$V_t = P_a Q_a - P_s Q_s,$$

where

V_t = Total variance.

P_a = Actual price.

Q_a = Actual quantity.

P_s = Standard price.

Q_s = Standard quantity.

The *two-way model* appraises both the price and quantity performance for a given activity. It is expressed by both a price and a quantity variance as follows:

$$V_p = Q_a(P_a - P_s)$$

and

$$V_q = P_s(Q_a - Q_s),$$

where

V_p = Price variance.

V_q = Quantity variance.

The *three-way model* formulates the price variance differently than the two-way model to pinpoint the joint responsibility through a joint price/quantity variance. The model is expressed by a price variance, a quantity variance, and a joint price/quantity variance as follows:

$$V_p = Q_s(P_a - P_s),$$
$$V_q = P_s(Q_a - Q_s),$$
$$V_{pq} = (P_a - P_s)(Q_a - Q_s),$$

where V_{pq} = joint price/quantity variance.

The usual breakdown of variances into only price and quantity variances, as advocated by the two-way model, is not conceptually correct because of the existence of a joint price/quantity variance. The graphic analysis of variance depicted in Figure 6.1 highlights these differences. The small area in the upper right corner may create problems, because a price-responsible agent may not accept responsibility for the price variance $Q_a(P_a - P_s)$, as computed in the two-way analysis of variances. However, any of

Figure 6.1   *Graphic Analysis of Variances*

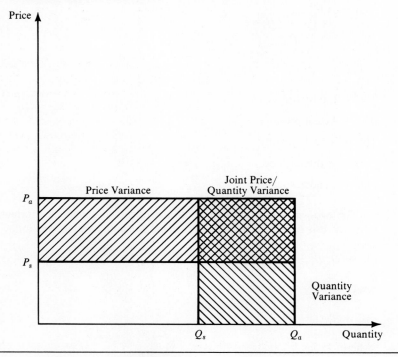

the three analyses of variance models can be used to assess the performance of operational activities pertaining to the acquisition and use of direct manufacturing inputs.

Direct-Material Variances

The master budget must include two standards for material costs: a material price standard and a material quantity standard. A comparison between actual and planned material costs, using a two-way analysis of variance, leads to the computation and evaluation of both a *material price variance* and a usage variance (material quantity variance). The material price standards set by the purchasing department reflect current market prices. They are intended to be both an indicator of efficient conduct of the purchasing activities and an indicator of the effects of price changes on the company's profits. The material price standards can be used to evaluate the purchasing department's general performance. The material price variance is computed as follows:

In a two-way model: $V_{MP} = Q_a(P_a - P_s)$,

In a three-way model: $V_{MP} = Q_s(P_a - P_s)$,

where V_{MP} = material price variance.

The material quantity standard set by the production department reflects basic material specifications for routine production operations. Either the quantity standard at the time of purchase or at the time of usage can be used, and both are indicators of the efficient conduct of production activities. The usage variance is computed in both two- and three-factor models as follows:

$$U = P_s(Q_a - Q_s),$$

where U = usage variance.

Direct-Labor Variances

The master budget specifies two standards for labor: a labor price standard, or rate standard, and a labor quantity standard, or labor efficiency standard. A difference between the actual and planned labor performance will lead—in a two-way analysis of variance—to the computation of both a labor price variance, or *labor rate variance*, and a labor quantity variance, or *labor efficiency variance*. The rate standard set by the personnel department is the result of collective bargaining agreements, government regulations, and other factors. Consequently, rate variances are rare and occur only in unusual situations. The rate variance is computed as follows:

In a two-way model: $R = Q_a(P_a - P_s)$,

In a three-way model: $R = Q_s(P_a - P_s)$,

where R = rate variance.

The labor efficiency standard set by the production department reflects production specifications. The production department uses it to evaluate labor management efficiency. The labor efficiency variance can be computed as follows:

$$E = P_s(Q_a - Q_s),$$

where E = labor efficiency variance.

Illustration of Direct-Cost Variances

The following data will be used to compute the direct-cost variances:

Input	Actual Quantity	Standard Quantity	Actual Price	Standard Price
Direct Material	5,000 Units	4,000 Units	$15	$20
Direct Labor	2,000 DLH	1,000 DLH	$20	$10

The formal calculation of direct-cost variances is shown in Table 6.1.

6.2.3 Factory Overhead Variances

Sources of Overhead Variances

Overhead variances occur only when standard values for factory overhead are used to record costs, which does not arise in all costing systems. Two differences in costing systems of significance to overhead variances should be examined:

1. Costing systems differ in terms of the inventory valuation techniques (absorption versus direct costing). This issue will be examined in chapter 9.

2. The valuation of costs can be in terms of actual, normal, or standard costing. An *actual costing system* applies to the units produced actual values for direct material consumed, direct labor used, and overhead. A *normal costing system* applies actual values for direct material consumed and direct labor used to the units produced, but it applies overhead on the basis of a predetermined overhead rate. Finally, a *standard costing system* applies standard values to the amounts of material, labor, and overhead used. Table 6.2 summarizes the three methods.

Application of Overhead in Normal and Standard Costing Systems

Factory overhead is applied on the basis of a predetermined overhead rate in both normal and standard costing. The computation of the factory overhead rate involves the following four steps:

1. Estimating the normal activity level and the corresponding factory overhead.

2. Classifying the factory overhead into fixed and variable components.

3. Determining the variable factory overhead rate, the fixed factory overhead rate, and the total factory overhead rate.

4. Applying the overhead rate to jobs and products on the basis of the actual activity level.

Table 6.3 illustrates the computation of the predetermined overhead rate and the resulting flexible budget. Assuming that 80 percent represents normal capacity, the predetermined or standard overhead rate can be computed as follows:

$$\text{Standard overhead rate} = \frac{\$10,000}{10,000 \text{ hours}} = \$1 \text{ per standard direct-labor hour (SDLH)}.$$

This determined rate may be divided into: (1) a fixed component: $3,000/10,000 = $.30 per SDLH, and (2) a variable component: $7,000/10,000 = $.70 per SDLH. Although straightforward, the steps for computing the predetermined overhead rate

Table 6.1   *Direct-Cost Variances*

I. Analysis of Variance

  A. *Total Material Variance*
    $(\$5,000 \times \$15) - (\$4,000 \times \$20)$ = $5,000 (Favorable)

  B. *Total Labor Variance*
    $(\$2,000 \times \$20) - (\$1,000 \times \$10)$ = $30,000 (Unfavorable)

  C. *Total Direct-Cost Variance*
    $\$5,000 + (\$30,000)$ = $25,000 (Unfavorable)

II. Two-Way Analysis of Variance

  A. *Material Variances*
    1. Material Price Variance
      $5,000 (\$15 - \$20)$ = $25,000 (Favorable)
    2. Usage Variance
      $\$20 (5,000 - 4,000)$ = $20,000 (Unfavorable)

  B. *Direct-Labor Variances*
    1. Rate Variance
      $2,000 (\$20 - \$10)$ = $20,000 (Unfavorable)
    2. Labor Efficiency Variance
      $\$10 (2,000 - 1,000)$ = $10,000 (Unfavorable)

III. Three-Way Analysis of Variance

  A. *Material Variances*
    1. Material Price Variance
      $4,000 (\$15 - \$20)$ = $20,000 (Favorable)
    2. Usage Variance (as above)   = $20,000 (Unfavorable)
    3. Joint Price/Quantity Material Variance
      $(5,000 - 4,000) \times (\$15 - \$10)$ = $5,000 (Favorable)

  B. *Direct-Labor Variances*
    1. Rate Variance
      $1,000 (\$20 - \$10)$ = $10,000 (Unfavorable)
    2. Labor Efficiency Variance
      $\$10 (2,000 - 1,000)$ = $10,000 (Unfavorable)
    3. Joint Price/Quantity Labor Variance
      $(2,000 - 1,000) (\$20 - \$10)$ = $10,000 (Unfavorable)

Table 6.2   *Comparison Summary of Product Costing Methods*

a. Actual Costing	b. Normal Costing	c. Standard Costing
Work-in-Process Inventory	**Work-in-Process Inventory**	**Work-in-Process Inventory**
Actual Direct Material	Actual Direct Material	Standard Direct Material
Actual Direct Labor	Actual Direct Labor	Standard Direct Labor
Actual Variable Factory Overhead	Applied Variable Factory Overhead	Standard Variable Factory Overhead
Actual Fixed Factory Overhead	Applied Fixed Factory Overhead	Standard Fixed Factory Overhead

Table 6.3   ***Flexible Factory Overhead Budget***

	40%	80%	100%
Capacity (Expressed as a Percentage of Normal)	40%	80%	100%
Direct-Labor Hours	5,000	10,000	15,000
Variable Factory Overhead			
Indirect Labor	$2,000	$ 3,000	$ 5,000
Indirect Material	1,000	4,000	5,000
Total Variable Factory Overhead	$3,000	$ 7,000	$10,000
Fixed Factory Overhead			
Machinery Depreciation	$1,000	$ 1,000	$ 1,000
Insurance	500	500	500
Property Taxes	500	500	500
Power and Light	800	800	800
Maintenance	200	200	200
Total Fixed Factory Overhead	$3,000	$ 3,000	$ 3,000
Total Factory Overhead	$6,000	$10,000	$13,000
Overhead Budget Formula	$3,000 + $.7 per Direct-Labor Hour		

present some conceptual problems in both the choice of the activity level, and the expression of the denominator level.

The choice of the activity level rests on the choice of an expression of capacity. Depending upon whether a long- or short-range viewpoint is adopted, the activity level can be expressed as either a normal capacity or an expected annual capacity.

The normal capacity is the level of capacity utilization that will meet average and trend variations. It covers a period long enough to average consumer demand over a number of years and includes seasonal, cyclical, and trend variations. Its timespan is sufficiently long to average out sizable changes in activity and allow a trend for sales. Under normal capacity, the overhead rate is uniform and does not change with changes in production levels. The use of normal capacity may result in overapplication in some years that is compensated by underapplication in other years.

The expected actual capacity, or expected annual capacity, is the anticipated level of capacity utilization for the coming year. Needless to say, the resulting overhead rate will vary from one period to another with changes in the short-term production levels. It may be easily argued that the use of the normal capacity avoids capricious changes in unit costs.

The denominator level expressing the activity level must be a useful common denominator for measuring production in all departments. Given the differences in the outputs of different departments, the activity level should be expressed uniformly. There must be a causal relationship between the denominator base and the overhead costs, and the denominator level should be measured in terms of outputs rather than inputs. In general, the denominator level is expressed in terms of *standard hours of input allowed for good output produced*. That is, if 1 unit of output requires 2 standard direct-labor hours, 800 units of output achieved may be expressed as 1,600 (800 × 2) standard hours of input allowed for good output produced.

One-Way Variance Model

Jobs and products in a *standard-cost system* are charged with overhead on the basis of standard direct-labor hours rather than actual hours. At the end of the period, the applied overhead is compared with the actual overhead. In the one-way variance model, the difference between the actual factory overhead and the applied factory overhead constitutes the total factory overhead variance.

Consider the following example. The Kahl Company has prepared the following estimates for 19XA:

Budgeted overhead: $3,000 + $.7 per DLH.

Normal capacity in DLH: 10,000 units × 1 DLH per unit = 10,000 DLH.

Standard total overhead rate: $\dfrac{\$3,000 + \$.7(10,000 \text{ DLH})}{10,000 \text{ DLH}}$ = $1 per DLH.

$$= \$.3 \text{ fixed per DLH} + \$.7 \text{ variable per DLH.}$$

In 19XA the actual data are

Variable Overhead	$4,500
Fixed Overhead	$4,000
Units Produced	8,000 Units
Direct-Labor Hours	8,700 DLH

Thus, during 19XB the factory overhead applied to production, based on standard labor hours for actual production, is equal to 8,000 units × 1 DLH per unit = 8,000 DLH.

The total factory overhead variance will be computed as follows:

Total factory overhead variance = Actual factory overhead − Applied factory overhead

The computation of the one-way variance model for the Kahl Company can be illustrated as follows:

Actual Factory Overhead (8,700 DLH)		**Applied Factory Overhead on the Basis of Standard Bonus** (8,000 DLH × $1 per DLH)
Fixed	$4,000	$2,400
Variable	$4,500	$5,600
Total	$8,500	$8,000

Factory Overhead Variance

$500 Unfavorable

This total unfavorable factory overhead variance needs further analysis to identify the exact causes of its incurrence and help management choose a corrective action. Further analysis may be made by (1) the two-way variance model A or B, (2) the three-way variance model A or B, or (3) the four-way variance model.

Two-Way Variance Model A

There are two possible two-way variance models. The two-way model A is analogous to that used for direct costs (material and labor). The total overhead variance is separated into an overhead price variance and an overhead efficiency variance. The computation of the two-way variance model A for the Kahl Company is as follows:

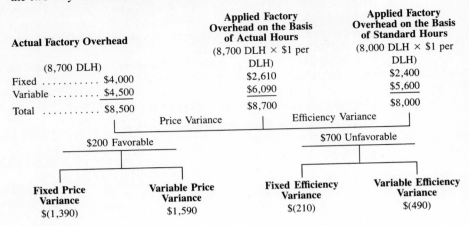

Two-Way Variance Model B

The two-way variance model B distinguishes between a controllable variance and a volume variance (uncontrollable). The computation of the two-way variance model B for the Kahl Company is as follows:

Actual Factory Overhead	Budgeted Overhead for Standard Hours	Applied Factory Overhead on the Basis of Standard Hours
(8,700 DLH)	$3,000 + $.7(8,000 DLH)	(8,000 DLH × $1 per DLH)
Fixed $4,000	$3,000	$2,400
Variable $4,500	$5,600	$5,600
Total $8,500	$8,600	$8,000

Controllable Variance | Uncontrollable Variance

$100 Favorable $600 Unfavorable

The controllable variance and the volume variance can be computed differently. The controllable variance is due to the variable overhead and can be computed as follows:

Variable Overhead at Normal Capacity	$7,000
Standard Hours Allowed (8,000 DLH)	× 80%
Allowable Variable Overhead	$5,600
Actual Variable Overhead ($8,500 − $3,000)	5,500
Controllable Variance	$ 100 (Favorable)

The uncontrollable (or volume) variance is due to the fixed overhead and can be computed as follows:

Normal Capacity	10,000 DLH
Standard Hours	− 8,000 DLH
Capacity Unused	2,000 DLH
Fixed Overhead Rate	×$ .3
	$ 600 (Unfavorable)

The controllable variance is the responsibility of the department manager, given that it is possible to control the causes of the variance. The uncontrollable or volume variance arises from the failure to use the total capacity or from inefficient use of the available capacity.

Three-Way Variance Model A

In the three-way variance model A, the total factory overhead variance is divided into (1) an *overhead spending variance*, (2) an overhead capacity variance (or *idle capacity variance*), and (3) an overhead efficiency variance. The three-way variance model A for the Kahl Company can be computed as follows:

Actual Factory Overhead	Budgeted Overhead for Actual Hours	Applied Overhead on the Basis of Actual Hours	Applied Overhead on the Basis of Standard Hours
(8,700 DLH)	$3,000 +	(8,700 DLH	(8,000 DLH
	$.7(8,700 DLH)	× $1 per DLH)	× $1 per DLH)
Fixed $4,000	$3,000	$2,610	$2,400
Variable $4,500	$6,090	$6,090	$5,600
Total $8,500	$9,090	$8,700	$8,000

Spending Variance	Idle Capacity Variance	Efficiency Variance
$590 Favorable	$390 Unfavorable	$700 Unfavorable

The idle capacity variance can be computed as follows:

Normal Capacity	10,000 DLH
Actual Capacity	− 8,700 DLH
Capacity Unused in Planning	1,300 DLH
Fixed Overhead Rate	×$ .3
	$ 390 (Unfavorable)

The spending variance is again the responsibility of the departmental manager. Performance based on the spending variance appears more favorable than performance based on the controllable variance ($100 versus $590), because the budgeted overhead is based on the actual rather than the standard hours.

The idle capacity variance is due to the underabsorption or overabsorption of overhead arising from differences between the actual capacity and the normal capacity, on which the overhead rate was based. The efficiency variance results from the differences between the actual hours and the standard hours allowed for actual production. These differences reflect inefficiencies in labor usage if the capacity level is expressed in terms of labor hours and they reflect inefficiencies in material usage if the capacity level is expressed in terms of machine hours.

Three-Way Variance Model B

The three-way variance model B makes a distinction between overhead spending variance, overhead efficiency variance, and overhead capacity variance. The computation of the three-way variance model B for the Kahl Company is illustrated as follows:

Actual Factory Overhead	Budgeted Overhead for Actual Hours $3,000 + $.7(8,700 DLH)	Budgeted Overhead for Standard Hours $3,000 + $.7(8,000 DLH)	Applied Overhead on the Basis of Standard Hours (8,000 DLH × $1 per DLH)
(8,700 DLH)			
Fixed $4,000	$3,000	$3,000	$2,400
Variable $4,500	$6,090	$5,600	$5,600
Total $8,500	$9,090	$8,600	$8,000

Spending Variance	Efficiency Variance	Idle Capacity Variance
$590 Favorable	$490 Unfavorable	$600 Unfavorable

Four-Way Variance Model

The four-way variance model is identical to the three-way variance model A, except the efficiency variance is separated into fixed efficiency variance and variable efficiency variance. The four-variance model for the Kahl Company is computed as follows:

Actual Factory Overhead	Budgeted Overhead for Actual Hours $3,000 + $.7(8,700 DLH)	Applied Overhead on the Basis of Actual Hours (8,700 DLH × $1 per DLH)	Applied Overhead on the Basis of Standard Hours (8,000 DLH × $1 per DLH)
(8,700 DLH)			
Fixed $4,000	$3,000	$2,610	$2,400
Variable $4,500	$6,090	$6,090	$5,600
Total $8,500	$9,090	$8,700	$8,000

Spending Variance	Idle Capacity Variance	Efficiency Variance
$590 Favorable	$390 Unfavorable	$700 Unfavorable

Fixed Efficiency Variance	Variable Efficiency Variance
$.3 × (8,700 − 8,000 DLH)	$.7 × (8,700 − 8,000 DLH)
$210 Unfavorable	$490 Unfavorable

Note that the sum of the spending variance ($590 favorable) and the variable efficiency variance ($490 unfavorable) equals the controllable variance ($100) of the two-way variance method B. Similarly, the sum of the idle capacity variance ($390 unfavorable) and the fixed efficiency variance ($210 unfavorable) equals the uncontrollable or volume variance ($600) of the two-way variance method B. Table 6.4 summarizes the factory overhead variance analysis methods.

6.2.4   Mix and Yield Variances

In industries where more than one material is required to produce 1 unit of the company's product, material mix and material yield are important in decisions related to setting the final product cost, determining which kind of raw material to use, and effecting cost reduction and profit improvements. Deviations from the standard mix and yield result in a mix (or blend) variance and a yield variance.

The mix variance results from using an actual mix in quantities of raw materials different than the standard material mix or specifications. The yield variance results from obtaining a yield (a measure of output) different than the one called for based on the standard input.

Consider the following simple example set up to show how the mix and yield variances can be derived. The ABC Company uses two different materials in the production of its product. Standard product and cost specifications per unit of finished product are as follows:

Material X: 1 Lb. @ $5 per Lb. = $ 5
Material Y: 2 Lb. @ $3 per Lb. = $ 6
Total Material Cost $11

The production of 1 unit of finished good requires 3 pounds of raw materials, or an expected yield of ⅓. Actual finished production for the month of January is 1,000 units, with the following materials used:

	Pounds	Cost
Material X	600	$ 4,800
Material Y	3,000	$12,000

Based on these figures, the material usage variance would be as follows:

Material X: (600 − 1,000)$5 = $2,000 Favorable
Material Y: (3,000 − 2,000)$3 = $3,000 Unfavorable
Unfavorable Usage Variance   = $1,000

The next step is to investigate whether this usage variance is due to a mix and/or a yield variance. These variances are calculated in the following manner:

Mix Variance

Formula		Ratio
Material X:	1 Lb.	⅓
Material Y:	2 Lb.	⅔
	3 Lb.	1

Actual Quantity		Actual Quantity Adjusted	
Material X:	600 Lb.	(⅓ × 3,600) =	1,200 Lb.
Material Y:	3,000 Lb.	(⅔ × 3,600) =	2,400 Lb.
	3,600 Lb.		3,600 Lb.

Mix Variance = (Actual quantity − Actual quantity adjusted) × Standard Price.
Material X = (600 − 1,200)$5 = $3,000 Favorable
Material Y = (3,000 − 2,400)$3 = $1,800 Unfavorable
Favorable Mix Variance $1,200

Yield Variance = (Actual Quantity Adjusted − Standard Quantity) × Standard Price.
Material X = (1,200 − 1,000)$5 = $1,000 Unfavorable
Material Y = (2,400 − 2,000)$3 = $1,200 Unfavorable
Unfavorable Yield Variance $2,200

Table 6.4   Summary of Factory Overhead Variance Analysis Methods

Method	Actual Factory Overhead	Budgeted Overhead for Actual Hours	Budgeted Overhead for Standard Hours	Actual Hours × Standard Rate	Standard Hours × Standard Rate
Two-Way Variance Method A	$8,500			$8,700	$8,000
Two-Way Variance Method B	8,500		$8,600		8,000
Three-Way Variance Method A	8,500	$9,090		8,700	8,000
Three-Way Variance Method B	8,500	9,090	8,600		8,000
Four-Way Variance Method	8,500	9,090	8,600	8,700	8,000

Dividing the material usage variance into a mix variance and a yield variance can guide the management of ABC Company toward the true cause of the unfavorable usage variance and toward a useful investigation and correction.

6.2.5   Standard Cost Accounting System

A standard cost accounting system includes at least two phases: (1) the recording of standard costs in the regular accounting system and the isolation of variances and (2) the disposition of variances.

Isolating the Direct-Material Variances

The general ledger entries to record and isolate the material variances arising in a standard cost accounting system generally fit into three categories:

1. Material purchase price variance is recognized at the time of the input purchases, while material usage variance is recognized at the time of the issuance of the input.

2. Material usage price variance and material usage (quantity) variance are both recognized at the time of the input issuance.

3. Material purchase price variance is recognized at the time of the input purchases, while both material usage price variance and material usage (quantity) variance are recognized at the time of the input issuance.

To illustrate the three methods, assume the following data:

Standard Material Cost per Unit	$3.00
Purchases	1,000 Units at $2.50
Issuance for Production	500 Units
Standard Quantity Allowed	450 Units

Table 6.4   continued

Variances for Each Method	Total Overhead Variance
Price Variance = Col. 1 − Col. 4 = $200 Favorable. Efficiency Variance = Col. 4 − Col. 5 = $700 Unfavorable.	$500 (Unfavorable)
Controllable Variance = Col. 1 − Col. 3 = $100 Favorable. Volume Variance = Col. 3 − Col. 5 = $600 Unfavorable.	$500 (Unfavorable)
Spending Variance = Col. 1 − Col. 2 = $590 Favorable. Idle Capacity Variance = Col. 2 − Col. 4 = $390 Unfavorable. Efficiency Variance = Col. 4 − Col. 5 = $700 Unfavorable.	$500 (Unfavorable)
Spending Variance = Col. 1 − Col. 2 = $590 Favorable. Efficiency Variance = Col. 2 − Col. 3 = $490 Unfavorable. Idle Capacity Variance = Col. 3 − Col. 5 = $600 Unfavorable.	$500 (Unfavorable)
Spending Variance = Col. 1 − Col. 2 = $590 Favorable. Idle Capacity Variance = Col. 2 − Col. 4 = $390 Unfavorable. Variable Efficiency Variance = Col. 2 − Col. 3 = $490 Unfavorable. Fixed Efficiency Variance = $210 Unfavorable.	$500 (Unfavorable)

Method 1   In the first method, the T accounts would appear as follows:

Material Inventory		Work-in-Process Inventory	
1. Beginning Inventory 2. Actual Quantity × Standard Price	3. Actual Quantity Requisitioned × Standard Price	3. Standard Quantity Requisitioned × Standard Price	

Accounts Payable		Direct-Material Purchase Price Variance		Direct-Material Usage Variance	
	2. Actual Quantity Purchased × Actual Price	2. Difference in Price × Actual Quantity		3. Difference in Quantity Issued × Standard Price	

The first method recognizes the material price variances at the time of incurrence or purchase and the usage variance at the time of issuance. Note that the variances are debited when unfavorable and credited when favorable.

The journal entry at the time of material incurrence would be

```
Material Inventory ......................   3,000
    Accounts Payable ....................          2,500
    Material Purchase Price Variance ........          500
To record the purchase of 1,000 units of direct material.
```

The journal entry at the time of material issuance would be

```
Work-in-Process .........................   1,350
Material Usage Variance ..................     150
    Material ...........................          1,500
To record the issuance of 500 units of direct material.
```

Method 2 In the second method the T accounts would appear as follows:

Material Inventory	
1. Beginning Inventory 2. Actual Quantity × Actual Price	3. Actual Quantity Requisitioned × Actual Price

Work-in-Process Inventory	
3. Standard Quantity Requisitioned × Standard Price	

Accounts Payable	
	2. Actual Quantity × Actual Price

Material Usage Price Variance	
3. Difference in Price × Actual Quantity	

Material Quantity Variance	
3. Differences in Quantity × Standard Price	

The second method recognizes both the material usage price variance and the material quantity variance at the time of issuance. The journal entry at the time of material incurrence would be

Material Inventory	2,500	
Accounts Payable		2,500

To record the purchase of 1,000 units of direct material.

The journal entry at the time of material issuance would be

Work-in-Process	1,350	
Material Quantity Variance	150	
Material		1,250
Material Usage Price Variance		250

To record the issuance of 500 units of direct material.

Method 3 In the third method, the T accounts would appear as follows:

Material Inventory	
1. Beginning Inventory 2. Actual Quantity × Standard Price	3. Actual Quantity × Standard Price

Work-in-Process Inventory	
3. Standard Quantity Requisitioned × Standard Price	

Accounts Payable	
	2. Actual Quantity × Actual Price

Direct-Material Purchase Price Variance	
2. Difference in Price × Actual Quantity Purchased	4. Difference in Price × Quantity Requisitioned

Direct-Material Usage Variance	
3. Difference in Quantity Issued × Standard Price	

Direct-Material Usage Price Variance	
4. Difference in Price × Quantity Requisitioned	

The third method recognizes the material purchase price variance at the time of purchase and both the material quantity and price variances at the time of issuance. The journal entry at the time of material incurrence would be

Material Inventory	3,000	
Accounts Payable		2,500
Material Purchase Price Variance		500

To record the purchase of 1,000 units of direct material.

The entry at the time of material issuance would be

Work-in-Process 1,350
Material Quantity Variance 150
    Materials   1,500
To record the issuance of 500 units of direct material.

The entry to record the material usage price variance would be

Materials Purchase Price Variance 250
    Materials Usage Price Variance   250

Isolating the Direct-Labor Variances

The general ledger entries to record and isolate the direct-labor variances arising in a standard cost accounting system generally fall under two categories: (1) direct labor incurred is recognized on the basis of actual values; and (2) standard direct labor distributed is recognized on the basis of standard values, and variances are isolated. To illustrate, assume the following data:

Actual Hours Worked   2,000 Hours
Actual Rate $5 per Hour
Standard Hours Allowed   1,500 Hours
Standard Rate $4 per Hour

To isolate the direct-labor variance, the T accounts would appear as follows:

Payroll		Work-in-Process Inventory		Accrued Payroll	
1. Direct Labor Incurred	2. Actual Hours × Actual Rate	2. Standard Hours Allowed × Standard Rate			1. Direct Labor Incurred

Labor Rate Variance		Labor Efficiency Variance	
2. Difference in Rates × Actual Hours Worked		2. Difference in Quantities × Standard Rate	

The two journal entries are as follows. The entry at the time of labor incurrence would be

Payroll 10,000
    Accrued Payroll   10,000
To record the incurrence of direct labor.

The entry at the time of labor distribution would be

Work-in-Process 6,000
Labor Rate Variance 2,000
Labor Efficiency Variance 2,000
    Payroll   10,000
To record the distribution of direct labor.

Isolating the Overhead Variances

The general ledger entries to record and isolate the overhead variances arising in a standard cost accounting system include the following three steps:

1. Factory overhead incurred is recognized on the basis of actual values.

2. Factory overhead is applied to the Work-in-Process Inventory (sometimes referred to as *Work-in-Process*) on the basis of standard or budgeted values.

3. Overhead variances are isolated.

To illustrate, assume the following data (used previously in section 6.2.3 to illustrate the computation of overhead variances).

Standard overhead = $3,000 + $.7 per SDLH.

Normal capacity = 10,000 SDLH.

Total predetermined overhead rate (TPOR) = $\dfrac{\$10,000}{10,000}$ = $1 per SDLH.

Variable predetermined overhead rate (VPOR) = $\dfrac{\$7,000}{10,000}$ = $.7 per SDLH.

Fixed predetermined overhead rate (FPOR) = $\dfrac{\$3,000}{10,000}$ = $.3 per SDLH.

Actual overhead = $4,000 fixed + $4,500 variable = $8,500.

Actual capacity = 8,700 DLH.

Standard hours for actual production = 8,000 SDLH.

The journal entries using the four-way variance method are as follows. At the time of factory overhead incurrence, the entry is

```
Factory Overhead Control . . . . . . . . . . . . . . . . . . . . . . . . . . . .   8,500
      Cash, Accounts Payable, Accrued Expenses  . . . . . . . .            8,500
To record the incurrence of actual factory overhead.
```

At the time of factory overhead application, the entry is

```
Work-in-Process  . . . . . . . . . . . . . . . . . . . . . . . . . . . . . . . .   8,000
Variable Efficiency Variance . . . . . . . . . . . . . . . . . . . . . . .     490
Fixed Efficiency Variance  . . . . . . . . . . . . . . . . . . . . . . . .     210
      Factory Overhead Control . . . . . . . . . . . . . . . . . . . . .              8,700
To record the application of factory overhead.
```

To record the other variances and close the $200 credit balance of Factory Overhead, the entry is

```
Factory Overhead  . . . . . . . . . . . . . . . . . . . . . . . . . . . . . . .     200
Idle Capacity Variance  . . . . . . . . . . . . . . . . . . . . . . . . . . .     390
      Spending Variance . . . . . . . . . . . . . . . . . . . . . . . . . . . .              590
```

Another possible accounting treatment for the second and third entries is as follows:

```
Work-in-Process  . . . . . . . . . . . . . . . . . . . . . . . . . . . . . . . .   8,000
      Factory Overhead Control . . . . . . . . . . . . . . . . . . . . .              8,000
Variable Efficiency Variance . . . . . . . . . . . . . . . . . . . . . . .     490
Fixed Efficiency Variance  . . . . . . . . . . . . . . . . . . . . . . . .     210
Idle Capacity Variance  . . . . . . . . . . . . . . . . . . . . . . . . . . .     390
      Spending Variance . . . . . . . . . . . . . . . . . . . . . . . . . . . .              590
      Factory Overhead Control . . . . . . . . . . . . . . . . . . . . .              500
```

Disposition of Variances

Both the normal and standard costing systems produce accounts valued at standard costs and a set of variances. At the end of the accounting period, the variances may be treated as follows:

1. They can be carried as deferred charges or credits on the balance sheet.
2. They can appear as charges or credits on the income statements.
3. They can be allocated to inventories and cost of goods sold.

Each of these will be dealt with in turn.

The deferral of variances is supported on the grounds that if the standards in use are based on normal levels of price, efficiency, and output, then positive and negative variances can be expected to offset one another in the long run. Because variance account balances at a given point in time are due to recurring seasonal and business cycle fluctuations, and because periodic reporting requirements result in arbitrary cutoff dates, variance account balances at a particular cutoff date are not assignable to the operating results of the period then ended. They will cancel out over recurring seasonal and business cycle fluctuations and, therefore, should be carried to the balance sheet. This method is appropriate for interim statements, no matter what method is used for annual statements.

If variances appear as charges or credits on the income statement, they are regarded as appropriate charges or credits in the period in which they arise, because they are considered to be the result of favorable or unfavorable departures from normal (standard) conditions. These variances are disclosed separately from cost of goods sold at standard cost and thus provide management with unobscured information permitting immediate corrective action. Inventory valuations and cost of goods sold should not be distorted by variances that represent abnormal efficiencies or inefficiencies. A standard cost represents the amount that is reasonably necessary to produce finished products and, therefore, should be considered the best measure of cost of goods manufactured and inventory valuation as long as the underlying operating conditions remain unchanged.

Those who advocate allocation of variances to inventories and cost of goods sold regard standard costs as a useful tool for purposes of managerial control rather than as substitutes for actual historical costs in the financial statements. These people believe that only actual historical costs should be used for financial reporting, even though these costs are greater or less than standard costs and without regard to the reasons for the historical costs' differences from standard costs. Standard cost variances are not gains or losses; they are costs (or reductions thereof) of goods manufactured and, as such, should be allocated to inventories and cost of goods sold. To treat standard cost variances as gains or losses in the period in which they arise distorts both the inventory and gross profit figures. This distortion would be even greater if the standards lacked accuracy or reliability. Further, to substitute standard costs for actual historical costs in the financial statements represents an unwarranted sacrifice of objectivity.

The decision to allocate variances to inventories and cost of goods sold depends on the following:

1. The type of variances—materials, labor, or overhead.
2. The materiality of the variances.
3. The sign of the variances—favorable or unfavorable, and controllable or uncontrollable.

4. The managerial policy concerning the nature of the cost giving rise to a variance—period cost or product cost.

To illustrate the *disposition of variances*, consider the Mercado Company, which began operations in 19X7 and had the following results:

Sales Price per Unit	$20 per Unit
Volume of Sales	9,000 Units
Direct Material Consumed	10,000 Units
Direct Labor Incurred	12,000 DLH at $5 per DLH = $60,000
Factory Overhead Incurred	$12,000
Predetermined Overhead Rate	$1 per DLH
Selling and Administrative Expenses	$10,000
Direct Material Purchased	15,000 Units at $6 per Unit = $90,000
Standard Price of Material	$5 per Unit
Standard Price of Labor	$4 per DLH
Production (in Units)	9,500 Units

The standard allowance per unit of finished output is 1 unit of material and 1 direct-labor hour. There are no beginning inventories of finished goods or work-in-process.

First Method: Variances Written Off Against Income   Under this method a separate variance analysis report is prepared, and the total variance is written off against income as a period cost. Both the income statement and the schedule of variances appear in Table 6.5.

Table 6.5   *Income Statement without Proration of Variances*

Sales (9,000 Units × $20)	$180,000
− Cost of Goods Sold at a Standard Cost of $12 per Unit	90,000
= Gross Profit at Standard	$ 90,000
+ Variances (See Schedule of Variances that Follows)	42,000
= Gross Profit at Actual	$ 48,000
− Selling and Administrative Expenses	10,000
= Operating Profit	$ 38,000

Schedule of Variances

Direct-Material Purchase Price = 15,000 Units ($6 − $5)	= $15,000
Direct-Material Usage = $5 (10,000 Units − 9,500 Units)	= 2,500
Direct-Labor Price = 12,000 DLH ($5 − $4)	= 12,000
Direct-Labor Efficiency = $4 (12,000 DLH − 9,500 DLH)	= 10,000
Total Overhead Variance = $12,000 − $9,500	= 2,500
Total Variances	= $42,000

Table 6.6 *Schedule of Proration of Variances*

	Total to Be Prorated	Usage Variance	Material Inventory	Finished Goods Inventory	Cost of Goods Sold
Standard Cost of Materials	$75,000	$2,500	$25,000	$2,500	$ 45,000
Proration of Variances					
Direct-Material Purchase Price	$15,000	$ 500	$ 5,000	$ 500	$ 9,000
Unadjusted Usage Variance	2,500	2,500			
Adjusted Usage Variance		$3,000		$ 158	$ 2,842
Direct-Labor Price	$12,000			632	11,368
Direct-Labor Efficiency	10,000			526	9,474
Total Overhead Variance	2,500			132	2,368
Total			$ 5,000	$1,948	$ 35,052
Standard Cost of Goods Sold					90,000
Actual Cost of Goods Sold					$125,052

Income Statement with Proration of Variances

Sales	$180,000
Cost of Goods Sold at Standard	90,000
+ Variances (See Schedule Above)	35,052
Actual Cost of Goods Sold	$125,052
Gross Profit	54,948
Selling and Administrative Expenses	10,000
Operating Profit	$ 44,948

The decision not to prorate variances can rest on different assumptions:

1. The variances are considered immaterial.

2. The standard costs are perceived to be the only product costs to be inventoried, and any variance is a period cost.

3. The variances are an indication of inefficiencies and should not be presented as assets.

Second Method: Proration of All Variances   Under such a method the variances will be prorated to the affected accounts (Material Inventory, Work-in-Process, Finished Goods, and Cost of Goods Sold) on some reasonable basis. In general, the variances are prorated on the basis of the determined proportion of standard costs in each affected account. Table 6.6 presents a schedule of the proration of variances and the resulting income statement. The material purchase price variance is prorated proportionally to the standard costs of materials in each affected account (Usage Variance, the Material Inventory, the Finished Goods Inventory, and the Cost of Goods Sold). The usage variance is then adjusted before being prorated to the Finished Goods Inventory and Cost of Goods Sold. Both the direct-labor variances and the overhead variances are also prorated in proportion to the related standard costs in the affected accounts (Finished Goods Inventory and Cost of Goods Sold).

Figure 6.2   *Feedback Control System*

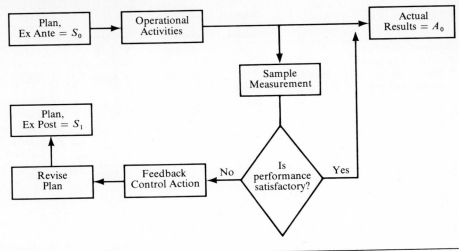

FEEDBACK CONTROL SYSTEM

In the traditional control system, costs are classified by responsibility, budgeted, and then compared at the end of the period with the actual results, using the techniques of standard cost variance analysis. The traditional system does not include any monitoring system to detect and correct errors arising during the accounting period. It is an almost fatalistic approach in which the budget is perceived as a static rather than a continuous and dynamic process. A net separation between the budgeting and control phases dismisses the obvious complementarity of both operations.

One possible method of alleviating these shortcomings is the feedback control system, whereby an error in the system becomes the basis for the correction of the budget estimates. It is used after an error is detected and, therefore, represents a reaction to the error. As Figure 6.2 shows, the feedback control system consists of first, an examination of a sample of operational activities; second, a feedback of observed errors or confirmation; and third, a revision of the budget in accordance with the deviations observed in the sample. Therefore, the feedback control system requires both the monitoring of errors and management action. R. N. Anthony and J. S. Reece observed:

Control reports are feedback devices, but they are only part of the feedback loop. Unlike the thermostat, which acts automatically in response to information about temperature, a control report does not by itself cause a change in performance. A change results only when managers take actions that lead to change. Thus, in a management control, the feedback loop requires both the control report plus management action.[6]

Feedback control systems may be applied to any business operation. For example, in the control of the purchasing manager, the accountant examines the actual prices paid to the

---

[6]R. N. Anthony and J. S. Reece, *Management Accounting: Text and Cases* (Homewood, Ill.: Irwin, 1975), p. 780.

supplier (sensor) and compares them to the budgeted prices (controller). If a variance emerges, the purchasing manager is advised to revise the budgeted price (actuator) to correct for the error.

J. S. Demski distinguishes between three types of results:

1. The *ex ante budgeted performance* (the original budgeted estimates).

2. The *ex post budgeted performance* (the revised budgeted performance after the feedback).

3. The *observed performance* (the actual performance).[7]

The total traditional variance between the observed performance and the ex ante performance can be dichotomized as follows:

1. The difference between the ex ante and ex post results is a rough measure of the firm's forecasting ability. This is the difference between what the firm budgeted and what it should have budgeted.

2. The difference between the ex post and the observed results is a measure of the "opportunity cost to the firm" of not using its resources to maximum advantage.

Assuming

S_0 = Ex ante performance.

S_1 = Ex post performance.

A_0 = Observed performance.

then

$$(A_0 - S_0) = (A_0 - S_1) + (S_1 - S_0),$$

where

$S_1 - S_0$ = Indicator of the efficiency of the planning process.

$A_0 - S_1$ = "Opportunity cost of non-optimal capacity utilization."[8]

This feedback control system, also labeled the ex post control system, when based on a linear programming formulation of the planning process was reported to have been successfully applied in conjunction with a petroleum refinery model in an effort to examine the system's feasibility.[9]

The feedback control system does have some operational limitations. First, it depends heavily on the success of the error detection process. Second, there may be a time lag between the error detection, error confirmation, and error revision during which actual results may have changed again. The effectiveness of the feedback control system depends on the rapidity of the error response process.

---

[7] J. S. Demski, "An Accounting System Structured on a Linear Programming Model," *Accounting Review* (October 1967), pp. 701–712.

[8] Ibid., p. 704.

[9] Ibid., p. 709.

6.4   FEEDFORWARD CONTROL SYSTEM

Feedback control systems must sense a specific error from a specific standard result before initiating a correction, and the process always occurs after the fact. Feedforward control systems do not rely on the examination of errors to recommend a correction. Instead, any correction is based on the anticipation of an error. As Figure 6.3 shows, a feedforward control system consists of first, an examination of a "related" activity based on the anticipation of a possible deviation between the standard and actual performance; second, the feedforward or confirmation of the possibility of such an error; and third, taking a compensatory action to maintain or adjust the operational activities. In other words, the information from the related activity acts as a surrogate for the operational activity and is fed forward to adjust the actual results through a compensatory action. Thus, the feedforward control system implies the possibility of predicting the effects of future actions and the very existence of a related activity:

Anticipation of deviations from standards depends upon the correlation of two systems such as the change in one enables prediction of change in the other. A controlling ac-

---

Figure 6.3   Feedforward Control System

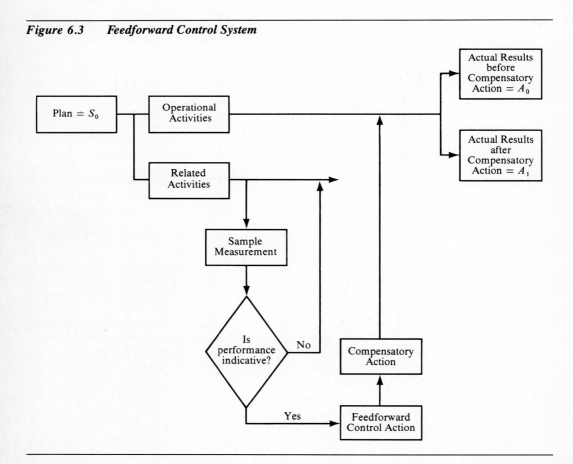

tivity, which we shall call the "related activity," is ahead of the primary activity and "feeds forward" information to it.[10]

Norbert Wiener, the father of cybernetics, recognized the limitations of feedback control systems. He pointed out that where there are lags in the system, corrections ("the compensator") must predict or anticipate errors. He referred to this system as an "anticipatory feedback" system. In fact, feedforward control systems have only been applied to specialized engineering processes, mainly chemical processes.[11]

The related activity acts as a signal and surrogate for the possible future performance of the operational activity. For example,

In a business setting, a feedforward control system might be used to adjust levels for inventories, production volume, purchase schedules, and employment as sales volume increases or decreases. A change in sales volume could automatically adjust the prescribed levels in the other factors in order to maintain a predetermined relationship of costs and activities to income.[12]

The typical feedforward control system goes through the following stages. At $t - 1$, an internal or external disturbance is detected by the controller (sensor). Given certain implied business relationships, the impact of such a disturbance on an organizational member's behavior at time t is postulated (controller). Appropriate information is fed forward to the given member for confirmation, and a compensatory action is taken that affects and governs the actual results (actuator).

To put such a system into operation, three figures are needed: the ex ante budgeted performance results (the originally budgeted results), the observed performance results (the actual results possible *before* the compensatory action), and the ex post actual performance results (the actual results *after* the compensatory action).

Feedforward control systems apply to management control as long as management can be provided information on forthcoming trouble in time for correction. For example, feedforward control can be used in cash planning, inventory control, and new product development. Mathematical models of these decisions programmed into a computer may be necessary to readily trace the influence of changes of input variables on cash flow, inventory level, and product development.[13] However, before feedforward can be applied as successfully in management control as it has been in engineering, several guidelines must be followed:

1. Thorough planning and analysis is required. . . .

2. Careful discrimination must be applied in selecting input variables. . . .

3. The feedforward system must be kept dynamic. . . .

---

[10] A. C. Filley, R. J. House, and S. Kerr, *Managerial Processes and Organizational Behavior* (Glenview, Ill.: Scott, Foresman, 1976), p. 441.

[11] E. C. MacMullen and F. G. Shinskey, "Feedforward Analog Computer Control of a Superfractionator," *Control Engineering*, no. 11 (1964), pp. 69–74; F. G. Shinskey, "Feedforward Control of pH," *Instrumentation Technology*, no. 15 (1968), pp. 65–69; and A. E. Nisenfield and Miyasaki, "Applications of Feedforward Control to Distillation Columns," *Proceedings of the IFAC* (June 1972), pp. 1–7.

[12] Filley, House, and Kerr, *Managerial Processes*, p. 443.

[13] Harold Koontz and Robert W. Bradspies, "Managing through Feedforward Control," *Business Horizons* (June 1972), pp. 25–36.

4. *A model of the control system should be developed.* . . .

5. *Data on input variables must be regularly collected.* . . .

6. *Data on input variables must be regularly assessed.* . . .

7. *Feedforward control requires action.* . . .[14]

The feedforward control system has two main limitations: It depends on the reliability of the relationship assumed between the related and operational activities, and it does not discriminate between usual or planned events and unusual events.

In fact, the feedforward and feedback control systems can be linked together, thus reducing the limitations attributed to each system. The general control process of usual events falls under the feedforward control system, while the control process for unusual events will be handled by the feedback control system:

Technical discussions also emphasize that while feedforward systems are useful in dealing with events which may be anticipated, such systems are best linked with feedback mechanisms to handle events which cannot be determined in advance.[15]

6.5   ASSESSING THE SIGNIFICANCE OF VARIANCES

Variances arising from differences between actual and standard performance results are investigated in conformity with the principle of management by exception, which states that significant variances should be corrected. To assess the significance of variances, a classic solution has been to devise rules of thumb based either on the absolute or relative size of the variance. For example, the decision rule may be to investigate all variances that exceed $2,000 or 20 percent of the standard values.

A more useful decision approach would be to separate the nonrandom from the random variances and then decide whether to investigate the nonrandom variances. Some statistical solutions can be used with a standard costing system to evaluate the significance of variances. Two basic solutions will be considered: (1) the *control chart method* and (2) the *decision theory method*.

6.5.1   *Control Chart Method*

Statistical quality control usually is used to monitor ongoing, repetitive operations in industrial processes and to pinpoint random variations. The control chart is the basic tool used. A standard (or average) is set within an acceptable range, bounded by an upper and lower control limit (UCL and LCL). Periodic samples from the output of the production process are plotted, and only observations falling beyond the control limits are considered nonrandom and worth investigating. In short, the control chart is a tool that signals when a variance is due to an assignable cause, and it separates random from nonrandom variances. There are at least four possible types of control charts: the $\bar{x}$ chart, the $\bar{R}$ chart, the P chart, and the C chart.

---

[14]Ibid., pp. 36–37.

[15]Filley, House, and Kerr, *Managerial Processes*, p. 463.

x̄ *Chart and* R̄ *Chart*

Both the $\bar{x}$ chart and the $\bar{R}$ chart are used for variable inspection, which is when a characteristic is measured on a continuous scale. The $\bar{x}$ chart shows variations in the arithmetic mean of the variable being measured, and the $\bar{R}$ chart shows variations in the range of the samples. Thus, while the $\bar{x}$ chart focuses on a control of the mean of the process, the $\bar{R}$ chart focuses on a control of the variability of the process.

The general procedure for establishing a control chart is first to draw twenty or more samples and second to compute the upper and lower control limits (generally set at ± 3 standard deviations), as follows. For $\bar{x}$:

Center line $= \bar{\bar{x}}$.

Upper control limit $= \bar{\bar{x}} + A_2\bar{R}$.

Lower control limit $= \bar{\bar{x}} - A_2\bar{R}$.

A_2 is given in column 2 of Table 6.7.

For $\bar{R}$ when σ is known:

Center line $= d_2\sigma$.

Upper control limit $= D_2\sigma$.

Lower control limit $= D_1\sigma$.

D_1 and D_2 are given in columns 3 and 4 of Table 6.7. d_2 is given in column 2 of Table 6.7.

For $\bar{R}$ when σ is unknown:

Center line $= \bar{R}$.

Upper control limit $= D_4\bar{R}$.

Lower control limit $= D_3\bar{R}$.

D_3 and D_4 are given in columns 5 and 6 of Table 6.7.

For example, assume that the individual weights of cereals for five boxes in each of ten samples are as shown in Table 6.8. To determine the $\bar{x}$ and $\bar{R}$ charts, the upper and lower control limits are set at three-sigma. Therefore, the control limits would be computed as follows. For $\bar{x}$:

Center line $= \bar{\bar{x}} = 7.35$.

Upper control limit $= \bar{\bar{x}} + A_2\bar{R} = 7.35 + 0.58(0.85) = 7.843$.

Lower control limit $= \bar{\bar{x}} - A_2\bar{R} = 7.35 - 0.58(0.85) = 6.857$.

For $\bar{R}$, assuming δ is unknown:

Center line $= \bar{R} = 0.855$.

Upper control limit $= D_4\bar{R} = 0.855(2.11) = 1.804$.

Lower control limit $= D_3\bar{R} = 0.855(0) = 0$.

Table 6.7   *Factors Determining Control Limits for x̄ and R̄ Charts*

Number of Observations in Subgroup (n)	Factor for x̄ Chart (A_2)	Factors for R̄ Chart (σ Known) LCL D_1	Factors for R̄ Chart (σ Known) UCL D_2	Factors for R̄ Chart (σ Estimated) LCL D_3	Factors for R̄ Chart (σ Estimated) UCL D_4
2	1.88	0	3.69	0	3.27
3	1.02	0	4.36	0	2.57
4	0.73	0	4.70	0	2.28
5	0.58	0	4.92	0	2.11
6	0.48	0	5.08	0	2.00
7	0.42	0.20	5.20	0.08	1.92
8	0.37	0.39	5.31	0.14	1.86
9	0.34	0.55	5.39	0.18	1.82
10	0.31	0.69	5.47	0.22	1.78
11	0.29	0.81	5.53	0.26	1.74
12	0.27	0.92	5.59	0.28	1.72
13	0.25	1.03	5.65	0.31	1.69
14	0.24	1.12	5.69	0.33	1.67
15	0.22	1.21	5.74	0.35	1.65
16	0.21	1.28	5.78	0.36	1.64
17	0.20	1.36	5.82	0.38	1.62
18	0.19	1.43	5.85	0.39	1.61
19	0.19	1.49	5.89	0.40	1.60
20	0.18	1.55	5.92	0.41	1.59

Source: Adapted from *Statistical Quality Control*, 3d ed., by E. L. Grant. Copyright © 1964, McGraw-Hill Book Company. Used with the permission of McGraw-Hill Book Company.

Table 6.8   *Weight of Cereals in Boxes (in Ounces)*

Sample Number	Box Number 1	2	3	4	5	Sum	Average	Range
1	6.50	7.30	7.10	7.00	7.10	35.00	7.00	0.80
2	7.05	7.25	7.25	7.95	7.59	37.09	7.41	0.90
3	6.85	7.31	7.61	7.81	7.38	36.96	7.39	0.96
4	7.15	8.01	7.49	7.39	7.21	37.25	7.45	0.86
5	6.90	6.15	6.35	6.70	6.40	32.50	6.50	0.75
6	7.95	7.06	7.11	7.31	7.55	36.98	7.39	0.89
7	7.10	6.45	7.35	7.10	7.00	35.00	7.00	0.90
8	7.55	7.50	7.06	7.59	8.00	37.70	7.54	0.94
9	7.90	x.90	8.75	7.85	7.95	40.25	8.05	0.90
10	7.27	7.92	7.87	7.87	7.92	38.85	7.77	0.65
						Totals	73.50	8.55

$$\bar{x} = \frac{\Sigma \bar{x}}{n} = \frac{73.50}{10} = 7.35.$$

$$\bar{R} = \frac{\Sigma R}{n} = \frac{8.55}{10} = 0.855.$$

Center line = 7.35.

UCL = 7.35 + 0.58 (0.85) = 7.843.

LCL = 7.35 − 0.58 (0.85) = 6.857.

Figure 6.4   **Control Chart for R̄**

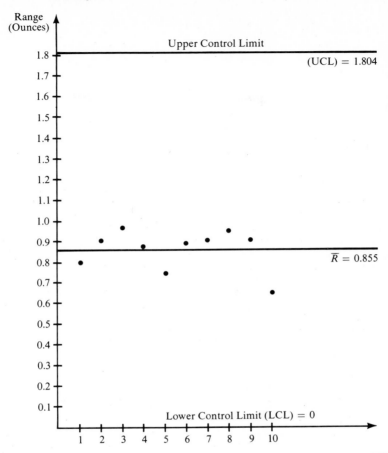

Figures 6.4 and 6.5 show the R̄ and x̄ charts. The x̄ chart shows that the system is out of control for samples 5 and 9.

P Chart and C Chart
Both the *P* and the *C* chart are used for attribute inspection. An attribute is a characteristic being measured that cannot be expressed as a continuous variable; that is, it is either present in the product, which is considered acceptable, or absent from the product, in which case the product is not acceptable.

When individual units are judged as either acceptable or defective, a *P* chart is used. If the attribute is expressed in terms of the number of defects per unit of output, a *C* chart is used.

P Chart   The *P* chart, where *P* is the fraction defective in the sample, shows whether the process fraction defective *P* is being maintained. If *P* is known and the sample size is *n*, the *P* chart has the following:

Figure 6.5   ***Control Chart for x̄***

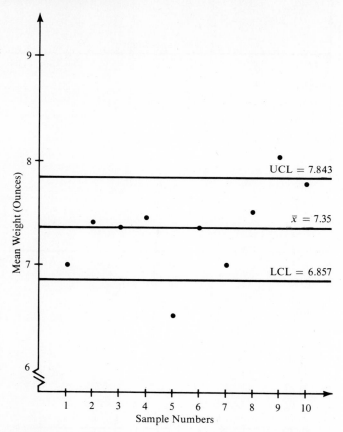

$$\text{Center line} = \bar{P} = \frac{\text{Total defective units}}{\text{Total inspected units}}.$$

$$\text{Upper control limit} = \bar{P} + 3 \sqrt{\frac{\bar{P}(1 - \bar{P})}{n}}.$$

$$\text{Lower control limit} = \bar{P} - 3 \sqrt{\frac{\bar{P}(1 - \bar{P})}{n}}.$$

For example, assume that a *P* chart is used for controlling the quality of operations in a soldering department. The fraction defective is the ratio of improperly soldered connections to total connections examined in ten samples containing thirty connections each. The control limits derived from data in Table 6.9 would be computed as follows:

$$\text{Center line} = 39/300 = 0.13.$$

$$\text{Upper control limit} = 0.10 + 3 \sqrt{0.13(1 - 0.13)/10} = 0.419.$$

Lower control limit = $0.10 - 3 \sqrt{0.13(1 - 0.13)/10} = -0.219$.

The *P* control chart is shown in Figure 6.6.

C *Chart* The *C* chart, where *C* is the number of defects per unit of output, is established as follows:

$$\text{Center line} = \bar{C} = \frac{\text{Total defects}}{\text{Number of samples}}.$$

$$\text{Upper control limit} = \bar{C} + 3 \sqrt{\bar{C}}.$$

$$\text{Lower control limit} = \bar{C} - 3 \sqrt{\bar{C}}.$$

For example, assume that a *C* chart is used for controlling the quality of the fabric woven for use as an armchair covering. The number of defects per square yard is represented by *C*. The control limits derived from the data in Table 6.10 would be computed as follows:

$$\text{Center line} = \frac{230}{10} = 23.$$

$$\text{Upper control limit} = 23 + 3 \sqrt{23} = 37.38.$$

$$\text{Lower control limit} = 23 - 3 \sqrt{23} = 8.61.$$

The *C* control chart is shown in Figure 6.7.

Table 6.9   *Reconciliation Samples*

Date Sampled	Sample Number	Number Sampled	Number Rejected	% Rejected
Jan. 3	1	30	5	0.166
Jan. 4	2	30	6	0.200
Jan. 5	3	30	6	0.200
Jan. 6	4	30	3	0.100
Jan. 7	5	30	2	0.066
Jan. 8	6	30	2	0.066
Jan. 9	7	30	2	0.066
Jan. 10	8	30	6	0.200
Jan. 11	9	30	6	0.200
Jan. 12	10	30	3	0.100
		300	39	

$$\bar{P} = \frac{\text{Total defective}}{\text{Total inspected}} = \frac{39}{300} = 0.13.$$

$$\text{UCL} = 0.10 + 3 \sqrt{0.13 (1 - 0.13/10)} = 0.419.$$
$$\text{LCL} = 0.10 - 3 \sqrt{0.13 (1 - 0.13/10)} = -0.219.$$

Figure 6.6   *Control Chart for P*

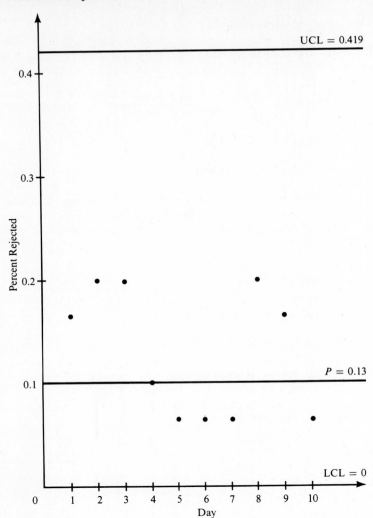

Decision Theory Method

Cost-Benefit Analysis and Breakeven Probability
Both the traditional approach and the control chart methods of evaluating the significance of variances are of limited value because they fail to explicitly consider the costs
and losses implicit in any control decision. The basis of any control decision, although
not explicitly stated, is that the benefits to be derived from investigation will exceed the
costs of investigation. Therefore, the decision to investigate a variance can be represented by a two-state–action problem as follows:

Table 6.10   Covering Samples

Sample Number	Number of Defects per Square Yard
1	21
2	22
3	23
4	25
5	26
6	23
7	20
8	26
9	22
10	22
	230

Figure 6.7   Control Chart for C

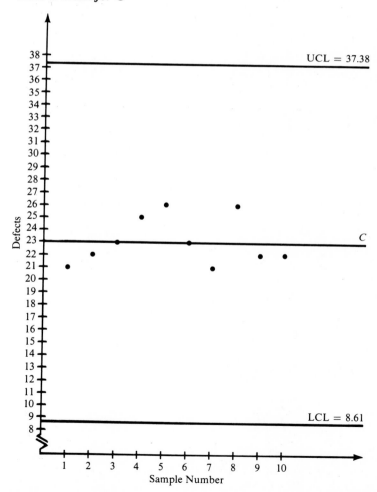

Actions	States of System	In Control, Random Variation	Out of Control, Nonrandom Variation
Investigate and Correct (a_1)		Cost = C Type I Error	Cost = $C + M$ Correct Decision
Do not Investigate (a_2)		Cost = 0 Correct Decision	Cost = L Type II Error
Probabilities		$_o\theta_2$	$_o\theta_2$

where

C = Cost of investigation of a variance.

M = Cost of correcting a variance.

L = Opportunity costs, which can be thought of as the future cost savings that might have been realized had the variance being investigated been found to be nonrandom and eliminated. This can be labeled as *out-of-control loss*.

$_o\theta_1$ = Prior probability that the process is in control or that the variance is due to random causes.

$_o\theta_2$ = Prior probability that the process is out of control or that the variance is due to nonrandom causes.

A firm would be indifferent toward investigation if the expected cost of each action were equal to the expected benefit; that is, when

$$C(1 - {_o\theta_2}) + (C + M)({_o\theta_2}) = 0({_o\theta_1}) + L_o\theta_2.$$

Solving for θ_2 yields the breakeven probability that equates the two actions as follows:

$$\theta_2^* = \frac{C}{L - M},$$

or alternatively, using θ_1,

$$\theta_1^* = 1 - \frac{C}{L - M}$$

for the breakeven probability. Therefore, if

$$\theta_1^* < 1 - \frac{C}{L - M},$$

the decision is to investigate, and if

$$\theta_1^* > 1 - \frac{C}{L - M},$$

the decision is to not investigate.

For example, assume the following:

C = \$3,600 = Cost of investigation.

L = \$16,000 = Present value of incremental costs that would have been incurred if corrective action were not taken.

M = \$10,000 = Cost of corrective action.

$_0\theta_1 = 0.8$ = Prior probability of the process being in control.

$_0\theta_2 = 0.2$ = Prior probability of the process being out of control.

Hence the breakeven probability is $\theta_1^* = 1 - 3,600/6,000 = 0.4$. Therefore, the variance is investigated when the probability of the system being in control drops below 0.4. Since $_0\theta_1 > 0.4$ (the critical probability), no investigation is indicated. The prior probabilities ($_0\theta_1$ and $_0\theta_2$) are based on past information. The manager observing an actual observation from current sample information must determine the revised or posterior probabilities of the states ($_1\theta_1$ and $_1\theta_2$) using the prior information and the actual cost. Bayes's theorem can be used to estimate the revised probabilities for the states.

Bayesian Analysis

The revision of the probabilities for the states follows, employing Bayes's theorem procedures. First, compute $P(\text{cost/in control})$, the probability of the actual cost observation if the process is in control. Next, compute $P(\text{cost/out of control})$, the probability of the actual cost observation if the process is out of control. Third, use Bayes's theorem to compute $_1\theta_1$, the revised probability of the process being in control, as follows:

$$_1\theta_1 = \frac{_0\theta_1 \times P(\text{Cost/In control})}{_0\theta_1 \times P(\text{Cost/In control}) + _0\theta_2 \times P(\text{Cost/Out of control})}.$$

The procedure will be explained using the previous example. Suppose further that a cost of \$8,000 has been incurred and that other variables remain unchanged. That is, $C = \$3,600$, $L = \$16,000$, $M = \$10,000$, $_0\theta_1 = 0.8$, and $_0\theta_2 = 0.2$. Assume also that the expected cost when the system is in control is \$6,000 with a standard deviation of 1,000, and the expected cost when the system is out of control is \$7,000 with a standard deviation of 1,000.

First, to compute $P(\text{cost/in control})$ or $P(\$8,000/\text{in control})$, compute the standardized value (Z) as follows:

$$Z = \frac{\$8,000 - \$6,000}{1,000} = \$2.$$

Table 6.11 shows a probability of 0.054 that an observation of \$8,000 will occur in a distribution with a mean of 6,000, yielding a Z value of 2. (The ordinate table in Table 6.11 shows the height of an ordinate of the normal curve at nZ_1, or n standard deviations from the mean.)

Next, to compute $P(\text{cost/out of control})$ or $P(\$8,000/\text{out of control})$, compute the standardized value (Z) as follows:

$$Z = \frac{\$8,000 - \$7,000}{1,000} = \$1.$$

Table 6.11   Ordinates of the Normal Curve

z	0.00	0.01	0.02	0.03	0.04	0.05	0.06	0.07	0.08	0.09
0.0	0.3989	0.3989	0.3989	0.3988	0.3986	0.3984	0.3982	0.3980	0.3977	0.3973
0.1	0.3970	0.3965	0.3961	0.3956	0.3951	0.3945	0.3939	0.3932	0.3925	0.3918
0.2	0.3910	0.3902	0.3894	0.3885	0.3876	0.3867	0.3857	0.3847	0.3836	0.3825
0.3	0.3814	0.3802	0.3790	0.3778	0.3765	0.3752	0.3739	0.3726	0.3712	0.3697
0.4	0.3683	0.3668	0.3653	0.3637	0.3621	0.3605	0.3589	0.3572	0.3555	0.3538
0.5	0.3521	0.3503	0.3485	0.3467	0.3448	0.3430	0.3411	0.3391	0.3372	0.3352
0.6	0.3332	0.3312	0.3292	0.3271	0.3251	0.3230	0.3209	0.3187	0.3166	0.3144
0.7	0.3123	0.3101	0.3079	0.3056	0.3034	0.3011	0.2989	0.2966	0.2943	0.2920
0.8	0.2897	0.2874	0.2850	0.2827	0.2803	0.2780	0.2756	0.2732	0.2709	0.2685
0.9	0.2661	0.2637	0.2613	0.2589	0.2565	0.2541	0.2516	0.2492	0.2468	0.2444
1.0	0.2420	0.2396	0.2371	0.2347	0.2323	0.2299	0.2275	0.2251	0.2227	0.2203
1.1	0.2179	0.2155	0.2131	0.2107	0.2083	0.2059	0.2036	0.2012	0.1989	0.1965
1.2	0.1942	0.1919	0.1895	0.1872	0.1849	0.1827	0.1804	0.1781	0.1759	0.1736
1.3	0.1714	0.1691	0.1669	0.1647	0.1626	0.1604	0.1582	0.1561	0.1540	0.1518
1.4	0.1497	0.1476	0.1456	0.1435	0.1415	0.1394	0.1374	0.1354	0.1334	0.1315
1.5	0.1295	0.1276	0.1257	0.1238	0.1219	0.1200	0.1182	0.1163	0.1145	0.1127
1.6	0.1109	0.1092	0.1074	0.1057	0.1040	0.1023	0.1006	0.0989	0.0973	0.0957
1.7	0.0941	0.0925	0.0909	0.0893	0.0878	0.0863	0.0848	0.0833	0.0818	0.0804
1.8	0.0790	0.0775	0.0761	0.0748	0.0734	0.0721	0.0707	0.0694	0.0681	0.0669
1.9	0.0656	0.0644	0.0632	0.0620	0.0608	0.0596	0.0584	0.0573	0.0562	0.0551
2.0	0.0540	0.0529	0.0519	0.0508	0.0498	0.0488	0.0478	0.0468	0.0459	0.0449
2.1	0.0440	0.0431	0.0422	0.0413	0.0404	0.0396	0.0387	0.0379	0.0371	0.0363
2.2	0.0355	0.0347	0.0339	0.0332	0.0325	0.0317	0.0310	0.0303	0.0297	0.0290
2.3	0.0283	0.0277	0.0270	0.0264	0.0258	0.0252	0.0246	0.0241	0.0235	0.0229
2.4	0.0224	0.0219	0.0213	0.0208	0.0203	0.0198	0.0194	0.0189	0.0184	0.0180
2.5	0.0175	0.0171	0.0167	0.0163	0.0158	0.0154	0.0151	0.0147	0.0143	0.0139
2.6	0.0136	0.0132	0.0129	0.0126	0.0122	0.0119	0.0116	0.0113	0.0110	0.0107
2.7	0.0104	0.0101	0.0099	0.0096	0.0093	0.0091	0.0088	0.0086	0.0084	0.0081
2.8	0.0079	0.0077	0.0075	0.0073	0.0071	0.0069	0.0067	0.0065	0.0063	0.0061
2.9	0.0060	0.0058	0.0056	0.0055	0.0053	0.0051	0.0050	0.0048	0.0047	0.0046
3.0	0.0044	0.0043	0.0042	0.0040	0.0039	0.0038	0.0037	0.0036	0.0035	0.0034
3.1	0.0033	0.0032	0.0031	0.0030	0.0029	0.0028	0.0027	0.0026	0.0025	0.0025
3.2	0.0024	0.0023	0.0022	0.0022	0.0021	0.0020	0.0020	0.0019	0.0018	0.0018
3.3	0.0017	0.0017	0.0016	0.0016	0.0015	0.0015	0.0014	0.0014	0.0013	0.0013
3.4	0.0012	0.0012	0.0012	0.0011	0.0011	0.0010	0.0010	0.0010	0.0010	0.0009
3.5	0.0009	0.0008	0.0008	0.0008	0.0008	0.0007	0.0007	0.0007	0.0007	0.0006
3.6	0.0006	0.0006	0.0006	0.0005	0.0005	0.0005	0.0005	0.0005	0.0005	0.0004
3.7	0.0004	0.0004	0.0004	0.0004	0.0004	0.0004	0.0003	0.0003	0.0003	0.0003
3.8	0.0003	0.0003	0.0003	0.0003	0.0003	0.0002	0.0002	0.0002	0.0002	0.0002
3.9	0.0002	0.0002	0.0002	0.0002	0.0002	0.0002	0.0002	0.0002	0.0001	0.0001
4.0	0.0001	0.0001	0.0001	0.0001	0.0001	0.0001	0.0001	0.0001	0.0001	0.0001

Table 6.11 shows a probability of 0.242 that an observation of \$8,000 will occur in a distribution with a mean of 7,000, yielding a Z value of 1.

Finally, to compute the revised probability of being in control, we use Bayes's formula as follows:

$$_1\theta_1 = \frac{0.8(0.054)}{0.8(0.054) + 0.2(0.242)} = 0.47.$$

Since $_1\theta_1 = 0.47$ is greater than the breakeven probability ($\theta_1^* = 0.4$), the decision is to not investigate.

6.6   *USE OF ACCOUNTING DATA IN PERFORMANCE EVALUATION*

A performance report showing, for example, a cost center's actual and standard costs can be used in various ways. How the information conveyed in the performance report is used can affect the efficiency of a company's operations. Similarly, the meaning and interpretation given to the variances as accounting measures of managerial performance depend on a given style of evaluation. A. G. Hopwood identified three styles of evaluation based on three distinct ways of using budgetary information in the evaluation of managerial performance. They are (1) the *budget-constrained style of evaluation*, (2) the *profit-conscious style*, and (3) the *nonaccounting style*, defined as follows:

1. Budget-Constrained Style of Evaluation. *Despite the many problems of using budgetary information as a comprehensive measure of managerial performance, the manager's performance is primarily evaluated upon the basis of his ability to continually meet the budget on a short-term basis. This criterion of performance is stressed at the expense of other valued and important criteria and the manager will receive unfavorable feedback from his superior if, for instance, his actual costs exceed the budgeted costs, regardless of other considerations.*

2. Profit-Conscious Style of Evaluation. *The manager's performance is evaluated on the basis of his ability to increase the general effectiveness of his unit's operations in relation to the long-term purposes of the organization. For instance, at the cost center level one important aspect of this ability concerns the attention which he devotes to reducing long-run costs. For this purpose however, the budgetary information has to be used with great care in a rather flexible manner.*

3. Nonaccounting Style of Evaluation. *The budgetary information plays a relatively unimportant part in the supervisor's evaluation of the manager's performance.*[16]

Hopwood suggests that a significant dimension of budget use is the relative importance attached to the budget in evaluating managerial performance. Empirical evidence indicates that a budget-constrained style of evaluation, based primarily on whether or not a manager has met the budget, results in a belief that the evaluation was unjust, widespread tension, worry on the job, distrust, rivalry, and manipulation of data. Such a situation can adversely influence long-term performance and success. Hopwood states:

The presence of this type of tension and conflict observed between members of a Budget Constrained department can often impede the cooperation, mutual help and assistance which are so essential for controlling independent activities and maintaining a flexible response to unusual circumstances.[17]

---

[16]A. G. Hopwood, *Accounting and Human Behavior* (Englewood Cliffs, N.J.: Prentice-Hall, 1974), p. 110.

[17]A. G. Hopwood, "An Empirical Study of the Role of Accounting Data in Performance Evaluation," *Journal of Accounting Research* supp., *Empirical Research in Accounting: Selected Studies 1972* (1972), p. 176.

A profit style of evaluation results in a higher general level of efficiency than a budget-constrained style. However, both the budget-constrained and profit-conscious styles lead to a higher degree of involvement with costs than the nonaccounting style. Hopwood primarily emphasizes the effect of budget use on the manager's beliefs and feelings rather than the overall effectiveness of operations. Empirical data is needed concerning the overall impact of the three different styles on the effectiveness of operations.

Hopwood's studies support the idea that the use of budgets and variance reports in performance evaluation reflects a supervisor's style. A reasonable hypothesis is that supervisory evaluation is a major determinant of aspiration, satisfaction, and performance levels. S. L. Ansari presented evidence that suggests employee satisfaction and performance are affected by both self-evaluation and supervisory evaluations.[18] In other words, employees are faced with two sets of perceptions—one about their performance and the other about their supervisor—and these may be contradictory. If this is the case, the employee must strive to reconcile the ambivalent reactions. Ansari presents this particular case:

If a supervisor is negative and the employee is positive toward performance, the latter will strive in some way to reconcile these dissonant cognitions. One possibility may be to reject the judgement of the supervisor. Another may be to discount one's own judgement. The first method is likely to reduce employee satisfaction with supervision; the second will lower his aspiration level. Both may, over time, reduce his productivity.[19]

6.7   CONCLUSION

This chapter elaborated on the following variance control issues:

1. The nature of the control process in terms of types, stages, and sources of control.

2. The various control processes, including the traditional, feedback, and feedforward control systems.

3. The statistical approaches to control, including the classical statistics and the decision theory approaches.

4. The behavioral control implications.

Control is a multidimensional activity. It includes the identification of the error to be controlled; the computation of the variance arising from the incurrence of error; the decision to investigate and correct the variance; and the behavioral implications of the reporting of errors, the assignment of responsibility for errors, and the reward or penalty given to the responsible agent.

To insure the success of the implementation of any control system, attention must be given to each of these dimensions of control.

---

[18] S. L. Ansari, "Behavioral Factors in Variance Control: Report on a Laboratory Experiment," *Journal of Accounting Research* (Autumn 1976), p. 192.

[19] Ibid.

GLOSSARY

Actual Costing A costing procedure based on actual prime costs and actual overhead.

Budget-Constrained Style of Evaluation The manager's performance is primarily evaluated on the basis of ability to continually meet the budget on a short-term basis.

Control A series of examinations of the deviations between actual and planned performances.

Current Standards Standard costs that can be attained in the prevailing business context by the efficient use of resources.

Disposition of Variances The classification and assignment of variances to accounts.

Efficiency Variance The difference between actual and standard quantities of labor or variable overhead for the level of activity times the standard price.

Feedback Control System A control system where management elects to bring about control by altering the planned results to conform to the actual results.

Feedforward Control System A control system where management elects to adjust the anticipated results through a compensatory action.

Idle Capacity The difference between the appropriate measure of a firm's productive capacity and the firm's current level of production.

Labor Rate Variance The difference between actual and standard wage rates times the actual hours of direct labor used.

Material Price Variance The difference between actual and standard unit prices for direct material times the actual number of units secured.

Nonaccounting Style of Evaluation Budgetary information plays a relatively unimportant part in the supervisor's evaluation of the manager's performance.

Normal Capacity The level of operations attainable by normal operating procedures, allowing for extraordinary events such as normal spoilage, ordinary machine breakdowns, and lost time.

Normal Costing A costing procedure based on actual prime costs and applied factory overhead.

Overhead Spending Variance The difference between actual overhead costs incurred and the sum of the actual number of units times the variable overhead rate plus the budgeted fixed overhead costs.

Profit-Conscious Style of Evaluation The manager's performance is evaluated on the basis of ability to increase the general effectiveness of the unit's operations in relation to the long-term purposes of the organization.

Standard-Cost System An organized set of procedures for using standard costs for work-in-process, raw materials, direct labor, and other costs so variances from the standard amounts can be identified separately as to cause and responsibility.

Standard Costing A costing procedure based on standard prime costs and standard overhead.

Standard Cost Expresses what costs should be.

Theoretical Capacity Denotes the level of operations possible under the best operating conditions without any unusual events.

Variance The deviation of actual performance from standard performance.

Variance Analysis The reconciliation and justification of a difference between actual events and planned events.

SELECTED READINGS

Barkman, Arnold, and Bodnar, George, "A Forecasting Approach to the Revision of Standard Costs," *Cost and Management* (May–June 1977), pp. 22–25.
Bather, J. A., "Control Charts and Minimization of Costs," *Journal of the Royal Statistical Society*, ser. B, vol. 25, no. 1 (1963), pp. 49–80.
Bierman, H. Jr.; Fouraker, L. E.; and Jaedicke, R. K., "A Use of Probability and Statistics in Performance Evaluation," *Accounting Review* (July 1961), pp. 409–417.
DeCoster, Don T., "Measurement of the Idle-Capacity Variance," *Accounting Review* (April 1966), pp. 297–302.

Demski, Joel S., "Analyzing the Effectiveness of the Traditional Standard Cost Variance Model," *Management Accounting* (October 1967), pp. 9–19.

Demski, Joel S., "Optimizing the Search for Cost Deviation Sources," *Management Science* (April 1970), pp. 486–494.

Duncan, A., "The Economic Design of x̄ Charts Used to Maintain Current Control of a Process," *Journal of the American Statistical Association* (June 1956), pp. 228–242.

Duvall, R. M., "Rules for Investigating Cost Variances," *Management Science* (June 1967), pp. 631–641.

Dyckman, T. R., "The Investigation of Cost Variances," *Journal of Accounting Research* (Fall 1969), pp. 215–244.

Ericson, Joseph H. Jr., "Standard Cost in Action," *Management Accounting* (August 1978), pp. 25–32.

Grinnell, D. Jacque, "Activity Levels and the Disposition of Volume Variances," *Management Accounting* (August 1975), pp. 29–32, 36.

Horngren, C. T., "A Contribution Margin Approach to the Analysis of Capacity Utilization," *Accounting Review* (April 1967), pp. 254–264.

Irvine, Bruce V., and Brennan, G. P., "The Components of Budget Pressure," *Cost and Management* (July–August 1979), pp. 16–22.

Kaplan, R. S., "The Significance and Investigation of Cost Variances: Survey and Extensions," *Journal of Accounting Research* (Autumn 1975), pp. 311–337.

Koehler, R. W., "The Relevance of Probability Statistics to Accounting Variance Control," *Management Accounting* (October 1968), pp. 35–40.

Koontz, Harold, and Bradspies, Robert W., "Managing through Feedforward Control," *Business Horizons* (June 1972), pp. 25–36.

Luh, F. S., "Controlled Cost: An Operation Concept and Statistical Approach for Standard Costing," *Accounting Review* (January 1968), pp. 123–132.

Miles, Raymond E., and Verger, Roger C., "Behavioral Properties of Variance Controls," *California Management Review* (Spring 1966), pp. 57–65.

Newman, W. H., *Constructive Control: Design and Use of Control Systems* (Englewood Cliffs, N.J.: Prentice-Hall, 1975).

Onsi, Mohamed, "Quantitative Models for Accounting Control," *Accounting Review* (April 1967), pp. 321–330.

Sayles, Leonard, "The Many Dimensions of Control," *Organizational Dynamics* (Summer 1972), pp. 21–31.

Solomons, David, "Flexible Budgets and the Analysis of Overhead Variances," *Management International*, no. 1 (1961), pp. 34–93.

Stallman, James C., "Approaching the Budget Variance Investigation Decision," *Managerial Planning* (March–April 1972), pp. 16–20.

QUESTIONS, EXERCISES, AND PROBLEMS

6.1   What are the different types of control?

6.2   What are the different sources of control?

6.3   Compare the traditional, feedback, and feedforward control systems.

6.4   What is the main difference between the two-way model and the three-way model to direct cost variances?

6.5   What are the likely effects of evaluation styles on a manager's beliefs and feelings?

6.6   *Direct-Cost Variances*   The Perrakis Co. has the following data for the month of June, when 5,000 finished units were produced. Direct material used was 13,000 pounds. The standard allowance per finished unit is 2 pounds at $10 a pound, and 15,000 pounds were purchased at $12 a pound. Actual direct labor amounted to 6,000 bonus hours at $10 per hour. The standard allowance per finished unit is 1 hour at $12 per hour.

Required:
Compute the direct-cost variances using the one-way model, the two-way model, and the three-way model.

6.7   ***Factory Overhead Variances***   The Moreau Company has prepared the following estimates for 19XA:

Budgeted overhead = $2,000 + $4 per DLH.

Normal capacity in direct-labor hours = 500 units × 40 DLH per unit = 2,000 DLH.

In 19XA the actual data were

Variable overhead = $10,000.

Fixed overhead   = $ 3,000.

Units produced   =   600 units.

Direct-labor hours =   2,700 DLH.

Required:
Prepare a schedule computing the overhead variances using

1. The one-way variance model.
2. The two-way variance model A.
3. The two-way variance model B.
4. The three-way variance model A.
5. The three-way variance model B.
6. The four-way variance model.

6.8   ***Budgeted Variable Cost per Unit of Output***   Total production costs for Gallop, Inc., are budgeted at $230,000 for 50,000 units of budgeted output and at $280,000 for 60,000 units of budgeted output. Because of the need for additional facilities, budgeted fixed costs for 60,000 units are 25 percent more than budgeted fixed costs for 50,000 units. What are Gallop's budgeted fixed costs for 50,000 units? What is Gallop's budgeted variable cost per unit of output?

(AICPA adapted)

6.9   ***Should a Process Be Investigated?***   The chief engineer at Random Corporation Ltd. is trying to determine if a particular production process is in control. The cost of investigation is $3,500, and if the process is out of control, it will cost the company $7,500 to correct the error. By correcting the error, the present value of the cost savings until the next scheduled routine intervention will be $20,000. The probability of the process being in control is 0.78, and the probability of the process being out of control is 0.22.

Required:
1. Should the process be investigated? Why or why not?
2. At what level of probability of the process being out of control would the engineer be indifferent about whether to investigate?

(SMA adapted)

6.10   ***Isolating the Direct-Material Variances***   Consider the following data compiled by the manufacturer of 9,000 records:

Standard Material Cost per Unit	$2
Actual Purchases (2,000 Units) at	$3 per Unit
Issuance for Production	600 Units
Standard Quantity Allowed	500 Units

Required:

1. Prepare journal entries for materials that recognize price variances at the time of purchase and usage variances at the time of issuance.

2. Prepare journal entries for materials that recognize price and usage variances at the time of issuance.

3. Prepare journal entries for materials that recognize price variances at both the time of purchase and issuance, as well as usage variances at the time of issuance.

6.11   ***Breakeven Probability of Investigation***   An unfavorable variance of $15,000 was reported for a manufacturing process. If no investigation is conducted and the process is out of control, the present value of excess production costs that could be avoided over the remaining budget period is an estimated $8,000. The cost of conducting an investigation is expected to be $1,400; if the process were actually out of control, the cost of correction would be an additional $1,000. There is a 0.75 probability that the $15,000 variance was caused by random uncontrollable events.

Required:

1. Should the process be investigated? Support your answer with (a) a payoff table and (b) an analysis of the expected costs of investigation versus no investigation.

2. At what probability level does the expected cost of investigating equal the expected cost of not investigating?

(SMA adapted)

6.12   ***Decision Theory Method***   The standard material cost for producing a conventional truck at the Fleetliner Company Limited is $28,000. Last week, several trucks were produced at an average material cost of $34,000. U. R. Able, a recent RIA graduate who joined the company as the cost analyst, has been asked to decide whether investigation was necessary.

Able feels that if nothing is done and the process is out of control, the present value of extra costs over the planning horizon will be $2,600. The cost to investigate is $380, and the cost to correct the process if it is out of control will be $850. Able feels there is an 80 percent chance that the process is in control.

Required:

1. Submit computations to show whether the process should be investigated.

2. What level of probability that the process is in control would be necessary to make Able indifferent about investigating the process?

3. If the process is out of control, why is the present value of the extra costs incurred substantially less than the current variance between the standard and actual costs of trucks produced?

(SMA adapted)

6.13   ***Decision Theory Method***   The Van Varenberg Company has the following costs:

Cost of investigating a variance = $1,500.

Cost of correcting a variance   = $500.

Out-of-control loss   = $3,000.

Actual cost   = $16,000.

Budgeted cost (in control)   = $10,000; S_e = $2,000.

Budgeted cost (out of control) = $20,000; S_e = $2,000.

The a priori probability of the system being in control was found to be 0.4.

Required:
1. Compute the following:
   a. P(cost/in control).   c. P(in control/cost).
   b. P(cost/out of control).   d. P(out of control/cost).
2. Determine whether or not an investigation of the process is justified.
3. Compute the breakeven probability.

6.14   ***Mix, Yield, and Usage Variances and Decision to Investigate***   A manufacturing process has the following standards for producing XRF, a chemical additive:

40 Pounds of Material P @ $2	$ 80
10 Pounds of Material Q @ $5	50
50 Pounds of Standard Mix @ $2.60	$130

Every 50 pounds of input should yield 40 pounds of the finished product. Production reports show that 21,000 and 4,800 pounds of raw materials P and Q, respectively, were used to manufacture 20,000 pounds of XRF during July. According to previous variance reports, the average material yield variance for XRF and its standard deviation are estimated to be $200 (unfavorable) and $1,350, respectively.

Required:
1. Calculate material usage, mix, and yield variances for the month of July. Submit computations.

2. Assume that management requires an investigation if an observed standard cost yield variance exceeds its standard deviation confidence interval of 2. Should the material yield variance for July be investigated? Why?

(SMA adapted)

6.15   ***Advantages of Standard Costs and Accounting for Standards***   Standard costing procedures are widely used in manufacturing operations and recently have become common in many nonmanufacturing operations.

Required:
1. Define standard costs. Distinguish between basic and current standards.
2. What are the advantages of a standard-cost system?

3. Present arguments in support of each of the following methods of treating standard-cost variances for purposes of financial reporting:
  a. They can be carried as deferred charges or credits on the balance sheet.
  b. They can appear as charges or credits on the income statements.
  c. They can be allocated to inventories and cost of goods sold.

(AICPA adapted)

6.16   ***Allocation of Standard-Cost Variances***   The Butrico Manufacturing Corporation uses a standard-cost system that records raw materials at actual cost, records material price variance at the time raw materials are issued to Work-in-Process, and prorates all variances at year-end. Variances associated with direct materials are prorated based on the direct-material balances in the appropriate accounts, and variances associated with direct labor and manufacturing overhead are prorated based on the direct-labor balances in the appropriate accounts.

The following information is available for Butrico for the year ended December 31, 19X2:

Raw Materials Inventory at December 31, 19X2	$ 65,000
Finished Goods Inventory at December 31, 19X2	
Direct Material	87,000
Direct Labor	130,500
Applied Manufacturing Overhead	104,400
Cost of Goods Sold for the Year Ended December 31, 19X2	
Direct Material	348,000
Direct Labor	739,500
Applied Manufacturing Overhead	591,600
Direct-Material Price Variance (Unfavorable)	10,000
Direct-Material Usage Variance (Favorable)	15,000
Direct-Labor Rate Variance (Unfavorable)	20,000
Direct-Labor Efficiency Variance (Favorable)	5,000
Manufacturing Overhead Incurred	690,000

There were no beginning inventories and no ending Work-in-Process Inventory. Manufacturing overhead is applied at 80 percent of standard direct labor.

Required:
Select the best answer for each of the following items:

1. The amount of direct-material price variance to be prorated to Finished Goods Inventory at December 31, 19X2, is a
  a. $1,740 debit.
  b. $2,000 debit.
  c. $2,610 debit.
  d. $3,000 credit.

2. The total amount of direct material in the Finished Goods Inventory at December 31, 19X2, after all variances have been prorated, is
  a. $86,130.
  b. $87,870.
  c. $88,000.
  d. $86,000.

3. The total amount of direct labor in the Finished Goods Inventory at December 31, 19X2, after all variances have been prorated, is
  a. $134,250.
  b. $131,850.
  c. $132,750.
  d. $126,750.

4. The total cost of goods sold for the year ended December 31, 19X2, after all variances have been prorated, is
  a. $1,682,750.   **c.** $1,683,270.
  b. $1,691,250.   **d.** $1,693,850.

(AICPA adapted)

6.17   *Standard-Cost Variances*   The Groomer Company manufactures two products used in the plastics industry: Florimene and Glyoxide. The company uses a flexible budget in its standard-cost system to develop variances. Selected data follow:

Data on Standard Costs	**Florimene**	**Glyoxide**
Raw Material per Unit	3 Pounds at $1 per Pound	4 Pounds at $1.10 per Pound
Direct Labor per Unit	5 Hours at $2 per Hour	6 Hours at $2.50 per Hour
Variable Factory Overhead per Unit	$3.50 per Direct-Labor Hour	$3.50 per Direct-Labor Hour
Fixed Factory Overhead per Month	$20,700	$26,520
Normal Activity per Month	$5,750 Direct-Labor Hours	7,800 Direct-Labor Hours
Units Produced in September	1,000	1,200
Costs Incurred for September		
Raw Material	3,100 Pounds at $.90 per Pound	4,700 Pounds at $1.15 per Pound
Direct Labor	4,900 Hours at $1.95 per Hour	7,400 Hours at $2.55 per Hour
Variable Factory Overhead	$16,170	$25,234
Fixed Factory Overhead	$20,930	$26,400

Required:
Select the best answer for each of the following items.

1. The total variances to be explained for both products for September are
  a. Florimene, $225 favorable; Glyoxide, $909 unfavorable.
  b. Florimene, $7,050 favorable; Glyoxide, $6,080 favorable.
  c. Florimene, $4,605 favorable; Glyoxide, $3,131 favorable.
  d. Florimene, $2,445 unfavorable; Glyoxide, $2,949 unfavorable.
  e. None of the above.

2. The labor efficiency variances for both products for September are
  a. Florimene, $195 favorable; Glyoxide, $510 unfavorable.
  b. Florimene, $1,700 favorable; Glyoxide, $1,000 favorable.
  c. Florimene, $200 favorable; Glyoxide, $500 unfavorable.
  d. Florimene, $195 favorable; Glyoxide, $510 favorable.
  e. None of the above.

3. The labor rate variances for both products for September are
  a. Florimene, $245 favorable; Glyoxide, $370 unfavorable.
  b. Florimene, $200 favorable; Glyoxide, $500 unfavorable.
  c. Florimene, $1,945 favorable; Glyoxide, $630 favorable.
  d. Florimene, $245 unfavorable; Glyoxide, $370 favorable.
  e. None of the above.

4. The spending variances for variable overhead for both products for September are
   a. Florimene, $490 unfavorable; Glyoxide, $666 favorable.
   b. Florimene, $167 unfavorable; Glyoxide, $35 unfavorable.
   c. Florimene, $170 unfavorable; Glyoxide, $34 unfavorable.
   d. Florimene, $1,900 favorable; Glyoxide, $1,960 favorable.
   e. None of the above.

(AICPA adapted)

6.18   ***Computation of Variances***   The Evans Co. Ltd. uses standard costs in recording and analyzing its manufacturing process. One product is produced in one department, and standard costs have been established as follows:

Material (4 Sheets @ $.50/Sheet)	$2
Direct Labor (1 Hour @ $3/Hour)	3
Variable Overhead	2
Fixed Overhead	1
	$8

Material is all added at the start of the process. Normal capacity is 25,000 units per month. Actual data for last month's operation follow:

Opening inventory	= 7,000 units, 60 percent complete.
Units started during the month	= 29,000.
Materials used	= 125,000 Sheets.
Direct-labor payroll	= $64,050 (21,000 hours).
Variable overhead	= $45,000.
Fixed overhead	= $24,500.
Ending inventory	= 12,000 units, 25 percent complete.

Required:
Compute all meaningful variances.

(CGA adapted)

6.19   ***Standard-Cost Variances***   Tolbert Manufacturing Company uses a standard-cost system in accounting for the production cost of its only product, product A. The standards for the production of 1 unit of product A are as follows:

Direct materials	= 10 feet of item 1 at $.75 per foot and 3 feet of item 2 at $1 per foot.
Direct labor	= 4 hours at $3.50 per hour.
Manufacturing overhead	= Applied at 150 percent of standard direct-labor costs.

There was no inventory on hand at July 1, 19X2. The following is a summary of costs and related data for the production of product A during the year ended June 30, 19X3:

100,000 feet of item 1 were purchased at $.78 per foot.

30,000 feet of item 2 were purchased at $.90 per foot.

8,000 units of product A were produced, which required 78,000 feet of item 1, 26,000 feet of item 2, and 31,000 hours of direct labor at $3.60 per hour.

6,000 units of product A were sold. At June 30, 19X3, there are 22,000 feet of item 1, 4,000 feet of item 2, and 2,000 completed units of product A on hand. All purchases and transfers are "charged in" at standard.

Required:
Select the best answer for each of the following items:

1. For the year ended June 30, 19X3, the total debits to the Raw Materials account for the purchase of item 1 would be
  a. $75,000.   **c.** $58,500.
  b. $78,000.   **d.** $60,000.

2. For the year ended June 30, 19X3, the total debits to the Work-in-Process account for direct labor would be
  a. $111,600.   **c.** $112,000.
  b. $108,500.   **d.** $115,100.

3. Before allocation of standard variances, the balance in the Material Usage Variance account for item 2 was
  a. $1,000 credit.   **c.** $600 debit.
  b. $2,600 debit.   **d.** $2,000 debit.

4. If all standard variances are prorated to inventories and Cost of Goods Sold, the amount of material usage variance for item 2 to be prorated to Raw Materials Inventory would be
  a. $0.   **c.** $333 debit.
  b. $333 credit.   **d.** $500 debit.

5. If all standard variances are prorated to inventories and Cost of Goods Sold, the amount of material price variance for item 1 to be prorated to Raw Materials Inventory would be
  a. $0.   **c.** $600 debit.
  b. $647 debit.   **d.** $660 debit.

(AICPA adapted)

6.20   ***Standard Costing***   Stanley Kusrick operates a medium-sized manufacturing establishment producing a number of regular stock items. The present accounting system is designed primarily for preparing the annual financial statements of the business, and Kusrick has relied on periodical income statements to indicate the degree of efficiency of the operations.

It has been suggested to Kusrick that he install a standard-cost system, since it would provide not only more effective control over the operations of the various plant departments, but also a practical basis for billing customers. Kusrick has had very little experience with cost accounting systems. He has come to Jean-Paul Duhamel, RIA, a personal friend and comptroller of another company, for assistance and an explanation of pertinent concepts should he decide to install a standard-cost system.

Required:
Take Duhamel's position and, in point form, explain each of the following:

1. Describe standard costs. Why and how are they used?

2. Describe the procedures that would be followed and considerations that must be taken into account in establishing adequate standard costs for Kusrick's operations.

3. Explain how standard costing could be used by Kusrick to effectively control the operations of the various plant departments and to provide a practical basis for billing customers.

(SMA adapted)

6.21   *Direct-Labor Variances*   The Clark Company has a contract with a labor union that guarantees a minimum wage of $500 per month to each direct-labor employee having at least twelve years of service. One hundred employees currently qualify for coverage. All direct-labor employees are paid $5 per hour.

The direct-labor budget for 19X0 was based on the annual usage of 400,000 hours of direct labor × $5, or a total of $2,000,000. Of this amount, $50,000 (100 employees × $500) per month (or $600,000 for the year) was regarded as fixed. Thus, the budget for any given month was determined by the formula $50,000 + ($3.50 × direct-labor hours worked). Data on performance for the first three months of 19X0 follow:

	January	February	March
Direct-Labor Hours Worked	22,000	32,000	42,000
Direct-Labor Costs Budgeted	$127,000	$162,000	$197,000
Direct-Labor Costs Incurred	$110,000	$160,000	$210,000
Variance (U = Unfavorable; F = Favorable)	$ 17,000 F	$ 2,000 F	$ 13,000 U

The factory manager was perplexed by the results, which showed favorable variances when production was low and unfavorable variances when production was high, because he believed his control over labor costs was consistently good.

Required:

1. Why did the variance arise? Explain and illustrate, using amounts and diagrams as necessary.

2. Does this direct-labor budget provide a basis for controlling direct-labor cost? Explain, indicating changes that could be made to improve control over direct-labor cost and to facilitate performance evaluation of direct-labor employees.

3. For inventory valuation purposes, how should per-unit standard costs for direct labor be determined in a situation such as this? Explain, assuming that in some months the company expects fewer than 10,000 hours to be utilized.

(AICPA adapted)

6.22   *Standard-Cost Variances*   The Harding Company Limited uses a standard-cost system for most of its product lines. The system is used exclusively for performance evaluation and the preparation of monthly (fixed) budgets. Standards reflect currently attainable costs and are revised every six months, if necessary.

The present standard unit cost for the ACDA product is as follows:

Direct Material	(2 Parts @ $1.50/Part)	$ 3.00
Direct Labor	(1.5 Hours @ $4/Hour)	6.00
Overhead		
Variable	(1.5 Hours @ $2/Hour)	3.00
Fixed	(1.5 Hours @ $4/Hour)	6.00
		$18.00

Annual volume for costing purposes is set at 240,000 units. Actual results for one month's production of the ACDA product are as follows:

Parts purchased   = 50,000 units for $ 74,200.

Parts used   = 42,600 units.

Direct labor   = 32,500 hours for $126,700.

Variable overhead = $ 64,500.

Fixed overhead   = $122,800.

Units produced   = 21,000.

Required:

1. Analyze all standard-cost variances. Show four variances for overhead.

2. Prepare a fixed budget for the next month, showing all costs for an expected production of 22,000 units. Identify any expected variance.

(SMA adapted)

6.23   ***Standard Costs and Responsibility***   The Carberg Corporation manufactures and sells a single product. The company uses a standard-cost system. The standard cost per unit of product is shown here:

Material (1 Pound Plastic @ $2/Pound)	$ 2.00
Direct Labor (1.6 Hours @ $4/Hour)	6.40
Variable Overhead Cost	3.00
Fixed Overhead Cost	1.45
	$12.85

The overhead cost per unit was calculated from the following annual overhead cost budget for a 60,000-unit volume:

Variable Overhead Cost	
Indirect Labor (30,000 Hours @ $4/Hour)	$120,000
Supplies: Oil (60,000 Gallons @ $.50/Gallon)	30,000
Allocated Variable Service: Department Costs	30,000
Total Variable Overhead Cost	$180,000
Fixed Overhead Cost	
Supervision	$ 27,000
Depreciation	45,000
Other Fixed Costs	15,000
Total Fixed Overhead Cost	$ 87,000
Total Budgeted Annual Overhead Cost at 60,000 Units	$267,000

The charges to the manufacturing departments for November, when 5,000 units were produced, are the following:

Material (5,300 Pounds @ $2/Pound)	$10,600
Direct Labor (8,200 Hours @ $4.10/Hour)	33,620
Indirect Labor (2,400 Hours @ $4.10/Hour)	9,840
Supplies: Oil (6,000 Gallons @ $.55/Gallon)	3,300
Other Variable Overhead Costs	3,200
Supervision	2,475
Depreciation	3,750
Other	1,250
Total	$68,035

The purchasing department normally buys about the same quantity as was used in production during a month. In November, 5,200 pounds were purchased at a price of $2.10 per pound.

Required:

1. Calculate the following variances from standard costs for the data given:

    a. Material purchase price.   **d.** Direct-labor efficiency.

    b. Material efficiency.   **e.** Overhead budget.

    c. Direct-labor wage price.

2. The company has divided its responsibility such that the purchasing department is responsible for the price at which materials and supplies are purchased, and the manufacturing department is responsible for the quantities of materials used. Does this division of responsibility solve the conflict between price and efficiency variances? Explain your answer.

3. Prepare a report that details the overhead budget variance. The report, which will be given to the manufacturing department manager, should display only the part of the variance that is the responsibility of the manager, and it should highlight the information in ways that would be useful to that manager in evaluating departmental performance and in considering corrective action.

4. Assume that the department manager performs the timekeeping function for this manufacturing department. From time to time, analysis of overhead and direct-labor variances has shown that the department manager deliberately misclassified labor hours (for example, listed direct-labor hours as indirect-labor hours, and vice versa), so only one of the two labor variances is unfavorable. It is not economically feasible to hire a separate timekeeper. What should the company do—if anything—to resolve this problem?

(CMA adapted)

6.24   ***Control of Government Services***   In late 19X1, Mr. Sootsman, the official in charge of the State Department of Automobile Regulation, established a system of performance measurement for the department's branch offices. He was convinced that management by objectives could help the department reach its objective of better service to citizens at a lower cost. The first step was to define the activities of the branch offices, to assign point values to the services performed, and to establish performance targets. Point values rather than revenue targets were employed because the department is a regulatory agency rather than a revenue-producing agency. Furthermore, the specific revenue for a service did not adequately reflect the differences in effort required. The analysis was compiled at the state office, and the results were distributed to the branch offices.

    The system has been in operation since 19X2. The performance targets for the branches have been revised each year by the state office. The revisions were designed to encourage better performance by increasing the target or reducing resources to achieve targets. The revisions incorporated noncontrollable events, such as population shifts, new branches, and changes in procedures.

Mr. Sootsman has been disappointed in the performances of branch offices because performance targets or budgets have not been met. He is especially concerned because the points earned from citizens' comments are declining.

The Barry County branch is typical of many branch offices. The following is a summary displaying the budgeted and actual performance for three years:

Barry County Branch
Performance Report

	19X2		19X3		19X4	
	Budget	**Actual**	**Budget**	**Actual**	**Budget**	**Actual**
Population Served		38,000		38,500		38,700
Number of Employees						
Administrative	1	1	1	1	1	1
Professional	1	1	1	1	1	1
Clerical	3	3	2	3	1½	3
Budgeted Performance Points[a]						
1. Services		19,500		16,000		15,500
2. Citizens' Comments		500		600		700
		20,000		16,600		16,200
Actual Performance Points[a]						
1. Services		14,500		14,600		15,600
2. Citizens' Comments		200		900		200
		14,700		15,500		15,800
Detail of Actual Performance[a]						
1. New Driver's License						
a. Examination and Road Test (3 Points)		3,000		3,150		3,030
b. Road Test Repeat—Failed Prior Test (2 Points)		600		750		1,650
2. Renew Driver's License (1 Point)		3,000		3,120		3,060
3. Issue License Plates (0.5 Point)		4,200		4,150		4,100
4. Issue Titles						
a. Dealer Transaction (0.5 Point)		2,000		1,900		2,100
b. Individual Transaction (1 Point)		1,700		1,530		1,660
		14,500		14,600		15,600

[a]The budgeted performance points for services are calculated using 3 points per available hour. One-half of the administrative employee's time is devoted to administration and one-half to regular service. The calculations for the services point budget are as follows:

19X2: 4½ people × 8 hours × 240 days × 3 points × 75% productive time = 19,440 rounded to 19,500.

19X3: 3½ people × 8 hours × 240 days × 3 points × 80% productive time = 16,128 rounded to 16,000.

19X4: 3 people × 8 hours × 240 days × 3 points × 90% productive time = 15,552 rounded to 15,500.

The comments targets are based on rough estimates by department officials.

The actual point totals for the branch are calculated by multiplying the weights, shown in parentheses in the report, by the number of such services performed or comments received.

Required:

1. Does the method of performance measurement properly capture the objectives of this operation? Justify your answer.

2. The Barry County branch office came close to its target for 19X4. Does this constitute improved performance compared with 19X3? Justify your answer.

(CMA adapted)

6.25   ***Choosing Labor Standards***   The Alton Company is going to expand its punch press department and is about to purchase three new punch presses from Equipment Manufacturers, Inc. Engineers at Equipment Manufacturers report that their mechanical studies indicate that for Alton's intended use, the output rate for one press should be 1,000 pieces per hour. Alton has very similar presses now in operation, and production from these presses now averages 600 pieces per hour.

A study of Alton shows this average is derived from the following individual outputs:

Worker	Daily Output
L. Jones	750
J. Green	750
R. Smith	600
H. Brown	500
R. Alters	550
G. Hoag	450
Total	3,600
Average	600

Alton management plans to institute a standard cost accounting system in the very near future. Company engineers support a standard based on 1,000 pieces per hour, the accounting department is arguing for 750 pieces per hour, and the department supervisor is arguing for 600 pieces per hour.

Required:

1. What arguments would each proponent probably use to support his or her case?

2. Which alternative best reconciles the needs of cost control and the motivation of improved performance? Explain your choice.

(CMA adapted)

6.26   ***Mix and Yield Variance***   Bright Business Machines Ltd. is marketing two of its latest models of computers, the Quick Speed and the Super Accuracy. Budgeted data for the two models are as follows:

	Quick Speed			Super Accuracy			Total		
	Units	Price ($)	Total ($)	Units	Price ($)	Total ($)	Units	Price[a] ($)	Total ($)
Sales	4,500	3,200	14,400,000	1,200	6,000	7,200,000	5,700	3,789	21,600,000
Variable Costs	4,500	2,800	12,600,000	1,200	4,800	5,760,000	5,700	3,221	18,360,000
Contribution Margin	4,500	400	1,800,000	1,200	1,200	1,440,000	5,700	568	3,240,000

[a] Numbers are rounded to the nearest dollar.

The target unit selling prices, unit costs, and unit contribution margins were all reached, and the actual results are as follows:

	Quick Speed			Super Accuracy			Total		
	Units	Price ($)	Total ($)	Units	Price ($)	Total ($)	Units	Price[a] ($)	Total ($)
Sales	4,200	3,200	13,440,000	1,800	6,000	10,800,000	6,000	4,040	24,240,000
Variable Costs	4,200	2,800	11,760,000	1,800	4,800	8,640,000	6,000	3,400	20,400,000
Contribution Margin	4,200	400	1,680,000	1,800	1,200	2,160,000	6,000	640	3,840,000

[a]Numbers are rounded to the nearest dollar.

Required:
1. Prepare an analysis for each product and in total, showing why the actual total contribution margin differs from the budgeted margin. Use only a physical volume variance, a quantity variance, and a mix variance.

2. Discuss the circumstances in which the use of the physical volume variance would suffice and situations where the quantity mix approach could yield additional insights.

(SMA adapted)

6.27   *Investigation of an Efficiency Variance*   The Folding Department supervisor must decide each week whether the department will operate normally the following week. The supervisor can order a corrective action if she feels the folding department will operate inefficiently; otherwise, she does nothing. The supervisor receives a weekly folding department efficiency variance report from the accounting department. A week in which the folding department operates inefficiently is usually preceded by a large efficiency variance. The graph in Figure 1 gives the probability that the folding department will operate normally in the following week as a function of the magnitude of the current week's variance reported to the supervisor.

Required:
Select the best answer for each of the following items:

1. An efficiency variance of $1,500 this week means that the probability of operating normally the following week is
    a. 0 percent.   **c.** 90 percent.
    b. 10 percent.   **d.** 100 percent.

Figure 1

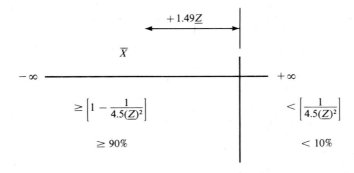

2. What are the possible relationships between the current efficiency variance and next week's operations?

   a. Large variance followed by normal operation, large variance followed by inefficient operation, small variance followed by normal operation, and small variance followed by inefficient operation.

   b. Large variance followed by normal operation, small variance followed by inefficient operation, and small variance followed by normal operation.

   c. Large variance followed by inefficient operation, small variance followed by normal operation, and small variance followed by inefficient operation.

   d. Large variance followed by 90 percent of normal operation, small variance followed by 10 percent of normal operation, large variance followed by inefficient operation, and small variance followed by inefficient operation.

3. If the supervisor can determine with certainty whether the folding department will operate normally next week, and the cost of corrective action is less than the extra cost of operating the folding department inefficiently, then the best decision rule for the supervisor to follow is

   a. If normal operations are predicted, do not take corrective action; if inefficient operations are predicted, take corrective action.

   b. Regardless of the current variance, do not take corrective action.

   c. If normal operations are predicted, take corrective action; if inefficient operations are predicted, do not take corrective action.

   d. Regardless of the current variance, take corrective action.

4. The following cost information is relevant to the folding department supervisor deciding whether corrective action is warranted: $500 = cost of corrective action that will insure normal operation of the folding department for the following week; and $3,000 = excess cost of operating the folding department inefficiently for one week. The supervisor receives a report that the folding department efficiency variance is $600. The expected cost of *not* taking corrective action is

a. $0.	**c.** $2,700.
b. $300.	**d.** $3,000.

(AICPA adapted)

6.28   ***Control Chart Method***   Robert Johnson was recently appointed chief cost accountant for a medium-sized manufacturing firm. His first assignment is to investigate whether material usage within the plant is under control. He recalled that he studied statistical quality control techniques in one of his management accounting courses and decided to apply it to his investigation. During the past few days, he took samples of 4 units each on an hourly basis. The following three samples are representative of a pattern that has been in effect for quite some time:

Sample Number	Cost of Each Item			
1	$94	$87	$85	$94
2	82	94	94	78
3	94	90	94	86

The control limits specified for the arithmetic mean are $88 ± $6. After preparing a control chart for $\bar{x}$ and one for the individual observations, Johnson detected some interesting results.

Required:

1. Prepare the two control charts using the designated control limits.

2. Comment on any differences between the two charts in regard to whether the process is in control.

3. What do you suspect may have happened?

(SMA adapted)

6.29   ***Regression and Assessing the Significance of Variance***   The Turgot Widget Company started operations in August 19X7. The management of the company tabulated the following data for the first six months of operation for the widget production process:

	Widgets Produced (Units)	Alloy Used (Kilograms)
August 19X7	800	3,200
September 19X7	900	3,590
October 19X7	1,000	3,960
November 19X7	1,100	4,380
December 19X7	1,200	4,900
January 19X8	1,000	4,050

Turgot can file a claim with the alloy supplier if the alloy is not up to specifications. The company established a provisional policy of investigating unfavorable variances when they exceed $+3\sigma$. Up to the end of January 19X8, no such investigation had been warranted because variances had been low. The cost of investigation is $100. If an investigation reveals that the material is faulty, the purchase will be replaced free of charge by the supplier, and Turgot will not encounter unexpected abnormal wastage in future production resulting from that purchase.

The alloy costs $1 per kilogram, and the company orders in lots of 1,000 kilograms. The benefit of the investigation which pinpoints the blame on the production staff alone would be equal to the cost of the investigation. A dual cause (alloy faulty and production negligent) would yield the sum of the benefits.

The following are the actual results after another three months of operation:

	Widgets Produced (Units)	Alloy Used (Kilograms)
February 19X8	1,300	5,500
March 19X8	1,100	4,500
April 19X8	1,200	5,030

The following regressions fit to this data for the usage of alloy where A = amount of alloy used, and W = number of widgets produced:

1. August 19X7 to January 19X8 (inclusive):

$$A = -176.7 + 4.190W. \quad S_e = 49.81.$$
$$R^2 = 0.994.$$

2. August 19X7 to February 19X8 (inclusive):

$$A = -491.5 + 4.523W. \quad S_e = 84.2.$$
$$R^2 = 0.990.$$

3. August 19X7 to March 19X8 (inclusive):

$$A = -494.2 + 4.528W. \; S_e = 77.1.$$
$$R^2 = 0.990.$$

4. August 19X7 to March 19X8 (excluding February 19X8):

$$A = -221.2 + 4.243W. \; S_e = 52.0.$$
$$R^2 = 0.993.$$

Required:
1. Compute the expected usage for February, March, and April separately, and state whether the individual variances for these months should be investigated. Specify the reasons for your choice of the regression equations.

2. Using the following joint probability distribution and assuming that each lot purchased is sufficient for an average level of production, compute the net benefit of investigation under the two following situations:
   a. If the variance is $< +3\sigma$.
   b. If the variance is $> +3\sigma$.

	If Variance $< +3\sigma$		If Variance $> +3\sigma$	
	Alloy Faulty	Alloy Acceptable	Alloy Faulty	Alloy Acceptable
Production Negligent	0.1	0.2	0.6	0.1
Production Acceptable	0.1	0.6	0.1	0.2

(SMA adapted)

6.30   ***Control Chart Method***   After considerable research, the chief engineer of the Extreme Precision Tool Company specified that the diameter of a certain part should have a tolerance limit of 0.4519 to 0.4521. Recently, the production process has caused occasional rejects upon inspection. The comptroller knows that U. R. Able, a new member of the company and recent RIA graduate, is versed in statistical quality control techniques and has asked him to determine whether the engineering tolerance limits are really attainable under current operating conditions.

Table 1

Sample Number	Diameter of Each of the Four Parts within the Sample				Arithmetic Mean ($\bar{x}$)	Range (R)
1	0.4516	0.4522	0.4520	0.4518	0.4519	0.0006
2	0.4521	0.4519	0.4524	0.4522	0.4521	0.0005
3	0.4524	0.4516	0.4517	0.4521	0.4519	0.0008
4	0.4521	0.4519	0.4520	0.4525	0.4521	0.0006
5	0.4524	0.4525	0.4520	0.4519	0.4522	0.0006
6	0.4517	0.4516	0.4522	0.4524	0.4520	0.0008
7	0.4516	0.4524	0.4517	0.4519	0.4519	0.0008
8	0.4517	0.4522	0.4518	0.4525	0.4520	0.0008
				Total	3.6161	0.0055
				Grand Arithmetic Mean	0.4520 ($\bar{x}$)	0.00069 ($\bar{R}$)

Table 2   **Factors for Determining from R̄ the Three-Sigma Control Limits for x̄ and R̄ charts**

Number of Observations in Subgroup (n)	Factor for x̄ Chart (A₂)	Lower Control Limit (D₃)	Upper Control Limit (D₄)
2	1.88	0	3.27
3	1.02	0	2.57
4	0.73	0	2.28
5	0.58	0	2.11
6	0.48	0	2.00
7	0.42	0.08	1.92
8	0.37	0.14	1.86

Upon receiving his first assignment, Able took two samples each day for four consecutive days. Each sample consisted of four parts, as shown in Tables 1 and 2.

Required:

1. Are the present engineering tolerance limits currently attainable? Show all computations and control charts.

2. If the engineering tolerance limits are not currently attainable, what alternatives are open to the company?

3. From the results of part 1, can you conclude that the production process is satisfactory? Why or why not?

4. The company specifies that any part out of the existing engineering tolerance limit should be rejected. Indicate the circumstances under which the cost of rejects should be treated as a loss or as a cost of normal production. Explain.

(SMA adapted)

The industrial learning curve thus embraces more than the increasing skill of an individual by repetition of a simple operation. Instead, it describes a more complex organism—the collective efforts of many people, some in line and others in staff positions, but all aiming to accomplish a common task progressively more efficiently.[1]

7.1   DEFINITION

Progress depends on people learning, and a conventional hypothesis in industry is that they learn according to a predictable pattern often called the *learning curve*. The learning curve describes the empirical relationships between output quantities and quantities of certain inputs (mainly direct-labor hours) where learning-induced improvement is present. It portrays the concept that the cumulative average unit cost decreases systematically by a common percentage each time the volume of production increases geometrically (that is, increases by doubling). The recognition of this phenomenon is helpful in the investigation of cost behavioral patterns, cost estimation, and decision making in general.[2] Synonyms for the learning curve include the manufacturing progress function, cost-quantity relationship, cost curve, production acceleration curve, improvement curve, performance curve, experience curve, and efficiency curve.

[1]Winfred B. Hirschmann, "Profit from the Learning Curve," *Harvard Business Review* (January 1964), p. 128.
[2]Ahmed Belkaoui, "Costing through Learning," *Cost and Management* (May–June 1976), pp. 36–40.

7.2   *HISTORY AND THEORY*

The learning curve was first recognized in the aircraft industry,[3] where any reduction in the considerable number of direct-labor hours needed for assembly work is quickly recognized and formalized. However, the learning curve was not translated into an empirical theory curve until 1925, when it was observed in a military manufacturing operation. Some eleven years later, T. P. Wright disclosed the results of empirical tests of the learning curve. He observed that on the average, when output doubled in the aircraft industry, the labor requirements decreased by about 20 percent; in other words, there was an 80 percent learning factor.[4]

Interested in such a discovery applied to a wartime situation, the United States Defense Department commissioned the Stanford Research Institute to study the direct-labor input required for aircraft production in a number of firms. The resulting learning curves had a common characteristic: an 80 percent improvement rate. From 1909, when the first Model T Ford was produced, until 1926, productivity improved along an 86 percent learning curve.[5] Evidence of improvement over sixteen years and on sixteen million items was found in a human-paced operation that involved assembling candy boxes. The learning continued for the production of tens of millions of units in a machine-paced operation.[6]

The learning curve theory is based on a simple principle of human nature: People learn from experience. As workers repeat a task, they become more efficient at it. The net result is a reduced use of direct-labor hours per unit. This improvement can be regular enough to follow a predictable pattern that should apply to any task or job in any industry. The early literature considered the learning improvement possible only in labor-intensive, discontinuous forms of manufacture, such as airframe assembly.[7] It was later proved, however, that the improvement could take place in continuous and capital-intensive forms of manufacture. Industries where the learning phenomenon is applicable include the petroleum, refining, and basic chemical industries. Finally, learning was found to exist in process-oriented contexts as well as job-order production,[8] and in mature phases of production as well as in start-up phases.[9]

As an example of the learning phenomenon, assume that the average labor hours required per unit are reduced by 30 percent as the quantity produced doubles. If the first unit takes 100 hours, then the average for 2 units is 70 hours (0.7 × 100 hours), or a total of 140 hours for 2 units. Therefore, the time required to complete the second unit equals 40 hours (140 − 100). Continuing this line of reasoning, 4 units would require an average of 49 hours per unit (0.7 × 70 hours), and a total of 196 hours (4 × 49 hours) for all 4 units. The third and fourth units require 56 hours (196 hours required for 4 units minus 140 hours required for 2 units).

The basic doctrine of the learning curve can be summarized as follows:

---

[3]Miguel Reguero, *An Economic Study of the Military Plane Industry* (Wright-Patterson Air Force Base, Ohio: Department of the Air Force, 1957), p. 213.
[4]T. P. Wright, "Factors Affecting the Cost of Airplanes," *Journal of Aeronautical Science* (February 1936), pp. 122–128.
[5]Hirschmann, "Learning Curve," p. 136.
[6]Ibid.
[7]Frank J. Andress, "The Learning Curve as a Production Tool," *Harvard Business Review* (January–February 1954), p. 87.
[8]Nicholas Baloff, "The Learning Curve: Some Controversial Issues," *Journal of Industrial Economics* (July 1966), p. 278.
[9]Hirschmann, "Learning Curve," p. 136.

1. Where there is life, there can be learning.

2. The more complex the life, the greater the rate of learning. Man-paced operations are more susceptible to learning or can give greater rates of progress than machine-paced operations.

3. The rate of learning can be sufficiently regular to be predictive. Operations can develop trends which are characteristic of themselves. Projecting such established trends is more valid than assuming a level performance or no learning.[10]

What factors account for the learning curve phenomenon? It is appropriate to distinguish between the impact of two factors: (1) the learning in the literal sense on the part of the workers, and (2) other factors, including management innovation. Although, these factors operate together, the presence of a consistent behavior indicates that of the various factors, learning in the literal sense is the predominant influence. The nonlearning factors, such as new machinery, time studies, or design changes, do bring some labor savings; however, they will probably have an irregular effect on the learning curve. Furthermore, the learning factors will be subject to two conditions: (1) the predisposition of an operation to an improvement, and (2) the extent to which the predisposition is used.

On one hand, the predisposition to an improvement is related to the *human content* of an operation. It is reflected in the ratio of assembly (human content) to machine work. In assembly work there are relatively large possibilities for learning; in machine work the improvement is constrained by the fact that the machines cannot "learn" to run any faster. The following rates are often employed as possible benchmarks:

75% assembly labor, 25% machine labor: 80% curve.
50% assembly labor, 50% machine labor: 85% curve.
25% assembly labor, 75% machine labor: 90% curve.[11]

On the other hand, the extent to which the predisposition is used may depend on the following two factors:

1. The effect of faith. A positive attitude toward the possibility of learning can reinforce progress. Winfred B. Hirschmann states:

If progress is believed *possible, it will likely be sought; and if it is looked for, there is some possibility of finding it. Conversely, if improvements are considered unlikely, there will be little urge to seek them. A defeatist philosophy can be engendered which so debilitates an effort that it helps to produce the very condition it assumes.*[12]

2. The presence of open-ended expectations. The absence of "ceiling psychology" may create a predisposition to learning and permit improvement to continue. Some companies obtain more rapid progress when the workers are not informed of the target rate.

[10] Ibid.
[11] Thomas G. Vayda, "How to Use the Learning Curve for Planning and Control," *Cost and Management* (July–August 1972), p. 28.
[12] Hirschmann, "Learning Curve," p. 134.

Figure 7.1   Cumulative Average Labor Time at 80 Percent Learning Rate

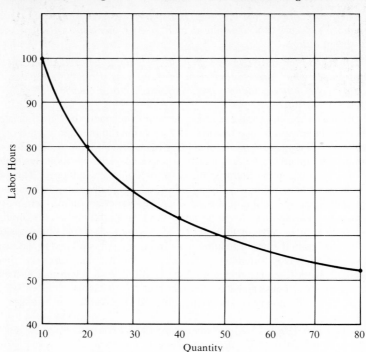

a. Plotted on arithmetic paper, it forms an abrupt,
    sloping path that is difficult to project.

7.3   CHARACTERISTICS OF THE CURVE

Assume that a company's rate of learning, like the aircraft industry's, is 80 percent. On an arithmetic chart with linear coordinates, the relationship between the cumulative average direct-labor hours and the cumulative units of production is portrayed by a curve showing a rapid decline that trails off (see Figure 7.1a). The same curve on a logarithmic chart will show a straight declining rate (see Figure 7.1b). The portrayal of the learning phenomenon as a straight line is generally preferred for practical reasons.

There are several variations to these forms, however, mainly with respect to the starting point. The steepness of the curves in Figure 7.1 may be due to an assumed high labor requirement. For example, if the proportion of assembly work was supposed to be lower, the downward slope of the curve would not be as steep. Hirschmann listed the following possible anomalies to the learning curve shape.

1. A *leveling off* or a *toe up* may occur due to such factors as the closing of operations at the end of a contract. The costs may increase, a condition known in industry as *reverse learning*.

2. An aberration also may occur in the middle of the curve. Hence if the production process is interrupted for a significant length of time, resumption of the work will reflect a sharp increase in the learning curve. The aberration may be due to inefficiencies result-

Figure 7.1   **(continued)**

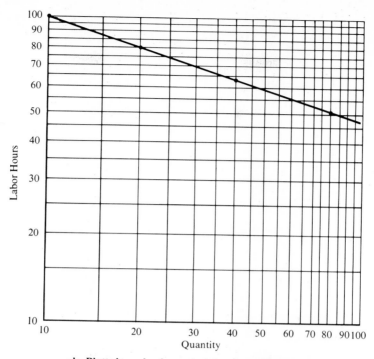

b. Plotted on a log-log scale, it is a descending straight
line, easy to extend and easy to read off.

ing from the employees' loss of skill and from the reorganization costs. Such a situation is called a *scallop*. It may also result from the change in the design of a product followed by two costs: (a) the cost of added design less the quoted cost of the design removed, and (b) a loss of learning resulting in not being able to produce an assembly at the full quantity contracted.

3. A *leveling down* or a *toe down* may result from major innovations or sudden improvements in the learning process.[13]

Figure 7.2 portrays the possible anomalies in the learning curve.

7.4   *LEARNING CURVE MODELS*

The learning curve phenomenon is generally expressed by

$$Y = KX^b,$$

[13] Ibid., pp. 126–127.

Figure 7.2   Anomalies in the Learning Curve

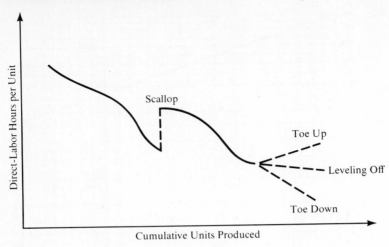

where

> X = Cumulative total units produced.
>
> K = Quantity of input required to produce the first unit of output.
>
> r = Learning rate.
>
> b = An index of learning, $b = \dfrac{\text{Log } r}{\text{Log } 2}$.[14]

$1 - r$ = Progress ratio.

There are two possible types of learning curve models, which differ in their definitions of Y:

1. The *average time model* specifies that the new cumulative average time per unit (Y) will decrease by a constant percentage (r) as cumulative production doubles.

2. The *marginal time model* specifies that the new marginal time per unit (Y) will decrease by a constant percentage (r) as cumulative production doubles.

---

[14] The formula is determined as follows:

$$r = \frac{Y_{2n}}{Y_n} ,$$

or

$$r = \frac{K2_n^b}{Kn^b}$$

$$= 2^b.$$

Log $r = b$ log 2,

and

$$b = \frac{\text{Log } r}{\text{Log } 2} .$$

It is necessary first to decide which model to use. Plotting both average time and marginal time on a log-log graph will determine the best choice.

7.4.1   *Average Time Model*

The learning curve relationships can be expressed mathematically, and important learning curve formulae follow.

Formula 1 computes the *average curve* (that is, the average cumulative labor hours, labor dollars, or material cost for all units produced up to any particular point):

$$Y = KX^b,$$

where

Y = Average cumulative labor hours, labor dollars, or material costs for X number of units.

K = Theoretical value or actual value (if known) of the first unit.

X = Cumulative number of units produced.

b = Slope coefficient, exponent, or learning index. It is always negative, since the cost or number of hours is decreasing.

A much-used logarithmic version of formula 1 is $\log Y = (\log K) + (b \log X)$.

Formula 2 computes the *total curve* (that is, the total labor hours or cost required to produce a predetermined number of units):

$$T = XKX^b = KX^{b+1},$$

where T = total labor hours or cost required to produce a predetermined number of units.

Formula 3 computes the *marginal curve* (that is, the xth unit cost or labor hours):

$$Y_x = (b + 1)KX^b,$$

where

Y_x = Cost of the xth unit.

$b + 1$ = Conversion factor arrived at by adding b to 1.

Formula 4 computes the value of the exponent b and the log of the learning percentage for any learning curve:

$$b = \text{Log of the learning percentage}/\text{Log 2},$$

and

$$\text{Log of the learning percentage} = b(\text{Log 2}).$$

To apply these formulae, assume that (1) it takes 800 hours to produce the first unit of a product, and (2) an 80 percent learning rate exists in the average assembly time when cumulative production doubles. Determine the value of b and the cumulative average labor hours for 4 units of output as follows.

First, determine the value of b:

$$b = \text{Log } (0.80)/\text{Log } 2.$$

Inserting the appropriate values obtained using the logarithmic key of a calculator,

$$b = \frac{9.9031 - 10}{0.301} = -0.322.$$

Next, insert the proper values in the average curve formula. The average cumulative labor hours for 4 units can be computed as follows:

$$Y = 800(4)^{-0.322},$$

or

$$\text{Log } Y = (\text{Log } 800) - (0.322 \log 4)$$
$$= 2.9031 - (0.322 \times 0.6021)$$
$$= 2.7092.$$
$$Y = 511.9.$$

The procedure can be extended to determine the average labor hours, total labor hours, and marginal labor hours for different numbers of units, as shown in Table 7.1 and as graphed in Figures 7.3 and 7.4.

Table 7.1   *Average, Total, and Marginal Hours (Average Time Model)*

Units	Cumulative Units	Average Time	Total Time	Marginal Time
1	1	$800(1)^{-0.322} = 800$	$800(1)^{0.678} = 800$	$800 \times 0.678(1)^{-0.322} = 542$
1	2	$800(2)^{-0.322} = 640$	$800(2)^{0.678} = 1280$	$800 \times 0.678(2)^{-0.322} = 434$
1	3	$800(3)^{-0.322} = 562$	$800(3)^{0.678} = 1680$	$800 \times 0.678(3)^{-0.322} = 381$
1	4	$800(4)^{-0.322} = 512$	$800(4)^{0.678} = 2048$	$800 \times 0.678(4)^{-0.322} = 347$
1	5	$800(5)^{-0.322} = 476$	$800(5)^{0.678} = 2380$	$800 \times 0.678(5)^{-0.322} = 322$
1	6	$800(6)^{-0.322} = 449$	$800(6)^{0.678} = 2694$	$800 \times 0.678(6)^{-0.322} = 304$
1	7	$800(7)^{-0.322} = 427$	$800(7)^{0.678} = 2980$	$800 \times 0.678(7)^{-0.322} = 289$
1	8	$800(8)^{-0.322} = 409$	$800(8)^{0.678} = 3272$	$800 \times 0.678(8)^{-0.322} = 277$
1	9	$800(9)^{-0.322} = 394$	$800(9)^{0.678} = 3548$	$800 \times 0.678(9)^{-0.322} = 267$
1	10	$800(10)^{-0.322} = 381$	$800(10)^{0.678} = 3811$	$800 \times 0.678(10)^{-0.322} = 258$

Figure 7.3   Eighty Percent Average Time Curve, Logarithmic Graph

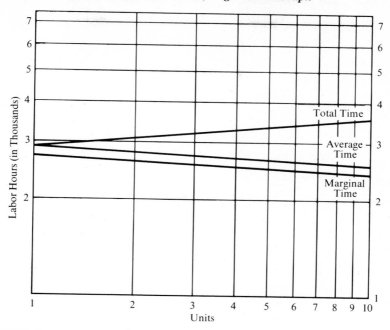

Figure 7.4   Eighty Percent Average Time Curve, Arithmetic Graph

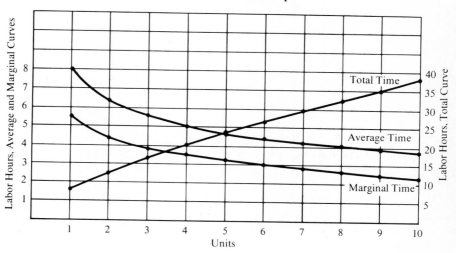

7.4.2   *Marginal Time Model*

The marginal time model depicts situations where there is a marginal time per unit rather than an average time per unit when production doubles. Again, there are several important formulae that express the learning curve relationships.

Formula 1 computes the *marginal time*:

$$Y = KX^b,$$

where

Y = Marginal time.

K = Number of labor hours to build the first unit.

X = Number of units completed.

b = Learning factor.

Formula 2 computes the *total time*:

$$T = \int_0^x Y$$

$$T = \frac{K}{b+1}\left(X^{b+1}\right),$$

where T = total labor hours required to build a predetermined number of units.

Formula 3 computes the *average time*:

$$A = \frac{T}{X} = \frac{K}{b+1}\left(X^b\right),$$

where A = average labor hours required to build a number of units.

To apply these formulae, assume that (1) it takes 700 hours to complete the first unit of output, and (2) an 80 percent learning curve exists in the marginal time when production doubles. Determine the value of b and the marginal time to complete 4 units. The analysis will be as follows:

1. $b = -0.322$ (as in the average time model example).

2. Inserting the proper values in the equation, compute the marginal labor hours for 4 units as follows:

$$Y = 700(4)^{-0.322}.$$

Log Y = (Log 7) − (0.322 log 4)

$\qquad$ = 2.8451 − [0.322(0.6081)] = 2.6493.

$$Y = 447.955.$$

Again, the procedure can be repeated to determine the marginal time, total time, and average time for different levels of production, as shown in Table 7.2. These results are

Table 7.2   Marginal, Total, and Average Hours (Marginal Time Model)

Units	Cumulative Units	Marginal Time	Total Time	Average Time
1	1	$700(1)^{-0.322} = 700$	$\dfrac{700}{0.678} \times (1)^{0.678} = 1{,}032$	$700(1)^{-0.322} = 1{,}032$
1	2	$700(2)^{-0.322} = 559$	$\dfrac{700}{0.678} \times (2)^{0.678} = 1{,}651$	$700(2)^{-0.322} = 825$
1	3	$700(3)^{-0.322} = 491$	$\dfrac{700}{0.678} \times (3)^{0.678} = 2{,}173$	$700(3)^{-0.322} = 724$
1	4	$700(4)^{-0.322} = 448$	$\dfrac{700}{0.678} \times (4)^{0.678} = 2{,}641$	$700(4)^{-0.322} = 660$
1	5	$700(5)^{-0.322} = 416$	$\dfrac{700}{0.678} \times (5)^{0.678} = 3{,}073$	$700(5)^{-0.322} = 614$
1	6	$700(6)^{-0.322} = 393$	$\dfrac{700}{0.678} \times (6)^{0.678} = 3{,}478$	$700(6)^{-0.322} = 579$
1	7	$700(7)^{-0.322} = 374$	$\dfrac{700}{0.678} \times (7)^{0.678} = 3{,}860$	$700(7)^{-0.322} = 551$
1	8	$700(8)^{-0.322} = 358$	$\dfrac{700}{0.678} \times (8)^{0.678} = 4{,}226$	$700(8)^{-0.322} = 528$
1	9	$700(9)^{-0.322} = 345$	$\dfrac{700}{0.678} \times (9)^{0.678} = 4{,}577$	$700(9)^{-0.322} = 508$
1	10	$700(10)^{-0.322} = 333$	$\dfrac{700}{0.678} \times (10)^{0.678} = 4{,}917$	$700(10)^{-0.322} = 491$

Figure 7.5   Eighty Percent Marginal Time Curve, Arithmetic Graph

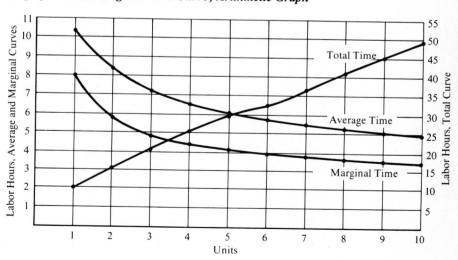

Figure 7.6   Eighty Percent Marginal Time Curve, Logarithmic Graph

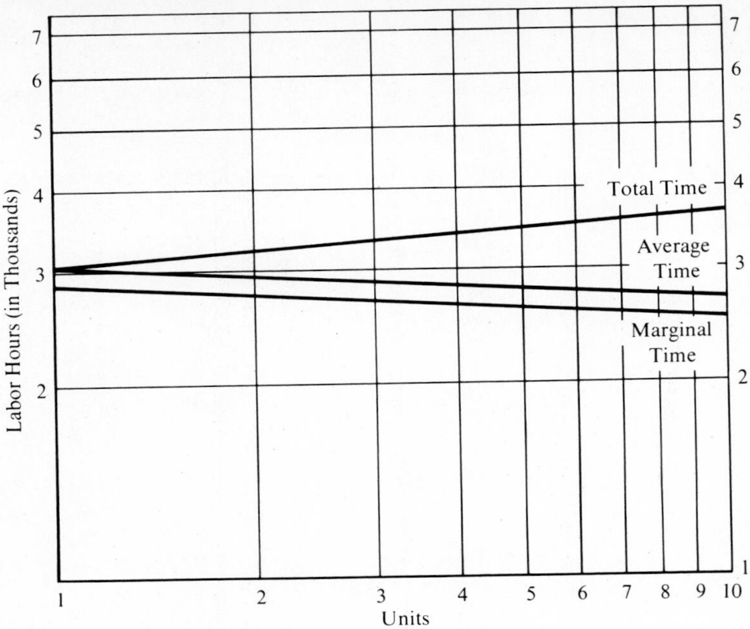

also portrayed in Figures 7.5 and 7.6. The arithmetic graph shows the amounts of change in time, whereas the logarithmic graph shows the rates of change in time.

7.4.3   *Relationship between Percentage of Learning and Parameter* b

To simplify the computations necessary in the applications of the learning curve, the relationships between the percentage of learning (r) and the exponent (b) can be established for all possible values of r. In general, the relationship is computed as $b = \log r / \log 2$.

For example, for $r = 80$ percent, b equals -0.322. Table 7.3 establishes this relationship for all values of r ranging from 51 through 100, and the table can be used as an expedient way to find the appropriate value of b.

7.5   *LEARNING CURVE APPLICATIONS*

As is evident from the learning curve formulae, the major technical problems confronting the cost accountant in constructing the learning curve are (1) the determination of the rate of learning, (2) the length of the learning period, and (3) the availability of the relevant accounting data. Thus, the learning curve theoretically is sound, and consideration must now be given to its practical construction and use.

Cost Estimation

The learning curve can be used in cost estimation. For example, suppose you are provided the data in Table 7.4 in the columns showing the week and the values for columns *a* and *c*. Once these data have been plotted on a log-log graph and the presence of a learning phenomenon has been indicated, the learning rate can be determined in one of two ways.

In one method, a regression analysis of the logarithmic data using the least squares method will provide a regression line. Its slope coefficient, exponent, or learning constant can be determined using the least squares method as follows:

$$b = \frac{N\Sigma(X \times Y) - (\Sigma X)(\Sigma Y)}{N \times \Sigma(X^2) - (\Sigma X)^2},$$

Table 7.3   *Relationship between* **r** *and* **b**

r	b	r	b	r	b	r	b
51	−0.97143	66	−0.59946	81	−0.30401	96	−0.05639
52	−0.94342	67	−0.57777	82	−0.28630	97	−0.04394
53	−0.91594	68	−0.55639	83	−0.26882	98	−0.02515
54	−0.88997	69	−0.53533	84	−0.25154	99	−0.01450
55	−0.86250	70	−0.51457	85	−0.23447	100	−0
56	−0.83650	71	−0.49411	86	−0.21759		
57	−0.81097	72	−0.47393	87	−0.20091		
58	−0.78588	73	−0.45403	88	−0.18442		
59	−0.76121	74	−0.43440	89	−0.16812		
60	−0.73697	75	−0.41504	90	−0.15200		
61	−0.71312	76	−0.39593	91	−0.13606		
62	−0.68966	77	−0.37707	92	−0.12029		
63	−0.66658	78	−0.35845	93	−0.10470		
64	−0.64396	79	−0.34000	94	−0.08927		
65	−0.62149	80	−0.32193	95	−0.07400		

Table 7.4   *Practical Example for Computing Learning Factor*

Week	Total Production (a)	Cumulative Units Completed (b)	Direct-Labor Hours (c)	Cumulative Direct Labor (d)	Cumulative Average Direct-Labor Hours per Unit (d/b)	Computation
1	10	10	174.0	174.0	17.40	
2	10	20	116.0	290.0	14.50	17.4 × 0.83
3	20	40	191.6	481.6	12.04	14.5 × 0.83
4	40	80	318.4	800.0	10.00	12.04 × 0.83
5	80	160	528.0	1328.0	8.30	10 × 0.83
6						8.3 × 0.83

where

N = Number of observations for which cost or hours are available.

$X \times Y$ = Product of log X and log Y.

X = Log of the quantity for each observation.

To apply the formula, we need the following information:

Week	X	Y_x	Log X	Log Y_x	Log X(Log Y)	(Log X)
1	10	17.40	1.00000	1.24054920	1.2405	1.0000
2	20	14.50	1.30103	1.16136800	1.5110	1.6926
3	40	12.04	1.60206	1.08062650	1.7312	2.5667
4	80	10.00	1.90309	1.00000000	1.9031	3.6218
5	160	8.30	2.20412	0.91907809	2.0258	4.8581
			8.01030	5.40162170	8.4116	13.7392

Inserting the correct values in the formula yields

$$b = \frac{5(8.4116) - 8.0103(5.4016)}{5(13.7392) - (8.0103)^2} = -0.267.$$

Next, the learning rate (r) can be determined as follows:

$$b = \frac{\text{Log } r}{\text{Log } 2}.$$

Log $r = b$ log 2

$$= -0.267(0.3010) = -0.080367.$$

$r = 83.3\%$.

The other method of finding the learning rate is simply to read the gain in time over any doubled quantity from a graph that could be drawn based on the data in Table 7.4.[15] The learning factor can be expressed as the ratio between the time taken to produce Z units and the cumulative time to produce $2Z$ units. Using the data from Table 7.4, the learning factor may be computed as follows. If the time to produce 10 units is 174 hours and the cumulative time for 20 units is 290 hours, the learning factor is equal to

$$\left(\frac{290}{20}\right) \div \left(\frac{174}{10}\right) \times 100\% = 83.3\%.$$

After determining the learning rate, any of the computational formulae described earlier can be used to compute the average cumulative labor hours, unit labor hours, or total labor hours required to produce a specific number of units. Table 7.4 shows the results of these computations. Finally, assuming the rate of learning will continue beyond the

---

[15] If doubled quantities are not available, use the formula

$$n = \frac{\text{Log (Cost 2/Cost 1)}}{\text{Log (Quantity 2/Quantity 1)}}.$$

Figure 7.7   Pattern of Costs and Prices

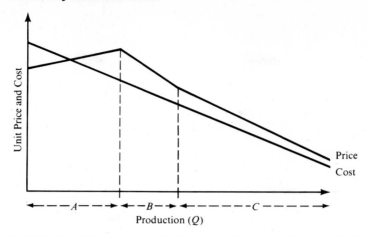

Figure 7.8   Pattern of Costs and Prices

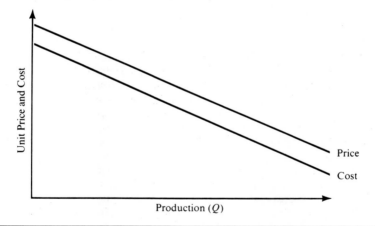

total estimated production of 80 units, the learning curves can be used to make cost estimates.

7.5.2   *Price Estimation*

The learning curve can be used for price estimation as well as cost estimation, using similar techniques. In general, there are two price patterns, as shown in Figures 7.7 and 7.8.[16]

---

[16]Patrick Conley, "Experience Curves as a Planning Tool," in *Essentials of Corporate Planning*, eds. S. Jain and S. Singhir (New York: Planning Executives Institute, 1973), pp. 292–303.

During phase A of the pattern shown in Figure 7.7, the dominant producer creates a price umbrella by keeping the price constant (or showing little decline), which may attract more producers. During phase B the prices decline as a result of a price war where aggressive competitors strive for dominance. Finally, during phase C the price war is over, and a more stable and competitive situation is established among the price war survivors. The weak producers may have been eliminated or have differentiated their product.

The pattern in Figure 7.8 is simpler. Given that the cost function (Y) follows the pattern $Y = KX^b$, the dominant producer may adopt a parallel stable pattern for the price function: $Y^1 = K^1X^b$, where Y^1 is the average price and K^1 the price of the first unit. This may discourage the entry of competitors.

Although other price patterns exist, the predictive ability of the learning curve generally can be used as a determinant in estimating the number of labor hours required for production. This facilitates the seller's pricing of the output, of course. Thus, given a knowledge of prime costs, the labor hours determined from the learning curve can be used as an allocation base for the other indirect costs. Furthermore, the buyer aware of the learning characteristics of the seller's costs may be willing initially to pay a higher price that is to be reduced as the supplier's production increases and its costs begin declining.

7.5.3   *Make or Buy Decisions*

Learning curves are very helpful in make-or-buy decisions, which involve a choice between the cost of producing an item and the cost of purchasing it. The learning curve can provide the data necessary for determining the necessary labor hours and the cost of producing the item. There are other costs involved, of course, but the labor costs are usually considered more illustrative. Once they have been determined, the make-or-buy decision is reduced to simpler terms.

7.5.4   *Production*

Knowing the time required to perform an operation is an important element in management decisions concerning work flow, equipment, and number of workers (to name just a few). The predictive ability of the learning curve can be applied to such production activities as forecasting output and forecasting worker requirements during periods of volume fluctuations. When these factors are unknown to a firm, unnecessary labor expenses may be incurred along with further losses due to poor estimation of production and a subsequent loss of sales.

7.5.5   *Financial Planning*

External financing is expensive, and the need for it often arises from a simple timing problem. A learning curve is useful here because it permits a comparison between costs and prices and allows an estimation of the period of financial drain. Such information facilitates preplanning and permits making early banking arrangements, which can reduce the costs of borrowing.

7.5.6   Capital Budgeting

For most companies capital budgeting is a very serious and precarious proposition, and any reduction in the uncertainty of the potential cash flow is desirable. First, in a capital budgeting situation the company is likely to be at the top of its learning curve; hence it can derive significant labor and time savings estimates from the curve. Second, the greater the proportion of labor assembly time, the more likely the curve will explain cost behavior. Third, the more advance planning the company does, the more useful will be the predictive aspects of learning curves.

On the basis of these three criteria, Frank J. Andress lists several industries that could apply the learning curve phenomena. The electronics industry, home appliance industry, residential home construction, shipbuilding, and machine shops can apply the criteria to varying degrees.[17]

7.5.7   Internal Reporting

Nicholas Baloff and John W. Kennelly argue that "explicit recognition and estimation of the entire productivity path of a start-up will result in more effective accounting, whereas the application of a constant cost or productivity standard may result in misleading internal or external reporting."[18] For cost or internal accounting, this assertion pertains mainly to the use of the start-up values as a basis for computing standards. Such use will generate important problems in effective motivation and control of operations.[19] An important contribution of the learning curve here is to point to the necessity of adapting the standard cost accounting system to higher productivity and lower cost functions.

7.5.8   External Reporting

As stated earlier, external accounting may also be affected. Nicholas Baloff and R. B. McKersie suggest that the cost savings due to the learning effect should be abstracted from the profit so actual increased productivity can be examined rather than productivity due to a repetition of tasks.[20]

A more important problem is the distortion of profit that can occur when production costs follow the learning curve phenomenon if two conditions exist:

1. The contract(s) covers two or more periods.

2. The unit price is based on a cumulative average cost per unit. To correct for the possible misstatement of the profit, Wayne J. Morse has shown that a cost allocation model based on the learning curve phenomenon will disclose the relationships between efforts and accomplishments better than the conventional method.[21]

---

[17] Andress, "Learning Curve," p. 91.
[18] Nicholas Baloff and John W. Kennelly, "Accounting Implications of Product and Process Start-ups," *Journal of Accounting Research* (Autumn 1967), p. 135.
[19] Nicholas Baloff and R. B. McKersie, "Motivating Start-ups," *Journal of Business* (October 1966), pp. 473–484.
[20] Ibid., p. 479.
[21] Wayne J. Morse, "Reporting Production Costs That Follow the Learning Curve Phenomenon," *Accounting Review* (October 1972), pp. 761–773.

To illustrate the problem of profit misstatement and the learning curve allocation model proposed by Morse, let us return to the data illustrated in Table 7.4 and assume that (1) 40 units are sold in 19X1, and 120 units are sold in 19X2; (2) the unit selling price is $50 per unit in both years; (3) the factory overhead and direct-labor cost are each incurred at the rate of $5 per direct-labor hour; and (4) the material cost is $1 per unit.

Table 7.5 shows the income statements for both years under both the conventional method of matching actual costs with revenues and Morse's method of using a learning curve cost allocation model. Under the conventional method the company shows a loss of $608 in the first year, followed by a profit of $1,168 in the second year; the learning curve cost allocation model shows a profit of $140 in the first year and a profit of $420 in the second year. Notice that the total profit for the two years is $560 under both methods.

To avoid such reporting differences, which may adversely affect the market image of the firm, Morse proposed the following reporting system:

As production takes place any excess of the projected cost of each unit over the expected average cost of all anticipated production is charged to a deferred production expense account and inventory is charged with an amount equal to the expected average unit cost of all anticipated production. When the projected unit cost is less than the expected average unit cost of all anticipated production this difference is deducted from the deferred production expense account and inventory is charged with an amount equal to the expected average unit cost of all anticipated production. As production takes place, any

Table 7.5   *Income Statements*

Prepared Matching Actual Costs with Revenues

19X1	(40 Units Sold)	19X2	(120 Units Sold)
Sales at $50 per Unit	$2,000		$6,000
Costs of Goods Sold			
Overhead and Labor			
($5 $\times \dfrac{481.6 \text{ hours}}{40} \times$ 40)	2,408	($5 $\times \dfrac{318.4 + 528}{120} \times$ 120)	4,232
Material at $5 per Unit	200		600
Costs of Goods Sold	$2,608		$4,832
Net Income	$ (608)		$1,168

Prepared Using Learning Curve Cost Allocation Model

19X1	(40 Units Sold)	19X2	(120 Units Sold)
Sales at $50 per Unit	$2,000		$6,000
Costs of Goods Sold			
Overhead and Labor			
($5 $\times$ 8.3 $\times$ 40)	1,660	($5 $\times$ 8.3 $\times$ 120)	4,980
Material at $5 per Unit	200		600
Costs of Goods Sold	$1,860		$5,580
Net Income	$ 140		$ 420

Figure 7.9   ***Cash Flows when Cost Difference due to Learning Is Deferred***

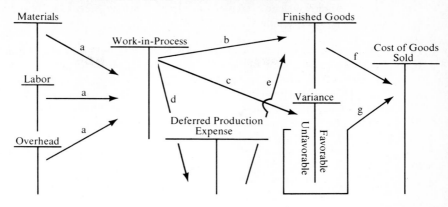

a. Actual costs.
b. Projected unit cost or expected average unit cost of all anticipated production, whichever is lower.
c. Actual less projected unit cost.
d. Excess of projected unit cost over expected average unit cost of all anticipated production.
e. Excess of expected average unit cost of all anticipated production over projected unit cost.
f. Period sold.
g. Period incurred.

Source: Reprinted by permission from Wayne J. Morse, "Reporting Production Costs that Follow the Learning Curve Phenomenon," *Accounting Review* (October 1972), p. 765.

differences between actual and projected costs are written off as a period variance unless a change in a parameter of the model occurs.[22]

Figure 7.9 shows graphically how such a deferring and averaging process can be accomplished.

Applying this reporting system to the previous problem yields the following journal entries:

Year 1

Deferred Production Expenses	748	
Work-in-Process		748

To defer the difference between the actual costs of $2,408 and average cumulative costs of $1,660.

Year 2

Finished Goods	748	
Deferred Production Expenses		748

To charge the difference between the actual costs of $4,232 and average cumulative costs of $4,980.

7.6   *LIMITS OF THE LEARNING CURVE*

Considering all the positive effects of the learning curve's application to industry cost estimation, why has the effect largely been ignored? Several limitations must be pointed

---

[22] Ibid., p. 764.

out. There are deficiencies within the model, but there are also factors that, when analyzed properly, can be overcome to make the learning effect a viable and necessary concept in cost accounting.[23]

Illusory Savings   Illusory savings may be the result of errors in selection of labor hour data to be used in plotting the curve.[24] First, automation may lead to a reduction in labor input per unit. Second, a direct-labor savings may disguise a greater use of indirect labor. Third, a change in the "labor mix" through hiring more qualified workers may lead to a savings in direct-labor hours and an increase in direct-labor cost. Finally, the savings in labor may be due to a change in volume rather than to learning.

Verification   The problem of verification pertains mainly to the possibility of obtaining inaccurate data for direct labor, and to the potential inability to isolate accurately the learning factor that led to the reduction in direct labor. As a result, the learning curve in its present state is not a "scientific tool."[25]

Barriers to Acceptance   Resistance to the use of the learning curve may be due to a lack of awareness that improvement patterns can be quantified, to a skepticism that improvement can continue, and to a lack of awareness that the learning factor can describe group as well as individual performance. On the other hand, the use of the learning curve and the effort to reduce the costs accompanying it may have unforeseen implications: a loss of innovative capability, reduced flexibility, and higher overhead.[26]

7.7   CONCLUSION

Given an accurate record of direct-labor hours used to produce specific units, the learning curve can be a very useful cost accounting technique in cost estimation. This chapter reviewed some of the possible computational formulae and provided examples of possible applications of the learning curve.

A knowledge of the learning curve provides savings useful in internal decision making, mainly in the areas of standard setting during start-up phases; pricing; and make-or-buy, production, and financial decisions. In general, the learning curve can be applied each time the skill of a worker is subject to improvement by repetition of operations. Accountants dealing with uncertain situations will find it a useful tool.

Although the derivation of the learning curve is straightforward, five possible problems could complicate the isolation of the learning curve slope decline:

1. The overestimation of initial costs for self-protection.

2. Shifting workers from direct to indirect status, and vice versa.

3. Changes in manufacturing methods and tooling.

[23] William J. Abernathy and Kenneth Wayne, "Limits to the Learning Curve," *Harvard Business Review* (September–October 1974), pp. 109–119.
[24] Andress, "Learning Curve," p. 90.
[25] E. L. Summers and G. A. Welsh, "How Learning Curve Models Can Be Applied to Profit Planning," *Management Sciences* (March–April 1970), pp. 45–50.
[26] Abernathy and Wayne, "Limits to the Learning Curve," pp. 109–119.

4. The manufacturing lot size and material availability.

5. Continuing engineering changes.[27]

GLOSSARY

Average Time Model Specifies that the new cumulative average time per unit (Y) will decrease by a constant percentage (r) as cumulative production doubles.

Learning Curve Portrays the concept that the cumulative average unit cost decreases systematically by a common percentage each time the volume of production increases geometrically (that is, increases by doubling).

Leveling Off or Toe Up A cost increase due to reverse learning.

Leveling Down or Toe Down A cost decrease as a result of major innovations or sudden improvements in the learning process.

Marginal Time Model Specifies that the new marginal time per unit (Y) will decrease by a constant percentage (r) as cumulative production doubles.

SELECTED READINGS

Abernathy, William J., and Wayne, Kenneth, "Limits of the Learning Curve," *Harvard Business Review* (September–October 1974), pp. 109–119.

Alchian, A., "Costs and Outputs," in *The Allocation of Economic Resources*, ed. N. Abramatovitz (Stanford, Calif.: Stanford University Press, 1959).

Andress, Frank J., "The Learning Curve as a Production Tool," *Harvard Business Review* (January–February 1954), pp. 87–97.

Arrow, Kenneth J., "The Economic Implications of Learning or Doing," *Review of Economic Studies* (April 1962), pp. 155–173.

Baloff, Nicholas, "The Learning Curve: Some Controversial Issues," *Journal of Industrial Economics* (July 1966), pp. 275–282.

Baloff, Nicholas, "Start-ups in Machine Intensive Manufacture," *Journal of Industrial Engineering* (January 1966), pp. 25–32.

Baloff, Nicholas, and Kennelly, John W., "Accounting Implications of Product and Process Start-ups," *Journal of Accounting Research* (Autumn 1967), pp. 131–143.

Baloff, Nicholas, and McKersie, R. B., "Motivating Start-ups," *Journal of Business* (October 1966), pp. 473–484.

Belkaoui, Ahmed, "Costing through Learning," *Cost and Management* (May–June 1976), pp. 36–40.

Berghell, A. B., *Production Engineering in the Aircraft Industry* (New York: McGraw-Hill, 1944).

Bhada, Y. K., "Dynamic Cost Analysis," *Management Accounting* (July 1970), pp. 11–14.

Billon, S. A., "Industrial Learning Curves and Forecasting," *Management International Review*, no. 6 (1966), pp. 65–96.

Boren, William H., "Some Applications of the Learning Curve to Government Contracts," *NAA Bulletin* (October 1964), pp. 21–22.

Brenneck, Ronald, "The Learning Curve for Labor Hours: For Pricing," *NAA Bulletin* (June 1958), pp. 77–78.

Broadston, James A., "Learning Curve Wage Incentives," *Management Accounting* (August 1968), pp. 15–23.

Bump, Edwin A., "Effects of Learning on Cost Projections," *Management Accounting* (May 1974), pp. 19–24.

---

[27] S. Young, "Misapplications of the Learning Curve Concept," *Journal of Industrial Engineering* (November 1966), pp. 410–415.

Carlson, J. G., "How Management Can Use the Improvement Phenomenon," *California Management Review* (Winter 1961), pp. 83–94.

Conway, R. W., and Schultz, A., "The Manufacturing Progress Function," *Journal of Industrial Engineering* (January–February 1959), pp. 39–53.

Gillespie, Jackson F., "An Application of Learning Curves to Standard Costing," *Management Accounting* (September 1981), pp. 63–65.

Harris, Le Brone C., and Stephens, W. L., "The Learning Curve: A Case Study," *Management Accounting* (February 1978), pp. 47–52.

Harvey, D. W., "Financial Planning Information for Production Start-ups," *Accounting Review* (October 1976), pp. 838–845.

Hirschmann, Winfred B., "Profit from the Learning Curve," *Harvard Business Review* (January 1964), pp. 125–139.

Imhoff, E. A. Jr., "The Learning Curve and Its Applications," *Management Accounting* (February 1978), pp. 44–46.

Jordan, Raymond B., "Learning How to Use the Learning Curve," *NAA Bulletin* (January 1958), pp. 27–39.

Morse, Wayne J., "Reporting Production Costs that Follow the Learning Curve Phenomenon," *Accounting Review* (October 1972), pp. 761–773.

Pegels, Carl C., "Start Up or Learning Curves: Some New Approaches," *Decision Sciences* (October 1976), pp. 705–713.

Shroad, Vincent J., "Control of Labor Costs through the Use of Learning Curves," *NAA Bulletin* (October 1964), pp. 15–20.

Summers, E. L., and Welsch, G. A., "How Learning Curve Models Can Be Applied to Profit Planning," *Management Services* (March–April 1970), pp. 45–50.

Taylor, Marvin L., "The Learning Curve: A Basic Cost Projection Tool," *NAA Bulletin* (February 1961), pp. 21–26.

Toole, Howard R., "The Learning Curve Model: Its Use and Implications," *Cost and Management* (March–April 1970), pp. 36–40.

Vayda, Thomas G., "How to Use the Learning Curve for Planning and Control," *Cost and Management* (July–August 1972), pp. 25–32.

Wyer, Rolfe, "The Learning Curve Technique for Direct Labor Management," *NAA Bulletin* (July 1958), pp. 19–27.

Yelle, Louis, "The Learning Curve: Historical Review and Comprehensive Survey," *Decision Sciences* (April 1979), pp. 302–328.

Young, Samuel L., "Misapplications of the Learning Curve Concept," *Journal of Industrial Engineering* (August 1966), pp. 410–415.

QUESTIONS, EXERCISES, AND PROBLEMS

7.1   Define the learning curve.

7.2   What factors may account for the learning curve phenomenon?

7.3   What are the differences between the learning curve models, and how can you decide which model to use?

7.4   What are the possible anomalies in the learning curve?

7.5   What is meant by a 90 percent learning factor?

7.6   Derive the learning constant for an 80 percent curve.

7.7   *Average Cumulative Unit Hour and Average Incremental Unit Hours*   Assume that a given process has an expected learning curve of 80 percent.

Required:
1. Complete the following table:

**Average Cumulative Unit Cost
with an 80 Percent Learning Curve**

Lot Number	Units Produced	Cumulative Production	Average Cumulative Unit Hours	Cumulative Total Hours
1	1	——	8.00	8.00
2	1	——	——	——
3	2	——	——	——
4	4	——	——	——
5	8	——	——	——
6	16	——	——	——

2. Determine the average incremental unit hours for the second unit produced.

3. Derive a formula for computing the average incremental unit hours.

4. Determine the average incremental unit hours for each of the six lots produced.

5. Is a learning curve of 50 percent possible?

7.8   ***Determination of the Learning Factor***   Marie Holland, the cost accountant at the Berry Company, suspects that the assembly time of their main product is subject to the learning phenomenon. She would like to determine the learning factor and has found that the costs required for the 100th unit and the 136th unit are $50 and $47.10, respectively.

Required:
Determine the learning factor (b).

7.9   ***Derivation of the Parameters of the Learning Curve Model***   The Baksi Company manufactures trivets. Its accounting records show that the total time to complete 6 units and 2 units were 183 hours and 72 hours, respectively. Assuming an average time learning curve exists, derive the values of K, b, and the percentage of learning (r).

7.10   ***Application of Learning Curves***   The XYZ Company found that 35,765 actual direct-labor hours were required to produce the first unit of a new aircraft. Evidence exists showing an average time learning curve of 80 percent. The major buyer of this new aircraft maintains that a 70 percent average time learning curve is attainable, based on a review of another vendor's proposals. What are the average hours' savings to the XYZ Company in accepting the other vendor's proposals if the buyer's potential cumulative purchases may be 20, 50, 100, 500, and 700 units?

7.11   ***Learning Curves***   Select the best answer for each of the following items:

1. The Green Company's new production process will be carried out in one department and has an expected learning curve of 80 percent. The costs subject to the learning effect for the first batch produced by the process were $10,000. Using the simplest form of the learning function, the cumulative average cost per batch subject to the learning effect after the sixteenth batch has been produced can be estimated as
    a. $3,276.80.   **c.** $8,000.00.
    b. $4,096.00.   **d.** $10,000.00.

2. The learning function's mathematical form, enabling it to be plotted as a straight line on log-log graph paper, is

    a. Trigonometric.   **c.** Linear.

    b. Cyclical.   **d.** Exponential.

(AICPA adapted)

7.12   *Learning Curves*   The average number of minutes required to assemble trivets is predictable upon an 80 percent learning curve. That is, whenever cumulative production doubles, cumulative average time per unit becomes 80 percent of what it was at the previous doubling point. The trivets are produced in lots of 300 units, and 60 minutes of labor are required to assemble each first lot.

Required:

Using the concept of the learning curve and the letters listed below, select the best answer to the following questions.

MT = Marginal time for the xth lot.

  M = Marginal time for the first lot.

  X = Lots produced.

  b = Exponent expressing the improvement; b has the range $-1 < b \le 0$.

1. A normal graph (that is, not a log or a log-log graph) of average minutes per lot of production, where cumulative lots are represented by the x-axis and average minutes per lot are represented by the y-axis, would produce a

    a. Linear function sloping downward to the right.

    b. Linear function sloping upward to the right.

    c. Curvilinear function sloping upward to the right at an increasing rate.

    d. Curvilinear function sloping downward to the right at a decreasing rate.

2. A log-log graph of average minutes per lot of production, where cumulative lots are represented by the x-axis and average minutes per lot are represented by the y-axis, would produce a

    a. Linear function sloping downward to the right.

    b. Linear function sloping upward to the right.

    c. Curvilinear function sloping upward to the right at a decreasing rate.

    d. Curvilinear function sloping downward to the right at a decreasing rate.

3. The average number of minutes required per lot to complete four lots is approximately

    a. 60.0.   **c.** 38.4.

    b. 48.5.   **d.** 30.7.

4. The average time to produce X lots of trivets could be expressed as

    a. MX^{b+1}.   **c.** MT^{b+1}.

    b. MX^{b}.   **d.** MX^{b-1}.

5. Assuming $b = -0.322$, the average number of minutes required to produce X lots of trivets could be expressed as

    a. $40.08X^{0.678}$.   **c.** $60X^{-0.322}$.

    b. $40.08X$.   **d.** $60X^{1.322}$.

(AICPA adapted)

7.13   ***Application of Learning Curves***   The Lande Company has accepted a contract for 5,000 units of its unique product, Zeta. Management earlier determined that labor hours for the 5,000 units of Zeta will follow a 75 percent average time learning curve. Time for the first unit is 45 minutes.

Required:
1. Estimate the total required labor.

2. While working on the production of the 5,000 units, the management of the Lande Company accepted another contract for 5,000 units of Zeta. Estimate the total hours required by the second contract.

7.14   ***Learning Curve and Costs of an Order***   The Anderson Company makes parts for the aircraft and missile industry. It has received an order for 500 units of an airplane part. Earlier, the Anderson Company produced 500 units of the same parts for the following costs:

Direct Materials	$15,000
Direct Labor (500 hours at $10/Hour)	5,000
Variable Overhead ($5/DLH)	2,500
Fixed Overhead	5,000
Total Costs	$27,500

The Anderson Company has noted that the part's manufacturing follows an 80 percent learning curve.

Required:
Assuming no changes in the unit labor cost, what are the additional costs of accepting the order?

7.15   ***Learning Curve and Bid Submission***   The Business Computing Manufacturing Company has received an invitation to bid on the production of 1,600 computer terminals. The cost department has estimated the costs of producing 200 terminals as follows:

Direct Materials at $100/Unit	$20,000
Direct Labor (2,000 Hours at $8/Hour)	16,000
Variable Manufacturing Costs ($5/DLH)	10,000
Fixed Manufacturing Costs	10,000
Total Costs	$56,000

The Business Computing Manufacturing Company has noted that manufacturing of the terminals follows an 80 percent learning curve. The fixed manufacturing costs are not expected to change as a result of the eventual acceptance of the bid.

Required:
What is the lowest cost per unit acceptable to the Business Computing Manufacturing Company?

7.16   ***Learning Curve and External Reporting***   The McMartin Co. manufactures and sells airplanes. Labor hours and production volume for the last five months, which you believe are representative of the entire year, were as follows:

Month	Total Production	Direct-Labor Hours
1	1,000 Units	1,000 Hours
2	1,000	8,000
3	2,000	14,400
4	4,000	25,920
5	8,000	46,656

The average number of hours required to produce a plane is based upon a learning curve.

The McMartin Co. sold 4,000 first units produced in 19X1 and the remaining units in 19X2 at $20,000 per unit. The factory overhead and direct-labor costs are each incurred at a rate of $1,000 per direct-labor hour. The material cost is $5,000 per unit.

Required:
1. Determine the learning percentage and the average cumulative direct-labor hours per unit for each month.

2. Determine the income statements for 19X1 and 19X2 based on the conventional matching of actual production costs with revenues.

3. Determine the income statements for 19X1 and 19X2 based on the learning curve cost allocation model.

4. Make the entries necessary to reconcile the results between parts 2 and 3.

7.17   *Make or Buy: Learning Curve Analysis* The Xyon Company purchases 80,000 pumps annually from Kobec Inc. The price has increased each year and reached $68 per unit last year. Because the purchase price has increased significantly, Xyon management asked that an estimate be made of the cost to manufacture the pumps in its own facilities. Xyon's products consist of stamping and castings. The company has little experience with products requiring assembly.

The engineering, manufacturing, and accounting departments prepared a report for management, which included the following estimate for an assembly run of 10,000 units. Additional production employees would be hired to manufacture the subassembly. However, no additional equipment, space, or supervision would be needed.

The report states that total costs for 10,000 units are estimated at $957,000, or $95.70 per unit. The current purchase price is $68 per unit, so the report recommends the continued purchase of the product.

Components (Outside Purchases)	$120,000
Assembly Labor[a]	300,000
Factory Overhead[b]	450,000
General and Administrative Overhead[c]	87,000
	$957,000

[a] Assembly labor consists of hourly production workers.
[b] Factory overhead is applied to products on a direct-labor dollar basis. Variable overhead costs vary closely with direct-labor dollars.

Fixed Overhead	50% of Direct-Labor Dollars
Variable Overhead	100% of Direct-Labor Dollars
Factory Overhead Rate	150% of Direct-Labor Dollars

[c] General and administrative overhead is applied at 10 percent of the total cost of material (or components), assembly labor, and factory overhead. It is fixed on an annual basis.

Required:
1. Was the analysis prepared by the engineering, manufacturing, and accounting departments of Xyon Company and the recommendation to continue purchasing the pumps

that followed from the analysis correct? Explain your answer, and include any supportive calculations you consider necessary.

2. Assume Xyon Company could experience labor cost improvements on the pump assembly consistent with an 80 percent learning curve. An assembly run of 10,000 units represents the initial lot or batch for measurement purposes. Should Xyon produce the 80,000 pumps in this situation? Explain your answer.

(CMA adapted)

COST ACCUMULATION FOR PRODUCT COSTING: JOB-ORDER AND PROCESS COSTING

A cost accounting system comprises a set of activities related to collecting and recording costs and assigning them to cost objects. The two major cost objects are the departments and the units of products, because a cost accounting system emphasizes the determination of unit costs and the control of costs. Thus, determination of unit costs for inventory valuation is essential to profit determination, and determination of departmental costs and assignment of responsibility is essential to the control process. Both objectives rely heavily on techniques of cost accumulation for product costing.

There are two basic approaches to product costing—the job-order cost system and the process cost system—and each has many variations. Before describing these two accounting systems, this chapter will describe the elements and techniques of cost recording. It will also include a discussion of standard costing; accounting for spoilage, waste, defective units, and scrap; and accounting for payroll.

8.1 TECHNIQUES OF COST RECORDING

Cost recording techniques involve accounting entries and the allocation of costs to costing objects by means of an averaging process. These two phases provide the data bank with recorded costs that can be used for both product costing and decision making.

8.1.1 General and Subsidiary Ledger Relationships

Cost accounting has two objectives: inventory valuation and control. Therefore, the accounting system and its supporting documents consist of two components: the *general ledger* and a set of *subsidiary ledgers*. (See Figure 8.1.)

The general ledger is a summary device that portrays the general accounting relationship of the cost accounting cycle in a system of financial accounts. Its ultimate output is inventory valuation and profit determination. Using double-entry bookkeeping, total costs are recorded first to show the transfer of inputs to a Work-in-Process Inventory account (sometimes referred to as Work-in-Process or *W-I-P*), and second to portray the

Figure 8.1   *Total Accounting System*

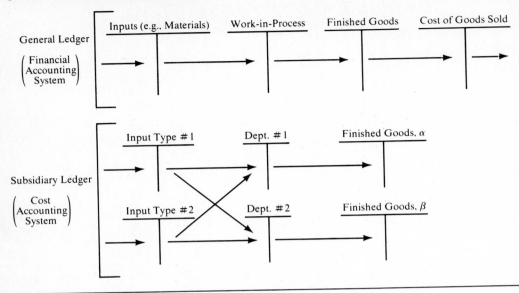

transfer of finished goods to a Finished Goods account. These total entries are supported by detailed entries in the subsidiary ledger. Thus, the general ledger, a part of the financial accounting system, is composed of a set of accounts to summarize the detailed operations of the costing system. Postings to it are made from subsidiary ledger totals.

In general, the control accounts in the general ledger and their corresponding subsidiary ledgers of records are as follows:

1. The *Materials account* controls the *materials cards* in a perpetual inventory system.

2. The *Factory Overhead account* controls the *expense ledger* or *departmental expense analysis sheet*.

3. The *Work-in-Process account* controls the *job-order cost sheet* in a job-order costing system and the *production reports* in a process costing system.

4. The *Finished Goods account* controls the *finished goods ledger cards*.

Although conceptually subordinate to the financial accounting system, the cost accounting system is more flexible in the sense that it can be adapted to produce information useful for decision making. Using the cost accounting system, it is always possible to record additional cost accounting information outside the constraints of double-entry bookkeeping, for example, to record memorandum data on opportunity costs. The control account–subsidiary ledger combination can be used to gather information on every possible segment of the firm.

8.1.2   *Averaging Process*

The association of costs with products depends on the degree of traceability to the product and the nature of the production center. The product costs are either direct or indirect in terms of their ease of traceability with regard to the product. The production center produces as output either *homogeneous* units (not distinguishable from one another during a production process) or *heterogeneous* units (identifiable as individual units or lots).

The direct costs in either homogeneous or heterogeneous cost accounting situations can be traced easily to the appropriate product accounts. However, a few calculations may be necessary in the allocation of the indirect costs.

First, with a homogeneous output, the indirect costs can be assigned directly to the appropriate product by an averaging process used on the physical output of the producing department. Hence if a producing department incurred a total indirect cost of $50,000 for a production volume of 5,000 widgets, the average indirect cost per widget is simply $50,000/5,000 = $10. Second, with a heterogeneous output, the indirect costs can only be assigned to each appropriate product by an averaging process applied to some identifiable and common basis of allocation, usually the direct-labor hours used by each product.

8.2   DIFFERENCES BETWEEN JOB-ORDER AND PROCESS COSTING

The two main product costing methods are *job-order costing* and *process costing*. Both can be used with an actual- or standard-cost system.

Job-order costing has been appropriately defined as a method of cost accounting whereby costs are accumulated for a specific quantity of products, equipment, repairs, or other services that move through the production process as a continuously identifiable unit. It is used by companies with heterogeneous products or where an order is produced to a customer's specifications (batch production). Whether the batch production is in the form of individual units or lots, it is characterized by the need to accumulate costs by job. Accordingly, job-order cost accounting can be defined as the system of cost accumulation by individual jobs. The method applies to such diverse industries as the construction, printing, aircraft, furniture, shipbuilding, foundry, and machine tool industries.

Process costing is used by companies with products manufactured in a relatively continuous operation or with homogeneous products. This method can be applied in such diverse industries as the textile, oil, brewery, food processing, paint, carpeting, paper, and many other industries. It is appropriate where there is mass production of standardized units requiring a continuous, uniform set of production processes or operations. Costs are accumulated by cost centers or processes periodically, rather than by jobs. Accordingly, process cost accounting can be defined as a system of cost accumulation for products undergoing a continuous production process.

The difference between the job-order and process costing methods centers on the nature of the demand, the product, and the production process. Process costing involves situations where (1) production is initiated by future market demand rather than a specific customer order; (2) the individual units are homogeneous, like units requiring the same input, technology, and effort; and (3) the production process can be characterized by mass production with task specialization under standard operating procedures.

8.3   JOB-ORDER COSTING

8.3.1   Job-Order Procedures

In job-order costing, each job is an object of costing in the sense that it is assigned materials, labor, and overhead. The cost information on each job is recorded in the appropriate column of a *job-order cost sheet*, the basic document for the accumulation of product costs which the cost accounting department sets up for each job. The totals in the file of cost sheets are periodically posted to the Work-in-Process account; the cost sheets are subsidiary records to the Work-in-Process account.

In the discussion that follows, assume that the ABEL Manufacturing Company uses a job-order costing system. Its main products are custom-made chairs and desks. To clarify the explanation, cost accounting procedures have been divided into accounting for materials, accounting for labor, accounting for overhead, and accounting for jobs completed and cost of goods sold. Each phase will be discussed in terms of the general ledger entries, the subsidiary ledger entries, and the nature of the supporting source documents. Assume that the ABEL Manufacturing Company accepts two orders to manufacture a custom-made chair and desk during January. It assigns job numbers 1 and 2 to these orders. The following transactions took place during January:

1. Materials are purchased as follows:

	Type A	Type B	Supplies	Total
Materials	$1,000	$1,000	$1,000	$3,000

2. Materials are issued to the factory as follows:

	Factory Overhead	Job 1	Job 2	Total
Materials, Type A		$500	$400	$ 900
Materials, Type B		200	400	600
Supplies	$300			300
	$300	$700	$800	$1,800

3. Labor costs are incurred as follows:

	Factory Overhead	Job 1	Job 2	Total
Direct Labor		$300	$300	$600
Indirect Labor	$200			200
Total	$200	$300	$300	$800
Labor Hours		25	25	

4. Other costs are incurred as follows:

Depreciation of Equipment	$ 50
Light, Heat, and Power	100
Miscellaneous	110
Total	$260

8.3.2   ## Accounting for Materials

Accounting for materials in a job-order costing system involves three main transactions: the purchase of materials and supplies, the issuance of direct materials for production use, and the issuance of supplies (indirect materials) for production use.

All entries start when, upon receipt of a *customer's order*, the sales department notifies the production department of all necessary production details. These data are then used by the production department to prepare a *production order* authorizing the manufacturing process. At the same time, the cost accounting department sets up the appropriate number of *job cost sheets* (in this case, job cost sheets 1 and 2). The production order, including detailed requirements for production, is used to prepare a schedule of the required materials in a document called a *bill of materials*. A copy of the bill of materials is forwarded to the storekeeper to verify the availability of an adequate amount of materials on hand for completing the order. At this stage procedures are implemented for the purchase of raw materials and supplies. These procedures originated when, through a *purchase requisition*, a warehouse clerk or a material ledger clerk notified the purchasing agent of the need for a particular material. On the basis of the purchase requisition, the purchasing agent issued a *purchase order* to a supplier. Upon receipt of the materials, the receiving department issued a *receiving report*. Finally, upon receipt of copies of the receiving report, the purchase order, and the *approved vendor's invoice*, the accounting department originated the following entries:

1. General Ledger

Materials Inventory Control	3,000	
Accounts Payable		3,000

To record the purchase of raw materials (types A and B and supplies).

2. Subsidiary Ledger

Materials Card A (Received Column)	$1,000
Materials Card B (Received Column)	1,000
Supplies Card (Received Column)	1,000

Each individual materials card shows at least the quantity on hand and the cost of the materials.

The purpose of this double counting procedure at the accounting department is to insure maximum control and to meet the two cost objectives, namely, the control objective and the product costing objective. The balance of the Materials Inventory account and the total of the materials card (in a materials ledger or stores ledger) are compared periodically to identify any discrepancies.

The issuance of materials originates when, through a *materials requisition card*, a production clerk notifies the storekeeper to deliver materials to a given department. Upon receipt of a sufficient number of materials requisitions, the accounting department originates the following entries:

1. General Ledger

Work-in-Process Inventory Control	1,500	
Materials Inventory Control		1,500

To record the issuance of direct material.

In the cost department, the materials requisition cards bearing the job numbers are used to assign the materials to the appropriate job by entering the amount in the Materials column of the appropriate cost sheet and the Issued column of the materials card as follows:

2. Subsidiary Ledger

Job-Order Cost Sheet 1 (Custom Chair) $700
Job-Order Cost Sheet 2 (Custom Desk)   800
Materials Card A (Issued Column)   900
Materials Card B (Issued Column)   600

The issuance of supplies for departmental use involves the same entries as the issuance of materials (direct materials), except the Factory Overhead Control account is debited instead of the Work-in-Process Control account. This treatment is justified by the "indirect" nature of supplies, which cannot be traced directly to a particular job. Similarly, in the subsidiary ledger, the amount is debited to an Indirect Material column of a department overhead cost sheet. Thus, the accounting department originates the following entries:

1. General Ledger

Factory Overhead Control   300
  Materials Inventory Control   300
To record the issuance of indirect materials.

2. Subsidiary Ledger

Department Overhead Cost Sheet (Indirect Material Column) $300
Supplies Card (Issued Column)   300

8.3.3   *Accounting for Labor*

Accounting for labor includes at least two phases: (1) the recording and payment of labor and (2) the distribution of labor. Time tickets, clock cards, and a payroll register usually are used to record the number of hours and the cost of direct and indirect labor. (Figure 8.2 shows a time ticket.) Time tickets are collected daily, checked with the clock cards, and used by the payroll clerk to post to the payroll record the number of hours worked by each employee the previous day. At the end of each payroll period, the payroll department determines the net amount payable to each employee. The general ledger entry follows, ignoring for the time being all labor deductions:

1. General Ledger

Factory Payroll   800
  Cash   800
To record the payment of payroll.

The information for the distribution of labor in the time tickets is first recorded in a *labor cost summary* (or labor distribution manual), which distinguishes between direct and indirect labor as well as regular time, overtime, and idle time. The labor cost summary is basically a summary of the time tickets that will be used by the cost clerk in the accounting department to originate the following entries:

1. General Ledger

Work-in-Process Inventory Control   600
Factory Overhead Control (Indirect Labor)   200
  Factory Payroll   800
To record the distribution of direct and indirect labor.

2. Subsidiary Ledger

Job-Order Cost Sheet 1 (Direct-Labor Column) $300
Job-Order Cost Sheet 2 (Direct-Labor Column)   300
Department Overhead Cost Sheet (Indirect-Labor Column)   200

Figure 8.2 Time Ticket

Clarkson Manufacturing Co.
Grinding Department

Employee No. _____ *1064*

Employee Name _____ *PAUL PSILOS*

Job	Time			
Job No. 101	0.15 1.50 2.50	0.5 1.75 2.75	1 ② 3	1.15 2.15 3.15
Job No. 102	0.15 1.50 2.50	0.5 1.75 2.75	1 2 3	1.15 ②.15 3.15
Job No. 103	0.15 1.50 2.50	0.5 ①.75 2.75	1 2 3	1.15 2.15 3.15
Job No. 104	0.15 1.50 2.50	0.5 1.75 2.75	1 2 3	1.15 ②.15 3.15

Superintendent
Signature _____ *John Monti*

Note that the Factory Payroll account is a temporary clearing account. It allows the recording of the labor costs indicated in the clock cards and the time tickets over the total payroll cycle. At the end of the period, the balance of the Factory Payroll account is zero.

8.3.4 Accounting for Manufacturing Overhead

Accounting for manufacturing overhead involves three phases: the purchase of overhead, the estimation of overhead, and the application of overhead.

Purchase of Actual Factory Overhead

Besides indirect material and indirect labor, other factory overhead expenses are incurred during the production cycle. Examples of indirect manufacturing expenses are rent, insurance, property taxes, utilities, depreciation, lubricants, and so forth. These factory expenses are recorded both on the departmental overhead cost sheet and in the Factory Overhead Control account in the general ledger. The accounting department originates the following entries:

1. General Ledger

Factory Overhead Control 260
        Accumulated Depreciation   50
        Cash, Payables, or Prepaids   210
To record the incurrence of factory overhead.

2. Subsidiary Ledger (Departmental Overhead Cost Sheet)

Depreciation Column .... $ 50
Heat, Light, and Power Column 100
Miscellaneous Column 110

Note that a single departmental cost sheet with individual columns to record each kind of expense is used in this example. A possible alternative would be to use separate expense ledger sheets for each kind of expense, with individual columns to show a departmental classification.

Estimation of Overhead

Given the heterogeneous nature of the output in a job-order costing situation, overhead cannot be directly traced to the particular jobs, so an averaging process is necessary. Thus, factory overhead will be entered in the job cost sheets on the basis of a predetermined overhead rate based on a justified relationship between the overhead costs and an activity index. The predetermined overhead rate is established based on past experience and the budget for the period. A popular activity index used in accounting for overhead is direct-labor hours. Direct-labor costs and machine hours are also frequently used. For example, suppose that the ABEL Manufacturing Company has estimated its manufacturing overhead to be $100,000 and direct labor to be 10,000 hours. The predetermined overhead rate is then equal to $100,000/10,000 = $10. This rate is used in charging a share of overhead to each job.

Application of Overhead

Overhead is then applied to each job by multiplying the job's direct-labor hours by the predetermined overhead rate and entering the resulting amount, which is the *applied factory overhead*, in the Overhead column of the job cost sheets. Similarly, the overhead rate is used to apply overhead to any job in process by the end of the accounting period. The total overhead assigned to all jobs is recorded in the general ledger by the following entry:

Work-in-Process Inventory Control 500
        Applied Factory Overhead ....   500 (50 Hours × $10)
To apply factory overhead to jobs at the rate of $10 per direct-labor hour.

Similarly, in the subsidiary ledger overhead is applied to the appropriate job by entering the amount of applied overhead in the Manufacturing Overhead column of the appropriate cost sheet:

Job-Order Cost Sheet 1 .... $250 (25 Hours × $10)
Job-Order Cost Sheet 2 .... 250 (25 Hours × $10)

8.3.5   Accounting for Jobs Completed and Cost of Goods Sold

Suppose jobs 1 and 2 for the custom-made chair and desk are completed; cost sheets 1 and 2 will be transferred in the subsidiary ledger to a finished goods file. In the general ledger an entry is originated as follows:

```
Finished Goods Inventory Control ........................................ 2,600
    Work-in-Process Inventory Control .................................          2,600
To record the completion of jobs 1 and 2.
```

If job 1 is sold, the sale is recorded as follows:

```
Accounts Receivable ..................................................... 2,000
Cost of Goods Sold ...................................................... 1,250
    Finished Goods Inventory Control ..................................          1,250
    Sales .............................................................          2,000
To recognize the sales revenue and the cost of goods sold of job 1.         .
```

8.3.6   *Disposition of Overapplied or Underapplied Overhead*

The actual overhead costs usually will differ from the total applied overhead because of estimation errors in the computation of the predetermined overhead rate. If the difference is a debit balance, it is known as an *underapplied overhead*; if it is a credit balance, it is an *overapplied overhead*. In the case of the ABEL Manufacturing Company, the balance of overapplied or underapplied overhead is determined by the following entry at the end of the accounting period:

```
Applied Factory Overhead ................................................ 500
    Factory Overhead Control ..........................................          500
To recognize the amount of applied overhead.
```

Different accounting treatments can be used for the disposition of the underapplied or overapplied overhead.

A first, expedient solution is to charge the total underapplied or overapplied overhead as an adjustment of the Cost of Goods Sold as follows:

```
Cost of Goods Sold ...................................................... 260
    Factory Overhead Control ..........................................          260
To close and charge underapplied overhead to the Cost of Goods Sold.
```

Note that if it were an overapplied overhead, it would instead be credited to Cost of Goods Sold.

A second solution would be to prorate the underapplied or overapplied overhead between the balance amounts of the Work-in-Process Control account, the Finished Goods Control account, and the Cost of Goods Sold account in the general ledger and the individual job orders in the subsidiary ledger. For ABEL Manufacturing Company, the Work-in-Process, Finished Goods Inventory, and Cost of Goods Sold accounts have balances equal to 0, $135, and $125, respectively. Consequently, the following entry is recorded in the general ledger to reflect the proportional allocation of the underapplied overhead:

Work-in-Process 0

Finished Goods .... $135 (260 \times \frac{1,350}{2,600})$

Cost of Goods Sold .... $125 (260 \times \frac{1,250}{2,600})$

    Factory Overhead Control 260

To close and prorate the underapplied overhead to the Work-in-Process Inventory, Finished Goods, and Cost of Goods Sold.

Table 8.1 A Summary of Cost Flows for ABEL Manufacturing Co.: General Ledger

Materials Inventory

Debit	Credit
(a.) 3,000	(b.) 1,500
	(c.) 300

Accounts Payable

Debit	Credit
	(a.) 3,000

Work-in-Process

Debit	Credit
(b.) 1,500	(i.) 2,600
(e.) 600	
(g.) 500	

Factory Overhead Control

Debit	Credit
(c.) 300	(h.) 500
(e.) 200	(k.) 260
(f.) 260	

Cash, Payables, Prepaids

Debit	Credit
	(f.) 210

Accumulated Depreciation

Debit	Credit
	(f.) 50

Factory Payroll

Debit	Credit
(d.) 800	(e.) 800

Accrued Payroll

Debit	Credit
	(d.) 800

Finished Goods

Debit	Credit
(i.) 2,600	(j.) 1,250
(k.) 135	

Cost of Goods Sold

Debit	Credit
(j.) 1,250	
(k.) 125	

Sales Revenue

Debit	Credit
	(j.) 2,000

Factory Overhead Applied

Debit	Credit
(h.) 500	(g.) 500

Accounts Receivable

Debit	Credit
(j.) 2,000	

Explanation of Entries
(a.) Purchase of materials and supplies.
(b.) Issuance of materials for production.
(c.) Issuance of supplies for production.
(d.) Recording of payroll.
(e.) Recording of distribution of direct and indirect labor.
(f.) Purchase of factory overhead.
(g.) Application of overhead.
(h.) Closing of Applied Factory Overhead.
(i.) Transfer of cost of goods manufactured into Finished Goods.
(j.) Sale of finished goods.
(k.) Proration of underapplied overhead.

The choice of either accounting treatment again depends on the magnitude and materiality of the overapplied or underapplied overhead and also on the particular managerial objective use of the resulting data.

Table 8.1 and Figure 8.3 summarize all the entries that have taken place in the ABEL Manufacturing Company example in both the general and subsidiary ledgers.

8.4 PROCESS COSTING

8.4.1 Process Costing Documents and Procedures

As discussed earlier, product costing is an averaging process. The basic difference between job-order and process costing is the size of the denominator, which is large for

Figure 8.3 *A Summary of Cost Flows for ABEL Manufacturing Co.: Subsidiary Ledger*

a. Job Cost Sheet #1

Job Number ___1___
Department ___Finishing___
Item ___Chair___

Materials		Direct Labor			Manufacturing Overhead		
Req. No.	Amount	Card	Hours	Amount	Hour	Rate	Amount
x1	700	13	100	300	250	$1	250

Cost Summary	
Materials	$ 700
Direct Labor	$ 300
Overhead	$ 250
Total Cost	$1,250

Figure 8.3   *(continued)*

b. Job Cost Sheet #2

Job Number _____2_____

Department ___Finishing___

Item ___Desk___

Materials		Direct Labor			Manufacturing Overhead		
Req. No.	Amount	Card	Hours	Amount	Hour	Rate	Amount
x1	800	15	100	300	250	$1	250

Cost Summary	
Materials	$ 800
Direct Labor	$ 300
Overhead	$ 250
Total Cost	$1,350

process costing. Process costing is used when production is characterized by a large volume of like units flowing in a constant stream through a series of manufacturing steps or processes. Each of the steps in a manufacturing process is accomplished in an autonomous department. Consequently, in a process cost system, costs are accumulated by departments in conformity with the existing product flow, which may be sequential, parallel, or selective.

In a sequential product flow, all units undergo transformation in each of the processing centers. As Figure 8.4 shows, the recording of cost goes from one work-in-process account to another and finally to a finished goods account when completed.

In a parallel product flow, units may undergo transformation in different processing centers. As Figure 8.5 shows, costs are initially recorded in different work-in-process accounts and then brought together in a final work-in-process before being transferred to a finished goods account.

Finally, in a selective product flow, costs are charged to different work-in-process accounts in conformity with the existing output mix. (See Figure 8.6.)

Whatever the product flow, costs are charged directly to the appropriate department.

Figure 8.3   **_(continued)_**

c. Department F, Overhead Cost Sheet

Indirect Material	Indirect Labor	Depreciation	Heat, Light, and Power	Miscellaneous
$300	$200	$50	$100	$110

d. Raw Materials Subsidiary Ledger

Material A

Received	Issued	Balance
$1,000	$900	$100

Material B

Received	Issued	Balance
$1,000	$600	$400

Supplies C

Received	Issued	Balance
$1,000	$300	$700

Figure 8.4   _Sequential Product Flow_

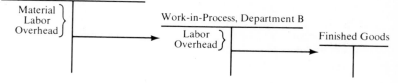

Figure 8.5   _A Parallel Product Flow_

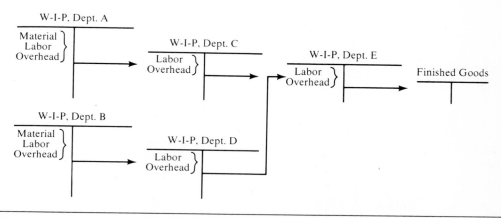

Figure 8.6   Selective Product Flow

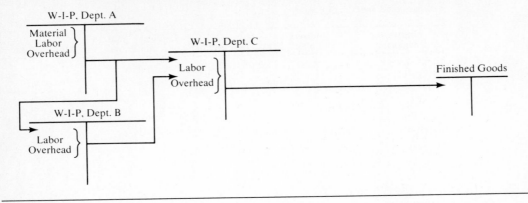

A cost per unit is computed per department, which enables the computation of the amount transferred from one department to another. A *cost of production report* is used to collect, summarize, and compute total and unit costs incurred in a given department. It will be used as a source document for general ledger entries. In general, a cost of production report shows (1) costs charged to a given department, (2) *equivalent unit* processing costs, and (3) the costs applicable to the work of the department.

The major difficulty in establishing a cost of production report arises when computing the equivalent units for a given department. At the end of a given period a certain number of units may remain incomplete. To compute a unit cost, the incomplete units must be converted to equivalent units on the basis of their degree of completion. For example, 200 units, 50 percent complete, make 100 equivalent units.

The process costing procedure consists of the following steps:

1. The costs of material, labor, and factory overhead are accumulated by department.

2. The equivalent units for each department are determined, resulting in the computation of the equivalent processing unit costs.

3. On the basis of the unit costs obtained in step 2, the costs are applied to the work in each department.

4. The costs of units completed in each department are transferred to either another work-in-process or to a finished goods account.

Although this procedure is straightforward, a difference may arise according to the choice of a given inventory flow method. Two common methods of tracing beginning inventory costs are the *weighted average* and *first-in, first-out* (*FIFO*) costing methods. The following discussion illustrates the process cost accounting system first under a weighted average method and second under a FIFO method. Both methods are described in terms of the following example.

The ABEL Manufacturing Company produces a product alpha as follows. Material A is introduced at the beginning of the process in the grinding department, after which it is transferred to a finishing department, where material B is added evenly throughout the process. The other processing costs, labor and overhead, are also added evenly during both the grinding and finishing operations. The output of the finishing department, alpha, is transferred to a finished goods account. Data for the January 19X5 cost period are as follows:

	Grinding Department	Finishing Department
Beginning Work-in-Process Inventory		
Units	3,000 (⅓)	2,000 (¼)
Material	$3,000	$9,250
Labor	$15,500	$9,750
Overhead	$15,000	$10,250
Transferred In		$19,000
Units Started in January	30,000	18,000
Units Completed and Transferred	18,000	14,000
Ending Work-in-Process Inventory		
Units	15,000 (⅔)	6,000 (⅓)
Current Costs		
Material	$30,000	$38,750
Labor	$40,500	$54,250
Overhead	$27,000	$69,750
Transferred In	—	?

8.4.2   Weighted Average Method

A company using the weighted average method can be characterized by two main characteristics from a product costing point of view:

1. The production equation is as follows:

$$
\begin{array}{c}
\text{Number of units} \\
\text{in the beginning} \\
\text{work-in-process} \\
\text{inventory}
\end{array}
+
\begin{array}{c}
\text{Units started} \\
\text{in the period}
\end{array}
=
\begin{array}{c}
\text{Units completed} \\
\text{in the period}
\end{array}
+
\begin{array}{c}
\text{Number of units} \\
\text{in the ending} \\
\text{work-in-process} \\
\text{inventory.}
\end{array}
$$

2. The average unit cost of the period is viewed as follows:

$$
\text{Average unit input cost} = \frac{\text{Beginning work-in-process inventory costs} + \text{Current costs of the period}}{\text{Number of equivalent units}}.
$$

In other words, the Beginning Work-in-Process Inventory is treated as if it were started in the current period.

The accumulation of process costs, the method of computing unit costs, and the application of costs to the work of the department are accomplished in a document called the *cost of production report* or a *process cost summary*. Tables 8.2 and 8.3 illustrate the cost of production reports for the grinding and finishing departments, respectively, for January 19X5 using the method of weighted average costing and the four steps outlined earlier.

In Table 8.2, the first step is to accumulate the costs of material, labor, and overhead for the grinding department. These costs include both the costs of the beginning work-in-process and the current costs. (Keep in mind this is one of the requirements of the

Table 8.2   **ABEL Manufacturing Company, Ltd., Grinding Department Process Cost Summary for the Month Ended January 31, 19X5 (Weighted Average Method)**

1. Costs Charged to the Department

	Material	Labor	Overhead	Total
Current Costs	$30,000	$40,500	$27,000	$ 97,500
Beginning Work-in-Process	3,000	15,500	15,000	33,500
Total Costs to Be Accounted for	$33,000	$56,000	$42,000	$131,000

2. Equivalent Unit Processing Costs

	Total Units	Equivalent Units		
		Material	Labor	Overhead
Beginning Work-in-Process (1/3)	3,000			
Units Started	30,000			
To Account for	33,000			
Units Completed	18,000	18,000	18,000	18,000
Ending Work-in-Process (2/3)	15,000	15,000	10,000	10,000
Equivalent Units	33,000	33,000	28,000	28,000
Total Costs to Be Accounted for		$33,000	$56,000	$42,000
Equivalent Unit Processing Costs		$1.00	$2.00	$1.50

3. Costs Applicable to the Work of the Department

Goods Completed: 18,000 ($1.00 + $2.00 + $1.50)	$ 81,000
Ending Work-in-Process	50,000[a]
	$131,000

[a]The ending Work-in-Process is computed by deducting the Costs of Goods Completed from the Total Costs. It is, however, appropriate to check the accuracy of the figure as follows:
Material: 15,000 × $1.00 = $15,000
Labor: 10,000 × $2.00 = 20,000
Overhead: 10,000 × $1.50 =   15,000
            $50,000

weighted average method.) The Beginning Work-in-Process of the grinding department includes $3,000 of direct material, $15,500 of direct labor, and $15,000 of overhead. The current costs include $30,000 of direct material, $40,500 of direct labor, and $27,000 of overhead.

The second step is to determine the equivalent units for the grinding department and the corresponding equivalent unit processing costs. Notice that the production equation used for the weighted average method specifies that the number of units in the beginning work-in-process inventory (3,000) plus the units started in the period (30,000) equal the units completed in the period (18,000) plus the number of units in the ending work-in-process inventory (15,000). The equivalent units are computed for both the units completed and the ending work-in-process inventory. Hence to complete 18,000 finished goods units, 18,000 equivalent units of material, labor, and overhead are required. Because the ending work-in-process is two-thirds complete, 15,000 units of material are

Table 8.3   **ABEL Manufacturing Company, Ltd., Finishing Department Process Cost Summary for the Month Ended January 31, 19X5 (Weighted Average Method)**

1. Costs Charged to the Department

	Material	Labor	Overhead	Transferred In	Total
Current Costs	$38,750	$54,250	$69,750	$ 81,000	$243,750
Beginning Work-in-Process	9,250	9,750	10,250	19,000	48,250
Total Costs to Be Accounted for	$48,000	$64,000	$80,000	$100,000	$292,000

2. Equivalent Unit Processing Costs

	Total Units	Equivalent Units			
		Material	Labor	Overhead	Transferred In
Beginning Work-in-Process (1/4)	2,000				
Units Started	18,000				
To Account for	20,000				
Units Completed	14,000	14,000	14,000	14,000	14,000
Ending Work-in-Process (1/3)	6,000	2,000	2,000	2,000	6,000
Equivalent Units		16,000	16,000	16,000	20,000
Total Costs to Be Accounted for		$48,000	$64,000	$80,000	$100,000
Equivalent Unit Processing Costs		$3.00	$4.00	$5.00	$5.00

3. Costs Applicable to the Work of the Department

Goods Completed: 14,000 ($3.00 + $4.00 + $5.00 + $5.00) $238,000
Ending Work-in-Process   54,000[a]
                                                                                          _____
                                                                                          $292,000

[a]Ending Work-in-Process:
Material: 2,000 × $3.00 = $ 6,000
Labor: 2,000 × $4.00 =   8,000
Overhead: 2,000 × $5.00 =   10,000
Transferred In: 6,000 × $5.00 =   30,000
                                              _____
                                              $54,000

required (keep in mind that the material is added at the beginning of the process), and only 10,000 equivalent units of labor and overhead are required (in other words, two-thirds of 15,000 units, because the ending work-in-process is two-thirds complete and because the labor and overhead are added evenly throughout the process; only 10,000 units—two-thirds of 15,000—are required). On this basis, the equivalent units are 33,000 units for material, 28,000 for labor, and 28,000 for overhead.

Using the total cost information obtained in step 1 and the equivalent units obtained in step 2, the equivalent unit processing costs can now be computed. They are $1 per unit for material, $2 per unit for labor, and $1.50 per unit for overhead.

The third step is to apply the cost to the work of the department—namely, the Goods Completed and the Ending Work-in-Process accounts—which in this case is $81,000 to the Goods Completed and $50,000 to the Ending Work-in-Process accounts.

In Table 8.3 the whole process is repeated. The only difference stems from the addition of a new column for an additional input, which is the transferred-in costs of $81,000 corresponding to the goods completed in the grinding department and transferred to the finishing department. Notice that in Table 8.3, the transferred-in cost is submitted to the same treatment as labor, material, and overhead.

8.4.3   *First-In, First-Out Method*

A company using the FIFO method can be distinguished by two main characteristics from a product costing point of view:

1. The production equation is viewed as follows:

$$
\begin{array}{c}\text{Number of units} \\ \text{in the beginning} \\ \text{work-in-process} \\ \text{inventory}\end{array} + \begin{array}{c}\text{Units started} \\ \text{in the period}\end{array} = \begin{array}{c}\text{Units completed} \\ \text{from the beginning} \\ \text{work-in-process} \\ \text{inventory}\end{array} + \begin{array}{c}\text{Units started} \\ \text{and completed} \\ \text{in the period}\end{array} + \begin{array}{c}\text{Number of} \\ \text{units in the ending} \\ \text{work-in-process} \\ \text{inventory.}\end{array}
$$

2. The average unit cost of the period is as follows:

$$
\text{Average unit input cost} = \frac{\text{Current costs of the period}}{\text{Number of equivalent units}}.
$$

In other words, a company using the FIFO method would consider the beginning work-in-process as completely separate and distinct from the units started and completed in the period. Consequently, only the current costs are used toward the computation of the equivalent unit processing costs.

Tables 8.4 and 8.5 illustrate the cost of production reports for the grinding department and the finishing department, respectively, for January using the FIFO method and the four steps outlined earlier.

In Table 8.4, the first step is to accumulate the costs of material, labor, and overhead. These costs include only the current costs, and the beginning work-in-process costs are considered as start-up costs incurred in the previous period. Keep in mind that this is a major requirement of the FIFO method. The current costs include $30,000 for material, $40,500 for direct labor, and $27,000 for overhead. A separate column for start-up costs includes the beginning work-in-process costs of $33,500.

The second step is to determine the equivalent units for the grinding department and the corresponding equivalent unit processing costs. Notice that the production equation used in the FIFO method specifies that the number of units in the beginning work-in-process inventory (3,000) plus the units started (30,000) equal the units completed from the beginning work-in-process inventory (3,000) plus the units started and completed in the period (15,000) plus the ending work-in-process inventory (15,000). The equivalent units are computed for the units completed from the beginning work-in-process inventory, the units started and completed in the period, and the ending work-in-process inventory. Therefore, to complete 3,000 units from the beginning work-in-process inventory which are one-third complete, no material is required (given that material is added in the beginning of the process and, hence, has already been added to the beginning work-in-process inventory in the previous period) and 2,000 equivalent units of both labor and overhead are required (in other words, two-thirds of 3,000 equivalent units are required to complete 3,000 units, one-third complete). For the units started and completed, 15,000 equivalent units of material, labor, and overhead are required. Finally,

Table 8.4   **ABEL Manufacturing Company, Ltd., Grinding Department Process Cost Summary for the Month Ended January 31, 19X5 (FIFO Method)**

1. Costs Charged to the Department

	Material	Labor	Overhead	Start-up	Total
Current Costs	$30,000	$40,500	$27,000	—	$ 97,500
Beginning Work-in-Process	—	—	—	$33,500	33,500
Total Costs to Be Accounted for	$30,000	$40,500	$27,000	$33,500	$131,000

2. Equivalent Unit Processing Costs

	Total Units	Equivalent Units Material	Labor	Overhead
Beginning Work-in-Process (1/3)	3,000			
Units Started	30,000			
To Account for	33,000			
Units Completed				
Beginning Inventory (1/3)	3,000	—	2,000	2,000
Started and Completed	15,000	15,000	15,000	15,000
Ending Work-in-Process (2/3)	15,000	15,000	10,000	10,000
Equivalent Units		30,000	27,000	27,000
Total Costs to Be Accounted for		$30,000	$40,500	$27,000
Equivalent Unit Processing Costs		$1.00	$1.50	$1.00

3. Costs Applicable to the Work of the Department

Goods Completed	
Beginning Work-in-Process: 33,500 + 2,000 ($1.50 + $1.00)	$ 38,500
Started and Completed: 15,000 ($1.00 + $1.50 + $1.00)	52,500
	$ 91,000
Ending Work-in-Process ($131,000 − $91,000)	40,000[a]
	$131,000

[a]Ending Work-in-Process:
Material: 15,000 × $1.00 = $15,000
Labor: 10,000 × $1.50 = 15,000
Overhead: 10,000 × $1.00 = 10,000
                         $40,000

the 15,000 units in the ending work-in-process inventory (two-thirds complete) require 15,000 units of material (because material is added at the beginning of the process) and 10,000 units of labor and overhead (two-thirds of 15,000). On this basis, the equivalent units are 30,000 units for material, 27,000 units for labor, and 27,000 units for overhead. The equivalent unit processing costs are $1 for material, $1.50 for labor, and $1 for overhead.

The third step is to apply the cost to the work of the department—namely, the Goods Completed and the Ending Work-in-Process accounts—which in this case is $91,000 to the Goods Completed and $40,000 to the Ending Work-in-Process accounts. Notice that

Table 8.5   **ABEL Manufacturing Company, Ltd., Finishing Department Process Cost Summary for the Month Ended January 31, 19X5 (FIFO Method)**

1. Costs Charged to the Department

	Material	Labor	Overhead	Transferred In	Start-up	Total
Current Costs	$38,750	$54,250	$69,750	$91,000	—	$253,750
Beginning Work-in-Process	—	—	—	—	$48,250	48,250
Total Costs to Be Accounted for	$38,750	$54,250	$69,750	$91,000	$48,250	$302,000

2. Equivalent Unit Processing Costs

	Total Units	Equivalent Units			
		Material	Labor	Overhead	Transferred In
Beginning Work-in-Process (1/4)	2,000				
Units Started	18,000				
To Account for	20,000				
Units Completed					
Beginning Inventory (1/4)	2,000	1,500	1,500	1,500	—
Started and Completed	12,000	12,000	12,000	12,000	12,000
Ending Work-in-Process	6,000	2,000	2,000	2,000	6,000
Equivalent Units		15,500	15,500	15,500	18,000
Total Costs to Be Accounted for		$38,750	$54,250	$69,750	$91,000
Equivalent Unit Processing Costs		$2.50	$3.50	$4.50	$5.0555

3. Costs Applicable to the Work of the Department

Goods Completed
Beginning Inventory: 48,250 + 1,500 ($2.50 + $3.50 + $4.50) $ 64,000
Units Started and Completed: 12,000 ($2.50 + $3.50 + $4.50 + $5.0555)   186,666

$250,666

Ending Work-in-Process: $302,000 − $250,666 =   51,334[a]

$302,000

[a] Ending Work-in-Process:
Material:	2,000 × $2.50 =	$ 5,000
Labor:	2,000 × $3.50 =	7,000
Overhead:	2,000 × $4.50 =	9,000
Transferred In:	6,000 × $5.0555 =	30,334

$51,334

the costs of the units completed from the beginning inventories include not only the start-up costs (from the previous period) of $33,500 but also the costs of 2,000 equivalent units of labor and overhead (see Table 8.4).

In Table 8.5 the whole process is repeated. The only difference stems from the addition of a new column for an additional input, the transferred-in costs of $91,000 corresponding to the goods completed in the grinding department and transferred to the finishing department. Notice that in Table 8.5 the transferred-in costs are submitted to the same treatment as labor, material, and overhead.

8.4.4 Journal Entries in a Process Cost System

The journal entries for the ABEL Manufacturing Company example are as follows:

	Weighted Average		**FIFO**	
Work-in-Process—Grinding Department	97,500		97,500	
Raw Material Inventory		30,000		30,000
Factory Payroll		40,500		40,500
Factory Overhead		27,000		27,000
To record the input of material and conversion costs.				
Work-in-Process—Finishing	81,000		91,000	
Work-in-Process—Grinding		81,000		91,000
To record the costs of goods finished and transferred to the finishing department.				
Work-in-Process—Finishing	162,750		162,750	
Raw Material Inventory		38,750		38,750
Factory Payroll		54,250		54,250
Factory Overhead		69,750		69,750
To record the input of material and conversion costs.				
Finished Goods Inventory	238,000		250,666	
Work-in-Process—Finishing		238,000		250,666
To record the cost of goods finished and transferred to Finished Goods.				

8.4.5 Reconciling the Computation of Equivalent Units

The difference in equivalent units obtained by the weighted average and the FIFO methods arises from the two different assumptions about the production equation and the average unit costs, as described at the beginning of sections 8.4.2 and 8.4.3. In brief, the beginning work-in process inventory in the FIFO method is viewed as a batch of goods separate and distinct from the units started and completed. Thus, the main difference between the equivalent units in the FIFO and the weighted average methods relates to the fact that the FIFO method excludes the old equivalent units for work done on beginning inventories. In other words,

$$\begin{array}{c}\text{Equivalent units} \\ \text{(weighted average)}\end{array} - \begin{array}{c}\text{Old equivalent} \\ \text{units for} \\ \text{work done on} \\ \text{beginning inventory}\end{array} = \text{Equivalent units (FIFO).}$$

The application of this reconciliation formula is illustrated in Table 8.6 based on the data from the ABEL Manufacturing Company example.

8.5 STANDARD COSTS AND PROCESS COSTING

Standard costing can be used in both job-order and process cost situations. It is more appropriate, however, in situations where operations are amenable to the establishment of physical standards, usually continuous mass production processes. One of the main advantages of standard costs used in process costing is the elimination of the conflicts between the weighted average and FIFO costing methods.

To illustrate the application of standard costs in process costing, assume that the fol-

Table 8.6   Reconciliation of the Computations of Equivalent Units

Equivalent Units

Grinding Department	Total Units	Material	Labor	Overhead	Trans-ferred In
Beginning Work-in-Process (1/3)	3,000				
Units Started	30,000				
To Account for	33,000				
Units Completed	18,000	18,000	18,000	18,000	
Ending Work-in-Process (2/3)	15,000	15,000	10,000	10,000	
Equivalent Units (Weighted Average)		33,000	28,000	28,000	
Less Old Equivalent Units for Work Done on Beginning Inventory		3,000	1,000	1,000	
Equivalent Units (FIFO)		30,000	27,000	27,000	
Finishing Department					
Beginning Work-in-Process (1/4)	2,000				
Units Started	18,000				
To Account for	20,000				
Units Completed	14,000	14,000	14,000	14,000	14,000
Ending Work-in-Process (1/3)	6,000	2,000	2,000	2,000	6,000
Equivalent Units (Weighted Average)		16,000	16,000	16,000	20,000
Less Old Equivalent Units for Work Done on Beginning Inventory		500	500	500	2,000
Equivalent Units (FIFO)		15,500	15,500	15,500	18,000

lowing standard costs have been determined for the grinding department of the ABEL Manufacturing Company:

	Per Unit
Direct Material	$1.50
Direct Labor	1.00
Overhead	2.00
	$4.50

The beginning work-in-process inventory = 3,000 units, one-third complete (material $4,500, labor $3,000, overhead $6,000) = $13,500. Units started and completed = 15,000 units. The ending work-in-process inventory = 15,000 units, two-thirds complete.

The process cost summary for the grinding department using standard costs is shown in Table 8.7. Not only does the use of standard costs eliminate the need to compute the equivalent unit cost, it also facilitates control through the computation of the summary of variances. Notice that the computation of equivalent units for standard costing corresponds to the FIFO-based equivalent units.

Table 8.7   ABEL Manufacturing Company, Ltd., Grinding Department Process Cost Summary for the Month Ended January 31, 19X5 (Standard Costs)

1. Standard Costs Charged to the Department

	Material	Labor	Overhead	Start-up	Total
Current Costs	$45,000	$27,000	$54,000	—	$126,000
Beginning Work-in-Process	—	—	—	$13,500	13,500
Total Costs to Be Accounted for	$45,000	$27,000	$54,000	$13,500	$139,500

2. Equivalent Unit Processing Costs

	Total Units	Equivalent Units		
		Material	Labor	Overhead
Beginning Work-in-Process (1/3)	3,000			
Units Started	30,000			
To Account for	33,000			
Units Completed				
Beginning Inventory (1/3)	3,000	—	2,000	2,000
Started and Completed	15,000	15,000	15,000	15,000
Ending Work-in-Process (2/3)	15,000	15,000	10,000	10,000
Equivalent Units		30,000	27,000	27,000

3. Costs Applicable to the Work of the Department

Goods Completed	
Beginning Inventory: $13,500 + 2,000 ($1.00 + $2.00)	$ 19,500
Units Started and Completed: 15,000 ($1.50 + $1.00 + $2.00)	67,500
	87,000
Ending Work-in-Process: ($139,500 − $87,000)	52,500[a]
	$139,500

[a]Ending Work-in-Process:
Material: 15,000 × $1.50 = $22,500
Labor: 10,000 × $1.00 =   10,000
Overhead: 10,000 × $2.00 =   20,000
                              $52,500

4. Summary of Variances (Actual Performance − Standard Performance)

Material: $30,000 − $45,000 $15,000 Favorable
Labor: $40,500 − $27,000   13,500 Unfavorable
Overhead: $27,000 − $54,000   27,000 Favorable

                              $28,500 Favorable

8.6   *ACCOUNTING FOR SCRAP, SPOILED GOODS, DEFECTIVE WORK, AND UNITS LOST IN PRODUCTION*

Most manufacturing operations are expected to be subject to possible production losses due to *scrap*, spoilage, or defective work. To be fully informative, a good cost accounting system must recognize such losses.

8.6.1   *Scrap and Waste*

Scrap and waste are material residues of manufacturing operations that are believed to have minor resale value to scrap dealers. If the amount of scrap is relatively significant, scrap tickets are prepared to support entries to scrap reports usually expressed in terms of quantities of scrap delivered to the storeroom. At the time of sale, the possible entries are as follows.

Cash (or Accounts Receivable) xxx
    Income from sale of scrap (or Department Factory Overhead Control account)   xxx

This entry shows that in case the scrap is not identifiable to a particular job or department, the credit entry can be made either to a special income account or to reduce the Department Factory Overhead account. The posting made to the subsidiary ledger is recorded in the Sale of Scrap column on the departmental cost sheet.

Cash (or Accounts Receivable) xxx
    Work-in-Process   xxx

If the scrap is identifiable to a specific job or department, an alternative treatment is to credit the appropriate work-in-process account. This treatment is justifiable when an agreement exists between the manufacturer and the customer that specifies the crediting of jobs with all scrap or spoilage losses. Accordingly, the posting made to the subsidiary ledger is recorded in the specific job-order cost sheet.

From a critical point of view, timely and continuous reporting of scrap losses is advisable for the proper functioning of a responsibility accounting system. At the time of occurrence, the recording of not only the scrap quantity but also the scrap value at an "estimated" resale value may even be advisable. The entry would be

Scrap Inventory xxx
    Factory Overhead (or Work-in-Process)   xxx

This last entry is more justifiable when there is a significant time lag between the incurrence and sale of scrap.

8.6.2   *Defective Work*

Defective goods result from failure to meet the production standard established for a good unit. When they occur, the supervisor can authorize either rework or resale. If the decision is to rework the defective units at added cost of materials, labor, and overhead, the accounting treatment will depend on whether the cost of defective units is to be charged to the total production and, consequently, debited to the Department Factory Overhead Control account, or if it is to be charged to a specific job and, consequently, debited to Work-in-Process. In either case, the entries will be as follows:

Department Factory Overhead (or Work-in-Process)................................. xxx
    Materials xxx
    Labor xxx
    Overhead Applied xxx

8.6.3   Spoilage

Spoilage and lost units result from either (1) production that does not meet the standard established for good units, that cannot be reworked, and, consequently, that is sold for disposal value, or (2) shrinkage or evaporation of the materials used so completed production has a smaller volume than the total of basic inputs. *Normal spoilage* is an expected, inherent result of the production process that cannot be controlled. It should be internalized logically in the computation of the predetermined overhead rate to be prorated to the total period production. *Abnormal spoilage* is an unexpected production loss resulting from controllable factors; as such, it should be recognized by a loss account called Loss from Abnormal Spoilage. To illustrate, assume the following example:

Units Completed: 2,200 Units

Good Units	2,000
Normal Spoilage	50
Abnormal Spoilage	150
Total	2,200 Units

Unit Cost: $3

The accounting entries for this example could be as follows:

Work-in-Process 6,600
    Material, Factory Payroll, Manufacturing Overhead 6,600
To record the input of material and conversion costs.
Cost of Spoiled Goods 600
    Work-in-Process 600
To record the spoilage of 200 units.
Finished Goods 6,000
    Work-in-Process 6,000
To record the completion of 2,000 units.
Finished Goods 150
    Cost of Spoiled Goods 150
To record the normal spoilage of 50 units.
Loss from Abnormal Spoilage 450
    Cost of Spoiled Goods 450
To record the abnormal spoilage of 150 units.

Note that the second entry recognizes a cost of spoiled goods and is, in a way, a clearing account that allows the recognition of both normal and abnormal spoilage as product costs first, and then as either a loss or an expense. In practice, such an entry can be skipped for expediency.

8.6.4   Lost Units

Accounting for lost units depends on whether the units were lost in the first department or after the first department. If the units are lost in the first department, the number of units decreases; this leads to a higher unit cost, and no adjustments are necessary. If the units are lost in subsequent departments, an adjustment for lost units must be made. Such an adjustment can be computed according to two possible methods.

Method 1 The adjustment for lost units is equal to the difference between the new unit cost and the old unit cost, where the unit cost is computed as follows:

$$\text{New unit cost} = \frac{\text{Transferred-in cost}}{\begin{array}{c}\text{Units transferred} \\ \text{from preceding department}\end{array} - \text{Lost units}}.$$

Method 2 The adjustment for lost units is computed by allocating the total cost lost over the number of units actually produced:

$$\text{Adjustment for lost units} = \frac{\text{Lost units} \times \text{Old unit cost}}{\begin{array}{c}\text{Units transferred} \\ \text{from preceding department} - \text{Lost units}\end{array}}.$$

As an example, assume the following information for departments 1 and 2:

Transferred-in Costs from Department 1	$120,000
Units Transferred from Department 1	30,000
Units Lost in Department 2	6,000

The adjustment for lost units is computed using method 1 as follows:

New unit cost: $120,000/(30,000 - 6,000) = \$5$.

Old unit cost: $120,000/30,000 = \$4$.

Adjustment: $\$5 - \$4 = \$1$.

Using method 2,

$$\text{Adjustment: } \frac{6,000 \times \$4}{30,000 - 6,000} = \$1.$$

Besides requiring an adjustment to the unit cost, the possibility of units lost in production or units added in the process requires an adjustment in the flow of units in the production equation. Hence the production equation will be as follows for the *weighted average method*:

$$\begin{array}{c}\text{Units in process} \\ \text{at the beginning}\end{array} + \begin{array}{c}\text{Units} \\ \text{started}\end{array} + \begin{array}{c}\text{Units} \\ \text{added}\end{array} = \begin{array}{c}\text{Units} \\ \text{completed}\end{array} + \begin{array}{c}\text{Units still} \\ \text{in process} \\ \text{at the end}\end{array} + \text{Units lost}.$$

For the *FIFO* method, the production equation will be

$$\begin{array}{c}\text{Units in process} \\ \text{at the beginning}\end{array} + \begin{array}{c}\text{Units} \\ \text{started}\end{array} + \begin{array}{c}\text{Units} \\ \text{added}\end{array} = \begin{array}{c}\text{Units} \\ \text{completed from the} \\ \text{beginning inventory}\end{array} + \begin{array}{c}\text{Units started} \\ \text{and completed}\end{array} + \begin{array}{c}\text{Units still} \\ \text{in process} \\ \text{at the end}\end{array} + \begin{array}{c}\text{Units} \\ \text{lost}.\end{array}$$

Notice that *units added* increases the left side of the production equation, while *units lost* increases the right side. Using method 1, the following adjustment for lost units is made for another example:

New unit cost: $300,000/(60,000 − 12,000) = \$6.25.

Old unit cost: $300,000/60,000 \qquad = \$5.00.

Adjustment for lost units: $6.25 − \$5 \quad = \$1.25.

Using method 2,

$$\text{Adjustment for lost units} = \frac{18,000 \text{ units} \times \$5}{60,000 - 12,000} = \$1.25.$$

8.6.5 Process Costing and Spoilage (Shrinkage, Evaporation, Waste, and Lost Units)

Process costing for spoilage (shrinkage, evaporation, waste, and lost units) differs depending on where in production the spoilage takes place. If spoilage occurs at the beginning of operations, the condition is called *initial spoilage*. The costs of spoiled goods from normal spoilage are allocated to good production and units in the Ending Work-in-Process Inventory. If spoilage occurs at the end of operations, the condition is called *terminal spoilage*, and the costs of spoiled goods from normal spoilage are only allocated to the Units Completed and Transferred Out of the Department. The following example illustrates the accounting treatment of spoilage in a process cost system under either the FIFO or the weighted average method and assuming either initial or terminal spoilage.

Assume that the ABEL Manufacturing Company produces a product alpha with costs accumulated on a process cost basis. Materials for alpha are added in at the beginning of the process, and the conversion costs are added evenly throughout the process. Normal spoilage represents about one-tenth of the good output. Additional relevant production statistics for December are as follows:

Beginning Inventory	
Number of Units	2,000 (¼ Complete)
Total Costs	$29,250
Material	$17,000
Labor	$ 8,500
Overhead	$ 3,750
Processing Costs	
Total Costs	$90,000
Material	$60,000
Labor	$24,000
Overhead	$ 6,000
Production	
Units Started	5,000
Units Completed	5,000
Ending Inventory (Units)	1,000 (½ Complete)
Normal Spoilage (Units)	500
Abnormal Spoilage (Units)	500

Table 8.8   **ABEL Manufacturing Company, Ltd., Process Cost Summary (Weighted Average Method)**

1. Costs Charged to the Department

	Material	Labor	Overhead	Total
Current Costs	$60,000	$24,000	$6,000	$ 90,000
Beginning Work-in-Process	17,000	8,500	3,750	29,250
Total Costs to Be Accounted for	$77,000	$32,500	$9,750	$119,250

2. Equivalent Unit Processing Costs

	Total Units	Equivalent Units		
		Material	Labor	Overhead
Beginning Work-in-Process (1/4)	2,000			
Units Started	5,000			
To Account for	7,000			
Units Completed	5,000	5,000	5,000	5,000
Ending Work-in-Process (1/2)	1,000	1,000	500	500
Spoilage	1,000	1,000	1,000	1,000
Equivalent Units		7,000	6,500	6,500
Total Costs to Be Accounted for		$77,000	$32,500	$9,750
Equivalent Unit Processing Costs		$11.00	$5.00	$1.50

3. Costs Applicable to the Work of the Department

Goods Completed:	5,000 ($11 + $5.00 + $1.50)		$ 87,500
Ending Work-in-Process			
Material:	1,000 ($11.00)	$11,000	
Conversion Costs:	500 ($6.50)	3,250	14,250
Normal Spoilage:	500 ($17.50)		8,750
Abnormal Spoilage:	500 ($17.50)		8,750
Total Costs Accounted for			$119,250

Tables 8.8 and 8.9 show the process cost summary under the weighted average method and the FIFO method, respectively. On the basis of these two process cost summaries, accounting for spoilage (either initial or terminal) can be initiated.

If the spoilage in the ABEL Manufacturing Company was an initial spoilage, the costs of spoiled goods from normal spoilage would be allocated to good production and units in the Ending Work-in-Process. The allocation using the weighted average results would be as follows:

1. Ending Work-in-Process before normal spoilage: $14,250.

2. Goods Completed before normal spoilage loss: $87,500.

3. Normal spoilage per unit ($8,750/6,000 units): $1.458.

4. Normal spoilage allocated to Goods Completed ($1.458 × 5,000): $7,292.

5. Normal Spoilage allocated to Ending Work-in-Process ($1.458 × 1,000): $1,458.
6. Goods Completed after normal spoilage (2 + 4): $94,790.
7. Ending Work-in-Process after normal spoilage (1 + 5): $15,708.

The allocation using the FIFO results would be as follows:

1. Ending Work-in-Process before normal spoilage: $14,500.
2. Goods Completed before normal spoilage loss: $87,750.
3. Normal spoilage per unit ($8,500/6,000 units): $1.416.
4. Normal spoilage allocated to Goods Completed ($1.416 × 5,000): $7,084.

Table 8.9   **ABEL Manufacturing Company, Ltd., Process Cost Summary (FIFO) Method)**

1. Costs Charged to the Department

	Material	Labor	Overhead	Start-up	Total
Current Costs	$60,000	$24,000	$6,000	—	$ 90,000
Beginning Work-in-Process	—	—	—	$29,250	29,250
Total Costs to Be Accounted for	$60,000	$24,000	$6,000	$29,250	$119,250

2. Equivalent Unit Processing Costs

	Total Units	Equivalent Units Material	Equivalent Units Labor	Equivalent Units Overhead
Beginning Work-in-Process (1/4)	2,000			
Units Started	5,000			
To Account for	7,000			
Units Completed				
Beginning Inventory	2,000	—	1,500	1,500
Started and Completed	3,000	3,000	3,000	3,000
Ending Work-in-Process (1/2)	1,000	1,000	500	500
Spoilage	1,000	1,000	1,000	1,000
Equivalent Units		5,000	6,000	6,000
Total Costs to Be Accounted for		$60,000	$24,000	$6,000
Equivalent Unit Processing Costs		$12.00	$4.00	$1.00

3. Costs Applicable to the Work of the Department

Goods Completed			
Beginning Inventory:	29,250 + 1,500 ($4.00 + $1.00)		$ 36,750
Started and Completed:	3,000 ($17.00)		51,000
Normal Spoilage:	500 ($17.00)		8,500
Abnormal Spoilage:	500 ($17.00)		8,500
Ending Work-in-Process			
Materials:	1,000 ($12.00)	$12,000	
Conversion Costs:	500 ($ 5.00)	2,500	14,500
Total Costs Accounted for:			$119,250

5. Normal spoilage allocated to Ending Work-in-Process ($1.416 × 1,000): $1,416.

6. Goods Completed after normal spoilage (2 + 4): $94,835.

7. Ending Work-in-Process after normal spoilage (1 + 5): $15,917.

The journal entries will be as follows:

	Weighted Average		FIFO	
Work-in-Process	90,000		90,000	
Raw Material Inventory		60,000		60,000
Factory Payroll		24,000		24,000
Factory Overhead		6,000		6,000
To record the input of material and conversion costs.				
Cost of Spoiled Goods	17,500		17,000	
Work-in-Process		17,500		17,000
To record the spoilage of 1,000 units.				
Finished Goods	87,500		87,750	
Cost of Spoiled Goods		87,500		87,750
To record the completion of 5,000 units.				
Finished Goods	7,292		7,084	
Work-in-Process	1,458		1,416	
Cost of Spoiled Goods		8,750		8,500
To allocate normal spoilage to good production and units in the Ending Work-in-Process.				
Loss from Abnormal Spoilage	8,750		8,500	
Cost of Spoiled Goods		8,750		8,500
To record the abnormal spoilage of 500 units.				

If the spoilage in the ABEL Manufacturing Company were a terminal spoilage, the costs of spoiled goods from normal spoilage would be only allocated to the units completed and transferred out of the department. In such a case, the journal entries would be as follows:

	Weighted Average		FIFO	
Work-in-Process	90,000		90,000	
Raw Material Inventory		60,000		60,000
Factory Payroll		24,000		24,000
Factory Overhead		6,000		6,000
To record the input of material and conversion costs.				
Cost of Spoiled Goods	17,500		17,000	
Work-in-Process		17,500		17,000
To record the spoilage of 1,000 units.				
Finished Goods	87,500		87,750	
Work-in-Process		87,500		87,750
To record the completion of 5,000 units.				
Finished Goods	8,750		8,500	
Cost of Spoiled Goods		8,750		8,500
To record the normal spoilage of 500 units.				
Loss from Abnormal Spoilage	8,750		8,500	
Cost of Spoiled Goods		8,750		8,500
To record the abnormal spoilage of 500 units.				

8.7 ACCOUNTING FOR LABOR

Accounting for labor involves (1) the distribution of labor costs to the appropriate cost objects such as jobs, processes, and so forth; (2) the withholding of different types of taxes and the payment of employees; and (3) the remittance of all the withholdings and the payments of different labor-related costs such as vacation pay, sick pay, retirement benefits, insurance benefits, employee training, and so forth. These entries can be illustrated as follows:

Factory Payroll	100,000	
Accrued Payroll		100,000
To record the incurrence of labor costs.		
Work-in-Process Control	50,000	
Factory Overhead Control	30,000	
Selling Expense Control	10,000	
Administrative Expense Control	10,000	
Factory Payroll		100,000
To record the distribution of labor costs.		
Accrued Payroll	100,000	
Withheld Income Taxes Payable (Assume 20%)		20,000
Withheld FICA Taxes Payable (Assume 5%)		5,000
Vouchers Payable or Cash		75,000
To record the withholding of taxes and the payment of earnings to employees.		
Withheld Income Taxes Payable	20,000	
Withheld FICA Taxes Payable	5,000	
Vouchers Payable or Cash		25,000
To record the remitting of withholdings.		
Work-in-Process Control	1,000	
Factory Overhead Control	500	
Liability for Vacation Pay, Bonuses, Etc.		1,500
To accrue vacation pay, bonuses, and other fringe benefits.		
Liability for Vacation Pay, Bonuses, Etc.	1,500	
Vouchers Payable or Cash		1,500
To record the payment of fringe benefits.		

It may also be expedient to regard the fringe benefits as essentially indirect costs, in which case the fifth entry will be as follows:

Factory Overhead Control	1,500	
Liability for Vacation Pay		1,500
To record the payment of fringe benefits.		

8.8 CONCLUSION

Cost accumulation provides the information essential for such internal decision making areas as product costing, inventory valuation, income determination, and planning and control. Consequently, the cost recording system and the supporting documents should be designed with the multidimensional use of accounting information as an objective. This chapter attempted to present cost characteristics and differences commonly encountered in the real world. It is the cost analyst's responsibility to design the unique cost system most useful to a particular firm and its environment.

GLOSSARY

Abnormal Spoilage Any spoilage in excess of what is considered to be normal and that is controllable and the result of inefficient operations.

Applied Factory Overhead Overhead assigned to units produced on the basis of a predetermined overhead rate.

Defective Goods Goods that do not meet production criteria and must be reworked to become salable.

Equivalent Unit The expression of output in terms of the amount of input applied thereto.

First-In, First-Out (FIFO) Costing A costing method in which units in the beginning inventory are completed before units started in the period are completed.

General Ledger A summary device to portray the general accounting relationship of the cost accounting cycle in a system of financial accounts.

Job-Order Costing A method of accounting whereby costs are accumulated for a specific quantity of products that move through the production process as a continuously identifiable unit.

Normal Spoilage Spoilage that would be expected in an efficient production process.

Process Costing A method of accounting used when production is characterized by a large volume of like units flowing in a constant stream through a series of manufacturing steps or processes.

Scrap Raw material residues of manufacturing operations that are believed to have minor resale value to scrap dealers.

Weighted Average Costing A costing method in which units in the beginning inventory are treated as if they were started during the period.

SELECTED READINGS

Anthony, Robert N., "The Rebirth of Cost Accounting," *Management Accounting* (October 1975), pp. 13–16.

Bergquist, Richard E., "Direct Labour versus Machine Hour Costing," *Management Accounting* (May 1971), pp. 25–28.

Bower, James B.; Schlosser, Robert E.; and Zlatkovich, Charles T., *Financial Information Systems: Theory and Practice* (Boston: Allyn & Bacon. 1972), chaps. 18–19.

Corcoran, A. Wayne, "A Matrix Approach to Process Cost Accounting," *Management Accounting* (November 1966), pp. 48–53.

Farag, Shawki M., "A Planning Model for the Divisionalized Enterprise," *Accounting Review* (April 1968), pp. 312–320.

Feltham, Gerald A., "Some Quantitative Approaches to Planning for Multiproduct Production Systems," *Accounting Review* (January 1970), pp. 11–26.

Frank, W., "A Computer Application to Process Cost Accounting," *Accounting Review* (October 1965), pp. 854–862.

Gambling, Trevor E., "A Technological Model for Use in Input-Output Analysis and Cost Accounting," *Management Accounting* (December 1968), pp. 33–38.

Grinnell, D. Jacques, "Activity Levels and the Disposition of Volume Variances," *Management Accounting* (August 1975), pp. 29–32, 36.

Handbook of Successful Operating Systems and Procedures with Forms (Englewood Cliffs, N.J.: Prentice-Hall, 1964).

Henrici, S. B., *Standard Costs for Manufacturing* (New York: McGraw-Hill, 1970).

Ijiri, Yuji, "An Application of Input-Output Analysis to Some Problems in Cost Accounting," *Management Accounting* (April 1968), pp. 49–61.

Koch, Alfred P., "A Fallacy in Accounting for Spoiled Goods," *Accounting Review* (July 1960), pp. 501–502.

Livingstone, John Leslie, "Input-Output: Analysis for Cost Accounting, Planning and Control," *Accounting Review* (January 1969), pp. 48–64.

National Association of Accountants, *Research Series No. 32*, "Accounting for Labor Costs and Labor-Related Costs," (New York: NAA, 1957).

National Association of Accountants Committee on Management Accounting Practices, "Concepts for Contract Costing," in *Management Accounting* (October 1972).

National Association of Accountants, *Accounting Practice Report No. 12*, "Cost Control of Spoiled Work," (New York: NAA, 1971).

Reimund, Franke, "A Process Model for Costing," *Management Accounting* (January 1975), pp. 45–47.

Schwan, E. S., "Process Accounting via Reaction Accounting," *Management Accounting* (September 1974), pp. 45–50.

Wise, Ronald L., "Cost Reporting for the Small and Medium Size Job-Shop Operations," *Management Accounting* (February 1970), pp. 20–22.

QUESTIONS, EXERCISES, AND PROBLEMS

8.1   Explain the dualistic nature of record keeping using general and subsidiary ledgers in a cost accumulation system.

8.2   How is overhead usually accounted for in a job cost situation?

(CGA adapted)

8.3   Distinguish between the weighted average and FIFO methods of process costing.

(CGA adapted)

8.4   The following three independent questions concern a typical manufacturing company that uses a process cost accounting system.

Required:

1. Briefly state and explain the difference between the use of process costing and job-order costing for product costing purposes.

2. Define *equivalent production* (or *equivalent units produced*). Explain the significance and use of equivalent production for product costing purposes.

3. Briefly state and explain the difference between the FIFO method of process costing and the weighted average method of process costing.

(SMA adapted)

8.5   In manufacturing activities, a portion of the units placed in process is sometimes spoiled and becomes practically worthless. Discuss two ways in which the cost of such spoiled units could be treated in the accounts, and describe the circumstances under which each method might be used.

(AICPA adapted)

8.6   The following information for a recent fiscal period pertains to a producing department of a company following process costing procedures:

Opening Work-in-Process (Materials 100% Complete, Conversion 40%)	100,000 Units
Materials Cost	$150,600
Conversion Cost	$ 68,100
Started in Production	420,000 Units
Materials Cost	$567,000
Conversion Cost	$675,324
Lost Units—at Final Completion Stage (15,000 Units Normal Spoilage)	30,000 Units
Closing Work-in-Process (Materials 100% Complete, Conversion 60%)	90,000 Units

Required:
Prepare a report showing the cost of production for the period using the FIFO method. This report should show equivalent production, unit costs, and a reconciliation of total costs between Goods Transferred, Spoilage (Normal and Abnormal), and Work-in-Process, showing the disposition of these items.

(SMA adapted)

8.7   ***Equivalent Production and Spoilage***   Process costing typically is used in manufacturing operations with long and repetitive production runs producing homogeneous units.

Required:
1. Accountants frequently use equivalent production in computing per-unit costs for inventory valuation.
   a. Define *equivalent production.*
   b. Why is equivalent production used in computing per-unit costs for inventory valuation?
2. Every manufacturing process operates at less than theoretical maximum capacity.
   a. List the important causes of productivity losses.
   b. Distinguish between normal and abnormal spoilage.
   c. What accounting treatment is most appropriate for abnormal spoilage?
3. Discuss the advisability of ignoring unavoidably spoiled units in the computation of equivalent production for developing per-unit costs. Consider in your discussion the possibility that the point of inspection, and hence the identification of spoiled units, occurs
   a. At the end of the processing sequence in the department.
   b. At the beginning of the processing sequence in the department.
   c. Throughout the processing sequence in the department.

(AICPA adapted)

8.8   ***Weighted Average and Spoilage***   Milton, Inc., had 8,000 units of work-in-process in its department M on March 1, 19X0, which were 50 percent complete as to conversion costs. Materials are introduced at the beginning of the process. During March, 17,000 units were started, 18,000 units were completed, and there were 2,000 units of normal spoilage. Milton had 5,000 units of work-in-process at March 31, 19X0, which were 60 percent complete as to conversion costs. Under Milton's cost accounting system, spoiled units reduce the number of units over which total cost can be spread. Using the weighted average method, the equivalent units for March for conversion costs were

1. 17,000.
2. 19,000.
3. 21,000.
4. 23,000.

(AICPA adapted)

8.9   ***Weighted Average Method***   Information for the month of May concerning department A, the first stage of Wit Corporation's production cycle, is as follows:

	Materials	Conversion Costs
Beginning Work-in-Process	$ 4,000	$ 3,000
Current Costs	20,000	16,000
Total Costs	$ 24,000	$19,000
Equivalent Units Based on Weighted Average Method	100,000	95,000
Average Unit Costs	$ 0.24	$ 0.20

Goods Completed: 90,000 Units
Ending Work-in-Process: 10,000 Units

Material costs are added at the beginning of the process. The ending work-in-process is 50 percent complete as to conversion costs. How would the total costs accounted for be distributed, using the weighted average method?

1. Goods Completed, $39,600; Ending Work-in-Process, $3,400.
2. Goods Completed, $39,600; Ending Work-in-Process, $4,400.
3. Goods Completed, $43,000; Ending Work-in-Process, $0.
4. Goods Completed, $44,000; Ending Work-in-Process, $3,400.

(AICPA adapted)

8.10   *Weighted Average Method and Equivalent Units*   The wiring department is the second stage of Flem Company's production cycle. On May 1, the beginning work-in-process contained 25,000 units, which were 60 percent complete as to conversion costs. During May, 100,000 units were transferred in from the first stage of Flem's production cycle. On May 31, the ending work-in-process contained 20,000 units, which were 80 percent complete as to conversion costs. Material costs are added at the end of the process. Using the weighted average method, the equivalent units were

1. Transferred-In Costs, 100,000; Materials, 125,000; Conversion Costs, 100,000.
2. Transferred-In Costs, 125,000; Materials, 105,000; Conversion Costs, 105,000.
3. Transferred-In Costs, 125,000; Materials, 105,000; Conversion Costs, 121,000.
4. Transferred-In Costs, 125,000; Materials, 125,000; Conversion Costs, 121,000.

(AICPA adapted)

8.11   *Process Costing, Spoilage, Weighted Average*   The Easygoing Company produced a single product in a continuous process in one department. During November, the company started 5,300 units and completed 3,600 good units only. The ending work-in-process inventory contained 1,000 units, 50 percent complete. (Materials are all put into process at the beginning of production, while labor and overhead are incurred uniformly throughout the process.)

Work-in-Process, November 1 (700 units)
    Direct Materials $2,030
    Direct Labor   310
    Overhead Applied   215

Cost Data for November
Direct Materials	15,970
Direct Labor	15,510
Overhead Applied	10,765

Spoilage is detected when the units are 90 percent complete. Normal spoilage allowance is expected to be 10 percent of normal input, or for each 10 units started the company expects to obtain a yield of 9 good units.

Required:

1. Prepare a cost of production report for November, using the average costing method.

2. Journalize all cost data affecting Work-in-Process during November.

(SMA adapted)

8.12   ***Process Costing, Weighted Average, Spoilage***   The Edmonton Co. Ltd. uses a weighted average process costing system in accounting for its three manufacturing departments. Department 2 receives units from department 1 and applies conversion costs to these units at a uniform rate. When the units are 80 percent complete they are inspected, and material is then added to the good units. A spoilage rate of 5 percent is built into the process in department 2.

The following information is available concerning department 2 for the month of December 19X7:

1. On December 1, 3,000 units were in process and were estimated to be 30 percent complete. Costs associated with these units were

Department 1 Costs	$16,000
Department 2 Costs	2,600
	$18,600

2. During December, 32,000 units were received from department 1 at a cost of $180,000.

3. Costs incurred by department 2 during December were materials, $12,000; and conversion costs, $96,700.

4. During December, 30,000 units were completed and transferred to department 3.

5. At the end of December, 4,500 units were still in process and were estimated to be 60 percent complete.

Required:

1. Prepare a cost of production report for department 2 for December 19X7.

2. Prepare the journal entry to record the transfer of 30,000 units to department 3.

(CGA adapted)

8.13   ***Manufacturing Accounting***   The Toronto Co. Ltd. operates under a job cost system and applies overhead at a predetermined rate of 50 percent of direct-labor cost. At the beginning of March 19X8, balances in factory-related accounts were as follows:

Stores	$12,000
Work-in-Process	6,000
Finished Goods	34,000
Accounts Payable (Used for Stores Purchases Only)	25,000
Accrued Factory Payroll	14,000
Accumulated Depreciation—Factory	95,000
Prepaid Insurance—Factory	3,000

The following information is available regarding March production:

Supplies Used in Production	$ 20,000
Direct-Labor Cost	160,000
Cost of Goods Sold	320,000
Payment of Factory Payroll	206,000
Miscellaneous Overhead	11,000
Stores Purchases	100,000

There was one job still in process on March 31, and materials of $500 and direct labor of $2,000 were charged to it. Relevant account balances at March 31 were as follows:

Finished Goods	$26,500
Accounts Payable	36,000
Accrued Factory Payroll	8,000
Accumulated Depreciation—Factory	105,000
Prepaid Insurance—Factory	2,000

Required:
Compute the following (the use of T accounts is recommended):

1. Overhead applied.
2. Ending inventory of Work-in-Process.
3. Cost of goods manufactured.
4. Materials used.
5. Ending inventory of Stores.
6. Payment of Accounts Payable.
7. Underapplied or overapplied overhead.

(CGA adapted)

8.14   ***Prorating Overapplied or Underapplied Overhead***   The Ritter Company Limited had budgeted the following performance for 19X5:

Sales (80,000 Units)	$400,000
Production Cost for 100,000 Units	
Materials	100,000
Labor (30,000 Hours)	120,000
Overhead	180,000

The actual results for the year were as follows: put into production, 100,000 units; completed, 90,000 units; finished goods inventory, 10,000 units; and work-in-process inventory, 10,000 units.

The 10,000 units left in the work-in-process inventory were 75 percent complete except for materials, which were used at the beginning of the production process. Actual costs for the year were materials, $100,000; labor, $117,000; and overhead, $187,200. Overhead was applied on the basis of direct-labor dollars. There were no beginning inventories.

Required:

1. Assuming that any overapplied or underapplied overhead is adjusted to the cost of goods sold at year-end, determine the balances in the Work-in-Process, Finished Goods, and Cost of Goods Sold accounts (after adjusting for overhead) at December 31, 19X5.

2. Determine the balances in the Work-in-Process, Finished Goods, and Cost of Goods Sold accounts (after the adjustments) at December 31, 19X5. Assume the company pro-rates any overapplied or underapplied overhead to inventories and Cost of Goods Sold at year-end, using the direct-labor dollar base.

(SMA adapted)

8.15   *Job-Order Costing*   The Monti Company specializes in the production of mobile homes. During January 19X1, the company produced four batches of mobile homes: one of type A, one of type B, one of type C, and one of type D. Each batch contains ten identical mobile homes. On December 31, the company had no inventories of materials, goods-in-process, or finished goods. The following transactions were completed and recorded by the cost accountant:

1. Purchased 2,000 units of material X at $10 each, 2,000 units of material Y at $15 each, and different supplies for $10,000. The invoices and receiving reports were used as supporting documents.

2. Issued materials for the completion of four batches of mobile homes as follows:

Requisition No. 1 for Job 1 (10 Type A Mobile Homes)   200 Units of Material X
Requisition No. 2 for Job 2 (10 Type B Mobile Homes)   300 Units of Material Y
Requisition No. 3 for Job 3 (10 Type C Mobile Homes)   300 Units of Material X
Requisition No. 4 for Job 4 (10 Type D Mobile Homes)   400 Units of Material Y
Requisition No. 5 for Supplies $2,000

3. Recorded the payment of factory payroll totaling $16,000.

4. Distributed the direct labor and indirect labor to jobs on the basis of the time tickets' information as follows:

Time Tickets Nos. 90–94 for Direct Labor on Job 1 . . . . $1,000
Time Tickets Nos. 95–100 for Direct Labor on Job 2 1,500
Time Tickets Nos. 101–110 for Direct Labor on Job 3 2,000
Time Tickets Nos. 111–125 for Direct Labor on Job 4 3,000
Time Tickets Nos. 125–130 for Indirect Labor 2,000

5. On January 1, established the company's annual overhead application rate based on direct-labor cost. Estimated that the company would incur $200,000 of overhead cost during 19X1 and $100,000 of direct-labor cost.

6. Made an adjusting entry to record:

Depreciation of Factory Equipment $1,500
Depreciation of Factory Building   5,000
Expired Factory Insurance   1,000
Accrued Factory Taxes Payable   500

7. Paid diverse overhead items as follows:

Heat, Light, and Power	$2,000
Repairs (Machinery)	1,000
Miscellaneous	1,000
Selling and Administrative Expenses	5,000

8. Jobs 1 and 4 were finished and transferred to the finished goods warehouse.

9. Job 1 was sold on credit for a total of $6,000.

10. At the end of January, applied overhead to the incomplete jobs.

11. Determined and disposed of overapplied or underapplied overhead.

Required:
1. Draw up T accounts for the general ledger and stores cards, job cost sheets, and finished goods cards for the subsidiary ledgers.

2. Enter the applicable information of items 1 through 11 in both the general ledger and subsidiary ledgers.

8.16   ***Weighted Average and FIFO Methods***   The Zribi Company has the following data for the month of January:

	Grinding Department	**Finishing Department**
Beginning Inventory	3,000 Units (½ Finished)	2,000 Units (½ Finished)
Start-up Costs	$ 0	$17,000
Material	$ 3,000	$19,000
Labor	$13,500	$11,500
Overhead	$ 2,250	$ 4,000
Units Started in January	30,000 Units	18,000 Units
Units Completed and Transferred	18,000 Units	14,000 Units
Ending Inventory	15,000 Units (½ Finished)	6,000 Units (½ Finished)
Processing Costs in January		
Material	$30,000	$32,000
Labor	$12,000	$48,000
Overhead	$36,000	64,000
Transferred In	—	?

Material is added at the beginning of the process in the grinding department. The other inputs in the grinding department and all the inputs in the finishing department are added evenly throughout the process.

Required:
1. Using weighted average costing, prepare a production report for each department. Show the cost of goods completed and transferred and also show the cost of the ending work-in-process.

2. Using FIFO, repeat the requirements of part 1.

8.17   ***Reconstruction of Manufacturing Entries***   The Smith Company commenced operations on July 1, 19X4. The following shows the gross debits and credits in each account of the ledger as of December 31, 19X4, except for the Work-in-Process and Finished Goods Inventory accounts. The company uses a cost system for its manufacturing operations.

Trial Balance
December 31, 19X4

	Transactions		Balance	
	Dr.	Cr.	Dr.	Cr.
Cash	$464,000	$370,000	$ 94,000	
Notes Receivable	20,000	12,000	8,000	
Accounts Receivable	340,000	302,000	38,000	
Raw Materials	125,000	118,000	7,000	
Finished Goods	Compute	Compute	30,000	
Work-in-Process	Compute	Compute	14,000	
Supplies	18,000	14,000	4,000	
Prepaid Insurance	1,900	1,500	400	
Plant and Equipment	95,000	0	95,000	
Mortgage Payable	0	50,000		$ 50,000
Accrued Mortgage Interest	0	750		750
Accrued Wages	145,100	147,000		1,900
Capital Stock	0	150,000		150,000
Vouchers Payable	325,000	365,500		40,500
Sales	0	360,000		360,000
Cost of Goods Sold	250,000	0	250,000	
Selling Expense	27,500	0	27,500	
Administrative Expense	29,000	0	29,000	
Financial Expense	6,250	0	6,250	
			$603,150	$603,150

You also are given the following information:

1. The ending work-in-process inventory consists of the following: materials, $6,000; direct labor, $4,500; and manufacturing expense, $3,500.

2. Insurance premiums apply two-thirds to the plant and one-third to the office.

3. The cost of the finished product is made up of materials, 40 percent; direct labor, 40 percent; and manufacturing expense, 20 percent.

Required:
Use T accounts to show the entries making up the transactions included in the figures shown on the trial balance. Key each entry (debit and offsetting credit) by use of a number.

(AICPA adapted)

8.18   *Job-Order Costing and Contract Pricing*   The Estes Corporation was awarded a federal government fixed-price incentive contract that called for the construction and delivery of ten digital computers within the next twelve months. Provisions of the contract included the following.

The total contract target price is $900,000, which includes a target cost of $775,000. The total adjusted price cannot exceed $1,100,000.

The total adjusted price is computed as follows:

When Total Adjusted Cost Is	**Allowance for Profit Is**
Equal to Total Target Cost	Total Target Profit
Greater than Total Target Cost	Total Target Profit Less 20 Percent of the Excess of Total Adjusted Cost over Target Cost
Less than Total Target Cost	Total Target Profit Plus 20 Percent of the Difference (Total Target Cost − Total Adjusted Cost)

At the end of six months, the corporation submitted the following report to the government:

Cost Accumulated on the Contract

Direct Materials	$150,000
Direct Labor	165,000
Overhead	200,000
Total	$515,000

Estimated Costs to Complete Contract

Direct Materials	$155,000
Direct Labor	170,000
Overhead	215,000
Total	$540,000

Five computers were completed and billed at the target price of $500,000.

Past experience has shown that approximately 1.5 percent of the allocated overhead costs are disallowed by government auditors as contract costs. No provision has been made for this disallowance. In addition to this 1.5 percent disallowance, the following costs will be disallowed: (1) depreciation of $1,500 on equipment that was not used for work on the contract and (2) $5,000 of nonrecurring costs of training personnel.

The Estes Corporation failed to take purchase discounts of $2,500 on materials charged to the contract. These "lost discounts" will be subtracted from the contract costs.

Required:
Prepare a schedule computing the estimated total adjusted price (the final contract price) for the fixed-price incentive contract.

(AICPA adapted)

8.19   *Weighted Average*   The following information pertains to the operation of a processing department.

	Materials	Conversion
Current Costs	$38,600	$421,300
Beginning Inventory (1,000 Units)	Complete	40% Complete
Costs	$10,000	$44,000
Units Transferred: 40,000 Total		
Ending Inventory (8,000 Units)	Complete	25% Complete
Spoilage (Detected when the Units are 50% Complete)		
Normal: 400 Units		
Abnormal: 200 Units		

Required:
1. Using the weighted average method, determine the costs that should be allocated to
   a. Normal and abnormal spoilage.
   b. Units transferred (including spoilage costs, if appropriate).
   c. Ending inventory (including spoilage costs, if appropriate).

2. Discuss the reasons underlying the different treatment of abnormal and normal spoilage.

(SMA adapted)

8.20   ***Standard Costing*** The Longhorn Manufacturing Corporation produces only one product, Bevo, and accounts for its production using a standard-cost system. At the end of
each year, Longhorn prorates all variances among the various inventories and cost of
sales. Because Longhorn prices its inventories on the FIFO basis and all the beginning
inventories are used during the year, the variances that had been allocated to the ending
inventories are immediately charged to Cost of Sales at the beginning of the following
year. This allows only the current year's variances to be recorded in the variance accounts in any given year.

The following are the standards for the production of 1 unit of Bevo: 3 units of item A
at $1 per unit; 1 unit of item B at $.50 per unit; 4 units of item C at $.30 per unit; and 20
minutes of direct labor at $4.50 per hour. Separate variance accounts are maintained for
each type of raw material and for direct labor. Raw material purchases are recorded
initially at standard. Manufacturing overhead is applied at $9 per actual direct-labor
hour and is not related to the standard-cost system. There was no overapplied or underapplied manufacturing overhead at December 31, 19X2.

After proration of the variances, the various inventories at December 31, 19X2, were
priced as follows:

	Raw Materials		
Item	Number of Units	Unit Cost	Amount
A	15,000	$1.10	$16,500
B	4,000	0.52	2,080
C	20,000	0.32	6,400
			$24,980

In the work-in-process inventory, 9,000 units of Bevo were 100 percent complete as
to items A and B, 50 percent complete as to item C, and 30 percent complete as to labor.
The composition and valuation of the inventory follows:

Work-in-Process	
Item	Amount
A	$28,600
B	4,940
C	6,240
Direct Labor	6,175
	$45,955
Overhead	11,700
	$57,655

The finished goods inventory was made up of 4,800 units of Bevo valued as follows:

Finished Goods	
Item	Amount
A	$15,180
B	2,704
C	6,368
Direct Labor	8,540
	$32,792
Overhead	16,200
	$48,992

The following is a schedule of raw materials purchased and direct labor incurred for the
year ended December 31, 19X3. Unit cost of each item of raw material and direct-labor
cost per hour remained constant throughout the year.

	Purchases Actual Number of		
Item	Units or Hours	Unit Price	Amount
A	290,000	$1.15	$333,500
B	101,000	0.55	55,550
C	367,000	0.35	128,450
Direct Labor	34,100	4.60	156,860

During the year ended December 31, 19X3, Longhorn sold 90,000 units of Bevo and had ending physical inventories as follows:

Raw Materials	
Item	Number of Units
A	28,300
B	2,100
C	28,900

In the ending work-in-process inventory, 7,500 units of Bevo were 100 percent complete as to items A and B, 50 percent complete as to item C, and 20 percent complete as to labor, as follows:

Work-in-Process	
Item	Number of Units or Hours
A	22,900
B	8,300
C	15,800
Direct Labor	800

In the finished goods inventory there were 5,100 units of Bevo, as follows:

Finished Goods	
Item	Number of Units or Hours
A	15,600
B	6,300
C	21,700
Direct Labor	2,050

There was no overapplied or underapplied manufacturing overhead at December 31, 19X3.

Required:
Answer each of the following questions. Supporting computations should be prepared in good form:

1. What was the charge or credit to Cost of Sales at the beginning of 19X3 for the variances in the December 31, 19X2, inventories?

2. What was the total charge or credit to the three material price variance accounts for items A, B, and C for the year ended December 31, 19X3?

3. What was the total charge or credit to the three material efficiency variance accounts for items A, B, and C for the year ended December 31, 19X3?

4. What was the total charge or credit to the Direct-Labor Price Variance account for the year ended December 31, 19X3?

5. What was the total charge or credit to the Direct-Labor Efficiency Variance account for the year ended December 31, 19X3?

(AICPA adapted)

8.21   ***Job-Order Costing***   The Separato Manufacturing Company uses a factory ledger that is maintained by the factory accountant at the plant site. The following accounts are included in the ledger: Stores, Work-in-Process, Finished Goods, Overhead Control, Overhead Applied, and Head Office Ledger Control.

Perpetual inventory ledger cards showing inventory costs are kept for both the Stores and the Finished Goods. The plant uses a job cost system and records all inventories by the moving average method. Two days after the June month-end closing, the factory accountant discovered the following:

1. Two material requisitions for the month of June were not recorded by the stockroom or the factory accountant: requisition #1091, for six bottles of cleaning solvent, part F65, $12 each, used by head office maintenance; and requisition #1092, for eighty motor mounting brackets, part M286, $2.50 each, used for job 75.

2. Job 68 (production of four hundred pressure meters, product PM16) was completed and sent to the warehouse. The job cost sheet was not processed by accounting, and the warehouse did not record receipt of these meters. The warehouse ledger card for PM16 showed a balance on hand of 100 units at $14 per unit. The cost of job 68 amounted to $5,920.

3. The daily time cards for Harry Brown for the last two days of June were not recorded on the factory accountant's distribution sheet nor were they sent to the head office payroll department. The company pays wages one week in arrears; therefore, corrections to Brown's pay can still be made in the current payroll. The company utilizes a combination clock card and time card. Brown's hourly pay is $5. The two cards show the following hours: operation H41, job 71: 8 hours; operation H45, job 73: 6 hours; and adjusting punch press, 2 hours.

4. The factory accountant applies overhead on the basis of $6 per direct-labor hour.

Required:
Prepare journal entries (without narratives) for the factory ledger to adjust for items 1 through 4, and explain what other entries or adjustments should be made to the subsidiary ledger records. Be specific for each item.

(SMA adapted)

8.22   ***Computation of FIFO Unit Costs***   Bisto Corporation manufactures valves and pumps for liquids. On December 1, 19X4, Bisto paid $25,000 to the Poplen Company for the patent for its watertight valve. Bisto planned to carry on Poplen's procedure of having the valve casing and parts cast by an independent foundry and doing the grinding and assembling in its own plant.

Bisto also purchased Poplen's inventory of the valves at 80 percent of its cost to Poplen. The purchased inventory was composed of the following:

	Units
Raw Material (Unfinished Casings and Parts)	1,100
Work-in-Process	
Grinding (25% Complete)	800
Assembling (40% Complete)	600
Finished Valves	900

Poplen's cost accounting system provided the following unit costs:

	Cost per Unit
Raw Materials (Unfinished Casings and Parts)	$2.00
Grinding Costs	1.00
Assembling Costs	2.50

Bisto's cost accounting system accumulated the following costs for the month of December, which do not include the cost of the inventory purchased from Poplen:

Raw Material Purchases (Casings and Parts for 5,000 Units)	$10,500
Grinding Costs	2,430
Assembling Costs	5,664

Bisto's inventory of watertight valves at December 31, 19X4, follows:

	Units
Raw Material (Unfinished Casings and Parts)	2,700
Work-in-Process	
Grinding (35% Complete)	2,000
Assembling (33⅓% Complete)	300
Finished Valves	2,250

No valves were spoiled or lost during the manufacturing process. Bisto uses the process costing method in its accounting system.

Required:
1. Prepare a schedule to compute the equivalent units produced and costs incurred per unit for the month of December 19X4.

2. Prepare a schedule of inventories on the FIFO basis as of December 1 and 31, 19X4, setting forth by layers the number of units, unit costs, and amounts. Show all supporting schedules in good form.

(AICPA adapted)

8.23   ***Weighted Average, Two Departments, Terminal Spoilage***   The Mantis Manufacturing Company manufactures a single product that passes through two departments: extruding and finishing-packing. The product is shipped at the end of the day on which it is packed. The production in the extruding and finishing-packing departments does not increase the number of units started.

The cost and production data for January are as follows:

Cost Data	Extruding Department	Finishing-Packing Department
Work-in-Process, January 1		
Cost from Preceding Department	—	$60,200
Materials	$ 5,900	—
Labor	1,900	1,500
Overhead	1,400	2,000
Costs Added during January		
Materials	20,100	4,400
Labor	10,700	7,720
Overhead	8,680	11,830

Percentage of Completion of Work-in-Process

January 1		
Materials	70%	0%
Labor	50	30
Overhead	50	30
January 31		
Materials	50	0
Labor	40	35
Overhead	40	35

January Production Statistics

Units-in-Process, January 1	10,000 Units	29,000 Units
Units-in-Process, January 31	8,000	6,000
Units Started or Received from Preceding Department	20,000	22,000
Units Completed and Transferred or Shipped	22,000	44,000

In the extruding department, materials are added at various phases of the process. All lost units occur at the end of the process, when the inspection operation takes place.

In the finishing-packing department, the materials added consist only of packing supplies. These materials are added at the midpoint of the process, when the packing operations begin. Cost studies have disclosed that one-half the labor and overhead costs apply to the finishing operation, and one-half apply to the packing operation. All lost units occur at the end of the finishing operation, when the product is inspected. All the work-in-process in this department at January 1 and 31 was in the finishing operation phase of the manufacturing process. The company uses the weighted average method in its accounting system.

Required:

1. Compute the units lost, if any, for each department during January.

2. Compute the equivalent units for the calculation of unit costs for each department in January.

3. Prepare a cost of production report for each department for January. The report should disclose the departmental total cost and cost per unit (for materials, labor, and overhead) of the units (a) transferred to the finishing-packing department and (b) shipped. Assume that January production and costs were normal. Submit all supporting computations in good form.

(AICPA adapted)

8.24   *Weighted Average and Spoilage*   The Ground Company manufactures a product MOP on a continuous process basis through one department. The product MOP requires the following parts: 1 subassembly K at the beginning of process, 1 part L at the beginning of process, and 2 parts M when 60 percent complete.

The subassembly K was formerly produced by the Ground Company in another department and then transferred in. For economical reasons, the company discontinued the manufacturing of the subassembly K a year ago and now buys it from a local supplier at a unit cost of $2.10.

Labor and overhead costs are added continuously throughout the process. Overhead is applied at 150 percent of direct-labor cost. The work-in-process inventory at the beginning of April consisted of 2,500 units at a cost of $7,520 (K, $5,250; L, $1,050; and conversion cost, $1,220).

During April 19X4, the following activities took place:

1. New units started: 21,000.

2. Parts usage: L, $8,350; M, $10,200.

3. Direct-labor cost: $18,520.

4. Units completed during the month: 16,000.

5. An unexpected loss occurred with all the beginning work-in-process units due to a mechanical failure in the calibrating machine. The loss was discovered when the units were 40 percent complete. The controller asked to show this loss separately.

6. Ending work-in-process: 4,000 units, 50 percent complete.

The normal spoilage was as expected. Since normal spoilage is detected at the 80 percent completion stage, it has been the company's practice to charge this normal loss to the cost of the completed units for the month.

Required:
Prepare a cost of production report for April. Show the output in equivalent units, and summarize the application of costs to products. Assume that the weighted average method is used.

(SMA adapted)

8.25   *Spoilage*   The D. Hayes Cramer Company manufactures product C, whose cost per unit is $1 of materials, $2 of labor, and $3 of overhead costs. During the month of May, 1,000 units of product C were spoiled. These units could be sold for $.60 each. The accountant said that one of the four entries shown in Table 1 could be made for these 1,000 lost or spoiled units.

Required:
Indicate the circumstance under which each of the four entries in Table 1 would be appropriate.

(AICPA adapted)

8.26   *Job-Order Costing*   The Custer Manufacturing Corporation, which uses a job-order cost system, produces various plastic parts for the aircraft industry. On October 9, 19X2, production was started on job 487 for one hundred front bubbles (windshields) for commercial helicopters.

    Production of the bubbles begins in the fabricating department, where sheets of plastic (purchased as raw material) are melted down and poured into molds. The molds are then placed in a room of special temperature and humidity to harden the plastic. The hardened plastic bubbles are then removed from the molds and worked by hand to remove imperfections.

    After fabrication, the bubbles are transferred to the testing department, where each bubble must meet rigid specifications. Bubbles that fail the tests are scrapped, and there is no salvage value. Bubbles passing the tests are transferred to the assembly department, where they are inserted into metal frames. The frames, purchased from vendors, require no work prior to installing the bubbles. The assembled unit is then transferred to the shipping department for crating and shipment. Crating material is relatively expensive, and most of the work is done by hand.

    The following information concerning job 487 is available as of December 31, 19X2 (the information is correct as stated):

Table 1	Entries

Entry 1

Spoiled Goods	600	
Work-in-Process: Materials		100
Work-in-Process: Labor		200
Work-in-Process: Overhead		300

Entry 2

Spoiled Goods	600	
Manufacturing Expenses	5,400	
Work-in-Process: Materials		1,000
Work-in-Process: Labor		2,000
Work-in-Process: Overhead		3,000

Entry 3

Spoiled Goods	600	
Loss on Spoiled Goods	5,400	
Work-in-Process: Materials		1,000
Work-in-Process: Labor		2,000
Work-in-Process: Overhead		3,000

Entry 4

Spoiled Goods	600	
Receivable	5,400	
Work-in-Process: Materials		1,000
Work-in-Process: Labor		2,000
Work-in-Process: Overhead		3,000

1. The following direct material was charged to the job. 1,000 square feet of plastic at $12.75 per square foot was charged to the fabricating department. This amount was to meet all plastic material requirements of the job, assuming no spoilage. Seventy-four metal frames at $408.52 each were charged to the assembly department. Packing material for 40 units at $75 per unit was charged to the shipping department.

2. Direct-labor charges through December 31, 19X2, were as follows:

	Total	Per Unit
Fabricating Department	$1,424	$16
Testing Department	444	6
Assembly Department	612	12
Shipping Department	256	8
	$2,736	

3. Differences between actual and applied manufacturing overhead were immaterial for the year ended December 31, 19X2. Manufacturing overhead is charged to the four production departments by various allocation methods, all of which you approve of. Manufacturing overhead charged to the fabricating department is allocated to jobs based on heat-room hours; the other production departments allocate manufacturing overhead to jobs on the basis of direct-labor dollars charged to each job within the department. The following reflects the manufacturing overhead rates for the year ended December 31, 19X2:

	Rate per Unit
Fabricating Department	$.45 per Hour
Testing Department	$.68 per Direct-Labor Dollar
Assembly Department	$.38 per Direct-Labor Dollar
Shipping Department	$.25 per Direct-Labor Dollar

4. Job 487 used 855 heat-room hours during the year ended December 31, 19X2.

5. The following is the physical inventory for job 487 as of December 31, 19X2. Fabricating department: 50 square feet of plastic sheet; 8 hardened bubbles, one-fourth complete as to direct labor; and 4 complete bubbles. Testing department: 15 bubbles that failed testing when two-fifths of testing was complete (no others failed); and 7 bubbles complete as to testing. Assembly department: 13 frames with no direct labor; 15 bubbles and frames, one-third complete as to direct labor; and 3 complete bubbles and frames. Shipping department: 9 complete units, two-thirds complete as to packing material, one-third complete as to direct labor; 10 complete units, 100 percent complete as to packing material, 50 percent complete as to direct labor; 1 unit complete for shipping that was dropped off the loading docks (there is no salvage); 23 units that have been shipped prior to December 31, 19X2; and no inventory of packing materials in the shipping department on December 31, 19X2.

6. Table 2 shows a schedule of equivalent units in production by department for job 487 as of December 31, 19X2.

Required:
Prepare a schedule for job 487 of ending inventory costs for (1) raw materials by department, (2) work-in-process by department, and (3) cost of goods shipped. All spoilage costs are charged to Cost of Goods Shipped.

(AICPA adapted)

8.27   *Job-Order Costing and Internal Control*   During an investigation of the receiving procedures of a large manufacturing company, the following information was found.

The receiving department prepares six copies of the receiving report for the following distribution: one copy to the stockroom, one copy to the purchasing department, two copies to the accounts payable department, one copy to be retained and filed in numerical order, and one copy to the inspection department. The goods are sent with a copy of the receiving report to the inspection department. After the quality control check, they are sent to the stockroom, and the inspection department's copy of the receiving report is destroyed.

If the goods do not meet specifications, the inspection department prepares a rejection report. The goods are returned to the receiving department together with one copy of the rejection report and the receiving report copy. Three other copies of the rejection report are sent to the stockroom and to the purchasing and accounts payable departments (one copy each) for cancellation of the receiving report.

The stockroom updates the inventory records from its copy of the receiving report, which is then destroyed. The purchasing department uses its receiving report copy to update purchase order records. The copy is then filed by receiving date. The accounts payable department attaches one of its copies to the vendor's invoice for vouchering. The other copy is used to maintain numerical control of the receiving reports.

Table 2   *Custer Manufacturing Corporation Schedule of Equivalent Units in Production for Job Number 487, December 31, 19X2*

	Fabricating Department (Units)			
	Plastic (Square Feet)	Bubbles		
		Materials	Labor	Overhead
Transferred In from Raw Materials	1,000	—	—	—
Production to Date	(950)	95	89	95
Transferred Out to Other Departments	—	(83)	(83)	(83)
Spoilage	—	—	—	—
Balance at December 31, 19X2	50	12	6	12

	Testing Department (Units)		
	Bubbles		
	Transferred In	Labor	Overhead
Transferred In from Other Departments	83	—	—
Production to Date	—	74	74
Transferred Out to Other Departments	(61)	(61)	(61)
Spoilage	(15)	(6)	(6)
Balance at December 31, 19X2	7	7	7

	Assembly Department (Units)			
	Transferred In	Frames	Labor	Overhead
Transferred In from Raw Materials	—	74	—	—
Transferred In from Other Departments . .	61	—	—	—
Production to Date	—	—	51	51
Transferred Out to Other Departments . . .	(43)	(43)	(43)	(43)
Balance at December 31, 19X2	18	31	8	8

	Shipping Department (Units)			
	Transferred In	Packing Material	Labor	Overhead
Transferred In from Raw Materials	—	40	—	—
Transferred In from Other Departments . .	43	—	—	—
Production to Date	—	—	32	32
Shipped	(23)	(23)	(23)	(23)
Spoilage	(1)	(1)	(1)	(1)
Balance at December 31, 19X2	19	16	8	8

Required:
What improvement, if any, can be made to the receiving report procedure?

(SMA adapted)

8.28   ***Standard-Cost System: Job Order and No Spoilage***   The Justin Company has recently installed a standard-cost system to simplify its factory bookkeeping and to aid in cost control. The company makes standard items for inventory, but because of the many products in its line, each is manufactured periodically under a production order. Prior to the installation of the system, job-order cost sheets were maintained for each production order. Since the introduction of the standard-cost system, however, they have not been kept.

The fabricating department is managed by a general supervisor, who has overall responsibility for scheduling, performance, and cost control. The department consists of four machine/work centers. Each work center is staffed by a four-person work group, or team, and the centers are aided by a twelve-person support group. Departmental practice is to assign a job to one team and expect the team to perform most of the work necessary to complete the job, including acquisition of materials and supplies from the stores department as well as machining and assembling. This has been practical and satisfactory in the past and is readily accepted by the employees.

Information regarding production cost standards, products produced, and actual costs for the fabricating department in March is presented as follows:

		Part	
Unit Standard Costs	**A7A**	**C6D**	**C7A**
Material	$2.00	$3.00	$1.50
Direct Labor	1.50	2.00	1.00
Overhead (per Direct-Labor Dollar)[a]			
Variable	3.00	4.00	2.00
Fixed	0.75	1.00	0.50
	$7.25	$10.00	$5.00

[a] The departmental standard overhead rates are applied to the products as a percentage of direct-labor dollars. The labor base was chosen because nearly all of the variable overhead costs are caused by labor activity. The departmental overhead rates were calculated at the beginning of the year as follows:

	Variable (Including Indirect Labor)	Fixed
Estimated Annual Cost	$360,000	$ 90,000
Estimated Annual Department Direct-Labor Dollars	$180,000	$180,000
Overhead Rate	200%	50%

Separate control accounts are maintained for variable and fixed factory overhead. An analysis of the Fabricating Department account for March follows:

Costs to Be Accounted for

Materials		
Job No. 307-11	$ 5,200	
Job No. 307-12	2,900	
Job No. 307-14	9,400	$17,500
Labor Charges		
Job No. 307-11	$ 4,000	
Job No. 307-12	2,100	
Job No. 307-14	6,200	
Indirect Labor	12,200	24,500
Variable Overhead Costs (e.g., Supplies and Electricity)		18,800
Fixed Overhead Costs (e.g., Supervisor's Salary, Depreciation, Property Tax, and Insurance)		7,000
Total Charges to Department for March		$67,800

Accounting for Costs

Completed Jobs

Job No. 307-11 (2000 Units, Part A7A @ $7.25)	$14,500	
Job No. 307-12 (1000 Units, Part C6D @ $10)	10,000	
Job No. 307-14 (6000 Units, Part C7A @ $5)	30,000	$54,500

Variances Transferred to Factory Variance Accounts

Materials[a]	$ 1,500	
Direct Labor[b]	1,300	
Variable Overhead	9,000	
Fixed Overhead	1,500	13,300
		$67,800

[a] Material price variances are isolated at acquisition and charged to the stores department.
[b] All direct labor was paid at the standard wage rate during March.

Required:

1. The Justin Company assumes that its efforts to control costs in the fabricating department would be aided if variances were calculated by jobs. Management intends to add this analysis next month. Calculate all the variances by job that might contribute to cost control under this assumption.

2. Do you agree with the company's plan to initiate the calculation of job variances in addition to the currently calculated departmental variances? Explain your answer.

3. Prepare standard-cost journal entries summarizing activity in the fabricating department. (*Hint:* There is no beginning or ending work-in-process inventory.)

(CMA adapted)

DIRECT VERSUS ABSORPTION COSTING: INVENTORY VALUATION AND DECISION MAKING

The issue of whether inventories should be costed at variable or full cost remains a subject of debate in both the academic and business worlds. The controversy centers mainly on two inventory valuation methods: the *direct* or *variable costing* method and the *absorption* or *full costing* method. The costing problem encompasses many conceptual and operational dimensions, mainly in the areas of asset valuation, income determination, and decision making. This chapter elaborates on (1) a definition of the problem, (2) the arguments in the controversy, (3) the reconciliation of the two inventory valuation methods, and (4) the relevance for decision making.

9.1 NATURE OF THE PROBLEM

9.1.1 Asset-Expense Dichotomy

The central problem in asset valuation, and particularly in inventory valuation, is making a clear distinction between assets and expenses. A cost is recognized as an asset if it results from the acquisition of future potential services. A determinant of an asset lies in its *revenue-producing powers*. The term *asset* has been approximately defined as follows:

Assets are economic resources devoted to business purposes within a specific accounting entity; they are aggregates of service potential available for or beneficial to expected operation. The significance of some assets may be uniquely related to the objectives of the business entity and will depend upon enterprise continuity.[1]

---

[1]Committee on Concepts and Standards Underlying Corporate Financial Statements, "Accounting and Reporting Standards for Corporate Financial Statements, 1957 Revision," *Accounting Review* (October 1957), p. 538.

For example, inventories and prepaid expenses are viewed as assets, since they both constitute realizable aggregates of service potential.

An expense, however, results from the use or expiration of a resource that is an asset. In other words, when assets no longer have service potential, they are expired and called *expenses*. For example, the prepaid rent of $3,000 for three years, recognized initially as an asset, is reduced by $1,000 rent expense at the end of the first year to reflect the expiration of some of the rights to use the property.

The central problem in the *asset-expense dichotomy* is that while the definition of *asset* as an acquisition of an aggregate of service potential is accepted, the definition of *expense* as the expiration of some of this service potential is subject to different interpretations. The accounting profession has adopted two principles to resolve the expiration problem: the "costs attach" principle and the matching principle.[2] A proper conceptual definition of these principles is necessary for an understanding of the asset-expense dichotomy or, more precisely, the acquisition-expiration process.

Costs Attach Principle

The costs attach principle implies that if accounting is to be a good description of events occurring in the real world, all the related costs should "attach" to the units produced. In other words, all costs actually expended in the production process are to be attached directly to the product. A. W. Paton and A. C. Littleton stated:

It is a basic concept of accounting that costs can be marshalled into new groups that possess real significance. It is as if costs had a power of cohesion when properly brought into contact. Accounting assumes that acquisition costs are mobile and may be reapportioned or regrouped, and that costs reassembled have a natural affinity for each other which identify them with the group. Some costs, like manufacturing overhead, in which an affinity with a product can be detected, are allocated directly to a product. . . .

The purpose of reassembling is to trace the efforts made to give materials and other components additional utility.[3]

The costs attach principle specifies that those costs that are essential to the very existence of the product are to be inventoried with the product. They constitute the economic attributes of the product and would only expire with the loss of these attributes.

Matching Principle: Product versus Period Matching

While the costs attach principle specifies the requirements for a cost to be inventoried and attached to a product or asset, the matching principle specifies the requirements for the recognition of the expense. Consider the following definition:

Costs (defined as product and service factors given up) should be related to revenues realized within a specific period on the basis of some discernible positive correlation of such costs with the recognized revenues.[4]

[2]George H. Sorter and Charles T. Horngren, "Asset Recognition and Economic Attributes: The Relevant Costing Approach," *Accounting Review* (July 1962), pp. 391–399.

[3]A. W. Paton and A. C. Littleton, *An Introduction to Corporate Accounting Standards* (Evanston, Ill.: American Accounting Association, 1940), pp. 13–14.

[4]American Accounting Association 1964 Concepts and Standards Research Study Committee, "The Matching Concept," *Accounting Review* (April 1965), p. 369.

Thus, the matching principle requires the determination of a proper association between expenses and the revenues of the period.

Two methods conventionally used are the direct, or *product matching*, method and the indirect, or *period matching*, method. The direct, or product matching, method consists of at least two steps. First, some costs (known as *product costs*) are attached to the product or asset and inventoried according to a costs attach criteria. Second, some of these product costs are released as expenses at the time of reporting the associated revenues. The indirect, or period matching, method consists of reporting some costs (known as *period costs*) as expenses during the period they are used. The rationale lies in the association of these expenses with the period rather than with the revenues. Whether an item constitutes a product cost (and hence an asset) or a period cost (and hence an expense) depends on the choice between the two inventory valuation methods: absorption costing and direct costing.

9.1.2   *Accounting for Fixed Manufacturing Overhead*

The main issue in the inventory valuation controversy is the classification of costs as either product or period costs. Thus,

1. The absorption costing method is a *total input concept* in the sense that all the manufacturing costs, whether variable or fixed, are treated as product costs and hence inventoried with the products. The cost of an item, then, includes the cost of direct material, the cost of direct labor, and an apportioned share of manufacturing overhead. Consequently, under absorption costing the period costs are limited to both selling and administrative overhead.

2. The direct costing method is a *variable input concept* in the sense that only the variable manufacturing costs are treated as product costs and inventoried. The period costs include not only the selling and administrative overhead, but also the fixed manufacturing overhead.[5]

The main difference between product costing methods lies in the accounting treatment of the fixed manufacturing overhead. Under the direct costing method, the fixed manufacturing overhead is regarded as a period cost (that is, an expired cost to be immediately charged against the period sales). Figure 9.1 highlights the differences between these two inventory valuation techniques.

To illustrate the operational differences, consider the following example. The XYZ Company produces 4,000 units of a single product per year. The costs related to the product are

	Cost per Unit of Product
Direct-Material Cost	$ 5
Direct-Labor Cost	$ 3
Variable Manufacturing Overhead	$ 2
Fixed Manufacturing Overhead	$20,000

[5]Under the third approach, known as *prime costing*, manufacturing overhead is not considered to be a product cost, and both variable and fixed manufacturing overhead are considered period costs. Although not recognized in North America, this approach is considered appropriate for various circumstances in the United Kingdom.

Figure 9.1   Comparison of the Flow of Costs

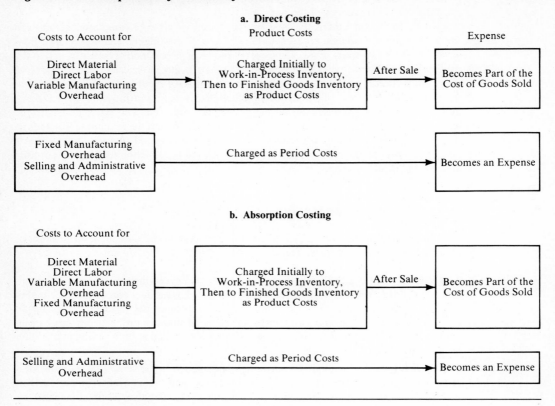

Assume you are required to compute the unit cost of a product under both the absorption costing method and the direct costing method. Correct computations follow:

Absorption Costing

Direct Material	$ 5
Direct Labor	3
Variable Manufacturing Overhead	2
Fixed Manufacturing Overhead ($20,000 ÷ 4,000)	5
Total Cost per Unit	$15

Direct Costing

Direct Material	$ 5
Direct Labor	3
Variable Manufacturing Overhead	2
Total Cost per Unit	$10

The items in the ending inventory of finished goods will be valued at $15 under the absorption costing method and at $10 under the direct costing method. The $20,000 fixed manufacturing overhead will be released as period expenses against income under the direct costing method.

9.1.3   Comparison of Absorption and Direct Costing Results

This section will illustrate the impact of absorption and direct costing on inventory valuation and income determination. For consistency, the income determination format resulting from the use of absorption costing for inventory valuation will be labeled as the *traditional method*, and the format resulting from the use of direct costing will be called the *contribution method*. Income statements prepared under both methods are presented in Tables 9.1 and 9.2 The cost characteristics used to prepare these statements follow:

Normal Capacity	10,000 Units
Standard Direct-Material Cost per Unit	$ 1
Standard Direct-Labor Cost per Unit	$ 2
Standard Variable Manufacturing Overhead per Unit	$ 4
Standard Fixed Manufacturing Overhead per Year	$50,000
Standard Fixed Manufacturing Overhead per Unit ($50,000 ÷ 10,000)	$ 5
Fixed Selling and Administrative Overhead per Year	$20,000
Work-in-Process Inventories	0 Units
Sales Price per Unit	$ 20
Variable Selling and Administrative Overhead per Unit	$ 1

Table 9.1   Profit Figures under the Traditional Method (Absorption Costing)

Income Statement	First Year	Second Year	Third Year	Three Years Together
Sales	$200,000	$200,000	$160,000	$560,000
Direct Material	$ 10,000	$ 12,000	$ 6,000	$ 28,000
+ Direct Labor	20,000	24,000	12,000	56,000
+ Variable Factory Overhead	40,000	48,000	24,000	112,000
+ Fixed Factory Overhead	50,000	60,000	30,000	140,000
Cost of Goods Manufactured	$120,000	$144,000	$ 72,000	$336,000
+ Beginning Inventory @ $12	0	0	24,000	0
Available for Sale	$120,000	$144,000	$ 96,000	$336,000
− Ending Inventory @ $12	0	24,000	0	0
Cost of Goods Sold	$120,000	$120,000	$ 96,000	$336,000
+ Volume variance[a]	0	(10,000)[c]	20,000	10,000
Adjusted Cost of Goods Sold	$120,000	$110,000	$116,000	$346,000
Gross Margin	$ 80,000	$ 90,000	$ 44,000	$214,000
− Selling and Administrative Expenses	30,000[b]	30,000[b]	28,000[d]	88,000[e]
Net Operating Income	$ 50,000	$ 60,000	$ 16,000	$126,000

[a] Volume variance resulting from a normal capacity of 10,000 units: Second year: (12,000 − 10,000) × $5 = $10,000 overapplied. Third year: (10,000 − 6,000) × $5 = $20,000 underapplied. Three years together: (30,000 − 28,000) × $5 = $10,000 underapplied.
[b] $20,000 + ($1.00 × 10,000 units sold).
[c] Another possible alternative is to prorate the volume variance between the Inventory and Cost of Goods Sold.
[d] $20,000 + ($1.00 × 8,000 units sold).
[e] ($20,000 × 3) + ($1.00 × 28,000 units sold).

Table 9.2   Profit Figures under the Contribution Method (Direct Costing)

Income Statement	First Year	Second Year	Third Year	Three Years Together
Sales	$200,000	$200,000	$160,000	$560,000
Direct Material	$ 10,000	$ 12,000	$ 6,000	$ 28,000
+ Direct Labor	20,000	24,000	12,000	56,000
+ Variable Manufacturing Overhead	40,000	48,000	24,000	112,000
Variable Cost of Goods Manufactured	$ 70,000	$ 84,000	$ 42,000	$196,000
+ Beginning Inventory @ $7	0	0	14,000	0
Available for Sale	$ 70,000	$ 84,000	$ 56,000	$196,000
− Ending Inventory @ $7	0	14,000	0	0
Variable Cost of Goods Sold	$ 70,000	$ 70,000	$ 56,000	$196,000
+ Variable Selling and Administrative Overhead	10,000	10,000	8,000	28,000
− Total Variable Expenses	$ 80,000	$ 80,000	$ 64,000	$224,000
Total Contribution Margin	$120,000	$120,000	$ 96,000	$336,000
Fixed Manufacturing Overhead	$ 50,000	$ 50,000	$ 50,000	$150,000
+ Fixed Selling and Administrative Overhead	20,000	20,000	20,000	60,000
Total Fixed Expenses	$ 70,000	$ 70,000	$ 70,000	$210,000
Net Operating Income	$ 50,000	$ 50,000	$ 26,000	$126,000

Similarly, the actual production, sales, and finished goods inventory in units are

	Year 1	Year 2	Year 3	Three Years Together
Beginning Inventory	0	0	2,000	0
Production	10,000	12,000	6,000	28,000
Sales	10,000	10,000	8,000	28,000
Ending Inventory	0	2,000	0	0

There were no variances from the standard variable costs, and volume variance is written off directly at year-end as an adjustment to Cost of Goods Sold.

The following generalizations can be made from the results shown in Tables 9.1 and 9.2:

1. When the sales and production volumes are equal, the profits under absorption and direct costing are equal. In year 1, the profit under both methods is equal to $50,000 due to the fact that under both methods, the $50,000 fixed manufacturing overhead is charged off in total against income as a period expense.

2. When the production volume exceeds the sales volume, absorption costing yields a higher profit, as shown in the results for year 2. The reason is that while the total fixed manufacturing overhead of $50,000 is released as a period expense under direct costing, only a portion of it is charged off as a period expense, and the rest is charged to inventory to be deferred to future periods under absorption costing.

3. When the sales volume exceeds the production volume, direct costing yields a higher profit, as seen in the results for year 3. Fixed costs previously deferred to inventory under direct costing are now charged off against income as a period expense.

4. The profit under direct costing fluctuates in proportion to sales, as shown by a comparison of the results of year 1 and year 2. Hence, given a constant sales volume in year 1 and year 2, the profit under direct costing is constant in both years, while the profit under absorption costing from year 1 to year 2 is affected by the direction and amount of the changes in inventory.

5. The difference in profits between the two methods in each of the three years is attributable to the differences in accounting for fixed manufacturing overhead and the imbalances between sales and production. Under absorption costing, the fixed manufacturing overhead is transferred from one year to another as a product or inventoried cost. Under direct costing, the fixed manufacturing overhead is indirectly charged as a period expense. The following formula computes the differences between the net profits of absorption and direct costing:

$$\begin{array}{c}\text{Absorption}\\\text{costing}\\\text{profit}\end{array} - \begin{array}{c}\text{Direct}\\\text{costing}\\\text{profit}\end{array} = \begin{array}{c}\text{Fixed}\\\text{manufacturing}\\\text{overhead}\\\text{per unit}\end{array} \times \begin{array}{c}\text{Changes in}\\\text{inventory}\\\text{in units.}\end{array}$$

When applied to the XYZ Company example, the formula yields the following results:

	Year 1	Year 2	Year 3	Three Years Together
Absorption Costing Profit	$50,000	$60,000	$ 16,000	$126,000
− Direct Costing Profit	50,000	50,000	26,000	126,000
= Difference in Profit	$ 0	$10,000	$(10,000)	$ 0
Fixed Manufacturing Overhead per Unit	$ 5	$ 5	$ 5	$ 5
× Changes in Inventory Units	0	2,000	(2,000)	0
= Difference in Profit	$ 0	$10,000	$(10,000)	$ 0

These generalizations do not hold in all cases and, as will be indicated, depend on the cost flow assumptions.[6]

The real controversy between the direct and absorption costing methods concerning income fluctuations is whether income should be affected by the production or inventory policies. While direct costing advocates say income should not be affected, the absorption costing advocates maintain that the profit is the result of the total activity of the firm, including both production and sales.

---

[6]Furthermore, the accuracy of the generalizations are subject to the additional assumptions that there are no variations in the unit fixed manufacturing cost.

Table 9.3   *Differences between Full- and Direct-Cost Profit Inventory Costing Methods (PF−PD)*

Inventory Costing Methods	(PF−PD)
Average	$\dfrac{ws}{w+s}\left[\dfrac{MN}{s}-\dfrac{BN}{w}\right]$
FIFO with $s \geqslant w^-$	$w\left[\dfrac{MN}{q}-\dfrac{BN}{w}\right]$
FIFO with $s \leqslant w^-$	$s\left[\dfrac{MN}{s}-\dfrac{BN}{w^-}\right]$
LIFO with $s \leqslant q$	$(w-w^-)\dfrac{MN}{q}$
LIFO with $s \geqslant q$	$(w-w^-)\dfrac{BN}{w^-}$
Standard	$\alpha^*(w-w^-)$

Notation is as follows:

PF = Profit under full costing (absorption costing).
PD = Profit under direct costing.
MN = The fixed cost portion of the current period's manufacturing cost.
BN = The fixed portion of beginning inventory.
w = Ending inventory quantity.
w^- = Beginning inventory quantity.
s = Current period's quantity sold.
q = The quantity produced in the current period.
α^* = Standard fixed cost per unit.

Source: Yuji Ijiri, Robert K. Jaedicke, and John L. Livingstone, "The Effect of Inventory Costing Methods on Full and Direct Costing," *Journal of Accounting Research* (Spring 1965), pp. 63–74. Reprinted by permission.

9.2   RECONCILIATION OF DIRECT AND ABSORPTION COSTING PROFITS

9.2.1   Differences between Direct and Absorption Costing Profits

The difference between the full- and direct-cost profits was defined as being equal to the changes in inventory multiplied by the unit fixed manufacturing cost. This generalization holds only under the last-in, first-out (LIFO) and the standard-cost methods of inventory costing.[7] Table 9.3 shows the correct generalizations for the various inventory costing methods.

[7] Yuji Ijiri, Robert K. Jaedicke, and John L. Livingstone, "The Effect of Inventory Costing Methods on Full and Direct Costing," *Journal of Accounting Research* (Spring 1965), pp. 63–74.

9.2.2   *Formats for Reconciliation*

Given the relative merit of and the controversy surrounding the use of the direct and absorption costing methods, a format providing a reconciliation of both methods may be appropriate. In fact, firms can elect to keep their accounting records on a direct costing basis and make a reconciliation of both methods at the end of the year.

One-Factor Model

Table 9.4 presents a format for reconciling both direct and absorption costing. Up to the entry "Total Contribution," it is based on a direct costing approach. The section following "Total Contribution" reconciles both methods.

The example assumes an opening inventory of 5,000 units, a production volume of 10,000 units, a sales volume of 6,000 units, and an ending inventory of 9,000 units. Assume also that (1) a first-in, first-out (FIFO) actual inventory valuation method is used; (2) the variable cost per unit is $50 for the previous and current periods; and (3) the fixed manufacturing cost per unit decreased from $15 in the previous period to $10 in the current period. The sales price per unit is $100.

The adjustment to absorption costing equals the difference between the fixed overhead charged to Ending Inventory and the fixed overhead charged to Beginning Inventory. Consequently, the following results can be noted:

1. When the fixed overhead charged to Ending Inventory is equal to the amount in Beginning Inventory, both inventory valuation methods will charge the same amount of fixed costs against revenues.

2. When the fixed overhead charged to Ending Inventory is greater than the amount in Beginning Inventory, absorption costing will yield a higher profit than direct costing.

3. When the fixed overhead charged to Ending Inventory is less than the amount in Beginning Inventory, direct costing will yield a higher profit than absorption costing.

Table 9.4   *Modified Direct Costing Format (Fictional Example), One-Factor Model*

Net Sales (6,000 × $100)		$600,000
minus Variable Cost of Goods Sold (6,000 × $50)		300,000
equals Contribution Margin		$300,000
minus Fixed Costs		100,000
equals Total Contribution		$200,000
plus Adjustment to Absorption Costing Fixed Costs for Ending Inventory (9,000 × $10)	$90,000	
Less: Fixed Costs for Beginning Inventory (5,000 × $15)	75,000	15,000
equals Net Profit under Absorption Costing		$215,000

Table 9.5   *Modified Direct Costing Format, Two-Factor Model*

Net Sales (6,000 × $100)		$600,000
minus Variable Costs of Goods Sold		300,000
equals Contribution Margin		$300,000
minus Fixed Costs		100,000
equals Total Contribution		$200,000
plus Adjustment to Absorption Costing		
Changes in Fixed Cost Due to a Decrease in Fixed Manufacturing		
Overhead Rate (5,000 × $5) $25,000		
Changes in Fixed Cost Due to an Increase in Inventory		
(4,000 × $10) 40,000		15,000
equals Net Profit under Absorption Costing		$215,000

Two-Factor Model

The reconciliation format presented in Table 9.5 takes into account only the difference in profits during the time periods in which the fixed manufacturing overhead costs incurred in a given period are charged as a period cost. This format considers only a single determinant of the difference in the profits under both inventory valuation techniques. This profit difference can be separated into two components: (1) the change due to the difference in the physical quantity of inventory and (2) the change due to the difference in the fixed manufacturing overhead rate between the two periods.

Using the same example as the one-factor model, the two-factor model shows the change in fixed costs due to (1) an increase (or decrease) in the fixed manufacturing overhead rate and (2) an increase (or decrease) in the inventory volumes.

9.3   ARGUMENTS IN THE CONTROVERSY

Inventory valuation focuses on a product and its costs and, consequently, affects both the external and internal uses of the resulting data. The external uses include asset measurement, income determination, and external reporting, whereas the internal uses refer to internal decision making. Thus, the arguments in the controversy between absorption and direct costing center mainly on the methods' relative merits to income determination, asset measurement, external reporting, and decision making.

9.3.1   Period/Product Question for Income Determination

The central issue affecting income determination is whether fixed manufacturing costs are product or period costs. Two views exist in the literature.[8]

---

[8] James M. Fremgen, "The Direct Costing Controversy: An Identification of Issues," *Accounting Review* (January 1964), pp. 43–51.

According to one view, known as the *period cost concept*, the fixed manufacturing costs are viewed as period costs. This view associates the expiration of fixed manufacturing costs with the passage of time rather than with flow of units produced. Its main assumption is that the fixed manufacturing costs are continuously incurred for each time period to create a productive capacity, regardless of the state of the production process:

Proponents of variable costing maintain that fixed factory overhead provides capacity to produce. Whether that capacity is used to the fullest extent or not used at all is usually irrelevant insofar as the expiration of fixed cost is concerned.
. . . As the clock ticks, fixed costs expire, to be replenished by new bundles of fixed costs that will enable production to continue in succeeding periods.[9]

According to the other view of fixed manufacturing costs, known as the *product cost concept*, all manufacturing costs are viewed as product costs. They are assumed to be associated with and assigned to the product rather than the period. An extreme position in support of the product cost concept follows:

In theory, there is no such thing as a true period cost. All costs incurred by a firm, including non-manufacturing costs, are costs of the product. For the product of a firm is not merely a physical commodity from a production line, it is a bundle of economic utilities, which include time and place as well as form. Thus, in theory, distribution and administrative costs are just as much costs of the product as are factory costs. The product is not complete until it is in a form and place and at a time desired by the customer; and this product completion involves distribution just as essentially as it does manufacturing.[10]

9.3.2   Nature of Service Potential for Asset Measurement

The product cost method of costing pertains mainly to the choice of an inventory valuation method and, consequently, to the choice of an asset valuation method. Assets have been defined as "aggregates of service potential available for or beneficial to expected operation." The link between assets and service potential can be used to resolve the controversy between absorption and direct costing. In other words, the test for determining whether fixed manufacturing overhead is a product or period cost is to determine whether the costs are beneficial to the operations of future periods. There are two possible interpretations of the concept of *service potential*: the *cost obviation concept* and the *revenue production concept*.

According to the cost obviation concept, the measurement of assets should include those costs that will be obviated in the future as a result of their incurrence in the past. In other words, assets have service potential if the costs included will not need to be incurred in the future. Advocates of direct costing point out that the incurrence of variable manufacturing costs avert their future incurrence, while the incurrence of fixed manufacturing costs does not. They maintain that the production of goods for inventory may create a revenue potential for the future without a reincurrence of the variable costs of producing the same inventory of goods. Only the variable costs of production should be

[9] Charles T. Horngren and George H. Sorter, " 'Direct' Costing for External Reporting," *Accounting Review* (January 1961), p. 88.
[10] James M. Fremgen, "Variable Costing for External Reporting: A Reconsideration," *Accounting Review* (January 1962), p. 78.

inventoried, given that the fixed costs of production do not result in future cost avoidance. Robert B. Wetnight argued as follows:

If this test of future benefit is applied to the two methods of costing under discussion, it can be seen that direct costing most closely fits the requirements. In the first place, there is a future benefit from the incurrence of variable costs. These costs will not need to be incurred in a future period. However, in the case of fixed costs, no future benefits exist, since these costs will be incurred during the future period, no matter what the level of operations. [11]

According to the revenue production concept of service potential, the measurement of assets should include those costs that will contribute to the production of revenues in the future. This concept defines a product cost as a cost conducive to the realization of revenue in the future. James M. Fremgen contended:

Any cost essential to the production of a product that may reasonably be expected to be sold and, thus generate revenue, is a cost of obtaining such revenue and should be deferred in inventory so that it may be matched with the revenue in the determination of income for the period of sale. [12]

This revenue production concept can be used to argue for either direct or absorption costing, depending on whether or not an association—logical or empirical—can be established between fixed manufacturing costs and revenue. Thus, any costs essential to the production of goods that reasonably can be expected to be sold in the future should be considered product costs.

9.4   RELEVANCE FOR DECISION MAKING

Proponents of direct costing base their beliefs mainly on its relevance to internal decision making. They assume that separate reporting of fixed and variable costs facilitates incremental profit analysis and removes from income the effect of inventory changes. These advantages have been summarized in the NAA *Research Series No. 23* as follows:

1. Cost-volume-profit relationship data wanted for profit planning purposes is readily obtained from the regular accounting statements. Hence management does not have to work with two separate sets of data to relate one to the other.

2. The profit for a period is not affected by changes in absorption of fixed expenses resulting from building or reducing inventory. Other things remaining equal (e.g., selling prices, costs, sales mix), profits move in the same direction as sales when direct costing is in use.

3. Manufacturing cost and income statements in the direct cost form follow manage-

---

[11] Robert B. Wetnight, "Direct Costing Passes the 'Future Benefit Test,'" *NAA Bulletin* (August 1958), p. 84.
[12] Fremgen, "Direct Costing Controversy," p. 50.

ment's thinking more closely than does the absorption cost form for these statements. For this reason, management finds it easier to understand and to use direct cost reports.

4. The impact of fixed costs on profits is emphasized because the total amount of such cost for the period appears in the income statement.

5. Marginal income figures facilitate relative appraisal of products, territories, classes of customers, and other segments of the business without having the results obscured by allocation of joint fixed costs.

6. Direct costing ties in with such effective plans for cost control as standard costs and flexible budgets. In fact, the flexible budget is an aspect for direct costing and many companies thus use direct costing methods for this purpose without recognizing them as such.

7. Direct cost constitutes a concept of inventory cost which corresponds closely with the current out-of-pocket expenditure necessary to manufacture the goods.[13]

As a result of these advantages, various firms elect to adopt a cost accounting system based on direct costing. This system, known as *contribution margin reporting*, consists of reporting variable and fixed costs separately to facilitate decision making, for example, analysis of special price contracts, segment analysis, and make-or-buy analysis.

9.4.1   *Analysis of Special Price Contracts*

The differentiation between the fixed and variable components of costs is useful in the appraisal of the impact of changes in activity volume. It can be applied in decisions sensitive to volume changes, such as the acceptance of special orders.

For example, every year the ABEL Manufacturing Company produces and sells 100,000 units of a product for $10 per unit. The variable manufacturing cost per unit and the total fixed manufacturing costs are $6 and $200,000, respectively. The fixed selling and administrative expenses are $100,000. The absorption costing profit follows:

Sales (100,000 Units @ $10/Unit)	$1,000,000
Cost of Goods Sold (100,000 Units @ $8/Unit)	800,000
Gross Profit	$ 200,000
Selling and Administrative Expenses (Fixed)	100,000
Net Income	$ 100,000

The ABEL Manufacturing Company has received an order for an additional 50,000 units at $7 per unit, and acceptance would not require additional capacity. On the basis of the absorption costing results, the order would not be accepted, given that the unit production cost of $8 is higher than the offered contract price of $7. However, under direct costing it can be assumed that the fixed manufacturing expenses are period expenses that would not be affected by the additional sale. The following table shows the net income with and without the special order:

---

[13] National Association of Accountants, *Research Series No. 23*, "Direct Costing," (New York: NAA, 1953) p. 55.

Contribution Income Statement

	Without Special Order	With Special Order	Combined
Sales	$1,000,000	$350,000	$1,350,000
Variable Cost of Goods Sold ($6 Each)	600,000	300,000	900,000
Contribution Margin	$ 400,000	$ 50,000	$ 450,000
Fixed Manufacturing Costs			200,000
Fixed Selling and Administrative Costs			100,000
Net Income			$ 150,000

The direct costing approach to the problem shows that the net income will increase by $50,000 as a result of the acceptance of the special order.

9.4.2 Segment Analysis

A *segment* of a firm is any portion of the organization about which costs and/or reve-nues can be accumulated, such as a division, product line, sales territory, region of the country, or a portion differentiated by the degree of domestic and foreign operations. In examining the profitability of a company's segments, management may have to decide whether or not to discontinue a particular segment.

To illustrate the usefulness of contribution margin reporting to segment analysis, con-sider this example. The Poduch Company produces and sells three different products: Ex, Why, and Zee. Cost analysis reveals that (1) production costs are 50 percent vari-able and 50 percent fixed; and (2) selling and administrative costs are 60 percent vari-able and 40 percent fixed. Projected income statements by product line and prepared on an absorption costing basis follow:

	Ex	Why	Zee	Total
Revenues	$400,000	$300,000	$200,000	$900,000
Cost of Goods Sold	200,000	150,000	150,000	500,000
Gross Profit	$200,000	$150,000	$ 50,000	$400,000
Selling and Administrative Expenses	100,000	100,000	60,000	260,000
Net Income	$100,000	$ 50,000	$(10,000)	$140,000

When faced with a decision on whether or not to discontinue product Zee, management of the Poduch Company elected first to prepare the income statements on a direct costing basis, taking into account the fact that the fixed costs cannot be traced adequately to the individual products on a cause-and-effect basis. The contribution income statements follow:

	Ex	Why	Zee	Total
Revenues	$400,000	$300,000	$200,000	$900,000
Variable Costs and Expenses				
Production	$100,000	$ 75,000	$ 75,000	$250,000
Selling and Administrative Expenses	60,000	60,000	36,000	156,000
Total	$160,000	$135,000	$111,000	$406,000
Contribution Margin	$240,000	$165,000	$ 89,000	$494,000
Fixed Expenses (Not Traceable)				
Production				$250,000
Selling and Administrative Expenses				104,000
Total				$354,000
Net Income				$140,000

The direct costing approach to the problem reveals that product Zee contributes $89,000 to the total income rather than creating a $10,000 loss. Thus, if Zee is discontinued, not only will the net income drop drastically, but the productive capacity used by Zee will be idle.

9.4.3 *Make-or-Buy Analysis*

Management often faces the problem of whether to make or buy component parts or tools. When faced with a make-or-buy decision, management should evaluate the qualitative factors important to the decision. One factor supporting a decision to buy a part would be problems of availability of know-how, technology, skilled labor, materials, and so forth. A second factor favoring buying the part would be the desire to secure long-term relationships with suppliers rather than destroying them by an erratic decision to make the part in good (profitable) times and buy the part in bad (unprofitable) times. A factor supporting a decision to make a part would be the desire to secure and maintain high-quality parts.

Management should also evaluate the quantitative factors important to the make-or-buy decision. First they should compare the cost of making the part with the cost (or price) of buying it. For example, assume the following costs are reported:

Costs of Making Part No. 1200

	Total Costs for 1,000 Units	Cost per Unit
Direct Materials	$ 2,000	$ 2
Direct Labor	7,000	7
Variable Overhead	3,000	3
Fixed Overhead	7,000	7
Total Costs	$19,000	$19

Assume also that another manufacturer offers to sell the company that same part for $15. What should the company decide? It needs more information on the nature of the costs involved.

As a second step, management can determine whether some of the costs are unavoidable (that is, whether they will continue to be incurred regardless of the decision). Assume in this case that $3,000 of the fixed overhead is unavoidable. The comparison of the cost of making the part with the cost (or price) of buying it is as follows:

Per-Unit Costs

	Make	Buy
Direct Material	$ 2	
Direct Labor	7	
Variable Overhead	3	
Fixed Overhead ($4,000 ÷ 1,000 Units)	4	
Total Relevant Costs	$16	$15

Management should choose to buy the part, assuming that the capacity used to make the part will become idle.

Thus, as a third step in evaluating quantitative factors in make-or-buy decisions, management must investigate how to best use the idle capacity if they decide to buy the part. Essentially, the decision to buy or make becomes a decision of how to use the available facilities. More explicitly, management must determine the opportunity cost of resources that will be expended as a result of the decision to buy rather than make the product.

Assume the following courses of action are available:

	Make	Buy and Leave Facilities Idle	Buy and Lease the Facilities	Buy and Use Facilities for Other Products
Lease Revenue			$ 10,000	
Net Revenue from Other Products				$ 13,000
Cost of Making the Part	$(16,000)			
Cost of Purchasing the Part		$(15,000)	(15,000)	(15,000)
Net Relevant Costs	$(16,000)	$(15,000)	$ (5,000)	$ (2,000)

Management should decide to buy and use the facilities to make other products.

It is important to insure that the costs used to compare make-versus-buy situations are future costs that take fully into account what costs "should be" under all existing conditions.[14]

9.4.4   *Product Pricing*

Pricing decisions in most firms are preceded by and depend on pricing policies, which indicate the main factors to be considered in pricing decisions. Pricing policies must be congruent with the overall goals of the organization, such as profit maximization, achieving a target rate of return on investment, or reaching a target market share. When these goals and the corresponding pricing policies are determined, management can proceed with pricing decisions. It is useful to make a distinction between the economist's and the accountant's approaches.

Economist's Approach
As seen in section 4.4 (which explains the economic approach to breakeven analysis), the economist reasons on the basis of a nonlinear total revenue and cost function and assumes the existence of a profit-maximizing sales volume where marginal costs equal marginal revenues. Hence the optimal selling price for the economist would be the price necessary to reach the optimal sales volume. To illustrate the computation of such a price, assume the following example:

Demand function: $x = 22 - 10p$.

Total cost function: $y = 3.2 + 0.2x + 0.1x^2$.

1. Solving the demand function for p yields the price function as follows:

Price function: $p = 2.2 - 0.1x$.

2. The total revenue, marginal cost, and marginal revenue can be computed as follows:

---

[14]National Association of Accountants Committee on Management Practice, *Statement No. 5*, "Criteria for Make-or-Buy Decisions," (New York: NAA, 1965), p. 8.

Total revenue function: $R = 2.2x - 0.1x^2$.

Marginal cost $= MC = \dfrac{dy}{dx} = 0.2 + 0.2x$.

Marginal revenue $= MR = \dfrac{dR}{dx} = 2.2 - 0.2x$.

3. Setting the marginal cost equal to the marginal revenue and solving for x yields the optimal sales volume:

$$MR = MC = 0.2 + 0.2x = 2.2 - 0.2x \text{ where } x = 5.$$

4. Finally, solving the price function on the basis of the optimal sales volume yields the optimal sales price, as follows:

$$p = \$2.2 - 0.1(5)$$
$$= \$1.7.$$

Accountant's Approaches

The accountant's approaches can be based on either a target rate of return on investment or a cost-plus approach.

Target Rate of Return on Investment   Firms generally set a target rate of return on investment computed as follows:

$$\text{Return on investment } (ROI) = \frac{\text{Income}}{\text{Total investment}}.$$

Assuming p = price, Q = sales volume, v = variable cost, F = total fixed cost, t = tax rate, and C = investment, then the rate of return on investment can be computed as follows:

$$ROI = \frac{[Q(p - v) - F](1 - t)}{C}.$$

Solving for p yields

$$p = \frac{\dfrac{ROI \times C}{(1 - t)} + F}{Q} + v.$$

For example, assume that Fabiani Ltd. has a target rate of return on investment of 20 percent, a capital investment of \$300,000, a tax rate of 40 percent, a total fixed cost of \$300,000, an expected sales volume of 40,000 units, and a unit variable cost of \$100. The selling price can be determined as follows:

$$p = \frac{\dfrac{20\% \times \$300,000}{(1 - 0.4)} + \$300,000}{40,000} + \$100 = \$110.$$

Cost-Plus Approaches   The cost-plus pricing methods can be determined on the basis of either the full cost or the incremental cost. The markup will vary between the two methods as follows:

$$\text{Full cost markup} = \frac{\text{Target profit}}{\text{Estimated full costs}}.$$

$$\text{Incremental cost markup} = \frac{\text{Target profit} + \text{Estimated unallocated fixed costs}}{\text{Estimated incremental costs}}.$$

For example, assume that Fabiani Ltd. is instead using an accounting product pricing method. The target profit before tax is estimated to be $500,000, the variable costs to be $5,000,000, and the fixed cost to be $15,000,000. The markup for Fabiani Ltd. will be either

$$\text{Full cost markup} = \frac{\$500,000}{\$5,000,000 + \$15,000,000} = \$0.025.$$

or

$$\text{Incremental cost markup} = \frac{\$500,000 + \$15,000,000}{\$5,000,000} = \$3.1.$$

If we also assume that Fabiani Ltd. has an incremental cost per unit of $5 and a fixed cost per unit of $15, then the selling price would be as follows:

Full cost markup method: $(1 + 0.025)(\$15 + \$5) = \$20.5$.

Incremental cost markup method: $(1 + 3.1)(\$5) = \$20.5$.

The cost-plus pricing methods are generally favored by corporations, because they provide a practical benchmark in pricing decisions.

Pricing under the Robinson-Patman Act

The Robinson-Patman Act of 1936 prohibits certain kinds of price discrimination. Its purpose is

To make it unlawful for any person engaged in commerce to discriminate in price or terms of sale between purchasers of commodities of like grade and quality; to prohibit the payment of brokerage or commission under certain conditions, to suppress pseudo advertising allowances; to provide a presumptive measure of damages in certain cases; and to protect the independent merchant, the public whom he serves; and the manufacturer from whom he buys, from exploitation by unfair competitors.[15]

The legislation, however, does not prohibit price discrimination when it is justified by differences in costs of manufacturing, sales, or delivery. The act states:

That nothing herein contained shall prevent differentials which make only due allowances for differences in cost of manufacture, sale, or delivery resulting from the dif-

---

[15] Wright Patman, *The Robinson-Patman Act* (New York: Ronald Press, 1938), p. 3.

fering methods or quantities in which such commodities are to such purchasers sold or delivered.[16]

Because the act rests on the interpretation of *cost*, Patman defined *cost* as including all costs of manufacture and sale, excluding the return on invested capital but including a prorated share of all overhead costs. The courts and the Federal Trade Commission base their decisions accordingly—on the full cost rather than on the direct or differential cost.

9.5   *INVENTORY VALUATION AND REGULATION*

Various regulatory agencies encourage the adoption of the full absorption method of accounting for reasons similar to those that will be described in this section.

The general acceptability of direct costing as an accounting principle for external reporting purposes is ambiguously expressed in the AICPA *Accounting Research Bulletin No. 43*, which states:

The exclusion of all overhead from inventory costs does not constitute an accepted accounting procedure. The exercise of judgment in an individual situation involves a consideration of the adequacy of the procedures of the cost accounting system in use, the soundness of the principles thereof, and their consistent application.[17]

The ambiguity of that paragraph led first to the acceptance of various alternative methods of allocating overhead costs to inventory under absorption costing, and second to the possibility that direct costing could be recognized as a generally accepted accounting principle. In spite of this possible recognition of direct costing, absorption costing remains the predominant method for external reporting purposes, and it is preferred in generally accepted accounting principles.

The Securities and Exchange Commission (SEC) relies on the accounting profession to set generally accepted accounting principles and hence favors absorption costing as the basis of valuation in SEC filings. Any departure following the adoption of some form of direct costing must be fully disclosed:

Sometimes the omission of overhead from inventory does not have a material effect either on the financial position or on the results of the operations during the period under report. In that case the SEC has accepted registration statements containing financial statements which disclosed the facts and stated that the statements had not been adjusted.[18]

In September 1973, the Internal Revenue Service promulgated rules and regulations governing the allocation of indirect costs to inventories:

In order to conform as nearly as may be possible to the best accounting practices and to reflect income (as required by section 471 of the code) both direct and indirect produc-

[16] Ibid., p. 7.

[17] American Institute of Certified Public Accountants, *Accounting Research Bulletin No. 43* (New York: AICPA, 1953), chap. 4, par. 5.

[18] Louis H. Rappaport, *SEC Accounting Practice and Procedure*, 2d ed. (New York: Ronald Press, 1963), chap. 21, p. 2.

tion costs must be taken into account in the computation of inventoriable costs in accordance with the "full absorption" method of inventory pricing.[19]

These regulations specify which indirect costs should be included. Regulation 1.471.11 divides typical overhead costs into three classifications:

1. *Category 1 costs* include overhead items that must be capitalized (that is, included in the computation of cost inventory regardless of their financial statements treatment). The items are repair costs; maintenance; utilities; rent; indirect materials and supplies; tools and equipment not capitalized; quality control; inspection; and indirect labor and production supervision wages, including basic compensation, overtime pay, vacation and holiday pay, sick leave pay (with exceptions), shift differential, payroll taxes, and contributions to a supplemental unemployment benefits plan.

2. *Category 2 costs* include overhead items that can be included at the taxpayer's option, regardless of their financial statement treatment: marketing costs, advertising costs, selling costs, other distribution costs, interest, research and development, specified casualty and other losses, excess of percentage depletion over costs, excess of tax over book depreciation, income taxes on inventory sales, past service cost as pension contributions, general and administrative overall activities, and officers' salaries and overall management activities.

3. *Category 3 costs* include overhead items governed by the financial statements, provided that the statements are prepared in accordance with generally accepted accounting principles: property and other local and state taxes; book depreciation and cost depletion; costs attributable to strikes, rework labor, scrap, and spoilage; factory administrative costs; production officers' salaries; insurance costs; and employee benefits (current pension service costs; worker's compensation; wage continuation; nonqualified pension, profit sharing, and stock bonus—to an extent taxable to employees—life and health insurance premiums; safety and medical treatment; cafeteria; recreational facilities; and membership dues).

Despite the popular use of direct costing for internal segment reporting, the FASB seems to support absorption costing as a basis for segment profit reporting, as shown in *Statement No. 14.*[20]

9.6   CONCLUSION

This chapter presented two fundamentally conflicting methods of reporting the same information that are considered equally correct. The advocates of both direct costing and absorption costing support the usefulness of the results of their method with both practical and theoretical justifications.

From the theoretical point of view, both methods appear to be internally consistent. Under absorption costing, the fixed manufacturing overhead costs are perceived as product costs, inventoried as part of the cost of finished goods, and only released for matching with the revenues realized as part of the cost of goods sold. Similarly, under the

---

[19]*Internal Revenue Code* (September 1973), sec. 471, 1.471.11, par. 1.

[20]Financial Accounting Standards Board, *Statement of Financial Accounting Standards No. 14*, "Financial Reporting for Segments of Business Enterprises" (Stamford, Conn.: FASB, 1976).

direct costing approach, the fixed manufacturing overhead costs are perceived as period costs and released immediately against the revenues of the period. On one hand, the fluctuation of the profit with both sales and production volume and the inclusion of a fair share of fixed manufacturing overhead in asset valuation under absorption costing, and on the other hand, the fluctuation of the profit with sales volume only and the valuation of assets on the basis of variable costs only are consistent with one another.

From the practical point of view as well, both methods have merit. Thus, there is no absolute answer to whether a cost is a product or a period cost. Theoretically, all costs incurred are ultimately costs of the products produced and sold. The accountant is forced into the time period assumption to provide a rationale for differentiating between product and period costs.

Given that it is difficult to make a value judgment on which method gives proper recognition to the true nature of costs, either method can be used, and either maintains a full disclosure in the sense that a reconciliation is made to adjust the results from one method to the other. More research on the behavioral impact of both methods is necessary to ultimately assess the relevance of either method.

GLOSSARY

Absorption Costing A costing method under which all manufacturing costs are charged to product costs.

Contribution Method An income determination method resulting from the use of direct costing.

Cost Obviation Concept The measurement of assets should include those costs that will be obviated in the future as a result of their incurrence in the past.

Direct Costing A costing method under which only the variable manufacturing costs are charged to product costs.

Revenue Production Concept The measurement of assets should include those costs that will contribute to the production of revenues in the future.

Traditional Method An income determination method resulting from the use of absorption costing.

SELECTED READINGS

Amerman, Gilbert, "Facts about Direct Costing for Profit Determination," *Accounting Research* (April 1954), pp. 154–166. Reprinted in *Contemporary Issues in Cost Accounting*, eds. H. R. Anton and P. A. Firmin, 2d ed. (Boston: Houghton Mifflin, 1971).

Blum, J. D., "Decision Tree Analysis for Accounting Decisions," *Management Accounting* (December 1976), pp. 45–46.

Brumett, R. Lee, "Direct Costing: Should It Be a Controversial Issue?" *Accounting Review* (July 1955), pp. 439–443.

Canadian Institute of Chartered Accountants, *Overhead as an Element of Inventory Cost: A Research Study* (Toronto: CICA, 1965).

Fekrat, Ali M., "The Conceptual Foundations of Absorption Costing," *Accounting Review* (April 1972), pp. 351–355.

Fremgen, James M., "The Direct Costing Controversy: An Identification of Issues," *Accounting Review* (January 1964), pp. 43–51.

Gordon, A. Lawrence, and Cook, Henry Jr., "Absorption Costing and Fixed Factors of Production," *Accounting Review* (January 1973), pp. 128–130.

Green, David Jr., "A Moral to Direct Costing Controversy?" *Journal of Business* (July 1960), pp. 218–226.

Grinnell, D. J., "Product Mix Decisions: Direct Costing versus Absorption Costing," *Management Accounting* (August 1976), pp. 36–42, 53.

Heimann, S. R., and Lusk, E. J., "Decision Flexibility: An Alternative Evaluation Criterion," *Accounting Review* (January 1976), pp. 51–64.

Horngren, Charles T., and Sorter, George H., "'Direct' Costing for External Reporting," *Accounting Review* (January 1961), pp. 84–93.

Ijiri, Yuji; Jaedicke, Robert K.; and Livingstone, John L., "The Effect of Inventory Costing Methods on Full and Direct Costing," *Journal of Accounting Research* (Spring 1965), pp. 63–74.

Largay, James, "Microeconomic Foundations of Variable Costing," *Accounting Review* (January 1973), pp. 115–119.

National Association of Accountants, *Research Report No. 37*, "Current Application of Direct Costing," (New York: NAA, 1961).

Nielsen, Oswald, "Direct Costing: The Case 'For'," *Accounting Review* (January 1954), pp. 89–93.

Staubus, George J., "Direct, Relevant or Absorption Costing?" *Accounting Review* (January 1963), pp. 64–73.

Swalley, R. W., "The Benefits of Direct Costing," *Management Accounting* (September 1974), pp. 13–16.

Williams, Bruce R., "Measuring Costs: Full Absorption Cost or Direct Cost?" *Management Accounting* (January 1976), pp. 23–24, 36.

QUESTIONS, EXERCISES, AND PROBLEMS

9.1   Briefly explain the differences between absorption and direct costing.

9.2   Briefly explain the following generalizations:

1. When the sales volume is greater than the production volume, absorption costing will yield a lower profit than the direct costing alternative.

2. When the production volume is greater than the sales volume, direct costing will yield a lower profit than the absorption costing alternative.

9.3   ***Direct and Absorption Costing: Effects of Production and Sales***   The following data will be used to prepare income statements under both direct and absorption costing.

	Year 1	Year 2	Year 3	Three Years Together
Sales (in Units)	10,000	10,000	12,000	32,000
Beginning Inventory (in Units)	0	0	2,000	0
Production (in Units)	10,000	12,000	10,000	32,000
Ending Inventory (in Units)	0	2,000	0	0

Sales Price: $20
Standard Production Costs
   Variable ($5 per Unit)
   Fixed ($32,000 per Year)
Selling and Administrative Costs
   Variable ($3 per Unit Sold)
   Fixed ($20,000 per Year)
Fixed Production Costs Incurred: $32,000

There were no work-in-process inventories.

Required:
1. Prepare income statements for years 1, 2, 3, and the three years together under direct and absorption costing.

2. Reconcile the differences in the operating incomes.

9.4

Gyro Gear Company produces a special gear used in automatic transmissions. Each gear sells for $28, and the company sells approximately 500,000 gears each year. Unit cost data for 19X3 were direct material, $6; and direct labor, $5. Other unit costs included

	Variable	Fixed
Manufacturing	$2	$7
Distribution	4	3

Required:

1. The unit cost of gears for direct-cost inventory purposes is
   a. $13.   **c.** $17.
   b. $20.   **d.** $27.

2. Gyro has received an offer from a foreign manufacturer to purchase 25,000 gears. Domestic sales would be unaffected by this transaction. If the offer is accepted, variable distribution costs will increase by $1.50 per gear for insurance, shipping, and import duties. The relevant unit cost to a pricing decision on this offer is
   a. $17.00.   **c.** $28.50.
   b. $14.50.   **d.** $18.50.

A company had income of $50,000 using direct costing for a given period. Beginning and ending inventories for that period were 13,000 units and 18,000 units, respectively.

Required:

3. Ignoring income taxes, if the fixed overhead application rate was $2 per unit, what was the income using absorption costing?
   a. $40,000.   **c.** $60,000.
   b. $50,000.   **d.** Cannot be determined from the information given.

The following data apply to Frelm Corporation for a given period:

Total Variable Cost per Unit	$3.50
Contribution Margin (Percentage of Sales)	30%
Breakeven Sales (Present Volume)	$1,000,000

Frelm wants to sell an additional 50,000 units at the same selling price and contribution margin.

Required:

4. By how much can fixed costs increase to generate a gross margin equal to 10 percent of the sales value of the additional 50,000 units to be sold?
   a. $50,000.   **c.** $ 67,500.
   b. $57,500.   **d.** $175,000.

(AICPA adapted)

9.5

Direct and Absorption Costing   The following information is available for Keller Corporation's new product line:

Selling Price per Unit .... $	15
Variable Manufacturing Costs per Unit of Production	8
Total Annual Fixed Manufacturing Costs	25,000
Variable Administrative Costs per Unit of Production	3
Total Annual Fixed Selling and Administrative Expenses	15,000

There was no inventory at the beginning of the year. During the year, 12,500 units were produced and 10,000 units were sold.

Required:
Select the best answer for each of the following items.

1. Assuming Keller uses direct costing, the ending inventory would be
  a. $25,000.   **c.** $27,500.
  b. $32,500.   **d.** $20,000.

2. Assuming Keller uses absorption costing, the ending inventory would be
  a. $32,500.   **c.** $20,000.
  b. $27,500.   **d.** $25,000.

3. Assuming Keller uses direct costing, the total variable costs charged to expense for the year would be
  a. $110,000.   **c.** $117,500.
  b. $100,000.   **d.** $ 80,000.

4. Assuming Keller uses absorption costing, the total fixed costs charged against the current year's operations would be
  a. $35,000.   **c.** $25,000.
  b. $40,000.   **d.** $15,000.

(AICPA adapted)

9.6   *Income Statements*   The Mass Company manufactures and sells a single product. The following data cover the two latest operating years:

	19X3	19X4
Selling Price per Unit	$ 40	$ 40
Sales in Units	25,000	25,000
Opening Inventory in Units	1,000	1,000
Closing Inventory in Units	1,000	5,000
Fixed Manufacturing Costs	$120,000	$120,000
Fixed Selling and Administrative Costs	$ 90,000	$ 90,000
Standard Variable Costs per Unit		
Materials	$10.50	
Direct Labor	$ 9.50	
Variable Overhead	$ 4.00	
Variable Selling and Administrative	$ 1.20	

The denominator activity is 30,000 units a year. Mass Company's accounting records produce direct costing information, and year-end adjustments are made to produce external reports showing absorption costing data. Any variances are charged to Cost of Sales.

Required:
1. Ignoring income taxes, prepare two income statements for 19X4, one under the direct costing method and one under the absorption costing method. Present your answer in good form.
2. Briefly explain why the net income figures computed in part 1 agree or do not agree.
3. Give two advantages and two disadvantages of using direct costing for internal reporting.

(SMA adapted)

9.7

Absorption versus Direct Costing The following annual flexible budget has been prepared for use in making decisions relating to product X:

	100,000 Units	150,000 Units	200,000 Units
Sales Volume	$800,000	$1,200,000	$1,600,000
Manufacturing Costs			
Variable	$300,000	$ 450,000	$ 600,000
Fixed	200,000	200,000	200,000
Total	$500,000	$ 650,000	$ 800,000
Selling and Other Expenses			
Variable	$200,000	$ 300,000	$ 400,000
Fixed	160,000	160,000	160,000
Total	$360,000	$ 460,000	$ 560,000
Income (or Loss)	$(60,000)	$ 90,000	$ 240,000

The 200,000-unit budget has been adopted and will be used for allocating fixed manufacturing costs to units of product X. At the end of the first six months, the following information is available:

	Units
Production	120,000
Sales	60,000

All fixed costs are budgeted and incurred uniformly throughout the year, and all costs incurred coincide with the budget. Overapplied and underapplied fixed manufacturing costs are deferred until year-end. Annual sales have the following seasonal pattern:

	Portion of Annual Sales
First Quarter	10%
Second Quarter	20
Third Quarter	30
Fourth Quarter	40
	100%

Required:

1. The amount of fixed factory costs applied to product X during the first six months under absorption costing would be

 a. Overapplied by $20,000.

 b. Equal to the fixed costs incurred.

 c. Underapplied by $40,000.

 d. Underapplied by $80,000.

 e. None of the above.

2. Reported net income (or loss) for the first six months under absorption costing would be

 a. $160,000.

 b. $80,000.

 c. $40,000.

 d. $(40,000).

 e. None of the above.

3. Reported net income (or loss) for the first six months under direct costing would be

 a. $144,000.

 b. $72,000.

 c. $0.

 d. $(36,000).

 e. None of the above.

4. Assuming that 90,000 units of product X were sold during the first six months and that this is to be used as a basis, the revised budget estimate for the total number of units to be sold during this year would be

    a. 360,000.   **d.** 120,000.

    b. 240,000.   **e.** None of the above.

    c. 200,000.

(AICPA adapted)

9.8   ***Income Statement and the Costing Method***   The XYZ Company manufactures its own brand of cleaner. During 19X3, it had an opening inventory of 10,000 units, a production volume of 20,000 units, and an ending inventory of 18,000 units. The company uses a FIFO actual inventory valuation method. The variable cost per unit is $100 for both the previous and current periods. The fixed manufacturing cost per unit decreased from $25 in the previous period to $20 in the current period. The unit selling price is $500.

Required:

1. Draw up a direct costing income statement.

2. Draw up an absorption costing income statement.

3. Reconcile both results.

9.9   ***Reconciliation of FIFO Profit with Direct Costing Profit***   Zind Inc. records its inventory on a FIFO absorption costing basis. The data for the first three years of operations are as follows:

	Year 1	Year 2	Year 3
Absorption Costing Profits	$30,000	$ 60,000	$100,000
Tons Produced	3,000	4,000	5,000
Tons Sold	2,500	4,000	4,000
Fixed Costs	$60,000	$120,000	$250,000

Required:

1. Compute the direct costing profit for each year.

2. Reconcile the total profits under FIFO absorption and under direct costing for the three years.

9.10   ***Direct and Absorption Costing: Effects of Production and Sales***   The Landish Company had the following operating characteristics in 19X5 and 19X6:

Basic Production Data at Standard Cost

Direct Material	$ 4
Direct Labor	2
Variable Overhead	3
	$ 9
Fixed Overhead ($100,000 ÷ 100,000 Units of Denominator Volume)	1
Total Factory Overhead at Standard	$10

Sales Price: $20 per Unit

Selling and Administrative Expense
    Variable: $2 per Unit
    Fixed: $50,000 per Year

Production and Sales

Statistics (in Units)	19X5	19X6
Beginning Inventory	—	20,000
Production	100,000	120,000
Sales	80,000	130,000
Ending Inventory	20,000	10,000

There were no work-in-process inventories, and fixed production costs incurred were $100,000. The denominator variance is written off directly at year-end as an adjustment to Cost of Goods Sold.

Required:

1. Prepare income statements for the years 19X5 and 19X6 under direct costing and absorption costing.

2. Reconcile the differences in operating incomes.

9.11   ***Direct versus Absorption Costing: Income Statements***   The Quebec Co. Ltd. decided to use direct costing in accounting for its only product. Standard manufacturing costs per unit were as follows:

Materials	$ 5
Direct Labor	4
Variable Overhead	3
	$12

The fixed overhead budget was $160,000, and the company expected to produce 80,000 units during 19X7.

During 19X7, 85,000 units actually were produced, and 75,000 units were sold at $25 each. Actual costs incurred were

Materials Used	$434,000
Direct Labor	350,000
Variable Overhead	250,000
Fixed Overhead	162,000
Variable Selling and Administrative	75,000
Fixed Selling and Administrative	100,000

Required:

1. Prepare a direct costing income statement for 19X7, assuming all variances are charged to the period.

2. What net income would Quebec Co. Ltd. have reported if it had continued to use absorption costing? (An income statement is not required.)

(CGA adapted)

9.12   ***Direct versus Absorption Costing: Income Statements***   The S. T. Shire Company uses direct costing for internal management purposes and absorption costing for external reporting purposes. Thus, at the end of each year, financial information must be converted from direct costing to absorption costing to satisfy external requirements.

At the end of 19X1 the company anticipated that sales would rise 20 percent the next year, and it increased production from 20,000 units to 24,000 units to meet this expected demand. However, economic conditions kept the sales level at 20,000 units for both years.

The following data pertain to 19X1 and 19X2:

	19X1	19X2
Selling Price per Unit	$ 30	$ 30
Sales (Units)	20,000	20,000
Beginning Inventory (Units)	2,000	2,000
Production (Units)	20,000	24,000
Ending Inventory (Units)	2,000	6,000
Unfavorable Labor, Materials, and Variable Overhead Variances (Total)	$ 5,000	$ 4,000

Standard Variable Costs per Unit for 19X1 and 19X2	
Labor	$ 7.50
Materials	4.50
Variable Overhead	3.00
	$15.00

The overhead rate under absorption costing is based on practical plant capacity, which is 30,000 units per year. All variances and underabsorbed or overabsorbed overhead are taken to Cost of Goods Sold. All taxes are to be ignored.

Required:

1. Present the income statement based on direct costing for 19X2.

2. Present the income statement based on absorption costing for 19X2.

3. Explain the difference, if any, in the net income figures. Give the entry necessary to adjust the book figures to the financial statement figure, if one is necessary.

4. The S. T. Shire Company finds it worthwhile to develop its internal financial data on a direct-cost basis. What advantages and disadvantages are attributed to direct costing for internal purposes?

5. There are many who believe that direct costing is appropriate for external reporting and many who oppose its use for external reporting. What arguments for and against the use of direct costing are advanced regarding its use in external reporting?

(CMA adapted)

9.13   *Direct versus Absorption Costing: Income Statements*   During November 19X8, the Delta Co. Ltd. produced 7,000 units. Inventory at November 1, 19X8, was 3,000 units. During November, 9,000 units were sold for $450,000. Delta uses a standard-cost system with the following standard costs per unit:

Materials	$ 6
Direct Labor	14
Variable Overhead	7
Fixed Overhead	5
	$32

Other information available for November 19X8 is as follows:

Variable selling expenses were $2 per unit.

Fixed selling and administrative expenses were $20,000.

Denominator activity was 8,000 units.

Variable variances totaled $5,000 (unfavorable).

An unfavorable fixed overhead spending variance amounted to $2,000.

Required:

1. Prepare an income statement for November 19X8 using direct costing.

2. If Delta had used absorption costing, would the net income have been higher or lower? By how much?

(CGA adapted)

9.14   ***Standard Cost Computations and a Comparison of Absorption and Direct Costing***
Norwood Corporation is considering changing its method of inventory valuation from absorption costing to direct costing and has hired you to determine the effect of the proposed change on the 19X8 financial statements.

The corporation manufactures Gink, which is sold for $20 per unit. Marsh is added before processing starts, and labor and overhead are added evenly during the manufacturing process. Production capacity is budgeted at 110,000 units of Gink annually. The standard costs per unit of Gink are

Marsh (2 Pounds)	$3.00
Labor	6.00
Variable Manufacturing Overhead	1.00
Fixed Manufacturing Overhead	1.10

A process cost system is used employing standard costs. Variances from standard costs are now charged or credited to Cost of Goods Sold. If direct costing were adopted, only variances resulting from variable costs would be charged or credited to Cost of Goods Sold.

Inventory data for 19X8 follow:

	Units	
	January 1	**December 31**
Marsh (Pounds)	50,000	40,000
Work-in-Process		
⅔ Processed	10,000	
⅓ Processed		15,000
Finished Goods	20,000	12,000

During 19X8, 220,000 pounds of Marsh were purchased, and 230,000 pounds were transferred to work-in-process. Also, 110,000 units of Gink were transferred to finished goods. Actual fixed manufacturing overhead during the year was $121,000. There were no variances between standard variable costs and actual variable costs during the year.

Required:

1. Prepare schedules that present the computation of
  a. Equivalent units of production for material.
  b. Number of units sold.
  c. Standard unit costs under direct costing and absorption costing.
  d. Amount, if any, of overapplied or underapplied fixed manufacturing overhead.

2. Prepare a comparative statement of cost of goods sold using standard direct costing and standard absorption costing.

(AICPA adapted)

Table 1   *Eastern Company Statement of Operating Income for the Year Ended October 31, 19X6*

	All Three Products	Product C
Sales	$2,800,150	$350,000
Cost of Sales		
Raw Materials	565,000	80,000
Labor		
Direct	1,250,000	150,000
Indirect	55,000	18,000
Fringe Benefits (15% of Labor)	195,750	25,200
Royalties (1% of Product C Sales)	3,500	3,500
Maintenance and Repairs	6,000	2,000
Factory Supplies	15,000	2,100
Depreciation (Straight-Line)	25,200	7,100
Electrical Power	25,000	3,000
Scrap and Spoilage	4,300	600
Total Cost of Sales	2,144,750	291,500
Gross Profit	$ 655,400	$ 58,500
Selling, General and Administrative Expenses		
Sales Commissions	120,000	15,000
Officers' Salaries	32,000	10,500
Other Wages and Salaries	14,000	5,300
Fringe Benefits (15% of Wages, Salaries, and Commissions)	24,900	4,620
Delivery Expense	79,500	10,000
Advertising Expense	195,100	26,000
Miscellaneous Fixed Expenses	31,900	10,630
Total Selling, General and Administrative Expenses	497,400	82,050
Operating Income (Loss)	$ 158,000	$ (23,550)

9.15   *Eliminating a Product*   The president of Eastern Company wants guidance on the advisability of eliminating product C, one of the company's three similar products, or investing in new machinery to reduce the cost of product C in the hope of reversing product C's operating loss sustained in 19X6. The three similar products are manufactured in a single plant in about the same amount of floor space. The markets in which they are sold are very competitive.

Table 1 shows the condensed statement of operating income for Eastern Company and for product C for the year ended October 31, 19X6.

Required:
Disregard income taxes.

1. Prepare a schedule showing the contribution of product C to the recovery of fixed costs and expenses (marginal income) for the year ended October 31, 19X6. Assume that each element of cost and expense is entirely fixed or variable within the relevant range and that the change in inventory levels has been negligible.

2. Assume that in fiscal 19X6 the variable costs and expenses of product C totaled $297,500 and that its fixed costs and expenses amounted to $75,100. Prepare a schedule computing the breakeven point of product C in terms of annual dollar sales volume. Sales for 19X6 amounted to $350,000.

3. The direct-labor costs of product C could have been reduced by $75,000 and the indirect labor costs by $4,000 by investing an additional $340,000 (financed with 5 percent bonds) in machinery with a ten-year life and an estimated salvage value of $30,000 at the end of the period. However, Eastern Company would have been liable for total severance pay costs of $18,000 (to be amortized over a five-year period), and electrical power costs would have increased $500 annually. Assuming the information given in part 2, prepare a schedule computing the breakeven point of product C in terms of annual dollar sales volume if the additional machinery had been purchased and installed at the beginning of the year.

(AICPA adapted)

9.16   ***Profitability Analysis***   The officers of Bradshaw Company are reviewing the profitability of the company's four products and the potential effect of several proposals for varying the product mix. An excerpt from the income statement and other data follow:

	Totals	Product P	Product Q	Product R	Product S
Sales	$62,600	$10,000	$18,000	$12,600	$22,000
Cost of Goods Sold	44,274	4,750	7,056	13,968	18,500
Gross Profit	$18,326	$ 5,250	$10,944	$(1,368)	$ 3,500
Operating Expenses	12,012	1,990	2,976	2,826	4,220
Income before Income Taxes	$ 6,314	$ 3,260	$ 7,968	$(4,194)	$ (720)
Units Sold		1,000	1,200	1,800	2,000
Sales Price per Unit		$10.00	$15.00	$ 7.00	$11.00
Variable Cost of Goods Sold per Unit		$ 2.50	$ 3.00	$ 6.50	$ 6.00
Variable Operating Expenses per Unit		$ 1.17	$ 1.25	$ 1.00	$ 1.20

Required:
Each of the following proposals is to be considered independently of the other proposals. Consider only the product changes stated in each proposal; the activity of the other products remains stable. Ignore income taxes. Select the best answer for each of the following items:

1. If product R is discontinued, the effect on income will be
   a. A $900 increase.   **d.** A $1,368 increase.
   b. A $4,194 increase.   **e.** None of the above.
   c. A $12,600 decrease.

2. If product R is discontinued and a consequent loss of customers causes a decrease of 200 units in sales of product Q, the total effect on income will be
   a. A $15,600 decrease.   **d.** A $1,250 decrease.
   b. A $2,866 increase.   **e.** None of the above.
   c. A $2,044 increase.

3. If the sales price of product R is increased to $8 and the number of units sold decreases to 1,500, the effect on income will be
   a. A $2,199 decrease.   **d.** A $2,199 increase.
   b. A $600 decrease.   **e.** None of the above.
   c. A $750 increase.

4. The plant in which product R is produced can be utilized to produce a new product, T. The total variable costs and expenses per unit of product T are $8.05, and 1,600 units can be sold at $9.50 each. If product T is introduced and product R is discontinued, the total effect on income will be

   a. A $2,600 increase.
   b. A $2,320 increase.
   c. A $3,220 increase.
   d. A $1,420 increase.
   e. None of the above.

5. Part of the plant in which product P is produced can easily be adapted to the production of product S, but changes in quantities may make changes in sales prices advisable. If production of product P is reduced to 500 units (to be sold at $12 each) and production of product S is increased to 2,500 units (to be sold at $10.50 each), the total effect on income will be

   a. A $1,765 decrease.
   b. A $250 increase.
   c. A $2,060 decrease.
   d. A $1,515 decrease.
   e. None of the above.

6. Production of product P can be doubled by adding a second shift, but higher wages must be paid, increasing the variable cost of goods sold to $3.50 for each of the additional units. If the 1,000 additional units of product P can be sold at $10 each, the total effect on income will be

   a. A $10,000 increase.
   b. A $5,330 increase.
   c. A $6,500 increase.
   d. A $2,260 increase.
   e. None of the above.

(AICPA adapted)

9.17   *Cost Analysis for Managerial Decision Making*   Your client, Ocean Company, manufactures and sells three different products: Ex, Why, and Zee. Projected income statements by product line for the year ended December 31, 19X6, are presented here:

	Ex	Why	Zee	Total
Unit Sales	10,000	500,000	125,000	635,000
Revenues	$ 925,000	$1,000,000	$575,000	$2,500,000
Variable Cost of Units Sold	$ 285,000	$ 350,000	$150,000	$ 785,000
Fixed Cost of Units Sold	304,200	289,000	166,800	760,000
Gross Margin	$ 335,800	$ 361,000	$258,200	$ 955,000
Variable General and Administrative Expenses	$ 270,000	$ 200,000	$ 80,000	$ 550,000
General and Administrative Fixed Expenses	125,800	136,000	78,200	340,000
Income (Loss) before Tax	$ (60,000)	$ 25,000	$100,000	$ 65,000

Production costs are similar for all three products. The fixed general and administrative expenses are allocated to products in proportion to revenues. The fixed cost of units sold is allocated to products by various allocation bases, such as square feet for factory rent, machine hours for repairs, and so forth.

   Ocean management is concerned about the loss for product Ex and is considering two alternative courses of corrective action. Under alternative A, Ocean would purchase some new machinery for the production of product Ex, which would involve an immediate cash outlay of $650,000. Management expects that the new machinery would reduce variable production costs so that total variable costs (cost of units sold and general and administrative expenses) for product Ex would be 52 percent of product Ex revenues. The new machinery would increase total fixed costs allocated to product Ex to $480,000 per year. No additional fixed costs would be allocated to products Why or Zee.

Under alternative B, Ocean would discontinue manufacturing product Ex. Selling prices of products Why and Zee would remain constant. Management expects that product Zee production and revenues would increase by 50 percent. Some of the machinery now devoted to product Ex could be sold at scrap value, which equals its removal costs. The removal of this machinery would reduce the fixed costs allocated to product Ex by $30,000 per year. The remaining fixed costs allocated to product Ex include $155,000 of rent expense per year. The space previously used for product Ex could be rented to an outside organization for $157,500 per year.

Required:
Prepare a schedule analyzing the effect of alternative A and alternative B on projected total Ocean Company income before tax.

(AICPA adapted)

9.18   *Acceptance of an Order*   Day Co. has approached the general manager of the Lightening Division of Strom Company with an order for 100,000 bicycle light generators at $1.48 each. Lightening's price to its regular customers is $1.74.

The Lightening Division, operating at full capacity, costs the generator as follows:

Materials	$0.545
Direct Labor	0.495
Variable Overhead	0.100
Fixed Overhead	0.110
	$1.250

Strom Company, which is operating at 50 percent capacity overall, bases its divisional general managers' bonuses on return on investment and dollar profits.

Day Co. includes these generators in a packaged unit, for which its present costs are

Generator	$1.480
Front Light Unit	0.370
Rear Light Unit	0.130
Mounting Brackets	0.085
Wire and Miscellaneous	0.015
Fixed Overhead	0.100
	$2.180

Required:
Ignore income tax implications.

1. As general manager of Strom's Lightening Division, would you accept the order? Why or why not?

2. Suppose Day Co. offered to purchase the complete packaged unit from Strom Company. The Lightening Division of Strom Company would supply the generator, with Strom's other divisions completing the package. Day Co. would pay its equivalent cost of $2.18. Strom's records show a $2.39 cost for the packaged unit, including $.38 fixed charges. As president of Strom, would you now accept the order? Why or why not?

3. What other factors should Strom's president consider in deciding to accept or reject the order?

(SMA adapted)

9.19   ***Product-Line Analysis***   The following income statement has been prepared for the Wardwell Company:

The Wardwell Company
Income Statement
January 1, 19X5, to March 31, 19X5
(in Thousands of Dollars)

	Total	Product 1	Product 2
Sales	$3,000	$2,500	$ 500
Cost of Sales	2,300	1,900	400
Gross Profit	$ 700	$ 600	$ 100
Administrative Expenses	$ 150	$ 105	$ 45
Selling Expenses	312	156	156
	$ 462	$ 261	$ 201
Net Income (Loss) before Taxes	$ 238	$ 339	$(101)
Income Tax (40%)	95.2	135.6	40.4
Net Income (Loss) after Taxes	$ 142.8	$ 203.4	$ (60.6)

Mr. Wardwell is very disappointed in the performance of product 2, which was launched after an expenditure of $250,000 on research and development ($230,000 is still carried as an asset).

A review of the accounting and other records discloses the following:

Variable manufacturing costs are 60 percent of cost of sales for product 1 and 65 percent for product 2.

Of the total fixed manufacturing cost, 90 percent is direct costs to products 1 and 2, and the remaining 10 percent is allocated equally to each product. Except for this allocation, fixed manufacturing costs for product 2 can be avoided.

Variable selling expenses are 2 percent of sales. Fixed selling expenses increased $60,000 when product 2 was introduced.

The manufacturing equipment used for product 2 has no alternative use and no scrap value.

Opening and closing inventories were equal.

Administrative expenses include

Executive Salaries (Allocated on Sales)	$30,000
Building Expenses (Prorated ⅔ to Product 1 and ⅓ to Product 2)	$45,000

The space used for product 2 can be leased annually for $100,000.

Required:
Prepare an income statement for the first quarter of 19X5 assuming that product 2 had been discontinued on December 31, 19X4. Based only on your income statement, recommend whether or not the product should be continued.

(SMA adapted)

9.20   ***Profit Analysis***   Sun Company, a wholly owned subsidiary of Guardian, Inc., produces and sells three main product lines. The company employs a standard-cost accounting system for record keeping.

At the beginning of 19X4, the president of Sun Company presented its budget to the parent company and accepted a commitment to contribute $15,800 to Guardian's consolidated profit in 19X4. The president has been confident that the year's profit would exceed the budget target, since the monthly sales reports that she has been receiving have shown that sales for the year will exceed budget by 10 percent. The president is both disturbed and confused when the controller presents an adjusted forecast as of November 30, 19X4, indicating that profit will be 11 percent under budget. The two forecasts are presented here:

Sun Company
Forecasts of Operating Results

	Forecasts as of 1/1/X4	11/30/X4
Sales	$268,000	$294,800
Cost of Sales at Standard	212,000ª	233,200
Gross Margin at Standard	$ 56,000	$ 61,600
Overabsorbed (Underabsorbed) Fixed Manufacturing Overhead	—	(6,000)
Gross Margin	$ 56,000	$ 55,600
Selling Expenses	$ 13,400	$ 14,740
Administrative Expenses	26,800	26,800
Total Operating Expenses	$ 40,200	$ 41,540
Earnings before Tax	$ 15,800	$ 14,060

ª Includes fixed manufacturing overhead of $30,000.

There have been no sales price changes or product mix shifts since the January 1, 19X4, forecast. The only cost variance on the income statement is the underabsorbed manufacturing overhead. This arose because the company produced only 16,000 standard machine hours (budgeted machine hours were 20,000) during 19X4 as a result of a shortage of raw materials while its principal supplier was closed by a strike. Fortunately, Sun Company's finished goods inventory was large enough to fill all sales orders received.

Required:
1. Analyze and explain why the profit has declined in spite of increased sales and good control over costs.

2. What plan, if any, could Sun Company adopt during December to improve its reported profit at year-end? Explain your answer.

3. Illustrate and explain how Sun Company could adopt an alternative internal cost reporting procedure that would avoid the confusing effect of the present procedure.

4. Would the alternative procedure described in part 3 be acceptable to Guardian, Inc., for financial reporting purposes? Explain your answer.

(CMA adapted)

9.21   *Plant Expansion*   Aurora Manufacturing Limited produces and sells one product. During 19X4 the company manufactured and sold 50,000 units at $25 per unit. Existing production capacity is 60,000 units per year.

In formulating the 19X5 budget, management is faced with a number of decisions concerning product pricing and output. The following information is available. A market survey shows that the sales volume is heavily dependent on the selling price. For each $1 drop in selling price, sales volume would increase by 10,000 units.

The company's expected cost structure for 19X5 is as follows:

Fixed Cost (Regardless of Production or Sales Activities) $360,000
Variable Cost per Unit (Including Production, Selling,
    and Administrative Expenses) $16 per Unit

To increase the annual capacity from the present 60,000 units to 90,000 units, additional investment for plant, building, equipment, and so forth of $200,000 would be necessary. The estimated average life of the additional investment would be ten years. (The investment for expansion of less than 30,000 additional units of capacity would be only slightly less than $200,000.)

Required:
Indicate, giving reasons, what the production level and selling price of the product should be for the coming year. Also indicate if the company should approve the plant expansion. Ignore income tax considerations and the time value of money. Show your calculations.

(SMA adapted)

9.22   *Cost Analysis for Managerial Decision Making*   The management of the Forth Company is examining various alternatives for the production and distribution of its single product, a packaged fertilizer. The results of 19X5 operations follow:

	Eastern Plant	Central Plant	Western Plant	Total
Sales ($5 per Unit)	$500,000	$600,000	$700,000	$1,800,000
Variable Expenses	$250,000	$300,000	$350,000	$ 900,000
Fixed Expenses	80,000	100,000	90,000	270,000
Allocated Home Office Expenses[a]	20,000	24,000	28,000	72,000
Total Expenses	$350,000	$424,000	$468,000	$1,242,000
Net Income before Tax	$150,000	$176,000	$232,000	$ 558,000

[a] Allocation is based on sales dollar value.

The lease renewal for the Central Plant calls for an increase of $50,000 in the annual rent. In addition, a 10 percent wage increase for direct labor at the Central Plant was effective on January 1, 19X6. Based on the Central Plant's 19X5 production, the wage increase will cost $12,000.

The Central Plant supplies the export market. If this plant were closed, export sales could be met by one of the following alternatives:

1. With the expansion of capacity at the Eastern Plant, fixed costs would increase by 50 percent, and shipping costs on export sales would increase by $.50 per unit.

2. A long-term agreement with a competing manufacturer is also possible. A competitor would agree to fill Forth's export commitments and pay Forth a commission of 18 percent of the gross export sales value.

Required:
1. Prepare a schedule showing Forth's net income before tax under each of the two alternatives given if the Central Plant is closed.
Notes:
    a. A formal income statement is not required. You may start your schedule with the

reported 19X5 net income before taxes and make the necessary adjustments to arrive at the revised net income for each alternative.

b. Assume that the costs of shutdown of the Central Plant are exactly offset by the proceeds of disposal of the plant.

2. Management is considering a third alternative: keep the Central Plant operating in 19X6 and increase export selling prices. Looking at the operations of the Central Plant and allowing for 19X6 cost increases, what selling price per unit would yield an income of 30 percent of sales before taxes and allocated home office expenses for the Central Plant?

(SMA adapted)

9.23   ***Make-or-Buy Decision and Relevant Cost Analysis***   The Vernom Corporation, which produces and sells to wholesalers a highly successful line of summer lotions and insect repellents, has decided to diversify in order to stabilize sales throughout the year. A natural area for the company to consider is the production of winter lotions and creams to prevent dry and chapped skin.

After considerable research, a winter products line has been developed. However, because of the conservative nature of the company's management, Vernom's president has decided to introduce only one of the new products for this coming winter. If the product is a success, further expansion in future years will be initiated.

The product selected, Chap-off, is a lip balm that will be sold in a lipstick-type tube. The product will be sold to wholesalers in boxes of twenty-four tubes for $8 per box. Because of available capacity, no additional fixed charges will be incurred to produce the product. However, a $100,000 fixed charge will be absorbed by the product to allocate a fair share of the company's present fixed costs to the new product.

Using the sales and production estimate of 100,000 boxes of Chap-off as the standard volume, the accounting department developed the following costs per box:

Direct Labor	$2.00
Direct Materials	3.00
Total Overhead	1.50
Total	$6.50

Vernom has approached a cosmetics manufacturer to discuss the possibility of purchasing tubes for Chap-off. The purchase price of the empty tubes from the cosmetics manufacturer would be $.90 per twenty-four tubes. If the Vernom Corporation accepts the purchase proposal, it is estimated that direct-labor and variable overhead costs would be reduced by 10 percent, and direct-material costs would be reduced by 20 percent.

Required:

1. Should the Vernom Corporation make or buy the tubes? Show calculations to support your answer.

2. What would be the maximum purchase price acceptable to the Vernom Corporation for the tubes? Support your answer with an appropriate explanation.

3. Instead of sales of 100,000 boxes, revised estimates show sales volume at 125,000 boxes. At this new volume, additional equipment at an annual rental of $10,000 must be acquired to manufacture the tubes. However, this incremental cost would be the only additional fixed cost required, even if sales increased to 300,000 boxes (the goal for the third year of production). Under these circumstances, should the Vernom Corporation make or buy the tubes? Show calculations to support your answer.

4. The company has the option of making and buying at the same time. What would be your answer to part 3 if this alternative were considered? Show calculations to support your answer.

5. What nonquantifiable factors should the Vernom Corporation consider in determining whether it should make or buy the lipstick tubes?

(CMA adapted)

9.24   *Profitability Analysis for Each of Three Segmental Operations*   Ruidoso Ski Lodge operates a ski shop, restaurant, and lodge during the 120-day ski season from November 15 to March 15. The proprietor is considering changing the operation and keeping the lodge open all year.

Results of the operations for the year ended March 15, 19X9, were as follows:

	Ski Shop		Restaurant		Lodge	
	Amount	Percentage	Amount	Percentage	Amount	Percentage
Revenue	$27,000	100%	$40,000	100%	$108,000	100%
Costs						
Cost of Goods Sold . .	$14,850	55	$24,000	60		
Supplies	1,350	5	4,000	10	$ 7,560	7
Utilities	270	1	1,200	3	2,160	2
Salaries	1,620	6	12,000	30	32,400	30
Insurance	810	3	800	2	9,720	9
Property Taxes on						
Building	540	2	1,600	4	6,480	6
Depreciation	1,080	4	2,000	5	28,080	26
Total Costs	$20,520	76%	$45,600	114%	$86,400	80%
Net Income (or Loss) . .	$ 6,480	24%	$(5,600)	(14)%	$21,600	20%

The lodge has one hundred rooms, and the rate from November 15 to March 15 is $10 per day for one or two persons. The occupancy rate from November 15 to March 15 is 90 percent.

Ski shop and restaurant sales vary in direct proportion to room occupancy.

For the ski shop and restaurant, the cost of goods sold, supplies, and utilities vary in direct proportion to sales. For the lodge, supplies and utilities vary in direct proportion to room occupancy.

The ski shop, restaurant, and lodge are located in the same building. Depreciation on the building is charged to the lodge. The ski shop and restaurant are charged with depreciation on equipment only. The full cost of the restaurant equipment became fully depreciated on March 15, 19X9, but the equipment has a remaining useful life of three years. The equipment can be sold for $1,200, but it will be worthless in three years. All depreciation is computed by the straight-line method.

Insurance premiums are for annual coverage for public liability and fire insurance on the building and equipment. All building insurance is charged to the lodge.

Salaries are the minimum necessary to keep each facility open and are for the ski season only except for the lodge security guard, who is paid $5,400 per year.

Two alternatives are being considered for the future operation of Ruidoso Ski Lodge. The proprietor believes that during the ski season the restaurant should be closed because "it does not have enough revenue to cover its out-of-pocket costs." It is estimated that lodge occupancy would drop to 80 percent of capacity if the restaurant were closed during the ski season. The space utilized by the restaurant would be used as a lounge for lodge guests.

As an alternative, the proprietor is considering keeping the lodge open from March 15 to November 15. The ski shop would be converted into a gift shop if the lodge were operated during this period, with conversion costs each year of $1,000 in March and $1,000 in November. It is estimated that revenues from the gift shop would be the same per room occupied as revenues from the ski shop, that variable costs would be in the same ratio to revenues, and that all other costs would be the same for the gift shop as for the ski shop. The occupancy rate of the lodge at a room rate of $7 per day is estimated at 50 percent during the period from March 15 to November 15, whether or not the restaurant is operated.

Required:
Ignore income taxes and use thirty days per month for computational purposes.

1. Prepare a projected income statement for the ski shop and lodge from November 15, 19X9, to March 15, 19Y0, assuming the restaurant is closed during this period and all facilities are closed during the remainder of the year.

2. Assume that all facilities will continue to be operated during the four-month period of November 15 to March 15 of each year.
  a. Assume that the lodge is operated during the eight months from March 15 to November 15. Prepare an analysis that indicates the projected marginal income or loss of operating the gift shop and lodge during this eight-month period.
  b. Compute the minimum room rate that should be charged to allow the lodge to break even during the eight months from March 15 to November 15, assuming the gift shop and restaurant are not operated during this period.

(AICPA adapted)

9.25   ***Contribution Margin and Relevant Cost Analysis***   The Justa Corporation produces and sells three products, A, B, and C, which are sold in a local market and a regional market. At the end of the first quarter of the current year, the following income statement has been prepared:

	Total	**Local**	**Regional**
Sales	$1,300,000	$1,000,000	$300,000
Cost of Goods Sold	1,010,000	775,000	235,000
Gross Margin	$ 290,000	$ 225,000	$ 65,000
Selling Expenses	$ 105,000	$ 60,000	$ 45,000
Administrative Expenses	52,000	40,000	12,000
	$ 157,000	$ 100,000	$ 57,000
Net Income	$ 133,000	$ 125,000	$ 8,000

Management has expressed special concern about the regional market because of the extremely poor return on sales. This market was entered a year ago because of excess capacity. It was originally believed that the return on sales would improve with time, but after a year no noticeable improvement can be seen from the results as reported in the quarterly statement.

In attempting to decide whether to eliminate the regional market, management has gathered the following information:

	Products		
	A	**B**	**C**
Sales	$500,000	$400,000	$400,000
Variable Manufacturing Expenses as a Percentage of Sales	60%	70%	60%
Variable Selling Expenses as a Percentage of Sales	3%	2%	2%

Sales by Markets

Product	Local	Regional
A	$400,000	$100,000
B	300,000	100,000
C	300,000	100,000

All administrative expenses and fixed manufacturing expenses are common to the three products, and the two markets are fixed for the period. The remaining selling expenses are fixed for the period and separable by market. All fixed expenses are based upon a prorated yearly amount.

Required:

1. Prepare the quarterly income statement showing contribution margins by markets.

2. Assuming there are no alternative uses for the Justa Corporation's present capacity, would you recommend dropping the regional market? Why or why not?

3. Prepare the quarterly income statement showing contribution margins by products.

4. It is believed that a new product can be ready for sale next year if the Justa Corporation decides to go ahead with continued research. The new product can be produced by simply converting equipment presently used in producing product C. This conversion will increase fixed costs by $10,000 per quarter. What must be the new product's minimum contribution margin per quarter to make the changeover financially feasible?

(CMA adapted)

9.26   *Contribution Approach to Pricing*   E. Berg and Sons builds custom-made pleasure boats that range in price from $10,000 to $250,000. For the past thirty years, Ed Berg, Sr., has determined the selling price of each boat by estimating the costs of material, labor, and a prorated portion of overhead, and adding 20 percent to these estimated costs.

For example, he determined a recent price quotation as follows:

Direct Materials	$ 5,000
Direct Labor	8,000
Overhead	2,000
	$15,000
Plus 20%	3,000
Selling Price	$18,000

He determined the overhead figure by estimating total overhead costs for the year and allocating them at 25 percent of direct-labor costs.

If a customer rejected the price and business was slack, Ed Berg, Sr., would often be willing to reduce his markup to as little as a 5 percent markup over estimated costs. Thus, the average markup for the year is estimated at 15 percent.

Ed Berg, Jr., just completed a course on pricing, and he believes the firm could use some of the techniques discussed in the course. The course emphasized the contribution margin approach to pricing, and Ed Berg, Jr., feels such an approach would be helpful in determining the selling prices of the custom-made pleasure boats.

Total overhead, which includes selling and administrative expenses for the year, has been estimated at $150,000, of which $90,000 is fixed and the remainder is variable in direct proportion to direct labor.

Required:

1. Assume the customer in the example rejected the $18,000 quotation as well as a $15,750 quotation (5 percent markup) during a slack period. The customer countered with a $15,000 offer.

    a. What is the difference in net income for the year between accepting or rejecting the customer's offer?

    b. What is the minimum selling price Ed Berg, Jr., could have quoted without reducing or increasing net income?

2. What advantages does the contribution margin approach to pricing have over the approach used by Ed Berg, Sr.?

3. What pitfalls are there, if any, to contribution margin pricing?

(CMA adapted)

9.27   ***Effect of Changed Costs and Selling Price on Profit***   The Dawn Mining Company mines selum, a commonly used mineral. The company's report of operations follows:

Dawn Mining Company
Report of Operations
for the Years Ended December 31, 19X2 and 19X3

	19X2	19X3	Increase (Decrease)
Net Sales	$ 840,000	$891,000	$ 51,000
Cost of Goods Sold	945,000	688,500	(256,500)
Gross Profit (Loss)	$(105,000)	$202,500	$ 307,500

The following information pertains to the company's operations:

The sales price of selum was increased from $8 per ton to $11 per ton on January 1, 19X3.

New mining machinery was placed in operation on January 1, 19X3, that reduced the cost of mining from $9 per ton to $8.50 per ton.

There was no change in ending inventories that were valued on the LIFO basis.

Required:

1. Prepare an analysis that accounts for the change in the gross profit of the Dawn Mining Company. The analysis should account for the effects of the changes in price, volume, and volume-price factors upon sales and cost of goods sold.

2. Assume that the inventory was carried at FIFO and consisted of 10,000 tons at both the beginning and the end of the year. How would this alter the 19X3 statement?

(AICPA adapted)

9.28   ***Cost-Plus Contract***   In January 19X4, the Graystone Electronics Company was awarded a fixed-price incentive by the federal government. Provisions of the contract include the following:

1. The total contract price of $780,000 includes a target cost of $700,000 and an estimated profit of $80,000.

2. The incentive clause states that the total adjusted price (final contract price) shall be established by adding to the total allowed cost an allowance for profit determined as follows:

When the Total Allowed Cost Is	The Allowance for Profit Is
Equal to the target cost	Total target profit
Greater than the target cost	Total target profit less 20 percent of the amount by which the allowed costs exceed the target cost
Less than the target cost	Total target profit plus 20 percent of the amount by which the allowed costs are less than the target cost

3. In no event shall the adjusted price exceed a ceiling of $810,000.

Graystone assigned the following costs to the contract:

Direct Materials	$200,000
Direct Labor	240,000
Overhead	300,000
Total	$740,000

However, based on past experience, management believes that the government will disallow the following items included in the computations:

One percent of overhead costs.

An additional $1,000 of depreciation on special equipment sold at a profit after the contract was completed.

Direct-labor costs of $4,000 that are attributed to idle time.

Cash discounts of $2,000 that Graystone failed to take on materials charged to the project. The company treats cash discounts, when taken, as a reduction of costs.

Required:
1. Based on the provisions of the contract, prepare a graph illustrating the relationship between allowed costs and revenues. Label the vertical axis "Allowed Costs and Revenues (000)," and label the horizontal axis "Allowed Costs (000)."

2. Determine the total adjusted price (allowed cost plus profit) of the contract.

3. Determine Graystone's profit or loss on the contract, as Graystone would record it on its books.

(AICPA adapted)

9.29   *Product Pricing: Revenue and Profit Maximization*

1. Determine the price and quantity for which revenue is maximized in the following two cases:
   a. If the price function $= (12 - x)^{1/2}$ for $0 \leq x \leq 12$.
   b. If the price function $= 15e^{-x/3}$ or $0 \leq x \leq 8$.

2. Determine the maximum profit for the following two cases:
   a. If the price function is $p = 26 - 2x - 4x^2$ and the average cost of producing and selling the product is $\bar{y} = x + 8$.

b. If the price function is $p = 28 - 5x$ and the average cost of producing and selling the product is $\bar{y} = x + 4$.

3. Determine the maximum profit and the value of the tax rate for which tax revenue is maximized in the following case:

Price function: $p = 20 - 4x$.

Average cost: $\bar{y} = 2$.

> *Cost Allocation at best is loaded with assumptions and in many cases highly arbitrary methods of apportionment are employed in practice. Certainly it is wise not to take the results of the usual process of internal cost consumption too seriously.*[1]

The nature of cost allocation has not changed significantly since this statement was made in the 1940s. The methods used are still arbitrary and their utility open to question. In fact, in two American Accounting Association studies, A. L. Thomas has argued against allocations in general because they are not only arbitrary, but also "incorrigible" or incapable of verification.[2]

In spite of these criticisms and limitations, in practice costs continue to be allocated to serve a variety of needs, such as inventory value determination, income determination, price and production determination, and meeting regulatory requirements. Various reports filed with the Securities and Exchange Commission require that joint costs be allocated. Similarly, when manufacturing firms deal with the government for contracts, they must adhere to a set of standards in arriving at a cost-plus contract figure. The United States has established the Cost Accounting Standards Board to establish cost accounting procedures for such firms. In addition, to avoid price discrimination among classes of customers, a firm must justify its actions based on cost data. Joint cost allocation is also required to facilitate the approval of bids on commercial contracts and contract negotiations. It is also useful in labor negotiations.

Cost allocation involves tracing and assigning costs to specific cost objects for internal reporting and for aiding in decision making within the firm. In general, a cause-and-effect relationship between cost and variations in activity level is the criterion for allocation. Direct costs such as material and labor are good examples of cause-and-effect

---

[1] W. J. Vatter, "Limitations of Overhead Allocation," *Accounting Review* (April 1945), pp. 163–176.
[2] A. L. Thomas, *Studies in Accounting Research No. 3*, "The Allocation Problem in Financial Accounting Theory" (Sarasota, Fla.: American Accounting Association, 1969); and A. L. Thomas, *Studies in Accounting Research No. 9*, "The Allocation Problem: Part 2," (Sarasota, Fla.: American Accounting Association, 1974).

relationships. However, this direct relationship between cost and cost object is not always apparent due to the joint nature of costs.

The joint cost problem of allocation is observable in accounting for overhead and for common product costs. This chapter fully discusses these two problems and emphasizes the different cost allocation methods used in practice and in the related literature.

10.1   ACCOUNTING FOR OVERHEAD

As discussed in chapter 2, *overhead* refers to the operating costs other than direct labor and direct material. It includes all costs with an indirect relationship to the cost object. Thus, overhead can be associated with the cost object only through a process of allocation. Before being allocated, overhead is distributed to the various departments; after being allocated, it is applied to the products. In other words, three steps are required for recording overhead: *cost distribution*, *cost allocation*, and *cost absorption* or *application*. Costs are first *distributed* to the corresponding departments, hence establishing responsibility. The service departments' costs then are *allocated* to various operating departments, thereby insuring proper matching of costs and cost objects. Finally, the costs are *applied* to the product, which insures product costing, inventory valuation, and income determination. For the sake of clarity in this discussion, cost distribution will be examined first, then cost application and, finally, cost allocation.

10.1.1   Overhead Distribution

Any transaction can be recorded using both the general and subsidiary ledgers, as discussed in chapter 8. Accordingly, overhead distribution takes place using first the subsidiary ledger accounts and, second, the general ledger accounts.

In the subsidiary ledger accounts, the overhead distribution takes place in the departmental cost ledgers. These ledgers are set up for each department and include as many columns as the number of detailed accounts required. For example, assume the indirect labor incurred was as follows:

Service Department I $100
Operating Department I   200
Operating Department II   200

Indirect material issued was used as follows:

Service Department I $200
Operating Department I   300
Operating Department II   300

These transactions will be recorded in both the Indirect Labor and Indirect Material columns of each of the three departments, as illustrated in Table 10.1. Notice that each departmental cost ledger includes a column for allocation from other departments, whether producing or service departments, and other columns for the other possible overhead items such as depreciation, cost, repairs, and so forth.

In the general ledger, a summary entry is made in the corresponding accounts: a debit of $1,300 to the manufacturing overhead control accounts and a credit to the appropriate accounts (Cash, Accounts Payable, or Prepaid Expenses). Notice that the information is "pooled" in the general ledger, while at least two classifications are provided in the sub-

Table 10.1   *Subsidiary Cost Ledgers*

Service Department

Indirect Material	Indirect Labor	Allocation from Other Departments	(Other Columns for Other Overhead Items)
$200	$100		

Operating Department I

Indirect Material	Indirect Labor	Allocation from Other Departments	(Other Columns for Other Overhead Items)
$300	$200		

Operating Department II

Indirect Material	Indirect Labor	Allocation from Other Departments	(Other Columns for Other Overhead Items)
$300	$200		

sidiary ledger: a natural classification and a departmental classification. Other refinements are possible in the subsidiary ledgers.

The example in this section covered only the indirect department charges that can be associated and charged directly to a given department. In most cases, however, indirect expenses incurred benefit more than one department and should be distributed in proportion to the services used. The selection of the distribution bases is important; however, it is also arbitrary, given the state of the art. Among the more likely choices for a distribution base are the following:

Type of Overhead	Distribution Bases
Power, Heat, and Cooling	Square Footage, Rated Horsepower Hours, Cubic Volume of Space Used
Factory Rent	Square Footage
Inspection	Number of Units Completed
Depreciation—Buildings	Square Footage
Superintendence	Number of Employees
Lighting	Kilowatt Hours or Number of Bulbs
Telephone and Telegraph	Number of Telephones or Number of Employees
Depreciation—Equipment	Number of Operating Hours
Property Tax	Square Footage
Worker's Compensation Insurance	Departmental Payroll
Freight In	Materials Used
Building Repairs	Square Footage

Other alternatives may exist and should be considered to insure equity and fairness through allocation. In general, firms can elect to distribute the pooled overhead over a single basis.

10.1.2   *Overhead Absorption (Application)*

Assuming first that overhead has been distributed to the various departments and second that the service department overhead costs have been allocated to the various operating departments, the next step is to apply the overhead to the various work-in-process inventories.

Overhead is applied to the products on the basis of a predetermined overhead rate computed as follows:

$$\text{Predetermined overhead rate} = \frac{\text{Estimated overhead for the cost period}}{\text{Estimated level of activity for the cost period}}.$$

The cost period for the determination of the predetermined overhead rate is generally one year, although it may be different. The application of overhead to the job-order cost sheets or the process summary reports in the subsidiary ledgers and to the Work-in-Process in the general ledger was illustrated in chapter 8. This chapter concentrates on the distribution base (*capacity index*) and the activity level (*capacity level*) to be used.

Capacity Index
Given that the cost object in overhead allocation is the product, the capacity index, or base that offers the best physical association with the product, could be the units of production, direct-labor hours, direct-labor dollars, machine hours, or direct-material dollars.

No specific rule exists for the choice of the optimal allocation base, but the actual situation can be used as a determinant. The following rules can be proposed:

1. Where only one product is manufactured, the units of production method of allocation is adequate. If the firm manufactures several products that are alike except for one characteristic such as weight or volume, an allocation method based on the weights of the units is more satisfactory than the units of production method.

2. Where the departmental tasks are heavily automated, machine labor hours or machine labor dollars can be chosen.

3. Where the departmental tasks include a large proportion of human assembly work, direct-labor hours or direct-labor dollars can be chosen.

4. Where the allocation base information is readily available, it should be assigned first priority.

5. Where the direct material constitutes a major part of the input mix, direct-material dollars can be chosen.

These are not normative rules; each situation should dictate to the cost accountant the allocation base most easily traceable to the product according to such criteria as information availability, accuracy, and reliability. Note, however, that using the estimation techniques presented in chapter 3 (especially least squares regression analysis), each capacity index could be regressed against overhead. The one providing the largest coefficient of determination would be selected as the best capacity index.

Capacity Level
The capacity size, or production capability of a firm, usually can be classified as practical (or attainable) capacity, normal (or average) capacity, expected annual capacity, or actual capacity.

The *theoretical (or ideal) capacity* represents the maximum level of production at which a firm can operate efficiently, assuming an absence of human or engineering inefficiencies. It represents 100 percent of the firm's capacity.

The *practical (or attainable) capacity* represents a firm's maximum level of production with sufficient allowances for normal human and engineering inefficiencies. Allowances for unavoidable work stoppage for repairs, strikes, unreliable material, vacations, and other factors reduce the theoretical capacity to a practical capacity. In general, a firm's practical capacity levels range from 75 to 85 percent of its theoretical capacity.

The *normal (or average) capacity* represents the production level necessary for a firm to satisfy average commercial demands or sales over a period long enough to cover cyclical, seasonal, and trend variations. It provides a trade-off between the technical capacity of a firm and the sales demand, and it usually spans several periods and encompasses past, present, and future ones. Thus, long-term management inefficiencies reduce the practical capacity to a normal capacity. In other words, management's failure to account for variations in sales demand reduces the practical capacity to a normal capacity.

The *expected annual capacity* represents an estimate of a firm's production level for the actual period as defined by the planning process. It can also be called the *master-budgeted capacity*. Thus, allowances for the factors that cause production to vary from one year to another change the normal capacity to an expected annual capacity.

Finally, the *actual capacity* represents the level of production attained in the actual period. Allowances for the forecast errors change the expected annual capacity to an actual capacity.

Given the differences in these measures of capacity level, one can expect wide differences in the overhead applied. Consequently, the choice of an allocation base may center on the nature of overapplied or underapplied overhead the accountant desires to obtain. For example, a choice of the expected annual capacity, based on the rationale that sales do not fluctuate considerably from year to year, would enable the association of the incurrence of an overapplied or underapplied overhead with short-term economic or managerial factors. Similarly, a choice of the normal capacity, based on the rationale that sales are affected by cyclical, seasonal, and trend variations, would associate the overapplied or underapplied overhead not only with short-term factors, but with medium-term factors as well.

In general, the normal capacity is considered a good trade-off between the rigidity imposed by the theoretical or practical capacity and the wide fluctuations that can be generated by the use of the expected annual capacity or actual capacity. When normal capacity is used, the predetermined overhead rate can be referred to as a *normalized overhead rate*.

The computation of the predetermined overhead rate under the various expressions of capacity is illustrated in the following table:

	Theoretical Capacity	Practical Capacity	Normal Capacity	Expected Annual Capacity	Actual Capacity
Percentage of Plant Use	100%	80%	70%	60%	50%
Direct-Labor Hours	10,000 Hrs.	8,000 Hrs.	7,000 Hrs.	6,000 Hrs.	5,000 Hrs.
Budgeted Manufacturing Overhead					
Fixed	$ 8,400	$ 8,400	$ 8,400	$ 8,400	$ 8,400
Variable	5,000	4,000	3,500	3,000	2,500
Total	$13,400	$12,400	$11,900	$11,400	$10,900
Variable Overhead Rate	$0.84	$1.05	$1.20	$1.40	$1.68
Fixed Overhead Rate	0.50	0.50	0.50	0.50	0.50
Total Overhead Rate	$1.34	$1.55	$1.70	$1.90	$2.18

Budget overhead formula = $8,400 + 0.5x$, where x is direct-labor hours.

From this schedule, the following observations can be made:

1. The overhead absorbed by Work-in-Process using a total overhead rate and based on actual activity is

Using theoretical capacity: $1.34 \times 5,000$ hrs. $= \$ 6,700.$

Using practical capacity: $1.55 \times 5,000$ hrs. $= \$ 7,750.$

Using normal capacity: $1.70 \times 5,000$ hrs. $= \$ 8,500.$

Using expected annual capacity: $1.90 \times 5,000$ hrs. $= \$ 9,500.$

Using actual capacity: $2.18 \times 5,000$ hrs. $= \$10,900.$

The large difference in the applied overhead rate indicates the importance of the choice of a capacity level best suited to a specific situation and managerial expectations.

2. The total overhead rate can be separated into a variable overhead rate and a fixed overhead rate. While the variable overhead rate remains unchanged, the fixed overhead rate tends to change from one expression of capacity to another. The absorption or application of the fixed overhead, therefore, should influence the selection of the capacity level. Two solutions, however, are possible. A budget formula can be used for the application of overhead. In this example, the formula is $\$8,400 + 0.5x$, where x is direct-labor hours used. Another solution, advanced in chapter 9, is to treat the fixed manufacturing overhead as a period cost rather than a product cost.

3. Although this example uses a total factorywide overhead rate, for accuracy some firms elect to use departmental overhead rates. The procedures and problems of overhead application are the same, except they may differ from one department to another and thus may be more detailed.

10.1.3   *Overhead Allocation*

Principles of Overhead Allocation
Firms generally have service departments in addition to producing or operating departments. By definition, the producing or operating department is primarily involved in the actual manufacturing process. A service department is not involved directly in any manufacturing process but provides viable services or assistance to the manufacturing process. Overhead of service departments includes the cafeteria; the purchasing, payroll, cost accounting, personnel, medical, maintenance, power, heat, and water departments; the repair shop, the production planning and control, the toolroom, the stores, and so forth. Because these departments are not directly associated with a product, there is no way of applying their costs directly to a product through a predetermined overhead rule. Instead, the service departments' costs are allocated to other departments (service and/or producing) in proportion to the amount of services rendered to those departments before the application of total manufacturing overhead to the products. This allocation of service department costs to other departments and the application of manufacturing overhead to products is illustrated in Figure 10.1.

The allocation of service department costs to operating departments is as follows:

1. The budgeted service department costs are established for each service department.

2. A reallocation base is determined.

3. A reallocation rate is computed:

Figure 10.1   Allocating Service Department Costs

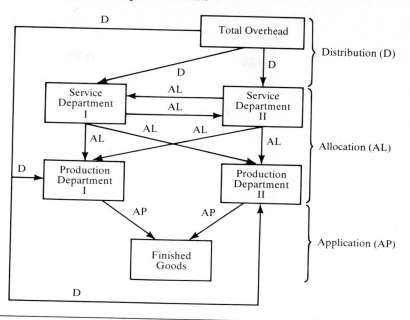

$$\text{Reallocation rate} = \frac{\text{Budgeted service department cost}}{\text{Reallocation base}}.$$

4. The service department costs are reallocated to each producing department on the basis of their proportional use of the services provided, as measured in terms of the reallocation base.

For example, suppose a firm's medical services are allocated to the two production departments on the basis of the number of their employees. The budgeted-cost behavior pattern of the service department is $20,000 plus $1 per employee operating in departments I and II. In January, the firm had 2,000 employees, three-fourths of them employed in department I and one-fourth in department II. When the allocation procedures are applied to service department costs,

1. The budgeted service department costs are equal to $22,000 [$20,000 + ($1 × 2,000)].

2. The reallocation base is equivalent to 2,000 employees.

3. The reallocation rate is equal to $22,000 ÷ 2,000 = $11 per employee.

4. The service department costs are reallocated as follows:

Department I: $\left(\dfrac{2,000 \times 3}{4}\right) \times \$11 = \$16,500$

Department II: $\left(\dfrac{2,000 \times 1}{4}\right) \times \$11 = \$\ 5,500$

Total service department costs $= \$22,000$.

Although straightforward, this principle of allocating service department costs is subject to the improvements described in the following paragraphs.

Whenever possible, it is conceptually more appropriate to separate the cost allocation rate for variable and fixed costs and to allocate the costs by behavior. By definition, fixed costs are incurred to provide a service capacity based on the needs of the operating departments, while variable costs are a function of the actual activity base. Consequently, it is more appropriate to allocate the fixed costs on the basis of the "normal" capacity to serve and the variable costs on the basis of the actual services used. Accordingly, if in the previous example the service departments had provided a basic maximum capacity to serve other departments with the assumption that department I would employ 1,600 employees and department II, 400 employees, the fixed costs would have been allocated to the two departments on the basis of the capacity to serve, as follows:

$$\text{Department I: } \frac{\$20,000 \times 1,600}{2,000} = \$16,000.$$

$$\text{Department II: } \frac{\$20,000 \times 400}{2,000} = \$4,000.$$

The variable costs would have been allocated to the two departments on the basis of the services utilized:

Department I: $\$1 \times 1,500 = \$1,500.$

Department II: $\$1 \times 500 = \$500.$

The total costs allocated would have been

Department I: $\$16,000 + \$1,500 = \$17,500$

Department II: $\$4,000 + \$500 = \$4,500$
Total service department costs $= \$22,000$.

Whenever possible, it is advisable also to avoid a reallocation of actual costs rather than budgeted costs. Thus, reallocation of the actual costs may result in imputing the inefficiencies of the service department to the producing departments. Using the previous example, assume that the actual service department costs were $30,000 because of inefficiencies and uncontrollable price changes. Reallocating the actual costs on the basis of the actual hours would lead to the following results:

$$\text{Department I: } \frac{\$30,000 \times 1,500}{2,000} = \$22,500$$

$$\text{Department II: } \frac{\$30,000 \times 500}{2,000} = \$7,500$$
Actual service department costs $= \$30,000$.

The following arguments can be advanced against these allocation procedures:

1. They result in a reallocation of the inefficiencies of the service department costs to the operating departments.

2. One department may be heavily penalized for a greater use of the services. In this example, department I has a greater proportion of costs solely because it uses more employees.

Allocation Bases

The choice of an appropriate allocation base facilitates the allocation of service department costs. A well-defined relationship between the activity of the operating departments and the services provided by the service department should guide the selection of the allocation base. In general, cause-and-effect relationships are preferred for cost allocation. The main criteria for determining such relationships used in practice and also advocated in the literature include the criterion of origin, the criterion of use, the criterion of facilities provided, the criterion of ability, and the criterion of fairness.

The *criterion of origin* favors the allocation of costs on the basis of their physical identification with the operating departments. This criterion is more applicable to overhead that does not tend to be organized in service centers.

The *criterion of use* allocates costs on the basis of the actual use or actual benefits received. This criterion implies that the cost of the services is related to the actual use, which may not necessarily be the case.

Using the *criterion of facilities provided*, costs are allocated on the basis of the estimated use of facilities rather than their actual use. This criterion of estimated use rather than actual use is more equitable in the sense that it emphasizes the capacity to serve rather than the actual performance.

The *criterion of ability* favors allocating costs on the basis of the ability of the operating departments to bear or to recover costs, such as allocation on the basis of sales or revenue. From a logical point of view, this criterion does not constitute an adequate criterion of a cause-and-effect relationship in spite of its popularity in practice.

Finally, the *criterion of fairness* favors the allocation of costs on the basis of equitable relationships. In other words, the amount allocated to each operating department should be reasonable enough to be understood and accepted by the managers of each department.

Although these criteria seem arbitrary, they provide possible choices for different actual situations. Their relative merit should be ascertained by the relative ease they provide in making an allocation.

The following general observations apply to everyday allocation procedures:

1. Criteria for overhead cost allocation that are capable of statistical verification have not yet been developed. The criteria that have been discussed have not been tested sufficiently to be considered objective.

2. The bases chosen for cost assignment are frequently imperfect expressions of the criteria. The choice of bases often consists of accepting or adapting available statistics to the problem. Expediency is the major factor that determines the choice of bases for cost assignment.

Allocation bases advocated in both practice and in the literature include the following:

Service Department	Allocation Base
Cafeteria	Number of Employees, Direct-Labor Hours Worked, Meals Served
Personnel	Number of Employees, Labor Turnover
Showroom	Weight, Units, Size
Maintenance	Number of Machines, Machine Hours
Material Handling	Tonnage, Units Carried
Toolroom	Requisitions
Medical	Number of Cases, Number of Employees
Cost Accounting	Labor Hours
Production Planning and Control	Machine Hours, Labor Hours

Allocation Procedures

There are four basic procedures for allocating the service department costs: the direct reallocation method, the step (step-down) allocation method, the reciprocal services method or normal equation method, and the matrix approach method. The last two procedures are the same and are the best methods for allocating service department costs. The other procedures are mentioned because of their use in practice, although they generally do not result in the full costing of the service department costs.

The following example will be used to illustrate the allocation procedures. Assume the ABEL Manufacturing Company has three production departments (P_1, P_2, and P_3) and two service departments (S_1 and S_2). The following data are provided for January:

Department	Direct Departmental Expense	Square Footage	Number of Employees
Processing (P_1)	$ 1,200	1,800	1,600
Fabricating (P_2)	2,800	1,800	2,400
Finishing (P_3)	3,000	2,700	1,600
Building and Grounds (S_1)	600	1,800	800
Personnel Services (S_2)	4,650	900	1,600
	$12,250	9,000	8,000

This example is illustrated in Figure 10.2. The allocation bases to be used are as follows:

1. Personnel services are allocated on the basis of the number of employees.

2. Building and grounds are allocated on the basis of the square footage.

Direct Reallocation Method

The *direct reallocation method* ignores the services provided by one service department to itself or to another service department and allocates only to the production departments. In other words, it ignores both reciprocal services and self-consumption. The results of this procedure using the ABEL Manufacturing Company example are presented in Table 10.2. The following steps are taken.

Figure 10.2   **ABEL Manufacturing Company, Service Department Allocation**

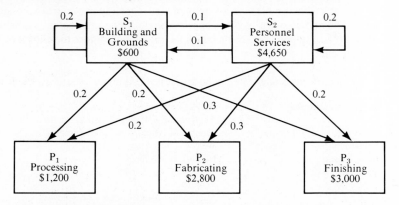

Table 10.2   Direct Method of Reallocation

	Building and Grounds	Personnel Services	Processing	Fabricating	Finishing	Total
				Departments		
Direct Costs before Reallocation	$ 600	$ 4,650	$1,200	$2,800	$3,000	$12,250
Reallocation						
1. Building and Grounds Basis: Square Footage 1,800, 1,800, 2,700	(600)		171	171	258	
2. Personnel Services Basis: Number of Employees 1,600, 2,400, 1,600		(4,650)	1,329	1,992	1,329	
Total			$2,700	$4,963	$4,587	$12,250
Basis of Application: DLH			1,000	2,000	2,000	5,000
Overhead Rate			$2.7	$2.4815	$2.2935	$2.45

Step 1 The building and grounds costs are allocated on the basis of the square footage in the processing, fabricating, and finishing departments. Given that the total square footage in departments P_1, P_2, and P_3 is 6,300 square feet, the allocation will be as follows:

$$\$171 = \left(\frac{1,800}{6,300} \times \$600\right) \text{ is allocated to the processing department.}$$

$$\$171 = \left(\frac{1,800}{6,300} \times \$600\right) \text{ is allocated to the fabricating department.}$$

$$\$258 = \left(\frac{2,700}{6,300} \times \$600\right) \text{ is allocated to the finishing department.}$$

(The figure $258 has been rounded.)

Step 2 The personnel service costs are allocated on the basis of the number of employees in the processing, fabricating, and finishing departments. Given that the total number of employees in these three departments is 5,600, the allocation will be as follows:

$$\$1,329 = \left(\frac{1,600}{5,600} \times \$4,650\right) \text{ is allocated to the processing department.}$$

$$\$1,992 = \left(\frac{2,400}{5,600} \times \$4,650\right) \text{ is allocated to the fabricating department.}$$

$$\$1,329 = \left(\frac{1,600}{5,600} \times \$4,650\right) \text{ is allocated to the finishing department.}$$

(The figure $1,329 has been rounded.)

Step (Step-Down) Allocation Method

The *step* or *step-down allocation method* ignores a service department's self-consumption while it recognizes the services rendered by one service department to other departments. The general rule is to proceed by a sequence of reallocations. There are two

Table 10.3   **Step Method Reallocations**

	Departments					
	Building and Grounds	**Personnel Services**	**Processing**	**Fabricating**	**Finishing**	**Total**
Direct Costs before Reallocation	$ 600	$ 4,650	$1,200	$2,800	$3,000	$12,250
1. Personnel Services Basis: Number of Employees 800, 1,600, 2,400, 1,600	581	(4,650)	1,163	1,743	1,163	
2. Building and Grounds Basis: Square Footage 1,800, 1,800, 2,700	(1,181)		337	337	507	
Total			$2,700	$4,880	$4,670	$12,250
Basis of Application: DLH			1,000	2,000	2,000	5,000
Overhead Rate (per DLH)			$2.7	$2.44	$2.335	$2.45

possible sequences: to distribute the costs of the service department with the "highest" cost first and continue the sequence in a step-by-step fashion, or to distribute the costs of the service department that provides services to the greatest number of other departments first and continue the sequence in a step-by-step fashion.

Table 10.3 uses the ABEL Manufacturing Company example to illustrate this method. The steps taken are as follows.

Step 1   The personnel services are allocated on the basis of the employees in the building and grounds, processing, fabricating, and finishing departments. The allocation will be as follows:

$$\$581 \ = \ \left(\frac{800}{6,400} \times \$4,650 \right) \text{ is allocated to the building and grounds department.}$$

$$\$1,163 = \left(\frac{1,600}{6,400} \times \$4,650 \right) \text{ is allocated to the processing department.}$$

$$\$1,743 = \left(\frac{2,400}{6,400} \times \$4,650 \right) \text{ is allocated to the fabricating department.}$$

$$\$1,163 = \left(\frac{1,600}{6,400} \times \$4,650 \right) \text{ is allocated to the finishing department.}$$

Step 2   The building and grounds costs are allocated on the basis of the square footage in the processing, fabricating, and finishing departments. Note that there is no further allocation made to the personnel services department. In other words, service department costs are not allocated back to accounts of service departments previously closed. Accordingly, the allocation will be as follows:

$$\$337 \ = \ \left(\frac{1,800}{6,300} \times \$1,181 \right) \text{ is allocated to the processing department.}$$

$$\$337 \ = \ \left(\frac{1,800}{6,300} \times \$1,181 \right) \text{ is allocated to the fabricating department.}$$

$$\$507 \ = \ \left(\frac{2,700}{6,300} \times \$1,181 \right) \text{ is allocated to the finishing department.}$$

Reciprocal Services, Algebraic, or Normal Equation Method

The *reciprocal services*, *algebraic*, or *normal equation allocation method* recognizes both reciprocal services and self-consumption. It is definitively superior to the methods previously introduced. The steps of the method applied to the ABEL Manufacturing Company example are as follows.

Step 1 A service distribution matrix summarizing all the relationships is established as follows:

Costs	Producing Departments			Service Departments		Costs to Be Allocated	Allocation Base
	Processing (P_1)	Manufacturing (P_2)	Finishing (P_3)	Building and Grounds (S_1)	Personnel Services (S_2)		
Building and Grounds (S_1)	0.2	0.2	0.3	0.2	0.1	$ 600	Square Footage
Personnel Services (S_2)	0.2	0.3	0.2	0.1	0.2	$4,650	Number of Employees

Step 2 The cost equations for the service departments are as follows:

$$S_1 = \$600 + 0.2S_1 + 0.1S_2,$$
$$S_2 = \$4,650 + 0.1S_1 + 0.2S_2,$$

where

S_1 = Cost of building and grounds.

S_2 = Cost of personnel services.

Step 3 Simplification of these equations will yield the results for S_1 and S_2 as follows:

$$S_1 - 0.2S_1 = \$600 + 0.1S_2$$
$$0.8S_1 = \$600 + 0.1S_2$$
$$S_1 = (\$600 + 0.1S_2) \div 0.8.$$

Therefore,

$$S_2 = \$4,650 + 0.1 \left(\frac{\$600 + 0.1S_2}{0.8} \right) + 0.2S_2$$
$$= \$6,000,$$

and

$$S_1 = (\$600 + 0.1 \times 6,000) \div 0.8 = \$1,500.$$

Step 4 Using the results obtained in steps 1, 2, and 3, the following normal equations, expressing the relationships between the service and producing departments, are established as follows:

$$P_1 = 0.2S_1 + 0.2S_2,$$

$$P_2 = 0.2S_1 + 0.3S_2,$$

$$P_3 = 0.3S_1 + 0.2S_2,$$

or

$$P_1 = 0.2(\$1,500) + 0.2(\$6,000) = \$1,500$$

$$P_2 = 0.2(\$1,500) + 0.3(\$6,000) = \$2,100$$

$$P_3 = 0.3(\$1,500) + 0.2(\$6,000) = \underline{\$1,650}$$
$$\$5,250.$$

Step 5   The final results in the allocation of service department costs to producing departments appear in Table 10.4

Matrix Approach to Cost Allocation

The reciprocal services method involves the application of traditional algebra in the form of simultaneous equations. However, where there are a great number of variables involving a complex system of equations, the use of matrix algebra provides a solution more expediently and efficiently.

From the previous example, the total costs of each operating department as well as the allocation from each service department are as follows:

$$P_1 = 0.2S_1 + 0.2S_2 + EP_1. \tag{1}$$

$$P_2 = 0.2S_1 + 0.3S_2 + EP_2. \tag{2}$$

$$P_3 = 0.3S_1 + 0.2S_2 + EP_3. \tag{3}$$

$$S_1 = 0.2S_1 + 0.1S_2 + ES_1. \tag{4}$$

$$S_2 = 0.1S_1 + 0.2S_2 + ES_2. \tag{5}$$

The unallocated direct departmental expenses of the processing, manufacturing, finishing, building and grounds, and personnel departments are $EP_1 = \$1,200$, $EP_2 = \$2,800$, $EP_3 = \$3,000$, $ES_1 = \$6,000$, and $ES_2 = \$4,650$, respectively. Similarly, P_1, P_2, P_3, S_1, and S_2 are the corresponding costs after allocation of the service departments.

The first problem is to determine the values of S_1 and S_2. Equations 4 and 5 in matrix form become

$$[S] = [A][S] + [I][ES], \tag{6}$$

where

$$[S] = \begin{bmatrix} S_1 \\ S_2 \end{bmatrix}, \quad [A] = \begin{bmatrix} 0.2 & 0.1 \\ 0.1 & 0.2 \end{bmatrix}, \quad [ES] = \begin{bmatrix} ES_1 \\ ES_2 \end{bmatrix} = \begin{bmatrix} \$600 \\ \$4,650 \end{bmatrix},$$

and $[I] = \begin{bmatrix} 1 & 0 \\ 0 & 1 \end{bmatrix}.$

Table 10.4   The Algebraic Method of Cost Allocation (Reciprocal Services Method)

			Allocated to			
Costs from	Buildings and Grounds (S_1)	Personnel Services (S_2)	Processing (P_1)	Manufacturing (P_2)	Finishing (P_3)	Total
S_1	$ 300	$ 150	$ 300	$ 300	$ 450	
S_2	600	1,200	1,200	1,800	1,200	
Subtotal	900	1,350	1,500	2,100	1,650	
First Allocation	600	4,650	0	0	0	
Total	$1,500	$6,000	$1,500	$2,100	$1,650	
Direct Departmental Costs			1,200	2,800	3,000	
Total after Allocation			$2,700	$4,900	$4,650	$12,250
Basis of Application: DLH			1,000	2,000	2,000	5,000
Overhead Rate			$2.7	$2.45	$2.325	$2.45

The solution for equation 6 can be developed as follows:

$$[S] = [A][S] + [I][ES]$$

$$[S] - [A][S] = [I][ES]$$

$$[S][I - A] = [I][ES]$$

$$[I - A]^{-1}[S][I - A] = [I - A]^{-1}[I][ES]$$

$$[S] \qquad = [I - A]^{-1}[I][ES]. \qquad [7]$$

Substituting the values from our example, we obtain

$$S = \left[\begin{bmatrix} 1 & 0 \\ 0 & 1 \end{bmatrix} - \begin{bmatrix} 0.2 & 0.1 \\ 0.1 & 0.2 \end{bmatrix} \right]^{-1} \begin{bmatrix} 1 & 0 \\ 0 & 1 \end{bmatrix} \begin{bmatrix} \$600 \\ \$4,650 \end{bmatrix}$$

$$= \begin{bmatrix} \$1,500 \\ \$6,000 \end{bmatrix}.$$

$$[P] = [C][S] + [I][EP], \qquad [8]$$

where

$$[P] = \begin{bmatrix} P_1 \\ P_2 \\ P_3 \end{bmatrix}, \quad [C] = \begin{bmatrix} 0.2 & 0.2 \\ 0.2 & 0.3 \\ 0.3 & 0.2 \end{bmatrix}, \quad [I] = \begin{bmatrix} 1 & 0 & 0 \\ 0 & 1 & 0 \\ 0 & 0 & 1 \end{bmatrix},$$

$$[EP] = \begin{bmatrix} EP_1 \\ EP_2 \\ EP_3 \end{bmatrix} = \begin{bmatrix} \$1,200 \\ \$2,800 \\ \$3,000 \end{bmatrix}, \quad \text{and } [S] = \begin{bmatrix} S_1 \\ S_2 \end{bmatrix} = \begin{bmatrix} \$1,500 \\ \$6,000 \end{bmatrix}.$$

Substituting the values from our example, we obtain

$$[P] = \begin{bmatrix} 0.2 & 0.2 \\ 0.2 & 0.3 \\ 0.3 & 0.2 \end{bmatrix} \begin{bmatrix} \$1,500 \\ \$6,000 \end{bmatrix} + \begin{bmatrix} 1 & 0 & 0 \\ 0 & 1 & 0 \\ 0 & 0 & 1 \end{bmatrix} \begin{bmatrix} \$1,200 \\ \$2,800 \\ \$3,000 \end{bmatrix}$$

$$= \begin{bmatrix} \$1,500 \\ \$2,100 \\ \$1,650 \end{bmatrix} + \begin{bmatrix} \$1,200 \\ \$2,800 \\ \$3,000 \end{bmatrix} = \begin{bmatrix} \$2,700 \\ \$4,900 \\ \$4,650 \end{bmatrix}.$$

The format of the matrix approach can be varied as follows:

$$[P] = [C][S] + [I][EP], \tag{8}$$

where

$$[S] = [I - A]^{-1}[I][ES]. \tag{7}$$

By combining equations 8 and 7 we have

$$[P] = [C][I - A]^{-1}[I][ES] + [I][EP]. \tag{9}$$

Let matrix E be as follows:

$$[E] = [C][I - A]^{-1}.$$

Equation 9, then, can be expressed directly as

$$[P] = [E][I][ES] + [I][EP] \tag{10}$$

or

$$[P] = [E][ES] + [EP]. \tag{11}$$

Substituting from our example, we obtain

$$[E] = \begin{bmatrix} 0.2 & 0.2 \\ 0.2 & 0.3 \\ 0.3 & 0.2 \end{bmatrix} \left(\begin{bmatrix} 1 & 0 \\ 0 & 1 \end{bmatrix} - \begin{bmatrix} 0.2 & 0.1 \\ 0.1 & 0.2 \end{bmatrix} \right)^{-1} \begin{bmatrix} 0.2857143 & 0.2857143 \\ 0.3015873 & 0.4126984 \\ 0.4126984 & 0.3015873 \end{bmatrix}$$

and

$$[P] = \begin{bmatrix} 0.2857 & 0.2857 \\ 0.3015 & 0.4126 \\ 0.4126 & 0.3015 \end{bmatrix} \begin{bmatrix} 1 & 0 \\ 0 & 1 \end{bmatrix} \begin{bmatrix} \$600 \\ \$4,650 \end{bmatrix} + \begin{bmatrix} 1 & 0 \\ 0 & 1 \end{bmatrix} \begin{bmatrix} \$1,200 \\ \$2,800 \\ \$3,000 \end{bmatrix}$$

$$= \begin{bmatrix} \$2,700 \\ \$4,900 \\ \$4,650 \end{bmatrix}.$$

The advantage of the new format as defined by equation 11 is that for any given set of direct charges, the same coefficient matrix E can be used. This holds true as long as the allocation relationships and proportions remain stable. Similarly, matrix E is an effective matrix in the sense that the sum of each column is equal to 1. Each element in matrix E corresponds to the proportion of services rendered to the operating department by the service department.

10.2   ACCOUNTING FOR COMMON PRODUCT COSTS

10.2.1   Nature of Common Product Costs

In most of the previously considered cases, the inputs were associated either directly or indirectly with a single output. In the other possible cases where the manufacturing process yields more than one particular output, the problem of the common product costs, or joint costs, arises: For financial accounting purposes the joint costs, which are basically *indivisible costs*, must be allocated to each of the outputs, usually called *joint products*. A classic example of common product costs is the cost of copper ore, which may contain gold, copper, zinc, and silver in different amounts. What cost should be allocated to each of these products? Figure 10.3 illustrates the common product costs, the joint products, and the *by-products*. The costs of copper ore are *common costs (joint costs)* up to a separation point (*split-off point*), where additional costs (*separable costs*) are incurred to generate the identifiable products (in this case gold, copper, zinc, and silver). These separable costs are sometimes referred to as *specific costs*.

Although both joint products and by-products are generated by the same process, for accounting purposes they are distinguished on the basis of their relative sales value. The joint product is used to identify products having significant sales values and quantities (in other words, products that are commercially viable). By-products are products that in a given, specific situation have low sales value in comparison to the other joint products. In the example illustrated in Figure 10.3, gold can be considered a by-product, while copper, silver, and zinc are joint products.

Industries where common product costs exist include the chemicals, tobacco manufacturing, petroleum, meat packing, copper mining, fruit and vegetable canning, lumber milling, dairy, coal mining, flour milling, coke manufacturing, and many other industries for which joint costs must be allocated to establish the unit cost of their

Figure 10.3   Example of Common Product Costs

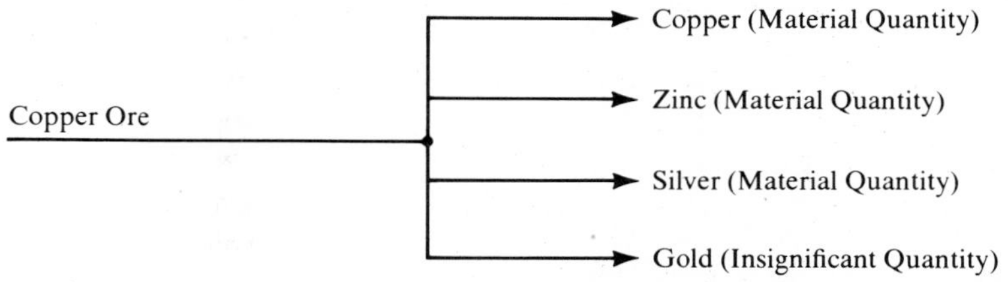

products. In all these cases, the joint costs must be allocated on a justifiable and acceptable base given the impact of such allocation on inventory valuation and income determination.

10.2.2   Joint Product Costing

Joint product costs are equal to the sum of the costs incurred in a single manufacturing process or in a series of processes that simultaneously yield two or more products of significant sales values and quantities. They include all costs incurred up to the point of separation of the joint products, or split-off point. For inventory valuation and income determination purposes, the question arises as to what amount of the joint product costs should be allocated to each of the individual joint products. Note again that the joint product costs cannot be physically identified or traced to any of the individual products, since the joint products were not separated before the split-off point. Nevertheless, the accountant is responsible for allocating the joint product costs to each of the joint products so ending inventories can be costed and income determined.

Several procedures exist in both the literature and in practice for the allocation of the joint costs to the individual products. The most popular are the following:

1. *Allocation by physical measure* (average unit cost method and weighted average method).

2. *Allocation by relative sales value.*

3. *Allocation by relative net realizable value.*

Other approaches identified in the literature deserve consideration and will also be presented.

The following example will be used to illustrate the procedures for the allocation of the joint product costs:

King Kong Company, January 19X3

Joint Costs	$30,000
Joint Products: Unit Output (Sales)	
King	2,000 Units
Kong	4,000 Units
Selling Price at the Split-off Point	
King	$ 4.00
Kong	$ 0.50
Additional Processing Costs per Unit	
King	$ 2.00
Kong	$ 3.00
Selling Price	
King	$ 12.00
Kong	$ 7.00
Joint Products: Weights	
King	2 Pounds
Kong	4 Pounds

Allocation by Physical Measure

The method of *allocation by physical measure* consists of allocating the joint costs on the basis of some unit of measure. In the King Kong example, the joint costs can be allocated on the basis of the units of output or on the basis of the weight of output. The first method will be labeled the *average unit cost method* and the second, the *weighted average method*.

Under the average unit cost method, the $30,000 joint costs are allocated on the basis of the 6,000 units produced, or a unit cost of $5 per unit. The costs allocated are $10,000 to King and $20,000 to Kong, with the following results:

Products	Units of Output	Percentage of Quantity (Units of Output ÷ Total Output)	Cost Allocation (% × Joint Cost)	Unit Cost (Allocation ÷ Output)
King	2,000	33.33%	$10,000	$5
Kong	4,000	66.66	20,000	$5
	6,000	100%	$30,000	

The average unit cost method does not always provide adequate results in cases where the joint products cannot be measured by the same basic measurement unit or where the products differ in terms of other factors such as weight, size, and so forth. In the King Kong example, since the joint products differ in size, a weighted average method may be more acceptable. Using this method, the $30,000 joint costs are allocated on the basis of a weight of output of 20,000 pounds. The costs allocated are $6,000 to King and $24,000 to Kong. The results are obtained as follows:

Products	Units of Output	Weight (Weight × Output), in Pounds	Percentage of Weight	Cost Allocation	Unit Cost
King	2,000	4,000	20%	$ 6,000	$3
Kong	4,000	16,000	80	24,000	$6
	6,000	20,000	100%	$30,000	

Allocation by Relative Sales Value

The most popular allocation method in practice is the method that allocates the joint costs on the basis of the market value at the split-off point. The rationale is based on the choice of a revenue-generating power criteria. In the King Kong example, the $30,000 joint product costs are allocated on the basis of a $10,000 market value. The costs are allocated as $24,000 to King and $6,000 to Kong, with these results:

Products	Units of Output	Selling Price at Split-off Point	Market Value	Percentage of Market Value	Cost Allocation	Unit Cost
King	2,000	$4.00	$ 8,000	80%	$24,000	$12.00
Kong	4,000	$0.50	2,000	20	6,000	$ 1.50
	6,000		$10,000	100%	$30,000	

Allocation by Net Realizable Value

Assuming that the selling prices at the split-off point are not available and that additional processing costs beyond the split-off point are needed to bring the joint products into salable form, the acceptable alternative to the allocation by relative sales value method is allocation by net realizable value. This method consists of determining the approximate market values of the joint products at the split-off point. Take the sales price of the final products at the point of sale and deduct the additional processing costs to approximate the sales prices at the split-off point. In the King Kong example, the $30,000 joint product costs are allocated on the basis of total net realizable value of $20,000. The costs are allocated as $16,667 to King and $13,333 to Kong, and the results obtained are as follows:

Products	Units of Output	Net Realizable Value per Unit	Total Net Realizable Value	Percentage of Net Realizable Value	Cost Allocation	Unit Cost
King	2,000	(12 − 2) = $10	$20,000	55.56%	$16,667	$8.33
Kong	4,000	(7 − 3) = $ 4	16,000	44.44	13,333	$3.33
	6,000		$36,000	100.00%	$30,000	

The following product line income statement results from the use of the net realizable value method of allocation:

Income Statement Resulting from the Use of the Net Realizable Value Method of Allocation

	Total	King	Kong
Sales	$52,000	$24,000	$28,000
Cost of Goods Sold[a]			
Joint Cost	30,000	16,667	13,333
Separable Costs	16,000	4,000	12,000
Total Cost of Goods Sold	$46,000	$20,667	$25,333
Gross Margin	$ 6,000	$ 3,333	$ 2,667
Gross Margin Percentage	11.54%	13.88%	9.52%

[a]It is assumed that there are no inventories.

The unit cost of each of the joint products will differ from one allocation procedure to another, as shown in Table 10.5. These differences will ultimately result in different product values for inventory valuation and income determination. However, these differences in unit costs are not important for decision making, namely, for cost planning and control problems.

Net Allocation by Overall Margin

Allocation by net realizable value can be criticized on the basis of its implicit assumption that the profit margin can be attributed entirely to the joint products without considering the separable costs. *Allocation by overall margin* is sometimes advocated as a method that corrects for this suggested anomaly. Under this procedure, the gross margin percentage for the total firm is computed. Next, the total cost that corresponds to each individual product is computed by applying the overall gross margin percentage to the sales of the individual products. Finally, the joint cost assigned to each individual product is computed by deducting the separable costs from the total costs obtained in the second step. The overall margin method is used with the King Kong example in Table 10.6.

Allocation by Cost Savings

In some cases the products or services obtained through the incurrence of a joint cost could also be directly obtained by the incurrence of a separable cost. In other words,

Table 10.5   Results of the Allocation Procedures for Products

	King	Kong
1st Weight		
Joint Cost	$ 3	$6.00
Add Separable Costs	2	3.00
	$ 5	$9.00
2nd Units		
Joint Cost	$ 5	$5.00
Add Separable Costs	2	3.00
	$ 7	$8.00
3rd Selling Price at Split-off		
Joint Cost	$12	$1.50
Add Separable Costs	2	3.00
	$14	$4.50
4th Net Realizable Value		
Joint Costs	$ 9	$3.00
Add Separable Costs	2	3.00
	$11	$6.00

Table 10.6   Overall Margin Method

	Total	King	Kong
Sales	$52,000	$24,000	$28,000
minus Overall Gross Margin Percentage (11.54%)	6,000	2,769	3,231
equals Total Cost	$46,000	$21,231	$24,769
minus Separable Costs	16,000	4,000	12,000
equals Joint Costs	$30,000	$17,231	$12,769

joint costs can be incurred to effect cost savings. In such a case, Shane Moriarity suggests *allocation by cost savings.*[3] He proposes the following procedures:

1. The costs that would be incurred if the products or services were obtained independently are summed. Assume they are represented by Σy_i.

2. The costs that would be incurred if the products or services were obtained jointly are also summed. Assume they are represented by X.

[3] Shane Moriarity, "Another Approach to Allocating Joint Costs," *Accounting Review* (October 1975), pp. 791–795.

3. The cost savings arising from the incurrence of a joint cost rather than the incurrence of separable costs are computed. Assume they are represented by $\Sigma y_i - X$.

4. The cost of each individual product or service will be equal to y_i less some allocation of the savings ($\Sigma y_i - X$). Moriarity suggests that this allocation may be proportional to the costs incurred to produce the products independently rather than jointly (that is, $y_i/\Sigma y_i$). Accordingly, the joint costs allocated to each product or service will be

$$y_i - \frac{y_i}{\Sigma y_i} (\Sigma y_i - X).$$

As an example, consider a company employing a consulting firm that has been charging $10,000 per year to provide advice to the accounting department and $5,000 per year to provide advice to the marketing department. It has been suggested that an in-house consulting department could provide the same services for a total cost of $13,500. Using Moriarity's alternative, calculations yield the following results:

Cost of consulting services purchased separately =	$\Sigma y_i = \$15,000$
Cost of consulting services purchased jointly =	$X = \$13,500$
Cost savings from joint purchase	$= \Sigma y_i - X = \$\ 1,500.$

Allocation to the accounting department would be

$$y_i - \frac{y_i}{\Sigma y_i} (\Sigma y_i - X).$$

$$\$10,000 - \frac{10,000}{15,000} (\$1,500) = \$9,000.$$

Allocation to the marketing department would be

$$y_i - \frac{y_i}{\Sigma y_i} (\Sigma y_i - X).$$

$$\$5,000 - \frac{5,000}{15,000} (\$1,500) = \$4,500.$$

The approach suggested by Moriarity fails to distinguish internal incremental costs from internal joint costs. A method proposed by J. G. Louderback explicitly considers the existence of incremental costs involved in providing a good or service internally, as well as joint costs. Hence "the departments (or any other segments, products, etc.) are charged with the incremental costs to provide the service internally plus a portion of the joint costs based on the *differences* between the incremental costs of buying the service outside and providing it internally. The result is that the total cost charged to the department is always equal or greater than the incremental cost to provide it inside and less than the incremental cost to buy the service outside." [4]

---

[4] J. G. Louderback, "Another Approach to Allocating Joint Costs: A Comment," *Accounting Review* (July 1976), pp. 683–685.

The formula for joint cost allocation under Louderback's approach is

$$(O_i - I_i)/(\Sigma O_i - \Sigma I_i) \times JC,$$

where

JC = Total joint cost.

O_i = Incremental cost outside for segment i.

I_i = Incremental cost inside for segment i.

To illustrate Louderback's approach, assume the same facts used for Moriarity's approach, except that there are joint costs of $6,500 involved in creating an in-house consulting department and incremental costs of $5,000 and $2,000 for the accounting and marketing departments, respectively. This makes the total cost $13,500 to provide the consulting service internally, which is the same as in the earlier example.

Under Louderback's approach the allocation would be as follows:

Department	O_i	I_i	$O_i - I_i$	$\dfrac{O_i - I_i}{\Sigma O_i - \Sigma I_i} \times$ Joint Cost	Joint Cost Allocation
Accounting	$10,000	$5,000	$5,000	⅝ × $6,500	$4,062.50 + $5,000 = $ 9,062.50
Marketing	5,000	2,000	3,000	⅜ × $6,500	$2,437.50 + $2,000 = $ 4,437.50
	$15,000	$7,000	$8,000		$6,500.00 + $7,000 = $13,500.00

10.2.3   By-product Costing

As stated earlier, by-products are identifiable products that in a given situation have low sales values in comparison to the joint products. In accounting for by-products, a common problem relates to timing the recognition of revenues and expenses. The by-product costing methods most common in practice and in the literature are as follows:

1. By-product revenue is recognized as other revenue.

2. By-product revenue is recognized as other income.

3. By-product revenue is recognized as a deduction from the cost of production.

4. The net realizable value of the by-product sold at the separation point is recognized as a deduction from the cost of goods sold. The net realizable value of the by-product sold is equal to the by-product revenue less separable costs incurred.

5. The net realizable value of the by-product produced at the separation point is recognized as a deduction from the cost of production. The net realizable value of the by-products produced is equal to the by-product revenues less separable costs incurred and to be incurred.

These methods are illustrated in Table 10.7. The variations in the net profits arising from the use of these methods should not be considered an important problem. First, these results tend to disappear in the long run, assuming equality between production and sales. Second, by definition, by-products are minor products with an immaterial impact on management decisions.

Table 10.7   Accounting Methods for By-products

Accounting Methods Income Statement	By-product Revenue Recognized as				Net Realizable Value Recognized as	
	Other Revenue	Other Income	Deduction from Cost of Goods Sold	Deduction from Cost of Production	Deduction from Cost of Goods Sold	Deduction from Cost of Production
Sales from Major Products	$ 20,000	$ 20,000	$ 20,000	$ 20,000	$ 20,000	$ 20,000
Revenue from By-products	1,000					
Total Revenue	$ 21,000	$ 20,000	$ 20,000	$ 20,000	$ 20,000	$ 20,000
Cost of Goods Sold						
Beginning Inventory	—	—	—	—	—	—
Production Costs	10,000	10,000	10,000	10,000	10,000	10,000
Revenue from By-products				(1,000)		
Net Realizable Value Produced						(600)
Ending Inventory	(5,000)	(5,000)	(5,000)	(5,000)	(5,000)	(5,000)
Cost of Goods Sold	$ 5,000	$ 5,000	$ 5,000	$ 4,000	$ 5,000	$ 4,400
Revenue from By-product			(1,000)			
Net Realizable Value Sold					(500)	
Gross Margin	16,000	15,000	16,000	16,000	15,500	15,600
Other Income		1,000				
Net Income	$ 16,000	$ 16,000	$ 16,000	$ 16,000	$ 15,500	$ 15,600

Main Product	**By-product**
Production = 1,000 units	Production = 1,200 units
Sales = 500 units	Sales = 1,000 units
Unit Cost = $10	Sales Price = $1
Sales Price = $40	Separable Cost Incurred per Unit = $.5

10.2.4   Joint Products and Decision Making

The preceding discussion centered on the problem of joint product allocation as it relates to the inventory valuation needed for income and balance sheet determinations. Information on joint products is also needed for making at least two types of internal decisions:

1. An *output decision* involves the impact that increases or decreases in the output of joint products have on total cost and profit. Examples are the decision to expand or discontinue total production and the determination of the most profitable mix of jointly produced products. Output decisions vary according to whether the joint products are produced in fixed or variable proportions.

2. A *depth-of-processing decision* involves whether to sell a joint product at the split-off point or to process it further.

Fixed Proportion Output Decisions[5]

Where joint products are produced in fixed proportions, increases or decreases in the volume of one product affect the volume of the other product. Product mix, therefore, is beyond management control, and the allocation of joint costs is irrelevant to internal decision making. In fact, output decisions should rest on a comparison between the total joint products revenue less the total joint costs and additional processing costs beyond the split-off point.

As an example, suppose a firm makes two products (X and Y) from a raw material that costs $4 per pound. Every 20 pounds of this raw material will yield 12 pounds of product X and 8 pounds of product Y after the incurrence of a joint cost of $14. Additional separable costs of $3 per pound of product X and $4 per pound of product Y are required after the split-off point.

Using this data, only the costs of making both products X and Y can be determined, rather than the individual cost of either product X or product Y. Hence the costs of producing 12 pounds of product X and 8 pounds of product Y are as follows:

Raw Material Cost (20 Pounds at $4)	$80
Joint Cost	14
Separable Cost of Product X (12 Pounds at $3)	36
Separable Cost of Product Y (8 Pounds at $4)	32
Total	$162

On the basis of this information, the following results can be obtained:

1. If the revenues from the sale of both products X and Y are higher than $162, both products X and Y should be produced.

2. If the revenues from the sale of product X are higher than $130, product X should be produced. Product Y should only be produced if revenues from the sale of product Y exceed $32.

3. If the revenues from the sale of product Y are higher than $126, product Y should be produced. Product X should be produced if the revenues from the sale of product X exceed $36.

4. If the revenues from the sale of both products X and Y are less than $130 for each product and less than $162 for both products, neither product X nor product Y should be produced.

Variable Proportion Output Decisions[6]

There are two cases in practice where the proportions in which joint products are produced could be variable: (1) when proportion produced of each product is *materials determined* (depends on the quality or composition of the joint material input) and (2) when the proportion produced of each product is *process determined* (depends on the changes in the processing methods used). In both cases, output decisions rest on a comparison between the total cost differentials and the total sales differentials for each alternative product mix considered.

To illustrate, suppose a firm produces two products (X and Y) from a single process.

---

[5]H. Bierman, Jr., and T. R. Dyckman, *Managerial Cost Accounting*, 2d. ed. (New York: Macmillan, 1976), pp. 173–174.

[6]G. Shillinglaw, *Cost Accounting: Analysis and Control* (Homewood, Ill.: Irwin, 1972), pp. 243–244.

Products X and Y sell for $10 a pound and $6 a pound, respectively. The processing method used yields ratios of 20 percent product X and 80 percent product Y. Another processing method can also be used that yields 80 percent product X and 20 percent product Y. The new processing method results in a total cost of $80. The application of the new processing method is equivalent to exchanging 60 pounds of product Y plus $80 for 20 pounds of product X. To determine the desirability of the new processing method, proceed with the following comparison:

Revenues after Processing		
Product X (60 Pounds at $10)		$600
Product Y (20 Pounds at $ 6)		120
Total		$720
Less: Processing Cost	$80	
Market Value of Product Y Processing (80 Pounds × $6)	480	560
Incremental Profit		$160

Put another way, the new processing method results in an incremental cost of another 60 pounds of product X at a processing cost of $80 plus the $360 sales value of the 60 pounds of product Y lost by the application of the new process, or $440, which is lower than the $600 incremental revenues generated by the additional 60 pounds of product X. As Nurnberg notes:

Thus, where increasing the production of one joint product has no effect on the production of the others, the incremental revenues should exceed the incremental costs; and where increasing the production of one joint product causes a reduction in the production of others, the incremental revenues of the former should exceed the sum of the incremental costs of the former and the net decremental revenues of the latter. [7]

Depth-of-Processing Decisions

The allocation of joint product costs is used for inventory valuation, which is necessary for both balance sheet and income determination. However, the choice of any allocation technique and the results obtained should not influence the decision making process in any way. In decisions regarding whether a product should be sold at the split-off point or processed further, joint costs are irrelevant. They have already been incurred prior to the decision and, therefore, constitute sunk costs. The only information relevant to the decisions are the incremental revenues and the incremental costs (including the cost of capital) from the additional processing. In general, the decision should be to process further if the incremental revenue exceeds the incremental costs.

To illustrate, return to the King Kong example and assume that the company is faced with the decision of selling Kong at $7 per unit or processing it further into a more refined product (Pong) selling at $10 per unit. In such a case, 44,000 units of Pong would be produced at an additional cost of $10,000. To solve this problem, proceed in three stages.

Stage 1 Show that joint cost allocations are not only irrelevant but may lead to inconsistent results. For example, while the weighted average method shows a loss, the net realizable value method shows a profit:

[7] H. Nurnberg, "Joint and By-Product Costs," in *Handbook of Cost Accounting*, eds. S. Davidson and R. L. Weil (New York: McGraw-Hill, 1978), chap. 18.

By Weighted Average		By Net Realizable Value	
Sales (4,000 × $10)	$40,000		$40,000
Joint Cost ($12,000 + $24,000)	$36,000	($12,000 + $13,333)	$25,333
Incremental Cost	10,000		10,000
Total Cost	$46,000		$35,333
Profit (Loss)	$(6,000)		$ 4,667

Stage 2   The incremental analysis is as follows:

Incremental Revenue (4,000 × $3)	$12,000
Incremental Cost	10,000
Incremental Profit	$ 2,000

As long as the incremental revenue exceeds the incremental cost by $2,000, Kong should be processed further into Pong.

Stage 3   Opportunity costs can be introduced into the analysis as follows:

Product Pong Revenues (4,000 × $10)	$40,000
Incremental Cost	$10,000
Opportunity Cost Resulting from Not Selling Kong (4,000 × $7)	28,000
Total Cost	$38,000
Difference	$ 2,000

The positive difference between Pong revenues and the total cost (including the opportunity costs) again shows that Kong should be processed further.

10.2.5   *Joint Products, Federal Income Tax Laws and Regulations*

The federal income tax laws and regulations are rather broad in attempting to resolve the joint cost problem. The most relevant statement is section 1.471-7 of the *Internal Revenue Code*, which states the following:

Inventories of miners and manufacturers. *A taxpayer engaged in mining or manufacturing who by a single process or uniform series of processes derives a product of two or more kinds, sizes, or grades the unit cost of which is substantially alike, and who in conformity to a recognized trade practice allocates an amount of cost to each kind, size, or grade of product, which in the aggregate will absorb the total cost of production, may, with the consent of the Commissioner use such allocated cost as a basis for pricing inventories, provided such allocation bears a reasonable relation to the respective selling values of the different kinds, sizes, or grades of a product.*

Although this regulation implies the required use of only the relative sales value method, the weighted average cost method has been effectively used under some circumstances. The regulations say that (1) the relative sales value is the suggested method "in conformity to a recognized trade practice . . . with the consent of the Commissioner" and (2) other methods can be proposed to the commissioner to decide whether they will be allowed.

10.3   SEGMENT PERFORMANCE AND THE CONTRIBUTION APPROACH TO COST ALLOCATION

The determination of the segment performance may require the allocation of the income statement items of a company as a whole to the various segments of the company. To facilitate such an allocation and emphasize cost behavioral patterns, a contribution approach can be used. Table 10.8 illustrates the contribution approach to segment performance. This approach differentiates between the allocation of items that vary with the activity level and those that do not.

First, the allocation of revenues, variable costs, and the contribution margin to the various segments is accomplished in a straightforward manner on the basis of the activity level of each segment. The contribution margin of each segment is a first performance evaluation measure that can be used to assess the impact of changes in the level of activity on the segment's income.

Second, the fixed costs can be divided into those controllable and those not controllable by the segments' managers, and the fixed costs considered controllable by the division can be easily traced to the segments. A second performance evaluation measure, the contribution controllable by the managers of the segments, can be obtained by deducting the fixed controllable costs from the contribution margin. This measure may be helpful in assessing the performance of the segments' managers by focusing only on the revenues and expenses items that are controllable by the managers.

Third, assuming that the fixed costs controllable by persons other than the segments' managers can be traced to the various segments, a third performance evaluation measure can be obtained by deducting the fixed costs controllable by others from the contribution controllable by the managers. This measure may be helpful in assessing the performance of the segments rather than of the segments' managers.

Table 10.8   The Contribution Approach to Segment Performance

		Region		Division			
	Company as a Whole	Region A	Region B	Division I	Division II	Division III	Division IV
1. Net Sales	$100,000	$60,000	$40,000	$24,000	$36,000	$8,000	$32,000
2. Variable Manufacturing Cost of Sales	60,000	36,000	24,000	14,400	21,600	4,800	19,200
3. Manufacturing Contribution Margin	$ 40,000	$24,000	$16,000	$ 9,600	$14,400	$3,200	$12,800
4. Variable Selling and Administrative Costs	10,000	6,000	4,000	2,400	3,600	1,000	3,000
5. Contribution Margin	$ 30,000	$18,000	$12,000	$ 7,200	$10,800	$2,200	$ 9,800
6. Fixed Costs Controllable by Segment Managers	10,000	6,000	4,000	3,000	3,000	1,000	3,000
7. Contribution Controllable by Segment Managers	$ 20,000	$12,000	$ 8,000	$ 4,200	$ 7,800	$1,200	$ 6,800
8. Fixed Costs Controllable by Others	6,000	3,600	2,400	2,000	1,600	400	2,000
9. Contribution by Segments	$ 14,000	$ 8,400	$ 5,600	$ 2,200	$ 6,200	$ 800	$ 4,800
10. Unallocated Costs	4,000	—	—	—	—	—	—
11. Income before Income Taxes	$ 10,000						

Finally, there may be some fixed costs, such as general company costs, that cannot be easily traced and allocated to the various segments. Allocating such costs may be difficult, arbitrary, and "incorrigible."

10.4   BEHAVIORAL CONSIDERATIONS IN COST ALLOCATION

Internal decisions, such as the decision to produce various joint products or the extent of their processing, are not dependent on any allocation method but on a comparison between the incremental revenues and the incremental costs. However, if accountants continue to allocate and base decisions on the results of the methods, it will merely lead to incorrect decision making. A. L. Thomas has constantly argued that most joint cost allocation approaches generate dysfunctional decisions, confuse decision makers, or are otherwise perverse.[8] As an alternative, he suggests devising allocation methods that are neutral or "sterilized" with respect to a particular decision:

Although a sterilized allocation is preferable to one that potentially generates poor decisions, it would be even better to make no allocation at all. Decision makers would be no worse off, accounting efforts would be slightly reduced, and the dangers of inappropriately employing the allocation in a context where it was not sterilized would be eliminated. Sterilized allocations, therefore, should be employed only in situations where decisions are better made from allocation-free data, but institutions compel allocations to be made or decision makers insist upon thinking in terms of allocated data. . . . Otherwise potentially obnoxious allocations can be rendered harmless if we know exactly what will be done with them. But the best that can be said of a sterilized allocation is that in some circumstances it will be entirely ineffectual.[9]

Thus, given that a joint cost allocation method cannot be sterilized for all kinds of decisions and that joint cost allocations will continue to be made to provide management control data and/or expense measurement, the cost accountant's main concern should be to determine how cost allocation can be used to motivate users. A. G. Hopwood states:

For however sophisticated the procedures of management accounting may be, and they are continually getting more sophisticated, their fundamental rationale always remains behaviourale in nature. The accountant contributes to the success of an enterprise primarily by the way in which he influences the behavior of other people and, at least in theory, his procedures should be designed to stimulate managers and employees to behave in a manner which is likely to contribute to the effectiveness of the enterprise as a whole.[10]

Allocation methods should be chosen with concern for the motivational dimension present in any allocation that affects financial performance. In short, the allocation method should be behavior congruent with respect to a particular decision. If it is behavior con-

---

[8] A. L. Thomas, *A Behavioral Analysis of Joint-Cost Allocation and Transfer Pricing* (Champaign, Ill.: Stipes, 1980), p. 9.

[9] Thomas, *Studies in Accounting Research No. 9*, p. 46.

[10] A. G. Hopwood, *Accounting and Human Behavior* (Englewood Cliffs, N.J.: Prentice-Hall, 1976), p. xiv.

gruent with respect to more than one decision, it is a welcome case of multiple congruence.

The problem of how a behavior-congruent allocation method should be chosen is in need of empirical evidence. Among the rare suggestions in the literature are those of G. Bodnar and E. J. Lusk.

We suggest that management would a priori specify a set of performance measures, a set of bases for cost allocation and an allocation criteria functional, such as fairness or ability to bear. During the period, data concerning performance and activity relative to the set of allocation bases would be accumulated. Alternative cost allocations then would be generated based on activity statistics. The specific allocation scheme would be selected ex post based on a review of subunit performance relative to the allocation criteria functional.[11]

In other words, they suggest that subunit activity be evaluated as it affects particular nonfinancial measures of performance. This evaluation then leads to the cost allocation scheme.

10.5   CONCLUSION

The joint cost problem of allocation can be observed in accounting for overhead and for common product costs.

Accounting for overhead requires three steps: cost distribution, cost allocation, and cost application. This chapter examined the cost allocation problem, namely, the allocation of service department costs. It presented four basic procedures: the direct reallocation method, the step method, the reciprocal services method, and the matrix approach method.

Accounting for common product costs involves accounting for both joint products and by-products. The chapter explained six procedures for the allocation of the joint costs to the individual products: the average unit cost method, the weighted average method, the relative sales value method, the net realizable value method, the overall margin method, and the cost savings method.

Internal decision making, such as the decision to produce various joint products or the desired extent of their processing, has been shown to be independent of any allocation method. However, it relies on a comparison between the incremental revenues and the incremental costs.

Finally, management should determine how cost allocation can be used to motivate users.

GLOSSARY

Actual Capacity The production level attained by a plant in the actual period.

Allocation by Cost Savings Allocating costs on the basis of the cost savings resulting from joint production rather than independent production.

---

[11]G. Bodnar and E. J. Lusk, "Motivational Considerations in Cost Allocation Systems: A Conditioning Theory Approach," *Accounting Review* (October 1977), p. 860.

Allocation by Net Realizable Value Allocating costs on the basis of net realizable value at the split-off point.

Allocation by Overall Margin Allocating costs by applying the overall gross margin percentage to the sales of individual products.

Allocation by Physical Measure Allocating costs on the basis of some unit of measure.

Allocation by Relative Sales Value Allocating costs on the basis of the market value at the split-off point.

By-product A product of limited sales value produced simultaneously with joint products.

Capacity Index The allocation base that offers the best physical association with the product.

Common Cost *(Joint Cost)* A cost incurred up to the split-off point, where individual joint products are identified.

Direct Reallocation Method This method ignores the services provided by one service department to itself or to another service department and allocates only to the production departments.

Expected Annual Capacity An estimate of the production level for the actual period as defined by the planning process.

Joint Products Individual products of significant sales value that are produced by a common process.

Normal Capacity The production level necessary to satisfy a plant's average commercial demand or sales over a period long enough to cover cyclical, seasonal, and trend variations.

Practical Capacity The maximum production level of a plant, with sufficient allowances for normal human and engineering inefficiencies.

Reciprocal Services Allocation Method This method recognizes both the reciprocal services and self-consumption.

Separable Cost A cost incurred beyond the split-off point to generate the joint products.

Step Allocation Method This method ignores the self-consumption by a service department while it recognizes the services rendered by one service department to other service departments.

Theoretical Capacity The maximum production level at which a plant can operate efficiently, assuming an absence of human or engineering inefficiencies.

SELECTED READINGS

Bierman, H. Jr., "Inventory Valuation: The Use of Market Prices," *Accounting Review* (October 1967), pp. 731–737.

Blamey, Richard L., "Setting Sewage Treatment User Charge Rates: A Cost/Benefit Approach," *Management Accounting* (December 1978), pp. 32–36.

Bodnar, G., and Lusk, E. J., "Motivational Considerations in Cost Allocation Systems: A Conditioning Theory Approach," *Accounting Review* (October 1977), pp. 857–868.

Butler, J. J., "Joint Product Analysis," *Management Accounting* (December 1971), pp. 12–14.

Callen, J. L., "Financial Cost Allocations: A Game Theoretic Approach," *Accounting Review* (April 1978), pp. 303–308.

Dun, L. C., "Product Costs: The Allocation Problem," *Chartered Accountant in Australia* (December 1972), pp. 18–22.

Feller, R. E., "Accounting for Joint Products in the Petroleum Industry," *Management Accounting* (September 1977), pp. 41–44, 48.

Fremgen, James M., and Liao, Shu S., "The Allocation of Corporate Indirect Costs," *Management Accounting* (September 1981), pp. 66–67.

Hamlen, S. S.; Hamlen, W. A. Jr.; and Tschirhart, J. T., "The Use of Core Theory in Evaluating Joint Cost Allocation Schemes," *Accounting Review* (July 1977), pp. 616–627.

Harris, W. T., and Chapin, W. R., "Joint Product Costing," *Management Accounting* (April 1973), pp. 43–47.

Hartley, Ronald V., "Decision Making When Joint Products Are Involved," *Accounting Review* (October 1971), pp. 746–755.

Hartley, Ronald V., "A Note on Quadratic Programming in a Case of Joint Production: A Reply," *Accounting Review* (October 1973), pp. 771–774.

Jensen, Daniel L., "A Class of Mutually Satisfactory Allocations," *Accounting Review* (October 1977), pp. 842–856.

Jensen, Daniel L., "Hartley's Demand-Price Analysis in a Case of Joint Production: A Comment," *Accounting Review* (October 1973), pp. 768–770.

Loehman, E. T., and Whinston, A. B., "A New Theory for Price and Decision Making for Public Investment," *Bell Journal of Economics and Management Science* (Autumn 1971), pp. 606–625.

Louderback, J. G., "Another Approach to Allocating Joint Costs: A Comment," *Accounting Review* (July 1976), pp. 683–685.

Manes, R. P., and Smith, L. Vernon, "Economic Joint Cost Theory and Accounting Practice," *Accounting Review* (January 1965), pp. 31–35.

Moriarity, Shane, "Another Approach to Allocating Joint Costs," *Accounting Review* (October 1975), pp. 791–795.

National Association of Accountants, *Research Series No. 31*, "Costing Joint Products" (New York: NAA, 1957).

Nurnberg, H., "Joint and By-Product Costs," in *Handbook of Cost Accounting*, eds. S. Davidson and R. L. Weil (New York: McGraw-Hill, 1978), chap. 18.

Thomas, A. L., *A Behavioral Analysis of Joint-Cost Allocation and Transfer Pricing*, (Champaign, Ill.: Stipes, 1980).

Thomas, A. L., *Studies in Accounting Research No. 3*, "The Allocation Problem in Financial Accounting Theory" (Sarasota, Fla.: American Accounting Association, 1969).

Thomas, A. L., *Studies in Accounting Research No. 9*, "The Allocation Problem: Part Two" (Sarasota, Fla.: American Accounting Association, 1974).

Vatter, William J., "Limitations of Overhead Allocation," *Accounting Review* (April 1945), pp. 163–176.

Vatter, William J., "Tailor-Making Cost Data for Specific Uses," *NACA Bulletin* (August 1954), pp. 1691–1707.

Weil, R. L. Jr., "Allocating Joint Costs," *American Economic Review* (December 1968), pp. 1342–1345.

Wells, M. C., "Is the Allocation of Overhead Costs Necessary?" *Australian Accountant* (November 1970), pp. 479–486.

QUESTIONS, EXERCISES, AND PROBLEMS

10.1   Differentiate between cost distribution, cost allocation, cost absorption, and cost application.

10.2   What are the main expressions of a capacity index, and what rules should guide its selection?

10.3   What are the main expressions of a capacity level, and what rules should guide its selection?

10.4   What is meant by a *normalized overhead rate*?

10.5   List and discuss some of the criteria used for the selection of an allocation base.

10.6   When is it necessary to allocate joint costs to joint products? In making a decision about the further processing of joint products, which costs will be relevant?

(CGA adapted)

10.7   What is a service department? How are service department costs accounted for?

(CGA adapted)

10.8   *Joint Costs*   From a particular joint process, Watkins Company produces three products (X, Y, and Z). Each product can be sold at the point of split-off or be processed further. Additional processing requires no special facilities, and production costs of further processing are entirely variable and traceable to the products involved. In 19X3, all three products were processed beyond split-off. Joint production costs for the year were $60,000. Sales values and costs needed to evaluate Watkins's 19X3 production policy follow:

Product	Units Produced	Sales Values at Split-off	Additional Costs and Sales Values if Processed Further Sales Values	Added Costs
X	6,000	$25,000	$42,000	$9,000
Y	4,000	41,000	45,000	7,000
Z	2,000	24,000	32,000	8,000

Joint costs are allocated to the products in proportion to their relative physical volume of output.

Required:
Select the best answer for each of the following items:

1. For units of product Z, the unit production cost most relevant to a decision to sell or process further is

    a. $5.

    b. $12.

    c. $4.

    d. $9.

2. To maximize profits, Watkins should subject the following products to additional processing:

    a. X only.

    b. X, Y, and Z.

    c. Y and Z only.

    d. Z only.

(AICPA adapted)

10.9   ***Joint Costs*** O'Connor Company manufactures product J and product K from a joint process. For product J, 4,000 units were produced having a sales value at split-off of $15,000. If product J were processed further, the additional costs would be $3,000, and the sales value would be $20,000. For product K, 2,000 units were produced having a sales value at split-off of $10,000. If product K were processed further, the additional costs would be $1,000, and the sales value would be $12,000. Using the approach of relative sales value at split-off, the portion of the total joint product costs allocated to product J was $9,000. Were the total product costs (1) $14,400, (2) $15,000, (3) $18,400, or (4) $19,000?

(AICPA adapted)

10.10   ***Joint Costs*** Andy Company manufactures products N, P, and R from a joint process. The following information is available:

	Product N	Product P	Product R	Total
Units Produced	12,000	?	?	24,000
Sales Value at Split-off	?	?	$50,000	$200,000
Joint Costs	$ 48,000	?	?	$120,000
Sales Value if Processed Further	$110,000	$90,000	$60,000	$260,000
Additional Costs if Processed Further	$ 18,000	$14,000	$10,000	$ 42,000

Required:
Assuming that joint product costs are allocated using the approach of relative sales value at split-off, what was the sales value at split-off for products N and P?

1. Product N, $66,000; and product P, $84,000.
2. Product N, $80,000; and product P, $70,000.
3. Product N, $98,000; and product P, $84,000.
4. Product N, $100,000; and product P, $50,000.

(AICPA adapted)

10.11   ***Joint Costs***   Superior Company manufactures products A and B from a joint process, which also yields a by-product (X). Superior accounts for the revenues from its by-product sales as a deduction from the cost of goods sold of its main products. Additional information follows:

	Product A	Product B	Product X	Total
Units Produced	15,000	9,000	6,000	30,000
Joint Costs	?	?	?	$264,000
Sales Value at Split-off	$290,000	$150,000	$10,000	$450,000

Required:
1. Assuming that joint product costs are allocated using the approach of relative sales value at split-off, what was the joint cost allocated to product B?
  a. $79,200.   c. $90,000.
  b. $88,000.   d. $99,000.

Stellar Corporation manufactures products R and S from a joint process. Additional information follows:

	Product R	Product S	Total
Units Produced	4,000	6,000	10,000
Joint Costs	$36,000	$ 54,000	$ 90,000
Sales Value at Split-off	?	?	?
Additional Costs if Processed Further	$ 3,000	$ 26,000	$ 29,000
Sales Value if Processed Further	$63,000	$126,000	$189,000
Additional Margin if Processed Further	$12,000	?	$ 40,000

Required:
2. Assuming that joint costs are allocated on the basis of relative sales value at split-off, what was the sales value at split-off for product S?
  a. $72,000.   c. $ 98,000.
  b. $82,000.   d. $100,000.

(AICPA adapted)

10.12   ***Fixed Proportion Output Decisions***   The JABEL Manufacturing Company makes two products (Alpha and Gamma) from a raw material costing $8 per pound. Each 10 pounds of this raw material will yield 6 units of Alpha and 4 units of Gamma after the additional incurrence of a joint cost of $25. Additional separable costs of $6 per pound of Alpha and $8 per pound of Gamma are required after the split-off point. Which product mix should the JABEL Manufacturing Company choose?

10.13   ***Variable Proportion Output Decisions***   The Zeghal Manufacturing Company produces two products (Taki and Tako) from a single process. Taki and Tako sell for $15 a pound and $10 a pound, respectively. The processing method used yields ratios of 80 percent Taki and 20 percent Tako. Another processing method can also be used, which results in a yield of 20 percent Taki and 80 percent Tako. The new processing method results in a total cost of $180. Should the new processing method be used?

10.14   ***Matrix Approach to Cost Allocation***   In a Chicago Heights hospital, the cafeteria and the personnel department service the pediatrics, maternity, and emergency room departments of the hospital. Allocations from the cafeteria are made on the basis of the number of meals served, whereas allocations from the personnel department are made on the basis of the number of employees in each department. The following data are provided for December 19X5:

Department	Direct Department Expenses	Number of Meals Served	Number of Employees
Pediatrics	$ 7,000	200	20
Maternity	6,000	200	30
Emergency Room	5,000	300	20
Cafeteria	1,200	200	10
Personnel	3,000	100	20
Total	$22,200	1,000	100

Required:
1. Allocate the costs of the service department using the direct method.
2. Allocate the same costs using the step method.
3. Allocate the same costs using the normal equation method.
4. Allocate the same costs using the matrix method.

10.15   ***Cost Allocation in a Hospital***   The administrator of Wright Hospital has presented you with a number of service projections for the year ending June 30, 19X2. Estimated room requirements for inpatients by type of service are

Type of Patient	Total Patients Expected	Average Number of Days in Hospital		Percentage of Regular Patients Selecting Types of Service		
		Regular	Medicare	Private	Semi-private	Ward
Medical	2,100	7	17	10%	60%	30%
Surgical	2,400	10	15	15	75	10

Of the patients served by the hospital, 10 percent are expected to be Medicare patients, all of whom are expected to select semiprivate rooms. Both the number and proportion of Medicare patients have increased over the past five years. Daily rentals per patient are $120 for a private room, $100 for a semiprivate room, and $80 for a ward.

Operating room charges are based on labor minutes (number of minutes the operating room is in use multiplied by the number of personnel assisting in the operation). The charges per labor minute are $0.25 for inpatients and $0.50 for outpatients. Studies for the current year show that operations on inpatients are divided as follows:

Type of Operation	Number of Operations	Average Number of Minutes per Operation	Average Number of Personnel Required
A	800	30	4
B	700	45	5
C	300	90	6
D	200	120	8
	2,000		

The same proportion of inpatient operations is expected for the next fiscal year, and 180 outpatients are expected to use the operating room. Outpatient operations average 20 minutes and require the assistance of three persons.

The budgeted expenses for the year ending June 30, 19X2, by department, follow:

General Services
Maintenance of Plant	$ 100,000
Operation of Plant	55,000
Administration	195,000
All Others	384,000

Revenue-Producing Services
Operating Room	136,880
All Others	1,400,000
	$2,270,880

The following information is provided for cost allocation purposes:

	Square Feet	Salaries
General Services		
Maintenance of Plant	12,000	$ 80,000
Operation of Plant	28,000	50,000
Administration	10,000	110,000
All Others	36,250	205,000
Revenue-Producing Services		
Operating Room	17,500	30,000
All Others	86,250	605,000
	190,000	$1,080,000

Basis of Allocations
Maintenance of Plant: Salaries
Operation of Plant: Square Feet
Administration: Salaries
All Others: 8 Percent to Operating Room

Required:
Prepare schedules showing the computation of

1. The number of patient-days (number of patients multiplied by average stay in hospital) expected by type of patient (medical and surgical) and service (private, semiprivate, and ward).

2. The total number of labor minutes expected for operating room services for inpatients and outpatients. For inpatients, show the breakdown of total operating room labor minutes by type of operation.

3. Expected gross revenue from room rentals.

4. Expected gross revenue from operating room services.

5. Cost per labor minute for operating room services, assuming that the total labor minutes computed in part 2 is 800,000 and that the step method of cost allocation is used. (*Hint: All* budgeted expenses are to be allocated to revenue-producing activities.)

(AICPA adapted)

10.16   *Cost Finding in a University*   Regional University is a state-supported university with a total enrollment of 5,000 full-time students and a faculty of 350. State appropriations are the sole source of operating funds, as all tuition and fees collected from students are required to be remitted to the state treasurer. The 19X6 operating appropriation was $12.5 million, which represents an average cost of $2,500 per student.

The basic product of the university is the granting of degrees to students who complete degree requirements in a particular program. The departments granting degrees are somewhat analogous to production departments, and the various support departments (for example, facilities services, academic support services, and administrative services) are similar to overhead departments in a manufacturing environment.

The administration has implemented a model used by a nearby university to analyze operating costs. The university's central administration believes that the new cost model will provide information that will be helpful in assessing the effectiveness of internal resource utilization, in assisting budget preparation and the related budget justification before the legislature, and in providing data for examining options for allocating funds based on current program costs and projected university enrollments. The cost model is designed to provide information about the traceable direct costs incurred by academic departments and allocated support costs charged to academic departments. The sum of the traceable direct and allocated support costs is considered the total costs of an academic department. Various cost measures are calculated for each academic department and for the student degree programs (majors) offered by each department.

The following schedules for the electrical engineering department of Regional University's College of Engineering have been prepared according to the new cost model. These are examples of schedules that are prepared for academic departments and degree programs in the university. The following definitions for student activity measures assist in the interpretation of the cost data:

1. A student credit hour (SCH) is the standard measure of instructional activity equivalent to 1 student enrolled in an academic course for which 1 credit hour is granted (for example, a 3-credit-hour course with 20 students equals 60 SCH of instructional activity).

2. A full-time student is a student enrolled for 30 credit hours in an academic year.

3. Equivalent full-time students equal the number of credit hours taken by students divided by 30 credit hours.

Schedule 1 presents the total instructional costs (traceable direct and allocated support) and the instructional costs per SCH taught by the electrical engineering department. Schedule 2 presents the traceable direct and total costs of the electrical engineering degree program (major); the cost per SCH taken and per student major is also presented there.

Schedule 1
Regional University, College of Engineering
Instructional Costs for the Electrical Engineering Department
For the 19X6–19X7 Academic Year

Traceable Direct Costs	Total Cost (000 Omitted)	Cost per SCH Taught[a]
Salaries and Benefits	$ 600	$ 73.20
Travel Expenses	25	3.00
Printing and Advertising	3	0.40
Supplies	29	3.50
Equipment	16	1.90
Rentals	12	1.50
Total Direct Costs	$ 685	$ 83.50
Allocated Support Costs		
Facilities Services (Utilities, Building and Grounds, Etc.)[b]	$ 180	$ 22.00
Academic Support Services (Library, Computer, Etc.)[c]	206	25.10
Administrative Services (Admissions, Placement, Etc.)[c]	103	12.60
Office of Engineering Dean[c]	15	1.80
Total Allocated Support Costs	$ 504	$ 61.50
Total Department Instruction Costs	$1,189	$145.00

[a] In the electrical engineering department, 8,200 student credit hours (SCH) were taught.
[b] Cost allocated on the basis of square feet occupied.
[c] Cost allocated on the basis of the number of student majors.

Schedule 2
Regional University, College of Engineering
Program Costs of Students Majoring in Electrical Engineering
For the 19X6–19X7 Academic Year

Department Providing Instruction	Traceable Direct Costs[a]		Total Costs[a]	
Chemical	($92.90 × 200)	$ 18,580	($169.60 × 200)	$ 33,920
Civil	($69.80 × 100)	6,980	($147.30 × 100)	14,730
Electrical	($83.50 × 6,500)	542,750	($145.00 × 6,500)	942,500
Mechanical	($74.80 × 1,150)	86,020	($126.50 × 1,150)	145,475
All Nonengineering[b]		112,500		202,500
Costs Associated with Students Enrolled as Electrical Engineering Majors		$766,830		$1,339,125
Electrical Engineering Degree Program Costs per SCH Taken[c]		$ 49.60		$ 86.70
Electrical Engineering Degree Program Costs per Student Majors[d]		$ 1,489		$ 2,600

[a] The costs of each academic department used by students majoring in electrical engineering are determined by multiplying the cost per SCH taught in that department by the number of SCH taken by students enrolled in the electrical engineering degree program from that department.
[b] Students majoring in electrical engineering were enrolled in 7,500 SCH from various nonengineering departments. Each nonengineering department has its own traceable direct and total cost per SCH, and the cost to the electrical engineering program is charged according to these rates. However, the details of these charges have been omitted from this schedule.
[c] A total of 15,450 SCH were taken by students in the electrical engineering degree program.
[d] The electrical engineering degree program has 515 full-time equivalent student majors.

Required:

1. The total traceable direct costs per SCH taught in the electrical engineering department are $83.50 (schedule 1). Is this an approximation of the variable costs per SCH taught in that department? Explain your answer.

2. The annual traceable direct cost per student majoring in electrical engineering is $1,489 (schedule 2). Is this an approximation of the annual variable cost per student majoring in electrical engineering? Explain your answer.

3. The allocated support costs per SCH taught are $61.50 for the electrical engineering department and $76.70 for the chemical engineering department. Does this mean that more support costs were allocated to the chemical engineering department? Explain your answer.

4. Should traceable direct and total department instructional costs per SCH taught (as presented in schedule 1) be used by the electrical engineering department in preparing its budget for presentation to the university administration? Explain your answer.

(CMA adapted)

10.17   ***Allocation Bases***   The Uptown Manufacturing Company incurred the following costs for the month of October:

Materials Used	
Direct Materials	$6,500
Indirect Materials	1,200
Payroll Costs Incurred	
Direct Labor	7,000
Indirect Labor	1,700
Salaries	
Production	2,400
Administration	5,100
Sales	3,200
Others	
Rent (Production Uses ½ of Building)	1,400
Rent for Molding Machine	400 per Month Plus $.50 per Unit Processed
Royalty (Calculation Based on Deliveries from Production to Finished Goods Stores, $.80 per Unit)	
Indirect Expenses, Accruals, Etc.	
Production	2,700
Sales and Administration	1,800

The company processed 1,200 units and obtained 1,000 good units. The 200 spoiled units are considered normal spoilage without resale or scrap value.

Required:

1. Determine the unit cost.

2. Assuming the data given represent normal monthly capacity and average monthly costs, calculate overhead rates on three different bases.

(SMA adapted)

10.18   ***Joint Product Costing and Decision Making***   The Charlottetown Co. Ltd. produces three products (C, L, and T) as the result of a joint process situation. During May 19X8, joint costs incurred totaled $200,000. The following information about each of the products is available:

	Product C	Product L	Product T
Production	15,000	10,000	20,000
Sales (in Units)	13,000	9,000	16,000
Sales Price	$ 20.00	$ 15.00	$ 9.50
Separable Processing Costs	$75,000	$25,000	$40,000

Required:

1. Compute the May gross profit for each of the products and in total. Use the approximate relative sales value approach.

2. A customer has offered to buy all of the output of product T at the split-off point for $7 per unit. Should Charlottetown accept this offer?

(CGA adapted)

10.19   *Net Realizable Value of Joint Products*   Miller Manufacturing Company buys zeon for $.80 per gallon. At the end of processing in department 1, zeon splits off into products A, B, and C. Product A is sold at the split-off point, with no further processing. Products B and C require further processing before they can be sold: Product B is processed in department 2, and product C is processed in department 3. The following is a summary of costs and other related data for the year ended June 30, 19X3:

	Department 1	Department 2	Department 3
Cost of Zeon	$96,000	—	—
Direct Labor	$14,000	$45,000	$65,000
Manufacturing Overhead	$10,000	$21,000	$49,000

	Product A	Product B	Product C
Gallons Sold	20,000	30,000	45,000
Gallons on Hand at June 30, 19X3	10,000	—	15,000
Sales (in Dollars)	$30,000	$96,000	$141,750

There were no inventories on hand at July 1, 19X2, and there was no zeon on hand at June 30, 19X3. All gallons on hand at June 30, 19X3, were complete as to processing. There were no manufacturing overhead variances. Miller uses the net realizable value method of allocating joint costs.

Required:

1. For allocating joint costs, the net realizable value of product A for the year ended June 30, 19X3, is
a. $30,000.   c. $21,000.
b. $45,000.   d. $ 6,000.

2. The joint costs for the year ended June 30, 19X3, to be allocated are
a. $300,000.   c. $120,000.
b. $ 95,000.   d. $ 96,000.

3. The cost of product B sold for the year ended June 30, 19X3, is
a. $90,000.   c. $88,857.
b. $66,000.   d. $96,000.

4. The value of the ending inventory for product A is
a. $24,000.   c. $ 8,000.
b. $12,000.   d. $13,333.

(AICPA adapted)

10.20

Depth-of-Processing Decisions The Crumble Company buys a chemical compound and refines it into three distinctively different compounds (X, Y, and Z), which are separated only at the final stage of the refining process. The yield of 100 pounds of input is

Compound X   50 Pounds
Compound Y   30
Compound Z   10

The remaining 10 pounds are waste and have no resale value at all.

The Crumble Company has been selling compounds X, Y, and Z after the final refining stage at $8 per pound for compound X, $10,000 per pound for compound Y, and $20,000 per pound for compound Z. The marketing manager recently suggested that compound X be processed further and then sold for $12 per pound. Cost data includes (1) raw chemical material at $1.80 per pound, (2) direct labor and variable overhead at $3.60 per pound of compound processed, and (3) fixed overhead at $540,000 per annum. The annual volume of sales (normal capacity) is

Compound X   100,000 Pounds
Compound Y   60,000
Compound Z   20,000

If compound X were processed further, additional direct-labor and variable costs of $3.50 per pound would be incurred. No additional fixed overhead would be incurred, but one-sixth of the present production facilities would be assigned to this further processing. The plant has been operating below its maximum capacity for some years.

Required:

1. What value per pound should be assigned to the year-end inventory for compounds X (without further processing), Y, and Z, assuming there are 1,000 pounds of each on hand. (Use the relative sales value method.)

2. Should compound X be processed further? Show calculations and give reasons for your answer.

3. Assuming that the Crumble Company has decided to process compound X further, what would be the cost per pound for the ending inventory, assuming there are 1,000 pounds of each product? (It is sufficient to express your answer in fractions.)

(SMA adapted)

10.21

Matrix Algebra Allocation A manufacturer's plant has two service departments (S_1 and S_2) and three production departments (P_1, P_2, and P_3) and wishes to allocate all factory overhead to production departments. The company distributes overhead from service departments to production departments on a reciprocal basis, recognizing the fact that services of one service department are utilized by another. Data regarding costs and allocation percentages are as follows:

| Service Department | S_1 | Percentages to Be Allocated to Departments | | | |
		S_2	P_1	P_2	P_3
S_1	0%	10%	20%	40%	30%
S_2	20	0	50	10	20

		Overhead to Be Allocated			
S_1	S_2	P_1	P_2	P_3
$98,000	$117,600	$1,400,000	$2,100,000	$640,000

Matrix algebra is to be used in the allocation process. The amount of overhead to be allocated to the service departments is expressed in two simultaneous equations, as follows:

$$S_1 = \$\ 98,000 + 0.20S_2, \text{ or } S_1 - 0.20S_2 = \$98,000.$$

$$S_2 = \$117,600 + 0.10S_1, \text{ or } S_2 - 0.10S_1 = \$117,600.$$

Required:
1. The system of simultaneous equations can be stated in which of the following matrix forms?

a. $\begin{array}{c} A \\ \begin{bmatrix} 1 & -0.20 \\ -0.10 & 1 \end{bmatrix} \end{array} \begin{array}{c} S \\ \begin{bmatrix} S_1 \\ S_2 \end{bmatrix} \end{array} = \begin{array}{c} b \\ \begin{bmatrix} 98,000 \\ 117,600 \end{bmatrix} \end{array}.$

b. $\begin{array}{c} A \\ \begin{bmatrix} 1 & 98,000 \\ -0.20 & 117,600 \end{bmatrix} \end{array} \begin{array}{c} S \\ \begin{bmatrix} 1 & S_1 \\ -0.10 & S_2 \end{bmatrix} \end{array} = \begin{array}{c} b \\ \begin{bmatrix} 98,000 \\ 117,600 \end{bmatrix} \end{array}.$

c. $\begin{array}{c} A \\ \begin{bmatrix} 1 & S_1 \\ -0.20 & S_2 \end{bmatrix} \end{array} \begin{array}{c} S \\ \begin{bmatrix} 1 & S_1 \\ -0.10 & S_2 \end{bmatrix} \end{array} = \begin{array}{c} b \\ \begin{bmatrix} 98,000 \\ 117,600 \end{bmatrix} \end{array}.$

d. $\begin{array}{c} A \\ \begin{bmatrix} 1 & 1 & S_1 \\ -0.20 & -0.10 & S_2 \end{bmatrix} \end{array} \begin{array}{c} S \\ \begin{bmatrix} S_1 \\ S_2 \end{bmatrix} \end{array} = \begin{array}{c} b \\ \begin{bmatrix} 98,000 \\ 117,600 \end{bmatrix} \end{array}.$

2. For the correct matrix A in part 1, there exists a unique inverse matrix, A^{-1}. Multiplication of the matrix A^{-1} by the matrix A produces
   a. The matrix A.
   b. Another inverse matrix.
   c. The correct solution to the system.
   d. An identity matrix.

3. Without prejudice to your previous answers, assume that the correct matrix form in part 1 is

$$\begin{array}{c} A \\ \begin{bmatrix} 1 & -0.20 \\ -0.10 & 1 \end{bmatrix} \end{array} \begin{array}{c} S \\ \begin{bmatrix} S_1 \\ S_2 \end{bmatrix} \end{array} = \begin{array}{c} b \\ \begin{bmatrix} 98,000 \\ 117,600 \end{bmatrix} \end{array}.$$

Then the correct inverse matrix A^{-1} is

a. $\begin{bmatrix} 1/0.98 & 0.20/0.98 \\ 0.10/0.98 & 1/0.98 \end{bmatrix}.$

b. $\begin{bmatrix} 1/0.98 & 1/0.98 \\ 0.20/0.98 & 0.10/0.98 \end{bmatrix}.$

c. $\begin{bmatrix} 1/0.30 & 0.20/0.30 \\ 0.10/0.30 & 1/0.30 \end{bmatrix}.$

d. $\begin{bmatrix} 1/0.98 & -1/0.98 \\ -0.20/0.98 & 0.10/0.98 \end{bmatrix}.$

4. The total overhead allocated to department S_1 after receiving the allocation from department S_2 is

    a. $141,779.

    b. $124,000.

    c. $121,520.

    d. $117,600.

5. The total amount of overhead allocated to department S_2 after receiving the allocation from department S_1 is

    a. $392,000.

    b. $220,000.

    c. $130,000.

    d. $127,400.

6. Without prejudice to your previous answers, assume that the answer to part 4 is $100,000 and the answer to part 5 is $150,000. The total amount of overhead allocated to production department P_1 then is

    a. $1,508,104.

    b. $1,495,000.

    c. $1,489,800.

    d. $ 108,104.

(AICPA adapted)

10.22   ***Various Bases for Allocating Service Department Costs***   Thrift-Shops, Inc., operates a chain of three food stores in a state that recently enacted legislation permitting municipalities within the state to levy an income tax on corporations operating within their respective municipalities. The legislation establishes a uniform tax rate that the municipalities can levy and regulations providing that the tax is to be computed on income derived within the taxing municipality after a reasonable and consistent allocation of general overhead expenses. General overhead expenses have not been allocated to individual stores previously and include warehouse, general office, advertising, and delivery expenses.

    Each of the municipalities in which Thrift-Shops, Inc., operates a store has levied the corporate income tax as provided by state legislation, and management is considering two plans for allocating general overhead expenses to the stores. The 19X9 operating results before general overhead and taxes for each store were as follows:

	Store			
	Ashville	**Burns**	**Clinton**	**Total**
Sales (Net)	$416,000	$353,600	$270,400	$1,040,000
Less: Cost of Sales	215,700	183,300	140,200	539,200
Gross Margin	$200,300	$170,300	$130,200	$ 500,800
Less: Local Operating Expenses				
Fixed	$ 60,800	$ 48,750	$ 50,200	$ 159,750
Variable	54,700	64,220	27,448	146,368
Total	$115,500	$112,970	$ 77,648	$ 306,118
Income before General Overhead and Taxes	$ 84,800	$ 57,330	$ 52,552	$ 194,682

General overhead expenses in 19X9 were as follows:

Warehousing and Delivery Expenses		
Warehouse Depreciation	$20,000	
Warehouse Operations	30,000	
Delivery Expenses	40,000	$ 90,000
Central Office Expenses		
Advertising	$18,000	
Central Office Salaries	37,000	
Other Central Office Expenses	28,000	$ 83,000
Total General Overhead		$173,000

Additional information includes the following:

One-fifth of the warehouse space is used to house the central office, and depreciation on this space is included in other central office expenses. Warehouse operating expenses vary with the quantity of merchandise sold.

Delivery expenses vary with distance and number of deliveries. The distances from the warehouse to each store and the number of deliveries made in 19X9 were as follows:

Store	Miles	Number of Deliveries
Ashville	120	140
Burns	200	64
Clinton	100	104

All advertising is prepared by the central office and is distributed in the areas in which stores are located.

As each store was opened, the fixed portion of central office salaries increased $7,000, and other central office expenses increased $2,500. Basic fixed central office salaries amount to $10,000, and basic fixed other central office expenses amount to $12,000. The remainder of central office salaries and the remainder of other central office expenses vary with sales.

Required:

1. For each of the following plans for allocating general overhead expenses, compute the income of each store that would be subject to the municipal levy on corporation income:

a. Plan 1 is to allocate all general overhead expenses on the basis of sales volume.

b. Plan 2 is to first allocate central office salaries and other central office expenses evenly to warehouse operations and each store. Second, allocate the resulting warehouse operations expenses, warehouse depreciation, and advertising of each store on the basis of sales volume. Third, allocate delivery expenses to each store on the basis of delivery miles times the number of deliveries.

2. Management has decided to expand one of the three stores to increase sales by $50,000. The expansion will increase local fixed operating expenses by $7,500 and require ten additional deliveries from the warehouse. Determine which store management should select for expansion to maximize corporate profits.

(AICPA adapted)

10.23   *Adding a Department*   The management of Bay Company is considering a proposal to install a third production department within its existing factory building. With the company's present production setup, raw material is passed through department I to produce materials A and B in equal proportions. Material A is then passed through department II to yield product C. Material B is now being sold "as is" at a price of $20.25 per pound. Product C has a selling price of $100 per pound.

The per-pound standard costs now being used by the Bay Company are as follows:

	Department I (Materials A and B)	Department II (Product C)	Material B
Prior Department Costs	—	$53.03	$13.47
Direct Material	$20.00	—	—
Direct Labor	7.00	12.00	—
Variable Overhead	3.00	5.00	—
Fixed Overhead			
Attributable	2.25	2.25	—
Allocated (⅔, ⅓)	1.00	1.00	—
	$33.25	$73.28	$13.47

These standard costs were developed by using an estimated production volume of 200,000 pounds of raw material as the denominator volume. The company assigns department I costs to materials A and B in proportion to their net sales values at the point of separation, computed by deducting subsequent standard production costs from sales prices. The $300,000 of common fixed overhead costs are allocated to the two producing departments on the basis of the space used by the departments.

Attributable overhead is the amount of fixed overhead that could be avoided if a given product or activity were discontinued. The proposed department III would be used to process material B into product D. It is expected that any quantity of product D can be sold for $30 per pound. Standard costs per pound under this proposal were developed by using 200,000 pounds of raw material as the denominator volume and are as follows:

	Department I (Materials A and B)	Department II (Product C)	Department III (Product D)
Prior Department Costs	—	$52.80	$13.20
Direct Material	$20.00	—	—
Direct Labor	7.00	12.00	5.50
Variable Overhead	3.00	5.00	2.00
Fixed Overhead			
Attributable	2.25	2.25	1.75
Allocated (½, ¼, ¼)	0.75	0.75	0.75
	$33.00	$72.80	$23.20

Required:

1. If sales and production levels are expected to remain constant in the foreseeable future, and there are no foreseeable alternative uses for the available factory space, should the Bay Company install department III and thereby produce product D? Show calculations to support your answer.

2. Instead of constant sales and production levels, suppose that under the present production setup, $1,000,000 in additions to the factory building must be made every ten years to accommodate growth. Suppose also that proper maintenance gives these factory additions an infinite life and that all such maintenance costs are included in the standard costs set forth in the text of the problem. How would the analysis that you performed in part 1 be changed if the installation of department III shortened the interval at which the $1,000,000 in factory additions are made from ten years to six years? Be as specific as possible in your answer.

(CMA adapted)

10.24   ***Joint Products and By-products***   The Harrison Corporation produces three products (Alpha, Beta, and Gamma). Alpha and Gamma are joint products, whereas Beta is a by-product of Alpha. No joint cost is to be allocated to the by-product. The production processes for a given year are as follows.

In department 1, 110,000 pounds of raw material (Rho) are processed at a total cost of $120,000. After processing in department 1, 60 percent of the units are transferred to department 2, and 40 percent of the units (now Gamma) are transferred to department 3.

In department 2, the material is further processed at a total additional cost of $38,000. Seventy percent of the units (now Alpha) are transferred to department 4, and 30 percent emerge as Beta, the by-product, to be sold at $1.20 per pound. Selling expenses related to disposing of Beta are $8,100.

In department 4, Alpha is processed at a total additional cost of $23,660. After this processing, Alpha is ready for sale at $5 per pound.

In department 3, Gamma is processed at a total additional cost of $165,000. In this department, a normal loss of units of Gamma equals 10 percent of the good output of Gamma. The remaining good output of Gamma is then sold for $12 per pound.

Required:
1. Prepare a schedule showing the allocation of the $120,000 joint cost between Alpha and Gamma using the net realizable value approach. The net realizable value of Beta should be treated as an addition to the sales value of Alpha.

2. Independent of your answer to part 1, assume that $102,000 of total joint costs were appropriately allocated to Alpha. Assume also that there were 48,000 pounds of Alpha and 20,000 pounds of Beta available to sell. Prepare a statement of gross margin for Alpha using the following facts:

During the year, sales of Alpha made up 80 percent of the pounds available for sale. There was no beginning inventory.

The net realizable value of Beta available for sale is to be deducted from the cost of producing Alpha. The ending inventory of Alpha is to be based on the net cost of production.

All other cost, selling price, and selling expense data are those listed in the text of this problem.

(AICPA adapted)

10.25   ***Service Department Costs***   The Parker Manufacturing Company has two production departments (fabrication and assembly) and three service departments (general factory administration, factory maintenance, and factory cafeteria). A summary of costs and other data for each department prior to the allocation of service department costs for the year ended June 30, 19X3, appears here:

	Fabrication	Assembly	General Factory Administration	Factory Maintenance	Factory Cafeteria
Direct-Labor Costs	$1,950,000	$2,050,000	$90,000	$82,100	$87,000
Direct-Material Costs	$3,130,000	$ 950,000	—	$65,000	$91,000
Manufacturing Overhead Costs	$1,650,000	$1,850,000	$70,000	$56,100	$62,000
Direct-Labor Hours	562,500	437,500	31,000	27,000	42,000
Number of Employees	280	200	12	8	20
Square Footage Occupied	88,000	72,000	1,750	2,000	4,800

The costs of the general factory administration department, factory maintenance department, and factory cafeteria are allocated on the basis of direct-labor hours, square footage occupied, and number of employees, respectively. There are no manufacturing overhead variances.

Required:
Choose the best answer to the following questions. Round all final calculations to the nearest dollar.
1. Assume that Parker elects to distribute service department costs directly to production departments without interservice department cost allocation. The amount of factory maintenance department costs that would be allocated to the fabrication department would be
  a. $0.   **c.** $106,091.
  b. $111,760.   **d.** $91,440.

2. Assume the same method of allocation as in part 1. The amount of general factory administration department costs that would be allocated to the assembly department would be

a. $0.
b. $63,636.
c. $70,000.
d. $90,000.

3. Assume that Parker elects to distribute service department costs to other service departments (starting with the service department with the greatest total costs) as well as to the production departments. What amount of factory cafeteria department costs would be allocated to the factory maintenance department? (*Note:* Once a service department's costs have been reallocated, no subsequent service department costs are recirculated back to it.)

a. $0.
b. $96,000.
c. $3,840.
d. $6,124.

4. Assume the same method of allocation as in part 3. The amount of factory maintenance department costs that would be allocated to the factory cafeteria would be

a. $0.
b. $5,787.
c. $5,856.
d. $6,124.

(AICPA adapted)

10.26   *Allocation of Common Cost by Joint and By-product Methods*   During 19X1 the Juno Chemical Company started a new division whose operation consists of processing a mineral into commercial products A, B, C, and D. Each product passes through identical processing operations. However, product D is classified as a second, or reject, and is sold at a lower price. The following information is available regarding the company's operation for 19X1:

Sales (Including Product D) $24,480
Production Costs 49,769
Selling Costs Allocated to Division 1,224

	Total	Product A	Product B	Product C	Product D
Quantity (Tons)					
Beginning Inventory	—	—	—	—	—
Production	634	305	137	22	170
Sales	285	132	83	10	60
Ending Inventory	349	173	54	12	110
Sales Price per Ton (Constant throughout the Period)	—	$100	$100	$100	$33

Required:

1. Compute the inventory valuation at December 31, 19X1, under the joint cost method of accounting at the lower of cost or market applied on an individual item basis.

2. Compute the inventory valuation at December 31, 19X1, under the by-product method of accounting at the lower of cost or market applied on an individual item basis. The company has elected to recognize income in the period in which the by-products are produced. No selling costs are assigned to the by-products.

(AICPA adapted)

10.27   *Joint Costs: Relative Sales Value*   By-products that require no additional processing after the point of separation are often accounted for by assigning to them a value of zero at the point of separation and crediting Cost of Production as sales are made.

Required:
1. Justify the treatment.
2. Discuss the possible shortcomings of the treatment.

The LaBreck Company's joint cost of producing 1,000 units of product A, 500 units of product B, and 500 units of product C is $100,000. The unit sales values of the three products at the split-off point are product A, $20; product B, $200; and product C, $160. Ending inventories include 100 units of product A, 300 units of product B, and 200 units of product C.

Required:
3. Compute the amount of joint cost that would be included in the ending inventory valuation of the three products (a) on the basis of their relative sales value and (b) on the basis of physical units.
4. Discuss the relative merits of each of these two bases of joint cost allocation (a) for financial statement purposes and (b) for decisions about the desirability of selling joint products at the split-off point or processing them further.

(AICPA adapted)

10.28   *Joint Costs*   The Harbison Company manufactures two sizes of plate glass, which are produced simultaneously in the same manufacturing process. Since the small sheets of plate glass are cut from large sheets that have flaws in them, the joint costs are allocated equally to each good sheet produced, large and small. There is a material difference in costs after split-off for large and small sheets.

In 19X6 the company decided to increase its efforts to sell the large sheets, because they produced a larger gross margin than the small sheets. Accordingly, the amount of the fixed advertising budget devoted to large sheets was increased, and the amount devoted to small sheets was decreased. However, no changes in sales prices were made.

By midyear the production scheduling department had increased the monthly production of large sheets to stay above the minimum inventory level. However, it also had cut back the monthly production of small sheets, because the inventory ceiling had been reached.

At the end of 19X6, the net result of the change in product mix was a decrease of $112,000 in gross margin. Although sales of large sheets had increased 34,500 units, sales of small sheets had decreased 40,200 units.

Required:
1. Distinguish between joint costs and
   a. Costs after split-off.
   b. Fixed costs.
   c. Prime costs.
   d. Indirect costs.
2. Discuss the propriety of allocating joint costs for general-purpose financial statements on the basis of
   a. Physical measures, such as weights or units.
   b. Relative sales or market value.
3. In the development of weights for allocating joint costs to joint products, why is the relative sales value of each joint product usually reduced by its costs after split-off?
4. Identify the mistake that the Harbison Company made in deciding to change its product mix. Explain why this caused a smaller gross margin for 19X6.

(AICPA adapted)

10.29

Joint Product Costing, Depth-of-Processing Decisions, and Accounting for By-products The Dual Company produces two products from the same raw materials. The first operation is a refining process of the raw materials. At the final stage of the first operation the processed materials are screened, resulting in an output of two different product grades (A and B). The proportions of output of products A and B remain constant, that is, 3:2 (every 100 pounds of input yields 60 pounds of A and 40 pounds of B).

At the end of this operation, product A can be sold immediately for $4 per pound and product B for $8 per pound. However, product B can be processed further and then sold for $10 per pound. Only 90 percent of the materials processed in this second operation emerge as final products. The remaining 10 percent can be sold only as a by-product for $2.40 per pound.

The Dual Company has been operating for one year at 50 percent capacity, and it sold all of its production at the end of the refining process. All costs of the refining process are charged to Cost of Goods Sold. Next year, the company expects to work at full capacity and anticipates some inventory buildup of finished products.

The anticipated costs for the refining process at full capacity are

Raw Materials	$ 96,000
Direct Labor	144,000
Variable Overhead	84,000
Fixed Overhead[a]	180,000
Total	$504,000
Total Pounds of Input	120,000 Pounds

[a]The fixed overhead is not expected to change whether product B is processed further or not.

Required:

1. Compute the cost per pound under two different methods of assigning joint costs to products A and B, assuming B is not processed further. State which method is more appropriate to the situation described, and give a reason for your choice.

2. For the evaluation of further processing of product B, advise management as to maximum costs that could be spent per pound. (Be specific, for example, pounds of input or output.)

3. List two methods of accounting for revenue from by-products.

(SMA adapted)

10.30

Joint and By-products, Process Further Gossett Chemical Company uses comprehensive annual profit planning procedures to evaluate pricing policies, finalize production decisions, and estimate unit costs for its products. One particular product group, which involves two joint products and two by-products, is separately analyzed each year to establish appropriate production and marketing policies.

The two joint products (ALCHEM-X and CHEM-P) emerge at the end of processing in department 20. Both chemicals can be sold at this split-off point—ALCHEM-X for $2.50 per unit and CHEM-P for $3 per unit. By-product BY-D20 also emerges at the split-off point in department 20 and is salable without further processing for $.50 per unit. Unit costs of preparing this by-product for market are $.03 for freight and $.12 for packaging.

CHEM-P is sold without further processing, but ALCHEM-X is transferred to department 22 for additional processing into the refined chemical ALCHEM-XF, sold for $5 per unit. No additional raw materials are added in department 22. By-product BY-D22 is created by the additional processing in department 22, and it can be sold for $.70 per unit. Unit marketing costs for BY-D22 are $.05 for freight and $.15 for packaging.

Gossett Chemical Company accounts for by-product production by crediting the net realizable value of by-products produced to production costs of the main products. The company uses the net realizable value method to allocate net joint production costs for inventory valuation purposes.

A portion of the 19X5 profit plan established in September 19X4 is presented here:

| | Units of Production | |
	CHEM-P	ALCHEM-XF
Estimated Sales	400,000	210,000
Planned Inventory Change	8,000	6,000
Required Production	392,000	204,000
Minimum Production Based on Joint Output Ratio	392,000	210,000

By-product Output
  BY-D20: 90,000 Units
  BY-D22: 60,000 Units

| | Costs | |
	Department 20	Department 22
Budgeted Production Costs		
Raw Material	$160,000	—
Costs Transferred from 20[a]	—	$225,000
Hourly Direct Labor	170,000	120,000
Variable Overhead	180,000	140,800
Fixed Overhead	247,500	188,000
	$757,500	$673,800

Budgeted Marketing Costs
  CHEM-P: $196,000
  ALCHEM-XF: $105,000

[a]The cost transferred to department 22 is calculated as follows:

Sales Value of Output		
ALCHEM-X (210,000 × $2.50)	$ 525,000	31%
CHEM-P (392,000 × $3)	1,176,000	69
	$1,701,000	100%

Department 20 Costs	$ 757,500
Less: By-product (90,000 × $.35)	31,500
Net Costs	$ 726,000

ALCHEM-X	31%	$ 225,000 or $1.07 per Unit
CHEM-P	69	501,000 or $1.28 per Unit
Allocated net costs	100%	$ 726,000

Shortly after this budget was compiled, the company learned that a chemical that would compete with ALCHEM-XF was to be introduced. The marketing department estimated that this would require a permanent price reduction to $3.50 per unit for the ALCHEM-XF to be sold in the present quantities. Gossett must now reevaluate the decision to further process ALCHEM-X. The market for ALCHEM-X will not be affected by the introduction of the new chemical, so the quantities of ALCHEM-X that are usually processed into ALCHEM-XF can be sold at the regular price of $2.50 per unit. The costs for marketing ALCHEM-X are estimated to be $105,000. If the further processing is terminated, department 22 will be dismantled, and all costs will be eliminated except equipment depreciation, $18,400; supervisory salaries, $21,200; and general overhead, $35,200.

Required:

1. Should Gossett sell ALCHEM-X at the split-off point or continue to process it further in department 22? Prepare a schedule of relevant costs and revenues to support your answer.

2. During discussions of the possible dropping of ALCHEM-XF, one person noted that the manufacturing margin for ALCHEM-X would be 57.2 percent, or (2.50 − 1.07) ÷ 2.50, and for CHEM-P, 57.3 percent. The normal markup for products sold in the market with ALCHEM-X is 72 percent. For the CHEM-P portion of the line, the markup is 47 percent. This person argued that the company's unit costs must be incorrect, because the margins differ from the typical rates. Briefly explain why Gossett's rates for the two products are almost identical, when "normal" rates are not.

(CMA adapted)

Management must often decide whether to add a product or buy a new machine. They make many general, nonrecurring investment decisions involving fixed assets, or *capital budgeting* decisions. Capital budgeting involves a current outlay or a series of outlays of cash resources in return for anticipated benefits to be received beyond one year in the future. The capital budgeting decision has three distinguishing characteristics: anticipated benefits, a time element, and a degree of risk associated with the realization of the benefits. In general, these characteristics can be described more specifically as anticipated cash benefits, a time lag between the initial capital investment and the realization of the cash benefits, and a degree of risk. Ideally, a firm with a profit maximization motive will seek an investment that will generate large benefits in a short period and with a minimum of risk. However, investments with potentially large benefits are generally possible only with high risk and may require more time than investments with lower benefits.

Given these less-than-ideal relationships between the dimensions of a capital budgeting decision, management should desire a trade-off between these elements in making a capital budgeting decision that will meet their objectives. Although various objective functions may be chosen by firms, the most useful for evaluating capital budgeting decisions is the stockholders' wealth maximization model (SWMM).[1] Despite the fact that it represents a normative model, the SWMM provides a generally acceptable and meaningful criterion for the evaluation of capital budgeting proposals: the maximization of owners' wealth.

11.1   *ADMINISTRATION OF CAPITAL BUDGETING*

Although the administrative process of capital budgeting may differ from one firm to another, it involves five basic steps. The first step is the planning, or origination and

---

[1] Ahmed Belkaoui, *Conceptual Foundations of Management Accounting* (Reading, Mass.: Addison-Wesley, 1980), pp. 58–60.

specification, of capital investments. Because capital investments are considered essential to a firm's profitable long-run growth, managers constantly search for new methods, processes, plants, and products. These projects usually come from various sources, including the following:

1. New products or markets, and the expansion of existing products or markets.

2. Research and development.

3. Replacement of fixed assets.

4. Other investments to reduce costs; improve the quality of the product; improve morale; or comply with government orders, labor agreements, insurance policy terms, and so forth.

The second step in capital budgeting is the evaluation of the proposed capital investments. Firms differ in their routine for processing capital budgets, but most evaluate and approve the projects at various managerial levels. For example, a request for capital investment made by the production department may be examined, evaluated, and approved by (1) the plant managers, (2) the vice-president for operations, and (3) a capital budget committee or department, which may submit recommendations to the president. The president, after adding recommendations, may submit the project to the board of directors. This routine is often complemented and simplified by a uniform policy and procedure manual presenting in detail the firm's capital budgeting philosophy and techniques.

The third step in capital budgeting is the decision making based on the results of the evaluation process. Depending on the size of the projects, some decisions may be made at a high level, such as the board of directors (if they are large projects), or at a lower level if they are small- to medium-sized projects.

The fourth step is control. The firm includes each of the accepted projects in the capital budget and appropriates funds. Periodically, control is exercised over the expenditures made for the project. If the appropriated funds are insufficient, a budgetary review can be initiated to examine and approve the estimated overrun. The control step can be extended to include a continuous evaluation process to incorporate current information and check the validity of the original predictions.

The fifth capital budgeting step is the postaudit. This involves a comparison of the actual cash flows of a capital investment with those planned and included in the capital budget.

11.2   ESTIMATING CASH FLOWS

One of the most important capital budgeting tasks for the evaluation of the project capital investments is the estimation of the *relevant cash flows* for each project, which refers to the incremental cash flow arising from each project. Because companies rely on accrual accounting rather than cash accounting, adjustments are necessary to derive the cash flows from the conventional financial accounting records.

11.2.1   Cash and Accrual Accounting

Capital budgeting determines a project's potential incremental cash inflows and outflows compared with the flows if the project were not initiated. The receipt and payment of cash is the significant event in recording the cash inflows and outflows and determining the cash income of a project. This cash income, however, differs in the following ways from the accounting income due to the timing differences arising from the use of accrual accounting for external reporting:

1. The first difference arises from the capitalization of the cost of a capital asset at the time of purchase and the recognition of depreciation expenses over the asset's economic life. In a capital budgeting context, the cost of a capital asset is a cash outflow when paid.

2. Accrual accounting rests on the application of the matching of revenues and expenses, which leads to the recognition of revenues when earned and costs when incurred, even if no cash has been received or paid. This leads to the recognition of accounts receivable, accounts payable, and various asset balances as the result of the timing differences between accounting income and cash income.

To determine the cash income, adjustments in the accounting income are necessary to correct for these timing differences. Some adjustments are illustrated in Table 11.1.

11.2.2   *Identifying the Project Cash Flows*

Project cash flows are incremental cash flows arising from a project and are equal to the difference between the cash inflows and the cash outflows. The cash inflows include (1) after-tax net cash revenues, (2) savings in operating expenses, and (3) the salvage value of equipment from each project. The cash outflows include the cost of investment in each of the projects.

11.2.3   *Effect of Charges on Cash Flows*

Various charges affect the computation of cash flows. *Depreciation* and *amortization charges* are noncash expenses. However, they have an indirect influence on cash flow. Because depreciation is tax deductible, it provides a tax shield by protecting from taxation an amount of income equal to the depreciation deduction. The after-tax proceeds of a project are increased by the allowable depreciation times the tax rate, as shown by the following relationships:

$$\text{After-tax cash proceeds} = \text{Revenues} - \text{Expenses other than depreciation} - \text{Income tax}. \qquad [1]$$

The income tax can be determined as follows:

$$\text{Income tax} = \text{Tax rate} \times \text{Taxable income} \qquad [2]$$

or

$$\text{Income tax} = \text{Tax rate} \times (\text{Revenues} - \text{Expenses other than depreciation} - \text{Depreciation}). \qquad [3]$$

Therefore, the higher the depreciation, the lower the income tax.

Table 11.1   Reconciliation of Cash Flow and Accounting Income

1. Accounting Income (Traditional Income Statement)

Assume that the purchase of a new machine costing $10,000 and having a ten-year life and zero disposal value is expected to earn the following for the first year:

Sales	$10,000
Less: Operating Expenses, Excluding Depreciation	$ 5,000
Depreciation (Straight-line)	1,000
Total expenses	$ 6,000
Operating Income before Income Taxes	$ 4,000
Less: Income Taxes at 40 Percent	1,600
Net Income after Taxes	$ 2,400

Other Accrual Information:
a. Sales are 40 percent cash.
b. The expenses, excluding depreciation, are 60 percent on credit.

2. Cash Flow (Cash Effects of Operations)

a. *Cash Inflow from Operations*	
Total Sales	$10,000
Less: Credit Sales: 60 Percent of $10,000 (Increase in Accounts Receivable)	6,000
Cash Collections from Sales	$ 4,000
b. *Cash Outflow from Operating Expenses*	
Total Expenses	$ 5,000
Less: Credit Expenditures: 60 Percent of $5,000 (Increase in Accounts Payable)	$ 3,000
Cash Payments for Operating Expenses	$ 2,000
c. *Net Cash Inflow:* $4,000 − $2,000	$ 2,000
d. *Income Tax Outflow*	$ 1,600
e. *After-Tax Net Cash Inflow*	$ 400
f. *Effect of Depreciation*	
Depreciation Expense	$ 1,000
Tax at 50%	500
Tax Shield	$ 500
g. *Total Cash Flow* (After-Tax Net Cash Inflow + Tax Shield)	$ 900

By substituting equation 3 into equation 1, the after-tax proceeds can be expressed as follows:

$$\text{After-tax cash proceeds} = \left[(1 - \text{Tax rate})\left(\text{Revenues} - \substack{\text{Expenses} \\ \text{other than} \\ \text{depreciation}}\right)\right] + (\text{Tax rate} \times \text{Depreciation}).$$

Financing charges are excluded from the cash flow computation used in capital budgeting. First, the interest factor would be counted twice by the use of present value methods of evaluation (to be presented in the next section). Second, the evaluation of a capital project is separate from and independent of the financing aspects.

Opportunity costs of scarce resources diverted from other uses because of the capital project should be charged against the investment project. They can be measured by estimating how much the resource (personnel time or facility space) would earn if the investment project were not undertaken.

11.3   RANKING CAPITAL PROJECTS

The project evaluation phase consists of evaluating the attractiveness of the investment proposals. Managers first choose the project evaluation methods best suited to the capital budgeting decision. The most common are the *discounted cash flow (DCF) methods* (*internal rate of return (IRR) method, net present value (NPV) method*, and profitability index, or PI), the *payback method*, and the *accounting rate of return (ARR) method*. Each of these methods will be examined in the following sections.

11.4   DISCOUNTED CASH FLOW METHODS

The discounted cash flow methods consider the *time value of money* in the evaluation of capital budgeting proposals. A dollar received now is worth more than a dollar received in the future; a dollar in the hand today can be invested to earn a return. Hence, to understand the discounted cash flow methods, it is necessary to grasp the time value concepts included in appendices 11.A to 11.E.

The discounted cash flow methods focus on cash flows generated over the life of a project rather than the accounting income. These methods involve discounting the cash flow of a project to its *present value* using an appropriate discount rate. There are two basic discounted cash flow methods: (1) the internal rate of return (or time-adjusted rate of return) method and (2) the net present value method.

11.4.1   Internal Rate of Return Method

The IRR is the interest rate that equates the present value of an investment's cash flows and the cost of the investment. The IRR equation follows:

$$\sum_{t=0}^{n} \left[\frac{C_t}{(1 + r)^t} \right] = 0,$$

where

C_t = Cash flow for period t, whether it be a net inflow or a net outflow, including the initial investment at $t = 0$.

n = Investment life, that is, the last period in which a cash flow is expected.

r = IRR as the discount rate that equates the present value of cash flow C_t to zero.

If the initial cash outlay or cost occurs at a time 0, the IRR equation becomes

$$\sum_{t=1}^{n}\left[\frac{C_t}{(1 + r)^t}\right] - C_0 = 0.$$

Solving for r is on a trial-and-error basis; the procedures differ depending on whether the cash flows are uniform or nonuniform.

Uniform Cash Flows

To illustrate, assume a project considered by the Camelli Corporation requires a cash outlay of $39,100 and has an expected after-tax annual net cash savings of $10,000 for six years and no salvage value. Find the interest rate (r) that equates the present value of future annual cash flows of $10,000 and the initial outlay of $39,100 at time 0. Experimenting with two discount rates, 12 and 14 percent, you find

Discount Rate	Discount Factor (Appendix 11.E)	Cash Flow	Present Value of Stream
12%	4.1110	$10,000	$41,110
14%	3.8890	$10,000	$38,890

Thus, the IRR that equates the present value of the stream of annual savings and $39,100 is between 12 and 14 percent. This rate can be found by interpolating between 12 and 14 percent:

12% $41,110 (Too large)
14   38,890 (Too small)
 2% $ 2,220

$$\frac{\$41,110 - \$39,100}{\$2,220} = 0.905.$$

IRR = 12% + (0.905 × 2%) = 13.81%.

A trial-and-error process determines that 13.81 percent is the IRR that equates the present value of the stream of savings and the cost of the investment. This indicates that the investment will yield a return of 13.81 percent per year in addition to recovering the original cost of $39,100. Table 11.2 depicts the amortization schedule of the invest-

Table 11.2   Amortization Schedule: Proof for the Internal Rate of Return

Year	Unrecorded Investment at Beginning of Year	Annual Cash Savings	13.81% Return or Interest[a]	Cost Recovery[b]	Unrecovered Investment at End of Year[c]
1	$39,100.00	$10,000	$5399.71	$4600.29	$34,499.71
2	34,499.71	10,000	4764.41	5235.59	29,264.12
3	29,264.12	10,000	4041.38	5958.62	23,305.50
4	23,305.50	10,000	3218.49	6781.51	16,523.99
5	16,523.99	10,000	2281.96	7718.04	8,805.95
6	8,805.95	10,000	1216.10	8783.90	22.05[d]

[a] Return = Unrecorded investment × 13.81%.
[b] Cost recovery = Annual cash savings − Return.
[c] Unrecovered investment at the end of the year = Unrecorded investment at the beginning of the year − Cost recovery.
[d] Rounding error.

ment: The six-year cash savings of $10,000 recovers the original investment plus an annual return of 13.81 percent on the investment.

The computation of the IRR does not determine if the project is to be accepted or rejected. To do so, the IRR generally is compared with a required rate of return. For example, if the IRR exceeds the required rate of return, the project is acceptable. The required rate of return, also known as a *cutoff rate* or *hurdle rate*, is the firm's cost of capital (the cost of acquiring funds). Passing this test does not mean the project will be funded, as funds may be rationed.

Nonuniform Cash Flows

The following example illustrates a project yielding cash flows that are not equal for all the periods of the project's life. We assume the machine considered by the Camelli Corporation costs $39,100 and yields the following cash savings:

Year	Cash Savings
1	$20,000
2	14,000
3	10,000
4	6,000
5	5,000
6	4,000

Solving for the IRR that equates the present value of these savings and the cost of the investment also requires trial and error. First, experimenting with an interest rate of 16 percent, we find

Year	Discount Factor × (Appendix 11.C)	Cash Savings =	Present Value of Cash Savings
1	0.862	$20,000	$17,240
2	0.743	14,000	10,402
3	0.641	10,000	6,410
4	0.552	6,000	3,312
5	0.476	5,000	2,380
6	0.410	4,000	1,640
Present Value of Cash Savings			$41,384
Present Value of Cash Outflow (Cost of the Machine)			39,100
Difference			$ 2,284

Given that the present value of cash savings is $2,284 higher than the present value of the cash outflow, the IRR must be higher than 16 percent.

Second, experimenting with an interest rate of 20 percent, we find

Year	Discount Factor × (Appendix 11.C)	Cash Savings =	Present Value of Cash Savings
1	0.833	$20,000	$16,660
2	0.694	14,000	9,716
3	0.579	10,000	5,790
4	0.482	6,000	2,892
5	0.402	5,000	2,010
6	0.335	4,000	1,340
Present Value of Cash Savings			$38,408
Present Value of Cash Outflow (Cost of the Machine)			39,100
Difference (NPV)			$ (692)

Given that the present value of cash savings is $692 lower than the present value of the cash outflow, the IRR must be *between* 16 and 20 percent, and closer to 20 percent.

Third, experimenting with 19 percent we obtain

Year	Discount Factor (Appendix 11.C)	× Cash Savings	= Present Value of Cash Savings
1	0.840	$20,000	$16,800
2	0.706	14,000	9,884
3	0.593	10,000	5,930
4	0.499	6,000	2,994
5	0.419	5,000	2,095
6	0.352	4,000	1,408

Present Value of Cash Savings	$39,111
Present Value of Cash Outflow (Cost of the Machine)	39,100
Difference (NPV)	$ 11

Given that the present value of cash savings is only $11 higher than the cost of the machine, the IRR is approximately 19 percent.

Net Present Value Method

The NPV method compares the cost of an investment with the present value of the future cash flows of the investment at a selected rate of return, or hurdle rate. The NPV of an investment is

$$NPV = \sum_{t=1}^{n} \left[\frac{C_t}{(1 + r)^t} \right] - C_0,$$

where

C_t = Project cash flows.

r = Selected hurdle rate.

n = Project life.

C_0 = Cost of the investment.

If the NPV is greater than or equal to zero, the project is deemed acceptable, but it may not be funded if there is rationing. The required rate of return, or hurdle rate, is usually the cost of capital. The NPV procedure differs depending upon whether the cash flows are uniform or nonuniform.

Uniform Cash Flows

To illustrate the NPV method, let us return to the Camelli Corporation example in which a new machine costing $39,100 would yield an annual cash savings of $10,000 for the six years of its life. Assuming a cost of capital of 10 percent, the NPV of the project can be stated as follows:

$$NPV = \sum_{t=1}^{6} \left[\frac{\$10,000}{(1 + 0.10)^6} \right] - \$39,100.$$

Appendix 11.E shows the present value of a constant stream of $1 received at the end of each year for N years at r percent. The appropriate discount factor for the Camelli Corporation is 4.355. Thus, the NPV is computed as follows:

$$NPV = (\$10,000 \times 4.355) - \$39,100 = \$4,450.$$

Given that the NPV is greater than zero, the Camelli Corporation should accept the new machine proposal. The positive NPV indicates that the Camelli Corporation will earn a higher rate of return on its investment than its cost of capital.

Different NPVs result from different hurdle rates. For example,

NPV at an 8% required rate = $(\$10,000 \times 4.623) - \$39,100 = \$7,130.$

NPV at a 14% required rate = $(\$10,000 \times 3.889) - \$39,100 = \$(210).$

Thus, given a stream of uniform cash flows, the higher the hurdle rate, the less attractive any investment proposal becomes.

The NPV method rests on two assumptions: (1) The cash flows are *certain* (this applies also to the IRR), and (2) the original investment can be viewed as either borrowed or loaned by the Camelli Corporation at the hurdle rate.

Thus, if the Camelli Corporation borrows $39,100 from the bank at 10 percent and uses the cash flows generated to repay the loan, it will obtain the same return as if it had invested $4,450 at the same rate. (See Table 11.3.)

Table 11.3 *Amortization Schedule Underlying the Net Present Value*

Option 1: Borrow and Invest in the Project

Year	Loan Balance at Beginning of Year	Interest at 10% per Year	Loan and Interest at End of Year	Cash Flow to Repay the Loan	Loan Balance at End of Year
1	$39,100.00	$3,910.00	$43,010.00	$10,000	$ 33,010.00
2	33,010.00	3,301.00	36,311.00	10,000	26,311.00
3	26,311.00	2,631.10	28,942.10	10,000	18,942.10
4	18,942.10	1,894.21	20,836.31	10,000	10,836.31
5	10,836.31	1,083.63	11,919.94	10,000	1,919.94
6	1,919.94	191.99	2,111.93	10,000	(7,888.06)

Option 2: Invest $4,450 at 10 Percent Rate of Return

Year	Investment Balance at Beginning of Year	Interest at 10% per Year	Investment and Interest at End of Year
1	$4,450.00	$445.00	$4,895.00
2	4,895.00	489.50	5,385.50
3	5,384.50	538.45	5,922.95
4	5,922.95	592.30	6,515.95
5	6,515.25	651.53	7,166.78
6	7,166.78	716.68	7,883.46[a]

[a]The $4.60 difference between $7,888.06 and $7,883.46 is a rounding error.
Note:
The above result for option 2 could also be computed using Appendix 11.B by simply multiplying $4,450 by the appropriate compound sum factor.

Nonuniform Cash Flows
The following example illustrates a project yielding cash flows that are not equal for all periods of the project's life. Assume again that the machine considered by the Camelli Corporation yields annual cash savings of $20,000, $14,000, $10,000, $6,000, $5,000, and $4,000 for the six years, respectively, and the cost of capital is 10 percent. The computation of the NPV follows:

Year	Discount Factor × (Appendix 11.C)	Cash Savings =	Present Value of Cash Savings
1	0.909	$20,000	$18,180
2	0.826	14,000	11,564
3	0.753	10,000	7,530
4	0.683	6,000	4,098
5	0.621	5,000	3,105
6	0.564	4,000	2,256

Present Value of Cash Savings	$46,733
Present Value of Cash Outflow (Cost of the Machine)	39,100
Difference (NPV)	$ 7,633

The NPV method is easier to apply than the IRR method with nonuniform cash flows, because it does not require iterative numerical methods.

Profitability Index
The PI, or benefit cost ratio, is another form of the NPV method. It is generally expressed as

$$PI = \frac{\text{Present value of cash inflows}}{\text{Present value of cash outflows}} .$$

For the Camelli Corporation example with uniform cash flows, the PI would be

$$PI = \frac{\$43,550}{\$39,100} = 1.114.$$

For the Camelli Corporation example with nonuniform cash flows, the PI would be

$$PI = \frac{\$46,733}{\$39,100} = 1.195.$$

The decision rule when evaluating different projects is to choose the project with the highest PI.

The NPV and the PI result in the same acceptance or rejection decision for any given project. However, the NPV and the PI can give different rankings for mutually exclusive projects. In such a case, the NPV method is the preferred method; it expresses the absolute profitability of a project, whereas the PI expresses the relative profitability.

11.4.3   Comparison between Net Present Value and Internal Rate of Return

Acceptance or Rejection Decision
The IRR and NPV methods lead to the same acceptance or rejection decisions for independent projects with one or more periods of outlays followed *only* by periods of net

Figure 11.1 **Relationship between Net Present Value (NPV) and Internal Rate of Return (IRR)**

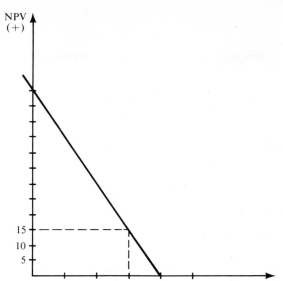

cash inflows. Figure 11.1 illustrates both the NPV and IRR applied to a capital project. At the zero discount rate, the NPV is equal to the sum of the total cash inflows less the total cash outflows. As the discount rate increases, the NPV decreases. Where the NPV reaches zero, the discount rate corresponds to the IRR, which is 20 percent in the fictional example depicted in Figure 11.1. The following situations are possible:

1. If the required rate of return used as a discount rate is less than the IRR, the project is acceptable under both methods. For example, if the required rate of return is 15 percent, the project is acceptable under both methods, given that at that rate Figure 11.1 shows an NPV superior to zero and a required rate inferior to the 20 percent IRR.

2. If the required rate of return is equal to the IRR, the project is acceptable under both methods. In such a case the NPV is equal to zero, and the required rate of return is equal to the IRR.

3. If the required rate of return is higher than the IRR, the project is not acceptable under either method.

Conflicts between Net Present Value and Internal Rate of Return
The NPV and the IRR methods may lead to conflicting rankings. Which method provides the best result? To answer this question, the main conflicts between NPV and IRR must be examined, along with the problems associated with each of the methods.

The conflicts arise mainly in comparing mutually exclusive projects (projects capable of performing the same function). The evaluation of mutually exclusive projects by the NPV and the IRR methods can lead to at least three problems:

1. The problem when the mutually exclusive projects have different initial outlays is called the *scale effects problem*.

2. The problem when the mutually exclusive projects have a different timing of cash flows is called the *timing effects problem*.

3. The problem when the mutually exclusive projects have different lives is called the *live effects problem*.

Other problems arise from possible *multiple rates of return* when using the IRR method.

Both the conflicts and problems identified will be examined before we judge which method provides the best ranking.

Scale Effects   The NPV and the IRR methods yield conflicting rankings when mutually exclusive projects having different initial outlays are compared. Consider the example in Table 11.4, where project X is ranked better with the IRR method, and project Y is ranked better with the NPV method.

Given this conflicting result, which project should be chosen? Projects X and Y are incorrectly ranked by the IRR method because of the large difference in the cost of the projects. The incremental cost of $8,616 for project Y can be seen as an additional project W, which yields a positive NPV of $79.70 and an IRR of 15.10 percent, which is greater than the required rate of return of 15 percent. The incremental cost is acceptable under both the IRR and the NPV methods; thus, project Y should be selected. Since the NPV method has selected project Y, the NPV method is preferable.

Timing Effects   The NPV and IRR methods also yield conflicting results when mutually exclusive projects of equal size but with different timing of cash flows are compared. Consider the example in Table 11.5, where project Y is ranked better with the IRR method, and project X is ranked better with the NPV method.

Given this conflicting result, should project X or Y be chosen? Again, use the incremental approach:

Year 0: $0 cash outlays for both projects.

Year 1: $1,000 project Y cash flow exceeds that of project X.

Year 2: $1,212 project X cash flow exceeds that of project Y.

This situation also can be conceived as an investment of $1,000 in year 1 yielding $1,212 in year 2. Such a project W will yield a positive NPV of $101.81 and an IRR of 21.19 percent. Thus, project X should be selected. Since the NPV method selected project X, it can again be concluded that the NPV method is preferable.

Live Effects: The Reinvestment Rate Assumption   The NPV and the IRR methods may yield conflicting results when mutually exclusive projects of equal sizes but with different lives are compared. For example, consider the example in Table 11.6, where project X is ranked better with the IRR method, whereas project Y is ranked better with the NPV method. This ranking difference is due to the differences in the investment rate assumption. The IRR method assumes a reinvestment rate equal to the internal rate, whereas the NPV method assumes a reinvestment rate equal to the required rate of return used as a discount factor.

The two reinvestment assumptions can be illustrated by calculating the terminal values of project X under each of the two assumptions. The terminal value using 15 percent for two years is equal to $7,601.50. The terminal value using the required rate of return of 10 percent is equal to $6,957.50. If we compare these two terminal values to the $7,025 terminal value of project Y, we obtain two situations:

1. Using the IRR method, the terminal value of project X, $7,601.50, is greater than the terminal value of project Y, $7,025. The IRR method favors project X.

Table 11.4   Mutually Exclusive Investments: Scale Effects

Project	Initial Outlay	Cash Inflow (End of Year 1)	NPV at 15%	IRR
X	$ 8,333	$10,000	$362.7	20%
Y	$16,949	$20,000	$442.4	18%
W	$ 8,616	$10,000	$ 79.7	15.10%

Table 11.5   Mutually Exclusive Investments: Timing Effects

Project	Initial Outlay	Cash Inflow (End of Year 1)	Cash Inflow (End of Year 2)	NPV at 10%	IRR
X	$2,310	$1,000	$2,000	$251.99	14%
Y	$2,310	$2,000	$ 788	$159.24	16%
W	$ 0	$1,000	$1,212	$101.817	21.19%

Table 11.6   Mutually Exclusive Investments: Different Lives

Project	Initial Outlay	Cash Inflow Year 1	Cash Inflow Year 2	Cash Inflow Year 3	NPV at 10%	IRR
X	$5,000	$5,750	—	—	$227.26	15%
Y	$5,000	—	—	$7,025	$277.95	12%

2. Using the NPV method, the terminal value of project X, $6,957.50, is lower than the terminal value of project Y, $7,025. The NPV method favors project Y.

The assumption of reinvestment at the required rate of return implied in the NPV method is considered to be the better one, the cost of capital being the minimum return acceptable to the firm.

Multiple Internal Rates of Return   Another problem with the IRR method arises from the possibility of multiple IRRs for "abnormal" projects. A "normal" project has one or more outflows followed by a series of inflows. An abnormal project is one that has negative cash flows in periods after the first positive cash flow. With abnormal projects, there may be several different returns which fit the equation, one for each change of the sign of the cash flows.

For example, suppose a capital project requires the following cash flows:

Year	Cash Flow
0	$(1,600)
1	10,000
2	(10,000)

Solving for the IRR, we find two rates: 25 and 400 percent. Neither rate is correct, because neither measures investment value. Instead, the NPV method will give the correct decision and avoid the problem of multiple rates of return associated with some abnormal projects.

11.5   PAYBACK METHOD

The payback method, also called the *payout method*, is simply the number of years before the initial cash outlay of a project is fully recovered by its future cash inflows. For example, assume a firm is considering purchasing at $15,000 a delivery truck expected to save $5,000 per year in shipping expenses for four years. The payback formula is

$$\text{Payback} = \frac{\text{Initial cost of the project}}{\text{Annual net cash flows}}$$

$$= \frac{\$15,000}{\$\ 5,000}$$

$$= 3 \text{ years}.$$

In other words, the cost of the delivery truck will be recovered in three years. If the payback period calculated is less than an acceptable maximum payback period, the firm should accept the truck proposal.

For projects with nonuniform cash flows the procedure is slightly different. For example, assume the yearly cash savings are $4,000 in year 1, $5,000 in year 2, $3,000 in year 3, $3,000 in year 4, and $6,000 in year 5. It takes up to year 4 to recover a cumulative cash savings equal to the initial cost of the truck. Therefore, the payback period is four years.

An extension of the payback method is the *bailout method*, which takes into account both the cash savings and the salvage value needed to recover the initial cost of a project. Going back to the first example of the $15,000 truck with an expected savings of $5,000 per year in shipping expenses, assume also that the salvage value is estimated to be $8,000 at the end of year 1 and $5,000 at the end of year 2. The cash savings and salvage value of the truck for the next two years, then, are as follows:

Year	Cash Savings	Salvage Value	Cumulative Cash Savings and Salvage Value
1	$5,000	$8,000	$13,000 = $5,000 + $8,000
2	$5,000	$5,000	$15,000 = $5,000 + $5,000 + $5,000

Thus, at the end of year 2, the total of the cumulative cash savings and the salvage value is equal to the initial cost of the truck. The bailout period is two years.

Businesses commonly use the payback method to provide a quick ranking of capital projects. Some of its features follow, including both advantages and disadvantages:

1. It is easy to calculate and provide a quick answer to the question, How many years will it take before the initial cash outlay is completely recovered?

2. The payback method does not take into account the time value of money. The annual cash flows are given the same weight from one year to another. While the first feature can be interpreted as one of the strengths of the method, this feature is definitely a weakness.

3. The payback method ignores both the cash flows occurring after the payback period and the project's total physical life plan.

4. The payback period can be used to compute the *payback reciprocal*, which is equal to the IRR of the project, providing the project's expected cash flows are constant and are anticipated to continue until infinity. Although projects rarely, if ever, have a perpetual life, a rule of thumb states that the payback reciprocal yields a reasonable approximation of the IRR.[2] The formula for the payback reciprocal is

$$\text{Payback reciprocal} = \frac{r}{\text{Payback period}} .$$

11.6   ACCOUNTING RATE OF RETURN

The ARR method is a capital budgeting evaluation technique that uses the ratio of the average annual profit after taxes to the investment of the project. The ARR formula based on initial investment is

$$\text{ARR} = \frac{\text{Annual revenue from the project} - \text{Annual expenses of the project}}{\text{Initial investment}} .$$

The ARR formula based on average investment is

$$\text{ARR} = \frac{\text{Annual revenue from the project} - \text{Annual expenses of the project}}{\text{Average investment}} .$$

These computed ARR values are compared with a cutoff rate before an acceptance or rejection decision is made. For example, assume the Saxon Company is contemplating the purchase of a new machine costing $20,000 and having a five-year useful life and no salvage value. The new machine is expected to generate annual operating revenues of $7,000 and annual expenses of $5,000. The ARR can be computed as follows:

$$\text{ARR based on initial investment:} \frac{\$7,000 - \$5,000}{\$20,000} = 10\%.$$

$$\text{ARR based on average investment} = \frac{\$7,000 - \$5,000}{\dfrac{\$20,000 + 0}{2}} = 20\%.$$

The ARR, then, depends on the choice of an initial or average investment base. Using an average investment base leads to substantially higher rates of return. This can be corrected, however, by choosing a higher required cutoff ARR.

The principal strength of the ARR may be its simplicity. It can be computed easily from the accounting records. Since this same characteristic can be perceived as a weakness, the ARR relies on accounting income rather than cash flows. It fails to take into account the timing of cash flows and the time value of money.

---

[2] The exact rule, introduced by M. J. Gordon in 1955, states that provided the economic life of a project is equal to or greater than twice the payback period, the payback reciprocal yields a reasonable approximation of the project's IRR. Gordon also mentioned that if a project's life exceeds twice the payback period by two or three years (for projects with payoffs of no more than five years), the payback reciprocal will be incorrect by approximately 10 percent.

11.7   *METHODS OF CALCULATING DEPRECIATION*

The three widely used depreciation methods are the straight-line (SL), sum-of-the-years'-digits (SYD), and double declining balance (DDB) methods. Depreciation charges under the straight-line method are constant over an asset's useful life. Depreciation charges under the latter two methods are higher in the early years of an asset's useful life and taper off rapidly in later years. The best method for tax depreciation maximizes the present value of the depreciation tax shield (that is, reduces income taxes resulting from depreciation expense). The Economic Recovery Act of 1981 introduced new tax lives and an accelerated depreciation method labeled the *Accelerated Cost Recovery System (ACRS)* which in most cases result in the highest tax shield.

To determine which of the three depreciation methods maximizes the present value of the tax shield, let us use the example of a machine costing $100,000 with a ten-year useful life and no expected salvage value. The required rate of return (r) is 10 percent, and the marginal tax rate (T) is 40 percent.

11.7.1   *Straight-Line Depreciation*

The annual straight-line depreciation charge is the difference between the cost of an asset (C) and its future salvage value (S) divided by the asset's useful life (N), where $t =$ year:

$$\text{Annual SL depreciation charge} = SL_t$$

$$= \frac{C - S}{N}$$

$$= \frac{\$100,000}{10}$$

$$= \$10,000.$$

$$\text{Annual SL depreciation rate} = SLR_6$$

$$= \frac{SL_t}{C - S}$$

$$= \frac{\$10,000}{100,000} = 10\%.$$

$$\text{Depreciation tax shield} = \sum_{t=1}^{N} \frac{SL_t \times T}{(1 + r)^t}$$

$$= \sum_{t=1}^{N} \frac{\$10,000 \times 0.40}{(1 + 0.10)^t}$$

$$= \$24,580.$$

11.7.2   *Double Declining Balance Depreciation*

Under the double declining balance method, twice the straight-line rate is applied to the book value of the asset each year until the salvage value is reached:

$$\text{Annual DDB depreciation} = DDB_t = \frac{2}{N} \left(C - \sum_{i=1}^{t-1} DDB_i \right).$$

$$\text{Annual DDB rate} = \frac{2}{N} = \frac{2}{10} = 20\%.$$

$$\text{Depreciation tax shield} = \sum_{t=1}^{n} \frac{DDB_t \times T}{(1 + r)^t}.$$

Applying these formulae yields the following results:

1 Year	2 Book Value before Depreciation	3 Depreciation	4 Tax Shield (Col. 3 × 40%)	5 Discount Factor at 10% (Appendix 11.C)	6 Present Value (Col. 4 × Col. 5)
1	$100,000	$20,000	$8,000	0.909	$ 7,272
2	80,000	16,000	6,400	0.826	5,286
3	64,000	12,800	5,120	0.751	3,845
4	51,200	10,240	4,096	0.683	2,798
5	40,960	8,192	3,277	0.621	2,035
6	32,768	6,554[a]	2,622	0.564	1,479
7	26,214	6,553	2,621	0.513	1,345
8	19,661	6,554	2,622	0.467	1,224
9	13,107	6,553	2,621	0.424	1,111
10	6,554	6,554	2,621	0.386	1,012

Present Value of Tax Shield $27,407

[a]Under the general guidelines provided in the tax code, firms are permitted to switch from double declining balance to straight-line depreciation when it is to their advantage to do so. They switch at the point that minimizes the tax bill. From the seventh year in this case, straight-line depreciation charges are higher than double declining balance charges. This is because we are applying a constant rate to a declining balance, which will not carry to the end of the useful life.

11.7.3   *Sum-of-the-Years'-Digits Depreciation*

Under the sum-of-the-years'-digits method, a mathematical fraction is applied to the base. The numerator for a given year is the number of years remaining in the life of the project taken from the beginning of the year. The denominator is the sum of the series of numbers representing the years of useful life. The sum of the numbers 1 through 10 is equal to 55. N = useful life, t = year, S = salvage value, T = tax rate, and C = acquisition price.

$$\text{Annual SYD depreciation} = SYD_t$$

$$= (C - S)\, \frac{N - t}{\dfrac{N(N + 1)}{2}}$$

$$= (C - S)\, \frac{2(N - t)}{\dfrac{N(N + 1)}{2}}.$$

$$\text{Annual SYD rate} = \frac{SYD_t}{C - S}.$$

$$\text{Depreciation tax shield} = \sum_{i=1}^{N} \frac{SYD_t \times T}{(1 + r)^t}.$$

Applying these formulae yields the following results:

1 Year	2 Fraction	3 Depreciation	4 Tax Shield (Col. 3 × 40%)	5 Discount Factor at 10% (Appendix 11.C)	6 Present Value (Col. 4 × Col. 5)
1	$10/55$	$18,182	$7,273	0.909	$ 6,611
2	$9/55$	16,364	6,546	0.826	5,407
3	$8/55$	14,545	5,818	0.751	4,369
4	$7/55$	12,727	5,091	0.683	3,477
5	$6/55$	10,909	4,364	0.621	2,710
6	$5/55$	9,091	3,636	0.564	2,051
7	$4/55$	7,273	2,909	0.513	1,492
8	$3/55$	5,455	2,182	0.467	1,019
9	$2/55$	3,636	1,455	0.424	617
10	$1/55$	1,818	727	0.386	281
Present Value of Tax Shield					$28,033

The present value of the tax shield under each depreciation method has been found to be

Straight-Line	$24,580
Double Declining Balance	27,407
Sum-of-the-Years'-Digits	28,033

Therefore, the present value of the tax shield is highest under the sum-of-the-years'-digits method for this example, and this method should be used for tax depreciation.

11.8   REPLACEMENT DECISIONS

The examples used to illustrate capital budgeting techniques were based on expansion projects. The analysis for replacement projects is slightly different. The following sections illustrate the replacement decision first where the lives of the projects are equal and, second, where the lives of the projects are unequal.

11.8.1   Replacement Decisions: Equal Lives

Assume that a machine purchased ten years ago by the Litton Company at a cost of $20,000 had an expected twenty-year useful life when purchased and zero salvage value. A straight-line depreciation charge of $2,000 makes the machine's present book value equal to $10,000. A new machine now being considered to replace the old one can be purchased for $30,000 and is expected to reduce operating costs from $10,000 to $4,000 for its ten-year useful life. The old machine can be sold for $4,000. The new machine is expected to have a $6,000 salvage value. Taxes are 48 percent, and an investment tax credit of 10 percent of the purchase price can be claimed on the purchase of

Table 11.7   Replacement Decision Analysis

Net Outflow at the Time the New Machine is Purchased (t = 0)

	Amount before Tax	Effect, Net of Taxes	Time Even Occurs	PV Factor at 12%	Present Value
1. Cost of New Machine	$30,000	$30,000	0	1.0	$30,000
2. Salvage Value of Old Machine	(4,000)	(4,000)	0	1.0	(4,000)
3. Tax Effect of Sale of Old Machine[a]	(6,000)	(2,880)	0	1.0	(2,880)
4. Investment Tax Credit	(3,000)	(3,000)	0	1.0	(3,000)
5. Total Present Value of Outflows					$20,120

Net Inflows of the Life of the New Machine (t = 1 to 10)

6. Decrease in Operating Costs[b]	$ 6,000	$ 3,120	1 to 10	5.650	$17,628
7. Depreciation on New Machine	2,400	—	—	—	—
8. Depreciation on Old Machine	1,000	—	—	—	—
9. Net Changes in Tax Savings from Depreciation	1,400	672	1 to 10	5.650	3,797
10. Salvage Value of New Machine	$ 6,000	$ 6,000	1 to 10	0.322	1,932
11. Total Present Value of Inflows					$23,357

12. NPV = $23,357 − $20,120 = $3,237

[a] The tax effect of sale of old machine = Loss × t = [($10,000 − $4,000) × 0.48] = $2,880.
[b] Cost reduction = Decrease in cost × (1 − t) = $4,000 (1 − 0.48) = $2,080.

the new machine.[3] The cost of capital is 12 percent. Should the Litton Company replace the old machine?

The NPV of the replacement decision, computed in Table 11.7, is $3,237. The new machine should be purchased to replace the old machine, given that it increases the value of the firm by $3,237.

11.8.2   Replacement Decisions: Unequal Lives

The procedure generally used to choose between two mutually exclusive replacement proposals with unequal lives is to convert the number of years of analysis to a common termination year through a series of *replacement chains*. For example, to choose between a four-year project X and a six-year project Y, it is necessary to compare a three-chain cycle for project X and a two-chain cycle for project Y, bringing the common termination year to 12.

Assume that the Shields Company is considering replacing a fully depreciated machine with one of two replacement machines. Machine X has a cost of $15,000, a five-year useful life, and will generate after-tax cash flows of $5,000 per year for five years. Machine Y has a cost of $18,000, a ten-year useful life, and will generate after-tax cash flows of $4,000 per year for ten years. The company's cost of capital is 12 percent.

[3] This means that 10 percent of the investment cost can be deducted directly from taxes due in the year of the investment.

To determine which machine should be chosen, the NPV of each machine can be computed:

$$NPV\ (X) = \$5,000(3.605) - \$15,000 = \$3,025.$$

$$NPV\ (Y) = \$4,000(5.650) - \$18,000 = \$4,600.$$

From these computations it appears that machine Y should be chosen. The analysis is incorrect, however, since a second investment can be made after five years if machine X is chosen, and the second investment may be profitable. A better analysis would be based on the common denominator of ten years. Therefore,

$$NPV\ (X) = \begin{array}{c} \text{Present value} \\ \text{of first investment} \\ \text{of machine X} \end{array} + \begin{array}{c} \text{Present value} \\ \text{of second investment} \\ \text{of machine Y} \end{array}$$

$$= \$3,025 + \$3,025(0.567) = \$4,740.$$

$$NPV\ (Y) = \qquad\qquad\qquad = \$4,600.$$

The NPV of machine X is \$4,740, which is higher than the NPV of machine Y.

11.9   CAPITAL RATIONING

Capital rationing exists when a firm faces limited supplies of funds, which precludes the acceptance of potentially profitable projects. Among the causes cited for capital rationing are (1) limits imposed on new borrowing, (2) a debt limit imposed by an outside agreement (for example, bond covenants), (3) limits on capital spending imposed on divisional management, and (4) management's desire to maintain a given dividend policy or a specific earnings-per-share or price/earnings ratio.[4]

Conventional methods of evaluation with capital rationing consist of (1) ranking the projects under consideration from highest to lowest for whichever evaluation model is used, that is, IRR, NPV, or the profitability index (PI); and (2) selecting projects starting at the top of the ranking until funds are exhausted. Although these conventional methods based on either the IRR or the NPV techniques are simple, discontinuities or size disparities between projects prevent the choice of optimal projects. For example, a 20 percent return on \$1,000 is considered better than a 15 percent return on \$2,000, according to the conventional capital rationing method.

To correct the limitations of the conventional capital rationing methods, mathematical programming can be used to select the optimal combination of projects. In 1955, James H. Lorie and Leonard J. Savage were the first to suggest mathematical programming—in the form of a heuristic programming approach—to deal with capital rationing.[5] This attempt was followed by a more comprehensive treatment of the problem by H. Martin Weingartner, whose basic model follows:

---

[4] James M. Fremgen, "Capital Budgeting Practices: A Survey," *Management Accounting* (May 1973), pp. 23–24.

[5] James H. Lorie and Leonard J. Savage, "Three Problems in Rationing Capital," *Journal of Business* (October 1955), pp. 229–239.

Table 11.8 *Capital Rationing Example*

Investment Proposal	Present Value of Outlay (Period 1)	Present Value of Outlay (Period 2)	NPV
1	$10	$ 5	$20
2	20	10	30
3	30	10	40
4	40	30	50

Maximize

$$\sum_{j=1}^{m} b_j X_j,$$

Subject to

$$\sum_{j=1}^{m} C_{tj} X_j \leq C_t \text{ for } t = 1, \ldots, n.$$

$$0 \leq X_j \leq 1.$$

X_j is an integer,

where

b_j = Net present value of investment proposal j.

X_j = 0 if the project is accepted, and 1 if the project is rejected.

C_{tj} = Net cash needed for proposal j in period t.

C_t = Total budget for period t.[6]

Because of the use of the last two constraints, this mathematical programming model is known as *integer programming*.

To illustrate the integer programming approach to capital budgeting, let us use the data shown in Table 11.8. The present values of the two budget constraints are $90 in period 1 and $30 in period 2. The model will look like the following:

Maximize

$$20x_1 + 30x_2 + 40x_3 + 50x_4,$$

Subject to

$$10x_1 + 20x_2 + 30x_3 + 40x_4 \leq 90.$$

[6]H. Martin Weingartner, *Mathematical Programming and the Analysis of Capital Budgeting Problems* (Englewood Cliffs, N.J.: Prentice-Hall, 1963).

$$5x_1 + 10x_2 + 10x_3 + 30x_4 \le 30.$$

$$0 \le X_j \le 1 \text{ for } j = 1, 2, 3, \text{ and } 4.$$

X_j is an integer.

11.10   CAPITAL BUDGETING UNDER UNCERTAINTY

11.10.1   Nature of Risk

Because the cash flows of a project often may be estimated on the basis of incomplete information, the capital budgeting evaluation must be performed in a climate of uncertainty. Although *uncertainty* and *risk* are sometimes used synonymously, they are different in the strict mathematical sense. *Risk* refers to the possible outcomes of a project to which probabilities can be assigned, whereas *uncertainty* refers to outcomes to which it is difficult to assign probabilities. Thus, the real interest lies with risk, because it is measurable.

Most decision makers are risk averse and perceive risk in different ways:

1. The *dollar price risk* is the risk associated with a decline in the number of dollars used to acquire a financial asset.

2. The *purchasing power risk* is the risk associated with a decline in the purchasing power of the monetary unit.

3. The *interest rate risk* is the risk associated with changes in the interest rate, which affect market values of many types of securities.

4. The *business risk* is the risk associated with the operational cash flows of a firm.

5. The *financial risk* is the risk associated with financial leverage.

6. The *systematic risk* or *market risk* is the risk associated with the common stocks of a particular industry.

7. The *unsystematic risk* is the risk associated with a particular company.

Because the perception of risk by decision makers affects their decision, it should be taken into account in the decision making process. Capital budgeting under uncertainty should incorporate risk in the evaluation process.

11.10.2   Risk-Adjusted Discount Rate Method

One of the techniques for incorporating risk in the evaluation process is the risk-adjusted discount rate, which consists of manipulating the discount rate applied to the cash flows to reflect the amount of risk inherent in a project. The higher the risk associated with a project, the higher the discount rate applied to the cash flows. If a given project is perceived to be twice as risky as most acceptable projects to the firm and the cost of capital is 12 percent, then the correct risk-adjusted discount rate is 24 percent.

In spite of its simplicity, the risk-adjusted discount rate method is subject to the following limitations:

1. The determination of the exact risk-adjusted discount rate is subjective and, therefore, subject to error.

2. The method adjusts the discount rate rather than the future cash flows, which are subject to variability and risk.

11.10.3   Certainty Equivalent Method

Another technique for incorporating risk in the evaluation process is the certainty equivalent method, which involves adjusting the future cash flows so a project can be evaluated on a riskless basis. The adjustment is formulated as follows:

$$NPV = \sum_{t=1}^{n} \left[\frac{\alpha_t \, CF_t}{(1 + R_F)} \right] - I_0,$$

where

α_t = Risk coefficient applied to the cash flow of period t (CF_t).

I_0 = Initial cost of the project.

R_F = Risk-free rate.

As this formula shows, the method proceeds by multiplying the future cash flows by certainty equivalents to obtain a riskless cash flow. Note also that the discount rate used is R_F, which is a risk-free rate of interest.

To illustrate the certainty equivalent method, assume an investment with the following characteristics:

I_0 = Initial cost = $30,000.

CF_1 = Cash flow, year 1 = $10,000.

CF_2 = Cash flow, year 2 = $20,000.

CF_3 = Cash flow, year 3 = $30,000.

α_1 = Certainty equivalent, year 1 = 0.9.

α_2 = Certainty equivalent, year 2 = 0.8.

α_3 = Certainty equivalent, year 3 = 0.6.

The NPV of the investment using a risk-free discount rate of 6 percent is computed as follows:

Period	Cash Flow (CF_t)	Risk Coefficient (α_t)	Certainty Equivalent	Risk-free Rate (R_F)	Present Value
1	$10,000	0.9	$ 9,000	0.943	$ 8,487
2	20,000	0.8	16,000	0.890	14,240
3	30,000	0.6	18,000	0.840	15,120
Present Value of Cash Flows					$37,847
Initial Investment					30,000
Net Present Value					$ 7,847

Since the NPV is positive, the investment should be considered acceptable. The main advantage of the certainty equivalent method is that it allows the assignment of a different risk factor to each cash flow, given that risk can concentrate in one or more periods.

The certainty equivalent method and the risk-adjusted discount rate method are comparable methods of evaluating risk. To produce similar ranking, the following equation must hold:

$$\frac{\alpha_t \, CF_t}{(1 + R_F)^t} = \frac{CF_t}{(1 + R_A)^t} \, ,$$

where

α_t = Risk coefficient used in the certainty equivalent method.

R_F = Risk-free discount rate.

R_A = Risk-adjusted discount rate used in the risk-adjusted discount rate method.

CF_t = Future cash flow.

Solving for α_t yields

$$\alpha_t = \frac{(1 + R_F)^t}{(1 + R_A)^t} \, .$$

Given that R_A and R_F are constant and $R_A > R_F$, then α_t decreases over time, which means that risk increases over time. To illustrate, assume that in the previous example $R_A = 15\%$. Then

$$\alpha_1 = \frac{(1 + R_F)^1}{(1 + R_A)^1} = \frac{(1 + 0.06)^1}{(1 + 0.15)^1} = 0.921.$$

$$\alpha_2 = \frac{(1 + R_F)^2}{(1 + R_A)^2} = \frac{(1 + 0.06)^2}{(1 + 0.15)^2} = 0.848.$$

$$\alpha_3 = \frac{(1 + R_F)^3}{(1 + R_A)^3} = \frac{(1 + 0.06)^3}{(1 + 0.15)^3} = 0.783.$$

In many cases this assumption of increasing risk may not be realistic.

11.10.4   *Probability Distribution*

The probability distribution approach to the evaluation of risk assigns probabilities to each cash flow outcome. Various measures of risk then can be computed, giving information about the dispersion or tightness of the probability distribution. *Standard deviation* is a conventional measure of dispersion. For a single period, the standard deviation is computed as follows:

$$\sigma_t = \sqrt{\sum_{i=1}^{n} [X_{it} - E_t(X)]^2 \, P(X_i)_t},$$

where

σ_t = Standard deviation of period t's cash flows.

X_{it} = Cash flow for the ith outcome in period t.

$E_t(X)$ = Expected value of cash flows in period t.

$P(X_i)_t$ = Probability of occurrence of cash flow X_i in period t.

The expected cash flow $E_t(X)$ is computed as follows:

$$E_t(X) = \sum_{i=1}^{n} X_{it} P(X_i)_t.$$

All things being equal, the higher the standard deviation, the greater the risk associated with the expected value.

Another measure of relative dispersion is the *coefficient of variation* (CV), a measure that compares the expected value and risk of a probability distribution. The coefficient of variation is computed as follows:

$$CV = \frac{\sigma}{E(X)}.$$

All things being equal, the smaller the coefficient of variation, the better the project. To illustrate these risk concepts, assume that projects A and B have the following discrete probability distributions of expected cash flows in each of the next three years:

Project A		Project B	
Probability	Cash Flow	Probability	Cash Flow
0.2	$1,000	0.3	$1,500
0.5	2,000	0.3	1,000
0.2	3,000	0.2	3,500
0.1	4,000	0.2	3,750

The expected value of cash flows of both projects can be computed as follows:

$$E\,(A) = 0.2(\$1,000) + 0.5(\$2,000) + 0.2(\$3,000) + 0.1(\$4,000) = \$2,200.$$

$$E\,(B) = 0.3(\$1,500) + 0.3(\$1,000) + 0.2(\$3,500) + 0.2(\$3,750) = \$2,200.$$

On the basis of the expected values as a measure of central tendency in the distribution, projects A and B are equivalent. To determine which project is riskier, the standard deviations for both projects can be computed as follows:

$$\sigma\,(A) = [0.2(\$1,000 - \$2,200)^2 + 0.5(\$2,000 - \$2,200)^2 + 0.2(\$3,000 - \$2,200)^2 + 0.1(\$4,000 - \$2,200)^2]^{1/2} = \$871.77.$$

$$\sigma (B) = [0.3(\$1,500 - \$2,200)^2 + 0.3(\$1,000 - \$2,200)^2 + 0.2(\$3,500 - \$2,200)^2 + 0.2(\$3,750 - \$2,200)^2]^{1/2} = \$1,182.15.$$

Thus, project B has a significantly higher standard deviation, indicating a greater dispersion of possible cash flows.

The standard deviation is an absolute measure of risk. For comparison, the projects also should be evaluated on the basis of their coefficient of variation, which measures the relative dispersion within the distribution. The coefficient of variation for both projects can be computed now:

$$CV (A) = \frac{\sigma_A}{E(A)} \times 100 = \frac{\$871.77}{\$2,200} = 39.6\%.$$

$$CV (B) = \frac{\sigma_B}{E(B)} \times 100 = \frac{\$1,182.15}{\$2,200} = 53.7\%.$$

The coefficient of variation for project B is significantly higher than for project A, which indicates again that project B presents a greater degree of risk.

The coefficient of variation is an especially useful measure when the comparison between projects leads to the acceptance of a given project based on a comparison between means, or when the comparison leads to the acceptance of a different project based on a comparison between standard deviations.

11.10.5   *Multiperiod Projects*

The computation of the measures of risk becomes more complicated when several periods are involved. Some assumptions must be made regarding the relationships between the period cash flows, namely, whether the cash flows are independent or dependent.

To illustrate, let us return to project A and assume (1) that the applicable discount rate (R) is 10 percent and (2) that the project calls for a $5,000 investment.

Independent of the nature of the relationship between cash flows in the three periods, the NPV of project A can be computed as follows:

$$NPV = \sum_{i=1}^{3} \left[\frac{\$2,200}{(1 + 0.10)^i} \right] - \$5,000 = \$471.$$

The standard deviation of the project will be computed differently according to whether we assume that the cash flows are dependent, independent, or mixed.

Independent Cash Flows
If we assume serial independence of the cash flows between the periods, the standard deviation of the entire project is

$$\sigma = \sqrt{\sum_{i=1}^{n} \frac{\sigma_i^2}{(1 + r)^{2i}}},$$

where

σ_t = standard deviation of the probability distribution of the cash flows in period t.

Hence the standard deviation of project A, assuming serial independence, is

$$\sigma_A = \sqrt{\frac{(\$871)^2}{(1+0.10)^2} + \frac{(\$871)^2}{(1+0.10)^4} + \frac{(\$871)^2}{(1+0.10)^6}} = \$358.04.$$

Dependent Cash Flows

In general, the cash flows of a given period are expected to influence the cash flows of subsequent periods. In the case of perfect correlation, the standard deviation of the entire project is

$$\sigma = \sum_{i=1}^{n} \frac{\sigma_t}{(1+r)^t}.$$

Therefore, the standard deviation of project A, assuming perfect correlation between interperiod cash flows, is

$$\sigma_A = \sum_{i=1}^{3} \frac{\$871}{(1+0.10)^i} = \$2,166.17.$$

Note that the standard deviation under the assumption of independence is $358.04, while under the assumption of perfect dependency it is considerably higher ($2,166.17). If the cash flows are perfectly correlated there is more risk inherent in the project than if the cash flows are independent.

Mixed Correlation

A project may include some independent and some dependent cash flows. Frederick Hillier proposed a model to deal with a mixed situation:

$$\sigma = \sum_{t=0}^{T} \frac{\sigma_{Y_t}^2}{(1+r)^{2t}} + \sum_{j=1}^{m} \left[\sum_{j=1}^{T} \frac{6_{Z_{jt}}}{(1+r)^i} \right]^2,$$

where

Y_t = The independent component of the net cash flow in period t.

Z_{jt} = The jth perfectly correlated component of the net cash flow in period t.[7]

To illustrate the computation of the standard deviation of a project with mixed correlation, Hillier assumed the following project data for a new product addition:

[7]Frederick Hillier, "The Deviation of Probabilistic Information for the Evaluation of Risky Investments," *Management Science* (April 1963), pp. 443–457.

Year	Source	Expected Value of Net Cash Flows (in Thousands)	Standard Deviation
0	Initial Investment	$(600)	$ 50
1	Production Cash Outflow	(250)	20
2	Production Cash Outflow	(200)	10
3	Production Cash Outflow	(200)	10
4	Production Cash Outflow	(200)	10
5	Production Outflow − Salvage Value	(100)	$10\sqrt{10}$
1	Marketing	300	50
2	Marketing	600	100
3	Marketing	500	100
4	Marketing	400	100
5	Marketing	300	100

Source: Frederick Hillier, "The Deviation of Probabilistic Information for the Evaluation of Risky Investments," *Management Science* (April 1963), pp. 443–457.

Hillier also assumed that all the outflows were independent and that all marketing flows were perfectly correlated. If 10 percent is used as the risk-free rate, the expected value of the NPV for the proposal is

$$NPV = \sum_{t=1}^{s}\left[\frac{\bar{X}}{(1 + 0.10)^t}\right] - C_0$$

or

$$NPV = \frac{\$300 - \$250}{(1.10)} + \frac{\$600 - \$200}{(1.10)^2} + \frac{\$500 - \$200}{(1.10)^3} + \frac{\$400 - \$200}{(1.10)^4}$$

$$+ \frac{\$300 - \$100}{(1.10)^5} - \$600 = \$262.$$

The standard deviation is

$$\sigma = \sqrt{50^2 + \frac{20^2}{(1.10)^2} + \ldots + \frac{(10\sqrt{10})^2}{(1.10)^{10}} + \left[\frac{50}{(1.10)} + \ldots + \frac{100}{(1.10)^5}\right]^2} = \$339.$$

Moderate Correlation

In most cases, cash flows cannot be easily classified as either independent or perfectly correlated, and a decision tree approach can be used. In a capital budgeting context, this approach involves the multiplication of the conditional probabilities of correlated periods to obtain the joint probabilities that will specify the probabilities of multiple events. Table 11.9 illustrates the decision tree approach to compute the joint probabilities and the expected value of a project.

Simulation

The preceding methods of dealing with uncertainty apply only when two probability distributions are considered. In most realistic capital budgeting situations, more than

Table 11.9   Decision Tree Approach to Capital Budgeting

Period 1		Period 2					
Net Cash Flows A_1	Initial Probability $p(1)$	Net Cash Flows A_2	Conditional Probability $p(2/1)$	Number of Cases	Joint Probability[a] p_j	Total Net Cash Flows[b] A_j	Expected Value of Total Net Cash Flows
$30	0.6	$20	0.3	1	0.18	$50	$ 9.00
		30	0.4	2	0.24	60	14.40
		40	0.3	3	0.18	70	12.60
40	0.4	30	0.2	4	0.08	70	5.60
		40	0.5	5	0.2	80	16.00
		50	0.3	6	0.12	90	10.80
Mean Value							$68.40

[a] $p_j = p(1) \times p(2/1)$.
[b] $A_j = A_1 + A_2$.

two variables are significant, and more than two variables are subject to uncertainty. The simulation technique takes into account the interacting variables and their corresponding probability distributions. David B. Hertz proposed a simulation model to obtain the dispersion about the expected rate of return for an investment proposal. He established nine separate probability distributions to determine the probability distribution of the average rate of return for the entire project. The following nine variables were considered.

Market analysis:
1. Market size.
2. Selling price.
3. Market growth rate.
4. Share of market.

Investment cost analysis:
5. Investment required.
6. Residual value of investment.

Operating and fixed costs:
7. Operating costs.
8. Fixed costs.
9. Useful life of facilities.[8]

The computer simulates trial values of each of the nine variables and then computes the return on investment based on the simulated values obtained. These trials are repeated often enough to obtain a frequency distribution for the return on investment. This approach can also be used to determine the NPV or the IRR of a project.

[8]David B. Hertz, "Risk Analysis in Capital Investment," *Harvard Business Review* (January–February 1964), pp. 95–106; and David B. Hertz, "Investment Policies That Pay Off," *Harvard Business Review* (January–February 1968), pp. 96–108.

11.11   CAPITAL BUDGETING UNDER INFLATION

Beginning with seminal work by Irving Fisher, economists have shown fairly conclusively that market rates of interest include an adjustment of expected inflation rate—the nonexistent "homogeneous expectation." This consensus forecast, therefore, is built into the discount rate used in capital budgeting. When rates of inflation were relatively low (say 2 to 3 percent) this did not lead to serious distortions in the IRR or NPV models, because any error in the rate estimation was immaterial in most cases. With the higher rates of inflation we are now experiencing, it is desirable to explicitly consider the rate of inflation in developing cash flow forecasts. The correct analysis can be done in either of two ways: (1) using a money discount rate to discount money cash flows, or (2) using a real discount rate to discount real cash flows.

Before illustrating either approach, let us explore the differences between money cash flows and real cash flows, and between real discount rate and money discount rate. Money cash flows are cash flows measured in dollars from various periods having different purchasing power. Real cash flows are cash flows measured in dollars having the same purchasing power. The real cash flow for a given year, expressed in terms of dollars of year$_0$ (the base year) is equal to the money cash flow for that year, multiplied by the following ratio:

$$\frac{\text{Price level index in year}_0}{\text{Price level index in year}_t}.$$

For example, if an investment promises a money return of $100 for 3 years and the price index for years 0 through 3 is 100, 110, 121, and 133.1, respectively, then the real cash flows are as follows:

Year 1: $100 × 100/110   = 90.90.

Year 2: $100 × 100/121   = 82.64.

Year 3: $100 × 100/133.1 = 75.13.

The money discount rate, r, can also be computed. Assuming that f is the annual rate of inflation, i is the real discount rate, and the decision maker is in the zero tax bracket, then

$$r = (1 + f)(1 + i) - 1,$$

or

$$r = i + f + if.$$

For example, if the real return before taxes is 3 percent, and the rate of inflation is 10 percent, then the nominal discount rate is

$$0.03 + 0.10 + 0.003 = 0.133.$$

To illustrate the correct analysis under inflation, assume the same data as in the previous example. The correct analysis can be either of two, as follows:

1. The first analysis discounts the money cash flows using a money discount rate. The present value of the investment will be computed as follows:

Period	Money Cash Flow	Nominal Present Value Factor at 13.3%	Present Value
1	100	0.8826	88.26
2	100	0.7792	77.92
3	100	0.6874	68.74
			234.92

2. The second analysis discounts the real cash flows using a real discount rate. The present value of the investment will give the same present value, as follows:

Period	Real Cash Flow	Real Present Value at 3%	Present Value
1	90.90	0.9709	88.254
2	82.64	0.9426	77.896
3	75.13	0.9151	68.751
			234.901

Assuming a marginal tax rate t on nominal income, the nominal discount rate will be computed as follows:

$$1 + (1 - t)r = (1 + f) + 1 + i(1 - t),$$

or

$$r = i + if + f/(1 - t).$$

Assuming the tax rate to be 30 percent, the nominal rate is then computed as follows:

$$r = 0.03 + (0.03 \times 0.10) + 0.10/(1 - 0.30)$$
$$= 0.1758.$$

In other words, a nominal rate of 17.58 percent is needed for an investor in a 30 percent tax bracket and facing an inflation rate of 10 percent to earn a real discount rate of 3 percent.

11.12 CONCLUSION

Many capital budgeting techniques exist in the literature and in practice. The discounted cash flow methods take the time value of money into account to evaluate capital budgeting proposals. The two basic discounted cash flow methods are the internal rate of return and the net present value methods. Management should consider some of the conflicts between these two methods when choosing between them. Other problems in using capital budgeting techniques include problems with replacement decisions, problems with capital rationing, and problems with capital budgeting under uncertainty.

11.A   APPENDIX: TIME VALUE OF MONEY

When people must choose between receiving payment immediately or periodically over a number of periods, they show a preference for present satisfaction over future satisfaction. The preference for present payment is motivated by the possibility of either consuming the funds or investing them to provide greater amounts in the future, whereas the choice of receiving money in the future involves the sacrifice of waiting before it can be used. The compensation for waiting is the time value of money, called *interest*. Individuals require interest for postponing consumption.

11.A.1   Compound Value

The *compound value* (CDV) is the future value of funds received today and invested at the prevalent interest rate. For example, assume an investment of $1,000 at 10 percent per year. The compound value at the end of year 1 is computed as follows:

$$CDV_1 = \$1,000(1 + 0.10)^1 = \$1,100.$$

Similarly, the compound value at the end of year 2 is computed as follows:

$$CDV_2 = \$1,100(1 + 0.10)^1 = \$1,210$$

or

$$CDV_2 = \$1,000(1 + 0.10)^2 = \$1,210.$$

This can be generalized to yield the following formula, which applies to compute the compound value:

$$S_n = P(1 + r)^n,$$

where

S_n = Compound value at the end of year n = $1,210.

P = Beginning amount or present value   = $1,000.

r = Interest rate or rate of return   = 10%.

n = Number of years   = 2.

Thus, the future value (FV) of $1, with n corresponding to the number of compounding periods, is

$$FV = (1 + r)^n.$$

The FV can be computed for any interest rate (r) and any number of compounding periods (n). Appendix 11.B shows the future value of $1 for a variety of interest rates and compounding periods.

11.A.2   *Present Value*

In the previous example, if $1,000 compounded at 10 percent per year becomes $1,210 at the end of two years, then $1,000 is the present value (PV) of $1,210 due at the end of two years. Finding the present value of a future value involves *discounting* the future value to the present. Discounting, then, is the opposite of compounding. The formula for the present value is the same as the formula for the future value, except it solves for P instead of S_n, which is known. Thus, if

$$S_n = P(1 + r)^n,$$

then

$$P = \frac{S_n}{(1 + r)^n}.$$

Inserting the illustrative numbers yields

$$P = \frac{\$1,210}{(1 + 0.10)^2} = \$1,000.$$

Thus, the general formula for the present value of $1 is

$$PV = \frac{1}{(1 + r)^n}.$$

Appendix 11.C shows the present value of $1 for any interest rate (r) and any number of periods (n).

11.A.3   *Future Value of an Annuity in Arrears of $1*

An *annuity in arrears* is a series of periodic and equal payments (receipts) to be paid (received) at the end of successive similar periods. Assume, for example, that a firm is to receive annual payments of $1,000 at the end of each year for three years and charges an interest rate of 10 percent. Using Appendix 11.B, the pattern of compounding is as follows:

```
             0      1       2       3
Payments    ──────────────────────────────
                  $1,000  $1,000  $1,000
                     └──────┼──────→ 1,210
                            └──────→ 1,100
                                    ────────
                                     $3,310
```

In other words, the future value of an annuity in arrears of $1,000 for three years at 10 percent is equal to

$$1,000(1 + 0.10)^2 + 1,000(1 + 0.10) + 1,000 = \$3,310$$

or

$$1{,}000 \left[1 + (1 + 0.10) + (1 + 0.10)^2\right] = \$3{,}310.$$

Therefore, the future value of an annuity in arrears can be determined from the following basic relationship:

$$S_n = a \left[(1 + r)^{n-1} + (1 + r)^{n-2} + \ldots + (1 + r)^1 + 1\right]$$

or

$$S_n = a \left[\frac{(1 + r)^n - 1}{r}\right],$$

where

S_n = The future value to which an annuity in arrears will accumulate.

a = The annuity.

$\dfrac{(1 + r)^n - 1}{r}$ = Annuity compound interest factor.

The annuity compound interest factor for an annuity in arrears of $1 can be computed for any interest rate and compounding period, as shown in Appendix 11.D.

11.A.4   *Present Value of an Annuity in Arrears of $1*

Assume again that a firm is to receive annual payments of $1,000 at the end of each year for three years. At a 10 percent interest rate, what is the present value of those annual payments? Using Appendix 11.C, the pattern of discounting is as follows:

	0	1	2	3
Present Value		$1,000	$1,000	$1,000
$ 909 ←				
826 ←				
751 ←				
$2,486				

The present value of an annuity in arrears of $1,000 for three years at 10 percent is equal to

$$\$1{,}000(1 + 0.10)^{-1} + 1{,}000(1 + 0.10)^{-2} + 1{,}000(1 + 0.10)^{-3} = \$2{,}486$$

or

$$\$1{,}000 \left[(1 + 0.10)^{-1} + (1 + 0.10)^{-2} + (1 + 0.10)^{-3}\right].$$

Therefore, the present value of an annuity in arrears can be generalized by the following formula:

$$P_n = a \left[\frac{1 - \dfrac{1}{(1 + r)^n}}{r} \right],$$

where

P_n = Present value of the annuity in arrears.

a = Amount of the annuity.

r = Interest rate.

n = Number of years.

The annuity discount interest factor,

$$\frac{1 - \dfrac{1}{(1 + r)^n}}{r},$$

can be computed for an annuity of $1 in arrears for any interest rate and discounting period, as shown in Appendix 11.E.

Appendix 11.B   Future Value of $1 Payable in Period N

Year (N)	1%	2%	3%	4%	5%	6%	7%
1	1.010	1.020	1.030	1.040	1.050	1.060	1.070
2	1.020	1.040	1.061	1.082	1.102	1.124	1.145
3	1.030	1.061	1.093	1.125	1.158	1.191	1.225
4	1.041	1.082	1.126	1.170	1.216	1.262	1.311
5	1.051	1.104	1.159	1.217	1.276	1.338	1.403
6	1.062	1.126	1.194	1.265	1.340	1.419	1.501
7	1.072	1.149	1.230	1.316	1.407	1.504	1.606
8	1.083	1.172	1.267	1.369	1.477	1.594	1.718
9	1.094	1.195	1.305	1.423	1.551	1.689	1.838
10	1.105	1.219	1.344	1.480	1.629	1.791	1.967
11	1.116	1.243	1.384	1.539	1.710	1.898	2.105
12	1.127	1.268	1.426	1.601	1.796	2.012	2.252
13	1.138	1.294	1.469	1.665	1.886	2.133	2.410
14	1.149	1.319	1.513	1.732	1.980	2.261	2.579
15	1.161	1.346	1.558	1.801	2.079	2.397	2.759
16	1.173	1.373	1.605	1.873	2.183	2.540	2.952
17	1.184	1.400	1.653	1.948	2.292	2.693	3.159
18	1.196	1.428	1.702	2.026	2.407	2.854	3.380
19	1.208	1.457	1.754	2.107	2.527	3.026	3.617
20	1.220	1.486	1.806	2.191	2.653	3.207	3.870
25	1.282	1.641	2.094	2.666	3.386	4.292	5.427
30	1.348	1.811	2.427	3.243	4.322	5.743	7.612

Appendix 11.B *continued*

Year (N)	8%	9%	10%	12%	14%	15%	16%
1	1.080	1.090	1.100	1.120	1.140	1.150	1.160
2	1.166	1.188	1.210	1.254	1.300	1.322	1.346
3	1.260	1.295	1.331	1.405	1.482	1.521	1.561
4	1.360	1.412	1.464	1.574	1.689	1.749	1.811
5	1.469	1.539	1.611	1.762	1.925	2.011	2.100
6	1.587	1.677	1.772	1.974	2.195	2.313	2.436
7	1.714	1.828	1.949	2.211	2.502	2.660	2.826
8	1.851	1.993	2.144	2.476	2.853	3.059	3.278
9	1.999	2.172	2.358	2.773	3.252	3.518	3.803
10	2.159	2.367	2.594	3.106	3.707	4.046	4.411
11	2.332	2.580	2.853	3.479	4.226	4.652	5.117
12	2.518	2.813	3.138	3.896	4.818	5.350	5.936
13	2.720	3.066	3.452	4.363	5.492	6.153	6.886
14	2.937	3.342	3.797	4.887	6.261	7.076	7.988
15	3.172	3.642	4.177	5.474	7.138	8.137	9.266
16	3.426	3.970	4.595	6.130	8.137	9.358	10.748
17	3.700	4.328	5.054	6.866	9.276	10.761	12.468
18	3.996	4.717	5.560	7.690	10.575	12.375	14.463
19	4.316	5.142	6.116	8.613	12.056	14.232	16.777
20	4.661	5.604	6.728	9.646	13.743	16.367	19.461
25	6.848	8.623	10.835	17.000	26.462	32.919	40.874
30	10.063	13.268	17.449	29.960	50.950	66.212	85.850

Appendix 11.C   Present Value of $1 Received at the End of Period

Years Hence	1%	2%	4%	6%	8%	10%	12%	14%	15%	16%	18%
1	0.990	0.980	0.962	0.943	0.926	0.909	0.893	0.877	0.870	0.862	0.847
2	0.980	0.961	0.925	0.890	0.857	0.826	0.797	0.769	0.756	0.743	0.718
3	0.971	0.942	0.889	0.840	0.794	0.751	0.712	0.675	0.658	0.641	0.609
4	0.961	0.924	0.855	0.792	0.735	0.683	0.636	0.592	0.572	0.552	0.516
5	0.951	0.906	0.822	0.747	0.681	0.621	0.567	0.519	0.497	0.476	0.437
6	0.942	0.888	0.790	0.705	0.630	0.564	0.507	0.456	0.432	0.410	0.370
7	0.933	0.871	0.760	0.665	0.583	0.513	0.452	0.400	0.376	0.354	0.314
8	0.923	0.853	0.731	0.627	0.540	0.467	0.404	0.351	0.327	0.305	0.266
9	0.914	0.837	0.703	0.592	0.500	0.424	0.361	0.308	0.284	0.263	0.225
10	0.905	0.820	0.676	0.558	0.463	0.386	0.322	0.270	0.247	0.227	0.191
11	0.896	0.804	0.650	0.527	0.429	0.350	0.287	0.237	0.215	0.195	0.162
12	0.887	0.788	0.625	0.497	0.397	0.319	0.257	0.208	0.187	0.168	0.137
13	0.879	0.773	0.601	0.469	0.368	0.290	0.229	0.182	0.163	0.145	0.116
14	0.870	0.758	0.577	0.442	0.340	0.263	0.205	0.160	0.141	0.125	0.099
15	0.861	0.743	0.555	0.417	0.315	0.239	0.183	0.140	0.123	0.108	0.084
16	0.853	0.728	0.534	0.394	0.292	0.218	0.163	0.123	0.107	0.093	0.071
17	0.844	0.714	0.513	0.371	0.270	0.198	0.146	0.108	0.093	0.080	0.060
18	0.836	0.700	0.494	0.350	0.250	0.180	0.130	0.095	0.081	0.069	0.051
19	0.828	0.686	0.475	0.331	0.232	0.164	0.116	0.083	0.070	0.060	0.043
20	0.820	0.673	0.456	0.312	0.215	0.149	0.104	0.073	0.061	0.051	0.037
21	0.811	0.660	0.439	0.294	0.199	0.135	0.093	0.064	0.053	0.044	0.031
22	0.803	0.647	0.422	0.278	0.184	0.123	0.083	0.056	0.046	0.038	0.026
23	0.795	0.634	0.406	0.262	0.170	0.112	0.074	0.049	0.040	0.033	0.022
24	0.788	0.622	0.390	0.247	0.158	0.102	0.066	0.043	0.035	0.028	0.019
25	0.780	0.610	0.375	0.233	0.146	0.092	0.059	0.038	0.030	0.024	0.016
26	0.772	0.598	0.361	0.220	0.135	0.084	0.053	0.033	0.026	0.021	0.014
27	0.764	0.586	0.347	0.207	0.125	0.076	0.047	0.029	0.023	0.018	0.011
28	0.757	0.574	0.333	0.196	0.116	0.069	0.042	0.026	0.020	0.016	0.010
29	0.749	0.563	0.321	0.185	0.107	0.063	0.037	0.022	0.017	0.014	0.008
30	0.742	0.552	0.308	0.174	0.099	0.057	0.033	0.020	0.015	0.012	0.007
40	0.672	0.453	0.208	0.097	0.046	0.022	0.011	0.005	0.004	0.003	0.001
50	0.608	0.372	0.141	0.054	0.021	0.009	0.003	0.001	0.001	0.001	

Appendix 11.C   continued

20%	22%	24%	25%	26%	28%	30%	35%	40%	45%	50%
0.833	0.820	0.806	0.800	0.794	0.781	0.769	0.741	0.714	0.690	0.667
0.694	0.672	0.650	0.640	0.630	0.610	0.592	0.549	0.510	0.476	0.444
0.579	0.551	0.524	0.512	0.500	0.477	0.455	0.406	0.364	0.328	0.296
0.482	0.451	0.423	0.410	0.397	0.373	0.350	0.301	0.260	0.226	0.198
0.402	0.370	0.341	0.328	0.315	0.291	0.269	0.223	0.186	0.156	0.132
0.335	0.303	0.275	0.262	0.250	0.227	0.207	0.165	0.133	0.108	0.088
0.279	0.249	0.222	0.210	0.198	0.178	0.159	0.122	0.095	0.074	0.059
0.233	0.204	0.179	0.168	0.157	0.139	0.123	0.091	0.068	0.051	0.039
0.194	0.167	0.144	0.134	0.125	0.108	0.094	0.067	0.048	0.035	0.026
0.162	0.137	0.116	0.107	0.099	0.085	0.073	0.050	0.035	0.024	0.017
0.135	0.112	0.094	0.086	0.079	0.066	0.056	0.037	0.025	0.017	0.012
0.112	0.092	0.076	0.069	0.062	0.052	0.043	0.027	0.018	0.012	0.008
0.093	0.075	0.061	0.055	0.050	0.040	0.033	0.020	0.013	0.008	0.005
0.078	0.062	0.049	0.044	0.039	0.032	0.025	0.015	0.009	0.006	0.003
0.065	0.051	0.040	0.035	0.031	0.025	0.020	0.011	0.006	0.004	0.002
0.054	0.042	0.032	0.028	0.025	0.019	0.015	0.008	0.005	0.003	0.002
0.045	0.034	0.026	0.023	0.020	0.015	0.012	0.006	0.003	0.002	0.001
0.038	0.028	0.021	0.018	0.016	0.012	0.009	0.005	0.002	0.001	0.001
0.031	0.023	0.017	0.014	0.012	0.009	0.007	0.003	0.002	0.001	
0.026	0.019	0.014	0.012	0.010	0.007	0.005	0.002	0.001	0.001	
0.022	0.015	0.011	0.009	0.008	0.006	0.004	0.002	0.001		
0.018	0.013	0.009	0.007	0.006	0.004	0.003	0.001	0.001		
0.015	0.010	0.007	0.006	0.005	0.003	0.002	0.001			
0.013	0.008	0.006	0.005	0.004	0.003	0.002	0.001			
0.010	0.007	0.005	0.004	0.003	0.002	0.001	0.001			
0.009	0.006	0.004	0.003	0.002	0.002	0.001				
0.007	0.005	0.003	0.002	0.002	0.001	0.001				
0.006	0.004	0.002	0.002	0.002	0.001	0.001				
0.005	0.003	0.002	0.002	0.001	0.001	0.001				
0.004	0.003	0.002	0.001	0.001	0.001					
0.001										

Appendix 11.D   Future Value of an Annuity in Arrears of $1 for N Periods

Year (N)	1%	2%	3%	4%	5%	6%
1	1.000	1.000	1.000	1.000	1.000	1.000
2	2.010	2.020	2.030	2.040	2.050	2.060
3	3.030	3.060	3.091	3.122	3.152	3.184
4	4.060	4.122	4.184	4.246	4.310	4.375
5	5.101	5.204	5.309	5.416	5.526	5.637
6	6.152	6.308	6.468	6.633	6.802	6.975
7	7.214	7.434	7.662	7.898	8.142	8.394
8	8.286	8.583	8.892	9.214	9.549	9.897
9	9.369	9.755	10.159	10.583	11.027	11.491
10	10.462	10.950	11.464	12.006	12.578	13.181
11	11.567	12.169	12.808	13.486	14.207	14.972
12	12.683	13.412	14.192	15.026	15.917	16.870
13	13.809	14.680	15.618	16.627	17.713	18.882
14	14.947	15.974	17.086	18.292	19.599	21.051
15	16.097	17.293	18.599	20.024	21.579	23.276
16	17.258	18.639	20.157	21.825	23.657	25.673
17	18.430	20.012	21.762	23.698	25.840	28.213
18	19.615	21.412	23.414	25.645	28.132	30.906
19	20.811	22.841	25.117	27.671	30.539	33.760
20	22.019	24.297	26.870	29.778	33.066	36.786
25	28.243	32.030	36.459	41.646	47.727	54.865
30	34.785	40.568	47.575	56.085	66.439	79.058

Appendix 11.D   continued

Year (N)	7%	8%	9%	10%	12%	14%
1	1.000	1.000	1.000	1.000	1.000	1.000
2	2.070	2.080	2.090	2.100	2.120	2.140
3	3.215	3.246	3.278	3.310	3.374	3.440
4	4.440	4.506	4.573	4.641	4.770	4.921
5	5.751	5.867	5.985	6.105	6.353	6.610
6	7.153	7.336	7.523	7.716	8.115	8.536
7	8.654	8.923	9.200	9.487	10.089	10.730
8	10.260	10.637	11.028	11.436	12.300	13.233
9	11.978	12.488	13.021	13.579	14.776	16.085
10	13.816	14.487	15.193	15.937	17.549	19.337
11	15.784	16.645	17.560	18.531	20.655	23.044
12	17.888	18.977	20.141	21.384	24.133	27.271
13	20.141	21.495	22.953	24.523	28.029	32.089
14	22.550	24.215	26.019	27.975	32.393	37.581
15	25.129	27.152	29.361	31.772	37.280	43.842
16	27.888	30.324	33.003	35.950	42.753	50.980
17	30.840	33.750	36.974	40.545	48.884	59.118
18	33.999	37.450	41.301	45.599	55.750	68.394
19	37.379	41.446	46.018	51.159	63.440	78.969
20	40.995	45.762	51.160	57.275	72.052	91.025
25	63.249	73.106	84.701	98.347	133.334	181.871
30	94.461	113.283	136.308	164.494	241.333	356.787

Appendix 11.E   *Present Value of $1 Received Annually at the End of Each Period for N Periods*

Year (N)	1%	2%	4%	6%	8%	10%	12%	14%	15%	16%
1	0.990	0.980	0.962	0.943	0.926	0.909	0.893	0.877	0.870	0.862
2	1.970	1.942	1.886	1.833	1.783	1.736	1.690	1.647	1.626	1.605
3	2.941	2.884	2.775	2.673	2.577	2.487	2.402	2.322	2.283	2.246
4	3.902	3.808	3.630	3.465	3.312	3.170	3.037	2.914	2.855	2.798
5	4.853	4.713	4.452	4.212	3.993	3.791	3.605	3.433	3.352	3.274
6	5.795	5.601	5.242	4.917	4.623	4.355	4.111	3.889	3.784	3.685
7	6.728	6.472	6.002	5.582	5.206	4.868	4.564	4.288	4.160	4.039
8	7.652	7.325	6.733	6.210	5.747	5.335	4.968	4.639	4.487	4.344
9	8.566	8.162	7.435	6.802	6.247	5.759	5.328	4.946	4.772	4.607
10	9.471	8.983	8.111	7.360	6.710	6.145	5.650	5.216	5.019	4.833
11	10.368	9.787	8.760	7.887	7.139	6.495	5.988	5.453	5.234	5.029
12	11.255	10.575	9.385	8.384	7.536	6.814	6.194	5.660	5.421	5.197
13	12.134	11.343	9.986	8.853	7.904	7.103	6.424	5.842	5.583	5.342
14	13.004	12.106	10.563	9.295	8.244	7.367	6.628	6.002	5.724	5.468
15	13.865	12.849	11.118	9.712	8.559	7.606	6.811	6.142	5.847	5.575
16	14.718	13.578	11.652	10.106	8.851	7.824	6.974	6.265	5.954	5.669
17	15.562	14.292	12.166	10.477	9.122	8.022	7.120	6.373	6.047	5.749
18	16.398	14.992	12.659	10.828	9.372	8.201	7.250	6.467	6.128	5.818
19	17.226	15.678	13.134	11.158	9.604	8.365	7.366	6.550	6.198	5.877
20	18.046	16.351	13.590	11.470	9.818	8.514	7.469	6.623	6.259	5.929
21	18.857	17.011	14.029	11.764	10.017	8.649	7.562	6.687	6.312	5.973
22	19.660	17.658	14.451	12.042	10.201	8.772	7.645	6.743	6.359	6.011
23	20.456	18.292	14.857	12.303	10.371	8.883	7.718	6.792	6.399	6.044
24	21.243	18.914	15.247	12.550	10.529	8.985	7.784	6.835	6.434	6.073
25	22.023	19.523	15.622	12.783	10.675	9.077	7.843	6.873	6.464	6.097
26	22.795	20.121	15.983	13.003	10.810	9.161	7.896	6.906	6.491	6.118
27	23.560	20.707	16.330	13.211	10.935	9.237	7.943	6.935	6.514	6.136
28	24.316	21.281	16.663	13.406	11.051	9.307	7.984	6.961	6.534	6.152
29	25.066	21.844	16.984	13.591	11.158	9.370	8.022	6.983	6.551	6.166
30	25.808	22.396	17.292	13.765	11.258	9.427	8.055	7.003	6.566	6.177
40	32.835	27.355	19.793	15.046	11.925	9.779	8.244	7.105	6.642	6.234
50	39.196	31.424	21.482	15.762	12.234	9.915	8.304	7.133	6.661	6.246

Appendix 11.E   *continued*

18%	20%	22%	24%	25%	26%	28%	30%	35%	40%	45%	50%
0.847	0.833	0.820	0.806	0.800	0.794	0.781	0.769	0.741	0.714	0.690	0.667
1.566	1.528	1.492	1.457	1.440	1.424	1.392	1.361	1.289	1.224	1.165	1.111
2.174	2.106	2.042	1.981	1.952	1.923	1.868	1.816	1.696	1.589	1.493	1.407
2.690	2.589	2.494	2.404	2.362	2.320	2.241	2.166	1.997	1.849	1.720	1.605
3.127	2.991	2.864	2.745	2.689	2.635	2.532	2.436	2.220	2.035	1.876	1.737
3.498	3.326	3.167	3.020	2.951	2.885	2.759	2.643	2.385	2.168	1.983	1.824
3.812	3.605	3.416	3.242	3.161	3.083	2.937	2.802	2.508	2.263	2.057	1.883
4.078	3.837	3.619	3.421	3.329	3.241	3.076	2.925	2.598	2.331	2.108	1.922
4.303	4.031	3.786	3.566	3.463	3.366	3.184	3.019	2.665	2.379	2.144	1.948
4.494	4.192	3.923	3.682	3.571	3.465	3.269	3.092	2.715	2.414	2.168	1.965
4.656	4.327	4.035	3.776	3.656	3.544	3.335	3.147	2.752	2.438	2.185	1.977
4.793	4.439	4.127	3.851	3.725	3.606	3.387	3.190	2.779	2.456	2.196	1.985
4.910	4.533	4.203	3.912	3.780	3.656	3.427	3.223	2.799	2.468	2.204	1.990
5.008	4.611	4.265	3.962	3.824	3.695	3.459	3.249	2.814	2.477	2.210	1.993
5.092	4.675	4.315	4.001	3.859	3.726	3.483	3.268	2.825	2.484	2.214	1.995
5.162	4.730	4.357	4.003	3.887	3.751	3.503	3.283	2.834	2.489	2.216	1.997
5.222	4.775	4.391	4.059	3.910	3.771	3.518	3.295	2.840	2.492	2.218	1.998
5.273	4.812	4.419	4.080	3.928	3.786	3.529	3.304	2.844	2.494	2.219	1.999
5.316	4.844	4.442	4.097	3.942	3.799	3.539	3.311	2.848	2.496	2.220	1.999
5.353	4.870	4.460	4.110	3.954	3.808	3.546	3.316	2.850	2.497	2.221	1.999
5.384	4.891	4.476	4.121	3.963	3.816	3.551	3.320	2.852	2.498	2.221	2.000
5.410	4.909	4.488	4.130	3.970	3.822	3.556	3.323	2.853	2.498	2.222	2.000
5.432	4.925	4.499	4.137	3.976	3.827	3.559	3.325	2.854	2.499	2.222	2.000
5.451	4.937	4.507	4.143	3.981	3.831	3.562	3.327	2.855	2.499	2.222	2.000
5.467	4.948	4.514	4.147	3.985	3.834	3.564	3.329	2.856	2.499	2.222	2.000
5.480	4.956	4.520	4.151	3.988	3.837	3.566	3.330	2.856	2.500	2.222	2.000
5.492	4.964	4.524	4.154	3.990	3.839	3.567	3.331	2.856	2.500	2.222	2.000
5.502	4.970	4.528	4.157	3.992	3.840	3.568	3.331	2.857	2.500	2.222	2.000
5.510	4.975	4.531	4.159	3.994	3.841	3.569	3.332	2.857	2.500	2.222	2.000
5.517	4.979	4.534	4.160	3.995	3.842	3.569	3.332	2.857	2.500	2.222	2.000
5.548	4.997	4.544	4.166	3.999	3.846	3.571	3.333	2.857	2.500	2.222	2.000
5.554	4.999	4.545	4.167	4.000	3.846	3.571	3.333	2.857	2.500	2.222	2.000

GLOSSARY

Accounting Rate of Return (ARR) Method An evaluation process that uses the ratio of the average annual profit after taxes to the investment of a project.

Annuity An arrangement for a series of cash flows payable at fixed intervals as the result of an investment.

Capital Budgeting Long-term planning for proposed capital outlays and their financing.

Capital Rationing The process of placing constraints upon the acquisition or use of capital resources in a capital budgeting decision.

Cash Flow The amount of cash receipts and disbursements over a specific period of time for a given segment of a firm.

Discounted Cash Flow (DCF) Method An evaluation process that uses present value concepts to measure the profitability of a project.

Internal Rate of Return (IRR) Method An evaluation process that computes the interest rate equating the present value of an investment's cash flows and the cost of the investment.

Net Present Value (NPV) Method An evaluation process that compares the cost of an investment with the present value of the future cash flows of the investment at a selected rate of return, or hurdle rate.

Payback Method An evaluation process that computes the number of years before the initial cash outlay of a project is fully recovered by its future cash inflows.

Present Value The amount that should be paid for the right to receive a payment (or a series of payments) in the future (at an assumed interest rate) if the payment is to be received after a specific period of time.

Risk A measure of the probability that unforeseen occurrences will cause estimates to vary from projections.

Time Value of Money The ability of money to earn more money in the future.

SELECTED READINGS

Bailes, Jack C.; Nielsen, James F.; and Wendell, Steve, "Capital Budgeting in the Forest Products Industry," *Management Accounting* (July 1979), pp. 46–51, 57.

Bavishi, Vinod B., "Capital Budgeting Practices at Multinationals," *Management Accounting* (August 1981), pp. 32–35.

Bergeron, Pierre G., "The Other Dimensions of the Payback Period," *Cost and Management* (May–June 1978), pp. 35–39.

Doenges, R. Conrad, "The Reinvestment Problem in a Practical Perspective," *Financial Management* (Spring 1972), pp. 85–91.

Elliot, Grover S., "Analyzing the Cost of Capital," *Management Accounting* (December 1980), pp. 13–18.

Fremgen, James M., "Capital Budgeting Practices: A Survey," *Management Accounting* (May 1973), pp. 19–25.

Gaertner, James F., and Milani, Ken, "The TRR Yardstick for Hospital Capital Expenditure Decisions," *Management Accounting* (December 1980), pp. 25–33.

Glahn, Gerald L.; Fields, Kent T.; and Trapnell, Jerry E., "How to Evaluate Mixed Risk Capital Projects," *Management Accounting* (December 1980), pp. 34–38.

Hendricks, James A., "Capital Budgeting Decisions: NPV or IRR?" *Cost and Management* (March–April 1980), pp. 16–20.

Hertz, David B., "Investment Policies That Pay Off," *Harvard Business Review* (January–February 1968), pp. 96–108.

Hertz, David B., "Risk Analysis in Capital Investment," *Harvard Business Review* (January–February 1964), pp. 95–106.

Hespos, Richard F., and Strassman, Paul A., "Stochastic Decision Trees for the Analysis of Investment Decisions," *Management Science* (August 1965), pp. 244–259.

Hillier, Frederick, "The Deviation of Probabilistic Information for the Evaluation of Risky Investments," *Management Science* (April 1963), pp. 443–457.

Hing-Ling, Amy, and Lau, Hong-Shiang, "Improving Present Value Analysis with a Programmable Calculator," *Management Accounting* (November 1979), pp. 52–57.

Johnson, Robert W., *Capital Budgeting* (Belmont, Calif.: Wadsworth Publishing, 1970).

Kim, Suk H., "Making the Long-term Investment Decision," *Management Accounting* (March 1979), pp. 41–49.

Kim, Suk H., and Farragher, Edward J., "Current Capital Budgeting Practices," *Management Accounting* (June 1981), pp. 26–31.

Lerner, Eugene M., and Rappaport, Alfred, "Limit DCF in Capital Budgeting," *Harvard Business Review* (September–October 1968), pp. 133–139.

Norgaard, Corine T., "The Post-Completion Audit of Capital Projects," *Cost and Management* (January–February 1979), pp. 19–25.

Osteryoung, Jerome S., *Capital Budgeting: Long-term Asset Selection* (Columbus, Ohio: Grid, 1974).

Osteryoung, Jerome S.; Scott, Elton; and Roberts, Gordon S., "Selecting Capital Projects with the Coefficient of Variation," *Financial Management* (Summer 1977), pp. 65–70.

Pettway, Richard H., "Integer Programming in Capital Budgeting: A Note on Computational Experience," *Journal of Financial and Quantitative Analysis* (September 1973), pp. 665–672.

Puglisi, D. J., and Chadwick, L. W., "Capital Budgeting with Realized Terminal Values," *Cost and Management* (May–June 1977), pp. 13–17.

Raiborn, D. D., and Ratcliffe, Thomas A., "Are You Accounting for Inflation in Your Capital Budgeting Process?" *Management Accounting* (September 1979), pp. 19–22.

Roemmich, Roger A.; Duke, Gordon L.; and Gates, William H., "Maximizing the Present Value of Tax Savings from Depreciation," *Management Accounting* (September 1978), pp. 55–57, 63.

Sangeladji, Mohammad A., "True Rate of Return for Evaluating Capital Investments," *Management Accounting* (February 1979), pp. 24–27.

Suver, James D., and Neumann, Bruce R., "Capital Budgeting for Hospitals," *Management Accounting* (December 1978), pp. 48–50, 53.

Truitt, Jack F., "A Solution to Capital Budgeting Problems Concerning Investments with Different Lives," *Cost and Management* (November–December 1978), pp. 44–45.

Uhl, Franklin S., "Automated Capital Investment Decisions," *Management Accounting* (April 1980), pp. 41–46.

Weingartner, H. Martin, "Capital Budgeting of Interrelated Projects: Surveys and Synthesis," *Management Science* (March 1966), pp. 485–516.

William, H. Jean, "On Multiple Rates of Return," *Journal of Finance* (March 1968), pp. 187–191.

QUESTIONS, EXERCISES, AND PROBLEMS

11.1   Define capital budgeting.

11.2   Define the stockholders' wealth maximization model.

11.3   *Payback Method*   A project being planned will cost $30,000. The annual cash inflow net of income taxes for the next five years is as follows:

Period	Cash Flow
1	$ 8,000
2	4,000
3	12,000
4	14,000
5	6,000

Required:
Compute the payback period of the project.

11.4   *Multiple Internal Rate of Return*   A project calls for the outlay of $20,000,000 to develop a strip mine. The mine will produce a cash flow of $90,000,000 at the end of year 1. At the end of year 2, $80,000,000 will be used to restore the land to its original condition. Compute the IRR of the project.

11.5   ***Estimating Cash Flows***   A new machine acquired for $48,000 will be depreciated on a double declining balance basis of 20 percent per year. A full year's depreciation of 20 percent will be taken in the year of acquisition. The accounting (book value) rate of return will be 14 percent on the initial investment. If a uniform cash flow is assumed, what will be the annual cash flow for the second year?

(SMA adapted)

11.6   ***Net Present Value***   A project being planned will cost $22,000. The annual cash inflow net of income taxes will be $5,000 per year for each of the next seven years. Using a rate of return of 12 percent, what is the present value of the cash flows generated by the project and the NPV of the project?

(SMA adapted)

11.7   ***Internal Rate of Return***   A project offers an initial cash outflow of $33,000, an annual expected cash inflow of $10,000 for five years, and no salvage value. Compute the IRR for the project.

11.8   ***Certainty Equivalent Method***   A project offers an initial cash outlay of $40,000, an annual expected cash inflow of $20,000 for three years, and no salvage value. The risk coefficients for the three periods are estimated to be 0.90, 0.80, and 0.75, respectively. The risk-free rate of interest is estimated to be 6 percent. Compute the NPV of the project.

11.9   ***Probability Distribution and Capital Budgeting***   The Santini Company can invest in one of two mutually exclusive projects. The probability distribution of the two projects' NPVs is shown here:

Project X		Project Y	
Net Present Value	**Probability**	**Net Present Value**	**Probability**
0.3	$2,000	0.4	$3,000
0.6	4,000	0.4	2,000
0.1	6,000	0.2	7,000

Required:

1. Compute the expected value, the standard deviation, and the coefficient of variation of each project.

2. Which of these two mutually exclusive projects should the Santini Company choose? Why?

11.10   ***Mutually Exclusive Projects: Different Outlays***   The Baksi Company is considering two mutually exclusive, one-year projects. Projects A and B require outlays of $1,000 and $1,500, respectively. Project A will generate a return of $1,250 at the end of the first year, and project B will generate a return of $1,830 at the end of the second year. The cost of capital is 10 percent.

Required:

1. Utilizing the NPV method, which project would the Baksi Company accept?

2. Utilizing the IRR method, which project would the company accept?

3. Which ranking is better?

(Adapted with permission from James A. Hendricks, "Capital Budgeting Decisions: NPV or IRR?" *Cost and Management*, March–April 1980, pp. 16–20.)

11.11 **Mutually Exclusive Projects: Differential Timing of Cash Flows** The Beauchemin Company is considering two mutually exclusive, two-year projects. Projects A and B require an outlay of $1,000 each. Project A promises a return of $200 at the end of year 1 and $1,290 at the end of year 2. Project B promises a return of $1,100 at the end of year 1 and $245 at the end of year 2. The cost of capital is 10 percent.

Required:

1. Using the NPV method, which project would the Beauchemin Company accept?

2. Using the IRR method, which project would the Beauchemin Company accept?

3. Which ranking is better?

(Adapted with permission from James A. Hendricks, "Capital Budgeting Decisions: NPV or IRR?" *Cost and Management*, March–April 1980, pp. 16–20.)

11.12 **Capital Budgeting under Uncertainty** Mr. Brown, the president of Saba Enterprises, is evaluating whether to invest $3,000,000 in a research project designed to discover a method of converting industrial waste from the Clean Company into usable fuel. If the research project is successful, the revenues net of operating costs (excluding the $3,000,000 outlay for the research and an initial investment in equipment) are estimated to be as follows:

Anticipated Net Revenue	Probability
$10,000,000	0.10
20,000,000	0.25
25,000,000	0.35
30,000,000	0.20
35,000,000	0.10

However, Brown knows there is a 60 percent chance that the project will be unsuccessful.

Required:

Assuming Brown wishes to maximize the expected value of net cash flows, should the investment be made in the research project? Show all calculations.

(SMA adapted)

11.13 **Capital Budgeting under Uncertainty** The Uncertain Company is contemplating the evaluation of an investment with a future return subject to uncertainty. The company decides to approximate the effects of uncertainty by concentrating upon the most pessimistic, most likely, and most optimistic outcomes. It estimates the associated probabilities of these three outcomes to be 0.4, 0.5, and 0.1, respectively. Discounting the expected streams of cash under each of the three outcomes yields present value amounts of $14,000, $45,000, and $90,000, respectively.

Required:

1. If the Uncertain Company must invest $35,000 now to earn the expected return, what will be the expected NPV? Should it invest?

2. How much should the company pay for perfect information regarding the expected return?

3. Assume the company uses the expected return as an investment criterion, and the most pessimistic outcome is realized. What is the ex post forecast error that results (that is, the impact of the error in the forecast of net income)? What is the error if the most optimistic outcome is realized?

(SMA adapted)

11.14   *Mutually Exclusive Projects: Different Lives*   The Express Company is considering two mutually exclusive projects. Projects A and B require an outlay of $1,000 each. Project A promises a return of $1,200 at the end of year 1, and project B promises only a return of $1,520 at the end of year 3. The cost of capital is 10 percent.

Required:

1. Using the NPV method, which project would the Express Company accept?

2. Using the IRR method, which project would the company accept?

3. Which ranking is better?

(Adapted with permission from James A. Hendricks, "Capital Budgeting Decisions: NPV or IRR?" *Cost and Management*, March–April 1980, pp. 16–20.)

11.15   *Capital Rationing*   The Francis Company is considering eight projects. The cost of capital is 12 percent, and the capital constraint is $500. Each project has a one-year life. The initial outlay and the cash flow at the end of year 1 for each project are as follows:

Project	Initial Outlay	Cash Inflow, End of Year 1
A	$100	$122
B	100	118
C	100	115
D	200	238
E	200	234
F	300	348
G	400	468

Required:

1. Compute the NPV and the IRR for each project.

2. Assuming the eight projects are not mutually exclusive, which combination of projects should the Francis Company choose? (Use NPV.)

3. Assuming projects A, B, E, and G are mutually exclusive, which combination of projects should the company choose? (Use NPV.)

(Adapted with permission from James A. Hendricks, "Capital Budgeting Decisions: NPV or IRR?" *Cost and Management*, March–April 1980, pp. 16–20.)

11.16   *Accounting Treatment of Accelerated Depreciation*   The McIntosh Company is considering the purchase of a piece of equipment for $100,000. The equipment will have a ten-year useful life and no salvage value, and the tax rate is 10 percent. The equipment is expected to generate an annual net income before taxes and depreciation of $50,000.

The McIntosh Company expects to take advantage of double declining balance depreciation for tax purposes, and for reporting purposes it expects to issue financial statements based on straight-line depreciation. The two approaches are reconciled by setting up a deferred tax credit account.

Required:
1. Determine the annual tax liability under straight-line depreciation.
2. Determine the annual tax liability under double declining balance depreciation.
3. Make the annual entries to recognize the tax expense and the tax payable.

11.17   ***Cash Flow and Accrual Accounting***   The Slattery Corporation purchased a new machine, which is expected to earn an accounting profit of $2,000 in 19X1, computed as follows:

Sales	$18,000
− Operating Expenses ($8,000) and Depreciation ($6,000)	14,000
= Operating Income before Tax	$ 4,000
− Income Tax Expense (50%)	2,000
= Operating Income after Tax	$ 2,000

Related accrual information includes the following:

Uncollected sales total $400 at year-end.

Unpaid wages amount to $800 at year-end.

The tax return depreciation is $12,000 for 19X1.

Required:
Determine the cash flow for 19X1.

11.18   ***Mathematical Programming and Capital Budgeting***   The Perrakis Company is considering the following investment proposals:

Projects	Initial Outlay Required	Required in Period 1	Net Present Value
1	$17,000	$14,000	$30,000
2	22,000	26,000	50,000
3	15,000	15,000	24,000
4	25,000	16,000	55,000

Projects 1 and 3 are mutually exclusive. The company has a budget constraint of $40,000 in year 1 and $30,000 in year 2.

Required:
1. Set up the selection process as a mathematical programming problem to maximize the NPV available from investment subject to the two budget constraints.
2. Set up the dual program assuming projects 1 and 3 are no longer mutually exclusive.
3. Explain the meaning of the dual values.

11.19   ***Multiperiod Projects***   The Dickenson Company has determined the following discrete probability distributions for net cash flows generated by a contemplated project:

Period 1		Period 2	
Probability	**Cash Flow**	**Probability**	**Cash Flow**
0.10	$5,000	0.10	$6,000
0.20	4,500	0.10	2,000
0.10	3,000	0.25	5,000
0.20	3,500	0.25	3,000
0.40	4,000	0.30	4,000

The after-tax risk-free rate is 10 percent, and the project requires an initial outlay of $6,000.

Required:

1. Determine the expected value of the NPV.

2. Determine the standard deviation of the NPV, assuming that the probability distributions of cash flows for future periods are independent.

3. Determine the standard deviation of the NPV, assuming that the probability distributions of cash flows for future periods are dependent.

11.20   ***Probabilities, Discounted Cash Flow***   During your examination of the financial statements of Benjamin Industries, the president requested your assistance in evaluating several financial management problems in her home appliances division, which she summarized for you as follows.

Management wants to determine the best sales price for a new appliance that has a variable cost of $4 per unit. The sales manager has estimated probabilities of achieving annual sales levels for several selling prices, as shown in the following chart:

Sales Level (Units)	Selling Price $4	$5	$6	$7
20,000	—	—	20%	80%
30,000	—	10%	40%	20%
40,000	50%	50%	20%	—
50,000	50%	40%	20%	—

The division's current profit rate is 5 percent on annual sales of $1,200,000; an investment of $400,000 is needed to finance these sales. The company's basis for measuring divisional success is return on investment.

Management is considering the following two alternative plans submitted by employees for improving operations in the home appliances division:

1. Green believes that sales volume can be doubled by greater promotional effort, but his method would lower the profit rate to 4 percent of sales and would require an additional investment of $100,000.

2. Gold favors eliminating some unprofitable appliances and improving efficiency by adding $200,000 in capital equipment. Her methods would decrease sales volume by 10 percent but would improve the profit rate to 7 percent.

Black, White, and Gray, three franchised home appliance dealers, have requested short-term financing from Benjamin Industries. The dealers have agreed to repay the loans within three years and to pay Benjamin Industries 5 percent of their net income for the three-year period for the use of the funds. The following table summarizes by dealer the financing requested and the total remittances (principal plus 5 percent of net income) expected at the end of each year:

	Black	**White**	**Gray**
Financing Requested	$ 80,000	$40,000	$30,000
Remittances Expected at End of			
Year 1	$ 10,000	$25,000	$10,000
Year 2	40,000	30,000	15,000
Year 3	70,000	5,000	15,000
	$120,000	$60,000	$40,000

Management believes these financing requests should be granted only if the annual pre-tax return to the company exceeds the target internal rate of 20 percent on investment. Discount factors (rounded) that would provide this 20 percent rate of return are

Year 1   0.8
Year 2   0.7
Year 3   0.6

Required:

1. Prepare a schedule computing the expected incremental income for each of the sales prices proposed for the new product. The schedule should include the expected sales levels in units (weighted according to the sales manager's estimated probabilities), expected total monetary sales, expected variable costs, and expected incremental income.

2. Prepare schedules computing (a) the company's current rate of return on investment in the home appliances division, as well as the anticipated rates of return under the alternative suggestions made by (b) Green and (c) Gold.

3. Prepare a schedule computing the NPV of the investment opportunities of financing Black, White, and Gray. The schedule should determine if the discounted cash flows expected from (a) Black, (b) White, and (c) Gray would be more or less than the amounts of Benjamin Industries' investment in loans to each of the three dealers.

(AICPA adapted)

11.21   ***Probabilities and Discounted Cash Flow***   Vernon Enterprises designs and manufactures toys. Past experience indicates that the product life cycle of a toy is three years. Promotional advertising produces large sales in the early years, but there is a substantial sales decline in the final year of a toy's life.

Consumer demand for new toys placed on the market tends to fall into three classes. About 30 percent of the new toys sell well above expectations, 60 percent sell as anticipated, and 10 percent have poor consumer acceptance.

A new toy has been developed, and the following sales projections were made by carefully evaluating consumer demand for it:

Consumer Demand for New Toy	**Chance of Occurring**	**Estimated Sales in**		
		Year 1	**Year 2**	**Year 3**
Above Average	30%	$1,200,000	$2,500,000	$600,000
Average	60	700,000	1,700,000	400,000
Below Average	10	200,000	900,000	150,000

Variable costs are estimated at 30 percent of the selling price. Special machinery must be purchased at a cost of $860,000 and will be installed in an unused portion of the factory, which Vernon Enterprises unsuccessfully has been trying to rent for several years at $50,000 per year and which has no future utilization prospects. Fixed expenses for the new toy (excluding depreciation) of a cash flow nature are estimated at $50,000 per year. The new machinery will be depreciated by the sum-of-the-years'-digits method with an estimated salvage value of $110,000, and it will be sold at the beginning of the fourth year. Advertising and promotional expenses will be incurred uniformly and will total $100,000 the first year, $150,000 the second year, and $50,000 the third year. These expenses will be deducted as incurred for income tax reporting. Vernon believes that state and federal income taxes will total 60 percent of income in the foreseeable future and can be assumed to be paid uniformly over the year the income is earned.

Required:
1. Prepare a schedule computing the probable sales of Vernon Enterprises' new toy in each of the three years, taking into account the probability of above-average, average, and below-average sales occurring.

2. Assume that the probable sales computed in part 1 are $900,000 the first year, $1,800,000 the second year, and $410,000 the third year. Prepare a schedule computing the probable net income for the new toy in each of the three years of its life.

3. Prepare a schedule of net cash flows from sales of the new toy for each of the years involved and from disposition of the machinery purchased. Use the sales data given in part 2.

4. Assuming a minimum desired rate of return of 10 percent, prepare a schedule of the present value of the net cash flows calculated in part 3. The following data are relevant:

Year	Present Value of $1 Due at End of Each Year Discounted at 10 Percent	Present Value of $1 Earned Uniformly throughout Year Discounted at 10 Percent
1	0.91	0.95
2	0.83	0.86
3	0.75	0.78

(AICPA adapted)

11.22   ***Replacement Decisions: Unequal Lives***   The Hass Company is considering replacing a fully depreciated lathe for trimming molded plastic with a new machine. Two replacement machines are available. Lathe X has a cost of $50,000, will last five years, and will produce after-tax cash flows of $15,000 per year for five years. Lathe Y has a cost of $60,000, will last ten years, and will produce net cash flows of $12,000 per year for ten years. The company's cost of capital is 10 percent. Should lathe X or Y be selected to replace the old machine?

11.23   ***Replacement Decisions: Equal Lives***   The Davidson Company purchased a computer ten years ago with a cost of $20,000, a useful life of twenty years, and a zero salvage value at the end of its useful life. Straight-line depreciation is used. A new manager suggested that a new computer costing $30,000 be purchased. The new computer has a ten-year life and could reduce operating costs from $10,000 to $5,000. The old computer can be sold now at an estimated $4,000, and the new computer can be sold at the end of the ten years for $5,000. Taxes are at 48 percent rate, and the company's cost of capital is 10 percent. An investment tax credit of 10 percent of the purchase price can be used if the new machine is acquired. Should the Davidson Company buy the new computer?

11.24   ***Capital Budgeting***   Madisons, Inc., has decided to acquire a new piece of equipment. It can do so by an outright cash purchase at $25,000 or by a leasing alternative of $6,000 per year for the life of the machine. Other relevant information follows:

Purchase Price Due at Time of Purchase	....	$25,000
Estimated Useful Life	....	5 Years
Estimated Salvage Value if Purchased	....	$ 3,000
Annual Cost of Maintenance Contract to Be Acquired with Either Lease or Purchase	.....	$ 500

The full purchase price of $25,000 could be borrowed from the bank at 10 percent annual interest and could be repaid in one payment at the end of the fifth year. Additional information includes the following:

Assume a 40 percent income tax rate and use of the straight-line method of depreciation.

The yearly lease, rental, and maintenance contract fees would be paid at the beginning of each year.

The minimum desired rate of return on investment is 10 percent.

All cash flows are assumed to occur at the end of the year, unless otherwise stated.

Selected present value factors for a 10 percent return are

Year	Present Value of $1 Received at End of Year
0	$1.000
1	0.909
2	0.826
3	0.751
4	0.683
5	0.621

Required:
Select the best answer for each of the following items:
1. The present value of the purchase price of the machine is
    a. $25,000.   **d.** $2,500.
    b. $22,725.   **e.** None of the above.
    c. $22,500.

2. Under the purchase alternative, the present value of the estimated salvage value is
    a. $3,000.   **d.** $0.
    b. $2,049.   **e.** None of the above.
    c. $1,863.

3. Under the purchase alternative, the annual cash inflow (tax reduction) related to depreciation is
    a. $5,000.   **d.** $1,760.
    b. $4,400.   **e.** None of the above.
    c. $2,640.

4. Under the purchase alternative, the annual after-tax cash outflow for interest and maintenance would be
    a. $3,000.   **d.** $1,200.
    b. $2,500.   **e.** None of the above.
    c. $1,800.

5. If salvage value is not ignored, the before-tax interest rate implicit in the lease contract is
    a. 20 percent or more.
    b. More than 10 percent but less than 20 percent.

c. Precisely 10 percent.

d. Less than 10 percent.

e. Not determinable from the given facts.

(AICPA adapted)

11.25   ***Capital Budgeting Decision Models***   Capital budgeting has received increased attention in recent years. The quantitative techniques employed for capital budgeting decisions depend largely upon accounting data.

Required:

1. Distinguish between capital budgeting and budgeting for operations.

2. Three quantitative methods used in making capital budgeting decisions are the (a) payback period method, (b) unadjusted accounting rate of return method, and (c) discounted cash flow method. Discuss the merits of each of these methods.

3. Two variations of the discounted cash flow method are the (a) time-adjusted rate of return method and (b) net present value method (sometimes referred to as *excess present value method*). Explain and compare these two variations of the discounted cash flow method.

4. Cost of capital is an important concept in capital budgeting. Define the term *cost of capital*, and explain how it is used in capital budgeting.

5. The statistical term *expected value* is used to describe estimates of future receipts of a capital budgeting project. Explain the meaning of the term, and indicate how the method to which it applies is used in estimating future receipts.

(AICPA adapted)

11.26   ***Real and Money Discount Rates***   Dr. Eric Magnum is considering a $900 investment that is expected to yield a return of $133 for the first two years and $1,133 in the third year. A rate of inflation of 10 percent and a real rate of 3 percent are expected. Magnum is in the zero tax bracket. Determine the net present value of the investment using: (1) a nominal discount rate, and (2) a real discount rate.

11.27   ***NPV Technique***   The Stefanski Company is considering the initiation of a new project. This project has a three-year life and initial outflow, or project cost, of $60,000. Revenues and expenses for the first year are estimated to be $100,000 and $50,000, respectively. It is assumed that an inflation rate of 10 percent per year will cause similar increases in cash revenues and cash expenses. The tax rate is assumed to be 40 percent.

Required:

1. Compute the income statements of the new project for each of the three years. (Assume a straight-line depreciation and no salvage.)

2. Compute the after-tax cash inflow for each of the three years.

3. Assuming that the before-tax borrowing rate is 15 percent, determine the NPV of the project.

Leasing has recently become an important source of financing for many types of assets. The lessee acquires the use of an asset while the title is retained by the lessor. More specifically, a lease is a contract between an owner (the lessor) and another party (the lessee) that grants the lessee the right to use the lessor's property under certain conditions and for a specified period of time. Because of the contractual nature of lease obligations, a lease should be considered a financing device and an alternative to debt financing. Both the lease rental payments and the payments of principal and interest on debt are fixed obligations. Any default in the payment of either obligation can create serious problems for a firm.

The decision to lease an asset is generally evaluated by comparing it with the borrowing decision necessary for an outright purchase of the same asset. Different valuation models have been proposed, and any choice can be challenged because of the controversial issues surrounding a given model and its corresponding variables and parameters. The main purpose of this chapter is to explain leasing arrangements and the main issues in financial leasing, and to provide a methodology for analysis.

The lease as a new form of financing undergoes constant change, as shown by the number and variations of the sources of leasing arrangements. Financial institutions involved in leasing differ mainly in their degree of specialization and include independent leasing companies, service leasing companies, lease brokers, commercial brokers, and insurance companies.

12.1   TYPES OF LEASING ARRANGEMENTS

Although it is possible to describe major forms of lease arrangements, the options, terms, and conditions may vary from contract to contract, giving a firm great flexibility in the adaptation of leasing as a financing method.

12.1.1   *Operating versus Financial Leases*

The first distinction to be made in leasing is between *operating* and *financial leases*. Under both contracts, the lessee agrees to make periodic rental payments. An operating lease is a short-term contract that is cancelable given proper notice at the option of the lessee, whereby the lessor gives the lessee the use of property in exchange for rental payments and at the same time retains the usual ownership risks (such as obsolescence) and rewards (such as a gain from appreciation in value at the end of the lease period). To compensate the lessor for assuming the ownership risks, the periodic rental payments of an operating lease will include a return on investment plus most ownership costs, such as maintenance, taxes, depreciation, obsolescence, casualty losses, and so forth. Examples of operating leases include car rentals, apartment rentals, telephone service, and space rental in shopping centers.

A financial lease is a comparatively long-term contract that is noncancelable by the lessor, who assumes little or no ownership costs. As a result, the periodic rental payments include only a return on investment, and the lessee may be required to pay most of the ownership costs. At the termination of the lease, options may exist allowing the lessee to acquire the asset at either a nominal cost or no cost at all. The financial lease allows the lessor to recover the investment and even realize a profit through the lessee's continuous rental payments over the period specified by the contract. The financial lease gives the lessee continuous use of the asset at a certain cost and, consequently, is a means of financing the use (and not the ownership) of the asset. In other words, the difference between the operating and financial lease lies mainly in the cancellation and financing options. As opposed to an operating lease, a financial lease is noncancelable, and it can be perceived as a financing instrument.

12.1.2   *Sale and Leaseback, Direct Leasing, and Leverage Leases*

Another important distinction in lease financing is made between the *sale and leaseback* and *direct lease* arrangements. The difference lies in the nature of the prior ownership of the asset to be leased. Under the sale and leaseback arrangement, a firm sells an asset it owns to another party, which in turn leases it back to the previous owner. Under this popular arrangement, a company in need of liquidity receives cash from the sale of the asset while retaining the economic use of the asset during the lease period.

Under direct leasing, the lessee acquires the use of an asset it did not previously own. The lessee can enter into the leasing arrangement with a manufacturer, independent leasing company, or financial institution.

With the advent of direct leasing through commercial banks in 1963, a new lease arrangement appeared called a *leverage lease*. This is a tripartite arrangement whereby the lessor finances a portion of the acquisition of the asset (50 to 80 percent of the purchase price) from a lender (commercial bank), securing the loan by a mortgage of the leased property as well as by the assignment of the lease and lease payments. The leverage lease is a popular instrument for special-purpose leasing companies and partnerships of individuals in high tax brackets because of the tax benefits provided by the accelerated depreciation charges, the investment tax credit, and the interest on debt, and because of the favorable return on the equity participation by the lessor. From the point of view of the lessee, the leverage lease is similar to any other lease and, consequently, does not affect the method of valuation.[1]

---

[1]For a discussion of leverage leasing, see Robert C. Wiar, "Economic Implications of Multiple Rates of Return in the Leverage Lease Context," *Journal of Finance* (December 1973), pp. 1, 275–286; and

Figure 12.1   Leases according to Parties Involved

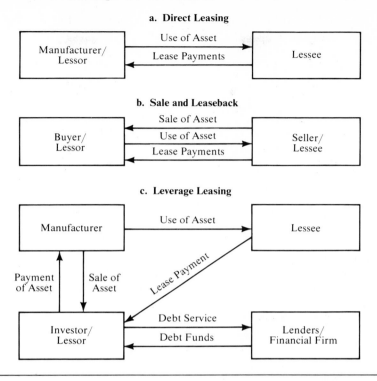

Leverage leasing involves at least four parties: a lessee, a manufacturer (or distributor), a lessor, and a lender. Arrangements are complex, and the parties enter into the agreement primarily for tax and financial cost savings rather than convenience. The lessee is able to obtain financial leasing from the lessor at a cost lower than the usual cost of capital; the lessor, being of a high income tax bracket, gains an investment tax credit (or capital cost allowance) benefit resulting in reduced taxes. The lessor passes on some of this benefit to the lessee through reduced lease costs.

Direct leasing, sale and leaseback, and leverage leasing are illustrated in Figure 12.1.

12.1.3   Maintenance, Nonmaintenance, and Net Leases

The assignment of responsibility for the maintenance of the asset during the life of a lease takes three forms: the *maintenance lease*, *nonmaintenance lease*, and *net lease*.

A maintenance lease assigns responsibility for the maintenance of a leased asset's good working order to the lessor. The lessor is required to incur the maintenance and repair expenses and the local and state taxes, and to provide insurance for the leased asset. The maintenance lease is preferable when the lessor is better equipped to provide low-cost repair than the lessee in terms of technology and skills. It is used mostly in

E. Richard Packham, "An Analysis of the Risks of Leverage Leasing," *Journal of Commercial Bank Lending* (March 1975), pp. 2–29.

rentals of automobiles, trucks, and specialized equipment, like computers, requiring a highly qualified maintenance staff.

A nonmaintenance lease assigns the responsibility for the maintenance of a leased asset to the lessee. The lessee is required to pay for all maintenance and repair costs and the local and state taxes, and to provide insurance. The nonmaintenance lease occurs principally in long-term leasing of land and buildings.

A net lease assigns total responsibility for an asset's maintenance to the lessee to the point that the lessee may be required to absorb all losses incurred by the sale of the asset at the end of the life of the lease. This is typical in fleet leasing of vehicles. In car leasing the net lease is sometimes referred to as an *open-end* lease: In return for a slightly lower monthly lease fee, the lessee agrees to make up the price differential if the leased car sells for less than the prearranged price when the lease expires because of excess mileage, poor maintenance, or any other reason.

12.2   ADVANTAGES OF LEASING

When a firm wishes to have the use and services of an asset, it either can purchase the asset or lease it. The decision to purchase the asset entails first borrowing the funds and then buying the asset. Thus, when evaluating the advantages of the leasing alternative, a firm should keep in mind the fact that the other alternative is to borrow and buy, rather than just buy. The lease-or-buy decision rests on the comparison between two methods of financing, both requiring a fixed obligation redeemable over a future period. The leasing alternative, then, should be evaluated by comparing its advantages and effects on the lessee's cash flow with those of the borrowing alternative. Often-cited advantages of leasing as opposed to borrowing include (1) shifting the risks of ownership, (2) the avoidance of restrictions associated with debt, (3) the effect on cash and borrowing capacity, and (4) tax advantages.

12.2.1   Shifting the Risks of Ownership

A firm that purchases an asset is subject to the risk of obsolescence due to innovation in the field. Generally, in the decision to lease or buy an asset subject to a high rate of obsolescence, the leasing alternative will appear more appropriate. Through leasing rather than buying the asset, the lessee can shift the risk of obsolescence and of ownership to the lessor.

This argument in favor of leasing relies heavily on the assumption that the lessor is not aware of the rate of obsolescence and innovation in the field. In most cases, however, the lessor is very knowledgeable and is in a better position to anticipate the rate of obsolescence than the lessee. The lessor, well aware of the risks of ownership, will attempt to recover the investment plus interest over the lease period and will probably include an implicit charge for obsolescence in the computation of the rental payments. Only when the lessor inaccurately estimates the rate of obsolescence does the lessee benefit from shifting the risks of ownership. If the asset becomes obsolete more rapidly than the lessor anticipated, the leasing alternative will be beneficial to the lessee. The lessor can keep the rental payments low by spreading the risk of obsolescence over many lease contracts. The diversification in this case will benefit both the lessor and the lessee.

12.2.2 *Avoidance of Restrictions Associated with Debt*

Leasing is assumed to offer fewer restrictions than debt and, consequently, to provide more flexibility. Most loan agreements and bond indentures include protective covenant restrictions, but similar limitations are not as common in leasing. One usual restriction accompanying leasing is in the use of the leased property. For example, the use of the leased equipment may be limited in terms of the number of hours per day. Changes and adjustments in the leased equipment may also be prohibited unless authorized by the lessor.

The advantage of fewer restrictions with leasing than with debt-financing will probably disappear in the near future. Most lenders impose restrictions on the amount to be leased for firms financed heavily by debt. Because leasing is becoming more and more accepted as a form of financing, protective covenants will probably be drafted for both leasing and bond indentures.

12.2.3 *Effect on Cash and Borrowing Capacity*

It is often said that leasing allows a firm to conserve cash and raise more funds than debt financing. This is based on the following claims—some supportable and some unsupportable—made on behalf of leasing.

People often argue that leasing allows the optimal use of cash leading to an improvement in a firm's total earning power. Thus, it is maintained, the capital intended for the purchase of fixed assets with low turnover is tied up for the acquisition of current assets with high turnover. Retailers most often are advised to rent their premises and allocate their capital to Inventory and Accounts Receivable. Although seemingly attractive, this claim on behalf of leasing is the result of confusion about the relationship between the investment and financing decisions. It assumes that the financing method is a determinant of the mix of assets. A firm actually decides first on the optimal mix of assets necessary for its line of business and then decides on the proper way of financing this mix by comparing the costs of buying and leasing. The firm can decide either to borrow or lease. In either case it decides to use the optimal mix of assets effectively and efficiently.

People also argue that leasing permits a firm not only to avoid buying an asset, but also to finance up to 100 percent of the cost of the asset. What is the impact on a firm's borrowing capacity? Does leasing provide more funds? The usual assumption is that leasing has no effect on a firm's borrowing power and a positive effect on its borrowing capacity. However, this line of reasoning is misleading. Given the fixed obligatory nature of the lease, it should be considered equivalent to an implicit loan of 100 percent of the funds needed. The borrowing capacity is definitely reduced, and the borrowing power must be compared with debt financing. The erroneous assumption that leasing provides more funds results from the conventional accounting treatment, whereby lease obligations are not shown by liabilities on the balance sheet. This situation has changed, and accounting treatments now tend to favor the capitalization of long-term leases.

Leasing permits the financing of capital additions on a piecemeal basis. To be practical, long-term debt financing must usually be arranged on a much larger scale than lease financing, which can be adjusted to each individual unit of property acquired. This can be a valid reason for using lease financing to make occasional asset acquisitions spaced over a period of time. However, this justification loses its validity when the total amount of capital additions over a given period is large enough to justify a debt issue. Long-term debt financing can be adapted to the timing of expenditures either through the use of interim bank borrowings with subsequent refunding or by a direct placement of securities with institutional investors, providing for a series of takedowns.[2]

12.2.4   *Tax Advantages*

A common argument in the lease-or-buy controversy is whether leasing offers tax advantages over ownership. Under present tax laws, rental payments are considered an operating expense and can be deducted from taxable income. This gives rise to two basic differences in the tax effects of leasing as compared with ownership:

1. Leasing makes it possible, in effect, to write off the depreciable portion of property over the basic term of a lease, which is generally shorter than the period that would be permitted for depreciation. The result is not a tax savings but a shift in the timing of deductions and tax payments similar to the effects of accelerated depreciation. To the extent that tax payments are deferred, the company benefits by having the use of these funds for the additional period.

2. Leasing makes it possible, in effect, to write off land values against taxable income, which is not allowed for depreciation purposes. The effect can be very significant where land represents a substantial portion of the total investment, as in urban department store properties. Although leasing provides a way of recovering part of the investment in land during the basic period of the lease, it also deprives the company of 100 percent of this value at the end of the period—which still leaves a net loss of 48 percent. Furthermore, if past trends in land value are any indication of the future trends, the loss could be considerably greater.[3]

Another cost implicitly packaged in the terms of any leasing contract is corrected with the federal income tax deduction. One of the frequently cited advantages of equipment leasing is that a leasing contract permits the lessee to enjoy a more advantageous stream of income tax expense deductions than would be possible with outright ownership of the equipment, where only depreciation and interest could be deducted. In fact, there may be some advantage if the lease payments are scheduled so they are higher in the earlier years of the lease than the sum of depreciation and interest and, conversely, lower in later years. Under these conditions, the present value of the tax deductions received under the lease plan is greater than the present value of the tax deductions under outright ownership. This advantage can be achieved in another way under financial leases. The agreement can be made for a relatively short initial term—say five years. During this time the lessor recovers the entire cost of the equipment; if the lessee purchased the equipment directly, it would have to be depreciated over a longer time span—say, seven to ten years.[4]

The Economic Recovery Tax Act of 1981 allows companies to transfer the tax benefits of tax credits and of the Accelerated Cost Recovery System (ACRS) on new plants and equipment bought between January 1 and August 13, 1981, through what is called *safe-harbor leasing*. Such transactions are safe as long as the letter of the Internal Revenue Service regulations is followed. This is possible in two cases:

---

[2]D. R. Gant, "Illusion in Lease Financing," *Harvard Business Review* (March–April 1959), p. 129.
[3]Ibid., p. 126.
[4]R. F. Vancil, "Lease or Borrow: New Method of Analysis," *Harvard Business Review* (September–October 1961), p. 127.

1. Under a reciprocal lease-sublease, the seller of the tax benefits (the lessor-sublessee) acquires new equipment for its own use and, within three months of purchase, leases it to the buyer of the tax credits (the lessee-sublessor). The seller transfers tax credits to the buyer via the lease, and the buyer simultaneously subleases the property back to the seller (the user) without those credits. The rentals payable by the buyer exceed the rentals to be received by the buyer. This differential is effectively the purchase price of the tax credits transferred.

2. Under a sale leaseback, the seller of the tax benefits (the seller and lessee of the property) acquires new equipment for its own use and, within three months of purchase, sells it to the buyer of the tax benefits (the buyer and lessor of the property). This enables the seller to transfer to the buyer the tax benefits related to the equipment. The consideration is composed of a cash down payment of at least 10 percent of the original cost of the property and a note for the remainder. The buyer then leases the property back to the seller for a lease term that is equal to the term of the note. If the rentals under the lease are equal to the payments on the note (principal and interest), the buyer's initial investment (the down payment) is the purchase price of the tax benefits. The seller continues to be the user of the property. The seller may retain title to the property or reacquire title at the end of the lease term for a nominal amount, such as $1.[5]

The intent of the legislation is that tax leases will allow firms that do not owe taxes or are unable to realize certain tax benefits to realize those benefits by making them transferable. Instead of receiving the benefits directly as a reduction of income taxes payable, firms not owing taxes can realize them by selling the right to those benefits to other firms that can use them to reduce taxes payable.

Shortly after the passage of the act, Ford Motor Company announced that it was selling to International Business Machines Corporation (IBM) its investment tax and depreciation deductions on "under $1 billion" worth of machinery, equipment, and tools acquired so far in 1981. Similarly, Bethlehem Steel Corp. and R. R. Donnelley & Sons Co. entered into a safe-harbor lease transaction that involves the exchange of tax credits. Donnelley will buy steel manufacturing equipment from Bethlehem and lease it back to the steelmaker.

12.3   A NORMATIVE MODEL FOR LEASE EVALUATION

Any model for lease evaluation is determined on a cash flow basis. The treatment of the variables in the model differ, depending on whether it is the lessee's or the lessor's model.

12.3.1   Lessor's Analysis

The lessor attempts to determine a rental payment amount that will insure that the present value of rental payments plus the present value of the salvage value of the asset equals or exceeds the original cost of the asset. The discount rate the lessor chooses will be adjusted for the recovery of both the cost of capital of the lessor and other ownership

---

[5] Financial Accounting Standards Board, *Accounting for the Sale or Purchase of Tax Benefits through Tax Leases*, Exposure Draft (Stamford, Conn.: FASB, November 30, 1981), p. 11.

costs before taxes. The lessee may have the option of paying the rental payments at the beginning or the end of each year. Both cases will be examined using the following sample problem.

Assume a firm has decided to lease an asset under the following conditions:

Purchase price of the asset (A_0) $= \$30,000.$

Expected salvage value of the asset (S) $= \$10,000.$

Before-tax rate of return (K_L) $= 8\%.$

Salvage value discount rate (K_s) $= 20\%.$

Lease period (n) $= 5$ years.

To compute the rental payment, proceed as follows:

1. The present value of the salvage value (S_{PV}) is

$$S_{PV} = \frac{S}{(1 + K_s)^n} = \frac{\$10,000}{(1 + 0.20)^5} = \$4,018.$$

2. The rental (R_j) if paid in advance is

$$A_0 - S_{PV} = R_1 + \sum_{j=2}^{5} \frac{R_j}{(1 + K_L)^{j-1}}$$

$$= R_1 + \sum_{j=2}^{5} \frac{R_j}{(1 + 0.08)^{j-1}}.$$

$$\$30,000 - \$4,018 = R_j(1 + 3.31213).$$

$$R_j = \$6,025.$$

3. The rental (R_j) if paid at the end of period is

$$A_0 - S_{PV} = \sum_{j=1}^{n} \frac{R_j}{(1 + K_L)^j}.$$

$$\$30,000 - \$4,018 = \sum_{j=1}^{5} \frac{R_j}{(1 + 0.08)^j}$$

$$= R_j(3.99271).$$

$$R_j = \$6,507.$$

12.3.2   Lessee's Analysis

The lessee's approach concentrates on how the asset is to be acquired, leaving to more conventional capital budgeting techniques the prior decision on whether the asset is to be acquired at all. Thus, the question the lessee examines is whether to borrow and buy or lease. The answer is found by comparing the respective costs of both alternatives. The summary measure used for the comparison can be either the net present value advantage of leasing (NAL) or the pretax interest rate on the lease (X_i). The NAL measure is expressed as follows:

$$NAL = A_0 - \sum_{j=1}^{n} \frac{R_j}{(1 + X_1)^j} + \sum_{j=1}^{n} \frac{TR_j}{(1 + X_2)^j} - \sum_{j=1}^{n} \frac{TD_j}{(1 + X_3)^j} - \sum_{j=1}^{n} \frac{TI_j}{(1 + X_4)^j}$$

$$\qquad [1] \qquad\qquad [2] \qquad\qquad\qquad [3] \qquad\qquad\qquad [4] \qquad\qquad\qquad [5]$$

$$+ \sum_{j=1}^{n} \frac{O_j(1 - T)}{(1 + X_5)^j} - \frac{V_n}{(1 + K_s)^j} \,.$$

$$\qquad\quad [6] \qquad\qquad\quad [7]$$

The variables included in the NAL equation are defined as follows:

A_0 = Purchase price of the asset.

R_j = Lease payment in period j.

D_j = Depreciation charge in period j.

V_n = Expected after-tax salvage value of the asset = $S_j - (S_j - B_j)T_g$.

S_j = Salvage value in period j.

B_j = Book value in period j.

X_i = Discount rates to apply to the various cash flow streams of the equation.

T_g = Tax rate applicable to gains and losses on the disposal of fixed assets.

T = Corporate income tax rate.

n = Number of years covered by the lease agreement.

I_j = Interest component of the loan payment.

K_s = Salvage value discount rate.

O_j = Incremental operating costs of ownership in period t.

The interpretation of the NAL equation is influenced by the treatment of the key variables in the lease evaluation decision. The seven terms in the NAL equation can be interpreted as follows:

1. The purchase price of the asset is an unavoidable cost of purchasing.

2. The present value of the rental payments is a cost of leasing.

3. The present value of the tax shield provided by the rental payments is a benefit of leasing and, consequently, an opportunity cost of purchasing.

4. The present value of the tax shield provided by the depreciation expense is a benefit of purchasing.

5. The present value of the tax shield provided by the interest expense on a "loan equivalent" to a lease is another benefit of purchasing.

6. The present value of the after-tax operating cost is a burden of ownership.

7. The present value of the after-tax residual value is a benefit of ownership.

Summing the seven terms, the basic equation provides the net present value advantage of leasing. Setting *NAL* equal to zero and solving for X_i provides the pretax interest rate on the lease. The NAL equation can also be explained as follows:

1. The present value of the borrow-and-buy alternative is

$$A_0 - \sum_{j=1}^{n} \frac{TD_j}{(1 + X_3)^j} - \sum_{j=1}^{n} \frac{TI_j}{(1 + X_4)^j} + \sum_{j=1}^{n} \left[\frac{O_j(1 - T)}{(1 + X_5)^j} \right] - \frac{V_n}{(1 + K_s)^j}.$$

2. The present value of leasing is

$$\sum_{j=1}^{n} \frac{R_j}{(1 + X_1)^j} - \sum_{j=1}^{n} \frac{TR_j}{(1 + X_2)^j}.$$

3. *NAL* = Present value of borrowing and buying − Present value of leasing.

Two problems in the applicability of the NAL equation lie in the choice of the appropriate discount rates to be used and the computation of the loan equivalent to the lease.

The discount rates X_1, X_2, X_3, X_4, and X_5 are those applied by the market to evaluate the streams of distribution of R_j, TR_j, TD_j, TI_j, and $O_j(1 - T)$. Possible alternatives are a single discount rate or an appropriate rate for each stream. We will first use the after-tax cost of debt as a single discount rate for all streams; later in the chapter, the other alternatives proposed in the literature will be discussed. Thus, the after-tax cost of debt will be used for each cash flow stream except V_n, which will be discounted at its own rate (K_s = 20 percent) due to the uncertainty associated with this "estimated" value.

The loan equivalent decision also has generated a debate in the literature. This chapter will propose a first alternative and later present the other proposed alternatives. For the first alternative, it assumed that

$$P_0 = A_0,$$

$$= \sum_{j=1}^{n} \frac{L_j}{(1 + r)^j},$$

where

P_0 = Present value of the loan equivalent.

L_j = Loan payment at the end of each period j.

r = Pretax interest rate on term loans "comparable" to the lease.

To illustrate the lessee's analysis, the same problem presented in the lessor's analysis will be used. The data required are as follows:

A_0 = \$30,000.

S = \$10,000.

$R_j = \$6,025$ (at the beginning of each period).

$R_j = \$6,507$ (at the end of each period).

$D_j = $ Straight-line depreciation at period $j = \dfrac{A_0 - S}{n} = \$4,000.$

$O_j = \$2,000.$

$B = 0.$

$T_g = 10\%.$

$V_n = S - [(S - B)T_g] = \$9,000.$

$r = 6\%.$

$T = 50\%.$

$n = 5$ years.

$K_s = 20\%.$

The lessee's analysis proceeds as follows:

1. For the loan payment computation, it has been assumed in this analysis that $P_0 = A_0,$ and

$$P_0 = \sum_{j=1}^{n} \frac{L_j}{(1 + r)^j} \, .$$

Given a 6 percent pretax interest rate on loans, the amount of the annual loan payment at the end of each year is found by solving the following equation for L_j:

$$\$30,000 = \sum_{j=1}^{5} \frac{L_j}{(1 + 0.06)^j} \, .$$

$$L_j = \$7,122.$$

2. When the rental payments are made in advance, the lease evaluation analysis proceeds by the computation of the NAL as follows:

$$NAL = \$30,000 - \left[\$6,025 + \sum_{j=1}^{4} \frac{\$6,025}{(1 + 0.03)^j} \right] + \sum_{j=1}^{5} \frac{(\$6,025)(0.5)}{(1 + 0.03)^j} - \sum_{j=1}^{5} \frac{(\$4,000)(0.5)}{(1 + 0.03)^j}$$

$$- \left[\frac{\$800(0.5)}{(1 + 0.03)^1} + \frac{\$1,480(0.5)}{(1 + 0.03)^2} + \frac{\$1,142(0.5)}{(1 + 0.03)^3} + \frac{\$783(0.5)}{(1 + 0.03)^4} + \frac{\$403(0.5)}{(1 + 0.03)^5} \right]$$

$$+ \sum_{j=1}^{5} \left[\frac{\$2,000(1 - 0.5)}{(1 + 0.03)^j} \right] - \frac{\$9,000}{(1 + 0.20)^5}$$

$$= \$30,000 - (\$6,025 + \$22,396) + \$13,796 - \$9,159 - \$2,130 + \$4,580 - \$3,617$$

$$= \$5,048 = NAL \text{ when rental payments are made in advance.}$$

3. The lease evaluation analysis when the rental payments are made at the end of the period is as follows:

$$NAL = \$30,000 - \sum_{j=1}^{5} \frac{\$6,507}{(1 + 0.03)^j} + \sum_{j=1}^{5} \frac{\$6,507(0.5)}{(1 + 0.03)^j} - \sum_{j=1}^{5} \frac{\$4,000(0.5)}{(1 + 0.03)^j}$$

$$- \left[\frac{\$800(0.5)}{(1 + 0.03)^1} + \frac{\$1,480(0.5)}{(1 + 0.03)^2} + \frac{\$1,142(0.5)}{(1 + 0.03)^3} + \frac{\$783(0.5)}{(1 + 0.03)^4} + \frac{\$403(0.5)}{(1 + 0.03)^5} \right]$$

$$+ \sum_{j=1}^{5} \left[\frac{\$2,000(1 - 0.5)}{(1 + 0.03)^j} \right] - \frac{\$9,000}{(1 + 0.20)^5}$$

$$= \$30,000 - \$29,800 + \$14,900 - \$9,159 - \$2,130 + \$4,580 - \$3,617$$

$$= \$4,774 = NAL \text{ when rental payments are made at the end of the period.}$$

These computations show the lease alternative to be preferable to the purchase alternative. Several points should be further emphasized:

1. Changing the depreciation method from straight-line to accelerated depreciation may change the outcome.

2. The timing of the rental payments has an impact on the NAL.

3. The analysis assumes that the acquisition price of the asset is equal to the principal of the loan.

4. All the cash flow streams except for the salvage value are discounted at the after-tax cost of debt.

5. It is assumed that the investment decision has been deemed acceptable. Only the financing decision remains to be evaluated in terms of a choice between borrowing and leasing.

12.4   ALTERNATIVE CALCULATIONS

12.4.1   The Johnson and Lewellen Approach

R. W. Johnson and W. G. Lewellen examined (1) whether the financing and investment decisions should be mixed in appraising lease possibilities and (2) which discount rate should be used.[6]

Johnson and Lewellen pose the decision problem as a lease-or-buy rather than a lease-or-borrow decision, since a lease contract is simply an arrangement for the long-term acquisition of service, which does not differ in financing terms from the alternative ac-

---

[6]R. W. Johnson and W. G. Lewellen, "Analysis of the Lease or Buy Decision," *Journal of Finance* (September 1972), pp. 815–823.

quisition-of-service arrangement called *purchase*. Hence the inclusion of a charge for interest as a "cost" of owning is viewed as a deficiency of current models for lease evaluation, and the concept of a loan equivalent is not necessary in the lease evaluation model.

The issue of the appropriate rate to use in discounting the cash flows relevant to the decision has been investigated by Johnson and Lewellen. They emphasize the following ideas:

1. The after-tax cash flows with predictability matching that associated with the firm's debt service obligations should be capitalized at the firm's after-tax borrowing rate (after-tax cost of debt). This will include the obligations incurred under the lease contract, such as lease payments and their respective tax savings.

2. The after-tax cash flows with uncertainty like the general risks faced by the firm in its line of business should be discounted at the firm's cost of capital. This will include the depreciation tax shield, the after-tax operating costs, and the salvage value.

The Johnson and Lewellen model now can be presented. It states

$$\Delta NPV = NPV(P) - NPV(L)$$

$$= \sum_{j=1}^{n} \left[\frac{D_j T - O_j(1 - T)}{(1 + K)^j} \right] + \frac{V_n}{(1 + K)^j} - A_0 + \sum_{j=1}^{n} \frac{R_j(1 - T)}{[1 + r(1 - T)]^j} \, ,$$

where

ΔNPV = Change in the firm's net present value.

$NPV(P)$ = The net present value of borrowing and buying.

$NPV(L)$ = The net present value of leasing.

K = Cost of capital at 12 percent.

A positive value of ΔNPV would imply that purchasing the asset is economically superior to leasing it. This would occur if the net salvage value exceeded after-tax operating costs or if the purchase price less depreciation tax savings were less than the burden of lease payments.

Using the data in the previous illustration, the Johnson and Lewellen model proceeds as follows:

1. If the rental payments are made at the beginning of the period,

$$\Delta NPV = \sum_{j=1}^{5} \left[\frac{\$2,000 - \$1,000}{(1 + 0.12)^j} \right] + \frac{\$9,000}{(1 + 0.12)^{-5}} - \$30,000$$

$$+ \left[\$6,025 + \sum_{j=1}^{4} \frac{\$6,025}{1.03^j} \right] - \sum_{j=1}^{5} \left[\frac{\$6,025(1 - 0.5)}{(1 + 0.03)^j} \right] = \$(6,664).$$

Thus, leasing is preferred.

2. If the rental payments are made at the end of the period,

$$\Delta NPV = \sum_{j=1}^{5} \left[\frac{\$2,000 - \$1,000}{(1 + 0.12)^j} \right] + \frac{\$9,000}{(1 + 0.12)^5} - \$30,000$$

$$+ \sum_{j=1}^{5} \left[\frac{\$6,507}{1.03^j} \right] - \sum_{j=1}^{5} \left[\frac{\$6,507(1 - 0.5)}{(1 + 0.03)^j} \right] = \$(6,388).$$

Leasing is preferred in this case as well.

As a result of discounting the costs of financing at $r(1 - T)$ and the ownership cash flows at K, the Johnson and Lewellen approach in this case creates a bias in favor of leasing. R. S. Bower contested the choice:

Johnson and Lewellen's selection of K as the discount rate is understandable but unappealing. It is understandable because K is the rate used in discounting depreciation shelters in conventional capital budgeting, where the shelter is part of the cash flow calculation. The selection of K is unappealing, though, because it involves discounting some of the tax shelter given up in leasing at a high rate, K, and discounting all of the tax shelter that comes with leasing at a low rate, r(1 − T). It is difficult to avoid the conclusion that a higher discount rate for the shelter element of lease cost does a great deal more to bias the analysis in favor of leasing than it does to recognize any real difference in risk.[7]

12.4.2   *The Roenfeldt and Osteryoung Approach*

The Roenfeldt and Osteryoung approach expanded on the Johnson and Lewellen approach by categorically separating the investment decision from the financing decision.[8] The methodology used consisted of (1) determining the desirability of the investment decision and (2) given that the investment decision was deemed desirable, evaluating the financing decision by comparing the after-tax cost of borrowing (r_b) with the after-tax cost of leasing (r_l).

Using the data from the illustration in the previous section, the Roenfeldt and Osteryoung approach proceeds as follows.

Step 1: The Investment Decision   The investment decision is made on the basis of a net present value or internal rate of return approach following traditional capital budgeting techniques. (See chapter 11.) The computation of a net present value or internal rate of return involves estimating the annual sales generated by the asset and computing the resulting net cash flows, as follows:

---

[7]R. S. Bower, "Issues in Lease Financing," *Financial Management* (Winter 1973), p. 29.

[8]R. L. Roenfeldt and J. S. Osteryoung, "Analysis of Financial Leases," *Financial Management* (Spring 1973), pp. 74–87.

	0	1	2	3	4	5
				Year		
1. Sales (Assumed)		$20,000	$20,000	$20,000	$20,000	$20,000
2. Depreciation		4,000	4,000	4,000	4,000	4,000
3. Cash Operating Costs		2,000	2,000	2,000	2,000	2,000
4. Taxable Income (Line 1 − Line 2 − Line 3)		14,000	14,000	14,000	14,000	14,000
5. Tax Liability (4 × T)		7,000	7,000	7,000	7,000	7,000
6. Net Cash Flow (Line 1 − Line 5 − Line 3)		11,000	11,000	11,000	11,000	11,000
7. Salvage Value (V_n)						9,000
8. Discount Factor ($K = 12$)						3.605
9. Discount Factor ($K_s = 20$)						0.402
10. Present Value of Cash Flow						39,655
11. Present Value of V_n						3,618
12. Total Present Value (Line 10 + Line 11)						$43,273

Thus, the net present value is equal to $13,273, or $43,273 − $30,000, and the investment is deemed desirable.

Step 2: The Financing Decision   The financing decision—to borrow or to lease—is made on the basis of a criterion of least cost by comparing the after-tax cost of borrowing (r_b) to the after-tax cost of leasing (r_l).

To compute r_b, the rate that equates the after-tax interest payments and amortization of the principal to the loan amount, the following formula is used:

$$A_0 = \sum_{j=1}^{n} \frac{L_j - I_j T}{(1 + r_b)^j} ,$$

or

$$\$30,000 = \sum_{j=1}^{5} \frac{\$7,122 - [0.5(I_j)]}{(1 + r_b)^j} .$$

The numerator (the net costs of borrowing) is computed as follows:

Year	Loan Payment	Interest	Interest Tax Shield ($I_j T$)	Net Cost of Borrowing
1	$7,122	$1,800	$900.0	$6,222.0
2	7,122	1,480	740.0	6,382.0
3	7,122	1,142	571.0	6,551.0
4	7,122	783	391.5	6,730.5
5	7,122	403	201.5	6,920.5

Solving for r_b yields

$$r_b = 3\%.$$

To compute r_l, the rate that equates the adjusted rental payments to the cost of the asset (A_0), Roenfeldt and Osteryoung make the following changes:

1. The rental payments are reduced by the amount of any operating costs assumed by the lessor.

2. The depreciation tax shield and after-tax salvage value are added to the cost of leasing.

3. Certainty equivalents are introduced into the operating and residual cash flows to adjust for risk.

The following formula is then used:

$$V_0 = \left\{ \sum_{j=1}^{n} \frac{[(L_j - \alpha_j O_j)(1 - T)] + D_j T}{(1 + r_l)^n} \right\} + \left[\frac{\alpha_n S_n - (\alpha_n S_n - B)T_g}{(1 + r_l)^n} \right],$$

where

α_j = Certainty equivalent for the operating costs.

α_n = Certainty equivalent for the salvage value.

Assuming $\alpha_j = 0.6$ and $\alpha_n = 0.99$, the cost of leasing (r_l) can be computed as follows:

1. If the rental payments are made at the end of the period,

$$\$30,000 = \left\{ \sum_{j=1}^{5} \frac{[\$6,507 - 0.6(\$2,000)](1 - 0.5) + [(\$4,000)(0.5)]}{(1 + r_l)^n} \right\}$$
$$+ \left\{ \frac{0.99(\$10,000) - [0.99(\$10,000) - 0](0.10)}{(1 + r_l)^n} \right\}$$
$$= \sum_{j=1}^{5} \left[\frac{\$4,653.5}{(1 + r_l)^n} \right] + \left[\frac{\$8,910}{(1 + r_l)^5} \right].$$

$r_l = 2\%$, and leasing is preferable to borrowing.

2. If the rental payments are made in advance,

$$\$30,000 = \left\{ \sum_{j=0}^{4} \frac{[\$6,025 - 0.6(\$2,000)](1 - 0.5) + [(\$4,000)(0.5)]}{(1 + r_l)^n} \right\} + \left[\frac{\$8,910}{(1 + r_l)^5} \right].$$

$r_l = 2.1\%$, and leasing is still preferable to borrowing.

12.4.3   Issues in Lease Financing

Bower summarized the following points of agreement and disagreement in the differing approaches to the lease-or-buy decision.[9] All the models require inputs that include the

---

[9] Bower, "Issues in Lease Financing," p. 27.

purchase price of the asset to be leased, (A_0), lease payments at the end or at the beginning of the period (R_j), a depreciation charge relevant for tax payments at the end of the period (D_j), a cash operating cost expected to occur in the period if the asset is purchased but not if it is leased (O_j), an expected after-tax salvage value of the asset at the end of the last period covered by the lease agreement (V_n), a pretax interest rate on the loan equivalent to the lease (r), an after-tax cost of capital for the corporation (k), a corporate income tax rate (T), and the number of periods covered by the lease agreement (n).

The points of disagreement relating to the lease-or-buy analysis include the following:

1. The choice of a summary measure, either the pretax interest rate on a lease (i) or the net advantage to a lease *(NAL)*.

2. The inclusion or exclusion of some of the terms previously presented in the normative model.

3. The computation of the loan equivalent.

4. The choice of a discount rate for each of the cash flows included in the normative model.

Table 12.1 summarizes the areas of disagreement.

12.4.4 The Bower Approach: A Decision Format

Bower has developed a decision format to reconcile the disagreements among the various approaches to the lease-or-buy analysis and still permit those interested to take advantage of the models' broad agreement on other points. The decision format examines the decision implications associated with different tax shelter discount rates.

The decision format uses the cost of capital (K) to calculate benefits that involve the purchase price, operating savings, and salvage value; it uses the appropriate interest rate (r) to calculate the present cost of the lease payments. The tax shelter effect is then calculated for rates of discount (X) from 0 through 14 percent.

The cost of purchasing (COP) depends on the purchase price, depreciation tax shelter, cash operating cost avoided by leasing, and salvage value:

$$COP = A_0 - \sum_{j=0}^{n} \left[\frac{TD_j}{(1+X)^j} \right] + \sum_{j=0}^{n} \left[\frac{O_j(1-T)}{(1+K)^j} \right] - \frac{V_n}{(1+K)^n} .$$

The cost of leasing (COL) depends on the lease payment, lease tax shelter, and the interest tax shelter lost by leasing:

$$COL = \sum_{j=0}^{n} \left[\frac{R_j}{(1+r)^j} \right] - \sum_{j=0}^{n} \left[\frac{TR_j}{(1+X)^j} \right] + \sum_{j=0}^{n} \left[\frac{TI_j}{(1+X)^j} \right] .$$

An illustrative example of Bower's decision format will be given using the data presented in the example in section 12.3.1. There is, however, one major change: The lease payment (R_j), as calculated in the lessor's analysis, will no longer be used. The equivalent loan is computed by Bower as follows:

Table 12.1   Approaches to Lease Evaluation

Approach	Summary Measure	Excluded Flows or Other Comments	Equivalent Loan Calculation[a]
Beechy	i	tL_j is used instead of tR_j in the third term of the equation.	$P_0 = A_0$ $B_0 = \sum_{j=0}^{n} (R_j/(1+r)^j)$ $L_j = R_j(P_0/B_0)$
Bower, Herringer, Williamson	NAL		$P_0 = A_0$ $B_0 = \sum_{j=0}^{n} (R_j/(1+r)^j)$ $L_j = R_j(P_0/B_0)$
Doenges, Mitchell, Wyman	$i(1-t)$	I_j is excluded. Wyman provides a probability distribution of rates.	None
Findlay	NAL	Certainty equivalents of O_j and V_n are used in the sixth and seventh terms.	$P_0 = \sum_{j=0}^{n} (R_j/(1+r)^j)$ $L_j = R_j$
Johnson and Lewellen	NAL	I_j is excluded.	None
Roenfeldt and Osteryoung	$i(1-t)$	I_j is excluded. Certainty equivalents of O_j and V_n are used in the sixth and seventh terms.	None
Vancil	NAL		$P_0 = A_0$ $L_j = R_j$

[a]Only the first two or three equations required to produce the equivalent loan flows are shown in each box. The remaining equations are the same for each approach. The full set of equations for Beechy's approach is:

$$P_0 = A_0 \qquad\qquad L_j = R_j(P_0/B_0) \qquad\qquad Q_j = L_j - I_j$$

$$B_0 = \sum_{j=0}^{n} (R_j/(1+r)^j) \qquad\qquad I_j = rP_{j-1} \qquad\qquad P_j = P_{j-1} - Q_j.$$

Source: R.S. Bower, "Issues in Lease Financing," *Financial Management* (Winter 1973), p. 27. Reprinted by permission.

$$\text{Loan equivalent } (P_0) = \sum_{j=1}^{n} \frac{R_j}{(1+r)^j} ,$$

where

R_j (Lease payment) = Loan payment (L_j).

r = Pretax interest rate on term loans "comparable" to the lease.

Table 12.1 *continued*

	Discount Rate Used for					
X_2	X_3	X_4	X_5	X_6	X_7
i	i	i	i	i	i
r	k	k	k	k	k
$i(1-t)$	$i(1-t)$	$i(1-t)$	—	$i(1-t)$	$i(1-t)$
r	$r(1-t)$	$r(1-t)$	$r(1-t)$	$r(1-t)$	$r(1-t)$
$r(1-t)$	$r(1-t)$	k	—	k	k
$r(1-t)$	$i(1-t)$	$i(1-t)$	—	$i(1-t)$	$i(1-t)$
r	k	k	k	k	k

Although most of the data supplied in the original example applies here, assume that as an alternative to purchasing, the asset can be leased for five years for a payment of $7,962 per annum.

In this case, the loan equivalent no longer equals the purchase price of the asset; instead, the following holds true:

$$\text{Loan equivalent } (P_0) = \sum_{j=1}^{n} \frac{\$7,962}{(1 + 0.06)^j} = \$33,538.$$

The loan equivalent is

Year	Loan Payment	Loan Balance (Year Start)	Interest (6%)	Principal Repayment	Loan Balance (Year-End)
1	$7,962	$33,538	$2,012	$5,950	$27,588
2	7,962	27,588	1,655	6,307	21,281
3	7,962	21,281	1,277	6,685	14,596
4	7,962	14,596	876	7,086	7,510
5	7,962	7,510	452	7,511	0

The decision format is presented in Table 12.2 and Figure 12.2. The columns at the right in Table 12.2 show that when the tax shelter is discounted at $r(1 - T) = 10$ percent, the net advantage of purchasing is $49. At all discount rates above 9.65 percent, the lease has a net disadvantage. Therefore, if a decision maker analyzing a graph such as Figure 12.2 believes that the proper tax shelter discount rate lies well below the intersection point, the decision to lease rather than purchase would provide the greater financial benefit to the company.

In developing this decision format, Bower has devised a composite approach to the lease-or-buy decision that enables the executive to make a judgment on the principal disagreement among academicians and on how the proper tax shelter discount rate, $r(1 - T)$, may affect the ultimate cost of a decision.

Table 12.2   Decision Format

Year t	Purchase Price A_0	Lease Payment $R_t = L_t$	Tax Shelter — Lease Payment TR_t	Tax Shelter — Depreciation TD_t	Tax Shelter — Loan Interest TI_t	After-Tax Operating Saving $O_t(1 - t)$	After-Tax Salvage V_n		
0	30,000								
1		7,962	3,981	2,000	1,006	1,000			
2		7,962	3,981	2,000	828	1,000			
3		7,962	3,981	2,000	638	1,000			
4		7,962	3,981	2,000	438	1,000			
5		7,962	3,981	2,000	226	1,000	9,000		
Present Value at									
$k = 0.12$	30,000						3,605	5,107	
$r = 0.06$		33,538							
								Cost of	
								Purchasing	Leasing
0			19,905	10,000	3,136			18,498	16,769
0.02			18,764	9,427	2,993			19,071	17,767
0.04			17,223	8,904	2,868			19,594	19,183
0.06			17,769	8,425	2,737			20,073	19,506
0.08			15,895	7,985	2,624			20,513	20,267
0.10			15,091	7,582	2,518			20,916	20,965
0.12			14,351	7,210	2,419			21,288	21,606
0.14			13,667	6,866	2,327			21,632	22,198

Figure 12.2   Decision Format

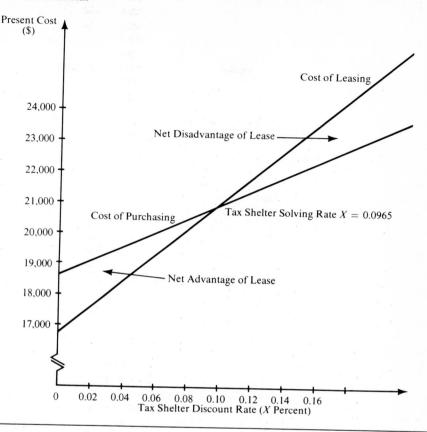

12.5   CONCLUSION

A firm may enter into a leasing arrangement for many reasons. Some of the primary motivations follow:

1. Leasing enables a firm to take advantage of tax shelters.

2. A leasing arrangement conserves working capital.

3. Cash budgeting benefits, because leasing permits accurate predictions of cash needs.

4. Leasing allows a company to retain a degree of flexibility lost by debt financing (that is, bond indenture sometimes imposes restrictions on future financing).

5. A leasing arrangement provides convenience.

6. Leasing can provide an economical means of obtaining excellent servicing and maintenance of equipment if a maintenance lease is included.

7. An operating lease provides more flexibility than ownership if the asset becomes unprofitable; it avoids part or all of the risk of obsolescence; and it can provide for modern equipment from year to year.

Most of the significant methods of analyzing lease-or-buy alternatives use the same basic formula for calculation, but there is considerable disagreement in the calculation methods. The disagreement lies with both relevant alternatives and the choice of the best summary measure of comparison. The relevant alternatives include the outstanding principal of the loan equivalent; loan payments at the end of the period; the interest component of the loan payment; the principal component; the present value of the lease claim; and the discount rates to be applied to cash flows in each category, which are intended to reflect opportunity cost. Summary measures are either the increment in net present value of owners' wealth or the after-tax interest rate on the lease.

The disagreement is more significant in the treatment of the terms, including lease payments and the tax shelter acquired or given up if the lease is accepted. This is most obvious in the decision to include or exclude the tax deduction associated with interest on the equivalent loan.

Bower's decision format of lease analysis is the most appropriate method to use today. It is a composite of the factors agreed upon by other theorists, and it enables decision makers to choose the cost of capital and interest rate they feel is most appropriate during the relevant period for making their lease-or-buy decision. Bower's decision format also enables decision makers to see the effects of other costs and rates and make their decision in light of the uncertainty of these factors.

GLOSSARY

Direct Lease A lessee acquires the use of an asset it did not previously own.

Financial Lease A long-term contract that is noncancelable by the lessor, who assumes little or no ownership costs.

Leverage Lease A tripartite arrangement whereby the lessor finances a part of the acquisition of an asset (50 to 80 percent of the purchase price) from a lender (commercial bank), securing the loan by a mortgage of the leased property as well as by the assignment of the lease and lease payments.

Maintenance Lease Assigns responsibility for the maintenance of a leased asset's good working order to the lessor.

Net Lease Assigns total responsibility for the maintenance of a leased asset to the lessee to the point that the lessee may be required to absorb all losses incurred by the sale of the asset at the end of the lease.

Nonmaintenance Lease Assigns the responsibility for the maintenance of a leased asset to the lessee.

Operating Lease A short-term contract that is cancelable given proper notice at the option of the lessee, whereby the lessor gives the lessee the use of property in exchange for rental payments and at the same time retains the usual risks and rewards of ownership.

Sale and Leaseback A firm sells an asset it owns to another party, which in turn leases it back to the original owner.

SELECTED READINGS

Beechy, T. H., "The Cost of Leasing: Comment and Correction," *Accounting Review* (October 1970), pp. 769–773.

Beechy, T. H., "Quasi-Debt Analysis of Financial Leases," *Accounting Review* (April 1969), pp. 375–381.

Billiam, Phillip L., "Lease versus Purchase: A Practical Problem," *Cost and Management* (September–October 1974), pp. 32–36.

Bower, R. S.; Herringer, F. C.; and Williamson, J. P., "Lease Evaluation," *Accounting Review* (April 1966), pp. 257–265.

Burns, Jane O., and Bindon, Kathleen, "Evaluating Leases with LP," *Management Accounting* (February 1980), pp. 48–53.

Doenges, E. C., "The Cost of Leasing," *Engineering Economist* (Winter 1971), pp. 31–44.

Duty, Glen L., "A Leasing Guide to Taxes," *Management Accounting* (August 1980), pp. 45–51.

Ferrara, William L.; Thies, James B.; and Dirsmith, Mark W., "The Lease-Purchase Decision," *Management Accounting* (May 1980), pp. 57–59.

Findlay, M. Chapman III, "Financial Lease Evaluation: Survey and Synthesis," mimeographed, abstracted in *Proceedings of the 1973 Annual Meeting of the Eastern Finance Association*, ed. Donald E. Fisher (Storrs, Conn.: April 12–14, 1973), p. 136.

Findlay, M. Chapman III, "A Sensitivity Analysis of IRR Leasing Models," *Engineering Economist* (Summer 1975), pp. 231–242.

Franks, Julian R., and Hodges, Stewart D., "Valuation of Financial Lease Contracts: A Note," *Journal of Finance* (May 1978), pp. 657–669.

Johnson, R. W., and Lewellen, W. G., "Analysis of the Lease or Buy Decision," *Journal of Finance* (September 1972), pp. 815–823.

Levy, Haim, and Sarnat, Marshall, "Leasing, Borrowing, and Financial Risk," *Financial Management* (Winter 1979), pp. 47–54.

Loretucci, Joseph A., "Financial Leasing: What's the Best Replacement Cycle?" *Management Accounting* (August 1979), pp. 45–48.

Millar, James A., "Hospital Equipment Leasing: The Breakeven Discount Rate," *Management Accounting* (July 1979), pp. 21–26.

Miller, M. H., and Upton, C. W., "Leasing, Buying and the Cost of Capital Services," *Journal of Finance* (June 1976), pp. 761–786.

Mitchell, G. B., "After-Tax Cost of Leasing," *Accounting Review* (April 1970), pp. 308–314.

Mokkelbost, Per B., "The Value of Leasing" (Paper presented at the 1976 meeting of the Canadian Association of Administrative Sciences, Université Laval, Quebec City, Quebec, May 31–June 2, 1976).

Myers, S. C.; Dill, D. A.; and Bautista, A. J., "Valuation of Financial Lease Contracts," *Journal of Finance* (June 1976), pp. 799–819.

Roenfeldt, R. L. and Osteryoung, J. S., "Analysis of Financial Leases," *Financial Management* (Spring 1973), pp. 74–87.

School, Lawrence D., "The Lease-or-Buy and Asset Acquisition Decision," *Journal of Finance* (September 1974), pp. 1, 203–211, 214.

Vancil, R. F., "Lease or Borrow: New Method of Analysis," *Harvard Business Review* (September 1961), pp. 122–136.

Wyman, H. E., "Financial Lease Evaluation under Conditions of Uncertainty," *Accounting Review* (July 1973), pp. 489–493.

QUESTIONS, EXERCISES, AND PROBLEMS

12.1   Why is leasing equivalent to borrowing?

12.2   List and define the main forms of leasing.

12.3   Show the normative model to the lease evaluation, and provide an interpretation of the model.

12.4   Using the normative model as a reference, what similarities and differences exist between the main lease evaluation models?

12.5   *Analysis of the Lease-or-Buy Decision: The Johnson and Lewellen Approach*   The Holland Consulting Company is considering obtaining a piece of equipment having a five-year useful life and costing $15,000. As an alternative to purchasing, the company can lease the equipment for five years for a payment of $4,200 per annum. The equipment, which would be fully depreciated on a sum-of-the-years'-digits schedule, is expected to command a $1,500 cash salvage value at the end of year 5 and will require $1,000 more in annual (pretax) operating costs if it is owned rather than leased. The Holland Consulting Company is also assuming the corporate income tax rate to be 50 percent, the capital gains tax rate to be 30 percent, the cost of capital after taxes to be 12 percent, and the pretax effective interest rate to be 8 percent.

Required:
Should Holland Consulting Company lease or buy the equipment? (Use the Johnson and Lewellen approach.)

(Adapted with permission from R. W. Johnson and W. G. Lewellen, "Analysis of the Lease or Buy Decision," *Journal of Finance*, September 1972, pp. 820–821.)

12.6   ***Analysis of the Lease-or-Buy Decision: A Decision Format***   Assume the same data as in question 12.5. This time, the Holland Consulting Company has decided to modify the Johnson and Lewellen approach as follows:

1. It will apply the cost of capital to the purchase price, after-tax operating savings, and after-tax salvage value.

2. It will apply the after-tax rate of interest to the lease payment, the lease payment tax shelter, and the depreciation tax shelter.

3. It will apply an after-tax rate of interest from 0 to 14 percent.

Required:
Should the Holland Company lease or buy the equipment?

12.7   ***Analysis of the Lease-or-Buy Decision: Another Decision Format***   Assume the same data as in question 12.5. This time, the Holland Consulting Company has decided to modify the Johnson and Lewellen approach as follows:

1. A loan equivalent is introduced in the evaluation. Findlay's loan equivalent formula is to be used. (See Table 12.1.)

2. The cost of purchasing depends on the purchase price, depreciation tax shelter, cash operating cost avoided by leasing, and salvage value.

3. The cost of leasing depends on the lease payment, lease tax shelter, and interest tax shelter lost by leasing.

4. The after-tax salvage and the after-tax operating savings are discounted at the cost of capital.

5. The lease payments are discounted at the pretax rate of interest.

6. The tax shelters are discounted at a rate of interest from 0 to 14 percent.

Required:
1. Determine the loan equivalent schedule using Findlay's equivalent loan.

2. Compute the costs of purchasing and costs of leasing, and determine if the Holland Consulting Company should lease or buy the equipment.

12.8   ***Lease or Borrow***   Madisons, Inc., has decided to acquire a new piece of equipment. It can do so by outright cash purchase at $25,000 or by a leasing alternative of $6,000 per year for the life of the machine. Other relevant information follows:

Purchase Price Due at Time of Purchase	$25,000
Estimated Useful Life	5 years
Estimated Salvage Value If Purchased	$ 3,000
Annual Cost of Maintenance Contract to Be Acquired with Either Lease or Purchase	$ 500

The full purchase price of $25,000 could be borrowed from the bank at 10 percent annual interest and could be repaid in one payment at the end of the fifth year.

The following additional information is available:

Assume a 40 percent income tax rate and use of straight-line depreciation for tax purposes.

Interest on the bank loan would be paid at the end of each year.

The yearly lease rental would be paid at the beginning of each year (the end of previous tax year).

The minimum desired rate of return on investment is 10 percent.

All cash flows, unless otherwise stated, are assumed to occur at the end of the year.

Required:
1. Should Madisons purchase or lease the equipment? (*Hint:* Determine the after-tax present value of net cash expenditures and any related salvage.)
2. What before-tax interest rate is implicit in the lease?

(CPA adapted)

12.9   *Lease-or-Buy Analysis*   Edwards Corporation is a manufacturing company that produces and sells a wide range of products. It not only mass-produces a number of products and equipment components but also is capable of producing special-purpose manufacturing equipment to customer specifications.

The firm is considering adding a new stapler to one of its product lines, and more equipment will be required to produce it. There are three ways to acquire the needed equipment: (1) purchase general-purpose equipment, (2) lease general-purpose equipment, or (3) build special-purpose equipment. A fourth alternative, purchase of the special-purpose equipment, has been ruled out because it would be prohibitively expensive.

The general-purpose equipment can be purchased for $125,000. This equipment has an estimated salvage value of $15,000 at the end of its useful life of ten years. At the end of five years the equipment can be used elsewhere in the plant or be sold for $40,000.

Alternatively, the general-purpose equipment can be acquired by a five-year lease for $40,000 annual rent. The lessor will assume all responsibility for taxes, insurance, and maintenance.

Special-purpose equipment can be constructed by the contract equipment department of Edwards Corporation. While this department is operating at a level that is normal for the time of year, it is below full capacity. Therefore, the department could produce the equipment without interfering with its regular revenue-producing activities.

The estimated departmental costs for the construction of the special-purpose equipment are

Materials and Parts	$ 75,000
Direct Labor	60,000
Variable Overhead (50% of Direct-Labor Dollars)	30,000
Fixed Overhead (25% of Direct-Labor Dollars)	15,000
Total	$180,000

The corporation's general and administrative costs average 20 percent of the labor dollar content of factory production.

Engineering and management studies have provided the following revenue and cost estimates (excluding lease payments and depreciation) for producing the new stapler, depending on the equipment used:

	General-Purpose Equipment		Self-Con- structed Equipment
	Leased	Purchased	
Unit Selling Price	$ 5.00	$ 5.00	$ 5.00
Unit Production Costs			
Materials	$ 1.80	$ 1.80	$ 1.70
Conversion Costs	1.65	1.65	1.40
Total Unit Production Costs	$ 3.45	$ 3.45	$ 3.10
Unit Contribution Margin	$ 1.55	$ 1.55	$ 1.90
Estimated Unit Volume	40,000	40,000	40,000
Estimated Total Contribution Margin	$62,000	$62,000	$76,000
Other Costs			
Supervision	$16,000	$16,000	$18,000
Taxes and Insurance	—	3,000	5,000
Maintenance	—	3,000	2,000
Total	$16,000	$22,000	$25,000

The company will depreciate the general-purpose machine over ten years using the sum-of-the-years'-digits method. At the end of five years the accumulated depreciation will total $80,000. (The present value of this amount for the first five years is $62,100.) The special-purpose machine will be depreciated over five years using the sum-of-the-years'-digits method. Its salvage value at the end of that time is estimated to be $30,000.

The company uses an after-tax cost of capital of 10 percent, and its marginal tax rate is 40 percent.

Required:

1. Calculate the net present value for each of the three alternatives Edwards Corporation has at its disposal.

2. Should Edwards Corporation select any of the three options? If so, which one? Explain your answer.

Discount Factors for 10% (Rounded)

Period	Present Value of $1	Present Value of $1 per Period Received at End of Period
1	0.91	0.91
2	0.83	1.74
3	0.75	2.49
4	0.68	3.17
5	0.62	3.79
6	0.56	4.35
7	0.51	4.86
8	0.47	5.33
9	0.42	5.75
10	0.39	6.14

(CMA adapted)

12.10   ***Lease and Inflation***   Dr. Eric Nagnum is considering leasing an asset that is expected to provide a real cash flow of $1,000 per year for three years. A rate of inflation of 10 percent and a real rate of interest of 3 percent are expected.

Required:
1. Determine the nominal rate of interest.
2. Determine the present value of the lease.

12.11   ***Comparison of Lease Evaluation Models***   The Richard Company is contemplating the addition of a truck to its commercial truck fleet. The truck costs $56,000, which does not include transportation costs of $4,000. The Richard Company has a policy of capitalizing freight in the determination of the acquisition cost. The truck has an estimated three-year useful life and a $2,000 residual value. Other relevant information for deciding whether to lease or buy the truck includes the following:

Borrowing rate: 6 percent.

Cost of capital before taxes: 20 percent.

Tax rate: 50 percent.

Depreciation method: sum-of-the-years'-digits method.

Rate of return on investment desired: 10 percent.

Salvage value discount rate: 20 percent.

Required:
1. From the lessor's perspective, determine the annual rental payment if paid in advance.

2. From the lessor's perspective, determine the annual rental payment if paid at the end of the period.

3. Present the normative model to be used by the lessee. What is required to express the model as an advantage to ownership?

4. Determine the loan payment on a loan equivalent to the lease.

5. From the lessee's perspective, should the Richard Company lease the equipment if the rental payment is made at the beginning of the period?

6. From the lessee's perspective, should the Richard Company lease the equipment if the rental payment is made at the end of the period?

7. Present the Johnson and Lewellen model that can be used by the lessee.

8. Repeat part 6 using the Johnson and Lewellen model.

DIVISIONALIZATION, PERFORMANCE MEASUREMENT, AND TRANSFER PRICING

The effective planning and control of an organization must be guided by a reporting system, or *responsibility accounting system*, that allows the optimal association of variances and such responsibility centers as *cost centers*, *profit centers*, and/or *investment centers*. The number of types of responsibility centers depends on the organizational structure used to accomplish corporate objectives.

Two types of organizational design are in general use: the centralized functional form and the decentralized divisional form. In response to the uncertainty created by technology and environment, most complex organizations decentralize (in other words, segment the organization into parts). Consequently, the growth of corporations and their need for a decentralization of operations has created the need for appropriate performance evaluation and transfer pricing.

This chapter introduces responsibility accounting, types of organizational design, performance evaluation methods, and transfer pricing methods in order to provide a planning and control system framework for a multiproduct firm.

13.1 AREAS OF RESPONSIBILITY

Areas of responsibility such as cost centers, profit centers, and investment centers are important to the efficient functioning of a responsibility accounting system. Consequently, the nature of responsibility accounting will be addressed first.

13.1.1 Responsibility Accounting

Responsibility accounting is a technique used within the total information system of an organization for classifying and reporting in accordance with managerial responsibilities. It is based on a system for reporting revenue and cost information to the manager responsible for the revenue-causing and/or cost-incurring functions. A responsibility accounting system is a reporting system designed to control expenditures by directly relating the reporting of controllable expenditures to the individuals in the company organization who are responsible for their control.[1]

Central to responsibility accounting is the assignment of responsibility and authority—first, in conformity with the relationships defined by the organizational structure and, second, for each activity in terms of expenses, income, capital expenditures, asset investment, and other criteria. Under the responsibility accounting system, information on the results of each activity is reported on the basis of where the results were incurred and who has responsibility for them.

The responsibility accounting system has the following characteristics:

1. The areas of responsibility are defined in conformity with the decision centers resulting from the organizational structure;

2. Items and responsibility are assigned to managers so that they are only charged with the items over which they can exercise a significant degree of direct control;

3. The information of significance to each area of responsibility is highlighted in the performance reports;

4. Heads of responsibility units participate in the preparation of their budgets. They must feel that the budget is their budget rather than some unrealistic and unworkable budget forced upon them.[2]

Thus, the most useful distinction in a responsibility accounting system is between controllable and uncontrollable costs for each responsibility center. Suggested guidelines for making this distinction follow:

1. A person who has authority over both the acquisition and the use of a service should be charged with the cost of such services.

2. A person who can significantly influence the amount of a cost through his or her own action may be charged with such costs.

3. Even a person who cannot significantly influence the amount of a cost through direct action may be charged with such costs when management wishes this person to influence those responsible.

To design a responsibility accounting system, management may have to rely on the formal organizational system, charts, and manuals to identify responsibility centers and determine the decisions and resources controllable by each center.[3] For example, Prince states:

The business organization under scrutiny contains a clearly defined organization chart with well established lines of authority for the conduct of the organization. Following these lines of authority the supervisory and administrative functions for the various groups of operations must be delegated to the various supervisory personnel. Concurrent with this delegation of responsibility . . . there is an accountability which flows in

---

[1]John A. Higgins, "Responsibility Accounting," *Arthur Anderson Chronicle* (April 1952), p. 1.

[2]Ibid.

[3]J. Pick, "Is Responsibility Accounting Irresponsible?" *New York Certified Public Accountant* (July 1971), pp. 487–494.

Figure 13.1   XYZ Company: Simplified Organizational Chart

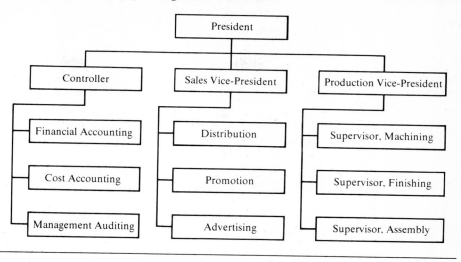

the reverse order . . . . [and later] since the organization chart is the backbone of a responsibility accounting system.[4]

The backbone of any company's responsibility accounting system is the organizational chart of the company. Figure 13.1 illustrates a simple organizational chart of the XYZ Company, which indirectly portrays the different levels of responsibility in the company. For example, each of the supervisors is responsible to the production department vice-president. The production vice-president, sales vice-president, and controller are responsible to the president.

The responsibility accounting system is based on a set of reports to the areas of responsibility as defined by the organizational chart. Hence each area of responsibility identified in Figure 13.1 will be the subject of a regular performance report outlining the nature of the difference between the actual and planned performance for a given control period. The information included in the performance report of a given level of responsibility is included in the reports of all the higher levels of responsibility. Examples of performance reports are shown in Table 13.1. The flow of responsibility starts with the assembly supervisor and goes to the production vice-president and the president. The information is sequentially integrated and can be traced from one report to another. The assembly supervisor reports only the $50,000 under his or her direct control. This amount figures in the production vice-president's report, given that the supervisor is under the vice-president's jurisdiction. The production vice-president reports a total of $150,000 under direct control. This amount figures in the president's report, given that the production vice-president is under the president's jurisdiction.

The success of the responsibility accounting system depends on at least the following factors:

[4]T. Prince, *Information Systems for Management Planning and Control* (Homewood, Ill.: Irwin, 1970), p. 15.

Table 13.1 *Responsibility Accounting Monthly Reports for the Assembly Supervisor, the Production Vice-President, and the President for the XYZ Company*

President's Performance Report

	Amount		Variance Favorable (Unfavorable)	
	This Month	Year to Date	This Month	Year to Date
President's Office	$300,000	$ 870,000	$ 26,000	$ 52,000
Controller	200,000	610,000	(12,000)	11,000
Production Vice-President	150,000	445,000	16,000	2,000
Sales Vice-President	100,000	290,000	4,000	13,000
Total Controllable Costs	$750,000	$2,215,000	$ 34,000	$ 78,000

Production Vice-President's Performance Report

	Amount		Variance Favorable (Unfavorable)	
Machining Department	$ 40,000	$ 115,000	$ (4,150)	$(13,120)
Finishing Department	60,000	185,000	20,630	27,280
Assembly Department	50,000	145,000	(480)	(12,160)
Total Controllable Costs	$150,000	$ 445,000	$ 16,000	$ 2,000

Assembly Supervisor's Performance Report

	Amount		Variance Favorable (Unfavorable)	
Direct Material	$ 20,000	$ 72,000	$ 1,800	$ (210)
Direct Labor	10,000	26,000	400	(2,975)
Manufacturing Overhead	20,000	47,000	(1,720)	(8,975)
Total Controllable Costs	$ 50,000	$ 145,000	$ 480	$ (12,160)

1. The system should emphasize exceptions or deviations and avoid unnecessary, voluminous reports on uncontrollable or immaterial variances. This factor is known as *management by exception.*

2. A necessary condition for the implementation of a responsibility accounting system is the creation of well-defined areas of responsibility, which can take the form of a cost center, a profit center, or an investment center.

3. Managers must be familiar with the reporting system concept and be trained to understand and use its results.

4. The reports must be prepared on a timely basis.

5. The general content and details of the reports must be relevant to the manager's responsibility and authority. A full knowledge of an individual's controllable costs was found to be positively correlated with the relevance of budgets, with positive attitudes toward budgets, and with a high level of cost consciousness.[5]

---

[5]C. H. Hofstede, *The Game of Budget Control* (Assen, The Netherlands: Royal Van Gorcum, 1968), p. 2.

6. The reports should focus on controllable items requiring management attention, including evidence of good, improving, or bad performance. The inclusion of non-controllable items in performance reports was found to produce unfavorable ratings for those reports, whereas favorable ratings occur when reports clearly establish an individual's responsibility.[6]

13.1.2   *Cost Centers, Profit Centers, and Investment Centers*

Cost centers, profit centers and investment centers differ in terms of the nature of the responsibility they assume.

Cost Center

A cost center is the smallest segment of activity or area of responsibility for which costs can be accumulated. Responsibility in a cost center is restricted to cost. For planning purposes, the budget estimates are cost estimates; for control purposes, performance evaluation is guided by a cost variance equal to the difference between the actual and budgeted costs for a given period. In general, cost centers are associated with segments of the firm that provide tangible or intangible services to line departments. For example, cost centers may include departments providing services such as legal advice and accounting, personnel, and data processing services. Cost centers may also be found in producing or line departments. Where a production process requires different types of machines and operations, cost centers are created to enhance the accumulation of costs by operation.

The method of evaluating the performance of a cost center can result in dysfunctional behavior. For example, a cost center manager may feel that to insure a budgeted amount in successive years similar to the present's, the present budget allowances should be spent. The manager may be inclined to authorize unnecessary expenditures at the end of the year to insure that "nothing is left in the budget." To minimize and/or prevent such a situation, a company should identify and assign costs so managers are motivated to act in a way beneficial to the firm. The American Accounting Association Committee on Cost Concepts and Standards gave the following advice:

> *The basis of measurement used in providing cost data for control is often a matter of management discretion and an important consideration in motivation. Different bases may significantly affect the way in which different individuals are motivated. For this reason, the basis of measurement selected should be consistent with the type of motivation desired. For example, different types of motivation may result when maintenance costs are charged to a responsibility center on the basis of: (1) a rate per maintenance labor hour, (2) a rate per job, or (3) a single amount per month.*[7]

Profit Center

A profit center is a segment of activity or area of responsibility for which both revenues and costs are accumulated. The manager holds responsibility for both revenues and ex-

---

[6]D. Cook, "The Psychological Impact of Certain Aspects of Performance Reports," *NAA Bulletin* (July 1968), pp. 26–34; and Graeme M. McNally, "Responsibility Accounting and Organizational Control: Some Perspectives and Prospects," *Journal of Business Finance and Accounting* (Summer 1980), p. 167.

[7]American Accounting Association, Committee on Cost Concepts and Standards, "Report of the Committee on Cost Concepts and Standards," *Accounting Review* (April 1956), p. 189.

penses. For planning purposes, the budget estimates are both revenue and cost estimates. For control purposes, performance evaluation is guided by both a revenue variance and a cost variance. In short, the objective function of a profit center's manager is to maximize the center's profit.

Although the profit center concept is vital to the implementation of *decentralization*, it can be also used in firms with *centralization*. In other words, the profit center concept leads essentially to a divisionalized firm, but not necessarily to a decentralized firm. As we will see later, decentralization implies the relative freedom to make decisions.

Investment Center

An investment center is a segment of activity or area held responsible for both profits and investment. For planning purposes, the budget estimate is a measure of the *rate of return on investment* (ROI) estimate. For control purposes, performance evaluation is guided by an ROI variance. In short, the objective function of an investment center is to maximize the center's ROI. The merits of the ROI measure and the possible problems associated with such a measure will be illustrated later in the chapter.

13.2   *TYPES OF ORGANIZATIONAL DESIGN*

To insure the implementation of responsibility accounting, responsibility centers and authority should be well defined. That is, the design of a formal organizational structure must contribute to the attainment of corporate objectives. Such design must take into account four process criteria and a design criterion.[8]

13.2.1   *Process Criteria*

The process criteria necessary in the design of a formal organizational structure include the following:

1. *Steady state efficiency* is achieved when the unit cost of output is minimized for a given level of activity. This involves analyzing such factors as economies of scale, of skills, and of overhead.

2. *Operating responsiveness* measures an organization's ability to make efficient changes in its production level in response to environmental changes. It involves inventory control and access to all information.

3. *Strategic responsiveness* measures an organization's ability to make efficient changes in the nature of its production process in response to environmental changes. It involves a possible expense for technological and market-related changes.

4. *Structural responsiveness* measures the ability of a firm to design and implement new structures when the first three criteria cannot be met.

Each of these criteria should be applied toward the evaluation of an organizational design's potential success in meeting the objectives of the firm.

---

[8]H. I. Ansoff and R. G. Brandenburg, "A Language for Organizational Design: Parts 1 and 2," *Management Science* 17 (1971), pp. 705–731.

13.2.2   *Structural Design*

The criteria just described can be met by at least two possible types of organizational designs: the centralized functional form and the decentralized divisional form.[9]

Centralized Functional Form

The centralized functional form consists primarily of a departmentalization by function. In a manufacturing firm, such functions include production, finance, sales, accounting, personnel, purchasing, research and development, and so forth. Such a design is justifiable in terms of steady state efficiency by allowing for economies of scale, of overhead, and of skills. It results, however, in relatively low strategic and structural responsiveness.

Decentralized Divisional Form

The decentralized divisional form consists primarily of a series of organizational units, or divisions, responsible for a specific product market under the direction of a manager having strategic and operating decision prerogatives. This form achieves steady state efficiency and operating responsiveness, because departmentalization by function is used within each division. This design is justifiable mainly in terms of strategic and structural responsiveness. Since World War II, the decentralized divisional form has become the most frequent in large firms. It is accomplished most often through either a departmentalization by location (geographical diversification) or a departmentalization by product.

The simplified organizational charts in Figure 13.2 illustrate the difference between a centralized and a decentralized company producing two products (X and Y). In the centralized concern, the production, marketing, personnel, and purchasing activities fall under the supervision and responsibility of a production, marketing, personnel and purchasing vice-president, respectively. In other words, the concern is departmentalized by function. In the decentralized concern, each of the products X and Y are produced and managed in a separate division.

13.2.3   *Decentralization through Divisionalization*

Nature of Decentralization

The diversification of the types of activities of many business entities has led to the realization that centralized control and coordinating mechanisms at corporate headquarters are not always in the best interests of the firm as a whole. A brief look at some types of organizational growth will show the necessity and main reasons for decentralizing the decision making process.

   The first type of organizational growth arises through the creation of new product lines. A second type arises from *vertical mergers* and consolidations in which firms involved in different stages of production of the same product are combined. As a result, the new, merged corporation achieves greater control over its production, purchasing, and distribution processes. Examples of this growth type can be found in the automotive

---

[9]H. I. Ansoff and R. G. Brandenburg considered two other possible designs, namely, the adaptive design and the innovative design. However, these designs are more applicable to program and project development than to a corporate firm.

Figure 13.2   Types of Organizational Designs

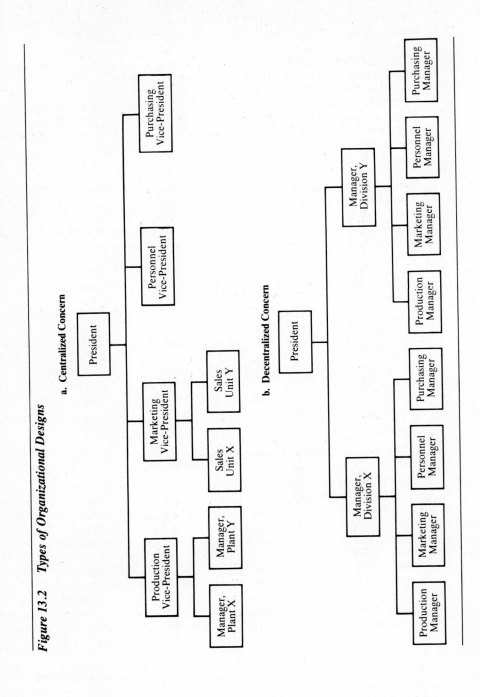

a. Centralized Concern

b. Decentralized Concern

and petroleum industries. Another type of growth, the *horizontal merger*, involves the merger of firms in the same line of business. This eliminates duplicate facilities and allows the establishment of auxiliary divisions that provide commonly needed goods or services to other subunits in the organization. The last major growth type is *conglomeration*, where firms of unrelated lines of business are combined. Interdependencies among the subunits are usually minimal. Practical factors, including lower taxes, lower transposition costs, and the increased security of belonging to a large organization, lead to the creation of conglomerates.

These types of organizational growth require the creation of decentralized organizational structures. Ideally, management will choose the degree of decentralization that will achieve corporate goals. Decentralization should not be confused with divisionalization, which is a major organizational device for decentralization, although it does not indicate to what degree. Decentralization is essentially the freedom to make decisions.

Benefits and Costs of Decentralization

Numerous arguments have been advanced in the literature in support of decentralization:

1. The modern, integrated, multiple-product firm will function best if it is made into a miniature of the competitive free enterprise system.[10]

2. Divisional managers may be more motivated, resulting in better decisions and greater efficiency. David Solomons summarizes the benefits as follows:

First, decentralized decision making is likely to result in better decisions because the people who make them are closer to the scene of action and have a smaller area of responsibility to worry about. Second, greater efficiency results from the sense the divisional managers have that they are running "their" businesses. In motivating these managers, divisional profit plays an important part. Third, giving a person responsibility for running a division is perhaps the best way of providing preparation for a top management role at the corporate level.[11]

3. The division manager is in a better position to process information concerning resource allocation.[12]

4. The division manager is in a better position to process and transmit information in general. This information economics advantage is reflected in the following two early observations:

Given realistic limits on human planning capacity, *the decentralized system will work better than the centralized.[13]*

[Decentralization] is advantageous in economizing on the transmission of information. In particular, the detailed technical knowledge of the process need not be transmitted to a central office but can be retained in the department. We may regard it as close to an

[10]Joel Dean, "Decentralization and Intracompany Pricing," *Harvard Business Review* (July–August 1955), pp. 65–74.

[11]David Solomons, "Divisional Reports," in *Handbook of Cost Accounting*, eds. S. Davidson and R. L. Weil (New York: McGraw-Hill, 1978), pp. 44–49.

[12]Nicholas Dopuch and D. F. Drake, "Accounting Implications of a Mathematical Programming Approach to the Transfer Price Problem," *Journal of Accounting Research* (Spring 1964), pp. 10–21.

[13]J. G. March and H. A. Simon, *Organizations* (New York: Wiley, 1958).

impossibility for individuals in close contact with the productive process to transmit their information in all its details to another office. This proposition, long recognized in practice, is the basis of the management literature on the questions of centralization and decentralization.[14]

5. The division manager's nearness to the marketplace provides relevant information regarding changes in the prices of output and input.[15]

6. Size and diversity of modern corporations and the promotion of morale (because of the decision making autonomy of managers) support the concept of decentralization.[16]

7. Decentralization represents a response to two major sources of uncertainty for a complex organization: its technology and its environment.

The costs associated with decentralization are also important:

1. Incongruence between the divisional goal and the corporate goal can result.

2. Decentralization can lead to dysfunctional decision making and, consequently, to *suboptimization* (that is, a decision that increases current divisional profit but limits the company profit as a whole).

3. Higher interdependence between the divisions will make every decision beneficial to one unit and harmful to another (and perhaps to the organization as a whole).

It can be concluded that decentralization is likely to be most beneficial and least costly when the organizational units are fairly independent.

Decentralization: Differentiation, Integration, and Accounting

The decentralization of an organization not only creates some independent subunits, but induces different behavioral patterns in the organizational members in terms of mental processes, working styles, decision criteria, and perceptions of reality.[17] To avoid suboptimization and insure that the efforts of all the subunits (now appropriately differentiated) contribute to the overall organizational goal, an integration process is required.

P. R. Lawrence and J. W. Lorsch showed empirically that successful firms are those that have achieved the right trade-off between integration and differentiation.[18] Some integrating mechanisms have been suggested by J. R. Galbraith:

Rules, routines, and standardization.

Organizational hierarchy.

Planning.

Direct contact.

---

[14] K. J. Arrow, "Optimization, Decentralization, and Internal Pricing in Business Firms," in *Contributions to Scientific Management* (California, 1959), pp. 9–18.

[15] Joshua Ronen and George McKinney III, "Transfer Pricing for Divisional Autonomy," *Journal of Accounting Research* (Spring 1970), pp. 99–112.

[16] J. T. Godfrey, "Short Run Planning in a Decentralized Firm," *Accounting Review* (April 1971), pp. 286–297.

[17] D. J. H. Watson and J. V. Baumler, "Transfer Pricing: A Behavioral Context," *Accounting Review* (July 1975), p. 467.

[18] P. R. Lawrence and J. W. Lorsch, *Organization and Its Environment* (Homewood, Ill.: Irwin, 1967), p. 13.

Liaison roles.

Temporary committees (task forces or teams).

Integrators (personnel specializing in the role of coordinating intersubunit activities).

Integrating departments (departments of integrators).

Matrix organization (an organization that is completely committed to joint problem solving and *shared* responsibility).[19]

The accounting system in a complex organization can be designed to achieve the trade-off between differentiation and integration. The differentiation can be achieved by an appropriate number of cost, profit, and investment centers equal to the number of differentiated units. Integration can be achieved by implementing some of the mechanisms suggested by Galbraith or by an adequate control system designed to (1) provide yard-sticks for divisional performance measurements and (2) contribute to intrafirm company transfer pricings.

Three criteria are helpful for designing or judging a particular accounting control system in a decentralized setting: goal congruence, performance evaluation, and autonomy.[20] Goal congruence focuses on harmonizing the objectives of the managers with the objectives of the organization as a whole. In other words, the divisional performance measures and the *transfer prices* must motivate the division managers to satisfy their individual goals in conformity with the organization's goals. Performance evaluation is needed to make predictions for future decisions, to appraise the abilities of the managers, and to assess the profitability of the capital invested in an organizational subunit as an economic investment. In other words, the divisional performance measures and the transfer prices must facilitate the profitability evaluation of the divisions of a firm. Finally, a preservation of the autonomy of each decentralized entity is necessary for a decentralized organization. In other words, the divisional performance measures and the transfer prices that create corporate as well as divisional profit maximization must at the same time preserve the operational autonomy of the division as a profit center.

13.3   APPRAISING DIVISIONAL PERFORMANCE

Investment centers can be evaluated using either an ROI or a residual income measure.

13.3.1   *Rate of Return on Investment*

Rather than using absolute dollar profits as a test of divisional profit, most financial control systems emphasize the use of a relationship of profit to invested capital. This relationship is usually expressed by the ROI and has received wide market acceptance.[21]

---

[19] J. R. Galbraith, "Organization Design: An Information Processing View," in *Organizational Planning: Cases and Concepts*, eds. J. W. Lorsch and P. R. Lawrence (Georgetown, Ontario: Irwin Dorsey, 1972), p. 20.

[20] Ronen and McKinney, "Transfer Pricing," pp. 99–112.

[21] In a survey of 3,525 companies, John J. Mauriel and Robert N. Anthony found that 92.36 percent of responding firms who had investment centers used ROI as a measure of performance. See John J. Mauriel and Robert N. Anthony, "Misevaluation of Investment Center Performance," *Harvard Business Review* (March–April 1966), p. 101.

E. I. du Pont de Nemours and Company is generally credited with the development of the ROI concept. Alfred P. Sloan evaluated the principle of ROI as follows:

I am not going to say that the rate of return is a magic word for every occasion in business. There are times when you have to spend money just to stay in business, regardless of the visible rate of return. Competition is the final price determinant and competitive prices may result in profits which force you to accept a rate of return less than you hoped for, or for that matter to accept temporary losses. And, in times of inflation, the rate-of-return concept comes up against the problem of assets undervalued in terms of replacement. Nevertheless, no other financial principle with which I am acquainted serves better than rate of return as an objective aid to business management.[22]

Measurement of Rate of Return on Investment

The ROI is found simply by dividing the net income by the amount of investment. It relates the profit to invested capital, both of which are important areas of management responsibility. The rationale lies in the belief that there is an optimal investment level in each asset leading to an optimal profit level. The ROI is the product of two components: *profit margin* and *investment turnover*. The profit margin equals net income divided by sales and indicates the segment's ability to transform sales into profit. The investment turnover equals sales divided by invested capital. Thus, the ROI can be expressed as follows:

$$ROI = \frac{\text{Net income}}{\text{Invested capital}} = \frac{\text{Sales}}{\text{Invested capital}} \times \frac{\text{Net income}}{\text{Sales}} \ .$$

This formula shows that the ROI can be increased by either an increase in the profit margin or the investment turnover, and it can be decreased by either a decrease in the profit margin or the investment turnover.

To illustrate, assume that a division desires to achieve a 25 percent return on invested capital. The present performance of the division is as follows:

$$\frac{\text{Sales}}{\text{Invested capital}} \times \frac{\text{Net income}}{\text{Sales}} = ROI,$$

or

$$\frac{\$200}{\$100} \times \frac{\$20}{\$200} = 20\%.$$

Two alternatives are possible to improve the ROI up to 25 percent:

1. A $5 decrease in expenses would increase net income to $25 such that

$$ROI = \frac{\$200}{\$100} \times \frac{\$25}{\$200} = 25\%.$$

2. A $20 decrease in inventories would decrease invested capital to $80 such that

---

[22]Alfred P. Sloan, Jr., *My Years with General Motors* (Garden City, N.Y.: Doubleday, 1964), p. 140.

$$ROI = \frac{\$200}{\$80} \times \frac{\$20}{\$200} = 25\%.$$

These are not the only alternatives. Figure 13.3 shows the factors that can affect the final ROI outcome.

The advantages of using the ROI to measure divisional performance include the following:

1. The ROI is a composite measuring tool combining both net income and investment features. It is useful for a comparison among the divisions of a given firm as well as for a comparison of divisional performance with that of companies in similar industries.

2. Use of the ROI encourages an effective use of resources and could serve as a corporate budgeting tool and aid in making short- and long-range plans.

3. Use of the ROI may have a positive behavioral effect on managers by creating a competitive spirit and by motivating increases in efficiency, effectiveness, and congruency with corporate goals.

Rate of Return on Investment Issues

Although the ROI may qualify as a good management tool, some potential problems must be recognized.

The net income figure used in calculating the ROI may require certain adjustments that do not conform with generally accepted accounting principles. Table 13.2 illustrates the format and content of a divisional income statement. Distinctions are made between sales to outside customers and sales to other divisions, between controllable and uncontrollable costs, and between variable and fixed costs. This format allows the possibility of distinguishing between the performance of the manager and the performance of the division. Two rates of return can be computed—the controllable ROI and the net ROI—as follows:

Controllable ROI = Controllable income ÷ Controllable capital investment.

Net ROI = Net income after taxes ÷ Total capital investment.

Another problem with the ROI is that the investment figure used in calculating the ROI may lead to an "unrealistic" ROI. Hence the most obvious figure is the net book value of assets, which is the original cost minus depreciation to date.[23] Such a measure has inherent weaknesses. For example, it enables divisions with old assets to earn a higher rate of return than divisions with newer assets, given the low book value resulting from greater depreciation charges.

Several solutions can overcome this limitation of the ROI method:

1. Gross book value can be used. However, this approach still enables a divisional manager to increase the ROI by scrapping nonprofitable assets that may be detrimental to the company.

2. Four nonhistorical cost valuation methods can be used: the economic value or capitalized value, the replacement cost, the net realizable value, and the general price level

---

[23]The Mauriel and Anthony study showed that of companies using ROI, 78 percent used net book value.

Figure 13.3   Relationship of Factors Influencing the Rate of Return on Investment

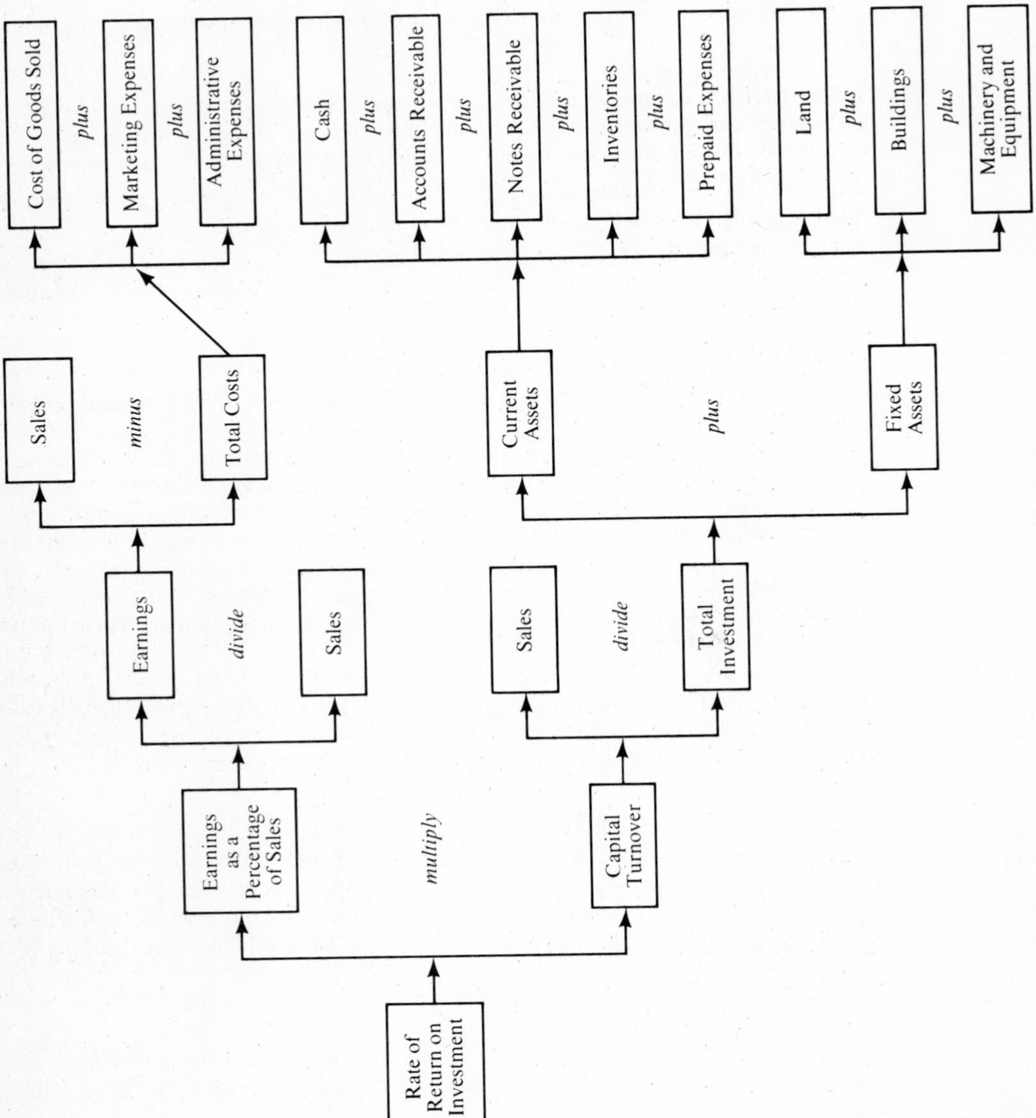

Table 13.2   ***Format and Content of a Divisional Income Statement***

Revenues		X
External Sales	X	
Internal Sales (Transfer Price Equal to Market Value)	X	
Internal Sales (Transfer Price Different from Market Value)	X	
Minus		
Variable costs		X
Variable Cost of Goods Sold	X	
Variable Selling and Administrative Divisional Expenses	X	
Total Contribution Margin		X
Add (Deduct)		
Fixed Costs Allocated to Other Divisions for Transfers Made at Other than Market Value	X	
Deduct		
Controllable Discretionary and Committed Fixed Costs	X	
Equals		
Controllable Operating Income		X
Deduct		
Uncontrollable Fixed Costs	X	
Operating Income before Taxes		X
Income Taxes	X	
Net Income (after Taxes)		X

Source: David Solomons, *Divisional Performance—Measurement and Control* (New York: Financial Executives Research Foundation, 1965), p. 82. Adapted by permission.

---

adjusted historical cost.[24] The first three methods approximate the current value, whereas the last merely adjusts historical cost. The replacement cost represents the amount of cash or other consideration that would be required to obtain the same asset or its equivalent. The net realizable value represents the amount of cash for which an asset can be sold. The capitalized value refers to the present value of net cash flows expected to be received from the use of the asset. The three current values are relevant to different types of decisions. For example a disposal, continuance, or expansion program would entail the following alternatives:

Table

	Alternatives		
	Disposal (Sell)	**Continuance (Hold)**	**Expansion (Buy)**
Decisions	Capitalized Value *versus* Net Realizable Value	Capitalized Value *versus* Net Realizable Value	Capitalized Value *versus* Replacement Cost

Although the capitalized value appears to be dominant, it is a subjective value based on the present value of expected cash flows. Replacement cost and net realizable value may be more available and constitute a better alternative to historical cost.

3. The use of an increasing-charge depreciation (annuity depreciation), the sinking-fund

---

[24]Ahmed Belkaoui, *Accounting Theory* (New York: Harcourt Brace Jovanovich, 1980), chaps. 5–7.

depreciation, can lead to a lower income being related to a smaller investment base. Sinking-fund depreciation is based on the financial concept that depreciation represents the return of investment. Suppose a company is considering buying an asset with a two-year life and no salvage value. If the cost of the asset is estimated to be $8,680 and the yearly cash flow to be $5,000, the ROI using a discounted cash flow method can be obtained by solving the following equation for r:

$$\$8,680 = \sum_{t=1}^{2} \frac{\$5,000}{(1 + r)^t} .$$

$$r = 10\%.$$

Given the knowledge of the ROI, sinking-fund depreciation assumes a capital recovery factor. Table 13.3 presents the results of sinking-fund depreciation, showing each cash payment to be equal to interest on investment plus principal. Table 13.4 shows the superiority of sinking-fund depreciation with the income statement and the ROI computations using either constant, increasing, or decreasing depreciation. The sinking-fund depreciation method results in a stable, constant ROI figure as compared with the fluctuating results obtained by the straight-line and accelerated methods. Therefore, sinking fund depreciation is preferred by many companies to measure divisional profitability.

An appropriate allocation of assets to divisions makes the ROI more meaningful and contributes to goal congruence. Such allocation differs from one company to another,

Table 13.3   Example of Sinking-Fund Depreciation

Year	Initial Investment (a)	Cash Earnings (b)	Return of 10% $(c = 10\% a)$	Depreciation $(d = b - c)$	Unrecovered Investment $(e = a - d)$
0					$8,680
1	$8,680	$5,000	$868.0	$4,132.0	$4,548
2	4,548	5,000	454.8	4,545.2	2.8[a]

[a] Due to rounding.

Table 13.4   Depreciation Methods and Rate of Return Computations

	Methods of Depreciation					
	Straight-Line		Accelerated Depreciation		Sinking-Fund Depreciation	
Year	1	2	1	2	1	2
Cash Earnings	$5,000	$5,000	$5,000	$5,000	$5,000	$5,000.0
Depreciation	4,340[a]	4,340[a]	5,786[b]	2,893[b]	4,132[c]	4,545.2[c]
Net Income	$ 660	$ 660	$ (786)	$2,107	$ 868	$ 454.8
Investment Base	$8,680	$4,340	$8,680	$2,894	$8,680	$4,548.0
Rate of Return on Investment	7.6%	15.2%	−9%	72%	10%	10%

[a] $8,680 ÷ 2 = $4,340.
[b] $8,680 × 2/3 = $5,786. $8680 × 1/3 = $2,983.
[c] See Table 13.3 for results.

given that some companies elect to centralize certain activities and decentralize others. For instance, in most decentralized companies the home office centralizes cash management, billing, or receivable collections.

As a general rule, the basis of allocation of assets to divisions should be *controllability*. That is, the amount of assets controllable by any given segment in its managerial activities should be the amount allocated to that segment in the computation of the rate of return on divisional investment.

To summarize, the ROI limitations can be corrected if the investment base is at current value net of depreciation and if a sinking-fund depreciation method is used.

13.3.2   *Residual Income*

Developed in the 1950s by General Electric Company, the concept of *residual income* to measure divisional performance is defined operationally as divisional income in excess of a prescribed interest on investment. This concept directs the manager toward the maximization of income above a charge for assets used. The interest rate used corresponds conceptually to the firm's cost of capital. For example, if a divisional income were $50,000 for a budgeted investment of $200,000 and a cost of capital of 10 percent, the residual income would be computed as follows:

Divisional Net Income	$50,000
Minus	
Imputed Interest at 10 Percent of Assets	20,000
Equals	
Residual Income	$30,000

There are two advantages to the residual income method for divisional performance evaluation:

1. The method enables the division to continue to expand as long as it meets the cost of capital requirement. For the previous example, the cost of capital was 10 percent, whereas the ROI was 25 percent ($50,000 ÷ $200,000). In other words, using the ROI of 25 percent as an investment criterion would eliminate projects whose returns might exceed the cost of capital and, consequently, would eliminate projects acceptable from the point of view of the corporation as a whole.

2. The method requires setting a rate of return target for every type of asset, regardless of the division's profitability. The end result is a yardstick for comparisons between divisions. However, the adequate determination of the cost of capital and/or the rate of return of individual assets is a possible problem.

13.4   TRANSFER PRICING

13.4.1   *Role of Transfer Pricing*

Transfer pricing is a major issue confronting decentralized organizations that expect division managers to operate their division as a semiautonomous business. These organizations face the problem of what price to charge for goods and services sold by one organizational unit to another in the same company. This situation prevails within vertically integrated organizations, where transactions often occur between the company's profit centers. When goods and services are transferred between divisions, the revenue of the supplying unit becomes the cost of the purchasing unit. These intracompany charges ultimately will be reflected in the profit and loss statements of the respective divisions. Since divisional performance is evaluated by a profit-based criterion such as ROI or residual income, the profit center managers will attempt to maximize their own center's profit. A conflict occurs when improved divisional performance is achieved at the expense of overall company profits.

In theory, to optimize an organization's profits, the transfer price should be selected so it motivates and guides managers to choose their inputs and outputs in coordination with the other subunits. Ideally, any intracompany pricing method should be consistent with the goals of maximizing both company and divisional profits: Transfer pricing should insure *goal congruence* between units.

Because of the potential conflicts that can arise in transfer price determination, three primary objectives can be used to establish a proper transfer price. The first objective of a transfer pricing system is to *assist top management in evaluating and guiding divisional performance* by providing adequate information on divisional revenues and expenses. The second objective is to *help the division manager in running the division*. The third objective is to *insure divisional autonomy* and allow each profit center to act as an independent agent.

In theory, the design of a transfer pricing scheme ultimately must point each division manager toward top management's goals. The scheme must reward divisional external economies and prevent and penalize diseconomies. Furthermore, a firm's transfer pricing divisions must acknowledge domestic and foreign legal and tax requirements, as well as antitrust and financial reporting constraints.

Developing a set of transfer pricing rules that can integrate the complex dimensions of an organization, insure divisional autonomy, and at the same time achieve overall corporate goals is a very difficult task. Consequently, a transfer pricing system must be developed with an awareness of these difficulties.

The main positive characteristics of a transfer pricing system include insuring goal congruence, being fair to all concerned parties, and minimizing conflicts between divisions. Some corporations set guidelines to insure an effective transfer pricing system.[25]

Various transfer pricing methods are used in practice. The most commonly used ones are market price, negotiated price, actual cost, standard cost, marginal or variable cost, target profit, and dual transfer price.

13.4.2   Market Price

A market-based transfer price is the price at which the producing division would sell the product externally. In other words, the producing division charges the same price to other divisions as it would charge to outside customers in open market transactions. The market price has the advantage of providing an objective measure of value for goods or services exchanged, and it may result in the best information for use in performance evaluation of the profit centers. A transfer pricing system based on market price requires a competitive intermediate market, minimal interdependencies of the profit centers, and the availability of dependable market quotations.

---

[25] *Setting Intercorporate Pricing Policies* (New York: Business International, 1973), p. 12.

There are also serious drawbacks to using a transfer price based on market price. First, in today's regulated economy, perfectly competitive markets are very rare. In an imperfect market, one seller or buyer, by itself, can affect the market price, rendering it inapplicable as an effective transfer price. Second, even if the intermediate market is perfect, there is no guarantee that the market price is for a product strictly comparable in terms of grade, quality, and other relevant characteristics. Third, a situation may arise in which the market price is a distress price. Should the transfer price be the distress price, or should it be a long-run average, or "normal," market price? Both prices are defensible. On one hand, the use of a distress price may lead managers of the supplying division to dispose of productive facilities to affect positively the short-run ROI. However, this may reduce the activities of the buying division, which would be disadvantageous to the company as a whole. On the other hand, the use of the long-run average market price may penalize the buying division by forcing it to buy at a price higher than the market price. If the objective is to preserve the spirit of decentralization and if safeguards exist to prevent the supplying division from disposing of productive facilities, the distress price should be chosen. Finally, there may be a problem if the goods or services transferred do not have a ready market price.

In spite of these limitations, the market price is considered the most effective transfer price because (1) it insures divisional autonomy, (2) it provides a good performance indication for use in performance evaluation, and (3) it creates a climate conducive to goal congruence.

13.4.3 Negotiated Price

A negotiated transfer price is the price set after bargaining between the buying and selling divisions. This system requires that these divisions deal with one another in the same way they deal with external suppliers and buyers. Thus, one basic requirement for the success of the bargaining process is the freedom of the divisions not only to bargain with one another, but also to deal with external markets if unsatisfied with the internal offers. This freedom will avoid the bilateral monopoly that exists when the divisions are only allowed to deal with themselves. In fact, the negotiated transfer price system works best when an intermediate market exists for the product or service transferred, providing the divisions with objective and reliable information for successful negotiations.

The literature contains several recommendations for the use of negotiated prices.[26] The writers maintain that prices negotiated in arm's-length bargaining by divisional managers help accomplish goal congruence. They view these prices as compatible with profit decentralization, insuring the division managers' freedom of action and increasing their accountability for profits. A survey conducted by R. K. Mautz indicates that about 24 percent of the participating diversified companies revealed *negotiation* as the basis for setting transfer prices between divisions.[27]

The negotiated transfer price system also may have a negative behavioral impact when personality conflicts arise between the bargainers; succeeding in the negotiation

---

[26] Dean, "Decentralization and Intracompany Pricing," pp. 65–74; David H. Li, "Interdivisional Transfer Planning," *Management Accounting* (June 1965), pp. 51–54; Timothy P. Haidinger, "Negotiate for Profits," *Management Accounting* (December 1970), pp. 23–24; James M. Fremgen, "Transfer Pricing and Management Goals," *Management Accounting* (December 1970), pp. 25–31; and H. James Shaub, "Transfer Pricing in a Decentralized Organization," *Management Accounting* (April 1978), pp. 33–36, 42.

[27] R. K. Mautz, *Financial Reporting by Diversified Companies* (New York: Financial Executives Research Foundation, 1968), p. 36.

may become a more important goal than the company's profitability. Another drawback of the negotiated price system is that it can be time-consuming. Division managers may lose an overall company perspective and direct their efforts to improve their divisional profit performance. In their attempts to obtain the best possible price, managers may find themselves in very lengthy argumentation.

When these conflicts arise, a transfer price should be set arbitrarily by a central decision of top management. This *arbitrary* or *imposed price* is the price felt to serve the overall company interests. Needless to say, the arbitrary price contradicts the spirit of decentralization, given the possible loss of divisional autonomy. Some authors in the accounting literature have fundamental objections to negotiation. Cyert and March viewed the organization as a coalition of interests and suggested that negotiation and renegotiation of transfer pricing can be expected to create conflict among the subunits constituting the coalition.[28] Nicholas Dopuch and D. F. Drake suggested that the negotiated price implies an evaluation of the power to negotiate rather than an evaluation of performance itself.[29]

13.4.4 Actual Cost

A transfer price based on actual cost is a price based on the historical full cost of the product or service exchanged. It has the obvious advantage of being measurable, verifiable, and readily available.

When the actual costs are accepted for the determination of transfer prices, the problem remains of motivating the selling division to sell internally at a price other than the market price. One way of motivating the selling division is to set the transfer price at full actual cost plus some markup as a way of approximating the market price. The resulting *synthetic market price* may be better than the actual market price when the product existing in the intermediate market differs in terms of quality, grade, and other relevant characteristics from the product transferred.

The full-cost-plus or synthetic market price has been found to be the most popular approach under the following conditions: (1) an absence of competitive prices, (2) the presence of an interest in saving the cost of negotiating prices, and (3) the presence of a need to implement a policy of pricing the final product.[30]

There are several limitations inherent in the implementation of a transfer pricing model based on actual cost:

1. A transfer price based on actual cost is actually based on absorption cost in the sense that it includes all direct and indirect expenses (variable and allocated joint and fixed costs). As a result, this type of transfer price may transfer the inefficiencies of the selling division to the buying division, making it unwise to use divisional profit for divisional performance evaluation.

2. A transfer price based on actual cost may lessen the selling division's incentive to control costs.

[28] R. Cyert and J. March, *A Behavioral Theory of the Firm* (Englewood Cliffs, N.J.: Prentice-Hall, 1963), p. 276.

[29] Dopuch and Drake, "Accounting Implications," p. 13.

[30] National Association of Accountants, *Research Report No. 30*, "Accounting for Intra-Company Transfers" (New York: NAA, 1954), pp. 31–36.

3. Martin Shubik notes that cost-plus pricing of transfer goods can impede the search for technological progress by the manufacturing division.[31]

13.4.5 Standard Cost

We have seen that a transfer price based on actual cost can reinforce the inefficiencies of the selling division and lessen its motivation to control costs. A transfer price based on standard cost can correct for these problems. It reflects a normative position by expressing what costs should be under certain circumstances. As a result, a transfer price based on standard cost eliminates the inefficiencies of the selling division; when compared with actual cost, it may create an incentive to control costs.

13.4.6 Marginal or Variable Cost

A company using a transfer price based on either the full actual cost or the full standard cost may face at least two situations:

1. The full actual cost and the full standard cost may be higher than the market price.

2. The full actual cost and the full standard cost include both direct and indirect costs (variable and fixed). The indirect costs can result from arbitrary allocation procedures. The fixed costs can be committed costs that are incurred whether the selling division operates at full or at less-than-full capacity. Thus, the buying division may feel that either the indirect costs and/or the fixed costs should not be included in the determination of the transfer price. When this situation arises, it may be more motivating and important to maintain the spirit of decentralization and resort to a *transfer price based on partial cost*, which charges only a portion of the full actual or, preferably, full standard cost. Conceptually, this partial cost includes values between full cost and zero cost and refers to either the marginal cost or the variable cost.

The *marginal cost* is the incremental cost of producing additional units. In general, the buying division will be willing to buy as long as the marginal revenue is superior to the marginal cost. Although conceptually appealing, a transfer price based on marginal cost requires available information on all production levels. Because such figures are not always available, a surrogate for the marginal cost may have to be used—the *variable cost*.

The variable cost or the variable cost plus a lump sum can be used either as a surrogate for marginal cost or as a way of encouraging the use of some facilities' services. First, the variable cost can be used when marginal cost cannot easily be computed because of the absence of adequate information. Second, the use of the variable cost can encourage divisions to use the services of facilities with excess capacity until it becomes more profitable or advantageous to the selling division to switch to a full cost (actual or standard).

---

[31]Martin Shubik, "Incentives, Decentralized Control: The Assignment of Joint Costs and Internal Pricing," in *Management Controls: New Directions in Basic Research*, eds. C. P. Bonini, R. K. Jaedicke, and H. M. Wagner (New York: McGraw-Hill, 1964), pp. 221–222.

13.4.7   *Dual Price*

From the preceding discussion of transfer pricing alternatives, it can be seen that (1) the best motivating transfer price for the selling division is the market price, and (2) the most acceptable price for the buying division is the variable cost.

One way of meeting both of these optimal situations is to use a dual transfer price rather than a single transfer price. The dual price system allows the selling division to sell either at a market price or at a synthetic market price, hence creating a profit and motivating the selling division to sell. This system allows the buying division to buy inside the company at variable cost, which prevents the selling division from having excess capacity when the buying division buys outside at market prices equal to or lower than the variable cost. In short, the dual price system motivates both the buying and selling divisions to operate in the best interests of the company as a whole. One possible drawback of this system is the possibility that the divisions may no longer be motivated to control costs.

13.4.8   *Transfer Pricing Systems Illustrated*

To illustrate the transfer pricing systems, assume the Dowbing Company has two divisions (X and Y). For one of the company's products, division X produces a major subassembly, and division Y incorporates this subassembly into a final product. In the open market, similar subassemblies can be purchased at $150 each. Division Y currently buys the total output of division X and wants to increase purchases by 500 units. The following are some recent cost data for division X:

Subassembly	Standard Cost	Actual Cost
Direct Material	$ 50	$ 60
Direct Labor	20	25
Variable Manufacturing Overhead	15	15
Fixed Manufacturing Overhead	15	20
	$100	$120

1. Using the current market price, division X would transfer the parts at $150 each:

500 units × $150 = $75,000.

2. Assume divisions X and Y agree after lengthy negotiations that the outside market price includes $10 of selling and advertising expenses. The negotiated price would be $140 ($150 − $10) each:

500 units × $140 = $70,000.

3. Assume that divisions X and Y cannot agree on the amount of selling and administrative expenses and that top management has set an arbitrary dictated price of $130 per unit:

500 units × $130 = $65,000.

4. Using the full actual cost, division X would transfer the parts at $120 each:

500 units × $120 = $60,000.

5. Using the full standard cost, division X would transfer the parts at $100 each:

500 units × $100 = $50,000.

6. Assume division X is already operating at full capacity, and to produce the additional 500 units it must incur additional standard fixed costs of $5 per unit. The marginal cost of production per unit is computed as follows:

Direct Material	$ 50
Direct Labor	20
Variable Manufacturing Overhead	15
Fixed Manufacturing Overhead ($15 + $5)	20
	$105

500 units × $105 = $52,500.

7. Using the actual variable cost, division X would transfer the parts at $100 each:

500 units × $100 = $50,000.

8. Using a dual price system, division X can be given credit for the market price of $150, and division Y is charged at the variable cost of $100. Assuming that the variable cost of Y is $30 per unit, the profit of the division will be as follows:

Division X	
Sales to Division Y at $150	$ 75,000
Variable Costs at $100	50,000
Contribution Margin	$ 25,000
Division Y	
Sales of Finished Product at $200 (Assumed)	$100,000
Variable Costs	
Division X at $100	50,000
Division Y at $30	15,000
Contribution Margin	$ 35,000

Note that the profit of the company as a whole is less than the sum of the divisional profits. Some eliminations must be made before the total company profit can be determined. The total profit of the company is actually only $35,000 ($200 unit selling price of the final product − $130 total unit variable cost incurred in both divisions X and Y = $70 contribution margin per unit; $70 contribution margin per unit × 500 units = $35,000 total contribution margin). The $25,000 additional contribution reflected in the income statement of division X is due to division X to allow it to sell at market price; this in fact constitutes a corporate subsidy to motivate division X to sell to division Y.

13.5   CONCLUSION

In 1967, the National Industrial Conference Board surveyed 190 U.S. firms to find the type of transfer price most often used by companies. The study classified all transfer prices into two main categories—cost- or market-based prices—and confirmed the use of more than one transfer price within a single enterprise.[32] No method emerged as the "preferred price." [33] This lack of agreement emphasizes the need for a better solution to the transfer pricing problem.

Legal restrictions are major considerations for companies establishing a transfer price. For internal tax purposes, a transfer price must make commercial sense. Transfers to foreign subsidiaries ideally should be justifiable and should not be made to achieve a more favorable tax climate. Antitrust regulations also force large companies to use realistic transfer prices.

Reliable information for use in determining transfer prices should be available through the accounting discipline. However, in the context of transfer pricing there is no one accounting solution that is simultaneously appropriate for performance evaluation, decision making, and general financial statement purposes. The dual pricing approach is the best solution accounting can offer. The use of a synthetic market price for the selling division and some form of variable cost charged to the buying division reflects most fairly a division's performance and permits the purchasing division to make decisions that are advantageous to the firm. The synthetic market price and variable cost must be determined by a third party who is knowledgeable about the relevance and reliability of these prices. The major deficiency in the dual pricing approach to the transfer pricing problem is the undermining of divisional autonomy through the introduction of a third party.

The economic analysis of divisionalized firms cannot provide a simple solution for transfer pricing of intermediate goods (see Appendix 13.A). The initial theory developed by Jack Hirschleifer in 1956 was considered a pathfinding approach to the problem. It outlined the risk of dysfunctional decisions if divisions were allowed to operate as autonomous units. Marginal costs and marginal revenues can be used to predict the optimal situation for a firm as a whole, and they provide the meeting ground for cost-based and market-oriented transfer prices.

The decomposition programming model (DPM) offers a systematic procedure for calculating the bonuses and penalties used in obtaining optimal use and pricing of resources (see Appendix 13.B). Using the central coordination of corporate headquarters, this method attempts to insure goal congruence by adjusting subprograms to the complexities of the overall firm. The DPM also eliminates interdivisional communication, thus minimizing the interpersonal conflicts that can otherwise arise. Performance evaluation focuses on the ability of division managers to adhere to the optimal plan. Although the degree of true divisional autonomy possible has been questioned, the decomposition procedure allows divisional responsibility and authority for the formulation and calculation of divisional programs.

It must be remembered that whatever solution is reached applies to a particular organizational environment. Each situation is unique and must be incorporated into the organizational philosophy. Without consideration for the behavioral aspect, no solution will succeed. "Users and uses must determine the transfer pricing technique to be selected." [34]

---

[32] *Interdivisional Transfer Pricing* (New York: National Industrial Conference Board, 1967).

[33] I. Sharav, "Transfer Pricing, Diversity of Goals and Practices," *Journal of Accountancy* (April 1974), pp. 56–62.

[34] Ibid., p. 61.

Figure 13.4   Transfer Pricing for Independent Divisions

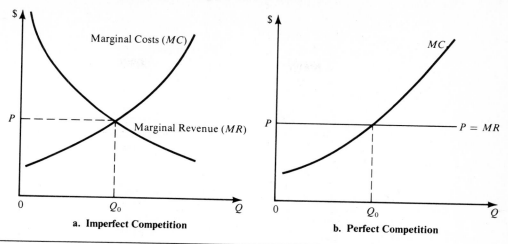

a. Imperfect Competition

b. Perfect Competition

13.A   APPENDIX: ECONOMIC SOLUTION TO TRANSFER PRICING[35]

The traditional economic answer to maximization of a firm's profits is to produce to the point where marginal cost (MC) equals marginal revenue (MR). Marginal cost in the economic sense is the additional cost of producing an additional unit, where cost includes returns to all factors of production, including capital. The problem in transfer pricing within a decentralized firm arises from the conflict between the objectives of each division and those of the organization. Once cost and demand dependencies between divisions are introduced, with the possibility of one unit being more dominant than another, transfer pricing becomes complex. The situation is further complicated if there is an external intermediate market in an environment of either perfect or imperfect competition. The following sections examine each of these possible cases.

13.A.1   Independent Divisions

If a firm is simply a conglomeration of independent, productive units, then transfer pricing is simple. Each division operates independently of the others and maximizes its profits according to the market situation. As Figure 13.4 shows, price (P) and output (Q) in each division are determined by its marginal cost and marginal revenue. A situation like this, while unusual, could apply to decentralized firms with a minimum of dependencies, such as a horizontally integrated firm. The market price would be the transfer price.

[35] Appendix 13.A draws heavily on Jack Hirschleifer's contributions to the transfer pricing problem. See his articles: "On the Economics of Transfer Pricing," *Journal of Business* (January 1956), pp. 172–184; and "Economics of the Divisionalized Firm," *Journal of Business* (April 1957), pp. 96–108.

13.A.2   *No Intermediate Markets and No Dominant Division*

Assume that two divisions—the buying and the selling—are cost independent, meaning that the level of operations in either division has no impact on the cost function of the other. Thus, the total marginal cost of the firm equals the marginal cost of the buying division plus the marginal cost of the selling division. To simplify the situation, assume there are no intermediate markets, or no demand or supply of the intermediate product (transferred product) except within the company. This assumption means that the output of both divisions must be coordinated exactly (excluding inventory buildup).

Figure 13.5 shows the determination of the transfer price in this case. The optimal output for the company as a whole is at the point where total marginal costs (MC) equal total marginal revenue (MR). The buying division, on one hand, pays a specified transfer price (P_t) to the selling division for the intermediate product; the buying division will maximize its profit by setting its output (Q_2) so its marginal cost ($P_t + MC_2$) equals its total marginal revenue. On the other hand, the marginal revenue of the selling division (MR_1) equals the transfer price, so it will set its output (Q_1) such that its marginal cost (MC_1) equals the transfer price.

The simplicity of the model disappears when an attempt is made to establish the optimal transfer price. Figure 13.6 depicts such a case. If management sets an initial transfer price, each division will respond by setting tentative outputs (Q_1 and Q_2). If Q_1 is greater than Q_2, too much of the intermediate product has been produced. The transfer price (P_t^h) is unattractive and should be lowered. Conversely, the transfer price (P_t^l) should be adjusted upward if Q_2 is greater than Q_1. Eventually the point (P_t^o) should be reached where Q_1 equals Q_2. At that point, net marginal revenue (nMR) equals the marginal cost of the buying division:

$$nMR(MR - MC_1) = MC_2.$$

This is the optimal output. To achieve optimality, however, both divisions are assumed to act like perfect competitors.

Figure 13.5   *No Intermediate Markets and No Dominant Division*

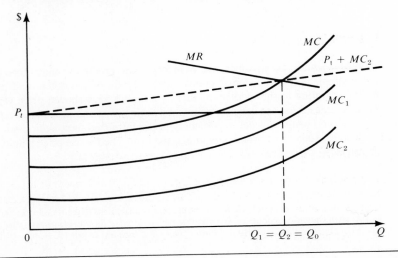

Figure 13.6   **No Dominant Division with No Intermediate Markets**
   a. Transfer Price Too High
   b. Transfer Price Too Low

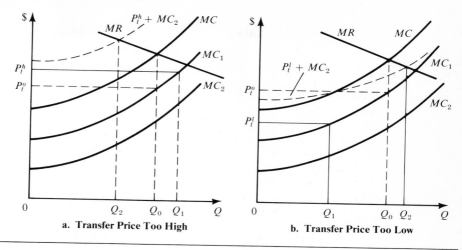

a. Transfer Price Too High   b. Transfer Price Too Low

Figure 13.7   **Dominant Division with No Intermediate Markets**
   a. Monopolistic Seller
   b. Monopolistic Buyer

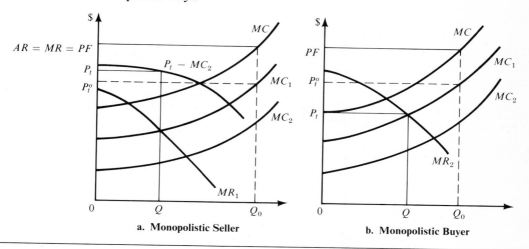

a. Monopolistic Seller   b. Monopolistic Buyer

13.A.3   Dominant Division with No Intermediate Markets

If the selling division sets the transfer price, it may be tempted to act as a monopolist, take advantage of the declining demand curve of the buyer, and maximize its profit at the cost of an overall loss to the firm. This case is illustrated in Figure 13.7a. On the other hand, if the buying division sets the transfer price, it may be tempted to be a monopolistic buyer and take advantage of the rising supply curve of the selling division (Figure 13.7b).

Even with a third-party negotiator, either division may attempt to suboptimize and sabotage cost information in the hopes of achieving a more favorable price. Consequently, these two situations—dominant selling division or dominant buying division—not only presuppose that some neutral umpire set the transfer price, but they also presuppose an awareness that one division may try to take advantage of the other.

13.A.4   *Perfectly Competitive External Intermediate Market with No Price Differences between Internal and External Markets*

If the original model is changed to include an external market for the intermediate product, then the outputs of the divisions no longer need to be coordinated. Furthermore, if this external market is perfectly competitive, neither division can affect the external price of the intermediate product, and both divisions will be indifferent as to where they buy or sell their products.

Actually, this situation could exist even if the external intermediate market were not perfectly competitive, as long as the firm itself were a negligible trader in a market dominated by a larger company fixing the price. In this case, the external market price is the transfer price. If the internal transfer price were higher, the buying division would buy outside; the reverse would occur if the internal price were lower. As a result, the internal transfer price will be set equal to the external market price.

Figure 13.8 illustrates the determination of the transfer price in this case. Quantity Q_1 will be produced so that

$$P_t = P_x = \text{Marginal cost of the selling division,}$$

where P_x = external market price. On the other hand, the buying division will buy only Q_2 until its marginal cost plus the transfer price equals the marginal revenue of the firm. The excess $(Q_1 - Q_2)$ will be sold externally at the transfer price.

Figure 13.8   *Perfectly Competitive External Intermediate Market with No Price Differences between Internal and External Markets*

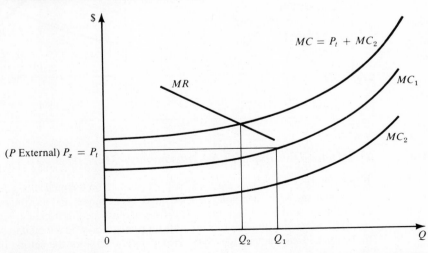

Figure 13.9 *Perfectly Competitive External Intermediate Market with Price Differences between External and Internal Markets*

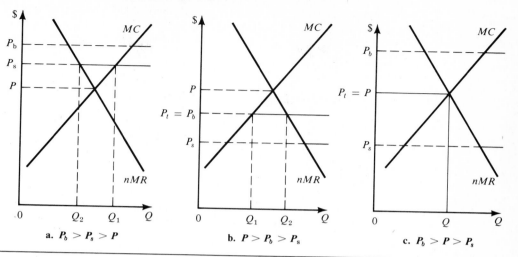

a. $P_b > P_s > P$ b. $P > P_b > P_s$ c. $P_b > P > P_s$

13.A.5 *Perfectly Competitive External Intermediate Market with Price Differences between External and Internal Markets*

Even in a perfectly competitive environment for an intermediate product there can arise price differentials between the buying and selling divisions. Therefore, cost is the imperfect aspect in buying and selling the intermediate product. As J. R. Gould points out, in such a case there may be three prices for the intermediate good: (1) the internal equilibrium price (P), which exists at the intersection of the net marginal revenue curve of the seller and the marginal cost curve of the seller; (2) the gross purchase price (P_b); and (3) the net selling price (P_s).[36]

Three possible situations, illustrated in Figure 13.9, show the necessity for management intervention to insure optimality. In Figure 13.9a, where $P_b > P_s > P$, profit maximization occurs when Q_1 is produced with Q_2 of it sold to the buying division at P_s. The remainder $(Q_1 - Q_2)$ is sold to the external market at P_s. Management first must insure that Q_2 is sold to the buying division and not to the external market; second, management must prevent the selling division from charging a higher price than P_s internally (one closer to P_b). As Gould notes,

The transfer price which insures these outputs is that central management should instruct the transferee to supply the quantity that the processing division demands at $P_{(s)}$. Subject to this constraint, autonomous profit-maximizing behavior on the part of the individual divisions will lead to the optimum for the firm. . . . It should be noted that at $P_{(s)}$ the transferee has not incentive to supply the processing division rather than outside customers. Thus it must be instructed to supply all the processing divisions at $P_{(s)}$.[37]

---

[36] J. R. Gould, "Economic Price Determination," *Journal of Business* (January 1964), pp. 61–67.
[37] Ibid., p. 63.

In Figure 13.9b, where $P > P_b > P_s$, the buying division is in the dominant position. The selling division should produce only Q_1 and sell it internally to the buying division at P_b. The remainder $(Q_2 - Q_1)$ should be bought externally at P_b. Once again, third-party direction will be required to insure optimality.

In Figure 13.9c, where $P_b > P > P_s$, the external market is irrelevant, and both divisions will trade Q at P, where $MC_1 = nMR$.

13.A.6 Imperfectly Competitive External Intermediate Market and a Dominant Supplier Division

If the model is altered so the perfectly competitive element of the external intermediate market disappears, further conflict arises between divisions. Assume that the internal supplier is a monopolist in the intermediate market. Since the marginal cost of the division is less than the external market price, the external market provides an alternative for the supplier but not for the buyer. If the higher external market price were used as the transfer price, then the buying division would have no alternative but to pay the higher price (to the detriment of the profits of the firm as a whole). Consequently, if we assume demand independence, wherein the demands of the internal market do not affect the external demand of the intermediate product, two prices should be established: a lower one for the buying division and a higher one for the outside demand. Consequently, the solution is twofold.

As seen in Figure 13.10, there is an external demand (d_x) and external marginal revenue (mr_x) line, and equilibrium is at the point where the external marginal revenue equals the internal transfer price (P_t), resulting in Q_x being produced for the external market.

However, to find the internal transfer price, it is necessary to superimpose this graph on one for both divisions (Figure 13.11). The Nmr line represents the marginal revenue of the firm less the marginal costs of the buying division, whereas the total revenue line of the selling division (smr) includes the additional revenue (mr_x) earned by the selling division on the external market. This smr line is equated to the selling division's mar-

Figure 13.10   Imperfectly Competitive External Intermediate Market and a Dominant Supplier Division

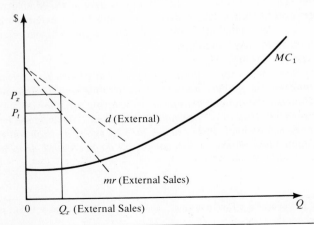

Figure 13.11 *Imperfectly Competitive External Intermediate Market and a Dominant Supplier Division*

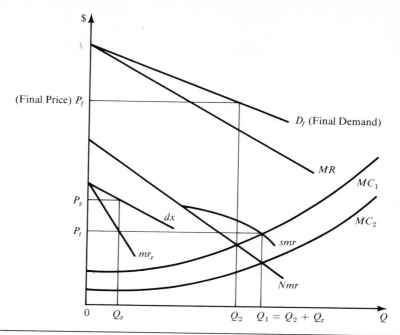

ginal costs (MC_1) to arrive at the internal transfer price. The P_t line, in turn, indicates both the amount to be sold externally (Q_x) and the amount required by the buying division for internal use (Q_2).[38]

The quantity Q_2 is determined at the point where the P_t line crosses the Nmr curve. Consequently, optimality occurs at the point where the selling division produces Q_1, Q_x for the external intermediate market to be transferred at price P_t. It is easy to see that the internal transfer price is set so $Q_1 = Q_2 + Q_x$. Again, a neutral umpire is needed to insure optimality. Otherwise, the selling division would use its powerful market position to exploit its internal customer, and the final output (Q_2) would be lower, with a resultant smaller overall profit for the firm.

13.A.7   *Buyer Division Dominant*

If the situation were reversed and the buying division were a monopolistic buyer in an imperfect market, it might be to the firm's overall benefit to discontinue production if the product could be bought in sufficient quantities and more cheaply externally. However, this is not a straightforward decision, and it would have to be examined for long-run ramifications. In a multidivisional company with interdependencies between several divisions, the situation would be very complex. In the final analysis, if the overall objec-

---

[38] This obviously assumes internal transfer is to be used for production. The buying division cannot turn around and sell the intermediate product to the external market for a profit.

tive of the firm were obtained by retaining the selling division, management would have to insist on internal purchase by the buying division.

13.A.8   Demand Dependence

If there is demand dependence between divisions and the demands of the internal market do affect the external demand, the price differential for internal and external customers should be less material. An internal transfer at marginal cost pricing now means a loss of more profitable sales to the supplier on the external market. Consequently, for marginal cost to apply, it should be redefined here to include the opportunity cost represented by the loss of external profit. In horizontal integration (where normally there is little exchange between divisions), if exchange does take place, demand dependence is more crucial than it is in vertical integration.

The demand for an intermediate product is primarily a derived demand: A solution only applies at the point of equilibrium. If the external intermediate market is not perfectly competitive, the elasticity of this derived demand will be a function of several variables: the extent of vertical integration, the elasticity of demand for the final product, and the elasticity of supply of the intermediate product. If there is cross-elasticity of demand, divisional marginal revenue should be adjusted. Since $R = P_1 Q_1 + P_2 Q_2$,

$$\frac{\delta R}{\delta Q_1} = \underbrace{P_1 + Q_1 \frac{\delta P_1}{\delta Q_1}}_{\substack{\text{Traditional} \\ \text{marginal} \\ \text{revenue}}} + \underbrace{Q_2 \frac{\delta P_2}{\delta Q_1}}_{\substack{\text{Cross marginal} \\ \text{revenue}}} .$$

$$\frac{\delta R}{\delta Q_2} = P_2 + \overbrace{Q_2 \frac{\delta P_2}{\delta Q_2}} + \overbrace{Q_1 \frac{\delta P_1}{\delta Q_2}} .$$

These equations represent the traditional marginal revenue for each product as additional units are sold *plus* the cross marginal revenue. In the first equation, for example, the third term expresses the effect on the revenue of Q_1 when an additional unit of Q_2 is sold. The true marginal revenue (MR^*) of each division should take into account this effect, and in the maximization of divisional profits, MC should be equated to MR^*.

To incorporate this into a divisional framework, a firm can set up a system of taxes if the cross-demand is competitive (for example, Pontiac and Chevrolet), or a system of bounties if the cross-demand is complementary (for example, cameras and film). This tax or subsidy would be equal to the cross marginal term in the equations. As a result, divisions with cross-elasticity of demand would still be motivated to use marginal costing.

13.A.9   Cost Dependence

Cost dependence is also more critical and common in horizontal integration than vertical integration. It is usually the effect of expanded or decreased operations on the price of common factors of two divisions. The interrelationship then concerns not only the external market, but also the internal production process. Obviously, management must decide on the optimal output of the divisions for the firm as a whole.

13.A.10   Limitations of Economic Analysis

In addition to the stated constraints in each situation that has been described, our economic analysis has assumed the model was static. This means we were concerned with a particular market situation at only one point in time. Changes in such factors as price discrimination over time were ignored. The models were also assumed to have linear production: The inputs of each of the buying and selling divisions were considered to be inputs of the final product.

Economic analysis of transfer pricing within a divisionalized firm is a complicated procedure, even in the simplest context. In our limited analysis, a two-division, vertically integrated firm—with no demand or cost dependencies, operating in a perfectly competitive, external intermediate market where the internal and external intermediate prices are the same—can use the market price for its optimal transfer price. Otherwise, a neutral umpire is needed to insure the optimal output for the firm.

Finally, the analyses provided by Hirschleifer and Gould demonstrate the existence of a transfer price along the marginal cost curve, but they fail to suggest an operational method of implementation.[39] Furthermore, the interpretation of marginal cost differs between economics and accounting. A. Rashad Abdel-Khalik and E. J. Lusk note:

> In summary, Hirschleifer suggests as a transfer pricing rule: price along the marginal cost curve. Hirschleifer has used the term 'marginal cost' in the context of economic theory, i.e., the additional cost of producing an additional unit where cost includes return to all factors of production including capital. In accounting, marginal cost has a different connotation; it is equated with the variable cost of producing one additional unit. Thus, pricing at the accounting marginal cost would not recover investments in fixed assets or returns to capital. Therefore, if the Hirschleifer system is to be implemented, modifications to the information generated by the accounting system become necessary.[40]

Joshua Ronen and George McKinney III feel Hirschleifer's analysis left three problems unanswered: (1) The apparent contribution of the divisions will not reflect the actual contribution to the firm's profits and, therefore, cannot be used for continuance-abandonment decisions; (2) Hirschleifer's system of transfer prices can be applied only after the firm's market situation has been determined, so the optimal transfer prices are contingent upon the specific environment; and (3) while Hirschleifer's rules are technically correct, they are not fully consistent with the decision making autonomy of the individual division managers.[41]

13.B   APPENDIX: OPERATIONS RESEARCH SOLUTION TO TRANSFER PRICING

The value of mathematical programming in the determination of transfer prices lies mainly in the information extracted from the shadow prices produced by various mod-

---

[39] Ronen and McKinney extend Hirschleifer's analysis and suggest a system for channeling information between divisions and headquarters so Hirschleifer's model can be implemented while maintaining divisional autonomy. See Ronen and McKinney, "Transfer Pricing," pp. 99–112.

[40] A. Rashad Abdel-Khalik and E. J. Lusk, "Transfer Pricing: A Synthesis," *Accounting Review* (January 1974), p. 13.

[41] Ronen and McKinney, "Transfer Pricing," pp. 99–112.

els. The shadow prices provide a measure of opportunity costs internal to the organization and are believed to be the most realistic measure of internal pricing for transactions between divisions. However, if market prices exist for the goods or services that are sold or bought, these are the most effective transfer prices. This is due to the fact that market prices best reflect opportunity costs and provide ideal conditions for the use of income figures as a control and evaluation device. The required competitive market is rare, however, and this unavailability of an adequate market price has prompted companies to use mathematical programming.

The basic mathematical programming approach is to design a system whereby all managers of a product or activity acting in their own interests also achieve the most profitable operation for the company as a whole.[42] Standard linear programming models are commonly applied to resource allocation problems, although they require a considerable amount of centralization. Based on the Dantzig and Wolfe decomposition principle, many decomposition programs have been established to decentralize the mathematical program.[43] The method essentially establishes a basis for negotiation between corporate headquarters and its divisions while eliminating the necessity for direct interdivisional communication. As pointed out earlier, this is in itself an advantage of the decomposition principle, because negotiations between division managers can lead to personal conflict detrimental to the company as a whole.

The decomposition programming model (DPM) will be illustrated primarily through a linear program to show how the procedure is used to attain a system of transfer prices. Mathematical expressions will be used only to clarify certain crucial aspects of the solution.

13.B.1   *Decomposition Programming Model*

The decomposition programming method can appropriately be called a *model* because its makeup can be adjusted as the user attempts to best approach reality. An explanation of the model's basic procedures will be followed by a discussion of its advantages and disadvantages.

Basic Structure
The structure of a DPM essentially represents a decentralized decision making process, because it decomposes into what can be regarded as separate problems.[44] A schematic model of the structure is presented in Figure 13.12. Each of the divisional constraint blocks (A_1 through A_n) represents a multiplicity of constraints corresponding to resource or input capacities (C_1 through C_n). In other words, each divisional constraint block (A_1 through A_n) can be seen as a matrix with a corresponding column vector of capacity (C_i). The corporate constraints are interpreted similarly to the divisional constraints, with one exception: The divisional constraints contain only data that are applicable solely to their own division. The corporate constraints, however, are in effect linking constraints, for they include resources that are not exclusively for use in a particular division. (This characteristic will be elaborated upon later in this appendix.) The objective function is an overall objective function containing the unit prices of all outputs in the organization.

---

[42] J. M. Samuels, "Opportunity Costing: An Application of Mathematical Programming," *Journal of Accounting Research* (Autumn 1965), pp. 182–191.

[43] G. B. Dantzig and P. Wolfe, "Decomposition Principle for Linear Programs," *Operations Research* (January–February 1960), pp. 101–111.

[44] W. Baumol and T. Fabian, "Decomposition, Pricing of Decentralization and External Economies," *Management Science* (Spring 1964), pp. 1–31.

Figure 13.12 Basic Structure of the Decomposition Programming Model

Objective Function:	P	
Corporate Constraints:	A_0	$\leq C_0$
	A_1	$\leq C_1$
Divisional Constraints:	A_2	$\leq C_2$
	A_n	$\leq C_n$

Figure 13.13 Basic Structure of the Decomposition Programming Model

Objective Function: $\text{Max. } P = p_1x_1 + p_2x_2 + p_3x_3 + p_4x_4.$
Subject to

Corporate Constraints:	$a_{11}x_1 + a_{12}x_2 + a_{13}x_3 + a_{14}x_4$	$\leq C_0.$
Division 1:	$a_{21}x_1 + a_{22}x_2$	$\leq C_1.$
	$a_{31}x_1 + a_{32}x_2$	$\leq C_2.$
Division 2:	$a_{43}x_3 + a_{44}x_4$	$\leq C_3.$
	$a_{53}x_3 + a_{54}x_4$	$\leq C_4.$
	All $x_i \geq 0.$	

Figure 13.14 Divisional Programs (Subprograms)

Division 1	Division 2
$\text{Max. } P^1 = p_1x_1 + p_2x_2.$	$\text{Max. } P^2 = p_3x_3 + p_4x_4.$
Subject to	Subject to
$a_{21}x_1 + a_{22}x_2 \leq C_1.$	$a_{43}x_3 + a_{44}x_4 \leq C_3.$
$a_{31}x_1 + a_{32}x_2 \leq C_2.$	$a_{53}x_3 + a_{54}x_4 \leq C_4.$
$x_1, x_2 \geq 0.$	$x_3, x_4 \geq 0.$

Figure 13.13 shows an example of the basic structure of the DPM for a company with two divisions with two outputs each. The corporate constraints are restricted to one for illustrative simplicity only. The variables are defined as follows:

P = Total company profit to be maximized.

p_j = Per-unit profit of output j (j = 1, 2, 3, 4).

a_{ij} = Amount of input i required to produce 1 unit of output j.

C_0 = Corporate resource capacity required by both divisions.

C_{is0} = Divisional resource limits.

X_j = Potential output j of divisions 1 + 2 (j = 1, 2, 3, 4).

Figure 13.14 shows the divisional programs for this example, which can be seen as independent programs for each division.

In decomposition programming, the DPM is divided into two programs. The already mentioned *divisional programs* are standard programs and need not be discussed further. The *executive program*, which is solved by corporate headquarters, will be discussed in detail.

Decomposition Procedure

Like the structure of the DPM, the basic decomposition procedure remains essentially the same regardless of the model's composition. The general procedure is as follows:

1. Every division is asked to submit an optimal plan of operations based on a unit profit figure assigned by the company for each product and based on each division's constraints, resources, and objectives.

2. Top management computes the impact of each division's activities on the other divisions' profit, in terms of how much benefit (external economy) or cost (external diseconomy) the activities of each division create for all other divisions.

3. Top management adds to each division's unit profit (a) a subsidy, for those activities leading to external economies, or (b) a tax, for those activities leading to external diseconomies. These subsidies and taxes are based on each division's initial plans.

4. As a result of the new inputs to their income statements, divisions submit new plans based on the objective of increasing their own divisional profit.

5. The entire process is repeated a number of times until the solution reached is the same optimal solution that would have been reached by solving the decomposed problem as one big linear programming problem (by using the simplex algorithm only once).

For a technical presentation of the procedure, the reader is directed to articles in the Selected Readings by W. Baumol and T. Fabian, and by J. E. Hass.

13.B.2   Evaluation of the Method

The major advantages and disadvantages of the decomposition programming method arise from the procedure itself. First, the divisional constraints are not included in the executive program. This greatly enhances the manageability of the computations and allows the programming of large problems, which would be cumbersome using a standard linear program. Second, the decomposition programming method provides a systematic basis for the calculation of bonuses and penalties. This is perhaps the most beneficial aspect of the method. Because the calculations are explicit (assuming the program is accepted by all concerned), the method may result in less conflict and be more acceptable to division managers. This is because the division managers have contributed to its calculation by proposing the various solutions from the programs they established. Third, the decomposition programming method has the advantage over other programming methods of being adaptable to a decentralized firm. The program can also be altered to encompass changing conditions. While another iteration is being performed, temporary production plans can be established that will not alter the situation drastically, provided the existing transfer prices are near optimal.

Unfortunately, the decomposition programming method is not without drawbacks. First, it relies on the ability of programmers to represent the existing conditions mathematically in the program. Division managers may purposely specify inaccurate data in their constraints (the output vectors) to gain more control over the allocation of scarce resources. The iterative process takes time, which managers in both headquarters and divisions may feel is unwarranted. The costs of gathering and processing appropriate data will also increase using the DPM. The complexity necessary in a program that represents the real situation may result in firms preferring to adopt much simpler approaches.

The DPM should be evaluated according to the three criteria: goal congruence, performance evaluation, and autonomy.

Goal Congruence

The possibility of specifying inaccurate output data, as has been mentioned, will result in goal incongruence. The decomposition programming method, while obtaining an optimal allocation of scarce resources, does not guarantee that the division managers will adhere to the optimal plan. Goal incongruence will occur, therefore, if the division managers are not motivated toward the achievement of the optimal corporate plan. Essentially, goal incongruence results from a behavioral problem.

Performance Evaluation

The measurement of the division managers' performance can be changed from one of profit maximization to a measurement of their ability to follow the optimal plan. This will have the effect of encouraging division managers to strive for overall profit maximization, thus decreasing interdivisional competition. A satisfactory reward system designed with this goal in mind could be quite beneficial.

Autonomy

Most criticism of the operations research method is based on the criterion of autonomy. Although division managers are responsible for their subprograms, the output decisions are made and enforced by top management. In this sense, divisional autonomy can be seen as artificial.

13.B.3   Conclusion

Like the other proposed solutions to the transfer pricing problem, the operations research solution is not without its share of problems. However, it does offer a viable approach to transfer pricing that cannot be disregarded. As the degree of sophistication of programming techniques continues to increase, the future prospects of operations research may improve greatly.

GLOSSARY

Centralization Departmentalization by function.

Cost Center An organizational unit used for collecting, organizing, and categorizing costs.

Decentralization A series of organizational units, or divisions, responsible for a specific product market under the direction of a manager having strategic and operating decision prerogatives.

Investment Center An organizational unit accountable for its rate of return on investment.

Investment Turnover Sales divided by invested capital.

Profit Center An organizational unit accountable for both its controllable costs and revenues.

Profit Margin Net income divided by sales.

Rate of Return on Investment (ROI) An indicator portraying the relationship of profit to invested capital.

Residual Income Divisional income in excess of a prescribed interest on investment.

Suboptimization A decision that increases current divisional profit but limits the company profit as a whole.

Transfer Price The price charged for goods and services sold by one organizational unit to another in the same company.

SELECTED READINGS

Abdel-Khalik, A. Rashad, and Lusk, E. J., "Transfer Pricing: A Synthesis," *Accounting Review* (January 1974), pp. 9–23.

Anthony, Robert N., and Dearden, J., *Management Control Systems*, 3d ed. (Homewood, Ill.: Irwin, 1976), chaps. 6–7.

Baumol, W., and Fabian, T., "Decomposition, Pricing of Decentralization and External Economies," *Management Science* (Spring 1964), pp. 1–32.

Benke, Ralph L.; Gibbs, Thomas E.; and Schroeder, Richard G., "Should You Use Transfer Pricing to Create Pseudo-Profit Centers?" *Management Accounting* (February 1979), pp. 29–34.

Berkwitt, G. J., "Do Profit Centres Really Work?" *Management Review* (August 1969), pp. 15–20.

Bernhard, R. H., "Some Problems in Applying Mathematical Programming to Opportunity Costing," *Journal of Accounting Research* (Spring 1968), pp. 143–148.

Bierman, H., "Pricing Intercompany Transfers," *Accounting Review* (July 1959), pp. 429–432.

Bierman, H., and Dyckman, T. R., *Managerial Cost Accounting*, 2d ed. (New York: Macmillan, 1976), chap. 19.

Cowen, Scott S.; Phillips, Lawrence C.; and Stillabower, Linda, "Multinational Transfer Pricing," *Management Accounting* (January 1979), pp. 17–22.

Dantzig, G. B., and Wolfe, P., "Decomposition Principle for Linear Programs," *Operations Research* (January–February 1960), pp. 101–111.

Dearden, J., "Interdivisional Pricing," *Harvard Business Review* (January–February 1960), pp. 117–125.

Dopuch, Nicholas, and Drake, D. F., "Accounting Implications of a Mathematical Programming Approach to the Transfer Price Problem," *Journal of Accounting Research* (Spring 1964), pp. 10–21.

Fremgen, James M., "Transfer Pricing and Management Goals," *Management Accounting* (December 1970), pp. 25–31.

Goetz, B. E., "Transfer Prices: An Exercise in Relevancy and Goal Congruence," *Accounting Review* (July 1967), pp. 435–440.

Gordon, Myron J., "A Method of Pricing for a Socialist Economy," *Accounting Review* (July 1970), pp. 427–443.

Hass, J. E., "Transfer Pricing in a Decentralized Firm," *Management Science* (February 1968), pp. B-310, B-333.

Hirschleifer, Jack, "Economics of the Divisionalized Firm," *Journal of Business* (April 1957), pp. 96–108.

Hirschleifer, Jack, "On the Economics of Transfer Pricing," *Journal of Business* (January 1956), pp. 172–184.

Jennergren, P., "Decentralization on the Basis of Price Schedules in Linear Decomposable Resource-Allocation Problems," *Journal of Financial and Quantitative Analysis* (January 1972), pp. 1407–1417.

Lucien, Kent, "Transfer Pricing for the Cost of Funds in a Commercial Bank," *Management Accounting* (January 1979), pp. 23–24.

Lusch, Robert F., and Bentz, William F., "A Variance Approach to Analyzing Changes in Return on Investment," *Management Accounting* (February 1979), pp. 29–33.

Madison, Roland L., "Responsibility Accounting and Transfer Pricing: Approach with Caution," *Management Accounting* (January 1979), pp. 25–29.

Onsi, M., "A Transfer Pricing System Based on Opportunity Cost," *Accounting Review* (July 1970), pp. 535–543.

Ronen, Joshua, and McKinney, George III, "Transfer Pricing for Divisional Autonomy," *Journal of Accounting Research* (Spring 1970), pp. 99–112.

Samuels, J. M., "Opportunity Costing: An Application of Mathematical Programming," *Journal of Accounting Research* (Autumn 1965), pp. 182–191.

Sharav, I., "Transfer Pricing, Diversity of Goals and Practices," *Journal of Accountancy* (April 1974), pp. 56–62.

Shubik, Martin, "Incentives, Decentralized Control: The Assignment of Joint Costs and Internal Pricing," in *Management Controls: New Directions in Basic Research*, eds. C. P. Bonini, R. K. Jaedicke, and H. M. Wagner (New York: McGraw-Hill, 1964), pp. 205–225.

Solomons, David, *Divisional Performance: Measurement and Control* (New York: Financial Executives Research Foundation, 1965).

Tang, Roger W., *Transfer Pricing Practices in the United States and Japan* (New York: Praeger, 1979).

Van Horne, J. C., *Financial Management and Policy*, 3d ed. (Englewood Cliffs, N.J.: Prentice-Hall, 1974), chap. 24.

Walker, W. E., "A Method for Obtaining the Optimal Dual Solution to a Linear Program Using the Dantzig-Wolfe Decomposition," *Operations Research* (March–April 1969), pp. 368–370.

Watson, D. J. H., and Baumler, J. V., "Transfer Pricing: A Behavioral Context," *Accounting Review* (July 1975), pp. 466–474.

Whinston, A., "Pricing Guides in Decentralized Organizations," in *New Perspectives in Organizational Research*, eds. W. W. Cooper et al. (New York: Wiley, 1964), chap. 22, pp. 411–417.

Whisler, T. L.; Meyer, H.; Baum, B. H.; and Sorenson, P. F., "Centralization of Control: An Empirical Study of Its Meaning and Measurement," *Journal of Business* (January 1970), pp. 10–26.

QUESTIONS, EXERCISES, AND PROBLEMS

13.1   Differentiate between a cost center, a profit center, and an investment center.

13.2   List some of the mechanisms that can be used to reach a trade-off between integration and differentiation in a decentralized firm.

13.3   In a review of the economic models of transfer pricing, what doubts may arise concerning the validity of the underlying assumptions and the adequacy of the prescribed procedures?

13.4   Contrast the economic model approach to transfer pricing with the mathematical programming approach.

13.5   ***Return on Net Worth as a Tool of Management Control***   A common measure of management's performance is *return on net worth*. This ratio is particularly important from the shareholder's point of view. It can be expressed as the product of three other ratios:

$$\frac{\text{Return on}}{\text{net worth}} = \frac{\text{Net income}}{\text{Net worth}} = \underset{[1]}{\frac{\text{Net income}}{\text{Sales}}} \times \underset{[2]}{\frac{\text{Sales}}{\text{Assets}}} \times \underset{[3]}{\frac{\text{Assets}}{\text{Net worth}}} \ .$$

Required:

1. Discuss the return on net worth as a management goal and as a measurement of management performance.

2. What management activities are measured by each of ratios 1, 2, and 3?

3. Would a separation of the return on net worth into the three ratios and the use of these ratios for planning targets and performance measures result in goal congruence (or improvement towards goal congruence) among the responsible managers? Explain your answer.

(CMA adapted)

13.6   Answer the following *independent* questions relating to decentralization:

1. Decentralization is likely to be most beneficial and least costly when the organizational units are independent. Name three criteria that should be met in order that a subunit can achieve complete independence.

2. A commonly used technique for measuring performance in a decentralized environment is the ROI method. Explain in terms of *margin* and *turnover* how a supermarket division with an average markup of 15 percent and a jewelry division with an average markup of 100 percent within the same conglomerate can achieve approximately the same ROI.

3. Name and briefly discuss three possible bases for computing the cost of invested capital.

4. Name and briefly discuss three basic methods for the control of internal operations.

(SMA adapted)

13.7   When we speak of decentralization with respect to organizations we are concerned not with physical dispersion of operations or personnel, but rather with the degree of dispersion of decision making within the organization.

Required:
Briefly discuss the benefits and costs of decentralization.

13.8   An important cost accounting concept is *responsibility accounting*.

Required:
1. Define the term *responsibility accounting*.

2. What conditions must exist for there to be effective responsibility accounting?

3. What benefits are said to result from responsibility accounting?

4. The following are three charges found in the monthly report of a division that manufactures and sells products primarily to outside companies. Divisional performance is evaluated by the ROI method. You are to state which, if any, of the following charges are consistent with the responsibility accounting concept. Support each answer with a brief explanation.

   a. A charge for general corporation administration at 10 percent of divisional sales.
   b. A charge for the use of the corporate computer facility. This charge is determined by taking actual annual computer department costs and allocating an amount to each user according to the ratio of its use to total corporation use.
   c. A charge for goods purchased from another division. This charge is based on the competitive market price for the goods.

(CMA adapted)

13.9   *Performance Evaluation Using ROI and Residual Income*   You are asked to compare the following two ventures:

	Venture A	Venture B
Capital Invested	$1,000	$5,000
Net Annual Return	200	750

Required:
1. Compute the ROI for each venture.

2. Compute the residual income for each venture assuming first that the cost of capital is 17½ percent and, second, that the cost of capital is 12 percent.

3. Which is the more successful venture?

(Adapted with permission from David Solomons, *Divisional Performance: Measurement and Control*, New York: Financial Executives Research Foundation, 1965.)

13.10   In the last two decades there has been a distinct tendency toward corporate decentralization. This has usually been accompanied by the establishment of profit centers and investment centers along with ROI objectives for corporate divisions.

Required:

1. Distinguish between cost, profit, and investment centers, and provide an example of each.

2. Three criteria are believed to be helpful for designing or evaluating a particular accounting system in a decentralized environment. What are they? Why are they important? From a behavioral point of view, how are they interrelated? Explain.

3. The ROI and its variants are acclaimed as management control devices for evaluating the performance of division managers. However, due to conceptual, measurement, and implementation problems, the ROI method has severe limitations. Briefly discuss the major problems and limitations of using the ROI.

13.11   In the evaluation of divisional performance in a decentralized environment, a number of approaches can be used, including the ROI and the residual income methods.

Required:

1. Discuss in point form the advantages and disadvantages of the ROI and residual income methods.

2. Discuss the advantages and disadvantages of using gross assets and net book values as investment bases in computing the ROI.

3. The ROI is basically a conventional accounting technique. Why are discounted cash flow techniques not used in performance evaluation?

(SMA adapted)

13.12   ***Appropriate Transfer Price Determination***   The Brown Motors Company has two major production divisions—parts and assembly—each of which is completely decentralized. The transfer price for the intermediate product of the parts division to the assembly division has been negotiated at $200. Both the intermediate and the final products have ready competitive markets. The final product currently is sold at $310 in the market; the variable costs are $135 and $150 in the parts and final assembly divisions, respectively.

Required:

1. If there is no excess capacity in the parts division, should transfers to the assembly division be made? If so, what would be the appropriate transfer price?

2. If the parts division has a maximum capacity of 1,200 units per month, and if sales to outsiders are not expected to exceed 1,000 units per month, should an excess over 1,000 units be produced and transferred by the parts division to the assembly division?

3. The market research department has determined that if the external price of the intermediate product were dropped to $193, all 1,200 units could be sold externally. Should the company reduce the selling price of its intermediate product? Show all calculations.

(SMA adapted)

13.13   ***Nature of Responsibility Accounting***   In recent years the distribution expenses of the Avey Company have increased more than other expenditures. To achieve more effective control, the company plans to provide the local managers with an income statement for their territory showing monthly and year-to-date amounts for the current and the previous year. Each sales office is supervised by a local manager, sales orders are forwarded to the main office and filled from a central warehouse, and billing and collections are also centrally processed. Expenses are first classified by function and then allocated to each territory in the following ways:

Function	Basis
Sales Salaries	Actual
Other Selling Expenses	Relative Sales Dollars
Warehousing	Relative Sales Dollars
Packing and Shipping	Weight of Package
Billing and Collections	Number of Billings
General Administration	Equally

Required:

1. a. Explain responsibility accounting and the classification of revenues and expenses under this concept.

b. What are the objectives of profit analysis by sales territories in income statements?

2. a. Discuss the effectiveness of the Avey Company's comparative income statements by sales territories as a tool for planning and control. Include in your discussion additional factors that should be considered and changes that may be desirable for effective planning by management and evaluation of the local sales managers.

b. Compare the degree of control that can be achieved over production costs and distribution costs, and explain why the degree of control differs.

c. Criticize the Avey Company's allocation and/or inclusion of other selling expenses, warehousing expense, and general administration expense.

(AICPA adapted)

13.14   ***ROI and Residual Income***   The following information is available:

	X Division	Y Division
Total Assets	$25,000	$125,000
Net Annual Earnings	5,000	18,750

The cost of capital for each division is 12 percent.

Required:

1. Using the ROI as a measure of management success, which is the more successful division? Why?

2. Using residual income as a measure of management success, which is the more successful division? Why?

(SMA adapted)

13.15   ***Limitations of ROI as a Measure of Performance***   You have been assigned the task of resolving a dispute between two divisional general managers of the Span Company. Span is a large company with highly decentralized decision making, and each division is treated as a profit center. The divisional general managers receive a substantial part of their remuneration in the form of a bonus based on the ROI of their divisions. Each manager is free to purchase and sell outside the company. However, over the years buying divisions traditionally have purchased within the company when possible. Selling divisions have always given a high priority to meeting intracompany orders, and many selling divisions have set aside substantial proportions of capacity (over 50 percent in many cases) to meet the needs of the buying divisions.

Each fall the divisional general managers meet with the president to discuss profit plans and to confirm interdivisional transfers of goods for the next year. The president is concerned about the growing volume of these internal transfers as a potential area of disputes among the divisional general managers.

At the current annual profit plan discussions there was a dispute between the divisional general managers of the lumber and furniture divisions. For the past four years, over 60 percent of the lumber division's output has been sold to the furniture division, with the balance sold to outsiders. Last year's operating data for the lumber division shows this relationship:

	Lumber Division To Furniture Division	To Outsiders
Sales		
5,000 Thousand Board Feet (TBF) @ $115 per TBF[a]	$575,000	
3,000 TBF @ $125 per TBF		$375,000
Variable Costs at $75 per TBF	375,000	225,000
	$200,000	$150,000
Fixed Costs	150,000	90,000
Gross Profit	$ 50,000	$ 60,000

[a]This price is based on market price less an allowance for selling and administrative costs normally incurred on outside sales.

The furniture division's general manager can purchase requirements for next year outside the company at a price of $105 per thousand board feet and refuses to pay a higher price to the lumber division. The lumber division's general manager, who cannot sell the 5,000 board feet elsewhere, states that if the lumber division sells material to the furniture division at $105 per thousand board feet, there will be no gross profit for the lumber division. In addition, the lumber division's capacity has been increased over the years to insure a steady supply for the furniture division's requirements.

Required:

1. Recommend to the president whether or not the furniture division should continue to purchase material from the lumber division. Support your recommendation with appropriate figures to the extent possible.

2. Discuss briefly the limitations of using ROI for the evaluation of the divisional general managers in this situation. What changes in the bonus system and/or the organization would you recommend to avoid or minimize future conflicts over internal prices?

(SMA adapted)

13.16   *Using ROI to Measure Divisional Performance*   T Limited consists of five operating divisions located throughout the country and a central corporate office. Each operating division produces and markets its own line of products and sells the product lines of other divisions within its region of the country. Each division prepares its own financial statements, and its manager is evaluated on the basis of the division's ROI. Since this system was started, the division's investment figure used in the calculation has included all the assets controlled by each division manager. Until last year, the investment figure of each division did not include two classes of assets: its headquarters's assets and research department's assets. The associated headquarters and research expenses were not included in the calculation of the ROI. The headquarters' assets were not material (2 percent of the company's total assets), since most of the headquarters' facilities were rented. Until recently, research assets also had been small, but by the spring of 19X5 they had grown to just over 10 percent of the company's total assets. It was expected that more funds would be invested in research facilities in the near future.

In late 19X5, the president of T Limited suggested that all the company's assets be distributed in some way to all the operating divisions. This, she stated, would make the reported ROI by the divisions more realistic indicators of how well the company was doing as a whole.

Required:
1. Outline the arguments for and against using ROI to measure divisional performance.
2. Evaluate the suggestion made by the president of T Limited.

(CICA adapted)

13.17   ***Transfer Pricing: Should Top Management Interfere?***   Recently there have been large quantities of shirt imports to Canada from the Far East, where the cost of labor is substantially lower. The sales division of a company now finds that at an imported cost of only $3.75 it can supply the Canadian market with shirts of its normal quality. Therefore, it wishes to purchase externally. The fixed costs of the manufacturing division will not change with a change in volume. The sales division's annual purchase is 150,000 shirts, and the manufacturing division's cost of producing a shirt is $4, consisting of a $3.25 variable cost and a $.75 fixed cost.

Required:
1. If the manufacturing division's facilities can be used for another contract that will generate a contribution margin of $50,000 per annum, will the company as a whole benefit from having its sales division purchase its shirt requirements from the external source?
2. Determine the appropriate transfer price, and state your reasons for choosing this price.
3. If the manufacturing division insists on charging $4.25 and the sales division wishes to purchase the shirts elsewhere, what factors should top management consider when deciding whether to interfere and impose a final decision?

(SMA adapted)

13.18   ***Performance Evaluation***   George Johnson was hired on July 1, 19A9, as assistant general manager of the Botel division of Staple, Inc. It was understood that he would be promoted to general manager of the division on January 1, 19B1, when its general manager would retire, and this was duly done. In addition to becoming acquainted with the division and the general manager's duties, Johnson was charged with the specific responsibility for developing the 19B0 and 19B1 budgets. As general manager in 19B1 he was, obviously, responsible for the 19B2 budget.

Staple, Inc., is a multiproduct company that is highly decentralized. Each division is quite autonomous. The corporate staff approves division-prepared operating budgets but seldom makes major changes in them. The corporate staff actively participates in decisions requiring capital investment (for expansion or replacement) and makes the final decisions. The divisional management is responsible for implementing the capital program. The major method used by Staple, Inc., to measure divisional performance is contribution return on division net investment. The budgets presented in Table 1 were approved by the corporation. Revision of the 19B2 budget is not considered necessary, even though the 19B1 actual departed from the 19B1 approved budget.

Table 1   **Botel Division (000 Omitted)**

Accounts	Actual 19A9	Actual 19B0	Actual 19B1	Budget 19B1	Budget 19B2
Sales	$1,000	$1,500	$1,800	$2,000	$2,400
Less: Division Variable Costs					
Material and Labor	250	375	450	500	600
Repairs	50	75	50	100	120
Supplies	20	30	36	40	48
Less: Division Managed Costs					
Employee Training	30	35	25	40	45
Maintenance	50	55	40	60	70
Less: Division Committed Costs					
Depreciation	120	160	160	200	200
Rent	80	100	110	140	140
Total	600	830	871	1,080	1,223
Division Net Contribution	400	670	929	920	1,177
Division Investment					
Accounts Receivable	100	150	180	200	240
Inventory	200	300	270	400	480
Fixed Assets	1,590	2,565	2,800	3,380	4,000
Less: Accounts and Wages Payable	(150)	(225)	(350)	(300)	(360)
Net Investment	$1,740	$2,790	$2,900	$3,680	$4,360
Contribution Return on Net Investment	23%	24%	32%	25%	27%

Required:

1. Identify Johnson's responsibilities under the management and measurement program described.

2. Appraise Johnson's performance in 19B1.

3. Recommend to the president any changes in the responsibilities assigned to managers or in the measurement methods used to evaluate divisional management you would make based on your analysis.

(CMA adapted)

13.19   ***Correct and Relevant Transfer Price***   The H & B Works has two divisions: hull and boat divisions. The company has markets for both the hulls (without sails) and the boats (complete with spars and sails). The divisions have been delegated profit responsibility, and the transfer price for hulls has been set at the long-run average market price.
    The following data are available:

Selling Price for Complete Boats	$3,000
Long-Run Average Selling Price for Hulls	2,600
Variable Cost for Completion in the Boat Division	500
Variable Cost for Completion in the Hull Division	1,700

Required:

1. If the hull division has no excess capacity, should it make transfers to the boat division? Is market price the correct transfer price? Explain your reasoning and show your calculations.

2. Assume that the hull division's maximum capacity is 1,000 units, and sales to the intermediate market are now 800 units. Should the hull division transfer 200 hulls to the boat division? At what relevant transfer price? Explain your reasoning and show your calculations.

(SMA adapted)

13.20   ***Transfer Pricing and Performance Evaluation***   A. R. Oma, Inc., manufactures a line of men's perfumes and after-shave lotions. The manufacturing process is basically a series of mixing operations with the addition of certain aromatic and coloring ingredients. The finished product is packaged in a company-produced glass bottle and packed in cases containing six bottles.

A. R. Oma feels that the sale of its product is heavily influenced by the appearance and appeal of the bottle. It has devoted considerable managerial effort to the bottle production process, which has resulted in the development of unique production processes in which management takes considerable pride.

The areas of perfume production and bottle manufacture have evolved over the years in an almost independent manner; in fact, a rivalry has developed between management personnel as to "which division is the more important to A. R. Oma." This attitude is probably intensified because the bottle manufacturing plant was purchased intact ten years ago, and no real interchange of management personnel or ideas has taken place (except at the top corporate level). Since the acquisition, all bottle production has been absorbed by the perfume manufacturing plant. Each area is considered a separate profit center and is evaluated as such.

As the new corporate controller, you are responsible for the definition of a proper transfer value to use in crediting the bottle production profit center and in debiting the packaging profit center. At your request, the bottle division's general manager has asked other bottle manufacturers to quote a price for the quantity and sizes demanded by the perfume division. These competitive prices follow:

Volume (in Equivalent Cases[a])	Total Price	Price per Case
2,000,000	$ 4,000,000	$2.00
4,000,000	7,000,000	1.75
6,000,000	10,000,000	1.67

[a] An *equivalent case* represents six bottles each.

A cost analysis of the internal bottle plant indicates that it can produce bottles at these costs:

Volume (in Equivalent Cases)	Total Price	Cost per Case
2,000,000	$3,200,000	$1.60
4,000,000	5,200,000	1.30
6,000,000	7,200,000	1.20

Your cost analysts point out that these costs represent fixed costs of $1,200,000 and variable costs of $1 per equivalent case.

These figures have given rise to considerable corporate discussion as to the proper value to use in the transfer of bottles to the perfume division. Interest is heightened because a significant portion of a division manager's income is an incentive bonus based on profit center results.

Volume	Total Price	Cost per Case
2,000,000 Cases	$16,400,000	$8.20
4,000,000	32,400,000	8.10
6,000,000	48,400,000	8.07

After considerable analysis, the marketing research department has furnished you with the following price/demand relationship for the finished product:

Sales Volume	Total Sales Revenue	Sales Price per Case
2,000,000 Cases	$25,000,000	$12.50
4,000,000	45,600,000	11.40
6,000,000	63,900,000	10.65

Required:

1. A. R. Oma has used market price transfer prices in the past. Using the current market prices and costs and assuming a volume of 6,000,000 cases, calculate the income for
   a. The bottle division.   **c.** The corporation.
   b. The perfume division.

2. Is this production and sales level the most profitable volume for
   a. The bottle division? (Explain your answer.)
   b. The perfume division? (Explain your answer.)
   c. The corporation? (Explain your answer.)

3. A. R. Oma uses the profit center concept for divisional operation.
   a. Define a profit center.
   b. What conditions should exist for a profit center to be established?
   c. Should the two divisions of A. R. Oma be organized as profit centers?

(CMA adapted)

13.21   ***Determination of the Appropriate Transfer Price***   Automobiles Canada is heavily decentralized, and each divisional vice-president has complete authority in setting transfer prices and making sales to external and internal customers. The Zany division has typically acquired automatic voltage regulators (AVRs) from the electrode division. Recently, however, with the entry of a new competitor in the field, the market price of AVRs dropped from $8.20 to $7.40 per unit. Since the electrode division's price of $8 exceeded the prevailing market price, Zany notified the electrode division of its intention to acquire AVRs from an outside supplier.

You are provided the following information. Zany's annual purchases of AVRs total 100,000 units. The electrode division's costs of producing AVRs follows:

Variable Cost per Unit	$7.00
Fixed Cost per Unit	0.80
Total Cost per Unit	$7.80

The electrode division's fixed costs are unavoidable.

Required:

1. Prepare an analysis to determine whether or not it would be in the best interests of Automobiles Canada if Zany acquired the AVRs from an external supplier.

   a. Assuming that the electrode division's facilities would be idle. Submit your calculations.

   b. Assuming that the electrode division's facilities would be used to manufacture resistors, resulting in cash savings of $35,000 per year. Submit your calculations.

2. Determine the appropriate transfer price under each of these assumptions, and justify your answers.

(SMA adapted)

13.22   ***Decentralized Decision Making***   The Ajax division of Cunnco Corporation, operating at capacity, has been asked by the Defco division of Cunnco to supply it with electrical fitting 1726. Ajax sells this part to its regular customers for $7.50 each. Defco, which is operating at 50 percent capacity, is willing to pay $5 each for the fitting. Defco will put the fitting into a brake unit that it is manufacturing on essentially a cost-plus basis for a commercial airplane manufacturer.

   Ajax has a variable cost of producing fitting 1726 of $4.25. The cost of the brake unit being built by Defco is as follows:

Purchased Parts—Outside Vendors	$22.50
Ajax Fitting 1726	5.00
Other Variable Costs	14.00
Fixed Overhead and Administration	8.00
	$49.50

Defco believes the price concession is necessary to get the job. The company uses return on investment and dollar profits in the measurement of division and division manager performance.

Required:

1. Assume you are the divisional controller of Ajax. Would you recommend that Ajax supply fitting 1726 to Defco? (Ignore any income tax issues.) Why or why not?

2. Would it be to the short-run economic advantage of the Cunnco Corporation for the Ajax division to supply the Defco division with fitting 1726 at $5 each? (Ignore any income tax issues.) Explain your answer.

3. Discuss the organizational and managerial behavior difficulties, if any, inherent in this situation. As the Cunnco controller, what would you advise the Cunnco Corporation president do in this situation?

(CMA adapted)

13.23   ***Transfer Pricing and Performance Evaluation***   North Star Guns is a high-technology enterprise making sophisticated products for the armaments market. North Star is made up of two independent profit centers: North Star Armor and North Star Engineering.

   North Star Armor makes two types of tanks: Light and Heavy. Light is a lightweight tank that has a potentially unlimited market and sells for $25,000 per unit. Heavy is a highly sophisticated main battle tank that uses a special type of radar equipment imported from West Germany at a cost of $10,000 per unit.

   North Star Engineering manufactures two types of electronic guidance units: Standard and Deluxe. These units require a high degree of skill in manufacturing. However, because of a shortage of trained engineers, North Star Engineering has only one hundred

Table 2   **North Star Armor**

	Light	Heavy
Materials (Parts)	$10,000	$50,000
Labor	100 Hr. @ $10	200 Hr. @ $10
Machine Hours	100 Hr. (1 Hr. per Labor Hr.)	200 Hr. (1 Hr. per Labor Hr.)
Variable Overhead per Machine Hour	$40	$40
Market Price	$25,000	$100,000

Fixed Overhead: $1,000,000

North Star Engineering

	Standard	Deluxe
Materials (Parts)	$1,000	$4,000
Labor	10 Hr. @ $20	100 Hr. @ $20
Variable Overhead per Labor Hour	$10	$10
Market Price	$1,500	$10,000

Fixed Overhead: $1,000,000

---

skilled employees, whose total labor capacity (allowing for sickness, leaves, and so on) is expected to be 100,000 hours per year. The data for the two divisions is given in Table 2.

Standard has a potentially unlimited market, but Deluxe has only the army as a customer. North Star Engineering has a standing order for 500 Deluxe units per year from the army. The research center at the headquarters has known for some time that Deluxe could be used to replace the West German radar in Heavy. The modifications would cost only $200 per unit for the additional labor at North Star Armor. However, the complete modifications required only recently have been specified, and this data plus the labor cost has been conveyed to North Star Armor. North Star Armor has requested North Star Engineering to declare a transfer price for Deluxe.

Required:

1. North Star Armor has a current order for 100 Heavy tanks. From the overall company's (North Star Guns') viewpoint, should North Star Engineering transfer Deluxe units to North Star Armor? Show your supporting calculations.

2. The tax rate for North Star Engineering is 50 percent of net income, and the capital investment is $10,000,000. Under which of the following performance evaluation schemes would the division transfer Deluxe at a price set by headquarters of $7,000 per unit?

   a. An ROI basis.

   b. A residual income basis with a desired ROI at 12 percent of invested capital. (There are no bonuses for performance exceeding 12 percent.)

(SMA adapted)

13.24   *Transfer Pricing Dispute*   The Lorax Electric Company manufactures a large variety of systems and individual components for the electronics industry. The firm is organized into several divisions with division managers given the authority to make virtually all operating decisions. Management control over divisional operations is maintained by a system of divisional profit and ROI measures, which are reviewed regularly by top management. The top management of Lorax has been quite pleased with the effectiveness of the system they have been using and believe it is responsible for the company's improved profitability over the last few years.

The devices division manufactures solid-state devices and is operating at capacity. The systems division has asked the devices division to supply a large quantity of integrated circuits IC378. The devices division currently is selling this component to its regular customers at $40 per one hundred. The systems division, which is operating at about 60 percent capacity, wants this component for a digital clock system. It has an opportunity to supply large quantities of these digital clock systems to Centonic Electric, a major producer of clock radios and other popular electronic home entertainment equipment. This is the first opportunity any of the Lorax divisions has had to do business with Centonic Electric. Centonic Electric has offered to pay $7.50 per clock system.

The systems division prepared an analysis of the probable costs to produce the clock system. The amount that could be paid to the devices division for the integrated circuits was determined by working backward from the selling price. The cost estimates employed by the division reflect the highest per-unit cost the systems division could incur for each cost component and still leave a sufficient margin so the division's income statement could show reasonable improvement. The cost estimates are summarized here:

Proposed Selling Price		$7.50
Costs Excluding Required Integrated Circuits IC378		
Components Purchased from Outside Suppliers	$2.75	
Circuit Board Etching—Labor and Variable Overhead	0.40	
Assembly, Testing, Packaging—Labor and Variable Overhead	1.35	
Fixed Overhead Allocations	1.50	
Profit Margin	0.50	6.50
Amount That Can Be Paid for Integrated Circuits IC378 (5 @ $20 per 100)		$1.00

As a result of this analysis, the systems division offered the devices division a price of $20 per one hundred for the integrated circuit. This bid was refused by the manager of the devices division, who felt the systems division should at least meet the price of $40 per one hundred that regular customers pay. When the systems division found that it could not obtain a comparable integrated circuit from outside vendors, the situation was brought to an arbitration committee that had been set up to review such problems.

The arbitration committee prepared an analysis that showed that $.15 would cover the variable costs of producing the integrated circuit; $.28 would cover the full cost, including fixed overhead; and $.35 would provide a gross margin equal to the average gross margin on all the products sold by the devices division. The manager of the systems division reacted by stating, "They could sell us that integrated circuit for $.20 and still earn a positive contribution toward profit. In fact, they should be required to sell at their variable cost—$.15—and not be allowed to take advantage of us."

Lou Belcher, manager of the devices division, countered by arguing, "It doesn't make sense to sell to the systems division at $20 per hundred when we can get $40 per hundred outside on all we can produce. In fact, Systems could pay us up to almost $60 per hundred, and they would still have a positive contribution to profit."

The recommendation of the committee—to set the price at $.35 per unit ($35 per one hundred) so the devices division could earn a "fair" gross margin—was rejected by both division managers. Consequently, the problem was brought to the attention of the vice-president of operations and her staff.

Required:
1. What would be the immediate economic effect on the Lorax Electric Company as a whole if the devices division were required to supply IC378 to the systems division at

$.35 per unit (the price recommended by the arbitration committee)? Explain your answer.

2. Discuss the advisability of intervention by top management as a solution to transfer pricing disputes between division managers such as the one experienced by the Lorax Electric Company.

3. Suppose that Lorax adopted a policy of requiring that the price to be paid in all internal transfers by the buying division must be equal to the variable costs per unit of the supplying division for that product, and the supplying division is required to sell if the buying division decides to buy an item. Discuss the consequences of adopting such a policy as a way of avoiding the need for an arbitration committee or intervention by the vice-president.

(CMA adapted)

13.25 *Transfer Pricing: Marginal Cost Approach* The Saba Company has three divisions: Eskot, Bruno, and Carla. Eskot division produces an intermediate product, Exo, which has no market whatsoever. Bruno and Carla divisions take Exo and process it further for sale. The operations of Eskot division have no effect on the cost functions of the other two divisions. The gross revenue before deducting further processing costs for Bruno and Carla divisions at various quantities of Exo are as follows:

Bruno Division

Quantity of Exo Processed (in Gallons)	Total Gross Revenue
1,000	$ 800
2,000	1,300
3,000	1,700
4,000	2,000

Carla Division

Quantity of Exo Processed (in Gallons)	Total Gross Revenue
2,000	$1,600
3,000	2,400
4,000	2,900
5,000	3,300
6,000	3,600

Eskot division has the following cost conditions:

Eskot Division

Quantity of Exo Produced (in Gallons)	Total Cost
4,000	$2,000
5,000	2,100
6,000	2,400
7,000	2,750
8,000	3,175
9,000	3,625
10,000	4,250

The processing costs in Bruno and Carla divisions are $200 per 1,000 gallons of Exo.

Required:
Determine the transfer price of Eskot division's output in this imperfect market. Submit detailed schedules. (Hint: Use a marginal-cost-equals-marginal-revenue approach.)

(SMA adapted)

A firm maintains inventories to create flexibility in manufacturing operations and to be able to supply customers' immediate demand for products. Ideally, a firm would be able to discover and maintain the optimal level of inventory, which would allow it to avoid the costs associated with both inadequate and excessive inventories. This chapter presents formal and informal *inventory control and valuation models*. These *inventory models* include deterministic inventory control models; probabilistic inventory control models; other, less formal inventory control models; and inventory valuation models.

14.1   *DETERMINISTIC INVENTORY CONTROL MODELS*

Management constantly faces tactical decisions of what to produce or buy, when, and in what quantity. Their objective is to maintain adequate control over production and inventory levels, because efficient inventory management can lead to better planning and business control. For firms with a large proportion of capital tied up in inventories, efficient inventory management is crucial.

A firm generally attempts to balance the costs of ordering and carrying inventory and the opportunity cost of not holding inventory. Companies hold inventories (as well as maintain cash balances) for transaction, precautionary, and speculative motives. The *transaction motive* arises from the need to hold inventories to meet demand requirements arising in the ordinary course of business. The *precautionary motive* for holding inventories arises from the need to meet unexpected contingencies that could result in stockouts. Finally, the *speculative motive* is a result of the desire to take advantage of expected future price changes.

14.1.1   *Relevant Costs for Inventory Decisions*

Three costs are relevant to the problem of inventory control: the costs of ordering inventory, carrying inventory, and not carrying sufficient inventory (stockout costs or *shortage costs*). *Ordering costs* are those costs associated with placing an order with a vendor (for example, clerical and transportation costs). In a production context, ordering costs are referred to as *setup costs* (that is, machine setup and production line start-up costs).[1] Some clerical costs are difficult to measure because of the joint services provided by the employees. A multiple regression cost estimation model (presented in chapter 3) can be helpful in the measurement of some clerical costs.

Carrying costs are those costs associated with holding inventories plus a desired rate of return on the investment (ROI) in inventories. The holding costs include storage and handling costs, property taxes, and insurance and obsolescence costs. The desired ROI in inventory includes interest plus an opportunity cost of having capital tied up in inventory.

Stockout or *shortage costs* represent the opportunity loss occurring when the demand for a good exceeds the supply. Examples of shortage costs include the loss of customer goodwill, lost sales, extra setup costs to process back orders (see section 14.1.7), quantity discounts foregone, and so forth.

14.1.2   Basic EOQ Model

The economic order quantity (EOQ) model determines the order size that minimizes the inventory carrying costs and ordering costs. The stockout costs are not included in the computation of total costs because of the assumption of no stockout situation. The EOQ model is applicable to both the purchase and the production of goods.[2]

The basic principle underlying the computation of the EOQ is the insuring of a balance between the ordering costs and carrying costs of inventory. We will adopt the following notation for our discussion:

D = Annual rate of the demand for the item (in units).

Q = Order size (in units).

C_0 = Ordering cost per order.

C_c = Carrying cost per unit of average inventory.

We can express the average inventory (A) and the number of orders (N):

$$A = \frac{Q}{2}, \text{ and } N = \frac{D}{Q} .$$

The ordering costs vary proportionally to N, and the carrying costs to A. As an example, assume the Archibald Company expects a demand for 7,200 widgets per year. It has determined the ordering cost to be $20 per order and the carrying costs to be $.20 per unit per year. Assume also that the *lead time*—the interval between when an order is placed and when the order is finally received from the supplier—is zero. Both the graphic approach (Figure 14.1) and the tabular approach (Table 14.1) show that the Archibald Company should place six orders of 1,200 units for the year.

---

[1] The acquisition cost per unit or the manufacturing cost per unit is assumed constant and would not be relevant to the inventory control decisions.

[2] When applied to the production of goods, the EOQ model is known as the economic lot size (ELS) model and includes a setup cost rather than an ordering cost.

Figure 14.1   Graphic Approach to the Determination of Economic Order Quantity (EOQ)

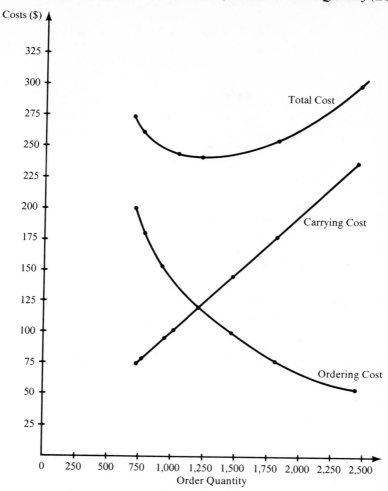

Table 14.1   Tabular Approach to the Determination of Economic Order Quantity (EOQ)

Number of Orders (N)	Order Quantity (Q = D/N)	Ordering Costs (N × C₀)	Carrying Costs (Q/2 × C꜀)	Total Costs
1	7,200	$ 20	$720	$740
2	3,600	40	360	400
3	2,400	60	240	300
4	1,800	80	180	260
5	1,440	100	144	244
6	1,200	120	120	240 *Least Cost*
7	1,028	140	102	242
8	900	160	90	250
9	800	180	80	260
10	720	200	72	272

This result also can be determined mathematically. The ordering, carrying, and total costs are expressed as

Ordering costs $= C_0\dfrac{D}{Q}$.

Carrying costs $= C_c\dfrac{Q}{2}$.

Total costs $= C_0\dfrac{D}{Q} + C_c\dfrac{Q}{2}$.

Differentiating the total costs (TC) with respect to Q and setting the result equal to zero yields

$$\dfrac{dTC}{dQ} = \dfrac{-C_0D}{Q^2} + \dfrac{C_c}{2} = 0.$$

Solving for Q yields

$$Q^* = \sqrt{\dfrac{2C_0D}{C_c}} = \text{Economic order quantity.}$$

Thus, the EOQ fluctuates directly with the square root of the demand and fluctuates inversely with the square root of the carrying cost per unit.

From the EOQ formula, it follows that

$$\text{Length of a cycle } (t_c) = Q^* \div \dfrac{D}{360} = 360\sqrt{\dfrac{2C_0}{C_cD}}.$$

$$\text{Optimal number of orders } (N) = D \div Q^* = \sqrt{\dfrac{DC_c}{2C_0}}.$$

$$\text{Average EOQ } (I_a) = Q^* \div 2 = \sqrt{\dfrac{C_0D}{2C_c}}.$$

The Archibald Company example shows that

$D = 7,200$ units per year.

$C_0 = \$20$ per order.

$C_c = \$.20$ per unit per year.

The EOQ formula yields the following results:

$$Q^* = \sqrt{\dfrac{2 \times 20 \times 7,200}{0.2}} = 1,200 \text{ units.}$$

$$t_c = 360\sqrt{\dfrac{2 \times 20}{0.2 \times 7,200}} = 60 \text{ days.}$$

$$N = \frac{7,200}{1,200} = 6 \text{ orders.}$$

$$I_a = \sqrt{\frac{20 \times 7,200}{2 \times 0.2}} = 600 \text{ units.}$$

$$\text{Total Cost} = \$20 \times \frac{7,200}{1,200} + \$.20 \times \frac{1,200}{2} = \$240.$$

It is important to remember that the results obtained so far are based on the following assumptions about the real world:

1. The demand is known with certainty and has a continuous (rather than a discrete) behavior over time.

2. The lead time also is known with certainty and is constant.

3. Both the ordering cost (C_0) and the carrying cost (C_c) are assumed to be constant, while the stockout cost (C_s) is assumed to be infinite. The system is never out of stock.

14.1.3   EOP Model

The *economic order point* (EOP) model determines the inventory level at which orders should be placed. The reorder point depends on three factors: (1) the EOQ, (2) the lead time, and (3) whether or not the usage rate during the lead time is constant or variable.

If there is a constant demand for the product during the lead time, the formula for computing the EOP is as follows:

EOP = Lead time in days or weeks $\times$ Average daily or weekly usage.

Using the Archibald Company example, assume that the lead time is 5 weeks and that the average weekly usage is 150 units. The reorder point in such a case would be 750 units. Figure 14.2 shows the graphic computation of the EOP.

If there is a variable usage during the lead time, some buffer stocks or safety stocks should be maintained. The buffer stock should equal the difference between the max-

Figure 14.2   *Graphic Determination of the Economic Order Point (EOP)*

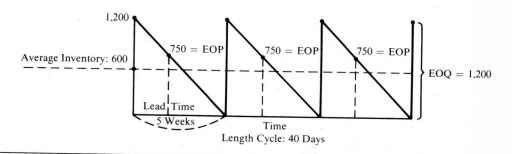

Figure 14.3   Graphic Determination of the EOP under a Variable Usage during Lead Time

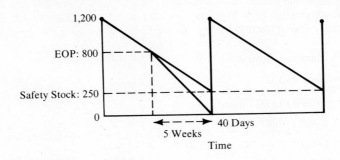

imum and average usage per week or per day multiplied by the lead time. In such a case the formula for computing EOP is

EOP = (Lead time in days or weeks × Average daily or weekly usage) + Safety stock.

Using the Archibald Company example, assume that the maximum usage per week is 160 units. The safety stock is then computed as follows:

Safety stock = (160 units − 150 units) × 5 weeks = 50 units.

The reorder point would be

EOP = (5 weeks × 150 units) + 50 units = 800 units.

Figure 14.3 shows the graphic determination of the EOP under a variable usage during the lead time.

14.1.4   *EOQ with a Capacity Constraint*

Suppose now that the Archibald Company tells us that its storage space is limited, and it can only store 1,000 units at a time. What is the new optimal inventory policy?

From Figure 14.1, we can see that as Q decreases from 1,200 units, the total cost increases. Hence 1,000 units is the optimal order quantity.

Intuitive reasoning leads us to state that if a capacity W exists, then

1. If $W \leq Q^*$, the new optimal order quantity is W.
2. If $W > Q^*$, the new optimal order quantity is Q^*.

For the Archibald Company, if $W \leq 1,200$, then W is optimal. If $W > 1,200$, then 1,200 units is optimal.

14.1.5   *EOQ with an Allowance for Stockouts*

In actuality, firms permit stockouts and receive back orders from customers to be filled when replenishment occurs. It is reasonable, then, to assume that firms incur back order costs or shortage costs (C_s). Figure 14.4 shows an inventory system with an allowance for stockouts. The following symbols are used, in addition to those already defined:

M = Maximum inventory.

$Q - M$ = Back orders.

t = Length of one order cycle.

T_s = Length of time for which inventory is held.

t_2 = Length of time for which there is a shortage.

The total cost (TC) function to be minimized is

TC = Ordering costs + Carrying costs + Stockout costs.

The following procedure can be used to determine the EOQ:

1. The ordering costs are a function of the number of orders. Thus,

Ordering costs = NC_0.

Figure 14.4   *EOQ with an Allowance for Stockouts*

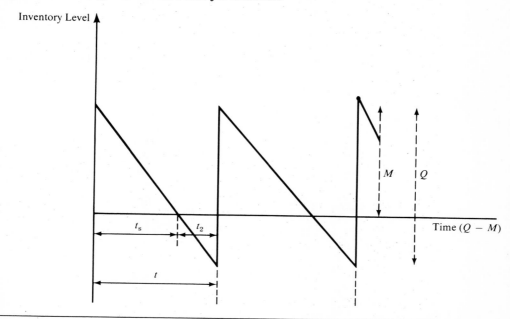

2. The carrying costs are a function of the average inventory. During t_s, the average inventory is $M/2$; during t_2, the average inventory is $Q - M/2$. In other words, the company is holding an average inventory Q/M percent of the time. Thus,

$$\text{Carrying costs} = \frac{M}{2} \times \frac{M}{Q} C_c$$

$$= \frac{M^2}{2Q} C_c.$$

3. The shortage costs are a function of the average inventory. During t_2, the shortage costs are equal to $Q - M/2$ for $Q - M/Q$ percent of the time. Thus,

$$\text{Shortage costs} = \frac{Q - M}{2} \times \frac{Q - M}{Q} C_s$$

$$= \frac{(Q - M)^2}{2Q} C_s.$$

4. TC will be equal to

$$TC = \frac{D}{Q} C_0 + \frac{M^2}{2Q} C_c + \frac{(Q - M)^2}{2Q} C_s.$$

5. Differentiating TC with respect to Q and M and setting the result equal to zero yields

$$\frac{\delta TC}{\delta M} = \frac{MC_c}{Q} + \frac{C_s(Q - M)}{Q} = 0,$$

and

$$\frac{\delta TC}{\delta Q} = \frac{-DC_0}{Q^2} - \frac{M^2 C_c}{2Q^2} + \frac{C_s}{2} - \frac{C_s M^2}{2Q^2} = 0.$$

6. Simplifying yields

$$Q^* = \sqrt{\frac{2C_0 D}{C_c}} \times \sqrt{\frac{C_c + C_s}{C_s}}.$$

$$M^* = \sqrt{\frac{2C_0 D}{C_c}} \times \sqrt{\frac{C_s}{C_c + C_s}}.$$

Thus, if $C_s = \$.80$, the EOQ is

$$Q^* = \sqrt{\frac{2 \times 20 \times 7,200}{0.2}} \times \sqrt{\frac{0.2 + 0.8}{0.8}} = 134 \text{ units.}$$

$$M^* = \sqrt{\frac{2 \times 20 \times 7,200}{0.2}} \times \sqrt{\frac{0.8}{0.2 + 0.8}} = 1,073 \text{ units.}$$

14.1.6   *EOQ with a Uniform Replenishment Rate*

The preceding discussions covered situations with instant deliveries; that is, if a quantity Q is ordered, it becomes immediately available. However, this is not always the case. Replenishment generally is taking place while demand is being met. This inventory system with a uniform replenishment rate is illustrated in Figure 14.5.

In the EOQ calculation for this situation, P is the inventory replenishment rate (production rate for the ELS model). The maximum inventory is $(P - D)(t_1/2)$. The average inventory $(\bar{I})$, then, is

$$\bar{I} = (P - D)\frac{t_1}{2}.$$

Since $Q = Pt_1$, then $\bar{I}$ can be expressed as

$$\bar{I} = (1 - \frac{D}{P}) \frac{Q}{2}.$$

The ordering costs are still expressed as follows:

$$\text{Ordering costs} = \frac{D}{Q} C_0.$$

The carrying costs are now expressed as

$$\text{Carrying costs} = (1 - \frac{D}{P})Q \frac{C_c}{2}.$$

Thus, the total cost of the inventory system becomes

$$TC = \frac{D}{Q} C_0 + (1 - \frac{D}{P})Q \frac{C_c}{2}.$$

Figure 14.5   *Uniform Replenishment Rate*

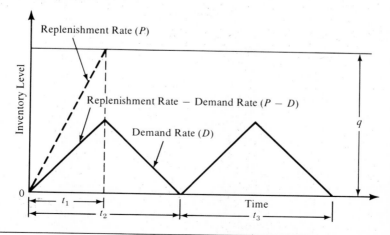

Differentiating TC with respect to Q and setting the result equal to zero yields the following formula for $Q*$:

$$\frac{dTC}{dQ} = \frac{-C_0 D}{Q^2} + \frac{(1 - \frac{D}{P})C_c}{2} = 0.$$

$$Q* = \sqrt{\frac{2C_0 D}{C_c}} \times \sqrt{\frac{P}{P - D}}.$$

Going back to the Archibald Company example and assuming that P equals 14,400 units per year, the EOQ can be found as follows:

$$Q* = \sqrt{\frac{2 \times 20 \times 7,200}{0.2}} \times \sqrt{\frac{14,400}{14,400 - 7,200}} = 1,697.$$

14.1.7   EOQ with a Uniform Replenishment Rate and Stockouts

So far our discussion of EOQ models has been restricted to the situation in which all demand must be serviced on time. However, if inventory carrying costs are high, it may be economically necessary to provide less prompt service in order to maintain lower inventory levels. This situation is common; for example, automobile dealerships do not carry all models of cars in all colors but instead order those not currently available when a customer provides specifications. Such customer orders that are serviced not immediately but after a procurement delay are called *back orders*. Back ordering is common in many industrial contexts. A paper producing corporation, for example, could find itself in a position in which production is trailing demand for many reasons. A period of unusually warm weather could cause a demand for soda cartons in excess of productive capacity. A strike of paper production workers could result in large back orders. Demand for a new product could exceed production capacity for a period of time.

It obviously is not always possible or desirable to back order. For example, if a grocery store's customers need milk for dinner, they cannot wait until tomorrow for a new shipment. In this case, the store would lose sales (and, presumably, these would be picked up by another store).

The inventory system with uniform replenishment rate and stockouts is depicted in Figure 14.6. The formula for the EOQ with a uniform replenishment rate and stockouts is as follows:

$$Q* = \sqrt{\frac{1}{1 - \frac{D}{P}}} \times \sqrt{\frac{2C_0 D}{C_c} + \frac{2C_0 D}{C_s}}.$$

Going back to the Archibald Company example, the EOQ can be found as follows:

$$Q* = \sqrt{\frac{1}{1 - \frac{7,200}{14,400}}} \times \sqrt{\frac{2 \times 20 \times 7,200}{0.2} + \frac{2 \times 20 \times 7,200}{0.8}} = 1,897.$$

Figure 14.6   *Stockouts and Uniform Replenishment Rate*

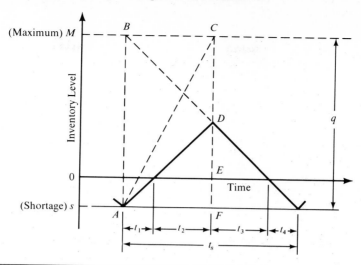

14.1.8   *Price Breaks or Quantity Discounts*

The purchase price per unit ordered often is not independent of the quantity ordered. For example, it is not unusual to have price structures such as the following:

$$\text{Cost per unit } (C_p) = \begin{cases} C_1 \text{ if } Q < Q_1. \\ C_2 \text{ if } Q_1 \leq Q < Q_2. \\ C_3 \text{ if } Q_2 \leq Q < Q_3. \\ \quad . \\ \quad . \\ \quad . \\ C_m \text{ if } Q_m - 1 \leq Q_m. \end{cases}$$

To illustrate the computation of the EOQ with price breaks, assume that D is to equal 25,000 units per year, ordering costs (C_0) are equal to \$400, and carrying costs (C_c) are equal to \$5 per unit per year. Assume also that the supplier quoted the following prices:

Unit Price (C_p)	Units
\$2.10	0–1,999
2.08	2,000–2,999
2.05	3,000–3,999
2.02	4,000–5,999

The total cost equation becomes

$$TC = \frac{D}{Q}C_0 + \frac{Q}{2}C_c + C_p D.$$

Table 14.2   Total Cost for Each of the Possible Unit Prices

Unit Price	Order Quantity	Purchase Cost	Inventory Cost	Total Cost
$2.10	1,999	$52,500	$10,000	$62,500
2.08	2,000	52,000	10,000	62,000[a]
2.05	3,000	51,250	10,833	62,083
2.02	4,000	50,500	12,500	63,000

[a] Minimum cost corresponding to economic order quantity.

Figure 14.7   Price Breaks

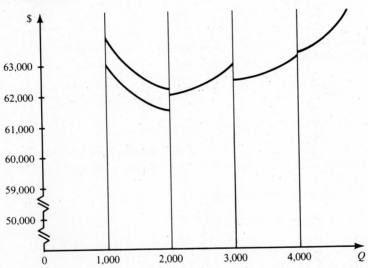

The total costs for each of the possible unit prices are computed in Table 14.2 and graphed in Figure 14.7. It appears that the EOQ is 2,000 units, taking into account the quantity discounts.

14.2   PROBABILISTIC INVENTORY CONTROL MODELS

The inventory model under uncertainty can be analyzed in a decision theoretical framework. The variables would be

1. A *set of actions*, namely, the different quantities that can be ordered.

2. A *set of states of nature*, namely, the demand distribution for the product.

3. The *a priori probability distribution* of the demand.

4. A *profit matrix* indicating the profit for each combination of action and state of nature.

The criterion for decision making can be either profit maximization or opportunity cost minimization. The following sections consider the static inventory problem under risk using each of these decision criteria.

14.2.1   *Profit Maximization*

Assume a store is considering how many Christmas trees to order for the Christmas season. Each Christmas tree costs $2 and sells for $5. The manager estimated the demand characteristics to be as follows:

Demand	Probability
10	0.20
15	0.30
20	0.30
25	0.20

There are four strategies available to order between 10 and 25 trees. Therefore, the payoff matrix will be as follows:

Orders \ Demand	10	15	20	25
10	$30	$30	$30	$30
15	20	45	45	45
20	10	35	60	60
25	0	25	50	75
Probability of Demand	0.20	0.30	0.30	0.20

Next, the expected profit associated with each order can be computed:

$E(10) = \$30(0.20) + \$30(0.30) + \$30(0.30) + \$30(0.20) = \$30.$

$E(15) = \$20(0.20) + \$45(0.30) + \$45(0.30) + \$45(0.20) = \$40.$

$E(20) = \$10(0.20) + \$35(0.30) + \$60(0.30) + \$60(0.20) = \$42.50.$

$E(25) = \$0(0.20) + \$25(0.30) + \$50(0.30) + \$75(0.20) = \$37.50.$

Therefore, the store should decide to order 20 units to maximize the expected profit.

14.2.2   *Opportunity Costs*

The same problem can be analyzed using the criterion of opportunity cost. The opportunity cost is equal to the difference between the profit made in the case where the right decision was acted upon minus the profit made as a result of the actual decision. The opportunity cost matrix for the Christmas tree store follows:

Orders \ Demand	10	15	20	25
10	$ 0	$15	$30	$45
15	10	0	15	30
20	20	10	0	15
25	30	20	10	0
Probability of Demand	0.20	0.30	0.30	0.20

The expected opportunity cost associated with each order can be computed:

$E(10) = \$0(0.20) + \$15(0.30) + \$30(0.30) + \$45(0.20) = \$22.50.$

$E(15) = \$10(0.20) + \$0(0.30) + \$15(0.30) + \$30(0.20) = \$12.50.$

$E(20) = \$20(0.20) + \$10(0.30) + \$0(0.30) + \$15(0.20) = \$10.$

$E(25) = \$30(0.20) + \$20(0.30) + \$10(0.30) + \$0(0.20) = \$15.$

Therefore, the store still should decide to order 20 units to minimize the expected opportunity cost.

Both the profit maximization and the opportunity cost analyses are a priori analyses, and an a posteriori analysis can be used to improve the decision. An example of the a posteriori analysis applicable to the inventory problem was presented in section 5.5.2.

14.3   OTHER INVENTORY CONTROL MODELS

Other inventory control methods, both informal and more formal, include the eyeball review method, two-bin method, order-cycling method, min.-max. method, and ABC method.

14.3.1   Eyeball Review Method

The informal eyeball review method consists of a periodic visual review of the inventory stock levels. On the basis of these reviews, orders are placed periodically, as needed.

14.3.2   Two-Bin Method

The two-bin method consists of keeping two bins that initially are filled with the items to be controlled. When the first bin is empty and use of the second bin has begun, it is time to reorder. A variation of the two-bin method is the "red line" method: A red line is painted at a reorder level, and consumption reaching the red line initiates the placing of an order.

14.3.3   Order-Cycling Method

Under an order-cycling system, the quantity level of each item on hand is examined periodically. High-value items and items critical to production usually require a short review cycle. Conversely, low-value items and items not critical to production can have a longer review cycle. At each review period, orders are placed to bring quantities up to some determined and desired level. The order-cycling method is appropriate when the cost of continuous inventory status surveillance is high or when transportation and ordering economies of scale can be gained through the regular ordering of several different items from the same supplier.

14.3.4   Min.-Max. Method

Under the min.-max. system, a maximum (which usage requirements normally will not exceed) is established for each item along with a minimum to provide the margin of safety necessary to prevent stockouts during a reorder cycle. The minimum level sets the reorder point, and the quantity to order is usually that quantity that will bring inventory up to the maximum level. The min.-max. system is appropriate where the cost of continuous inventory status surveillance is not high or where significant transportation and ordering economies of scale cannot be gained through regular ordering.

14.3.5   ABC Method

The ABC method consists of classifying inventory items into groups (A, B, and C) according to their average annual usage, weighted by their unit cost. Group A includes the items with the greatest percentage of total costs. It is the prime target for the application of a formal inventory control model to determine the EOQ, EOP, and safety levels. Group C includes the items with the lowest percentage of total costs. It may be controlled by less formal methods such as the eyeball review, two-bin, or red line method. Group B falls between groups A and C and can be controlled by a mix of formal and informal techniques.

To illustrate the use of the ABC method, assume that the Windsor Auto Plant has ten inventory items to be used for manufacturing a car component. The annual usage of these items, which must be purchased from outside suppliers, is shown in Table 14.3. Each of the items is classified as belonging to group A, B, or C, depending on the total dollar volume of the item's annual usage. The final analysis of the classification of the items is shown in Table 14.4. Group A represents only 20.83 percent of the total number of units; however, it includes 55 percent of the total inventory cost. Group C represents 50 percent of the total number of units and includes only 16.67 percent of the total inventory cost. It is clear that a large amount of continuous and formal planning and control should be exercised on the items in group A.

Table 14.3   Annual Usage, Total Cost, and Inventory Classification

(1) Item	(2) Average Usage	(3) Cost per Unit	(4) Total Cost	(5) ABC Classification
X2	2,000	$10	$ 20,000	C
YB3	5,000	2	10,000	C
RS4	10,000	5	50,000	B
A2	10,000	11	110,000	A
A16	2,000	30	60,000	B
B7	30,000	2	60,000	B
RD2	5,000	5	25,000	C
T1	20,000	11	220,000	A
R3	5,000	5	25,000	C
Z10	10,000	2	20,000	C

Table 14.4   ABC Analysis of Inventory Items

	Items		Dollars	
Classification	Number of Items	Percentage of Total	Total Costs	Percentage of Total
Group A	30,000	20.83%	$330,000	55.00%
Group B	42,000	29.17	170,000	28.33
Group C	72,000	50.00	100,000	16.67
	144,000	100%	$600,000	100%

14.4   INVENTORY VALUATION MODELS

Another control decision with respect to inventories is the choice of a *cost flow assumption* about the pattern of material utilization. This decision has an important effect on the way income is computed. Three inventory cost flow assumptions are widely accepted: the *weighted average method*, the *last-in, first-out (LIFO) method*, and the *first-in, first-out (FIFO) method*.

14.4.1   Weighted Average Method

The weighted average method uses the average price of the period to value inventories. For example, say XYZ Ltd. made the following purchases:

Date	Batch	Number of Units	Unit Price	Total
January 1 (Beginning Inventory)	1	500	$10	$ 5,000
February 10	2	200	15	3,000
June 15	3	300	20	6,000
Total		1,000		$14,000

Assume that 400 units are sold at $20 per unit. The weighted average price is $14,000/1,000, or $14. The weighted average method would assign value to the cost of goods sold and to the ending inventory as follows:

Cost of goods sold: 400 units × $14 = $5,600.

Ending Inventory: 600 units × $14 = $8,400.

14.4.2   Last-In, First-Out Method

The LIFO method cost flow assumption is that the units purchased last are sold first. Using the XYZ Ltd. example, this method would assign value to the cost of goods sold as follows:

From batch 3: 300 units × $20 = $6,000

From batch 2: 100 units × $15 = $1,500

Cost of goods sold   = $7,500

Value assigned to the ending inventory would be

From batch 2: 100 units × $15 = $1,500

From batch 1: 500 units × $10 = $5,000
Ending Inventory   = $6,500

14.4.3   First-In, First-Out Method

The FIFO method cost flow assumption is that the units are sold in the order in which they were purchased. Using the XYZ Ltd. example, this method would assign value to the cost of goods sold as follows:

From batch 1: 400 units × $10 = $4,000.

The FIFO method would assign value to the ending inventory as follows:

From batch 1: 100 units × $10 = $ 1,000

From batch 2: 200 units × $15 = $ 3,000

From batch 3: 300 units × $20 = $ 6,000
Ending Inventory   = $10,000

14.4.4   Comparison of First-In, First-Out; Weighted Average; and Last-In, First-Out Methods

The income statements made on the basis of the FIFO, weighted average, and LIFO cost flow assumptions would be as follows:

			FIFO	Weighted Average	LIFO
	Sales		$8,000	$8,000	$8,000
minus	Cost of Goods Sold				
		Beginning Inventory	$ 5,000	$ 5,000	$ 5,000
	plus	Purchases	9,000	9,000	9,000
	equals	Goods Available	14,000	14,000	14,000
	minus	Ending Inventory	10,000	8,400	6,500
	equals	Cost of Goods Sold	4,000	5,600	7,500
equals	Gross Profit		$4,000	$2,400	$ 500

Note that when prices are rising, the LIFO method shows less income than the other two methods, thus minimizing current taxes. Other important inventory valuation issues are more appropriately discussed in financial accounting texts.

14.5   CONCLUSION

Inventory models in accounting include both inventory control and inventory valuation models. The objective in using either model is to insure efficient inventory management so net income will be maximized. The study of these models leads to an understanding of cost analysis for inventory decisions in order to reach an optimal ordering policy taking into account assumptions regarding capacity constraints, allowances for stockouts, price breaks, a uniform replenishment rate, and a uniform replenishment rate with stockouts.

GLOSSARY

Carrying Cost The cost associated with holding inventories plus a desired rate of return on the investment in inventories.

Economic Order Point (EOP) The inventory level at which orders should be placed.

Economic Order Quantity (EOQ) The order size that minimizes the carrying and ordering costs of inventory.

First-In, First-Out (FIFO) Method Assumes that units are sold in the order in which they were purchased.

Inventory Control Model A model intended to control the levels of inventory stocks.

Inventory Model A model intended to resolve tactical decisions of what to produce or buy, when, and in what quantity.

Last-In, First-Out (LIFO) Method Assumes that the units purchased last are sold first.

Lead Time The time between the placement of an order for goods and the receipt of the goods.

Ordering Cost The cost associated with placing an order with a vendor.

Shortage Cost (Stockout Cost) The opportunity loss occurring when the demand for goods exceeds the supply.

Weighted Average Method Uses the average price of the period to value inventory.

SELECTED READINGS

American Institute of Certified Public Accountants, *Management Services Technical Study No. 6*, "Practical Techniques and Policies for Inventory Control" (New York: AICPA, 1968).

Backes, Robert W., "Cycle Counting: A Better Method for Achieving Accurate Inventory Records," *Management Accounting* (January 1980), pp. 42–46.

Buchan, J., and Keonigsberg, E., *Scientific Inventory Management* (Englewood Cliffs, N.J.: Prentice-Hall, 1963).

Bunch, Robert G., "The Effect of Payment Terms on Economic Order Quantity Determination," *Management Accounting* (January 1967), pp. 53–62.

Churchman, C. W.; Ackoff, R. L.; and Arnoff, E. L., *Introduction to Operations Research* (New York: Wiley, 1957).

Crossno, Garlon, "Programmed Requirements Planning," *Management Accounting* (March 1974), pp. 23–27.

Deakin, Edward B. III, "Finding Optimal Order Quantity When Quantity Discounts Are Offered," *Cost and Management* (May–June 1975), pp. 40–42.

Hadley, G., and Whiten, T. M., *Analysis of Inventory Systems* (Englewood Cliffs, N.J.: Prentice-Hall, 1963).

Hall, Thomas W., "Inventory Carrying Costs: A Case Study," *Management Accounting* (January 1974), pp. 37–39.

Lavery, K. R., *Special Study No. 4*, "Selective Inventory Management" (Hamilton, Ontario: Society of Management Accountants of Canada, 1978).

Lewin, R. I., and Kirkpatrick, C. A., *Quantitative Approaches to Management* (New York: McGraw-Hill, 1971).

Naddor, Eliezer, *Inventory Systems* (New York: Wiley, 1966).

National Association of Accountants, *Research Report No. 4*, "Techniques in Inventory Management" (New York: NAA, 1964).

Starr, M. K., and Miller, D. W., *Inventory Control: Theory and Practice* (Englewood Cliffs, N.J.: Prentice-Hall, 1962).

QUESTIONS, EXERCISES, AND PROBLEMS

14.1   What are the different types of inventory systems?

14.2   Give some of the reasons for maintaining an inventory.

14.3   Can you see how nuclear disarmament can be viewed as an inventory problem? Discuss. (*Note:* This certainly may not be the most useful way to model this situation.)

(Question suggested by Jeffrey B. Sidney, University of Ottawa.)

14.4   It is often very difficult to obtain the cost functions in an inventory problem, even though you may know the general type of costs involved. For example, consider the Knotstein Brothers Lumber Company, which is considering purchasing 100,000 acres of virgin forest in British Columbia. Trees of many sizes, ages, qualities, and species constitute the inventory of trees on this property.

Required:

1. What constitutes withdrawal from inventory? What constitutes inventory replacement?

2. What are the associated costs?

(Question suggested by Jeffrey B. Sidney, University of Ottawa.)

14.5   Lois Leanto, head of a local ecology group, is trying to prevent the sale of the 100,000 acres described in question 14.4 to Knotstein Brothers on ecological grounds.

Required:

1. How do you think Leanto's inventory evaluation differs from that of Knotstein Brothers?

2. Is there a general managerial principle to be learned from the fact that these two evaluations will presumably be quite different?

(Question suggested by Jeffrey B. Sidney, University of Ottawa.)

14.6   Suppose back orders are lost (that is, if an order occurs while you are out of stock, the order is never served). What is the optimal policy?

(Question suggested by Jeffrey B. Sidney, University of Ottawa.)

14.7   Firms sometimes use back orders as a substitute for sufficient inventory storage space. Explain how they can do so.

(Question suggested by Jeffrey B. Sidney, University of Ottawa.)

14.8   Suppose you have one machine that produces two products. The demand for product 1 is 1,000 units, and the demand for product 2 is 2,000 units. The production rate for product 1 is 1,500 units and product 2 is 3,000 units. (These are annual rates.)

Required:
1. Is it possible for one machine to service the demand for both products? Why or why not?
2. More generally, suppose there are K products, with production rates $P_1, P_2, \ldots, P_K$ and demand rates $D_1, D_2, \ldots, D_K$, where the production rates are rates on a particular machine. How many machines of this type are needed if demands are to be met?

(Question suggested by Jeffrey B. Sidney, University of Ottawa.)

14.9   *Need for Inventories and Types of Inventory Control Systems*   Inventories constitute an important part of the financial position of many business enterprises. For such firms, proper policies for inventory analysis and control are highly important in maintaining a sound financial condition.

Required:
1. Why do manufacturing firms maintain merchandise and materials inventories? (Your answer should state the reasons for physical stocks of goods rather than the accounting and auditing significance of inventories.)
2. Various types of inventory systems exist to control the ordering and amount of inventory on hand. For example, the ABC plan classifies high-carrying-cost and low-ordering-cost inventory as A items, low-carrying-cost and high-ordering-cost inventory as C items, and all other inventory as B items. This plan is appropriate for an inventory composed of a large number of items with a wide range of carrying and order costs. Explain the (a) order-cycling and (b) min.-max. method inventory control plans, and describe the conditions under which each is appropriate.
3. What factors should be considered in computing
   a. Optimum investment in inventory. (Identify both those costs that do and those that normally do not explicitly appear on formal accounting records.)
   b. Economic order quantity.
   c. Describe the advantages and disadvantages a manufacturer would obtain from stabilizing the production of a durable seasonal product.

(AICPA adapted)

14.10   *Comparison of Inventory Methods*   The Berg Corporation began doing business on January 1, 19X4. Information about its inventories under different valuation methods is shown here. Using this information, you are to choose the phrase that best answers each of the following questions.

	Inventory			
	LIFO Cost	FIFO Cost	Market	Lower of Cost or Market
December 31, 19X4	$10,200	$10,000	$ 9,600	$ 8,900
December 31, 19X5	9,100	9,000	8,800	8,500
December 31, 19X6	10,300	11,000	12,000	10,900

1. The inventory basis that would show the highest net income for 19X4 is
   a. LIFO cost.   **c.** Market.
   b. FIFO cost.   **d.** Lower of cost or market.

2. The inventory basis that would show the highest net income for 19X5 is
   a. LIFO cost.   **c.** Market.
   b. FIFO cost.   **d.** Lower of cost or market.

3. The inventory basis that would show the lowest net income for the three years combined is
   a. LIFO cost.   **c.** Market.
   b. FIFO cost.   **d.** Lower of cost or market.

4. For 19X5, how much higher or lower would profits be on the FIFO cost basis than on the lower-of-cost-or-market basis?
   a. $400 higher.   **e.** $1,000 higher.
   b. $400 lower.   **f.** $1,000 lower.
   c. $600 higher.   **g.** $1,400 higher.
   d. $600 lower.   **h.** $1,400 lower.

5. On the basis of the information given, it appears that the movement of prices for items in the inventory was
   a. Up in 19X4 and down in 19X6.
   b. Up in both 19X4 and 19X6.
   c. Down in 19X4 and up in 19X6.
   d. Down in both 19X4 and 19X6.

(AICPA adapted)

14.11   ***Economic Order Quantity***   The following information relates to the Gerald Company:

Optimal Production Run (in Units)	500
Average Inventory (in Units)	250
Number of Production Runs	10
Cost per Unit Produced	$5
Desired Annual Return on Inventory Investment	10%
Setup Cost per Production Run	$10

Required:
1. Assuming that the units will be required evenly throughout the year, what are the total annual relevant costs using the EOQ approach?
   a. $225.   **c.** $1,350.
   b. $350.   **d.** $2,625.

The following information relates to Eagle Company's material A:

Annual Usage (in Units)	7,200
Working Days per Year	240
Normal Lead Time (in Working Days)	20
Maximum Lead Time (in Working Days)	45

Required:
2. Assuming that the units of material A will be required evenly throughout the year, the safety stock and order point is
   a. Safety stock, 600; order point, 750.
   b. Safety stock, 600; order point, 1,350.

    c. Safety stock, 750; order point, 600.

    d. Safety stock, 750; order point, 1,350.

Light Company has 2,000 obsolete light fixtures that are carried in inventory at a manufacturing cost of $30,000. If the fixtures were reworked for $10,000, they could be sold for $18,000. As an alternate, the light fixtures could be sold for $3,000 to a jobber located in a distant city.

Required:

3. In a decision model analyzing these alternatives, the opportunity cost would be

    a. $ 3,000.   **c.** $13,000.

    b. $10,000.   **d.** $30,000.

The expected annual usage of a particular raw material is 2,000,000 units, and the standard order size is 10,000 units. The invoice cost of each unit is $500, and the cost to place a purchase order is $80.

Required:

4. The average inventory is

    a. 1,000,000 units.   **c.** 10,000 units.

    b. 5,000 units.   **d.** 7,500 units.

5. The estimated annual order cost is

    a. $ 16,000.   **c.** $32,000.

    b. $100,000.   **d.** $50,000.

The Polly Company wants to determine the amount of safety stock it should maintain for product D to result in the lowest cost. The following information is available.

Stockout Cost	$80 per Occurrence
Carrying Cost of Safety Stock	$2 per Unit
Number of Purchase Orders	5 per Year

The available options open to Polly are as follows:

Units of Safety Stock	Probability of Running Out of Safety Stock
10	50%
20	40
30	30
40	20
50	10
55	5

Required:

6. How many units of safety stock will result in the lowest cost?

    a. 20 units.   **c.** 50 units.

    b. 40 units.   **d.** 55 units.

                                                  (AICPA adapted)

14.12   *Economic Lot Size*   The Smith Manufacturing Co. produces and sells automotive parts to be used by an automobile assembly division. A three-week lead time is required if the division is to meet its expected demand of 200,000 units. The cost of setup is $20, and each unit carried in inventory costs the Smith Manufacturing Co. $.01 per year. Assume a production schedule of fifty weeks per year.

Required:

1. Determine the economic production lot size.

2. Determine the reorder point.

14.13 *EOQ with Uniform Replenishment Rate* The Eddy Corporation is currently purchasing sales units faster than it is able to sell them. As a result, management has requested a reevaluation of the company's order policy. An analysis of the current sales market reveals the following. Anticipated annual demand is 20,000 units; daily sales, 400 units; and daily arrivals of merchandise, 800 units. Other cost data include an order cost of $15 per order and a carrying cost of $.60 per unit.

Required:
Determine the EOQ.

14.14 *Price Break Model: Cost Comparison for Fixed Lot Discounts* Maheu, Inc., requires 1,000,000 pounds of oats for each year's operation. The ordering cost is $12.50 per order, the carrying cost is $.04 per pound, and the current purchase price is $.75 per pound. The supplier recently quoted the following prices:

Unit Price	Lot Size (in Pounds)
$.75	10,000
$.72	50,000
$.70	100,000
$.67	500,000

Required:
Should Maheu, Inc., purchase at one of the suggested lot sizes?

14.15 *Inventory Control* The Montreal Co. Ltd. has developed the following costs and other data pertaining to one of its raw materials:

Normal Use per Day (in Units)	400
Maximum Use per Day (in Units)	600
Minimum Use per Day (in Units)	100
Working Days per Year	250
Lead Time (in Days)	8
Cost of Placing One Order	$20
Carrying Cost per Unit per Year	$25

Required:
Compute the following:

1. The safety stock.

2. The reorder point.

3. The EOQ.

4. The normal maximum inventory.

5. The absolute maximum inventory.

6. The average inventory.

(CGA adapted)

14.16   ***Reorder Point***   Compute the reorder point in units and days, given the following:

1. A time period of 35 days, in which the full inventory is used (except the safety level).
2. A safety level of 150 units.
3. A maximum inventory level of 850 units.
4. A lead time of 12 days.

(SMA adapted)

14.17   ***Inventory Card, Moving Average***   Steel Stores Limited is a dealer in steel products. The company purchases its steel from various mills, and prices are FOB point of shipment. On January 1 freight costs were $5 per ton; however, on January 14 they advanced 10 percent. The steel industry uses the standard 2,000-pound ton.

During the month of January, the following transactions took place involving hot-rolled sheets 60 inches long and 36 inches wide:

January 1: Inventory	10 Tons at $6 per 100 Pounds
January 2: Purchased	3 Tons at $5.50 per 100 Pounds
January 3: Sold	2 Tons
January 5: Purchased	2 Tons at $5.60 per 100 Pounds
January 6: Sold	3 Tons
January 10: Purchased	8 Tons at $5.55 per 100 Pounds
January 12: Sold	8 Tons
January 15: Purchased	2 Tons at $5.55 per 100 Pounds
January 16: Sold	2 Tons
January 30: Purchased	5 Tons at $5.60 per 100 Pounds
January 31: Sold	7 Tons

Sales prices are determined by applying a markup of 30 percent to laid-down costs at the beginning of each month.

Required:
1. Show these transactions as they would appear on a perpetual inventory card, using the moving average cost method. Calculations should be made to the nearest cent. (In a moving average cost method, each purchase is combined with the former inventory balance so a new average unit price is used to price subsequent issues of inventory.)
2. Calculate the gross profit for the month.
3. Name two methods other than the moving average cost method that could have been used in pricing these issue transactions.

(SMA adapted)

14.18   ***Quantity Discounts***   The Micro Electronic Company produces testing devices that require 12 special sockets each. Annual production is 40,000 testing devices. Because of the large annual usage of 480,000 special sockets, the purchasing agent approached the present supplier in an effort to reduce the current net price of $1.05 per socket. After some intensive studies, the supplier replied that the price could be lowered to $1 per socket if the company were willing to increase its present order size from 40,000 units to 120,000 units, with 60 days' delivery rather than the present 30 days'.

The Micro Electronic Company estimated that additional space at $6,600 per annum would be required to stock the extra inventory. Safety stock should be increased by 10,000 units due to the greater time lag between deliveries. Inventory carrying costs are estimated at 10 percent per annum.

Required:
Evaluate the supplier's proposal by calculating the annual savings or losses.

(SMA adapted)

14.19   ***EOQ, Stockouts***   You have been hired to install an accounting system for the Kaufman Corporation. Among the inventory control features Kaufman desires as a part of the system are indicators of *how much* to order *when*. The following information is furnished for one item (Komtronic), which is carried in inventory:

Komtronics are sold by the gross (twelve dozen) at a list price of $800 per gross FOB shipper. Kaufman receives a 40 percent trade discount off the list price on purchases in gross lots.

Freight cost is $20 per gross from the shipping point to Kaufman's plant.

Kaufman uses about 5,000 Komtronics during a 259-day production year and must purchase a total of 36 gross per year to allow for normal breakage.

Normal delivery time to receive an order is twenty working days from the date a purchase request is initiated. A rush order in full gross lots can be received by air freight in five working days at an extra cost of $52 per gross. A stockout (complete exhaustion of the inventory) of Komtronics would stop production, and Kaufman would purchase Komtronics locally at the list price rather than shut down.

The cost of placing an order is $10; the cost of receiving an order is $20.

Space storage cost is $12 per year per gross stored.

Insurance and taxes are approximately 12 percent of the net delivered cost of average inventory, and Kaufman expects a return of at least 8 percent on its average investment. (Ignore return on order and carrying cost for simplicity.)

Required:
1. Prepare a schedule computing the total annual cost of Komtronics based on uniform order lot sizes of 1, 2, 3, 4, 5, and 6 gross of Komtronics. (The schedule should show the total annual cost according to each lot size.) Indicate the EOQ (economic lot size to order).

2. Prepare a schedule computing the minimum stock reorder point for Komtronics. The Komtronics inventory should not fall below this point without reordering to guard against a stockout. Factors to be considered include average lead time usage and safety stock requirements.

3. Prepare a schedule computing the cost of a stockout of Komtronics. Factors to be considered include the excess costs for local purchases and for rush orders.

(AICPA adapted)

14.20   ***EOQ and Reorder***   The Robney Company is a restaurant supplier that sells a number of products to restaurants in its area. One of its products is a special meat cutter with a disposable blade. The blades are sold in packages of twelve blades for $20 per package. After a number of years the company has determined that the demand for replacement blades is at a constant rate of 2,000 packages per month. The packages cost the Robney Company $10 each from the manufacturer and require a three-day lead time from the date of order to the date of delivery. The ordering cost is $1.20 per order, and the carrying cost is 10 percent per annum.

Required:
1. Calculate
   a. The EOQ.
   b. The number of orders needed per year.
   c. The total cost of buying and carrying blades for the year.

2. Assuming there is no reserve (for example, safety stock) and the present inventory level is 200 packages, when should the next order be placed? (Use 360 days to equal one year.)

3. Discuss the problems that most firms would have in attempting to apply the EOQ formula to their inventory problems.

(CMA adapted)

14.21   ***EOQ and Economic Savings***   Hermit Company manufactures a line of walnut office products. Hermit executives estimate the demand for the double walnut letter tray, one of the company's products, at 6,000 units. The letter tray sells for $80 per unit. The costs relating to the letter tray are estimated to be as follows for 19X7:

1. The standard manufacturing cost per letter tray unit is estimated at $50.

2. Costs to initiate a production run are estimated at $300.

3. Annual costs of carrying the letter tray in inventory are estimated at 20 percent of the standard manufacturing cost.

In previous years, Hermit Company has scheduled the production for the letter tray in two equal production runs. The company is aware that the EOQ model can be used to determine the optimal size for production runs. The EOQ formula as it applies to inventories for determining the optimal order quantity follows:

$$EOQ = \sqrt{\frac{2\,(\text{Annual demand})(\text{Cost per order})}{(\text{Cost per unit})(\text{Carrying cost})}}.$$

Required:
Calculate the expected annual cost savings Hermit Company could experience if it employed the EOQ model to determine the number of production runs that should be initiated during the year for the manufacture of the double walnut letter trays.

(CMA adapted)

14.22   ***EOQ Computations***   Evans Inc. is a large wholesale distributor that deals exclusively in baby shoes. Due to the substantial costs related to ordering and storing the shoes, the company has decided to employ the EOQ method to help determine the optimal quantities of shoes to order from the different manufacturers. The EOQ formula is

$$EOQ = \sqrt{\frac{2C_0 D}{PC_s}},$$

where

EOQ = Optimal number of units per purchase order.
   D = Annual demand.
   P = Purchase price per unit.

C_0 = Cost of placing an order.

C_s = Annual cost of storage per dollar of investment in inventory.

Before Evans Inc. can use the EOQ model, it must develop values for two of the cost parameters—ordering costs (C_0) and storage costs (C_s). As a starting point, management has decided to develop the values for the two cost parameters by using cost data from the most recent fiscal year, 19X5.

The company placed 4,000 purchase orders during 19X5. The largest number of orders placed during any one month was 400 orders in June, and the smallest number of orders placed was 250 orders in December. Selected cost data for these two months and the year for the purchasing, accounts payable, and warehousing operations follow:

	Costs for High-Activity Month (June, 400 orders)	Costs for Low-Activity Month (December, 250 orders)	Annual Costs
Purchasing Department			
Purchasing Manager	$ 1,750	$ 1,750	$ 21,000
Buyers	2,500	1,900	28,500
Clerks	2,000	1,100	20,600
Supplies	275	150	2,500
Accounts Payable Department			
Clerks	2,000	1,500	21,500
Supplies	125	75	1,100
Data Processing	2,600	2,300	30,000
Warehouse			
Supervisor	1,250	1,250	15,000
Receiving Clerks	2,300	1,800	23,300
Receiving Supplies	50	25	500
Shipping Clerks	3,800	3,500	44,000
Shipping Supplies	1,350	1,200	15,200
Freight Out	1,600	1,300	16,800
	$21,600	$17,850	$240,000

The purchasing department is responsible for placing all orders. The costs listed for the accounts payable department relate only to the processing of purchase orders for payment. The warehouse costs reflect two operations: receiving and shipping. The receiving clerks inspect all incoming shipments and place the orders in storage. The shipping clerks are responsible for processing all sales orders to retailers.

Evans Inc. leases space in a public warehouse, and the rental fee is priced according to the square feet occupied during a month. The annual charges during 19X5 totaled $34,500. Annual insurance and property taxes on the shoes stored in the warehouse amounted to $5,700 and $7,300, respectively. The company pays 8 percent per year for a small amount of short-term, seasonal bank debt. Long-term capital investments are expected to produce a rate of return of 12 percent after taxes. The effective tax rate is 40 percent.

The inventory balances tend to fluctuate during the year depending upon the demand for baby shoes. Selected data on inventory balances is shown here:

Inventory, January 1, 19X5	$160,000
Inventory, December 31, 19X5	120,000
Highest Inventory Balance (June)	220,000
Lowest Inventory Balance (December)	120,000
Average Monthly Inventory	190,000

The boxes in which the baby shoes are stored are all approximately the same size. Consequently, the shoes all occupy about the same amount of storage space in the warehouse.

Required:
1. Using the 19X5 data, determine the estimated values appropriate for
   a. C_0 (the cost of placing an order).
   b. C_s (the annual cost of storage per dollar of investment in inventory).

2. Should Evans Inc. use the cost parameters developed solely from the historical data in the employment of the EOQ model? Explain your answer.

(CMA adapted)

14.23   ***Decision Theory Approach***   The Starr Company manufactures several products. One of its main products requires an electric motor. The management of the Starr Company uses the EOQ formula to determine the optimal number of motors to order. Management now wants to determine how much safety stock to order.

The Starr Company uses 30,000 electric motors annually (300 working days). Using the EOQ formula, the company orders 3,000 motors at a time. The lead time for an order is five days. The annual cost of carrying one motor in safety stock is $10. Management has estimated that the cost of being out of stock is $20 for each motor the company is short.

The Starr Company has analyzed its usage during past reorder periods by examining the inventory records, which indicate the following usage patterns during the past reorder periods:

Usage During Lead Time	Number of Times Quantity Was Used
440	6
460	12
480	16
500	130
520	20
540	10
560	6
	200

Required:
1. Using an expected value approach, determine the safety stock level for electric motors that the Starr Company should maintain to minimize costs.

2. What would be the Starr Company's new reorder point?

3. What factors should the Starr Company have considered to estimate its stockout costs?

NAME INDEX

SUBJECT INDEX